Happy B

Mike

The black ribbon from the first Reunion of the
47th North Carolina Troop indicates you are a
descendent of a soldier killed or died from
war injuries. White ribbons were worn by those
whose family member survived the war - this ribbon,
to be used as a bookmark, should remain with the
book.

Love
Dad

Lee's Tar Heels

Civil War America

GARY W. GALLAGHER, EDITOR

Lee's TAR HEELS

The Pettigrew-Kirkland-MacRae Brigade

— EARL J. HESS —

THE UNIVERSITY OF NORTH CAROLINA PRESS   CHAPEL HILL AND LONDON

© 2002 The University of North Carolina Press
All rights reserved
Manufactured in the United States of America
Designed by April Leidig-Higgins
Set in Monotype Bulmer by Copperline Book Services, Inc.

The paper in this book meets the guidelines for permanence and
durability of the Committee on Production Guidelines for Book
Longevity of the Council on Library Resources.

Library of Congress Cataloging-in-Publication Data
Hess, Earl J.   Lee's Tar Heels: the Pettigrew-Kirkland-MacRae
Brigade / by Earl J. Hess.   p. cm.—(Civil War America)
Includes bibliographical references (p.   ) and index.
ISBN 0-8078-2687-1 (cloth: alk. paper)
1. Confederate States of America. Army. Pettigrew's Brigade.
2. North Carolina—History—Civil War, 1861–1865—Regimental
histories. 3. United States—History—Civil War, 1861–1865—
Regimental histories. 4. United States—History—Civil War,
1861–1865—Campaigns. 5. Pettigrew, James Johnston,
1828–1863. 6. Kirkland, William W. (William Whedbee),
1833–1915. 7. MacRae, William, 1834–1882. I. Title. II. Series.
E573.4.P48 H47 2002   973.7'456—dc21   2001048065

06 05 04 03 02   5 4 3 2 1

For Pratibha and Julie,
with love

CONTENTS

MAPS

ILLUSTRATIONS

ILLUSTRATIONS

PREFACE

Pettigrew's brigade was one of the most famous North Carolina units of the Civil War. Organized and led for nearly a year by James Johnston Pettigrew, a promising young officer, it spent the first nine months of its history operating in the backwaters of eastern North Carolina before it was thrust into the hard campaigning and tough fighting endured by Lee's Army of Northern Virginia. The brigade earned a bloody reputation for the work it did at Gettysburg, its first major battle. On July 1 it smashed two Union brigades (one of which was the famed Iron Brigade) and forced the Federal First Corps back to Seminary Ridge. The brigade took a leading role in Pickett's Charge on July 3; some of its men surged to within a few feet of the stone fence, going farther than did Pickett's Virginians. The brigade's losses at Gettysburg were astonishingly high, but that was not the end of its long battle history. It went on to participate in nearly every major engagement of Lee's army to the end of the war. The Tar Heels richly earned the praise of their superiors at Bristoe Station, the Wilderness, Spotsylvania, Cold Harbor, Globe Tavern, Reams Station, the Fifth Offensive at Petersburg, Burgess's Mill, and the final actions that led to the fall of Petersburg. The brigade trudged faithfully all the way to Appomattox, where it was one of the last units to lay down its arms in the official surrender ceremony on April 12.

The brigade consisted of five battle-tested regiments. The 11th North Carolina joined Pettigrew four months after he organized the brigade. It was nicknamed the Bethel Regiment because many of its members had served in the 1st North Carolina (six months), which was engaged in the first land battle of the war at Big Bethel. The 26th North Carolina, the oldest and most famous of the five regiments, was organized early in the war and led by Zebulon B. Vance, who was elected governor of North Carolina in the summer of 1862. It had seen combat at the battles of New Bern and Malvern Hill before joining the brigade. This regiment was always the largest and most powerful of the five regiments, and it compiled an impressive record during the war. The 44th North Carolina missed

Gettysburg because of an assignment to guard Lee's railroad lines near Richmond, but it became the reliable foundation of the brigade in the terrible campaigns of 1864–65. The 47th North Carolina and the 52nd North Carolina, like the 44th, were organized in the spring of 1862 and served the needs of the brigade with faithful devotion.

This study came about as the result of several inspirations. Much of my previous work has been devoted to studying the Northern side of the Civil War, and I felt the need to understand more deeply the experiences of Confederate soldiers and their officers. By a happy coincidence I had the opportunity to do that with a research fellowship from the Appalachian College Association in the fall of 1995. I spent that semester on the campus of the University of North Carolina at Chapel Hill, where I had access to the extremely rich holdings of the Southern Historical Collection. Equally rich holdings were within reach in the Special Collections department of the library at Duke University and in the North Carolina Division of Archives and History at Raleigh. Taken together, all three institutions have by far the largest collections of unpublished personal accounts by Confederate soldiers in the United States, and their holdings are heavily dominated by the papers of North Carolina soldiers.

Another thread of the story came into play the year before my fellowship period at Chapel Hill, when I visited Gettysburg for my first intensive examination of the battlefield. I noticed the newly placed monument to the 26th North Carolina, just in front of the stone fence, commemorating the advance of a small group of that regiment to within twenty yards of the Union position. There they were blasted by a charge of canister from a single Union artillery piece. It conjured up a dramatic and painful image that impressed me greatly. I wanted to learn more about the unit and the men who filled its ranks, and my residence at Chapel Hill allowed me to do that. Gathering material on the unit that fall, I also had a conversation with Greg Mast, a reenactor and historian of North Carolina's participation in the war, who suggested that a history of the brigade to which the 26th belonged might be a good idea. Thus the various influences that produced this book happily came together.

Studies like this one seem to have a timely necessity. It is astonishing that North Carolina and its people have played such a huge role in the Civil War, that there is such an abundance of primary material on that role, and yet that there are so few studies of that subject. When I began researching this project in 1995, one could literally count the number of significant books on North Carolina in the Civil War on the fingers of one, possibly two hands. Since then a few more books have appeared, but there are still far too few on such a large and important topic. Additional studies of other Tar Heel units, such as Lane's brigade,

Cooke's brigade, Clingman's brigade, and Barringer's cavalry, are needed. Biographies of Tar Heels such as William Dorsey Pender and Lawrence O'Bryan Branch would flesh out our understanding of the leadership of Lee's army. The major battles fought on North Carolina soil are being discovered by historians who have published recent books on Bentonville, but a number of secondary campaigns and engagements continue to exist in the shadows. It is my hope that this book will contribute to the growing awareness of the Old North State's contributions to the Confederate war effort and to its crucial role in the drama of the Civil War.

A unit history is a unique part of Civil War historiography. In some ways it has a fundamental quality lacking in other kinds of war studies. The ideal unit history should be complete and definitive, covering all aspects of its subject. Thus it is more than a mere recounting of the unit's battles; it should also describe the mobilization of manpower, the organization of the units, their acclimation to camp life, their initial combat experience, and the changing nature of the men's attitudes toward war and the cause they fought to uphold. Ties to the home front, food, medical care, logistical support, political attitudes, social background, postwar life experiences, and many other topics ought to be covered, as far as the available sources will allow. Fortunately there are numerous collections of unpublished personal accounts from members of the brigade, and I have been guided by them and many other sources I came across in shaping the contours of this book. While the wealth of sources still did not illuminate everything, I hope I have covered all important topics as thoroughly as possible.

While all these areas are legitimate topics for a unit history, battle remains the primary interest of most readers and the major reason for the existence of any unit. The history of Pettigrew's brigade is primarily the story of its battle experience. While it saw relatively little combat before Gettysburg, the brigade saw little else but combat after that terrible battle. During the course of the war the brigade engaged in twenty-one campaigns. It participated in at least twenty separate engagements, spread over as many days of fighting, during its two years and eight months of existence. In addition, three of its regiments fought in other battles separately. The 26th North Carolina participated in two extra campaigns, with four days of fighting, before it joined the brigade. The 44th Carolina and the 52nd North Carolina each had the equivalent of two extra campaigns and two days of fighting apart from the brigade.

All of this fighting led to enormous casualties. In a sense the unit was famous not so much for what it did on the battlefield (although that was in its own way very impressive), but for what was done to it by the Federals. A total of 8,256 men served in the five regiments; 58 percent of them became casualties. This figure was so high not only because the brigade suffered heavy losses at Gettysburg, at Bristoe Station, in the Overland campaign, at Burgess's Mill, and on April 2, 1865, but also because it had an unusually large number of men captured in battle. This component of the losses was particularly high on July 3 at Gettysburg, at Bristoe Station, at Burgess's Mill, and on April 2. In fact 35 percent of the members of the brigade were captured in battle, some more than once. The number of men who died as a result of combat was very high as well. The aggregate of those who were killed on the battlefield, died of their wounds, or died of disease or wounds while in Union prisons amounts to 1,202, or 14 percent of the total enrollment of the brigade.

In short, the Tar Heels fought hard and suffered a great deal. Thus I emphasize their battle experience above all other relevant topics covered in this book. The battle history of the brigade is absorbing and important, even without the high casualty rate. Gettysburg was its most famous battle, but the brigade really came into its own as a fighting unit in the Petersburg campaign. By then Pettigrew had long since departed; he was mortally wounded at the battle of Falling Waters during Lee's retreat from Pennsylvania. The next brigadier, William W. Kirkland, was a good battlefield commander but not an inspirational leader. He was wounded twice while commanding the brigade and thus spent many months convalescing. His influence on the character of the unit was minimal. But William MacRae had a different and decisive impact. He took charge of the brigade in June 1864 and turned it into one of Lee's most powerful striking units. MacRae and his men were primarily responsible for the stunning Confederate defeat of the Union Second Corps at the battle of Reams Station. They remained the foundation of Heth's division during the last few months of the war, retaining their battle efficiency despite shortages of food, the debilitating effects of increased desertion, and the gnawing realization that the war was lost. As was typical of Lee's army in general, the hard core of committed Southern patriots in MacRae's brigade trudged blindly toward Appomattox when all else was crumbling in the Confederacy.

The organization of this book proceeds chronologically. Because the 26th North Carolina had a fairly long history before it joined the brigade, Chapter 1 is devoted exclusively to its experiences from May 1861 until August 1862. Chapter 2 details the organization of Pettigrew's brigade, and subsequent chapters cover the unit's history to the end of the war. The final chapter briefly surveys the postwar lives of the survivors, and the appendix offers a statistical look at the service records of the brigade. Based on the records faithfully compiled and published by the North Carolina Division of Archives and History, the appendix attempts to present what might be termed a military profile of the brigade.

I would like to thank several people for their aid in preparing this book. Greg Mast discussed the shape of the project early in my work and shared information on available sources. Noah Andre Trudeau supplied a copy of a significant source from his research files. Patrick S. Brady generously shared material on the unit's role in the battle of Cold Harbor. Peter Cozzens also freely provided material that was relevant to my subject. Dale Floyd and Bruce E. Baker helped gather valuable sources. Steven Woodworth offered information; William Shea, A. Wilson Greene, and Arthur Bergeron encouraged me in pursuit of this topic; and Mark R. Terry shared his research on the capture of Confederate flags at Bristoe Station.

I wish to thank the staff members of all the archives listed in the bibliography for their help when I either visited their institutions or asked for material by mail. A special note of gratitude is due to John Coski at the Museum of the Confederacy, Richard Shrader of the Southern Historical Collection, and Nola Reed Knouse of the Moravian Music Foundation.

The Appalachian College Association's John B. Stephenson Fellowship was of enormous help in enabling me to have access to essential manuscript material. Also, a part of the James F. Haas Fellowship, offered to me by the Harrisburg Civil War Round Table in 1998, helped me to finish some loose ends of archival research for this project.

Finally, I owe more than I can say to my wife, Pratibha, who has supported me enormously in this and all other work. She makes it all worthwhile.

Chapter 1

The 26th North Carolina

The building blocks of every Civil War brigade were its component regiments, and the oldest, most experienced regiment of Pettigrew's brigade was the 26th North Carolina. It was organized on August 27, 1861, at Camp Crabtree, near Raleigh. The men came from eight different counties almost evenly divided between two geographic areas: the heartland of North Carolina, where the coastal plain met the piedmont, and the mountainous western side of the state.

The names of the individual companies that made up the 26th were colorful and expressive. The Jeff Davis Mountaineers from Ashe County became Company A; the Waxhaw Jackson Guards of Union County became Company B; the Wilkes Volunteers of Wilkes County became Company C; the Wake Guards of Wake County became Company D; the Independent Guards of Chatham County became Company E; the Hibriten Guards of Caldwell County became Company F; the Chatham Boys of Chatham County became Company G; the Moore Independents of Moore County became Company H; the Caldwell Guards of Caldwell County became Company I; and the Pee Dee Wild Cats of Anson County became Company K.[1]

These companies were part of a great wave of reaction against President Abraham Lincoln's call on April 15, 1861, for troops to suppress the rebellion. Like the rest of the Upper South states, North Carolina had refused to leave the Union before the firing on Fort Sumter, believing that the election of a Republican president was not sufficient cause to break up the nation. But the Confederate attack on Fort Sumter changed the dynamics of the secession issue. While the North unanimously supported a military solution to the breakup of the nation, most citizens of the Upper South refused to answer Lincoln's call for troops. As a result, North Carolina and three other slave states seceded from the Union and joined the original seven Deep South states. Most of the companies that made up the 26th were organized in July, but the Moore Independents, the first company of the regiment to form, assembled on May 13 at Carthage.[2]

As the companies assembled at Camp Crabtree and were selected for inclusion into the 26th, the personnel began to meet and form relationships that would see them through the remainder of the war. Maj. Henry King Burgwyn Jr., commander of the camp, would be elected lieutenant colonel of the new regiment. He came from a planter family of Northampton County, North Carolina, and was descended from English aristocratic stock. Born on October 3, 1841, while his parents vacationed in Boston, Harry, as he was known, attended Burlington College in North Carolina and was tutored to enter the U.S. Military Academy at West Point. The necessary appointment never came through, so Burgwyn entered the University of North Carolina; he graduated with a bachelor's degree in 1859. His taste for military training was so strong that he immediately enrolled in the Virginia Military Institute. Burgwyn was a staunch supporter of Southern rights. He advocated the state's secession even before the firing on Fort Sumter and threw himself into war preparations when North Carolina left the Union. He was given command of Camp Crabtree on July 5, but a commission in a field unit suited his temperament and ambition much more closely. His election to the lieutenant colonelcy on August 27 was a prayer answered. Burgwyn was only nineteen years, nine months, and twenty-seven days old, "probably the youngest Lt. Col. in the Confederate or U.S. service," he proudly noted in his diary.[3]

Capt. Abner B. Carmichael of the Wilkes Volunteers was elected major of the regiment; but the colonelcy went to a man who had no prior association with any of the companies at Camp Crabtree, and thus he would not even see his new regiment for several days after the election. Capt. Zebulon Baird Vance of the 14th North Carolina was given the nod by the company officers on August 27. He was a popular politician from the western counties of North Carolina and thus was well known by at least the three companies that hailed from the mountains. Born in Buncombe County near Asheville on May 13, 1830, Vance entered the University of North Carolina in 1852 but studied for only one year before he was admitted to the bar. He made a reputation as a lawyer, local politician, and editor of the *Asheville Spectator* before he was elected to the North Carolina House of Commons and the U.S. House of Representatives. Vance was a staunch Southern Whig, one of four Tar Heel Unionist congressmen before the attack on Fort Sumter. He deplored the pending breakup of the nation but was prepared to

Col. Henry King Burgwyn Jr. Pictured front center in this image of cadets, class of 1861, at Virginia Military Institute, Burgwyn became the second colonel of the 26th North Carolina and died at age twenty-one while leading his regiment in its famous charge at Gettysburg on July 1. (Preston Library, Virginia Military Institute, Lexington)

honor the Deep South's decision to leave. When Lincoln called for troops to restore the Union, Vance denounced the policy and enthusiastically joined the Confederate war effort. He volunteered as a private in the Rough and Ready Guards of Buncombe County but quickly was elected their captain when the unit became Company F, 14th North Carolina. Vance's men endured a summer of garrison duty at Suffolk, Virginia, before he was notified of his election to command the 26th. He was not unopposed. An anonymously published letter to the *Raleigh Register*, possibly authored by Burgwyn, urged the election of Rev. Cameron F. McRae, Burgwyn's brother-in-law, but this suggestion fell flat.[4]

Two other people who would rise to prominence before the war was half over entered the regiment in 1861 through the lower ranks. John Randolph Lane was born on Independence Day 1835 in what friends would later characterize as straitened circumstances. A contemporary, recalling that he was "reared with the advantages of self-denial," believed this helped to shape his character. Entering the Chatham Boys as a corporal, he soon was elected captain of Company G. His hard work and ability to learn the science of military affairs catapulted him into the lieutenant colonelcy when Burgwyn rose to command the regiment. Both men would be hit on July 1 at Gettysburg; Burgwyn died, and Lane suffered untold agony from a horrible head wound. Yet the pugnacious Lane would survive, return to rebuild the regiment, and be wounded several more times before the war was over. He lived to see the turn of the new century.[5]

John Thomas Jones was another quick riser in the ranks. He was a twenty-year-old student at the University of North Carolina when Fort Sumter was fired on, but like Burgwyn, he was a strong supporter of secession even before Lincoln's call for troops. The new Confederacy was "fighting for the institutions of the whole South," he wrote home, "and the South will yet sustain them. Who would rather be swung on to the tail end of a Northern . . . Republic than to be equals in a Southern confederacy[?] The safety of our institutions depend upon our being united; if we are divided where are we to look for success[?]" An alliance between the Upper South and the North would lead to "an abolition ticket here in this State. As for me I will never live in any such a country." Jones left the university just before graduation and volunteered as a private in the 1st North Carolina, a six-month regiment. He saw combat at the battle of Big Bethel on June 10, 1861, and organized the Caldwell Guards. Jones served the company as lieutenant and captain and was promoted major and lieutenant colonel by the midpoint of the war.[6]

The men who enlisted in the 26th North Carolina hardly spoke of their motivations to fight for the Confederacy, but defense of their native soil undoubtedly was the most important factor for the hundreds of men who made up the

Col. Zebulon Baird Vance. A prominent politician before the war, Vance led the 26th North Carolina in the battle of New Bern and then was elected governor of North Carolina, effectively leading the state for the remainder of the war. (Miscellaneous Photos, SHC-UNC)

regiment. Lt. Henry Clay Albright of Company G offered some insight into their thinking when he wrote to a North Carolina newspaper, "At the first sound of the war whoop, as it fell upon their ears from afar, these brave and chivalrous hearted men forsook the quiet of their farms, the happiness of the family circle, and all they held dear to them, and rushed as one man to the defence of their young Republic's bright and unsullied honor. . . . They resolved to sacrifice their lives rather than submit to the tyranny of a wrong and misguided tyrant." Albright privately assured his sister that "I'm willing to undergo any necessary hardship or privation . . . for my country's cause, which is the foremost and dearest companion of my heart."[7]

Noah Deaton of Company H summed up this attitude in a letter to one of his female friends when he criticized the men who continued to stay at home while their neighbors enlisted. "There are a great many young fellows that have no cares to keep them from going out in defense of their country but are such cowards that they would suffer subjugation rather than fight and I trust the ladies will not countenance such fellows." Deaton had the perfect remedy for anyone who was offended by his opinion: let them "take up arms to defend there homes and not wait for others to do what they should do." Deaton paid a price for his patriotism. He was captured at the battle of Bristoe Station on October 14, 1863, and was not paroled until nearly the end of the war.[8]

John Randolph Lane would commemorate the memory of the fallen at every opportunity for the rest of his long life. Speaking to the North Carolina Society of Baltimore in 1903, Lane eloquently remembered the men of his old regiment. They were "of good blood," he insisted. "I do not mean that their parents were aristocrats — far from it; many of them never owned a slave. They were the great middle class that owned small farms . . . who earned their living with honest sweat and owed not any man." Lane called each of his comrades a patriot who was "convinced that the cause for which he was fighting was just; he believed that he owed allegiance first to his home and his State. He was standing to combat an unjust invader."[9]

No sooner had the regiment completed its organization than orders arrived to move out. The Federals were responsible for the unit's hasty departure from Camp Crabtree. It was scheduled to be sent to Virginia, but a joint army and navy force under Maj. Gen. Benjamin Butler was even then attacking the outer banks of North Carolina. The state's long coastline, indented by a number of huge sounds protected by a string of tiny barrier islands, was vulnerable. If the Federals could take these outlying islands, they would have access to the relatively calm waters of the sounds. Most of the major rivers of the coastal plain drained into these sounds, offering avenues of invasion for seaborne Yankee armies. Fully one-third of the state's territory would be laid open to Northern incursions, a number of port cities would be cut off from European trade, and the Federals would be in a position to interrupt the Wilmington and Weldon Railroad, a vital link between North Carolina and Richmond.[10]

The 26th left Crabtree by rail early on the morning of September 2 and arrived later that day at New Bern, where it received orders to move south to Morehead City. The men were assigned to guard Fort Macon, a masonry fortification on the eastern end of Bogue Island that guarded Beaufort Inlet and the ports of Morehead City and Beaufort. Vance arrived on the evening of September 4 and took command of his new regiment as it made a difficult crossing of the sound. The men boarded a schooner that grounded well short of the beach, and they were forced to complete the journey in small boats. One Tar Heel was "mashed to death a geting on the Boat," and another was injured very badly. The regiment spent its first few days on the island setting up tents and digging wells. Vance and Burgwyn agreed to name their first encampment in the field Camp Burgwyn, after the lieutenant colonel's father, who was on Bogue Island acting as a volunteer aide for Governor Henry T. Clark.[11]

The logistical problem was immense. Vance was told to rely on the commissary stores at New Bern, but they were inadequate. He wrote an imploring letter to Governor Clark describing the 26th as "almost in a state of mutiny" because it had not been paid in four months. Most of the men suffered from the want of "ordinary articles of every day use" and had no way to buy them from local merchants. Vance urged Clark to pay the men something or "I fear I shall not be able to maintain discipline."[12]

Vance's men retained their spirit and enthusiasm despite the shortages. W. E. Setser of Company F put it more boldly: "the bois ar all aneious for a fight. we think we can whip six thousand yankees. the bois sais they can whip five a peace. i think i can whip six my self." If the Northerners landed on the island, "we will feed them on canon plates and grape and musketry." They needed all the spirit they could muster, for soon after setting up camp on Bogue Island, the 26th was hit by a wave of communicable diseases. Measles, malaria, typhoid fever, and mumps ravaged the camp, and a special hospital was created on the mainland near Carolina City, three miles west of Morehead City. Nine men from one company died in one week. The sickness raged from September through December before it finally subsided.[13]

Despite the illnesses and lack of supplies, Vance and his regiment devoted most of their attention to the prospect of a battle. There were numerous scares and false alarms. John A. Jackson of Company H informed a friend, "we cant tel what a day will bring forth[.] the next time you hear from us we may have had a hard battle or may be prisners bound for New York or some other port." The only contact with the enemy came as the result of an accident. A transport steamer, the USS *Union*, became separated from a fleet sailing south from Fortress Monroe and grounded on the shore of Bogue Island twelve miles west of Fort Macon on November 1. It broke apart, and several people on board were drowned. Eighty-one survivors approached Vance's regimental camp with a flag of truce on November 2 and gave themselves up. Vance was criticized by his superiors for not adequately picketing the approaches to his camp, illustrating the laxness with which he tended to run the regiment. Although the ship was broken up, it contained a load of valuable articles, and Companies D, F, H, and K were detached for salvage duty. The work began on November 4 and lasted until the nineteenth. Horses, muskets, whiskey, champagne, coal, mattresses, pillows, clothing, and two rifled cannon were recovered. At times the men were fired at by Federal ships; but they took shelter behind the sand hills, and no harm was done.[14]

When it became apparent that the Federals had no intention of attacking Fort Macon, the regiment left Bogue Island to establish winter quarters on the mainland on November 26. Camp Vance was laid out near Carolina City. The men's health improved with the onset of cooler weather, and the Christmas season passed quietly, save for several men who became drunk and rowdy and had to be placed in the guardhouse. While many enlisted men found their huts at Camp Vance to be clean and comfortable, Burgwyn thought the camp was in wretched shape when he returned from a stay in the hospital to recover from typhoid fever. Little care had been taken to police the area, so "you may imagine the filth," he complained to his mother. Discipline seemed worse than ever. Although Burgwyn drilled the men four hours every day, he was not satisfied with their proficiency. He heard recitations on tactics from officers each day as he slowly raised the standard in "my regiment." Burgwyn came to compare it favorably with all the other units in the area. "My own is the best & if it had a good Colonel would be a most capital reg. Col. Vance is however a man without any system or regularity whatever & has so little of an engineering mind. . . . His abilities appear to me to be more overated than those of any other person I know of." Burgwyn was critical of several other officers as well, calling them "exceedingly inefficient in tactics." He believed the quality of the 26th would be "much improved" if these officers could somehow be levered out of their positions.[15]

A long-awaited Union offensive into the sounds soon drew the regiment out of Camp Vance. Brig. Gen. Ambrose E. Burnside commanded a joint army and navy force to seal off port cities and establish a major Federal presence on the coastal plain. Roanoke Island and New Bern seemed to be the most likely targets, so Confederate authorities began rounding up all the troops they could spare. News of Burnside's expedition reached Camp Vance on January 24, and the order to move arrived two days later. Vance left immediately with six companies, and Burgwyn was to follow with the rest the next day. The regiment made Camp Branch their home for the next six weeks. Named for Brig. Gen. Lawrence O'Bryan Branch, commander of the District of the Pamlico, it was located four miles south of New Bern close to the Atlantic and North Carolina Railroad. Fort Thompson, on the west bank of the Neuse River, and a line of infantry works connecting it to the railroad were nearby. The threat to New Bern was real but not immediate. Rain set in with a vengeance, pouring down for four days running in mid-February. Sickness began to rise in the ranks; pneumonia and flux were among the afflictions, and Vance himself came down with a tough case of an undiagnosed illness. "Vance knows nothing about the manege of a Regmt," concluded Burgwyn when the colonel refused to move the regiment to better ground.[16]

As the men continued to wait for action, they were pressed to reenlist voluntarily for an additional two years of service as soon as their twelve months were up. John Thomas Jones did not believe it was possible for his Company I to reenlist willingly. "There are not more than 20 of my company that will go in without going home." William H. Glenn of Company B supported Jones's view. "I think I will go home befor I Stick mi name to a nuther paper," he wrote. Vance warned the reluctant soldiers that the Confederate Congress might pass a conscript law that would draft all soldiers to remain in the service.[17]

Ironically, the two highest-ranking officers were also eager to leave the regiment. The ambitious Burgwyn wanted a regiment of his own. "I am exceedingly disgusted with my present position," he complained to his father. "Vance is totally unsuitable in my opinion & I am heartily tired of being under his command. As for discipline not the faintest idea of it has ever entered his head." Vance himself wanted to recruit more men and form a legion, a unit that combined all arms. He dreamed of a second infantry regiment, two companies of cavalry, and a battery of artillery. "This would make a handsome brigade with which I would like to take the field on active service." The authorities in Richmond were happy to see him raise additional units but refused to promise a commission as brigadier general.[18]

Vance did accomplish one thing in this period, the recruitment of a regimental brass band, but it was only by accident that he secured a group of musicians. The band had no connection to any of the counties that contributed troops to the regiment; its roots lay in the rich Moravian heritage of Forsyth County. The Moravian denomination originated as a reform movement in Bohemia nearly a century before the beginning of the Protestant Reformation. It grew dramatically under the sponsorship of Saxon nobleman Nicholas Ludwig von Zinzendorf, who created a Moravian colony on his landed estate in the 1720s. The Unitas Fratrum, or United Brethren, expanded soon after that and established communities such as Bethlehem, Pennsylvania, in 1741, which became the center of the Moravian Church in the northern colonies. Salem, founded in Forsyth County in 1766, became the center of the Moravian Church in the southern colonies. A high regard for education and a love of choral and instrumental music were two of the distinctive characteristics of Moravian life in America.[19]

Moravians from Salem were already in the regimental bands of the 21st and the 33rd North Carolina, and Samuel Timothy Mickey wanted to organize men for a third unit. He was in New Bern trying to find a regiment that was stationed on Roanoke Island but was stymied when Burnside captured the island. Mickey happened to meet Vance in the lobby of the Gaston House in New Bern. Vance recognized Mickey immediately. "'You are the very man I am looking for,'" Vance told him. "'You represent the Salem Band.'" The colonel talked him into committing his group to the 26th. Vance bypassed red tape and agreed to receive Mickey's men "as an independent band, . . . without being regularly enlisted." The musicians would be paid not by the Confederate government but by the officers themselves.[20]

The group consisted of eight men, with Mickey elected as their "captain." Several members of the band were accomplished players, but others were neophytes, including Julius Linebach. He had worked as a bookkeeper for the Haw River Mills in Alamance County and had always wanted to do his duty for the Confederacy, but he "was not anxious to become a target for bullets fired by any one." So when someone suggested he quit his job and join the Salem Band, it seemed like a workable compromise. Linebach found that blowing a horn could be dangerous too. The mouthpiece of his brass instrument hurt his lips, and he thought his lung power was not up to the demands of the horn. His lips chapped, cracked, and bled at each practice, "so that after every piece we played I could pour a spoonful of bloody water from my crook." He solved this problem by trading instruments with Joe Hall, who had a cornet. The band acquired a uniform of sorts before leaving Salem: "cadet jeans with brass buttons, of which we were rather proud."[21]

Mickey's band left Salem on the morning of March 5 and reached the regiment by rail two days later. The musicians set up tents the next day just outside the guard line so they could come and go freely, and they bought caps in New Bern to complete their uniforms. The band had to play for guard mounting at 8:00 A.M.; perform at the daily evening dress parade; give a short concert each

Samuel Timothy Mickey. Organizer and leader of the Salem Band, the regimental band of the 26th North Carolina, Mickey was the dependable foundation of the Moravian musicians. He is seen here, in a photograph probably taken before the war, holding his E-flat cornet. When the band members were captured on April 5, 1865, and the Federals confiscated their equipment, Mickey saved this instrument by hiding it in his haversack. He is also holding the cornet in the 1862 band photograph. (MMF)

night; play at regimental inspections every Sunday morning; and play at each brigade review. They practiced every morning and afternoon. One of the most difficult things to learn was how to play and march at the same time, and they had to acquire the ability to divide their attention "between music, feet, & the ground." The condition of the parade ground did not help, for every stump, root, and hole tripped up a band member.[22]

The music that began to waft over Camp Branch failed to soften the news that Burnside was on the move. He landed on Roanoke Island and defeated the outnumbered Confederates there on February 8. The Federals now had access to the rivers that penetrated the coastal plain, and all of eastern North Carolina was seized with a panic. Burnside would launch the biggest attack of his campaign, using 8,000 men, in an effort to take New Bern. Branch had only about 4,000 volunteers and 2,000 hastily organized militia to defend it.[23]

Two lines of infantry works protected New Bern. Most of Branch's strength was gathered at the Fort Thompson Line, where the 26th was already stationed, but it ended at the railroad. Six miles farther south a work called the Croatan Line could easily be outflanked by troops disembarking at Fisher's Landing, between the two positions. Branch sent the 26th and a battery to reinforce the 35th North Carolina on the Croatan Line when word of Burnside's landing south of that earthwork reached New Bern. By the time the men got there by rail, the line had been evacuated, and the 26th, while retiring to the Fort Thompson Line, narrowly avoided a Federal force that had landed between the two lines.[24]

The Confederates worked feverishly in a deluge of rain on the night of March 13 to prepare the Fort Thompson works. The line ended about forty yards short of the track opposite the head of a swampy ravine called Bullen's Branch, which ran westward from the tracks for about one and a quarter miles into Brice's Creek. When Branch decided to extend the line west of the track, he had to retire it 150 yards to the rear to take advantage of the higher ground north of the branch. The terrain here was in the shape of narrow fingers of land, each about ten feet higher than the bottom, pointing southward. Vance planned and built a series of detached redans at the farthest edge of these fingers. He could not have constructed a continuous line of trench unless he moved the position at least a half-mile farther north than the rest of the line east of the railroad, creating an even bigger gap at the track.[25]

These redans, about eight in number, were hastily made and barely adequate for the task. The first was 200 yards west of the railroad, but the rest were only about 20 to 40 yards from one another and about 30 yards from the branch bed. Each one curved in a semicircle around the forward edge of each finger, was about 40 yards wide with no ditch or retrenchments, and had good parapets.

The trees had been cut down in front of the redans and in the swampy branch bottom, which had been made even wetter by the partial damming of Bullen's Branch and the rain that fell on March 13, so that three feet of water stood in front of the redans. Vance was put in charge of the irregular line west of the railroad. He stretched out the 26th North Carolina in the redans so that his right rested at Weathersby Road, and he divided responsibility for it among the regimental field officers. He posted himself in the center, placed Major Carmichael in charge of the left, and sent Burgwyn to see to the right. Carmichael had charge of Companies A, D, and G. Burgwyn had three companies of the 26th, two guns of Capt. T. H. Brem's battery; Companies A and E of the 19th North Carolina (better known as the 2nd North Carolina Cavalry), which was dismounted; and Capt. Walter G. McRae's independent company of North Carolina infantry.[26]

After a day and a night of heavy rain, the morning of Friday, March 14, dawned with a dark, gray overcast. Patches of fog hung low in the woods fronting the Confederate earthworks. Burnside's men advanced early in the morning with Brig. Gen. Jesse L. Reno's brigade deployed along and to the west of the railroad embankment. Reno hit Vance's line at 8:00 A.M., sending the 21st Massachusetts to slice through the gap in Branch's line along the railroad and aligning the 51st New York, 9th New Jersey, and 51st Pennsylvania west of the railroad. The 21st Massachusetts gained a foothold in the gap but was temporarily stalled by Confederate reinforcements. The air was still foggy when the rest of Reno's line approached Bullen's Branch and Carmichael's wing of the 26th opened fire. Vance was impressed by the very first volley his regiment fired in anger, calling it "especially magnificent. . . . The blaze at the muzzle of the guns was bright and glorious." The firing began on the left and was taken up company by company to the right; but Reno's line did not extend to Weathersby Road, and Burgwyn's wing never became engaged. Four companies of the 33rd North Carolina under Col. Clark M. Avery reinforced the 26th in the redans while two other companies under Lt. Col. Robert F. Hoke reinforced Burgwyn's men on the right.[27]

The 26th North Carolina was engaged in a hot fight against three times its numbers, but the Federals were reluctant to press home their attack because of the obstacles presented by Bullen's Branch. The heaviest fire took place on the left, where the Federals fired high at first, "cutting the boughs from the tops of the trees in our rear," recalled Capt. Oscar Rand of Company D. Carmichael conducted himself magnificently. A "quiet, nonobtrusive and rather slow" man, he was exalted by combat. "His face, form and bearing will remain in my memory as long as I live," remembered Rand, "as I saw him that morning, moving slowly from one end to the other of Rifle Pit No. 2, his head just above the bank, observing the enemy and quietly telling the men where to put their bullets."[28]

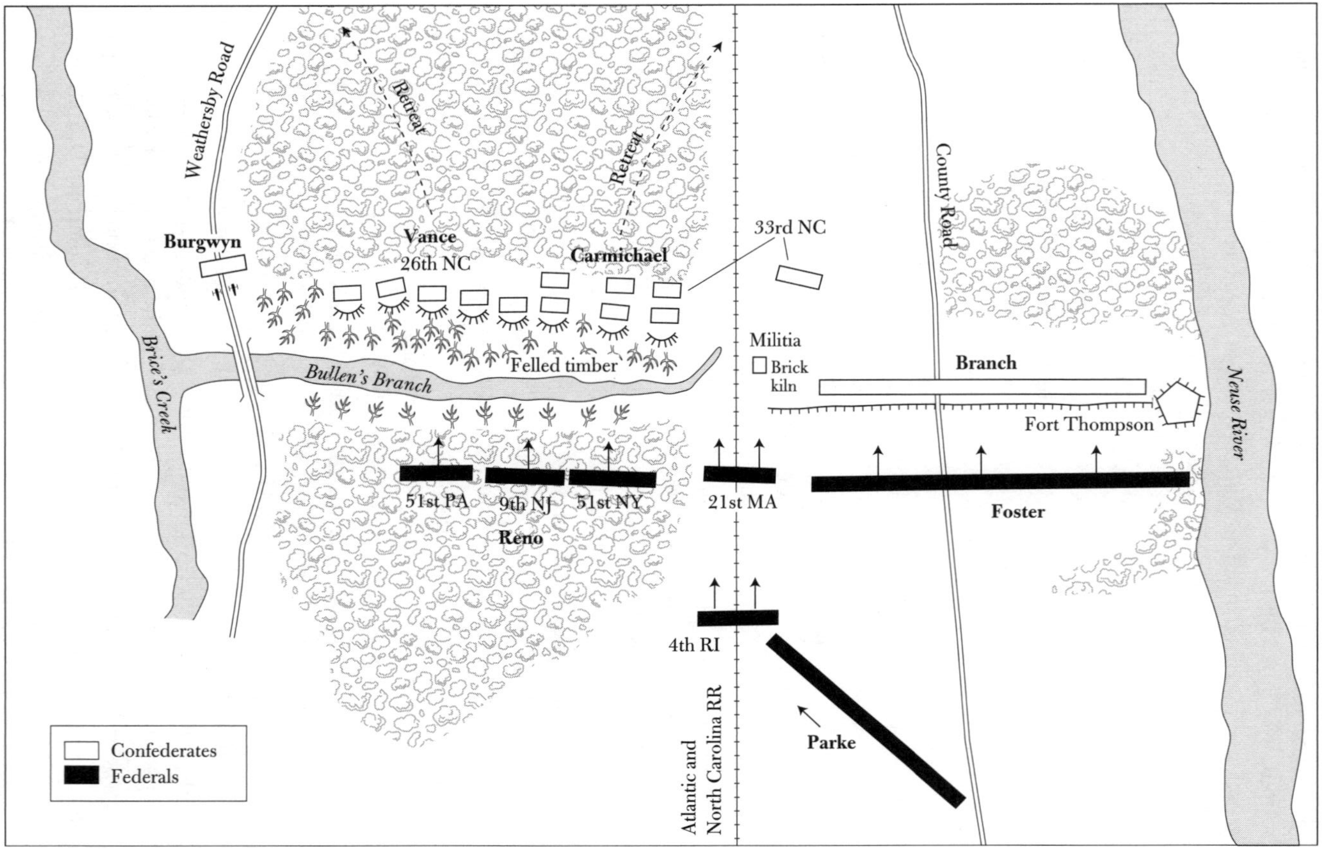

MAP 1.1 The Battle of New Bern, March 14, 1862

As soon as the Federals tried to cross the branch, the 26th met them with an "uninterrupted, fierce and deafening" fire. "Many of the Yankees tumbled over," wrote Vance, and "the rest toddled back into the woods." But the enemy began to gain the upper hand when reinforcements pushed forward along the railroad to help the 21st Massachusetts, and Major Carmichael was shot dead about 11:00 A.M. He and Colonel Avery were standing behind the left wing of the redan when a bullet entered Carmichael's mouth and exited the back of his neck. Rand was standing next to him and saw that death was instantaneous. "A feeling of bitter grief ran through the trenches as he fell, for there was not a man in the Twenty-sixth regiment who was not devotedly attached to him." It was possible that the Federal who fired this shot saw a small Confederate flag, three by four inches in size, that was mounted on a miniature staff attached to Carmichael's cap. A woman in New Bern had given it to him, and that may have distinguished him enough to draw the attention of a sharpshooter.[29]

To the east, the rest of Branch's line collapsed under the weight of Burnside's advance, and a general retreat ensued. Colonel Avery, in charge of the combined force on Vance's left, instantly realized that retreat was his only recourse. Orders were shouted at each of the redans, and the men "went out of the trenches amidst a perfect storm of bullets." Avery advanced northeast to the railroad embankment, where he was stunned to see four Federal guns and the 25th Massachusetts positioned across the track. The Yankees had succeeded in cutting off the retreat. Avery was forced to surrender 150 men. Rand later explained that the left wing of the regiment had received no orders from Vance to retreat, and it could have escaped capture if given more timely warning of the collapse of the rest of Branch's line.[30]

Vance received word of the deteriorating situation from Capt. Joseph J. Young, the regimental quartermaster, and ordered Burgwyn to retire, but he apparently ignored the left wing. The men in the center of the regiment jumped out of the redans and formed without confusion in the woods to the rear. Learning that the wagon bridge over Trent River, just south of New Bern, was already in flames, Vance struck out west to cross Brice's Creek. It was swollen by recent rains to a width of seventy-five yards and was unfordable. There was only one boat to be found, capable of hauling only three men, so several Tar Heels threw away their guns and tried to swim over; three of them drowned before officers could restrain the rest. Vance spurred his horse into the chilly water and was thrown when it panicked; the colonel nearly drowned before strong swimmers came to his rescue. After catching their breath, Vance and his saviors walked a half-mile before they found three boats and balanced them on their shoulders as they carried them all the way back to the creek.[31]

Burgwyn soon joined Vance's men on the east bank of Brice's Creek. He pulled out after receiving Vance's order to retire and naturally followed the colonel's route. "When I arrived at Brice's Creek my heart sank within me," he later wrote. "An impassable creek was [in front] of me & the enemy not far from us." He also searched up and down the stream for more boats and found one large enough to handle ten men. Everyone pushed and shoved to get aboard. The tension was eased somewhat when Vance arrived with his boats. Soon nearly everyone was over Brice's Creek. Burgwyn was the last man to leave the east bank; he and a black servant rode in the last boat while swimming his horse. The crossing had taken three hours, and Federal skirmishers came into sight just as Burgwyn bid adieu to the east bank.[32]

While the regiment narrowly made good its escape, the Moravian band was caught up in the anxiety that gripped New Bern. The musicians heard the heavy thud of artillery to the south while they waited with their baggage at the railroad depot. No word of the regiment's fate arrived all day, but the artillery sounded again the next morning, March 15, as Burnside cautiously approached New Bern. Julius Linebach knew it was time to get out of town. The musicians took a train to Goldsboro, where they stayed overnight, then retraced their way back to Kinston, where Branch's defeated army was assembling thirty-five miles from New Bern.[33]

The band reached Kinston just in time to meet the regiment, which had marched by way of Trenton Court House to bypass New Bern. The men pushed on "night and day," according to Vance, "stopping at no time for rest or sleep more than four hours." They had only the clothes on their backs and a few guns. The band walked out to greet them and filled the air with "Dixie," causing Vance to cry with emotion, when the 26th reached Kinston on March 16. The rest of Branch's command limped into town, and encampments were created in the surrounding countryside.[34]

The battle of New Bern was a disaster for the Confederacy, but the 26th North Carolina had performed well under difficult circumstances. The left wing had fired at least twenty rounds during the battle, the center had let fly at least ten rounds, and the regiment had stopped a Federal force three times its size. Vance found only one man who deserted his post in the redans before the order to retreat was issued. More than a month later two privates of Company D were court-martialed for cowardice at New Bern. One was "drummed out of service," but the other returned to duty by July. The regiment lost 9 killed, 9 wounded, 1 wounded and captured, and 71 missing, a total of 91 men. Four of the wounded returned to duty, while 2 others died of their injuries. Fifty of the captured were exchanged to resume duty in the regiment, 6 died in captivity, and 15 were released to reenter civilian life. The regiment's material losses were enormous. Most of its camp equipment and the personal belongings of its members were captured or destroyed by the Yankees.[35]

A change of commanders took place following the disastrous battle. Branch was demoted to brigade command and Brig. Gen. Samuel G. French took over the District of the Pamlico. Fresh troops were rapidly shifted from other areas of North Carolina, and the 26th found itself in a newly created brigade commanded by Brig. Gen. Robert Ransom. It included the 24th, 25th, 35th, 48th, and 49th, all North Carolina regiments.[36]

Members of the 26th tried to restore their spirits in the wake of the defeat. "I see no reason why we should be in the least downcast or disheartened," asserted Burgwyn. "The Yankees did not fight well & are no match for our men if properly led." Vance also tried to spread the word that his men were ready to fight again. "I believe they would every one follow me into the jaws of certain death if I lead the way," he crowed. It is possible that Vance was right. W. E. Setser felt pugnacious right after the battle: "we ar ready for the blasted thing again. . . . they may over pour us, but they cant Scear us."[37]

Vance supervised the election of Capt. Nathaniel P. Rankin of Company F to replace Carmichael as major, but his most pressing problem was to resupply the regiment. A flood of donations from well-wishers all over the state came to Kinston; in fact, so much clothing arrived that Vance informed the newspapers on March 26 that no more was needed. He also made certain that the men expressed their gratitude to all by printing in the *Raleigh North Carolina Standard* the names of each donor and the articles they contributed. Company officers filed requisitions to obtain equipment that was not available on the home front. Canteen straps, shoes, jackets, trousers, haversacks, knapsacks, and caps eventually were drawn from Confederate military stores to complete the regiment's refit.[38]

The strategic picture around Kinston settled into a dismal stalemate. Burnside diverted his force toward Fort Macon and Elizabeth City, canceling the anticipated attack on Goldsboro. With no Yankee advance on the horizon, the regiment addressed the reenlistment problem that had vexed its rank and file for months. The soldiers of the 26th North Carolina were still grumbling about the scarcity of furloughs and continued to cite this as their major cause for not signing the reenlistment papers. A good proportion of the men had never been home since they joined the army. The time for hesitation came to an end on April 16, when the government passed a conscript law. Under its provisions all men in the regiment who did not voluntarily reenlist were drafted into the Confederate army for further service. There was widespread "ranting about the tyrannical 'conscription bill'" among the rank and file at first, according to Henry Clay Albright. He could not decide if the act would ruin the Confederacy or serve as the "basis of our Independence." A member of Company K put the best face possible on this development, however, when he wrote a long letter to the Wadesboro *North Carolina Argus*: "The Conscript Law produces very little effect here. All cheerfully submit to it as a military necessity, and are more determined than ever, by the help of God, to make short work with old Abe." Any dissatisfaction among the regimental members was muted as everyone acquiesced to the inevitable. Vance helped to convince the men to accept their fate. He was such a persuasive speaker that other officers asked him to talk to their commands as well.[39]

The excitement of holding new elections for company and regimental officers helped to divert attention from the draft. The rank and file of each company elected their officers on April 21. Some incumbents retained their positions, but others "were thrown over-board" and left for home. Noncommissioned officers were appointed based on the recommendation of company captains. All company officers held elections for regimental officers on April 22. Vance had no trouble retaining his commission with a unanimous vote. Lt. George C. Underwood, an early historian of the regiment, stated that "Colonel Vance was always most popular with his men. He sought and obtained to the fullest extent the love of his soldiers, was always solicitous of their welfare and comfort, leaving chiefly to his second in command matters of drill and discipline. At no time was there any doubt as to his reelection."[40]

Burgwyn, however, was nearly replaced as lieutenant colonel. A considerable amount of dissatisfaction had been building because the young officer shouldered the responsibility of training and disciplining the regiment. "'I always found him strict in camp,'" recalled Sgt. Thomas J. Cureton of Company B, "'so much so, that up to the battle of New Bern he was very unpopular, and I often heard the men say if they ever got into a fight with him what they would do, etc., et.'" But that insistence on discipline stood the regiment well in the heat of battle. He earned the "entire confidence of his men and was their pride and love" because of his performance at that battle. Yet a "great deal of trickery & electioneering" took place for the lieutenant colonelcy, and Burgwyn had to rise from a sickbed to campaign for reelection. Lt. James S. Kendall of Company K was convinced to run against Burgwyn by an officer who wanted the captaincy of that company. Kendall did not want to oppose Burgwyn, but his ambition got the better of his judgment. He was "completely bamboozled by men who pretended to be his friends" and sheepishly confessed it to the lieutenant colonel. "I was completely disgusted myself," Burgwyn wrote home, "that in a matter where life

& death & what is even more to be valued reputation is at stake men should allow electioneering tricks to influance them." Kendall saved some face by being elected major instead, but his term of service was brief. Citing poor relations with the other members of the regimental field and staff, he offered his resignation on July 21 and died of yellow fever two months later. This led to John Thomas Jones's election to the majority in September.[41]

The regiment's reorganization was complete by the end of April, but Vance continued to push his scheme to form a legion. Promising to recruit the extra men within thirty days, he sent notices to newspapers across North Carolina offering a bounty of $100. "The best arms and equipments to be had in the Confederacy will be furnished. Recruits will be received singly or by companies. Turn out, and let's make short work with Abe." But Vance's efforts were stymied by state officials. Adj. Gen. James G. Martin was unwilling to cooperate because Vance had bypassed his office and had appealed to the Confederate government in his efforts to obtain permission to raise the legion. Martin refused to let Vance use state facilities to assemble and organize his recruits, and the colonel was unable to get a leave of absence to meet these men. This effectively killed his effort, for the thirty-day deadline arrived and Vance had collected the rolls of only four companies. An appeal to Secretary of War George W. Randolph and even to Gen. Robert E. Lee, who was serving as President Jefferson Davis's military adviser in Richmond, fell on deaf ears. Those men who had answered Vance's call were sent to other units, and the legion came to naught. Some newspapers criticized Vance's scheme to raise a legion, arguing that it was done merely to raise his reputation for a possible run at the governorship that summer.[42]

These furtive efforts at the top rank of the regiment's command structure had no effect on the Moravian band, which worked for the brigade and the community nearly as much as for the 26th. It performed for other units and for many civilian visitors to the camps. Mickey's musicians even staged three concerts to packed houses in Kinston to raise more than $420 for the military hospitals in town. Julius Linebach remembered these days near Kinston as "perhaps, the most pleasant time of all our army life." The musicians performed an *Aufblasen*, or blowing up, before dawn on Easter morning. It was traditional among Moravians to blast a festival day into daylight with chorales played by a brass ensemble. This was done to remind the community of the "spiritual nature of the day." In this and other ways Mickey's band was the descendant of the German *Stadtpfeiffer*, or town pipers. In the old country, brass ensembles like his band "announced special services, welcomed visitors, announced deaths, accompanied hymn singing at outdoor services and funerals, and marked events of note throughout the community." This heritage splendidly prepared the musicians for their present role, for these services to the civilian community closely paralleled their function in the army.[43]

In addition to restoring its stock of supplies, the 26th North Carolina recruited its ranks while at Kinston. From March 20 to 30, 114 men enlisted, and another 90 recruits joined in April and May. "You have no idea how much better it is to have a full regiment than a small incomplete battalion," Burgwyn informed his mother. "With 1000 men in line each one feels that he is to a considerable extent protected & aided. He is sure that no individual in a smaller regiment . . . can have his chances & hence feels much more capable of victorious effort."[44]

An unusual development caused ripples of excitement throughout the regimental camp when it was discovered that one of the new recruits streaming into Kinston was a woman. Sarah Malinda Pritchard had married William McKesson (Keith) Blalock in April 1861. Both were avowed Unionists from Caldwell County where they lived near Grandfather Mountain. Vance had met Blalock and his foster father in 1860, which probably accounted for Keith's decision to join the 26th North Carolina. Self-preservation rather than Southern patriotism was his motive. Keith wanted to avoid the draft, so he planned to volunteer, desert at the first opportunity, and make his way to Federal lines. Malinda decided to go with him. Whether Keith knew of this beforehand is uncertain, but she disguised herself as Keith's brother and enlisted as Samuel Blalock. Another recruit, James D. Moore, discovered the secret on the way to the rendezvous camp near Raleigh. Moore had previously served in the 26th North Carolina but had been discharged because of a stiff knee joint. Now he was ready to rejoin the regiment but decided to keep the Blalocks' secret; Malinda later said Keith had threatened him with physical violence if he informed on them. All three reached Company F on March 20. Sam was listed as sixteen years of age, 130 pounds, five feet, four inches tall, with dark hair. She managed to maintain her disguise by sleeping in the same tent with her "brother" and refusing to place herself in any situation where someone might detect her identity.

Yet the couple's plan failed. Keith developed a hernia and a great impatience to leave the Rebel army after only one month in camp. To further his chances of a medical discharge, he deliberately rubbed his body with poison sumac to create a terrible rash. The surgeons did not examine the rash closely, fearing it might be contagious. He was released on April 20; Sam suddenly announced to Capt. Joseph R. Ballew and to Colonel Vance that she was a woman and also received a discharge. Word quickly spread through the regimental camp and with it a lot of risque gossip. The woman soldier, Henry Clay Albright told his sister, "went to the creek the other day where some 500 were bathing and saw them cut their shines. I could tell you many other things she saw while here that would

Sarah Malinda Blalock. She served for one month in Company F, 26th North Carolina, under the alias Samuel Blalock to be with her husband, Keith Blalock. After their discharge, the couple fought as Unionist guerrillas in the mountains of North Carolina and Tennessee for the remainder of the war. (Miscellaneous Photos, SHC-UNC)

tickle any broad brim no matter how morose he might be." The couple went home to the mountains and began a wild life of marauding and attacking pro-Confederate residents in western North Carolina for the remainder of the war.[45]

Late in the regiment's stay at Kinston, Vance was offered the opportunity to reenter politics, a career he had merely put on hold when the war began. Supporters from all over the state began to clamor for his candidacy to fill the governor's chair. "You can do more for the Cause—and for the State—in the Executive Office than you can in the field," wrote Henry Watkins Miller, a member of the House of Commons from Wake County. "Your election is certain—there is great enthusiasm for you." Vance responded with an open letter to the *Fayetteville Observer*, explaining that he had sincerely wanted to remain in the army "until our independence was achieved." He professed to still believe that. "A true man should, however, be willing to serve wherever the public voice may assign him. If, therefore, my fellow-citizens believe that I could serve the great cause better as Governor than I am now doing, and should see proper to confer this great responsibility upon me without solicitation on my part, I should not feel at liberty to decline it, however conscious of my own unworthiness."[46]

Before the election, however, the 26th was thrown into a major campaign in Virginia and a bloody assault on the battlefield of Malvern Hill. Confederate authorities began to siphon troops from less threatened regions to reinforce the Army of Northern Virginia, now under General Lee, defending Richmond. Under Maj. Gen. George B. McClellan's cautious leadership, the Army of the Potomac had advanced along the Peninsula to the outskirts of the capital. Lee planned a bold offensive, the Seven Days campaign, to drive the Yankees away. The 26th received a telegram on the morning of June 18 ordering it to prepare for immediate departure. Everyone was in "high spirits at the prospect of some service." Vance gave a stirring address to the regiment when he announced the order at dress parade, and it had the desired effect on Henry Clay Albright. "I don't think I deviate from the truth when I say that I felt like rushing head long to victory or death." He could hardly suppress his feelings of pride "at the prospect of being enabled to stand up for right against wrong." But the trip to Richmond was not easy. The regiment set out on June 20, endured the slow, crowded trains and a derailment, and reached Petersburg two days later. It marched across the Appomattox River to join the rest of Ransom's brigade, which had preceded Vance's men. Ransom now had the 24th, 25th, 26th, 35th, and 49th North Carolina in his command. Another, shorter train ride to Richmond followed on June 24, and the regiment bivouacked on the grounds of the state capitol for the night of June 25.[47]

Vance's regiment was called on for immediate duty. McClellan launched a small, limited offensive of his own on Wednesday, June 25, along Williamsburg Road, his primary line of advance to the capital, in order to clear Confederate pickets from a large belt of woods called Oak Grove. Ransom's brigade was attached to Maj. Gen. Benjamin Huger's division, which held this sector of the Confederate line. The fighting swayed back and forth in the strip of woods all day as McClellan pushed his picket line 600 yards forward at a cost of more than 600 casualties. Huger lost more than 400 men as well.[48]

The 26th North Carolina left the capitol on the morning of June 25 and waited a mile and a half from Oak Grove for orders. Word arrived at 2:00 P.M. for it and two other regiments to occupy a section of the Confederate entrenchments. The band members played the "Marseilles" as the regiment marched off, but Vance told them to stay behind and help the surgeons. The other two regiments moved into the trenches, but the 26th was stopped by Huger himself, who wanted Vance's men to act as a reserve. The Tar Heels stood in line behind a strip of timber for two hours while Federal artillery rounds fell about their position. When the fighting ended at dusk, the regiment was ordered to relieve the 24th North Carolina as pickets south of Williamsburg Road, but no one gave either Vance or Burgwyn adequate information about the lay of the land or where the Federals were posted. Vance took charge of the five companies on the left, and Burgwyn took command of the other five companies on the right. "The woods were full of bogs, swamps, & bamboo, briars," Burgwyn remembered, and he became completely lost after guiding his men only 200 yards.[49]

The lieutenant colonel posted his men as best he could and went in search of Vance, whose wing had become separated from his own. Burgwyn heard scattered shots from the direction of his wing just as he located Vance's men, and he raced back to find that the Federals had opened a heavy fire along the picket line. The Tar Heels saw numerous musket flashes in the inky darkness; some were even to their rear, and others seemed to be as close as ten yards. Vance's wing also was startled by this close, unexpected fire. A member of Company B wrote that the bullets were "flying Among us as thick as hale fur awhile." Part of Vance's line was posted on one side of a fence that was lined with a hedge, and the Federals were on the opposite side, poking their muskets between the rails to fire at point-blank range. The fire was not well aimed, and few North Carolinians were injured; but it shattered the morale of the regiment. Without hesitation seven of the companies broke and fled. In the pitch-black swamp they became hopelessly scattered. Vance and Burgwyn could do nothing but retire with them and try to rally the fugitives at a safe distance. Only Companies G, H, and K, under Lane's direction on the far left of Vance's line, escaped the fire and remained in position.[50]

When Ransom, who was responsible for the failure to guide Vance and Burgwyn to their posts in the first place, sent a message to counterattack and re-form the picket line, Burgwyn gathered about 100 men and blindly slashed his way forward. He was fired on again and decided to halt and hold his ground until dawn. The tension-filled night passed without further incident, and the 26th was able to re-form and hold the position so inexpertly assigned it in the first place.

The regiment lost three killed and six wounded in the confusing night action that came to be known as the fight at King's School House. No one blamed the regiment for running. The 35th North Carolina, which was assigned to relieve the 25th North Carolina on picket, suffered the same misfortune.[51]

McClellan's little sally was completely overshadowed by Lee's strike at the Union right wing, north of the Chickahominy River, on June 26. There followed a series of battles as the Federals pulled back to Gaines's Mill, where Lee's men smashed their bridgehead north of the river and convinced McClellan to retreat all the way to a convenient base on the James River. The Army of Northern Virginia hammered the retreating Yankees, but McClellan conducted a masterful withdrawal, often inflicting heavy losses on the pursuers.[52]

The 26th North Carolina played a role only in the last of the Seven Days battles. It stood picket south of Williamsburg Road on June 26, enduring a scattering fire from the nervous Federals. The next day Vance was ordered out to support a Georgia regiment on a reconnaissance toward the Federal line. It proved that the works straddling Williamsburg Road were still held in force, so the regiment was relieved by the 24th North Carolina at dusk. At least part of the 26th had occupied some unfinished trenches dug by the Yankees. They jumped out and retired 100 yards to the rear before the Federals suddenly opened a heavy fire in their direction, wounding three Tar Heels. Vance was incensed that his men would be subjected to this fire when their backs were turned, and he lost his temper. The colonel ordered his men to race back to the trenches. He then stepped out in front of the works, waved his cap at the Federals, and challenged them "to come on, that he was ready for them." Of course, no attack was on the way. After a few minutes Vance ordered the men to the rear for a much-deserved rest.[53]

More picket duty awaited the regiment on the evening of June 28, but the apparent stalemate along Williamsburg Road soon changed. The men were ordered forward at dawn on June 29 and found the Federal camp empty of men but still filled with standing tents. Burgwyn quickly re-formed his wing after it crossed the earthwork so no one could leave the ranks and plunder the camp, but Vance allowed his men to roam about when they came upon the scene. "Our boys were eager to gather relics, and nearly all have something by which to remember the Yankees," reported Lt. Sidney P. Dula.[54]

Huger's division now set out in pursuit. The 26th left at 10:00 A.M. and bivouacked several miles down the Charles City Road that night. The march resumed on the morning of June 30, a day that saw two important battles, Glendale and White Oak Swamp, take place within hearing but out of reach of Ransom's brigade. The Confederates failed to stop McClellan's retreat or cut off a portion of his powerful army in either engagement. Huger's men found evidence of the Union retreat as they hurried along the road, for India rubber coats, knapsacks, and even some dead and wounded men were lying about. The 26th bivouacked that evening near White Oak Swamp.[55]

While Vance's regiment had been standing picket, taking Federal musket fire, and marching after the retreating enemy, its band members had been helping surgeons amputate limbs, dress wounds, chop wood, carry water, and feed the wounded of Glendale and White Oak Swamp. They had remained separated from the regiment since the morning of June 25. The Moravians scrounged some usable knapsacks from the abandoned Federal encampment along Williamsburg Road and also found sheet music, a bass tuba, and an E-flat alto horn abandoned along the road by the Federals. Julius Linebach thought the horn had a better sound than the one he had taken from home.[56]

The Seven Days campaign reached its climax on Tuesday, July 1, and the 26th played a direct role in it. The Federals established a strong defensive position at Malvern Hill, only a mile north of the James River, on an open plateau protected by Western Run on the east and Turkey Run on the west. The plateau was about sixty feet high; but its slope was gentle, and the Rebels would be exposed most of the way up. Only a few belts of trees were located here and there to frame the scene. The position was packed with thirty-seven guns halfway up the slope. Brig. Gen. George W. Morell's division of the Fifth Corps was to the left of Quaker Road, and Brig. Gen. Darius N. Couch's division of the Fourth Corps occupied the right. The two divisions would support the artillery concentration and bear the brunt of Rebel assaults.[57]

Despite its brilliant success to date, Lee's army had suffered heavy losses and much confusion in its pursuit of McClellan. It had its worst day of the campaign on July 1. Lee tried to bombard the Union position to soften it, but the Federal guns reigned supreme. Then uncoordinated assaults were sent in, and every one was repulsed with heavy slaughter. Ransom came up in time to take part in this tragic drama. The 26th left its bivouac early on the morning of July 1 and crossed the Glendale battlefield about noon. It was at Malvern Hill by 3:00 P.M. and took position in a belt of trees that straddled Western Run, just to the west of Quaker Road. The futile Confederate bombardment was still in progress, and the infantry attacks began some two hours later. Several brigades were fed into the escalating battle in piecemeal fashion, littering the open, ascending plain with more bodies. No one could get close enough to the roaring artillery to break the line. Morell's and Couch's infantrymen also added the weight of their musketry to the cannon fire.[58]

Ransom made one of the last efforts of the day. At 7:00 P.M., about an hour be-

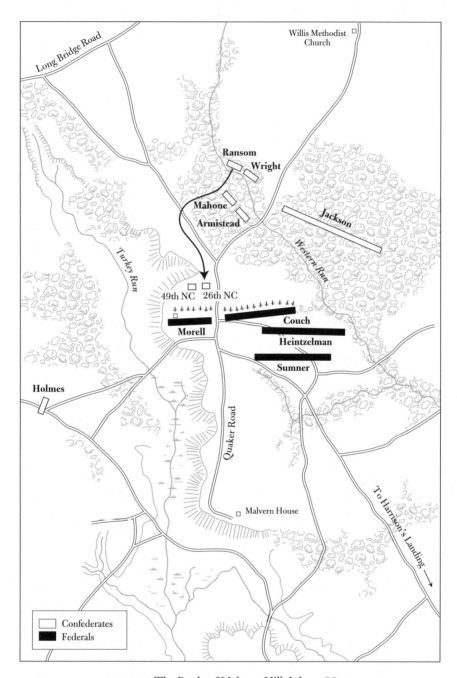

Long Bridge Road

Willis Methodist Church

Ransom
Wright

Mahone
Armistead

Jackson

Turkey Run

Western Run

49th NC   26th NC

Morell

Couch

Heintzelman

Sumner

Holmes

Quaker Road

Malvern House

To Harrison's Landing →

Confederates
Federals

MAP 1.2 The Battle of Malvern Hill, July 1, 1862

fore sunset, he sent the 24th North Carolina ahead as a vanguard and then accompanied the 26th and Col. Stephen D. Ramseur's 49th North Carolina as they brought up the rear. All the regiments moved at the double-quick to the extreme right of this seething battlefield. Many stragglers were retiring from the failed attacks, "telling everywhere their regiments had been cut to pieces," recalled Burgwyn.

Ransom stopped the 26th and 49th in the shade of the trees that bordered the west side of the plateau. Here, some 200 yards from the guns, regimental officers dressed their ranks and prepared for the final push. The foliage offered little shelter from the rain of shells that were "bursting over our heads & cutting down trees & lopping off huge limbs." Lt. Isaac Augustus Jarratt of Company C was awed by these projectiles that were "tearing through the trees" and wondered that anyone survived them. Burgwyn took out his watch and timed the discharges of the distant cannons, counting forty-eight in one minute and forty-nine in another.[59]

Orders were shouted, and the two regiments started out just as twilight began to descend. They received no directed fire for at least 100 yards, but then the Federal gunners spotted the two regiments and began to target them. Morell's infantrymen also saw them and prepared to deliver vollies of rifle fire in their direction. Vance walked well in front of his regiment as it encountered the human debris of previous attacks. This ground had already been traversed by the other regiments of Ransom's brigade, and many dead and wounded Tar Heels lay about. Some of the injured rose on one arm, waved their hats, and shouted encouragement to the 26th. Gus Jarratt felt a surge of patriotic feeling from this selfless act; "the fire of a thousand cannon would not have stopped the Regt then," he thought, but the weight of ordnance was incredible. Burgwyn described it later: "One shell burst immediately over me, and the way the Minie balls whistled was anything but pleasant." Henry Clay Albright thought the "balls fell thicker and a damned sight faster than any hail. I expected to be visited by one every minute." In the growing darkness, made worse by the thick smoke, some men in front of the brigade broke and retreated through the ranks of the 26th. This cut off several men of Company K on the extreme right wing. They fought with the 24th North Carolina for the remainder of the battle.[60]

Despite these difficulties, the two regiments managed to get within forty yards of the artillery line; Ransom believed that some men reached within twenty yards of the guns. They could do no more than that. The Tar Heels were compelled to stop, but they gamely fired a few rounds at the mass of Union metal and blue uniforms, aiming at the muzzle flashes that appeared in the dark. Then they plopped to the ground for cover. The darkness enabled them to stay close to the

Malvern Hill, looking toward the advance of the 26th North Carolina from the Union artillery line (Courtesy of the author)

enemy without enormous casualties. Even though the artillery continued to fire for another hour, the projectiles flew over their heads.[61]

Ransom finally ordered the two regiments to retire quietly at 10:00 P.M. The Federals retreated to Harrison's Landing on the James River that night, having given Lee his worst beating of the campaign. The 26th bivouacked near the starting point of its attack. "With lips parched, with thirst & bodies cold from the evaporating perspiration," the men drank from Western Run and rolled into their blankets by 2:00 A.M., but the wounded were scattered all along the line of attack. Burgwyn ordered forty men to collect them. Pitiful calls for help could be heard all night. It would be dawn before they were gathered and tended to by the overworked surgeons, even with the help of the Moravian musicians. "I was standing near our Surgeon as he was dressing the wounds," recalled Sam Mickey, "and was ready to do any thing he called for; several times, while Dr was working upon the wounds I thought he would drop asleep." Back on the battlefield, Gus Jarratt was so tired he "never slept sounder than I did there amongst the dead & wounded."[62]

Three of Ransom's five regimental leaders were wounded, and his command suffered a total of 499 casualties, the highest brigade loss in Lee's army that day. The 26th North Carolina lost 62 men—7 killed, 53 wounded, and 2 captured. Yet the Tar Heels were very proud of the part they played in the failed attack.

THE 26TH NORTH CAROLINA

Vance informed a friend at home, "My regiment acted gloriously. . . . They say it was the most terrific & bloody charge of the war, but was ill advised and murderous in its results." The morning of July 2 revealed a battlefield littered with bodies. "The dead reminded one more of the sheaves behind the reaper than anything I can compare it to," remarked Henry Clay Albright. W. E. Setser thought the battlefield "was a terable Sight to see," with "mens arms and legs and head shot of. they we a lying on won another. Some was Shot all to peases with canon Balls. the horses was ling thick." Yet Setser was proud of his unit's performance, crowing to relatives at home, "you art to a saw the old twenty six Stand up to the yankee Scoundrels."[63]

A cold rain set in on July 2 as the regimental officers of Ransom's brigade collected their men, scattered by the late evening assault. "The rainy weather & horrible sufferings which I have seen have made me low spirited to day," wrote Burgwyn to his father. The wandering band members rejoined their unit on July 3 just before Ransom made a short march south to observe McClellan's army at Harrison's Landing, where the men were subjected to sporadic artillery fire from the Federal gunboats. With no prospect of further action, Lee began to shift much of his army to other points. Orders reached the regiment on July 6 to march immediately to Drewry's Bluff, some twenty miles to the northwest. It was a commanding spot on the south bank of the James River about six miles below Richmond where heavy batteries had been built to protect the city against Yankee gunboats. The oppressive heat was made worse by Ransom's refusal to allow the men to stop so they could fill their canteens at convenient wells along the route. The marching was so rigorous that Cpl. George Welch of Company C asked Gus Jarratt to tell his father that "his feet have not got quite as much skin on them as he would like to have." Ransom bivouacked that night seven miles east of the James River and crossed a pontoon bridge on July 7.[64]

Drewry's Bluff seemed like an "oasis in the desert" to the "half worn out, famished soldiers." After a hurried rail journey from Kinston, two weeks of campaigning, two skirmishes, and one deadly assault, the regiment welcomed the rest. Soon, however, the men were put to work constructing fortifications to protect the river batteries. Sickness once again struck the 26th, and many of the afflicted were transferred from the Richmond hospitals to facilities at Lynchburg, Petersburg, and elsewhere, "where their wants may be better provided for," according to a member of the regiment who wrote for the *North Carolina Standard* under the pen name "Chatham." It was more likely that Lee's anticipated offensive to the north of the capital led the authorities to make room for battlefield casualties. Chatham also was happy to hear reports that conscripts would soon fill the ranks of the 26th, and he expressed guarded support for this policy. "Regretting the necessity of the law and protesting against it for fear that it will be used as a precedent, yet the blood of our fallen comrades, the desolated fields, deserted villages and plundered dwellings appeal to them to grasp the deadly firelock and come on to the rescue."[65]

The regiment was transferred to Petersburg after a few days of digging at Drewry's Bluff. Arriving on July 27, the men worked on the fortifications south of the Appomattox River as Vance began to deal with events that would dramatically change his career. He had allowed himself to be a candidate for governor, and the election was scheduled for August 7. The race became a contest between those North Carolinians who had supported secession before the firing on Fort Sumter and those who, like Vance, had hesitated. The Democrats called themselves the Confederate Party and nominated William Johnston, an "original Secessionist." They sought to retain control of both the governor's office and the state legislature. Whigs and pre-Sumter Unionists, led by William W. Holden, editor of the *Raleigh Standard*, called themselves the Conservative Party and nominated Vance. Neither candidate campaigned but let their partisan supporters fight the battle through speeches and newspaper editorials. While the Confederate Party argued that Vance's election would be a signal to the Yankees that North Carolina was lukewarm in its support of the Confederacy, the Conservatives tapped into popular discontent about the draft and President Davis's suspension of the writ of habeas corpus.[66]

Members of the 26th pushed hard for their colonel. Chatham, who served in either Company E or Company G, praised Vance's conduct at Malvern Hill. "Our gallant Colonel is all right, though ever exposed to the hottest of the enemy's fire, and by his bouyant courage and dauntless bravery has the entire confidence of the officers and soldiers under his command." Lt. Sidney P. Dula of Company I offered his commander the strongest endorsement: "Col. Vance is one of the men who always says, 'come, boys' and not 'go,' as a great many do, always keeping themselves out of danger. A braver man never lived—and he has a heart in his bosom that feels for the poor soldier, and he is ever ready to do any thing and every thing he can, to render his men pleasant and agreeable. We all love him, and will die round him if need be."[67]

Vance used the regimental band to enhance his electoral prospects by giving it a furlough to go home until after the election was over. He told them the good news on July 10 and paid their wages as well. The band traveled by rail to High Point, the station nearest Salem, and stopped three miles from their hometown early on the morning of July 14. Sam Mickey sent word to have the bandwagon brought out so they could arrive in style. It showed up with some relatives of band member W. H. Hall, who brought the sad news that his child had just died. His

26th North Carolina Regimental Band. This ferrotype was taken in Salem during its first furlough, July 14–August 14, 1862. Julius A. Linebach is second from right, and bandleader Samuel T. Mickey is far left. William Henry Hall, whose youngest son, "Gussie," died just before the band reached Salem, is fourth from left. Lewis Augustine Hauser, fifth from left, died the following November, the band's only fatality during the war. (Collection of Old Salem, Old Salem/Museum of Early Southern Decorative Arts, Winston-Salem, N.C.)

colleagues later played at the child's funeral. The Moravian musicians voted for Vance while at home, even though they were sorry to see him leave the regiment.[68]

Vance was sure he would "get a large majority of the army vote," even though some officers were politicking for his opponent. This was true even of the units in Ransom's brigade, for many officers in the 49th North Carolina refused to allow a group of 232 conscripts to vote when they expressed support for Vance. The soldiers cast their ballots on July 31; their votes were tallied by three men of each company, and regimental officers were responsible for certifying the returns. The civilian electorate cast their ballots on August 7. The next day Vance wrote with a mixture of relief and expectation to his wife. "I have every assurance that I will be governor by a large majority, but it is not certain — From 38 Regiments in the army I have recd more than two to one." His prediction was right. The statewide tally gave Vance 52,833 votes against Johnston's 20,174. Vance carried all but twelve counties in the state, and the Conservatives also gained control of the legislature. He received more than 75 percent of the 15,374 votes cast by Tar Heel soldiers. Only 7 of 700 votes cast by the 26th went for Johnston.[69]

Vance had done well as commander of the 26th North Carolina, but Burgwyn accurately pointed out his shortcomings: his refusal to be hard on the men even when it was necessary, his lack of interest in administrative detail, and his ignorance of proper sanitary conditions in camp. Yet Vance had the support of his men, who expected their leader to be a good fellow as well as a good soldier. They appreciated his leniency and admired his bravery in battle. Some members, such as Gus Jarratt, believed the regiment could not "fare near so well as it did while he was with us." Vance offered his resignation from the army on August 12 by assuring Confederate adjutant general Samuel Cooper that his "efforts to strengthen the Government in the prosecution of the war for liberty & independence" would be as tireless as his efforts to command the 26th North Carolina.[70]

The regimental band returned from its furlough on August 14 to the regiment's new encampment at Dunn's Hill, just north of the Appomattox River. Vance gave his farewell address to the 26th on the evening of August 15. More than 1,400 other soldiers joined the unit to honor Vance as he was presented with a ceremonial sword by the regimental officers. In the words of one who heard his speech, Vance, "with his usual truthfulness and sincerety, scorned to hold out any false promises to those who had been under his command, telling them plainly, that all they could expect was 'War! War!! War!!! Fight till the end.'" John Thomas Jones found the address so moving it "brought the tear to many an eye that had long been a stranger to such a thing."[71]

Vance left the regiment on August 16 for Raleigh and arrived there the next day. The new governor was worn out with illness. He needed rest in order to write his inaugural address, and he set out for two weeks "in our mountain air" at Buncombe County. Vance had done very well in his one year of military service, using the 26th as a springboard to the state's highest political office. He had come to the regiment a neophyte soldier and left it a celebrity. Years after the war John Randolph Lane remembered how Vance impressed him when they had met in 1861. "He had no appearance in the world of a soldier; his hair was long and flowing over his shoulders, and he was wearing a little sealskin coat, from which I judged him to be a Chaplain. He had not long been absent from the hustings of Western North Carolina, and had but little experience in war as Captain in the Fourteenth Regiment." He helped to mold the 26th North Carolina into what Lane called "almost a perfect instrument of war, devoted to their commander." Vance knew little of drill or discipline, shoving that responsibility onto Burgwyn's shoulders; his contribution to the regiment was in firming up its morale, inspiring the self-confidence of the men, and giving them a colorful and decisive figure to look up to.[72]

On August 17, just before he left Raleigh to recuperate in his mountain home,

Vance recommended Burgwyn to replace him as colonel. Describing the young planter aristocrat as "brave & intrepid in battle, but firm & judicious in the exercise of discipline," Vance also noted that he was "possessed moreover of considerable talent as an engineer." After pining for a full year for a command of his own, Burgwyn was on the verge of realizing his ambition.[73]

Chapter 2

Pettigrew's Brigade

Burgwyn would not have an easy time securing his new command. He was on sick leave when a storm of controversy broke. Ransom told Vance that he had no intention of recommending Burgwyn for the colonelcy, "on account of your age," reported John Thomas Jones to the lieutenant colonel. "He said he did not intend to have any more boys to command regiments in his Brigade." Ransom's motives were unclear. Jones believed that he "may have said this in one of his frets without meaning anything." Perhaps Ransom was jealous of his twenty-year-old subordinate. He was thirty-four years old, a graduate of the West Point class of 1850, and had served on the frontier before the war. Perhaps Ransom was stung by the fact that neither Burgwyn or many members of the 26th respected him. There was a widespread feeling that he was too strict in his discipline, ungenerous in his personal relations with subordinates, and a poor leader in the Seven Days campaign. For whatever hidden motives that might have existed, Ransom refused to consider Burgwyn a colleague.[1]

The officers of the 26th rallied to Burgwyn's defense. A committee pressed their case with Ransom on August 21, but he refused to yield. Ransom wanted Lt. Col. Thomas Ruffin of the 1st North Carolina Cavalry to become colonel of the 26th. Jones was beside himself. "For God's sake come to us as soon as you can," he wrote Burgwyn. "I wish you to resist to the last this usurpation of power. I am too angry to act. It is my intention to resign as soon as Ruffin arrives, if he should. I know nothing of him, have nothing against him, but to see you treated with such unheard of injustice is more than I am willing to submit to."[2]

The controversy came to a climax when Burgwyn returned to camp and had a long talk with Ransom on August 24. The brigade leader was forced to admit that the Conscript Act prevented him from denying the regiment its choice of officers. Burgwyn was relieved to hear this, and the conversation immediately turned to separating the regiment from Ransom's brigade. The lieutenant colonel arranged for a petition to be signed by all officers of the 26th requesting a transfer, "to relieve Ransom of a regiment, which he did not want & themselves of a Genrl. who was quite as distasteful to them." The transfer was approved, and Burgwyn was informed on August 27 that his regiment was to be shifted to a North Carolina brigade formerly commanded by Brig. Gen. James G. Martin and now led by Brig. Gen. James Johnston Pettigrew.[3]

Fortunately the regiment found a new and happy home. Pettigrew had just returned to duty after a severe wound suffered at the battle of Seven Pines the previous May. He had spent two months as a prisoner of the Federals and returned to duty in late summer. Now he took command of a brigade of newly raised North Carolina units formerly commanded by Martin, who also was adjutant general of North Carolina. It consisted of the 17th, 44th, 47th, and 52nd regiments. While the brigade was camped at Proctor's Station, halfway between Petersburg and the capital, Martin returned to North Carolina to wrap up some business relating to his adjutant general's office. He took the 17th North Carolina, which was commanded by his brother, with him. This left a vacancy in the brigade that the 26th could fill. There also was some discussion about adding a fifth regiment, the 57th North Carolina, which was scattered at Richmond, Drewry's Bluff, Salisbury, and Proctor's Station, but that never happened.[4]

The 26th separated itself from Ransom when the brigade moved out of its camp on August 26. The Moravian band played a serenade to send the former comrades off, and Ransom had the good grace to raise his hat as a goodbye to the regiment. Few men in the 26th missed the brigade leader due to his "severe discipline and rough manner," according to Julius Linebach, even though Gus Jarratt thought Ransom "had been very kind" to the regiment. The 26th stayed in camp one more might and on August 27 marched in the opposite direction, crossing the pontoon bridge over the James and heading for Pettigrew's camp near Drewry's Bluff. A few days after joining the brigade, Pettigrew moved his regiments south to within three miles of Petersburg and established Camp French on Prince George Court House Road.[5]

Pettigrew offered a stark contrast to Ransom. A product of a North Carolina planter family, as was Burgwyn, Pettigrew was born on Independence Day 1828 on one of three family plantations near Lake Phelps in Tyrrell County, deep in the coastal plain of North Carolina. He attended Bingham's Academy near Hillsborough and entered the University of North Carolina at Chapel Hill at age four-

James Johnston Pettigrew. Pictured here in civilian dress, Pettigrew was a scholarly, sensitive man who was widely loved for his warm personality and his immense accomplishments before the war. (Pettigrew Family Papers, SHC-UNC)

teen. His work there was outstanding, and he earned a mark of "excellent" in literally every subject for four years. Pettigrew graduated as valedictorian in 1847.

The young aristocrat's pre–Civil War life was unusually full. He was appointed a professor at the National Observatory by President James K. Polk, another graduate of the University of North Carolina, who had visited the campus in 1847 and had heard Pettigrew's valedictory address. Pettigrew left the observatory to study law and spent two years in Europe, where he took courses at the University of Berlin and traveled to all corners of the continent. He moved to Charleston, South Carolina, after he returned to America. His intellectual achievements were enormous. Proficient in four European languages, he also taught himself Hebrew and Arabic. He had impressive mathematical skills as well, was an accomplished military engineer, studied law, served in the South Carolina House of Representatives (where he strongly argued against reopening the slave trade), and visited Cuba to take part in an expected revolt against Spanish rule that never took place. A lifelong bachelor, he found time to serve in the South Carolina militia and traveled back to Europe in 1859 when war broke out in northern Italy. Pettigrew offered his services to the Italians, who were fighting for independence from their Austrian masters, but the conflict ended before he could take part in it. This second journey to Europe resulted in his most famous publication, *Notes on Spain and the Spaniards in the Summer of 1859, with a Glance at Sardinia*. Published in 1861, it was a warm, enthusiastic appraisal of Spanish culture.

Described by a modern-day author as "slender, fair-complexioned, with piercing eyes and a conspicuously high forehead," Pettigrew also was modest to a fault. He lived his ascetic life with a "medieval intensity," yet he quickly took an intimate part in the war. Pettigrew was made chief military aid to South Carolina governor Francis W. Pickens and later was elected colonel of the 1st South Carolina Rifles. He delivered a message to the Union garrison of Fort Sumter on December 27, 1860, and occupied Castle Pinckney, an abandoned Federal fort in the middle of Charleston harbor, later that day. He witnessed the bombardment of Fort Sumter on April 12 and soon after volunteered his services as a private in the Hampton Legion of South Carolina, then stationed in Virginia. His reputation led to his election as colonel of the 22nd North Carolina in August 1861.[6]

Pettigrew took his regiment to Richmond and brought along Louis G. Young, a South Carolina friend who had worked with him during the Fort Sumter crisis. Young had been a Charleston cotton merchant before the war and had strongly supported secession even before South Carolina left the Union. He became Pettigrew's most loyal friend and subordinate. While in Virginia, Pettigrew planned and built river batteries along the Potomac and was recommended for promotion to brigadier general, but he declined the commission because he believed he had not earned it. His acquaintance Mary Chesnut criticized him as being "too high and mighty" to accept preferment in his career. Pettigrew finally accepted a commission as brigadier general and command of a brigade on March 20. It consisted of the 22nd North Carolina, 2nd Arkansas Battalion, 35th Georgia, and 47th Virginia, and Pettigrew rigorously trained it. "Gen. Pettigrew knows every-

Brig. Gen. James Johnston Pettigrew. Pictured here in uniform, Pettigrew organized the brigade and led it longer than anyone else. (Pettigrew Family Papers, SHC-UNC)

thing about it," thought staff member John Wetmore Hinsdale of the drills, and "is teaching the brigade very fast."[7]

Pettigrew's first campaign was nearly his last. He went into action at Seven Pines on the Fair Oaks sector of the battlefield. Brig. Gen. John Sedgwick's division of the Federal Second Corps held this area, and it blasted every Confed-

PETTIGREW'S BRIGADE

erate attempt to dislodge the line, which was posted in a thick stand of timber. As dusk slowly descended on this bloody field, Pettigrew encountered Brig. Gen. Willis A. Gorman's brigade. Entering the woods to determine the exact position of the Federals, Pettigrew was alone, for his staff officers were busy hurrying his regiments. A rifle ball sliced through his throat and shoulder only ten minutes after the new brigadier plunged into the woods. Pettigrew dismounted but was already so weak from loss of blood that he needed help to lie down. Several privates tried to carry him away, but he refused, telling them to get back in line. Other men found him apparently dying; his eyes were fixed, and he was nearly insensible. The brigade was driven back soon afterward, and the Federals occupied the spot. Staff officer Louis G. Young was desperate to find his stranded commander. He tried to rally a handful of men to make a raid into the woods, but no one responded. They "could not stand up against the terrific storm of shot & shell which swept the wood & all the practicable approaches to it." The only option left to him was to ask for a flag of truce to search the woods, but Young remembered that Pettigrew had earlier told him it would not be proper to do such a thing: "no intercourse of this kind should be ever had with such an enemy as that we are now at war with."[8]

Young assumed Pettigrew was dead, and he was devastated. Writing to Pettigrew's brother only two days after the battle, Young offered his sympathy. "But in saying this my heart bleeds and I feel that I need more consolation than I can possibly give. I loved him with an earnestness the strength of which I can not express." Pettigrew's slave servant Peter was disconsolate over the loss of his master and perplexed about the staff's inability to help him. According to Hinsdale, Peter "thought it very strange that they could save themselves but not their general." Young gushed out his feelings for Pettigrew in a letter to his mother. "I have lost one of my most loved friends. Gladly would I have given my life for his. You cannot tell how I grieve his loss."[9]

But Pettigrew survived. His nearly fatal wound was bandaged just in time by Col. Augustus A. Bull of the 35th Georgia. Later Pettigrew was hit in the left shoulder by a spent ball and was bayoneted in the leg when the Federals recovered the ground. He was taken to the rear by the Unionists the next morning. The ball that initially hit him entered the lower part of his throat, struck his windpipe, and passed beneath his collarbone to exit from the top of his right shoulder. It cut an artery on the way out. For nearly two weeks he was tended by Dr. William G. Gaines at his home near what would later become the battlefield of Gaines's Mill. There a number of Federal officers visited the Confederate general. Pettigrew greeted these visitors on the condition that no one bring up the subject of politics. He was later transferred to Fort Delaware near Baltimore.[10]

Pettigrew's staff learned of their general's happy fate on June 4. The Tar Heel general was ashamed of having been taken prisoner and asserted that "if he had been able and in his mind he would never have been taken." By then Brig. Gen. William D. Pender of North Carolina had arrived to take over Pettigrew's brigade. Hinsdale found him "the coldest looking man I ever saw," but he was impressed by a bullet hole in his coat. Pender kept Pettigrew's staff intact and settled in for an indefinite stay as commander.[11]

Pettigrew was exchanged on August 6 and immediately attempted to get back into the field. One of Louis G. Young's brothers saw him later that day walking to Richmond from the boat landing to see if he was fit for duty. Pettigrew was quite bitter about his treatment at the hands of the Yankees. While McClellan's officers were "generally gentlemen" and had treated him well, the Federals at Fort Delaware had offended his sensibilities. Maj. Gen. John Wool had refused to parole him and had instead locked him in a cell. Worse still, the surgeon had admitted he was incapable of treating Pettigrew's wound properly, and it had not been dressed during his entire stay at Fort Delaware.[12]

When Pettigrew returned to duty, he expected to resume his old command, but that was not to be. Pender had already led the brigade through the Seven Days and the battle of Cedar Mountain. Higher authorities had decided he deserved to remain in charge. Pettigrew was assigned to command Martin's brigade on August 12 and immediately asked for Young's services. "We shall have a fine time," he assured the South Carolinian, "but the present regiments are strangers to me, and I to them." Young was only too happy to be reunited with Pettigrew. "Genl Pender is a good officer," he informed his mother, "and no one could treat me more pleasantly than he, but he is not Genl Pettigrew, and I feel that the boredom of camp life can be more easily borne when I am again under my old Commander."[13]

Young arrived in Richmond by August 17 and began to reassemble the old staff. Some were still with Pender but eager to return, while others had already resigned and resumed civilian life. Young had a very discerning eye and recommended to Pettigrew which men had done well. As it was finally formed, the staff of Pettigrew's brigade consisted of Capt. N. Colin Hughes as assistant adjutant general, Capt. Louis G. Young as aide de camp (a position that both Young and Pettigrew preferred so that they could remain close to each other), Lt. William Blunt Shepard as volunteer aide, Capt. Campbell T. Iredell as ordnance officer, Maj. George P. Collins as quartermaster, and Maj. William J. Baker as commissary. Later in the war Capt. W. W. McCreery and Lt. Walter H. Robertson joined as inspector general and ordnance officer, respectively. Three other volunteer aides, Capt. George White, Col. Thomas Galloway, and Capt. Starke Sutton, also served later at different times. Young, who was promoted to captain, was certainly the leader of the group and Pettigrew's right-hand man.[14]

Although "still partially paralyzed" from the bayonet wound, Pettigrew's right leg was improving. Even as he tended to paperwork in his quarters at Jarratt's Hotel in Petersburg, he received treatments of electrical current from a galvanic battery to strengthen his arm. "The yankees say that it is very hard to kill the North Carolinians entirely," Pettigrew wrote to a former staff member, "and it does seem so, though they wound a great many of us. Those of us, who had the bad luck to fall into their hands are more anxious than ever to have another trial."[15]

Pettigrew preferred a command in Lee's army rather than remaining in the Richmond and Petersburg area. "It will be a great relief to leave this country," he confided to a relative. "I think with proper energy the enemy might be routed out of Suffolk and North Carolina, and yet I am certain it will not be done." Following the failed Maryland campaign, Lee authorized Pettigrew's transfer to the Army of Northern Virginia to replace Lawrence O'Bryan Branch, who had been killed at the head of his North Carolina brigade at Antietam. But Pettigrew's superiors felt he could not be spared.[16]

Pettigrew never had any doubt that his new brigade would prove to be a fine body of soldiers. It had been organized in the frenzied days after the fall of New Bern. State authorities were so shocked by Branch's defeat on March 14 that they issued a call for more units. As a result, an additional twenty-eight regiments and several battalions were organized. The 44th, 47th, and 52nd North Carolina were among them; all three were assembled between April 21 and May 19. In mid-May Adjutant General Martin was given a commission as brigadier general in the Confederate army and sent to Kinston to command a brigade consisting of the 17th, 44th, 47th, and 52nd North Carolina. He was to watch Burnside's force at New Bern while the remaining regiments in the area were shifted to reinforce the Army of Northern Virginia.[17]

James Green Martin, the first commander of what would become Pettigrew's brigade, had a distinguished career. Born in Elizabeth City, North Carolina, on the north shore of Albemarle Sound, he was a graduate of West Point and had married the granddaughter of a signer of the Declaration of Independence. He had served well in the Mexican War and had lost an arm at the battle of Churubusco. As adjutant general, Martin had worked feverishly to receive, equip, and train the state's contribution to the Confederate army. His success in mobilizing supplies of all kinds for the troops was impressive. He accepted a Confederate commission as brigadier general on May 17 and assumed his post at Kinston by early June. His brigade remained there only one month, for on June 30

Lee ordered him to bring it to Richmond. Martin arrived too late to take part in the Seven Days campaign, and in July he returned to Raleigh with the 17th North Carolina in tow, leaving Pettigrew the remaining regiments.[18]

The brigade that Martin created would be molded by Pettigrew, who put his personal stamp on the unit. The three regiments were only three months in service when Pettigrew met them. The 26th North Carolina added a much needed leavening of experience to the brigade. Later, in December 1862, the 11th North Carolina was added to the brigade's complement. It too had been in service since the early months of 1862 but lacked the combat experience of the 26th. The makeup of the brigade would not change from December 1862 until it surrendered with Lee at Appomattox.

Although it had never seen action, the 11th was filled with men who had served in North Carolina's first Civil War regiment, the 1st North Carolina Infantry. The 1st was organized on May 13, 1861, for six months of service. Its commander was Daniel Harvey Hill, and the lieutenant colonel was James H. Lane, both destined to become Confederate generals. Until it participated in the battle of Big Bethel on June 10, 1861, the regiment was primarily engaged in fortifying the Yorktown Peninsula. The North Carolina government authorized the men to inscribe "Bethel" on their flag, and soon the unit was widely known as the Bethel Regiment.[19]

The men who served in the 1st North Carolina and who later joined the 11th were forthright in describing their motivation to fight. Egbert A. Ross was eager to repel the "ruthless invader" of Southern soil. Lewis Warlick also breathed enthusiasm for the cause, even though he admitted that he would not have joined if his girlfriend had consented to marry him the previous winter. Like Ross, Warlick was incensed by the invasion of the South. He reassured his girlfriend, who finally agreed to marry him before the war ended, that he would not expose himself needlessly while answering the call of "pure patriotism." "I knew before, that a soldier's life was a hard one, exposed to many hardships and severe trials," he wrote, "but a man should not look to that when his country is invaded with thieves and lawless persons, then every man should do all in his power for the protection of his much loved country and fireside."[20]

When the 1st was mustered out on November 12, many of its veterans enlisted in other regiments, such as the 36th North Carolina, which for a time took for itself the designation of Bethel Regiment. Anyone wishing to join a successor unit to the 1st had to wait four months. The 11th North Carolina assembled at Camp Mangum near Raleigh on March 31, 1862. So many enlistees were veterans of the old 1st that the 11th was authorized to call itself the Bethel Regiment. In fact, more than half of its officers had previously served in the 1st North Carolina.

Companies A, E, and H came from Mecklenburg County, in the piedmont; Companies B and D hailed from Burke County, in the mountains; Company C was recruited from Bertie County, in the coastal plain at the head of Albemarle Sound; Company F came from Chowan County, just east of Bertie on the north shore of Albemarle Sound; Company G originated in Orange County, at the edge of the coastal plain and the piedmont; and Company K came from Buncombe County, in the mountains. Thus the regiment represented all three geographic divisions of the state. Collett Leventhorpe was elected colonel, William J. Martin became lieutenant colonel, and Egbert A. Ross was the new major.[21]

Leventhorpe came to the regiment with an impressive past. Born at Exmouth, Devonshire, England, he was the descendant of a family that traced its heritage back to the fourteenth century and was intertwined with royalty through marriage and service. Leventhorpe studied at Winchester College and served as an ensign in the Fourteenth Regiment of Foot in Ireland, the British West Indies, and Canada. He resigned as captain in 1842 and traveled to South Carolina to do business for an English company. He fell in love with a young Southern lady from Rutherfordton, North Carolina, and was encouraged by her father to finish the medical studies he had earlier begun in England. After graduating from Charleston Medical College, he married his fiancée in 1849 and became a U.S. citizen later that year.[22]

Leventhorpe immediately offered his services to the Confederacy when the war broke out and was made colonel of the 34th North Carolina. He spent the winter of 1861–62 guarding the Roanoke River at Fort Branch, near Hamilton, to protect the Weldon Railroad bridge, and he was elected colonel of the 11th on April 2, 1862. It was quite an oddity to see a British aristocrat in charge of a regiment of North Carolina farm boys. The unit's introduction to Leventhorpe was a bit rowdy. It arrayed itself on dress parade, and the adjutant informed Leventhorpe that the men were ready to receive his orders. He shouted, "The Eleventh!" in "the most powerful voice we had ever heard from human lips." The volume of the shout, the cultured accent, and the men's utter naïveté about military etiquette led them to belt out a "loud laugh" when they heard "that potent voice." But as soon as Leventhorpe was able to demonstrate his ability to command, "that laugh was never heard again."[23]

William Joseph Martin was a well-educated son of an Irish immigrant. He graduated from the University of Virginia in 1854 and became a professor of natural science at Washington College in Pennsylvania. In 1857 he moved to the University of North Carolina, where he taught chemistry, mineralogy, and geology. Martin also became involved in preparations for the upcoming war by drilling students and instructing them in all areas of the military art. He obtained

Brig. Gen. Collett Leventhorpe. English-born commander of the 11th North Carolina, Leventhorpe was severely wounded and captured at Gettysburg. He rose in rank after his exchange but was no longer associated with the brigade. He undoubtedly would have succeeded Pettigrew but for his imprisonment. (Hickerson Papers, SHC-UNC)

a leave of absence to participate in the conflict and captained Company G, 28th North Carolina, for several months before he was promoted to major of that regiment in April 1862. Soon after, the officers of the 11th North Carolina elected him lieutenant colonel.

Maj. Egbert A. Ross came from a background much less distinguished than that of either Martin or Leventhorpe. Described as "an untried boy" by Martin, he had served as captain of Company C in the first Bethel Regiment and later was killed on the first day at Gettysburg.[24]

Leventhorpe had his work cut out for him. He was startled that the Tar Heel farm boys were lax in their personal hygiene and ordered company officers to "see that their men are regular in daily ablutions. On Saturday afternoon a cleansing of the whole person should be practised." Camp sanitation was a major concern. He also tried to clean up the conversation in camp, reminding the 11th "that the use of profane language is in breach of the Articles of War, and will not be permitted by the commanding officer."[25]

The regiment left Camp Mangum in early May 1862 to garrison Wilmington. On the way it stopped at Goldsboro to arm itself with a mixture of Enfield rifle muskets and smoothbore muskets that had been shipped on the *Nashville* through the Northern blockade. Training continued without interruption in the unit's new home, Camp Davis, near Wilmington. "Our Regiment is becoming very well drilled," reported Capt. Francis W. Bird of Company C to his sister, "and I think in quite a short time we will be in a condition not to disgrace our Bethel name."[26]

Maj. Egbert A. Ross. Mortally wounded in the 11th North Carolina attack on the Union Iron Brigade at Gettysburg, Ross was considered young and inexperienced by his colleagues. (Ross Papers, SHC-UNC)

The men persevered in their guard duties despite homesickness, agreeing with Pvt. William G. Parker of Company C that army life was not pleasant but they "would be willing to endure it all for the sake of our independence. I am fearfull that the vandalls will get possession of our county." Parker, a forty-two-year-old enlistee from Bertie County, had reason to fear a Federal incursion into his family's area, for he was a slave owner. He urged his wife to hire out the slaves to make money, for he had been inundated with requests from his comrades to hire them as cooks for the army. Parker also instructed Ema to move his slaves west if the Yankees showed any signs of invading Bertie.[27]

The 11th North Carolina moved from place to place during the next several months but always remained near Wilmington. In addition to garrisoning various points, the men were often detailed to unload blockade runners when they reached the docks. Leventhorpe was made commander of the District of the Cape Fear and was given additional units so that his combined strength amounted to about 3,500 men, a brigade-sized force. He wanted a promotion in rank to match it and blamed his failure to receive one on prejudice against his foreign birth. Leventhorpe's war against dirt continued. He reiterated orders for officers to have their men wash all Saturday afternoon. "Every man must be scrupulously clean, when inspected by Commanding officer on Sunday, both in person, arms, and accoutrements." Leventhorpe also issued detailed instructions for the maintenance of latrines. "Soldiers must repair to these sinks," he chided, "and not wander in the woods, which constitutes a nuisance in the neighborhood of a camp." He also prohibited the burial of offal, the remains of beef butchering, within the camp boundaries. Leventhorpe constantly observed how guards carried their muskets while on duty and urged all officers to help him in perfecting the style with which his regiment carried itself.[28]

The 11th was nearly struck by a serious outbreak of yellow fever in Wilmington during September 1862. Leventhorpe managed to move the regimental camp eight miles out of town when the disease began to manifest. The fever created panic in town, and people fled Wilmington by the hundreds "in every manner of conveyance that could be obtained," reported Sgt. Lemuel J. Hoyle to his mother. "Huge piles of tar and rosin were burning in every street, and the city was filled with a dense mass of black smoke. The sight was most distressing." Thirteen people died, and an additional forty-five new cases had appeared by the time the 11th was sent far from Wilmington on October 5. The regiment traveled by rail to Weldon and then took a branch line, the Seaboard and Roanoke, toward Union-held Suffolk. The bridge over the Nottoway River twenty-five miles southwest of Suffolk had been burned more than a year earlier when Confederate troops evacuated Norfolk. The 11th had to disembark, cross the stream on a flat boat, and march to Franklin, five miles east of the river on the rail line. A handcar was sent back to the Nottoway to pick up the regimental baggage, as there were no locomotives east of the stream. Leventhorpe took charge of all forces at Franklin, consisting of the 11th, a regiment of cavalry, and a battery of artillery. Federal patrols from Suffolk often wandered near Franklin, and several small skirmishes took place; but Leventhorpe's job was to observe the movements of the Yankees and alert the authorities to any major offensive toward Weldon, forty-five miles southwest of Franklin. He had to stretch his small force for thirty miles along the east side of the Nottoway. The 11th North Carolina would operate here for the next two and a half months before joining Pettigrew's brigade in late December.[29]

The other regiments in Pettigrew's new brigade could not lay claim to so distinguished an origin as that of the 11th. The 44th North Carolina was organized at Camp Mangum in March and consisted mostly of companies from the eastern part of the state. The Granville Regulators from Granville County, on the margin between the coastal plain and the piedmont, became Company A; Company B was enrolled in Edgecombe County, on the coastal plain; Company C came from Pitt County, also on the coastal plain; Company D was the Pitt Regulators, also from Pitt County; Company E started as the Turtle Paws of Chatham County, at the meeting of the coastal plain and the piedmont; Company F was the Trojan Regulators of Montgomery County, a piedmont area; Company G enlisted from Orange County, on the edge of the coastal plain and the piedmont, as well as from Alamance County in the piedmont; Company H originated as the Montgomery Guards of Montgomery County; Company I originated as the Eastern Tigers, which came from Pitt County and another coastal plain area, Craven County; and Company K was the Franklin Guides to Freedom, from Franklin County on the edge of the coastal plain and the piedmont. All ten companies had initially enlisted from January through March 1862, and all were mustered in at Camp Mangum on April 3.[30]

The company officers elected George B. Singletary as their colonel. He had been a captain in the Mexican War and resided in Greenville, North Carolina. After marrying a daughter of a former governor of the state, Singletary turned himself into "an able criminal lawyer" and served as a brigadier general in the state militia as well as a representative in the state legislature. After the war opened, he was elected colonel of the 27th North Carolina. Singletary was a bold officer prone to rash actions. He commanded the post at New Bern in the fall of 1861 and decided to launch an attack on the Federals occupying Hatteras Island contrary to the orders of his superior, Daniel Harvey Hill. Singletary loaded his regiment onto a steamer on November 8 and, to guide his ship, released two pilots from a New Bern jail who had been imprisoned on suspicion of disloyalty. He was forced to turn back before running into trouble and found himself the subject of a court-martial. Found guilty of disobeying orders, he was sentenced to suspension of rank and pay for two months. He resigned on December 16 before the sentence was served. Singletary's impetuous nature did not deter the officers of the 44th from wanting him as their leader. Other field and staff officers included Richard C. Cotton as lieutenant colonel and Elisha C. Cromwell as major.[31]

The regiment began to outfit itself before it was mustered into service. Capt. Lawrence Ruel Anderson requested 76 overcoats, blankets, canteens, caps, knapsacks, and haversacks, one for each member of his Company D. But he asked for 152 pairs of pants and drawers and 152 shirts. The company needed 80 camp kettles, 125 mess pans, 4 hatchets, 4 pick axes, 4 axes, 4 spades, and 1 drum. It also required 16 tents for privates and 2 tents for officers.[32]

The men who made up the 44th were devoted to defending their homeland, but many also joined at this time to avoid the impending draft. Sgt. Franklin Scarborough of Company H cheered the passage of the Conscript Act and was happy he volunteered just in time to avoid it. "I hope they will learn something of a soldier's life," he wrote of the conscripts, "for those that have never expirenced it can draw no ider[;] if it were not for the love of liberty no man would stay in camp." The payment of bounties also helped to spur voluntary enlistments.[33]

The 44th officially did not have a chaplain until October 8, 1862, when John H. Tillinghast was appointed to fill that post. He had studied at Virginia Theological Seminary in Alexandria before the Federals occupied that town, and then he had pastored an Episcopalian church in Rutherfordton, North Carolina, before he was offered the chaplaincy. Tillinghast's friend Capt. Robert Bingham was a son of the state's most distinguished family of educators. His father, William James Bingham, directed an academy, the Bingham School in Hillsborough, that had already turned out James Johnston Pettigrew. Robert received a bachelor's degree from the University of North Carolina in 1857 and went to work teaching at several academies and observing procedures at the University of Virginia. He received his master's degree at Chapel Hill in 1860. Robert had initially opposed secession but served in the Orange County militia and went to war when the state needed additional troops in the spring of 1862. Tillinghast reported that Bingham liked "his present mode of life, much better than teaching."[34]

Another well-educated member of the 44th was Charles Manly Stedman. A native of Pittsboro whose father had served in the state legislature and as state comptroller, Stedman attended the Pittsboro Academy and graduated from the University of North Carolina in 1861 with very high honors. He served as a private in Company H, 1st North Carolina, fought at Big Bethel, and was made lieutenant of Company E in the 44th North Carolina. He was elected captain of his company eight days later.[35]

The 44th North Carolina was sent to the field on May 19. It was stationed at Greenville, 100 miles east of Raleigh, on the Tar River. Greenville was the last Confederate-held town on the Tar, only twenty-five miles from Union-held

Washington. The regiment's job was to patrol and picket the area between the two towns, and it spent the next two months fending off Union patrols. Charles Stedman was involved in one such scrape during the last week of May. He led sixty men and a small detachment of cavalry to their picket posts when his command was surprised by Federal cavalry and infantry, and a melee ensued. Stedman rode up close to the Federals and shot a black man who was acting as a guide for them. A Union officer riding beside the guide shouted, "'D—n you I've got you now,'" but one of Stedman's cavalrymen killed him with a double-barreled shotgun. Stedman's horse was killed under him by more fire, and he injured his head on a tree trunk in falling. But this and other skirmishes resulted in very few casualties.[36]

One such skirmish cost the regiment its commanding officer, however. On May 31 Singletary took most of the 44th down the river toward Washington to Tranter's Creek, on the north side of the Tar River and about four miles upstream from Washington. He reinforced Stedman's company guarding a bridge over the creek at Myer's Mill. The regiment fought a skirmish with Union pickets on the east side of the stream on June 2 and took two prisoners. Three days later Singletary's 250 men were attacked by the 24th Massachusetts supported by two guns. The Tar Heels put up a good fight for forty-five minutes. Singletary sat on a log at the end of the bridge and shouted orders so his men would see that he was not frightened, but it cost him his life. A rifle bullet penetrated his skull and killed him instantly. "His last words, with the expiring gasp, were, 'Give it to them, boys.'" The regiment was forced to retreat, having suffered two killed and three wounded, while the Federals retired to Washington, having lost seven killed and eight wounded. Franklin Scarborough was impressed with this brief introduction to combat. "If I could see you," he wrote to his father, "I would tell you sumthing about how the bullets whistled, and the cannons roared." Scarborough felt "wasted from our fatigue in retreating." But no strategic result came from all the maneuvering and shooting between Greenville and Washington that spring.[37]

Singletary thus ended his brief and controversial career. His daughter later died at age ten, and his wife was so crushed by the quick passing of her small family that she died soon afterward. A shakeup of the regimental command followed his death. His brother, Thomas C. Singletary, had previously served under him as lieutenant colonel of the 27th North Carolina and now was elected colonel of the 44th. Lieutenant Colonel Cotton resigned because of his advanced age, seventy-six years, and was immediately replaced by Major Cromwell. But Cromwell resigned as lieutenant colonel on July 5 because of a "'disease of the kidneys.'" Tazewell L. Hargrove, former captain of Company A, had been elected major to replace Cromwell, and now he was promoted to replace him as lieutenant colonel on July 28. Stedman was promoted to major to replace Hargrove. This spell of rapid promotion led to a long, stable leadership for the regiment; Singletary, Hargrove, and Stedman would hold their posts for nearly the rest of the war.[38]

The remaining two regiments of the brigade were created at the same time and place as the 44th and had a similar early history. The 47th North Carolina was organized at Camp Mangum in March, but even before its organization was complete, some of its men were temporarily sent to the seat of war. New Bern was under attack, and the units that became Companies A, C, D, E, and I were sent from Raleigh under Sion H. Rogers without guns. They stayed below Kinston with Branch's defeated army for one week, then returned to Camp Mangum by the end of April. The regiment consisted of men mostly from the broad area where the coastal plain and the piedmont meet, around and to the north of Raleigh. Company A had been the Chicora Guards from Nash County, on the coastal plain. Company B was from Franklin County, also on the plain, while Company C was from Wake County. Company D was known as the Castalia Invincibles from Nash County. Company E also hailed from Wake County. The Sons of Liberty, from Franklin County, became Company F, while Company G was mostly recruited in Franklin County and partly in Granville County, where the plain and the piedmont meet. Company H was known as the North Carolina Tigers and hailed from Wake County, and Company I also was recruited from Wake. Company K was called the Alamance Minute Men from Alamance County. All of the companies were recruited from January through March; six were mustered in on April 11, three were mustered in on April 29, and the remaining company took the oath to the Confederate government on April 30.[39]

The regimental officers were elected on April 8 and 9. Sion Hart Rogers, former lieutenant of Company K, 14th North Carolina, was elected colonel; George H. Faribault, former captain of Company E, 14th North Carolina, was made lieutenant colonel; and John A. Graves, former captain of Company A, 13th North Carolina, was elected major.[40]

The regiment was ordered to Kinston about June 1 and became part of the brigade that Martin was organizing. It was stationed between Kinston and New Bern for some time, doing outpost duty and maneuvering to threatened points when Federal patrols moved too near. The regiment also suffered from illness, as recalled by Capt. John Houston Thorp of Company A. "It was here the men went through the sick period consequent upon the change from civil to military life; through measles and mumps and malarial fevers, from which quite a number died. Very few escaped sickness in passing through to the toughened condition."[41]

One man who survived the toughening process was Lt. Benjamin Wesley Justice, who served as the assistant commissary of subsistence for the regiment. A graduate of Wake Forest College and a tutor in classical literature, he had trouble adjusting to camp life and missed the home he shared with his wife and children in Wake County. "I am here in my tent, almost covered up with flies that tickle my hands & light on the tip end of my nose, hearing the almost incessant rub-a-dub of the drum, being compelled to listen to the profane oath, the vulgar slang, the coarse jests of rude men, having no soft, gentle hand to hold in mine, no white arm to encircle my neck when I lie down to rest, no warm, quiet, cozy little home, no sweet gentle wife, no innocent, prattling babes, no warm welcome at eve when fatigued by the toils of the day." Justice had no choice but to adjust; the regiment was shipped to the Richmond area with the rest of Martin's brigade but soon was detached to provost duty in Petersburg.[42]

The 52nd North Carolina was organized at Camp Mangum in April. Its component units represented mostly the piedmont region of the state. Company A was the Cabarrus Riflemen of Cabarrus County. The Randolph Guards of Randolph County became Company B. Company C was the Orapeake Guards of Gates County, in the coastal plain. Company D was formed in March, after Brig. Gen. Benjamin McCulloch was killed at the battle of Pea Ridge, Arkansas, and the men chose to call themselves McCulloch's Avengers. It came from Stokes County, in the piedmont. Company E, the Richmond Regulators, hailed from Richmond County on the dividing line between the coastal plain and the piedmont. Company F was the only mountain unit in the regiment, hailing from Wilkes County and calling itself the Wilkes Grays. Company G, the Dry Pond Dixies, was recruited from the piedmont county of Lincoln. The Spring Hill Guards, also from Lincoln County, became Company H. Company I called itself the Stanly Rebels from Stanly County, in the piedmont. Another piedmont region, Forsyth County, gave rise to the Fighting Boys, Company K.[43]

Although it came from a region with comparatively few slaves, the Stanly Rebels had a large number of slave owners within its ranks. Its commander, Capt. John C. McCain, owned fifteen slaves, and its first lieutenant, James D. Hearne, owned twenty-five slaves. Hearne was a delegate to the secession convention that took North Carolina out of the Union. Thomas K. Colson, owner of twenty-four slaves, joined the company but remained in Camp Mangum for only a few days before he "'got tired and went home.'" The roll books indicated he had never signed the enlistment papers anyway, so he was not arrested for desertion. His son, Thomas K. Colson Jr., enlisted at age eighteen in March 1863 and was wounded and captured during Pickett's Charge at Gettysburg. He returned home in February 1865. At least four other sons of slaveholders served in

Capt. Benjamin Wesley Justice. Regimental commissary of the 47th North Carolina, Justice wrote literate, moving letters to his wife. (Special Collections, Robert W. Woodruff Library, Emory University, Atlanta, Ga.)

the company, including Pvt. Julius A. Kendall, who was left mortally wounded on the field of Pickett's Charge.[44]

The election of regimental officers took place amid some controversy. The company officers elected Zebulon Baird Vance as colonel, James Keith Marshall as lieutenant colonel, and Marcus A. Parks as major. But Vance, understandably, was not interested in the position. As an alternative many officers wanted Lt. Col. Robert F. Hoke of the 33rd North Carolina, but there were not enough votes to put him into the position even if he had wanted to accept it.[45]

With Hoke and Vance out of the running, a new election brought James Keith Marshall into the colonelcy. He was a twenty-three-year-old Virginian, the grandson of former chief justice of the Supreme Court John Marshall. His family was related by blood or marriage to those of Thomas Jefferson, Robert E. Lee, and George E. Pickett. A royalist ancestor had fled to America in the wake of King Charles's execution in the English Civil War, and his great-grandfather had gone to school with George Washington and had commanded the 3rd Virginia Infantry during the War of Independence. Marshall's father was a slave owner. The young aristocrat graduated from Virginia Military Institute with a modest academic record and taught at a private school in Edenton, North Carolina, before the war broke out. He commanded Company M, 1st North Carolina, but missed the battle of Big Bethel. Thus he had no combat experience when elected colonel of the 52nd. Marcus A. Parks was elected lieutenant colonel, and John Q. Richardson was elected major.[46]

The regiment's early days at Camp Mangum saw a scramble for available equipment and housing. Capt. Benjamin Franklin Little of the Richmond Regulators managed to scrounge up enough planks to floor the tents of his sick men, and he sent servants out to collect dry broom sedge to serve as a foundation for his mattress and oilcloth. Sickness began to set in with measles, mumps, and colds. Little noticed that his men tended to eat inside their tents, allowing bits of crackers and meat to fall on the ground to rot and attract vermin. "I caution them to stop it & set them the example of bringing my own things out when I wish to eat," he informed his wife. The toughest part of adjusting to soldier life for Little was the separation from his family. He was called to a company officer's meeting at regimental headquarters where he began to read a letter from his wife and could not restrain the flow of tears. Little kept his head bowed to hide them. His wife and one of his children were sick, and another son was "missing his papa." He felt able to bear his fate in battle only as long as he was assured that his family could "get on without me."[47]

Sgt. Anderson C. Meyers, a farmer from Stokes County, also felt the pangs of homesickness. He began to miss his wife and children so much at dress parade one day that he cried. Meyers succeeded in hiding his tears from the men of Company D, but he felt so blue he could not to go sleep that night. "O if I could go to Bed tonight, with you I would give any thing. . . . I hope the time will soon come when we can have the opirtunity of sleeping together. I never go lie down to sleep without thinking of you."[48]

Officers such as Little had less time to be homesick than the privates, for they were plagued with paperwork. Filling out the muster rolls of his company was a gargantuan task. Little marveled at how slowly many of his recruits performed simple tasks like signing their names. He told his wife that he probably could write twenty names while some of his men wrote only their own on the roll sheet. Other men were unable to write at all and could only make their mark. At the same time, sickness immobilized over half of his men. The 52nd also received its weapons in late May. Two companies were armed with good Enfield rifle muskets, but the other eight companies were issued smoothbore muskets.[49]

The 52nd left Camp Mangum on June 6 for Kinston and went on picket duty ten days later. The regiment was shipped to Richmond too late to take part in Lee's offensive against McClellan, but it worked on the fortifications at Drewry's Bluff. Sickness spread through the ranks as the heat and humidity of August settled in. Benjamin Franklin Little was convinced that much illness, even death, could be avoided by "frequent bathing. But it seems it is no use to talk to *Some*. They can't muster courage to go through the *little trouble*, whereas many of the *same* would walk 5 miles for a half pint of mean whiskey, which would but render the cleansing of the skin still more necessary." The 52nd was moved from Drewry's Bluff to Petersburg on August 20 and went into Camp French one mile south of the Appomattox River and three miles east of Petersburg. "We will have to go to *digging* soon," wrote Little to his wife. "I expect *spades* will be *trumps*."[50]

The regiment had been in Virginia little more than a month, yet the desire to return home was strong for many men of Martin's brigade. They began to circulate a petition calling on the government to send them back to North Carolina. Little was appalled at this. He found the petition in his tent and "promptly & almost indignantly refused to sign it, & it did not get a signature in our Regt., and some who signed it in other Regts, regretted it." Little's refusal was based on a noble sense of fair play, for he "could not brook the idea for a moment of petitioning for *any* favor of the authorities not attainable by all with whom I am serving."[51]

Little need not have worried about the influence of soldier politics on the authorities, for the petition was ignored and Martin's brigade remained in Virginia. Many people assumed that in addition to the 44th, 47th, and 52nd, another regiment, the 42nd North Carolina, was part of the brigade, but they were mistaken. The 42nd was organized at Salisbury in April 1862, and its men had been detailed as prison guards at Lynchburg all summer. It was shipped to Richmond in August to report to Martin's brigade, but plans were changed when it arrived. The 42nd was not assigned to any brigade but remained under the direct control of the department commander, Maj. Gen. Gustavus W. Smith. It often operated with the regiments of Martin's and later Pettigrew's brigade, but usually was assigned to different duty away from it.[52]

The 26th North Carolina greatly strengthened Pettigrew's brigade. Its newly minted colonel wanted to shake up the officer corps by creating a regimental commission that would recommend candidates to President Davis for promotion. Pettigrew strongly supported Burgwyn in this scheme, which was sanctioned by a clause in the Conscript Act, and the young colonel felt "that with the exercise of a little judicious firmness I can succeed."[53]

The senior captain, John J. C. Steele of Company B, did not even apply to be examined by the commission for promotion to lieutenant colonel. He was suffering from chronic diarrhea and offered his resignation as captain from his hospital bed. Burgwyn suggested Capt. Oscar Rand of Company D for the vacant lieutenant colonelcy, but Rand was still being exchanged following his capture at the battle of New Bern. Capt. Joseph R. Ballew of Company F, the third-ranking captain in the regiment, argued that Steele's refusal to undergo examination by the regimental commission did not allow Burgwyn to recommend anyone for the lieutenant colonelcy. Also, Rand's repatriation dragged on much longer than expected. He was not officially declared exchanged until November 10 and could not hope to rejoin the regiment for many weeks.[54]

The commission, which consisted of Burgwyn, Colonel Singletary, and Lieutenant Colonel Hargrove of the 44th, now had to look elsewhere in the ranks to fill the post of lieutenant colonel left vacant by Burgwyn's promotion and the position of major made vacant by the resignation of James S. Kendall on July 21. Capt. John Randolph Lane of Company G passed his examination and became lieutenant colonel. Capt. John Thomas Jones of Company I became major. Burgwyn was pleased that Captain Ballew failed his examination; he was "always creating dissatisfaction & ill feeling in the Regt." The young colonel was very encouraged by Lane's and Jones's elevation. Their courage "has been often tried, & never failed. I have every confidence in them in that respect. Lane also, though greatly deficient in education, is exceedingly attentive & hard working, & I think I can educate him to fill his post very well."[55]

Burgwyn relied on Lane to refill the ranks of the 26th and sent him to North Carolina to round up draftees. "By all means," Burgwyn urged Lane with an overriding sense of urgency, "hasten the arrival of the conscripts as much as possible & select your men as well as you can." Burgwyn also concentrated on retrieving deserters. Pvt. John Vinson of Company G had enrolled on March 6 as a substitute from Chatham County. He was wounded at Malvern Hill but deserted from the hospital. A civilian named G. H. Vipperman apprehended and delivered Vinson and received thirty dollars from regimental headquarters.[56]

While Burgwyn busied himself with his new command, Vance was busy with his own new job. Wartime conditions prevented an elaborate inauguration ceremony, but the former colonel wanted the regimental band to perform. Burgwyn and Pettigrew readily granted permission and also authorized the band to play a series of concerts in eastern North Carolina before returning to camp. Gus Reich left camp early to get his "sleight of hand" act out of mothballs and use it as an added attraction at the festivities. The musicians polished their instruments and left Camp French on September 6; they reached Raleigh that evening. A large bus arrived, and the band played "some of our best music" as it conveyed them through the city. Suitable clothes arrived from Salem on September 8, inauguration day, to replace their "soiled army wear."[57]

The inauguration was the highlight of the band's war service. The group positioned itself on the west side of the capitol and played for the guests as they gathered. Vance's address was "short, but good," according to Julius Linebach, and then the band played as the crowd dispersed. That evening the musicians gave two performances to packed houses in the chapel of the institute for the deaf, dumb, and blind. Gus Reich performed his show, styling himself "The Southern Magician" and "The Wizard of the Blue Ridge." Much of the music the band played that memorable day was arranged or composed by Julius Linebach's brother, Edward. In fact, he wrote the official inauguration march for Vance. Edward never joined the band, but he instructed the members in their initial efforts to learn their instruments, provided music for them, and "in every way did what he could for our comfort and welfare all thru the wearying and trying years we spent in camp."[58]

While Vance settled into his new and demanding job, the band he had recruited for the 26th left for concert dates in eastern North Carolina. It played at Wilmington on September 10 and 11 and at Goldsboro on September 12. The latter town offered some unwanted excitement. A crowd of "rowdies pulled some of the seats down, and tried to break up the evening performance," according to bandleader Sam Mickey. They even roused the tired musicians at 3:00 in the morning and tried to cajole them into a serenade, but the Moravians refused. To make matters worse, yellow fever broke out in Goldsboro the day they left for Petersburg. The players were happy to rejoin their regiment on September 13, just as Pettigrew's brigade started on its first expedition into the field.[59]

Chapter 3

Back to Carolina

Pettigrew's brigade missed the campaigns in Virginia and Maryland in the last half of 1862 because the Federals continued to threaten strikes against Petersburg and other points on the railroad supply line between Wilmington and Richmond. This forced the Confederates to deploy forces south of the capital, and Pettigrew's brigade was a logical choice to remain south. It consisted mostly of untried troops, and as Tar Heels the men would naturally be more interested in defending the region than would troops from other parts of the Confederacy. As a result the brigade spent the rest of 1862 operating in southeastern Virginia and eastern North Carolina, guarding railroads, garrisoning towns, and concentrating to block threatened raids by the Federals. Pettigrew was forced to disperse his regiments to widely separated posts and was often unable to exercise command of a concentrated brigade during this time, but his men engaged in a few pitched battles and had the casualties to prove that they were playing an important role in the Confederate war effort.

Pettigrew initially chafed under his assignment. He proposed an attempt to recapture Suffolk in early September. The town was located on the Norfolk and Petersburg Railroad about fifty-five miles southeast of Petersburg and fifteen miles from Norfolk. Pettigrew believed it was vulnerable to a quick strike. He wanted to rebuild the railroad and telegraph to Zuni, fifteen miles short of Suffolk on the Blackwater River, reconstruct the bridge over the stream, and concentrate troops there. Then he would send a cavalry force ranging into the countryside to screen the advance. Pettigrew's proposal was limited by the reality that Suffolk could not be permanently held because it was so far from Petersburg and so close to Norfolk. Instead, he proposed taking the place simply to make a statement and to collect runaway slaves, ordnance, and medical stores. He believed at least 10,000 infantry, a battery, and four regiments of cavalry were needed if the Confederates hoped "to make a great capture at little cost." His superior, Maj. Gen. Gustavus W. Smith, liked the idea but pointed out that few troops were available. He also thought Pettigrew's chances of success, even with adequate troops, were "more than doubtful."[1]

Yet Pettigrew was allowed to try with his brigade, roughly 2,600 men, and a six-gun battery. He advanced to Wakefield Station, about ten miles northwest of the Blackwater River, by September 14. This was as far as the trains could go, for the track was wrecked farther along the line. A second battery and another North Carolina brigade commanded by Col. Junius Daniel joined Pettigrew at Wakefield.[2]

Pettigrew found that the difficulties Smith had foreseen were all too true. The wrecked bridge over the Blackwater was the most serious obstacle. Engineer officer Capt. Charles H. Dimmock failed to coordinate his efforts with Pettigrew, and as a result there were no timbers or tools available when the brigade reached Wakefield Station. Pettigrew ordered the men to move out of their comfortable bivouac at the station on September 19 and march parallel to the river toward Franklin. The weather was hot and dry that day, but rain set in on the twentieth. Pettigrew's and Daniel's brigades made it to within five miles of the point where the Seaboard and Roanoke line crossed the Blackwater, near Franklin, when orders arrived from Smith to call off the expedition and return by a network of back country roads to Petersburg. Pettigrew called the enterprise a "bust up." He left the 52nd North Carolina at Franklin, and the rest of the brigade returned to Camp French by September 23, having marched nearly seventy miles.[3]

Pettigrew was disgusted. "Instead of striking like the lightning of the tropics, we spent a whole week in rolling up our little thunder cloud, right before their faces, so that every fool would have raised his umbrella." He criticized the planning of what he called "our rather badly conceived expedition," ignoring the fact that his own plan was essentially followed. Gus Jarratt was equally disappointed. The men "accomplished literally nothing," he reported to his brother; they suffered from blistered feet and were "completely broken down, and in a bad humor because we had to march so far and did not get to whip the yankees."[4]

Pettigrew was forced to disperse his brigade as the need to guard a wide area of the Confederacy fell upon his shoulders. The 44th North Carolina was stationed at various points for the remainder of 1862, although neither surviving letters from its members or the regimental historian bothered to pinpoint exactly where or when. The whereabouts of the 47th North Carolina are nearly as obscure for these fall months.[5]

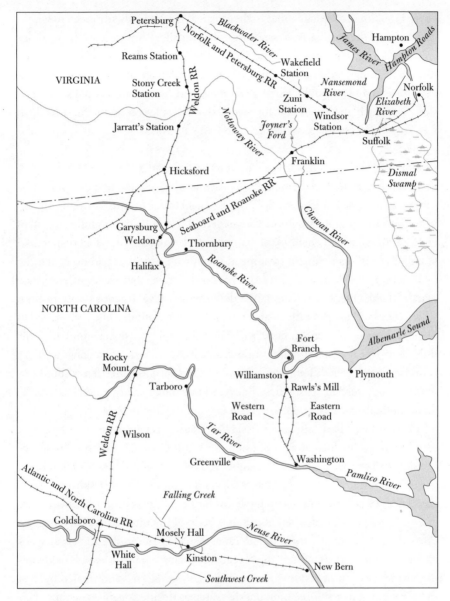

MAP 3.1 Southeastern Virginia and Eastern North Carolina

The 52nd North Carolina saw some action against the Federals, but it was fleeting. The regiment remained several days in the vicinity of Franklin after the rest of Pettigrew's brigade returned to Petersburg. The 52nd formed in line of battle to oppose a Federal force that had pushed out toward Franklin to shadow Pettigrew's march on September 23. The men formed west of the Blackwater to cover Franklin, a couple of miles to their rear, as the Federals advanced to within 400 yards of the east bank. Several rounds of artillery fire were exchanged, inspiring about twenty-five "Excited men" of the 52nd to fire their muskets, even though nothing could be accomplished at that distance. After a while the Yankees retreated. That night Marshall's men stood down and bivouacked. They were kept at a high level of alert for several days. Besides the 52nd, the 11th North Carolina, three regiments of cavalry, and two batteries were stationed at or near Franklin.[6]

Marshall's men again were called on to help save the town on October 3. A Federal force under Col. Samuel P. Spear consisting of 1,300 men supported by three gunboats sailed from Suffolk up the Blackwater toward Franklin. Its objective was to wreck the pontoon bridge there. The gunboats, mounting a total of eight cannons, began shelling the banks at daybreak, and Marshall dispatched Company A of his regiment to snipe at them from a bluff. It had no effect; the boats simply sped up and entered a part of the river that was bordered by a marsh. Marshall sent more companies downriver to advantageous positions from which they could pepper the boats on their return to Suffolk. The boats failed to push all the way to town. Marshall's regiment lost only one man wounded in this little affair. Spear's infantry and cannon came close enough to exchange artillery rounds with the Rebels for about two hours that afternoon, then left without suffering or inflicting any casualties. The 52nd was inexplicably called back to Petersburg that same day, and it arrived at Camp French on October 5.[7]

The regiment had only a short stay at Camp French. After one month it moved back to its former area of operations and took post seven miles above Franklin on the Blackwater by November 2. The men moved their camp to Black Creek Church on November 15 and engaged in another minor skirmish three days later. Twenty men of Company E, under Lt. Thomas Roper Baldwin, were guarding Joyner's Ford when about 300 Federal infantry and cavalry tried to cross the river. Initially the Confederates managed to repulse the cavalry advance, but a second attempt by the bluecoated infantry was successful. Baldwin's little band was compelled to give way. Marshall was alerted and rushed the rest of his regiment to reinforce him, but the Yankees decided against pressing their advance and retired across the river.

They moved to a point opposite Franklin and began to shell the town. Leventhorpe's Bethel Regiment bore the brunt of this confrontation. He told the men he was "determined to hold the place at all hazards and he hoped the Bethel regiment would still retain the reputation she had for valor." They responded with "three hearty cheers" and took position under the Yankee artillery for two hours. The men dodged shells until Leventhorpe ordered them to lie down for safety, which almost was more trying for Lewis Warlick than standing. He "had to lie and take it all and couldn't get a shot." No opportunity for engaging the Federal infantry materialized, yet five men of Company A were wounded before the Yankees retired to Suffolk. Marshall's 52nd North Carolina shifted about from one camp along the Blackwater to another for the next three weeks, always providing pickets for the fords and threatened points along the stream.[8]

Although not yet a part of Pettigrew's brigade, the 11th North Carolina operated with the 52nd North Carolina at Franklin. Colonel Leventhorpe provided patrols, pickets, and guards for river crossings just as Colonel Marshall did, and he continued to hone his men to a high level of proficiency. Sgt. Francis Calhoun Harris of Company H had left the ranks during the skirmish on November 18, but Leventhorpe came to realize that it was due to a misunderstanding of orders, not cowardice. Harris's demotion to private was therefore reversed. Leventhorpe was exceedingly proud of his own part in the November 18 fracas, crowing to his wife that "*my* management saved the Black water."[9]

The 26th North Carolina spent much of the fall at Camp French, but it was ready to go almost anywhere its services were needed. Everyone in the regiment left behind family members who were either exposed to enemy action or struggling to make ends meet. Sgt. Maj. Leonidas Lafayette Polk had a wife and children back home in Anson County, and he worried about their welfare. They lived alone and "unprotected," and he tried to find someone trustworthy to stay with them. "It is bad enough indeed to be away from my family, but it makes it worse to know that probably they will be compelled to leave home for safety. They live in a dangerous place, & I wish I could be with them." In addition to these family concerns, Polk was fed up with Burgwyn. "The Regt is very much dissatisfied. We all want old Zeb back with us. I hope I will not Stay with it long." Polk never explained the trouble, but he successfully secured promotion to lieutenant and transfer to the 43rd North Carolina on February 2, 1863.[10]

The band of the 26th continued to entertain the whole brigade. It performed two concerts in Petersburg, charging one dollar admission for adults and half that amount for children. Included in the selections were "Annie Laurie," "Capt. Horton's Waltz," "Lulu Is Gone," and "Here's Your Mule." The program was rounded out by a medley of "Dixie" and "Bonnie Blue Flag." Gus Rich enlivened the bill with his magic show, which included comic singing, "Mechanical Fantocine Figures," and "Quaint, Queer, Cute and Comical Magical Mystifications." The entertainment was a great success. The musicians were able to pay their expenses, over $200 for renting the theater and for hotel accommodations, and each player received $15 as well. The rest, $253.35, was distributed among the patients in the North Carolina hospitals at Petersburg. Band member

Edward Peterson accurately called it a regular business affair that, unlike the concert at Kinston, was designed to make a profit in addition to providing charitable relief for the wounded. Burgwyn was so taken by the success of these concerts that he began to ask the band to play for anyone he wanted to impress. Pettigrew also was "very kindly disposed towards us," recalled Julius Lineback. He gave the band the piano music to "The Rifle Regiment Quickstep." It was Pettigrew's favorite piece, and he insisted it be played as often as possible.[11]

The 26th saw action in early November when it participated in an expedition through the North Carolina coastal plain and was nearly gobbled up by a superior Union force. Maj. Gen. Samuel G. French sent the 17th North Carolina, the 59th North Carolina, some cavalry, and a battery, under Col. James D. Radcliffe, to attack the Yankee garrison at Plymouth. Burgwyn was to move toward Washington to keep the enemy from cutting off Radcliffe. The 26th left Camp French and reached Tarboro by rail on October 25, then it marched to Williamston, fifteen miles west of Plymouth and twenty-two miles north of Union-occupied Washington. This town was the key to Burgwyn's mission, for it was the junction of roads that connected his detached force with Radcliffe's command. He pushed south of Williamston toward Washington, detailing Capt. J. C. McLauchlin with two companies to build an earthwork at Rawls's Mill, near the intersection of two roads that led to Washington. He then moved to a point in Beaufort County sixteen miles south of Williamston by October 31. A small detail moved farther south to a point only eight miles below Washington on the Pamlico River to collect bacon. The detail passed within sight of town and could see the Yankee sentinels standing on their earthworks. The men of the 26th were isolated, and some were nearly barefoot.[12]

Burgwyn was highly critical of Radcliffe for puttering around in the vicinity of Plymouth and displaying a marked reluctance to attack the garrison. To make matters more complicated, Radcliffe ordered Burgwyn to send five companies back to Williamston under Lt. Col. John R. Lane while the remaining three companies and fourteen attached cavalrymen patrolled both roads to Washington.[13]

Burgwyn's pickets reported the arrival in Washington of twelve steamers carrying Federal troops on October 31. Maj. Gen. John G. Foster had decided to counter the Confederate move against both Plymouth and Washington with a quick strike that could capture all three Confederate regiments. He gathered three brigades under Col. Thomas G. Stevenson, Col. Horace C. Lee, and Col. T. J. C. Amory at Washington. Setting out on November 2, Foster took 5,000 men and twenty-one guns along the eastern road toward Williamston instead of the western road along which Burgwyn's three companies were bivouacked.

Burgwyn rushed his small command northward to Rawls's Mill, at a bridge over Ready Branch about five miles south of Williamston. He felt this was the decisive point in Foster's march, that the Federals would try to cut off his detachment here before it reached the town. Burgwyn had prepared for this contingency by making detailed maps of the area and cutting down trees and burning some bridges on the eastern road. Before he began his retreat, he sent a courier to Lane ordering the lieutenant colonel to bring the rest of the regiment to Rawls's Mill. He also sent a messenger to Radcliffe informing him of Foster's advance.[14]

Burgwyn reached Rawls's Mill more than an hour before sunset on November 2 and rested his men while he surveyed the area. It was an admirable position. The eastern road intersected the western road just south of the mill but crossed Little Creek one mile before the junction. There was a ford here with water two feet deep that was easily defensible, as shallow water and briars flanked both sides of the road. The land was very flat all around and partly cultivated, with the creek valley about ten feet deep. Burgwyn was riding past the intersection when he looked down the eastern road and saw Foster's cavalry van approaching. He barely had time to send McLauchlin with Companies I and K to stop them. McLauchlin's men raced down the road and took position just before the troopers tried to push across the ford. The Tar Heels waited until their targets were only twenty yards away, then they fired a volley right into their faces, emptying about twenty saddles and sending the survivors scampering back across Little Creek. Stevenson's brigade came up, and Belger's Rhode Island battery fired at the little band. Under cover of this artillery fire Stevenson ordered two companies of the 44th Massachusetts over the creek, but the Rebels fired so well that the Yankees were driven back, losing one killed and six wounded. After that the Federals made no more attempts to force a passage but simply relied on their artillery to flail the bushes with canister. McLauchlin's troops suffered little from the fire and were reinforced by Companies D and F under Major Jones, acting under Burgwyn's order. The young colonel realized it would only be a matter of time before Foster overwhelmed the tiny force at the creek, so he instructed the four companies to retire to the mill. By this time Lane had rejoined Burgwyn with the other five companies, uniting the 26th once again.[15]

Foster again relied on his artillery to minimize casualties, posting Belger's battery and some guns of a New York battery to shell the earthwork at Rawls's Mill for a half-hour in the descending darkness. Having delayed the Federals twice, Burgwyn now decided to retire under cover of night before they had a chance to outflank his position. He set fire to the bridge over Ready Branch next to the mill and pulled out. Just as he left, however, Radcliffe's entire force of two regiments and a battery arrived. Burgwyn quickly ordered two guns to deploy and fire a few rounds into the darkness, "simply for the moral effect."[16]

The skirmish at Rawls's Mill was over, but the campaign continued. Radcliffe took charge of the combined force, much to the disgust of Burgwyn. "You never saw such confusion & disorganization," he told his father; "there was no plan no order & no management." As the Rebels disengaged, Foster's men took possession of the mill and began to rebuild the bridge. Radcliffe ordered a retreat. The Confederates retired to Williamston and then took the road to Tarboro, marching most of the night with the 26th in front, and bivouacked at Spring Green Church. Brig. Gen. James G. Martin arrived to take command from Radcliffe, and more troops arrived, including the 44th and 47th North Carolina. The latter regiment had left Petersburg on November 5, bivouacked near Weldon that night, and reached Martin by November 13.[17]

Foster had failed in his objective, but he pushed out from Rawls's Mill on November 3 and pursued Martin for a few miles before giving up the chase. The Federals returned to Williamston on November 7 under an early and heavy fall of snow. Foster rested his footsore command for a day then marched to Plymouth, where transports loaded the men and left for New Bern on November 11.[18]

The Rebels also suffered under the storm that dumped up to six inches of snow on the night of November 7. Eleven men of Company I, 26th North Carolina, were barefoot, but Sgt. J. A. Bush Sr. was able to find space in the regimental wagons for them to ride. Several shoeless men in other companies groaned and shouted when forced to march in these conditions, until their officers ordered them to bear it silently. Brandy was issued to the men to warm them that night, leading to considerable tipsiness, but the residents of Tarboro rushed out pairs of shoes for soldiers who needed them. While Foster declared himself pleased with the results of his foray, the reality was that neither side could claim much from this adventure. The Federals lost 6 killed and 8 wounded, while Burgwyn lost 1 killed, 9 wounded, and 3 captured. Lt. William S. Ingram of Company K suffered a brain concussion from the explosion of a shell and was off duty for nearly a year trying to recover. He was finally allowed to resign because of " 'frequent attacks of convulsions' " brought on by the injury. Ironically, Burgwyn had matched wits with an old teacher in this campaign. Foster had tutored the teenager in 1856 when Burgwyn was trying to enter West Point, where Foster held a professorship.[19]

Martin's command quickly dispersed when the Union threat receded. The 26th and 47th entrained at Tarboro and reached Camp French on November 14 and 16, respectively. The 44th boarded cars at Weldon the next day for the return to Petersburg. The Moravian band nearly missed the campaign. It had remained at Camp French when the regiment left for North Carolina and did not set out until several days later. The musicians caught up with Burgwyn just before Foster struck. On the night of November 7, when the snow began to fall, Burgwyn gave the band members a large hospital tent so they could ride out the storm in relative comfort.[20]

The 26th North Carolina settled in for what the men assumed would be a long winter at Camp French. They asked for heavier clothing from home, especially socks. Gus Jarratt, recently promoted to captain of Company C, sent a man to Wilkes County to collect all the clothing he could find for his men. "They need it bad enough," he wrote; "some have not even a blanket and others are bare-footed. I hope their friends will be able to send them something." The regiment's health was good, but desertion became a problem. Nine men left the 26th in late November, two from Jarratt's company. He thought most of the deserters were conscripts. "I can't see why they desert so fast," Jarratt naively wrote his father; "some of the regiments have lost fifteen [to] twenty at one time."[21]

Throughout the fall of 1862 the regiments of Pettigrew's brigade relied on the Conscript Act to maintain their strength, but it was a controversial law that thousands of men ignored or evaded. A former sergeant of the 26th North Carolina, discharged for medical reasons and living in Union County, described to Governor Vance how some residents of his area avoided conscription. He noted during an enrollment of conscripts on December 19 that local officials aided friends by allowing them to create "the most flimsey excuse" for exemptions. One man bought a contract to deliver mail ten miles into an isolated area once a week and even hired another draft evader to help him do it. Another man talked several acquaintances into falsely swearing that he was an overseer of at least twenty slaves for them. Someone else obtained a false certificate of disability from "a hired Physician." Still another evader was a "pretended 'Doctr' . . . a near-quack, who had been trying to practice physic in a very obscure neighborhood," even though he had no diploma and "never heard a Medical lecture." All this deception was too much for the disabled soldier: "I saw enough . . . to disgust a member of the Old 26th N.C."[22]

Despite evasions, the conscript system netted many men for the army. The different regiments of Pettigrew's brigade sent officers to Raleigh to "collect" them. Benjamin Franklin Little performed this duty for the 52nd North Carolina. He found that the draftees were allowed some latitude in choosing their regiments, but draft officials tried to steer as many as possible to older, more depleted units. Little was able to persuade forty-five conscripts to join the 52nd and felt he could have had more if the conscription officer, Maj. Peter Mallett, had not interfered by telling him that the regiment already was pretty strong. Since most of these men were from Wilkes County, Little assumed they would be assigned to Company F. He returned to Camp French with his draftees to find that the regiment was still near Franklin. With no regimental officers available, Little reported to Pettigrew and was told to "'take charge of the conscripts & drill & get them trimmed up.'" The captain was greatly impressed by Pettigrew, believing he saw in his face "the eye of intelligence & of quick penetration." The brigade leader was dressed in civilian clothes and wore a military cap as he walked to and fro on the porch of the house that was his headquarters.[23]

Burgwyn was even more energetic than Little in using the Conscript Act to beef up his ranks. Lane delivered 110 draftees in September, bringing regimental strength to 1,150 men. Burgwyn was very proud of the 26th and hoped to create a glee club to lift the men's spirits as they were dismissed from drill. "I have a number of first rate singers," he assured his father.[24]

Many Quakers were forced into the conscript system in violation of their beliefs. Thomas Hinshaw, a Quaker residing in Randolph County with his wife and several children, was called up as a draftee, but he decided to ignore the notice. His faith led him to believe that war was "not in accordance with true Christianity." He continued living his quiet farm life for several months before the government acted. Militiamen were sent into the area to round up everyone who had failed to respond. One morning in the last week of October, Hinshaw was making shoes and his wife was preparing breakfast when the soldiers barged into their home and told him "in a hasty manner" that he would have to go to the militia camp two miles away. Hinshaw's wife was distraught. She begged the soldiers to allow Thomas his breakfast and condemned the war in general. The men would have none of it; one of them told her "in a very passionate manner to hold her tongue and mind her own business, with some other unpleasant expressions, which was hard to bear at that trying time," Hinshaw wrote, but he was taken from his family that morning.

Hinshaw found many relatives and acquaintances in the camp. His brother Jacob, brothers-in-law Cyrus and Nathan Barker, and friends Nathaniel Cox and Simon Piggott refused to pay for their own transportation to Asheboro, fifteen miles away. Their recalcitrance put the militia officer in a quandary; he felt guilty about forcing them to walk and therefore decided to work out a deal. The draftees could go home for a week to arrange their affairs, and he would find some way to pay for their transportation if they promised to return to duty on time. None of them could promise this, but their older relatives posted a bond for their return. Thus the unhappy men spent a final week with their loved ones and then left them "in a world of trouble." They reached Asheboro the next day and found a group of seventy draftees. Two Friends left when the group reached Raleigh; one was in poor health, and the other, Simon Piggott, promised to pay a commutation fee of $500. None of the other Quakers felt they could pay this in good conscience.

The men rode the train to Petersburg with no food or water and were packed so closely in the cars that they had to sit on one another's knees to rest. They reached Camp French on November 6 and were assigned to the 52nd North Carolina, then near Franklin. The draftees rested a few days and were shipped to the regiment, where they were told to choose a company. Hinshaw and his brother were remarkably consistent in their stand, refusing to make even this small concession to the military system. They stated that they "were brought out as prisoners or conscripts, and that our religious principles would not allow us to go into any service in the army, neither would we choose any company there." They again refused to pay the commutation fee. Colonel Marshall was forced to choose a unit for them, and he picked Capt. James M. Kincaid's Company G. It was either a mark of kindness on Marshall's part or a stroke of luck, for Hinshaw found Kincaid "to be a friend to us." Most members of the regiment were tolerant if not sympathetic about the plight of the Quakers, but not Lt. James Daniel Wells, "who seemed harsh towards us." Wells asked them why they did not draw knapsacks, as they could not possibly carry all their possessions and a rifle without one. "We told him we had no need for guns there, we did not believe in fighting, and did not expect to carry guns, and reasoned our case pretty clearly to him, stateing over passages of scripture to show that we were standing out only on what we thought to be true Christian principles." Wells argued that those scriptures were unreliable, that they had been "translated by men who did not understand the languages and they drawed them off to suit their own notions." He then threatened the Quakers, but this hardly impressed the Friends.

Their trials had only begun. The day after they joined the 52nd, the regiment moved its camp three miles. When Wells ordered the Quakers to help clear a new camping ground, they refused. The lieutenant was "in a passion" and vowed they would do duty. He ordered his men to fix bayonets and force the reluctant draftees to work. All of the soldiers were loath to do this. Some excused themselves by telling Wells they had no bayonets, others protested that their guns were elsewhere, and even those without an excuse did not press their bayonets closely. Fortunately Captain Kincaid noticed what was going on and took Wells aside for a dressing-down. Even more fortunate for the Hinshaws was the fact that there were Quakers living in the neighborhood of Franklin who asked

Marshall to allow these men to stay in their homes and attend their worship services. It was a most welcome respite from the pressures of army life, which began to increase in intensity.

Kincaid tried to see if there was any duty the Quakers were willing to do. They had earlier refused to take the oath as soldiers and now adamantly refused to cook, drive wagons, or tend the sick in hospitals. Kincaid threw up his hands and let Marshall handle the problem. The colonel insisted they help unload fodder being transported across the Blackwater in canoes to keep it out of Federal hands, but they said no. Marshall did not even pretend to listen to them but rode away as they protested. Junior officers then began to mete out the most harsh treatment Hinshaw and his brother received while in the army. They threatened to shoot or bayonet the Friends, then tied them to the forage wagons and drove three miles to the river, forcing the pair to walk through mud and water. The wagons were loaded, without Quaker help, and driven back to camp, where the two were untied. The Quakers paid a heavy price for their principled stand. They were subjected to repeated threats for weeks afterward, but gradually the officers reached a grudging accord with them. Marshall only asked that they keep up with the regiment, walking behind it on the march rather than within its ranks. "We thought it best to go along peacebly with them," remembered Thomas, "though it was very trying to us being in such a condition so long, and seeing so much carried on that we could not hold with." Conscription was a tragic burden for men such as the Hinshaws. These modern Jobs put their trust in God and endured a hated service. They were of no use to the cause but deserved enormous respect for their commitment to their ideals.[25]

The 26th North Carolina enrolled 178 men in September and October, and the conscripts were pretty evenly distributed to all the companies. They represented 6 percent of all the men who enrolled in the regiment after the Conscript Act was passed, but a lot of these draftees refused to serve. Of the 44 men enrolled in Company D those two months, 31 percent deserted. A few of them returned to duty voluntarily, making the permanent desertion rate 25 percent for these enrollees. Company B saw 51 percent of its 27 enrollees desert. When those who returned were subtracted, the permanent desertion rate was 33 percent. These figures were far higher than the average for the regiment's entire complement of men during the war years, which was 12 percent. The permanent desertion rate of the 26th North Carolina for the war was 9 percent.[26]

Although conscription drew in a lot of questionable recruits, it filled Pettigrew's brigade. In November, when Hinshaw and his brother "joined" the 52nd, Pettigrew had 4,417 men in his command. Adequately clothing them was another problem. Lt. R. R. Crawford was sent to Raleigh to round up supplies. All the clothing due the brigade, except overcoats, was on its way by late October, along with 300 pairs of shoes for each regiment. Crawford suggested that Pettigrew contract directly with private manufacturers for more shoes, as they would be of much better quality than those issued by the government.[27]

Most of Pettigrew's brigade tried to settle in winter camps near Petersburg by mid-December. The 26th North Carolina, with 1,160 men, was located five miles south of town, and the 44th North Carolina, with 780 men, was encamped two miles west of Petersburg. The 47th North Carolina numbered 878 men and pitched its camp near Burgwyn's regiment. The medical facilities were not up to standard, although not far below it. The medical inspector of Richmond area hospitals, Surg. Peter Lyons, reported that the 26th and 44th did not yet have their hospital tents pitched when he visited the camps on December 12. This forced surgeons to treat the sick in their own quarters until the men finished their winter huts and had time to erect the tents. Each regiment had two ambulances and from five to eight hospital tents. None of the regiments had a hospital fund from which they could buy necessities for the sick, and at least two of the regiments did not keep proper records. The surgeons of the 44th reported that they had requested proper record books long ago and had never received them. They were forced to make their monthly reports "from memory and no copies kept." The same surgeons maintained operating instruments that were "in not very good condition." Lyons found fault with the camp sanitation of the 26th as well. Only the 47th fared well in his report, with its hospital tents up and filled and its books properly kept.[28]

Soon after the regiments beefed up their ranks and supplied their material needs, the largest campaign of the fall took place. Union general Foster launched a major raid toward Goldsboro with the intention of cutting the rail line between Wilmington and Richmond. He set out from New Bern on December 11 with 10,000 infantrymen, 40 guns, and 640 cavalrymen. Two days later the Unionists fought a sharp battle at the crossing of Southwest Creek just south of Kinston. A South Carolina brigade under Brig. Gen. Nathan G. Evans held the earthworks there for a short while before Foster forced the Confederates to fall back to Kinston. The next day, December 14, Evans vainly tried to save the town and hold the bridge over the Neuse River. The Confederates were unable to burn the structure before the Federals took possession of it.[29]

At this point the first of Pettigrew's regiments arrived. The 47th North Carolina left Camp French on the evening of December 13, and the 44th North Carolina followed it the next morning. The 26th North Carolina left on December 15, while the 52nd North Carolina entrained at Franklin the next day. The 11th North Carolina had left Franklin two days earlier.[30]

Col. Sion H. Rogers's 47th arrived at Kinston late on the evening of December 14, just as Evans was retiring across the bridge. "In a jiffy," recalled John H. Thorp, "we were unloaded from the cars, which were run off immediately, ordered to pile our knapsacks, overcoats and blankets, which we never heard of afterwards, and doublequicked to the rescue." Evans ordered the regiment to cover his retreat from the bridge as Foster began to push two regiments and a battery over it to the north side of the Neuse. Rogers's men exchanged a few shots with the Yankees but suffered no casualties. Evans evacuated Kinston and established a defensive position two miles from town, placing the 47th prominently in his front. Soon after, Rogers received a message from Foster under a flag of truce. The Federal general wanted to know if Evans was ready to surrender. "'Tell General Foster I will fight him here,'" replied Evans. Foster bombarded the Confederate position for several hours, but nightfall and Evans's decision to retreat meant the 47th North Carolina would not be tested in battle that day.[31]

Evans fell back to Waters Mill on Falling Creek under cover of darkness. The men cooked cornmeal on shingles and pieces of bark laid on the ashes of their campfires. Company A of the 47th marched two miles toward Kinston to locate the Federals the next day, December 15, while the rest of the regiment remained in line at Falling Creek. That night Company K reinforced Company A, and both entered Kinston to find that Foster was gone. He had retreated to the south side of the Neuse on the morning of December 15 and continued on the most direct route to Goldsboro after destroying stores in Kinston and burning the bridge. Foster bivouacked near White Hall that night. The 47th left Evans's position at Falling Creek at 2:00 A.M. on December 16 to recover its two companies. Foster had stolen a full day's march on his cautious opponent.[32]

The 11th North Carolina was the next unit to arrive. Leventhorpe had taken his regiment from Franklin in company with a North Carolina brigade under Brig. Gen. Beverly H. Robertson. The combined force reached Mosely Hall, nine miles short of Kinston, where the president of the railroad informed them that Evans had evacuated the town. The men were told to wait there while Robertson and Leventhorpe boarded a tender and rode an additional five miles along the track to locate Evans. The South Carolina general was relieved to have help. He ordered Robertson to take the 11th and three other regiments to White Hall, sixteen miles west of Kinston. The men backtracked and arrived there at 3:00 P.M. on December 15. They broke open barrels of rosin to set fire to the bridge, while Foster's tired soldiers were still trudging forward several miles away. Skirmishers from the 11th were deployed along the riverbank, which was rather low and swampy on the north side, and Capt. Francis W. Bird's Company C deployed as pickets near the bridge. Federal cavalry supported by artillery came up that evening and shelled the position for two hours, destroying a gunboat that was under construction. Some Union cavalrymen tried to swim across but were easily repulsed by Company C.[33]

Foster waited until the morning of Tuesday, December 16, to make a serious attempt to cross the river. As a result the 11th experienced "its first real baptism of fire." Foster deployed the 9th New Jersey and Amory's brigade on the south bank of the river, occupying a range of low hills or river bluffs that were several feet above the low ground the Confederates held, and the infantry and artillery opened fire at 9:00 A.M. Robertson saw that the skirmishers needed help, so he called up the 31st North Carolina to hold the river side. For a time only this regiment, the artillery, and Companies B, C, and F of the 11th bore the brunt of Foster's fire. The Union artillery barrage was "so terrific," in Robertson's words, that the 31st North Carolina broke and retreated without orders. At 10 A.M. Robertson ordered the remaining eight companies of the 11th to replace the 31st.[34]

Leventhorpe shouted the order to move out, and the regiment suddenly felt "a perfect storm of lead and iron hail" descend on it. The men rushed across an open space of a half-mile so quickly they lost only one man, then they entered the swampy woods and took shelter behind logs and tree stumps. While the Federal infantry fired in volleys and by regiments, Leventhorpe ordered his men to fire at will. They had an advantage in that the Federals were on high ground and thus were silhouetted against the sky. Several batteries of Union artillery, only 250 yards from the 11th, continued to shell the swampy position for six hours. Lemuel Hoyle reported with some exaggeration that the "firing was terrific, indeed it is said by many that no troops during the war have been under a heavier fire. The swamp in which we lay was literally torn all to pieces." The Bethel soldiers also took shelter behind piles of pine logs at a sawmill near the riverbank. Lewis Warlick was hiding behind a stump when a shell hit the root of it and threw dirt and chips into the air. He saw comrades who were hit by shell fragments bleed to death before help could arrive. Robertson had inadequate artillery to counter this fire, and one of his two guns was disabled by the Federals. Yet Hoyle believed that the "whizzing & peculiar 'zip-zip' sound of the rifle balls was quite as scary and more dangerous than the artillery."[35]

After finding that there was no way to force a crossing of the Neuse here, Foster disengaged, left skirmishers behind, and tried to reach the railroad bridge at Goldsboro. The Confederates were pinned in place all night, but the 11th had done very well in its first battle. Robertson could not praise the regiment enough in his report and referred to its "gallant bearing" under fire. "No veteran soldiers ever fought better or inflicted more terrible loss upon an enemy considering the numbers engaged. . . . The conduct of this regiment reflects the greatest credit upon its accomplished and dauntless commander." The Bethel unit lost 7 killed and 24 wounded, and Leventhorpe counted 126 dead Federals on the battlefield. Foster did not note his losses at White Hall and thus failed to deny or verify Leventhorpe's rather high report of Federal casualties.[36]

The campaign was rapidly coming to a climax at Goldsboro, and the 52nd North Carolina would be a key player in the drama. Marshall reached Goldsboro at midnight on December 16, the day Leventhorpe's soldiers were holding the line at White Hall. He crossed the river and reported to Brig. Gen. Thomas L. Clingman, who was commanding on the south side of the Neuse. The 52nd rode the train across the bridge and jumped off but was told to bivouac along the railroad embankment. County Road came up from the east and crossed the track here as well.[37]

At dawn on Wednesday, December 17, scouts brought word to Marshall that the Yankees were coming up County Road. He formed a line straddling the road to cover its junction with the railroad. Soon after, about 8:00 A.M., Marshall sent out skirmishers. The regiment held on for at least a half-hour, then Marshall received orders to move by the left flank to the river and guard the bridge. As the Tar Heels executed this maneuver, Foster vigorously followed it up. He sent the 9th New Jersey and 17th Massachusetts forward to the rail line and then along the track, following the 52nd directly toward the bridge. Three other Massachusetts regiments moved by the right flank over the fields toward the bridge.[38]

Marshall repositioned the 52nd astride the railroad embankment in front of the structure and waited for the onslaught. Five bluecoated regiments bore down on his lone regiment, opening a scattering fire as soon as they came within range. Marshall deployed Companies A and D as skirmishers, but they were soon "nearly surrounded" and fell back to the regimental line. Clingman tried to rush support to the 52nd, placing the 8th North Carolina a half-mile upriver to guard County Road Bridge over the Neuse and positioning the 51st North Carolina between the two bridges, but neither unit was close enough to connect with Marshall's men. Both flanks of the 52nd were therefore exposed. The three Massachusetts regiments began to work their way around Marshall's left while the 9th New Jersey and 17th Massachusetts sent men to the west of the railroad to work their way around his right. The left wing of the 52nd fell back first, apparently without orders, forcing the entire regiment to retire westward over the embankment and on to the riverbank. Marshall ordered the men to move rapidly to County Road Bridge, a half-mile away, to escape Foster's converging columns. He faced another threat when the 51st mistook his men for Unionists and one company fired a volley. Fortunately few, if any, men were injured because a tall fence forced the mistaken Tar Heels to aim high. Having escaped both the Yankees and the Rebels, Marshall took his men, along with the 8th and 51st, across the bridge to the north side of the river.[39]

Foster had reached the ultimate goal of his campaign, and his men wasted no time in torching the bridge. It burned rapidly in the cold winter air and soon was beyond saving. Now it was nearly noon, and the five Union regiments came under Confederate artillery fire from across the Neuse. Foster directed his own artillery to rain projectiles on the enemy batteries and around the blazing bridge so no one could extinguish the flames. Satisfied with the job and feeling exposed some seventy miles from New Bern, Foster decided to retreat. He did not have the strength to seize and hold Goldsboro on a permanent basis. Most of his men retraced their steps to County Road and re-formed into marching columns, but Horace Lee's brigade and several artillery batteries remained in place on the low hill south of the bridge to cover Foster's rear. A forward line also was established at the intersection of County Road and the railroad, the first position the 52nd held that morning.[40]

The Confederate commanders were determined to make Foster pay for his success. By this time Evans had arrived with what was left of his South Carolina brigade after a long march from Mosely Hall. As ranking officer on the field, he assumed command of both his own and Clingman's units. Evans quickly ordered Clingman to cross the river and attack the Federals. The 52nd, along with the 8th, 51st, and 61st North Carolina, pushed over County Road Bridge with two guns to find the forward line of Yankees at the railroad crossing. Clingman split his small force in two, sending the 51st and 52nd along the riverbank to the railroad. Their assignment was to move within 500 yards of the Federal position but to keep covered by the embankment and then attack the Federal right flank when they heard the sound of Clingman's other wing attacking the left. Clingman himself led the remaining three regiments and two guns along County Road. At the right point this force turned left and advanced over an open field toward the Federals behind the embankment. The Yankees did not try to hold their position at the railroad crossing but quickly retreated to the top of the hill before either Confederate wing came in contact. Clingman's divided command moved up to the embankment by separate routes and waited while the brigade leader surveyed the situation.[41]

The Federal position was quite strong. For three-quarters of a mile in front of Lee's men the ground was open and sloped up gently to the Union guns. Battery B, 3rd New York Artillery, was positioned directly in front of the 51st and 52nd, with Battery F of the same regiment a short distance to its left. Several regiments of infantry were within easy supporting distance of the guns. Against this force Clingman tried to organize an attack. Although Marshall and Lt. Col. William A.

Allen of the 51st were several hundred yards away and had no word from him, they prepared to cross the railroad and engage the enemy at the sound of Confederate artillery.[42]

At this moment, about 4:00 P.M., Evans rode across County Road Bridge and impetuously ordered the two regiments to attack. This stunned Marshall and Allen. They explained that coordination with Clingman's other two regiments was essential, but Evans blurted, "'I rank Clingman: move forward at once; I will support you with the Holcombe Legion.'" It was true that Evans's small South Carolina brigade, which included the legion, was on its way across the river to join the offensive, but it had been handled roughly at Kinston. Clingman was too far away for consultation and, as the historian of the 52nd later put it, "commands must be obeyed." The two regiments dressed their ranks, the men shouted to steel their nerves, and then several hundred Tar Heels climbed the railroad embankment and saw the open slope before them, crowned with artillery and infantry.[43]

The attack was a much smaller repetition of the Confederate assault at Malvern Hill five months earlier. The two regiments stumbled over the railroad embankment and began to climb a "high rail fence." Union artillery fire pounded them as the men struggled across, even though the Yankee gunners had been surprised by the assault. Lt. Samuel Clarke Day of Battery B was lolling about among the guns, waiting for the rest of Foster's command to march eastward, when he heard "a rousing cheer." He looked to the west and saw Marshall's and Allen's men cross the railroad and clear the fence. It was an impressive sight: "They looked *splendid* their flags flying, and they came up bravely." The 52nd was in front and the 51st was just behind it. The men double-quicked over the open field in an effort to minimize casualties, but the shellfire "tore huge gaps in their ranks," reported Day. As the range lessened, the Yankees changed to canister, "and you can think what a storm of iron must have fell on the Rebel ranks."[44]

The 52nd pulled far ahead of the 51st, although more and more men were falling with each discharge from the six guns of Battery B. Its support, Battery F, also opened fire at the regiment, and still there was no artillery support from Clingman's two guns. The flag of Marshall's regiment went down three times, according to Day, but it was picked up each time and kept waving. When the regiment got within 200 yards — one Federal observer imagined it was so close he could throw a stone onto the heads of Marshall's men — the Tar Heels fell to the ground for cover. Here they waited for a half-hour, hoping for support that never came, for Allen's regiment had already fallen back. The descending twilight, which was early now that winter had arrived, offered the men a chance to retreat with relative safety. They were also helped by the fact that Battery B was nearly out of ammunition. Clingman managed to engage his artillery and send his two regiments into the open field east of the railroad, all of which diverted Federal attention. Marshall was able to pull his men to the safety of the railroad embankment, ending the battle of Goldsboro.[45]

The 52nd suffered heavily during its heroic but foolish assault. Marshall reported eight killed, forty-nine wounded, and eight captured. Allen's 51st suffered slightly less, with fifty-seven casualties in all. Everyone agreed that the attack should not have been ordered by Evans. John Robinson, the regimental historian, characterized the charge as a "simply reckless disregard" of the men's lives. Sgt. A. C. Meyers put the best cast he could on it by calling the attack "the most daring & dangerous . . . that has been made since the war comenced." But the most eloquent commentary actually came from Union hands. Samuel Clarke Day admired the pluck of the Tar Heels even as he mowed them down with his guns. "I must own I felt bad, for the poor reb's, for we slaughtered them awfuly. every time our guns discharged, I could see them go down for all the world like . . . grass before the scythe." Another Yankee, Hale Wesson of the 25th Massachusetts, described the attack for his father: "God forbid that we Ever Kill men So fast *again*," he moaned. "I tell you Old N.C. weeps and is in mourning to day, on account of that last 2 Short hours fighting at Goldsboro Bridge. This is a terrible war indeed. I am pretty cool and hard hearted but the thoughts of it make me *shudder*."[46]

Marshall found help at the railroad, for the rest of Pettigrew's brigade had assembled at Goldsboro. The 26th had reached White Hall too late to take part in Robertson's defense of the crossing on December 16, but Burgwyn pushed on to reach Goldsboro by morning. His regiment crossed County Road Bridge late in the day to support Clingman. Pettigrew and his staff also had reached Goldsboro by this time, but there is no evidence that they directed the movements of the different regiments. The 44th and the 47th missed the engagement at White Hall but were at Goldsboro by December 17. Both regiments endured the heavy shelling Foster's guns laid down around the burning bridge and crossed the river with Burgwyn an hour before dusk. The 44th suffered one killed and one wounded, but the 47th lost no men. The three regiments greeted the 52nd as it returned from its attack.[47]

The men of Pettigrew's brigade were appalled at the terrible waste of manpower, especially when rumors began to circulate that Evans was drunk when he ordered the charge. The Confederates remained in position behind the embankment for some time before they realized that the Federals had slipped away. The temperature had been "bitterly cold" all day, and the night was even worse. Marshall's men suffered the most, for they had worked up quite a sweat on their double-quick charge across the field and the air chilled their wet clothes. The generals took pity and allowed the regiments of Pettigrew's brigade to stand down and bivouac at County Road Bridge by 11:00 P.M. The wounded from the battle were shipped to the hotels in Goldsboro, where patrons were roused from their beds at midnight to make room for them. The Moravian musicians of the 26th North Carolina, who had been staying at Granger's Hotel, slept on the floor of the hotel's bar.[48]

Foster had achieved the minimum of his objectives. He cut the railroad to Virginia, but because Confederate troops still held the line, engineers could easily repair the damage. The Northern high command kept just enough men in the state to scare the Confederates but not enough to do more serious damage than Foster had achieved at Goldsboro. Nevertheless, this had been the most dangerous raid in the state since Burnside's campaign the previous winter.[49]

The Goldsboro campaign led to the transfer of the 11th North Carolina to Pettigrew's brigade. On December 19, when the troop concentration at Goldsboro was at its peak, Leventhorpe's regiment was made part of the brigade. Pettigrew's command was "the finest Brigade in the C.S.A." thought Burgwyn. It numbered more than 3,700 men on December 20. Julius Linebach was happy to see the 11th join the brigade, for it had a band filled with musicians from his home county. "They had much of the same music as ourselves . . . so that we could 'join forces,' & make a large band, playing with fine effect." For their part, the men of the Bethel Regiment had wanted to be part of the brigade for some time. "Both officers and men were equally won by Genl Pettigrew's great and rising reputation," recalled Leventhorpe. Pettigrew reviewed the brigade on December 21, and the 11th displayed itself for the first time before its new comrades.[50]

With Foster back in New Bern, Pettigrew was ordered to disperse his units again. The men began to leave on the evening of December 22 but were delayed by a massive train collision that fortunately injured no one. Leventhorpe's regiment reached Weldon that night. Weldon, rather than Franklin, was to be his post. Lemuel Hoyle was not impressed; he called it "unquestionably one of the filthiest, dirtiest and meanest places in the South." The 11th stayed on the parked railroad cars for two days and then marched a mile outside town to a suitable campground.[51]

Only three days after it established Camp Robertson, the 11th demonstrated that local inhabitants had cause to rue the day the regiment arrived in their midst. Leventhorpe received daily complaints from civilians about his soldiers stealing their property. "It is a matter of much surprise to the comdg officer, that men who have acted so nobly on the battle field, should act so dishonorably.

Such conduct if persisted in will soon deprive you of the laurels earned upon the field." Leventhorpe doubled the guards around camp to stop this thievery.[52]

The rest of the brigade went to its assigned posts. The 47th and 52nd left Goldsboro on December 23 for Franklin. Three days later they were in the field again, crossing Blackwater River on a foraging expedition under Brig. Gen. Roger A. Pryor, the new commander in this region. Pryor also took the 42nd North Carolina and some artillery and cavalry. After marching and gathering food for five days, he moved quickly to Windsor Station, several miles from Suffolk. Pryor easily chased away two companies of Federal cavalry with a little artillery fire, rested his men for the night, and returned to Franklin on January 1, 1863. No one liked this kind of campaigning. John Thorp recalled that the men had to march thirty miles a day. "All foot logs and small bridges are cut away ahead of us that the men may lose no time in breaking from column of fours, and we must take the mud and water in the roads through the boggy section." The 47th and 52nd were taken away from Pryor on January 3 when they broke camp on the Blackwater and marched to Garysburg. From there the two regiments traveled by rail to Rocky Mount on the night of January 5. Pettigrew had begun to move several regiments of his brigade to this town, situated on the railroad about halfway between Weldon and Goldsboro and where the line crossed the Tar River. The 47th rejoined the brigade after a brief absence, but the 52nd had not been physically near the other regiments for more than a few days since the previous September. The 47th also underwent a change of commanders when Sion H. Rogers resigned on Christmas Eve to become North Carolina's attorney general. He was succeeded by Lieutenant Colonel Faribault.[53]

While the 11th went to Weldon and the 47th and 52nd went to Rocky Mount, the 44th North Carolina remained for the time being at Goldsboro. The 26th moved back to its winter quarters at Camp French on December 23. Pettigrew did not like this dispersal of his command. He suggested to French that half of it be drawn back to Petersburg and the rest be stationed at Weldon so Pettigrew could divide his time between both places and help "preserve the esprit du corps of his Brigade." Leventhorpe certainly was capable of commanding the enlarged garrison at Weldon; he was already laying plans to fortify the approaches to the town. Pettigrew's suggestion was a halfway measure between total concentration and complete dispersal, thus reducing the confusion on the rail line if the entire brigade had to be quickly brought together.[54]

The Goldsboro campaign inspired Pettigrew to issue a set of "regulations" for his men to follow in future engagements. He ordered that anyone who left the ranks without permission should be bayoneted by the file closers. "The safety of the brave men who do their duty, requires that the cowards also should be forced to do theirs, even at the risk of their lives." The wounded were to be helped to the rear only by men given permission to do so by company officers, and even then they were to be escorted to a safe spot no more than 100 yards from the regiment. From there, ambulance corpsmen were to transport them to field hospitals. These corpsmen were to be selected from the companies, one man out of seventy-five, and were to wear a distinctive badge. In addition to helping the injured, the corpsmen were charged to "be vigilant to prevent stragglers from leaving the field under pretense of belonging to their corps, using for this purpose any amount of force that may be necessary." Pettigrew wanted no surrenders; every attempt to fight out of a trap should be made. Also, the ammunition of the fallen should be salvaged and distributed among the living. Pettigrew's orders reflected a determination to fight the war with vigor.[55]

The men of Marshall's regiment had little need for such orders. Some were still dying from their wounds as Christmas arrived. Reuben A. Rash of Company F had been hit by a rifle ball in both legs below the knee and endured a double amputation. He died on January 8. Capt. Nathaniel A. Foster informed Reuben's father that the "Grim monster Death has no Respector of Persons." Rash had left behind only a watch and four months' back pay, but Foster admitted he had no opportunity to collect the arrears for any deceased men in his company.[56]

Pettigrew was forced to shuffle his units in early January as the Rebel high command reacted to rumors of renewed Federal activity. Burgwyn moved the 26th to Garysburg, just north of Weldon, on January 4, and the 44th joined the 47th and the 52nd at Rocky Mount. The 26th remained at Garysburg for several weeks while Pettigrew established his headquarters at Rocky Mount. This gave Burgwyn an opportunity to lead French and Leventhorpe on a tour of the countryside around Thornbury, his family plantation ten miles east of town, to evaluate the condition of roads and the terrain in view of defending against a Yankee incursion.[57]

The band went on a Christmas furlough on December 23; it reached High Point in the middle of the night and walked under a bright, full moon to Salem. The Moravians rode the bandwagon into the village, playing loudly as they entered. The holidays passed quickly, and the band started back to the field on January 5. The Moravians reached camp in the middle of the night as snow began to fall. It did not dampen their spirit; at dawn the band struck up the tune "Git out the Wilderness!" and the whole camp woke up with a "shout of welcome" for the musicians.[58]

It had been a long and frustrating fall for the men of Pettigrew's brigade, assigned as they were to tedious duty in a significant but obscure theater of oper-

ations. As 1862 merged into a new year, there was a slight change. The Goldsboro campaign influenced Rebel commanders to concentrate their available
manpower and even lay plans to press the Yankees close to their occupied towns.
There would be no repetition of the Foster raid in 1863; instead, Confederate
forces would take the offensive against their enemy.

Chapter 4

New Bern and Washington

Pettigrew's command was one of five brigades stationed in North Carolina during the winter and spring of 1863. The 26th North Carolina was moved from Garysburg to Magnolia, on the railroad halfway between Goldsboro and Wilmington, on January 19, but the other regiments remained at Weldon and Rocky Mount. When departmental headquarters authorized leaves of absence, a flood of applications reached Pettigrew. He was surprised that his men seemed to believe active operations were over for the winter and stressed to his officers "the importance of Keeping their commands in constant readiness to move on very short notice."[1]

Desertion had been growing since the passage of the Conscript Act, and the 26th North Carolina was given a heavy-handed demonstration of its consequences on January 26. Pvt. Andrew Wyatt of Company B was to be shot for desertion. He had left camp on December 10 and was arrested while crossing the Roanoke River. Sergeant Major Polk thought the sentence was unjustified, and he prevailed on one of the brigade's colonels to start a petition for his pardon. No one knew if the petition was being considered when the day of execution arrived. Several chaplains took Wyatt into the woods and convinced him to profess his faith. He was then placed beside a coffin, and the entire brigade formed on three sides in front of him. His own company was given the responsibility of composing the firing squad. A "painful silence" settled over everyone as Captain Hughes, the assistant adjutant general of the brigade, stepped forward to read the sentence of the court-martial. To the surprise of all, he then read a reprieve of the sentence. The officers were convinced that Wyatt only wanted to see his family and would have returned soon. "The poor fellow," recalled Polk, "as if shocked by electricity—Straightened up . . . a wild hollow glance from his swollen eyes told that he doubted his senses." Wyatt immediately wrote a letter home to his family and vowed never to desert again. He was later killed at Gettysburg.[2]

Besides Andrew there were three other Wyatts from Wilkes County who enlisted on September 21, 1862; they likely were relatives, all caught up in the conscription system. Adam Wyatt deserted on January 17 but returned in time to be killed at Gettysburg. Jonas W. Wyatt also deserted on January 17 but returned to duty the following October and survived the war. Another Jonas Wyatt died on December 16, 1862, of typhoid.[3]

Pvt. William H. Glenn of Company B was very happy the reprieve came in time to save Andrew, for he had no stomach for shooting his own comrade. Glenn believed this dramatic event would put a stop to further desertions, and he was largely right. Thirty-seven men deserted from the 26th in December 1862 and January 1863, but only nine left from February through April 1863. The regimental and brigade officers probably staged the aborted execution to have this effect. Pettigrew later detailed fifty men to go home and search for runaways, offering fifty dollars and a furlough for whoever caught a deserter.[4]

The men of the 11th North Carolina tried to make themselves comfortable at Weldon, building bunks and chimneys for their tents that finally arrived from storage on December 30. They received an order to move out, and Lemuel Hoyle recalled the grumbling. " 'I knew it' says one. 'I told you so,' says another, 'I told you when you commenced building that chimney you'd have to move.' 'It won't do for soldiers to fix up so well, for they're bound to move.' " When another order arrived the next day reversing the previous instruction, the men quickly reconstructed their camp. With the addition of bed ticks filled with straw the tents were quite comfortable, even with a half-inch of ice and snow covering the canvas roofs.[5]

Smallpox began to appear in various towns throughout eastern North Carolina that winter, so Hoyle decided to inoculate himself. He took a smallpox scab from a man in Weldon and placed it into a small incision he made in his skin. Hoyle avoided the disease, and his unorthodox vaccination also saved him from the fate suffered by Sgt. William M. Hoggard of Company C. Hoggard was vaccinated with a syringe, developed erysipelas, and died on January 18. Capt. Francis W. Bird, Hoggard's commander, also vaccinated himself in the same way as Hoyle and survived; it "took very well indeed," he reported.[6]

The men of Leventhorpe's regiment amused themselves by playing baseball and attending a local Baptist church, mostly to look at the unmarried women who worshiped there. But they were forced to give up their comfortable quarters at Weldon and move to Magnolia by January 26. Leventhorpe had to issue another regimental order reminding them not to steal wood from the local civilians. His morale sank when he contemplated his frustrated hopes for higher rank. "I feel very keenly the *injustice* done me about promotion," he complained to his wife. Leventhorpe was not "a political hack," he admitted, and therefore was "quite ignored as regards reward." For their part, the troops were frustrated at the slow approval of furloughs, and there was quite a bit of loose talk among the members of Company C about deserting. The 44th, 47th, and 52nd moved to join their brigade comrades at Magnolia on the evening of January 26. Like the Bethel Regiment, these troops also had to wait for furloughs and began to steal wood belonging to civilians.[7]

The winter camp at Magnolia grew uncomfortable as lice became a problem for the 44th North Carolina. The railroad cars so frequently used by the brigade were full of them, "the branch where men wash & drink is full, the clothes that one gets washed are washed in lousy tubs, and so the chances are very small against keeping clear" of the vermin. The men took their minds off this problem by staging a mock battle when three inches of snow fell. They brought their regimental flags into play, organized sides, charged, took prisoners, and captured colors from their opponents. The 44th and 52nd resupplied their equipment with large quantities of cartridge boxes, cap pouches, bayonet scabbards, haversacks, canteens, and ammunition.[8]

The monotony of life at Magnolia was broken by General French, commander of the brigade's division. He wanted to send Pettigrew toward Union-occupied Plymouth to gather supplies in Washington, Martin, and Tyrrell Counties. Pettigrew was to protect the citizens from Yankee raiders and encourage them to plant crops in the spring. He was to move first to Goldsboro and Greenville. French hoped to keep the Federals penned up in their towns, protect the Confederate army's source of food, and help those citizens who had long been complaining about the lack of attention from their government. He initiated the first attempt by the Confederates to take an aggressive strategy of defending their interests in eastern North Carolina.[9]

Unfortunately for the citizens of the state, the move fell apart. Pettigrew set out from Magnolia with all five regiments, roughly 2,800 men, on the morning of February 13. The band of the 26th serenaded the citizens of the town as the soldiers marched through. Rather than travel on the train, the brigade walked to town along a wagon road that paralleled the tracks. It covered a low, swampy countryside made wetter by the winter weather. Julius Linebach recalled that in many spots there was only a log or a few poles covering deep mud holes, and the men got very dirty and wet when they slipped off this "pavement" into the muck.

NEW BERN AND WASHINGTON

Many men in the 47th did not even try to keep dry; they "boldly waded through" these wet places. The difficulties did not dampen the spirit of the band, which played a tune at several of the better houses along the route, "especially if there were several ladies in sight." Averaging fourteen to eighteen miles each day, the brigade reached Goldsboro on February 16 and marched an additional twelve miles from town before stopping for the night. Orders arrived to halt until further instructions were sent. The offensive was abandoned the next day, and Pettigrew was ordered to Goldsboro. He kept the 11th North Carolina in camp but marched the rest of his brigade back to Goldsboro the same day. The reason for this change was never reported, but French's original purpose would soon be put into operation in a much larger way against several occupied towns.[10]

Leventhorpe's regiment received orders to move out on February 20, but not back to Goldsboro; it moved on to Greenville and camped at the edge of town. Lemuel Hoyle thought Greenville had the appearance of a community that was "pretty well worn *out*, becoming thread bare and seedy." It was about twenty-five miles from Union-occupied Washington. Maj. Gen. Daniel Harvey Hill, the newly appointed commander of the Department of North Carolina, visited the post on February 27 and was serenaded by the band of the 11th. He gave a short speech that Lemuel Hoyle thought was "characteristic of the man. He gave the '*exempts*' particular fits."[11]

Although closer to the enemy than any of Pettigrew's regiments, the 11th was in little danger. Leventhorpe's men had plenty of bread, meat, and even liquor. The duty at Greenville was so undemanding that Sgt. William G. Parker of Company C worried more about his slaves back home than about the Federals. "I would like to know if the negroes have changed in any respect—in there manners or obedience-do they go to there business cheerful or not—I hope they will behave well, if they doo not I should like to have them all sent away that is suspicious and sold—you will have to doo it all," he informed his wife, "and be the judge for I cannot doo it for you."[12]

The furlough policy allowed the Quaker draftees of the 52nd North Carolina to go home on leave. One of them, Nathaniel Cox, received enough money from home to "pay out," in Thomas Hinshaw's words, so he went home to stay. But Thomas and his brother Jacob left camp on February 27. Their two weeks rolled by quickly, and then it was time to return to the army. Thomas and Jacob found it "a great temptation" simply to pay the $500 commutation fee, but their consciences would not allow it. The brothers left home on March 12, "I think it being as hard a trial as we ever have had," recalled Thomas. He wrote a petition to the officers of the 52nd, once again stating that he and his fellow Friends were not "willing to go in to any service whatever for the express purpose of aiding war," and they did not want to "buy [their] religious liberty." Thomas implored the officers to send them home for the entire summer so they could grow crops for the civilians who would suffer because their families were in the army. The petition was never acted on even though some of the regimental officers privately confessed their sympathy for the Quakers.[13]

In addition to granting his men furloughs, Pettigrew initiated a thorough inspection of his command during the idle weeks he spent in different camps that winter. He ordered his aide-de-camp, Louis G. Young, to inspect thoroughly each company in the brigade and report to him. Young began his work on February 9 and did not finish until March 5. He found the 11th North Carolina with good arms and ammunition, but seven companies that had Enfield rifles did not thoroughly clean them. Officers did not inspect their men's ammunition often enough; Young thought it should be looked at more than once per week. The officers also had no interest in the quality of their men's food. The regiment was moderately proficient in company drill but failed to meet Young's standards in skirmish drill. He found the bearing and cleanliness of the men to be slightly better than that of other commands he had seen since he entered the service. Young believed the regiment's spirit was excellent and the officers encouraged the troops to engage in athletics; "games of Ball" were among their favorite sports. Young was appalled that Company B loudly gave its opinion "as to the correctness of the orders & movements" when it was on skirmish drill. Company K had the least spirit in the regiment because its officers were " 'easy men.' " The 11th was well supplied with clothes and blankets, but it suffered a shortage of haversacks and canteens. Half of its officers were absent on sick leaves or furloughs.[14]

Young inspected the 26th North Carolina with particular attention to detail. He found Company A to be defective in discipline. The officers did not consistently enforce army regulations and failed to encourage athletics, but the men seemed "to be obedient & orderly." They were well acquainted with company drill and police guard but not skirmish drill or outpost duty, and they could not estimate distances very well. The appearance of Company A was as good as the average Confederate soldier, Young thought. The men had good weapons but did not take care of them. Ten soldiers in the company were without guns at all, and those who were armed carried only thirty-five rounds in their cartridge boxes. Some men needed canteens and haversacks, and Young found that no one in the company was held to strict accountability for lost equipment. The men were well clothed and comparatively clean. The company commander, Capt. Samuel P. Wagg, was a "tolerably good officer," but his second, Lt. Ambrose B. Duvall, was very young and in need of more vigor and knowledge.

The verdict was much the same with the other nine companies of the 26th.

Young believed that Gus Jarratt, commander of Company C, needed vigor but was moderately well informed of his duties. Six or seven men in Company E were barefoot. Young thought Company H was "excellent" in military appearance. Some men in this company were armed with smoothbores, while others had rifles. Two lieutenants in Capt. James D. McIver's Company H were knowledgeable "but do not give their orders with sufficient emphasis." McIver excused his subordinates, explaining that he always drilled the men and therefore his lieutenants did not have enough practice at it. Company I, on the other hand, displayed "indifferent" discipline, poor instruction, and "unsoldierly" appearance. This company also was partially armed with smoothbore muskets. Lt. Milton B. Blair lacked "dignity of manner" but was "anxious to do his duty," while Lt. James C. Greer was "very ignorant." Company K impressed Young. He gave it highly favorable ratings in all categories.

Young concluded that the spirit of the 26th was high, except in Company F. The regiment was the best informed and most proficient in skirmish drill among the brigade's units, yet it needed improvement. It was "composed for the most part of active young men well fitted to make very effective light troops." Young recommended that all men in the regiment be armed with the same weapons and that they be compelled to keep them cleaner. He found that each company had plenty of good clothing but most needed up to a dozen canteens, cartridge boxes, haversacks, knapsacks, or bayonets.[15]

The 52nd North Carolina fared significantly worse than the 26th. In all companies the commanders gave only general attention to enforcing regulations, while the lieutenants did little more than drill the men. Noncommissioned officers were surprised that seeing to the cleanliness of their men was part of their duties. Ammunition was not properly inspected, and officers paid slight attention to holding the men accountable for lost property. Young found that the privates simply claimed they had lost it in battle and thus were not held responsible for it. The level of knowledge and vigor among the officers was very low, thought Young; none of them deserved a higher command. They studied Hardee's manual and sometimes looked at the army regulations but did little beyond running the men through company drill. Company D was less proficient in drill because, claimed Capt. Leonidas R. Gibson, of the large number of conscripts in his unit. Young found that the men of the 52nd were constantly playing baseball. They also were very dirty due to the pine tar in their firewood. The regiment had a reputation for good marching, and Young was convinced that it could become a fine unit if the officers were willing to work harder at their jobs. The clothing was poor, and many men had no change of underwear. Twenty-five men in Company F alone were without shoes. At least ten men in each company did not have a bayonet, and there were shortages of blankets, knapsacks, canteens, and haversacks. Young admitted he had to take the word of the officers that these shortages existed, for they refused to make the men display their equipment for his inspection.[16]

Young discovered that the 44th North Carolina, like the other regiments, had a poor knowledge of skirmish drill but was proficient in company drill. It had good equipment but bad clothing. Much of the regiment's clothing had been lost at Rocky Mount when Col. Thomas Singletary told the men to throw it away just before they set out for Magnolia. He believed they would lose it anyway while marching. Young was appalled by the men of Company H. It was composed of "very ignorant & illiterate men, whom it is hard to teach," although the officers tried. The men told Young that they washed their faces and hands every day, but he knew the officers did not inspect them to make sure it was done. The conscripts in the 44th were "entirely untaught," and Young recommended they be temporarily separated from their companies and drilled intensely to bring them up to par with the rest of the regiment. A few guns and bayonets and a lot of clothing, haversacks, knapsacks, and canteens were wanting. As in the other regiments, officers paid too little attention to making the men accountable for lost property. The spirit of the 44th was unremarkable.[17]

The situation was much the same in the 47th North Carolina as in the other units. Young reported that each company needed a lot more equipment; for example, Company A needed thirty-five haversacks, sixty-five canteens, eighteen knapsacks, and forty-nine bayonets. But Young inspected the regiment just before it received a large shipment of supplies. The men were relatively clean and, unlike the other units, could perform the skirmish drill very well.[18]

Soon after taking stock of his command, Pettigrew prepared for an active campaign. Lt. Gen. James Longstreet brought two divisions from the Army of Northern Virginia and assumed command of the region, while Hill continued to command the Department of North Carolina. Both men wanted not only to protect the rail line between Wilmington and Richmond but to take the offensive against Union forces in southeastern Virginia and eastern North Carolina. They also wanted to gather as much food and forage as possible. Hill and Longstreet began to implement the basic idea suggested by French in his abortive Greenville expedition of mid-February. Confederate strategy in the region was focused on logistical considerations as the war dragged on and the South found it increasingly difficult to support its troops in the field.[19]

While Longstreet planned a move on Suffolk with his men from Lee's army, Hill turned his attention to New Bern, the key to the Federal presence in eastern North Carolina. He planned a three-pronged approach with 12,000 men. Pettigrew's brigade, 3,399 strong, would advance from Goldsboro by way of Kinston and continue along the north side of the Neuse River. Its job was to capture an isolated Union earthwork, Fort Anderson, on the north bank of the Neuse opposite New Bern and then shell the town and the gunboat fleet. Daniel's brigade was to advance south of the Neuse on the Trent Road, which paralleled the north bank of the Trent River as it approached and joined the Neuse at New Bern. Robertson's cavalry brigade was to advance south of the Trent and cut the railroad that led from New Bern to the coast at Morehead City. Pettigrew's role was crucial. If he could take Fort Anderson and open a heavy fire with the artillery that Hill had accumulated, he could make the difference between victory or defeat.[20]

Pettigrew started out from Goldsboro early on the morning of March 9 with four regiments. The 11th North Carolina was still at Greenville. Instead of accompanying the brigade, it would cooperate with Brig. Gen. Richard B. Garnett's Virginia brigade in a supporting move against Plymouth. The Tar Heel brigade reached Kinston on March 10, and Pettigrew received detailed instructions from Hill about his part in the attack. Maj. John C. Haskell was to join him with fifteen cannon. Two breech-loading Whitworth rifles, recently imported from England through the blockade, were due to arrive from Wilmington for his use. He was to capture Fort Anderson and begin bombarding New Bern on Thursday, March 12. The sound of his fire would be the signal for Daniel's brigade to attack the town from the south. Pettigrew was to insist on a combined surrender of the land forces and the gunboats. Hill sought to inspire Pettigrew to do his best: "It is proper for you to know that there is to be a combined movement from the James to the Cape Fear, and you are to begin it. Upon your success depends very much the success of the scheme. . . . Everything is intrusted to your skill, prudence, and good management."[21]

The brigade set out from Kinston on March 11 stripped for action, with only one blanket allowed for each man and no knapsacks. The march was terrible. Constant rain clogged the dirt roads of the lowland plain with thick mud, and the streams and swamps were a major obstacle. The bridge over Contentnea Creek was so weak the infantry had to walk across it in single file. The artillerymen suffered the most. Haskell's bigger guns were too heavy for the crude bridges and often broke through the flooring. It took time to free the pieces and repair the structures. No matter how hard they marched, the infantry could not reach New Bern early enough to attack on March 12. They encountered a ford over a swampy stream that was two and a half feet deep. The men of the 26th plunged into it laughing and joking to keep up their spirits. "They had been marching so much in the rain that it seemed a rather agreeable change to get a good soaking from

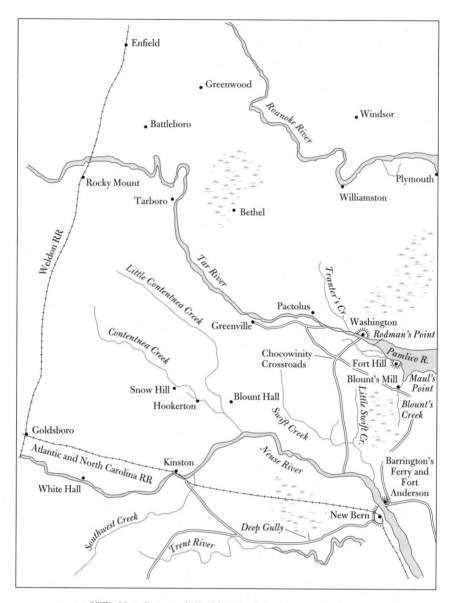

MAP 4.1 Hill's New Bern and Washington Campaigns, March–April 1863

below," thought Linebach, "and besides, a good quantity of real estate that they had been carrying for several days on their feet & legs, was gotten rid of." The band members, however, "were a little more shy of water" and rode in the wagons to avoid getting their feet wet. The 26th went to bed hungry because the commissary wagons were still miles away, bogged down on the muddy road with the artillery.[22]

Pettigrew had marched fifty miles thus far and had only eight miles to go, but he was forced to rest his men for much of March 13 to allow the trains and guns to catch up. When they started at 1:00 P.M., the regimental wagons and the Moravian band were left at the bivouac site. Pettigrew had earlier hoped to move to the fort the night before and capture it with a bayonet attack at dawn on the thirteenth. Now he told Burgwyn that the 26th would be responsible for attacking the earthwork. But Pettigrew admitted that he was undecided whether to "storm the fort or to shell them out by a concentrated fire of artillery." The 47th North Carolina initially was slated to support Burgwyn's men, but later the 44th North Carolina was substituted for it. The 26th, which was in the van of Pettigrew's column, neared the Federal pickets about dusk, and the whole brigade went into bivouac.[23]

A series of bad decisions on the morning of Saturday, March 14, robbed Pettigrew of a spectacular victory. Burgwyn encountered the Federal picket line about a quarter-mile from Fort Anderson at dawn as the rest of the brigade formed behind the 26th. Then he pushed forward to Barrington's house about 400 yards from the earthwork. Fort Anderson was well situated a short distance from Barrington's Ferry and was garrisoned by 350 men of the 92nd New York under Lt. Col. Hiram Anderson Jr. It was built at the end of a small peninsula flanked by a large swamp on one side and a creek on the other. The ground over which Burgwyn would have to advance sloped slightly upward and had a shallow undulation that might have provided some protection for anyone who lay prone in it. When the 26th appeared at Barrington's house, only one gunboat was in sight, anchored a bit upriver from the fort.[24]

Pettigrew made a fateful decision. Rather than rush the fort, which he estimated would cost 50 to 100 men, he decided "to display my force, demoralize them by a heavy fire, and demand a surrender, thus saving my own men and not unnecessarily killing theirs." The gunners fired about forty rounds before Pettigrew sent Louis G. Young with a flag of truce to demand Anderson's surrender. The Yankee hesitated, then asked for a half-hour to consult Foster, who was in New Bern. A boat was dispatched to inform the general, and Pettigrew waited. After the time had passed, Anderson informed him that he had no intention of surrendering. It became obvious that the delay was a ploy to give the gunboat an opportunity to move into place and cover the fort with its fire. Pettigrew ordered his own guns to resume their work, and a fierce artillery duel began that would last for four hours.[25]

This was a duel the Confederates could not win. The four twenty-pounder Parrotts proved to be utterly inadequate, but they were the only artillery available that had a chance with the gunboat. Their ammunition was so defective that about half of the shells burst prematurely just beyond the muzzles. The axle of one of the twenty-pounders broke during firing, while another gun burst, wounding two men and mortally injuring another. This made the crews on the remaining two guns very distrustful of their weapons, and their fire slackened considerably. Burgwyn thought it was unfortunate that the twenty-pounders were forced to concentrate on the gunboat, for he was convinced they could have reduced the fort with their concentrated fire.[26]

Eventually the Confederate guns were withdrawn, but Burgwyn's regiment remained in place. It occupied open, level land and had to take anything the Yankees threw at it. The other regiments were less exposed than the 26th. Benjamin Franklin Little assured his wife that he was never afraid or nervous while enduring this hail of iron. "I felt serious, as I wish always to feel under such circumstances, Sometimes my effort was to re-alize the danger to which I was exposed more than my feelings led me." Pettigrew deliberately exposed himself during this bombardment but remained unhurt. Two of his staff members were less fortunate. Louis G. Young was half asleep on the ground with a blanket over his head when a shell exploded nearby and threw sand on him. Captain Hughes was seriously injured when another shell exploded immediately in front of him and threw sand into his face, temporarily blinding him.[27]

Pettigrew was faced with a hard decision. It had become painfully obvious that the "principal object of the expedition" had "utterly failed." He now considered sending Burgwyn's men in anyway but felt the gunboats would make Fort Anderson untenable even if they captured it. He decided to withdraw. "I felt that my duty to the country required me to save my men for some operation in which sacrifices would be followed by consequences, not in capturing . . . and holding temporary possession of breastworks, however brilliant the operation might be." He withdrew his regiments by echelon about a mile over an open field at 12:30 P.M. The barrage ended when Pettigrew withdrew to his camp of the previous night, arriving there at midnight.[28]

The attack on New Bern was a dismal failure, and Pettigrew bore most of the blame for it. He was an amateur soldier with little experience handling troops in battle. His gentle nature got the better of him early in the confrontation at Barrington's Ferry. He would have been well advised to launch an immediate attack with little artillery preparation and accept the casualties. Pettigrew made a serious mistake in allowing Anderson time to consider his surrender demand, giving the Federals an opportunity to bring up their gunboats. In addition, the Rebel artillerists were hampered by the shoddy condition of their ammunition and the poor quality of the twenty-pounder tubes.[29]

Pettigrew lost two killed and twenty-one wounded. No one was lost in the 47th and 52nd, but three men were wounded in the 44th. The 26th suffered the most, with two killed, one mortally wounded, and twelve wounded. All of the injured were hit by naval gunnery, as there was no exchange of small arms fire. The mortally wounded man had his leg sliced off at the thigh by a shall fragment, and several others were injured by the concussion of a shell that exploded nearby; but most of the wounded were slightly injured by small fragments that hit their shoulders, backs, legs, or arms. The injured were laid on beds of fodder inside a nearby church with a large fire to keep them warm. Federal losses were only two killed and four wounded.[30]

The other columns of Hill's command fared no better than Pettigrew's. Daniel captured a fortified Union position at Deep Gully along the Trent Road on the evening of March 13. Hill waited at Deep Gully the next morning to see how Pettigrew fared. By early afternoon he could tell by the sound of the gunfire at Barrington's Ferry that Pettigrew had been repulsed. He ordered both Daniel and Robertson to retire some twenty miles from New Bern by nightfall.[31]

Everyone in the 26th North Carolina was aware that their repulse occurred on the first anniversary of the battle of New Bern, when the regiment had received its baptism of fire. The symbolism of timing was so strong that it intensified the disappointment felt in the ranks of the 26th. Gus Jarratt spoke for all when he wrote, "I wish we could have done something there for it was just twelve months since they run us off." Foster had participated in the battle and was also acutely aware of the timing of Pettigrew's attack. He even assumed the Rebels had planned it that way. What was intended to be a major assault turned into what Foster termed a "feeble, very feeble" attempt, "ineffective and weak, inflicting no damage and accomplishing no object."[32]

The repulse did not end the brigade's work. It reached camp at midnight on March 14 exhausted and in need of rest. Pettigrew's men rested in camp for much of March 15 until rumors of a Federal landing upriver from New Bern to cut off the brigade forced them to move westward to Swift Creek. The twelve-mile march exhausted the men, many of whom nodded off while riding or marching along the muddy road. The brigade took position at Swift Creek about dusk, deploying artillery behind brush to mask it and preparing for any contingency, but there was no enemy in sight.[33]

Orders came to move out again at midnight of March 15 for Greenville. The roads were awful, and the trains and artillery constantly bogged down, delaying the column. Pettigrew's men had to wade numerous cold streams in the darkness and shivered while waiting for the trains to move on. The way was lighted by hundreds of torches passed out to the men. "It was quite picturesque," recalled Julius Linebach, "to look forward & backward & see the lights flashing amongst the trees. When we made our one stop to rest, some one set fire to a dead pine tree aside of the road, that blazed up into an immense torch." Despite the hardships, the men marched seventeen miles that day and entered Greenville on March 17. They had covered 127 miles in seven days, Pettigrew reported to Hill, and had "waded swamps, worked in them by night and day, bivouacked in the rain, sometimes without fire, never enjoyed a full night's rest after the first, besides undergoing a furious shelling, and discharging other duties. All this without murmuring or even getting sick."[34]

While Pettigrew had been vainly trying to capture Fort Anderson, the 11th North Carolina was joined at Greenville by Garnett's Virginia brigade. The two units moved on to Plymouth to keep the Yankees penned up while foragers collected food in the countryside. Garnett and Leventhorpe left Greenville on March 15 with a total of 2,500 infantrymen, one battery, and a regiment of cavalry. While retreating from Barrington's Ferry, Pettigrew wrote to Garnett asking for support. The Virginians and Tar Heels were temporarily diverted to his aid, but Hill countermanded the move after the men had marched only five miles in Pettigrew's direction. The department commander sarcastically told Longstreet that Pettigrew "got a panic in him." After this little detour, Garnett reached a point within three miles of Plymouth on the evening of March 18, drove in the Federal pickets, and went into camp. Some 35,000 pounds of bacon and much corn, potatoes, and lard were hauled out of Washington and Tyrrell Counties.[35]

Hill ordered Pettigrew to support Garnett by keeping the Federals penned up in Washington. Pettigrew obeyed, but he worried about his mission. He was too far from Garnett to come to his aid if he was attacked by the Plymouth garrison, and Garnett could not come quickly to his support if the Washington Yankees moved out to attack him. A large swamp intervened, and Pettigrew would have to march for three days to get around it. He also feared for the safety of Daniel's brigade, all alone at Kinston, if Foster decided to move out of New Bern and attack it. Yet Pettigrew's brigade moved out of Greenville on March 18. Despite the rain, the boys of the 47th marched along the flooded roads with spirit. The brigade reached Tranter's Creek on March 19, the same spot where Col. George B. Singletary of the 44th North Carolina had been killed in a skirmish on June 5, 1862.[36]

There was no need for Pettigrew to worry about his exposed position, for the Federals were not inclined to move out of Plymouth, Washington, or New Bern to engage the Rebels. The brigade's stay at Tranter's Creek was punctuated by sporadic picket firing but little else. Six companies of the 47th escorted a Whitworth rifle to the south side of the Tar River at Pactolus, but Pettigrew had no intention of attacking the garrison at Washington. The town was protected by heavy fortifications, and two or three gunboats plied the river. With the retirement of Garnett's command from the vicinity of Plymouth, Pettigrew pulled out of his advanced position and marched toward Greenville on March 21. The journey was wet and muddy, as usual, for both commands. The 11th North Carolina had to wade in knee-deep, sometimes waist-deep water, or to march miles out of the way to avoid the truly flooded spots on the road. Pettigrew reached the town on March 21, and Garnett arrived three days later.[37]

The men needed a few days of rest and drying out. W. E. Setser of the 26th reported that he had no change of clothing for several days, "only what we have on. we ar tolerable Black about this time, But the Bois Seem to be in good har." Setser was tired of the privations. "I tell you it is a hard way to Serve the Lord in theas low lands. . . . I am giting tierd of Eastern NC. I had Rather be any whear Els." Burgwyn was disgusted with all the fruitless marching, and he blamed Hill for mismanaging the campaign.[38]

The brigade had little time to rest, for Hill quickly launched an expedition against Washington. Longstreet advised against a direct attack on the fortified town, but he wanted Hill to gather supplies from the region while penning the Federals in place. Garnett's brigade, minus the 11th North Carolina, was to march on the north side of the Tar River and deploy opposite the fortifications, keeping the Yankees behind their earthworks. Pettigrew's and Daniel's North Carolina brigades were to operate south of the Tar and position themselves so as to block a Union relieving column from New Bern. The Tar Heels also were to establish artillery positions downriver to prevent transports and gunboats from relieving the town.[39]

Some of Hill's troops moved out early. The 52nd North Carolina left Greenville on March 28 and reached its assigned post, seven miles downriver from Washington, the next day. The rest of Pettigrew's brigade left Greenville early on the morning of March 30. As Pettigrew approached the town, a small skirmish broke out about noon near Washington. Company K of the 47th North Carolina took shelter behind a barricade of cypress logs in the road and fired at a company of Federal infantry that was advancing along a dike through a neighboring swamp. Three Yankees were wounded and fell into Rebel hands when the Federals retreated. Burgwyn's command supported the 47th in this affair.

The brigade reached its destination, Chocowinity Crossroads, about three and a half miles south of town, at 4:30 P.M. All the roads approaching Washington from the south joined at this key junction. While the 47th deployed pickets at Rodman's Point on the south bank of the river, the rest of Pettigrew's brigade bivouacked at Chocowinity.[40]

Burgwyn relieved the 47th on March 31, dividing his regiment into two battalions. Four companies under Major Jones went to Rodman's Point, and Burgwyn took the rest to Grist's Farm, north of Chocowinity. Another small skirmish took place just before Jones's men relieved the 47th at Rodman's Point. The Federals tried to land 100 men from a flatboat, but the 47th stopped them with a well-aimed volley. Two Confederates were slightly wounded by the return fire. Burgwyn later detailed 300 men to dig entrenchments at Rodman's Point for the guns. They started at dusk and finished well before dawn. That same night other Confederate forces took possession of an abandoned Rebel fort at Hill's Point about seven miles downriver from Washington and called it Fort Hill. It was located at a strategic bend of the Pamlico River, the tidal stream that drained the Tar. As the 47th relieved the 26th on picket duty at dawn of April 1, the cannon at Rodman's Point opened up on the Union gunboats that were near town. The Confederates suffered bad luck from the beginning, for one of the Whitworth guns at Rodman's Point burst and another artillery piece exploded later in the day. It was an ominous sign.[41]

Pettigrew's regiments took up their assigned positions for the siege of Washington on April 2. The 11th, 44th, and 52nd were placed near Fort Hill to guard it against an attack by land. Burgwyn was ordered to report to Leventhorpe, whose regiment was holding the road from Blount's Mill to Washington. The mill was located where the road crossed Blount's Creek about four miles southeast of Fort Hill and was on one of two most likely routes that a relief column from New Bern would take to Washington. Leventhorpe ordered Burgwyn to place the 26th four miles west of the mill so he could watch other crossings of the creek to his right and to reinforce the 11th at the mill or support the 52nd North Carolina, which was picketing the riverbank west of Fort Hill. Leventhorpe was also placed in charge of the fort. He later noted that Pettigrew was responsible for choosing Blount's Mill as a defensive position and even planned the fortifications there, which Leventhorpe built. The Englishman thought it a strong post, with better defensive potential than his position at White Hall the previous December.[42]

Hill almost completely cut off Washington from the outside world. The garrison there was fully blocked by land, and the Confederate batteries at Rodman's Point and Fort Hill greatly reduced river traffic to the town. On the north side of the Tar, Garnett dug artillery positions opposite the heavily fortified line that curved around the land side of Washington and opened a daily bombardment that kept the Federals safely behind their defenses. Daniel's brigade deployed near Pettigrew's men between Blount's Mill and Chocowinity to guard the remaining road from New Bern.[43]

The Union garrison was comparatively small but well fortified. Foster himself had traveled by boat to Washington with a few staff officers before Hill began the siege. He was outnumbered three to one by the Confederates but managed to silence some of Garnett's artillery positions. A few transports bringing more supplies made their way through the Rebel blockade now and then, but Union naval commanders chose not to challenge the guns in Fort Hill.[44]

The strength of Foster's fortifications and the inadequacy of Hill's artillery would be the key factors in determining the outcome of the siege. The same problem that bedeviled Pettigrew at Barrington's Ferry haunted Hill. His artillery tubes were bursting right and left, and soon there were only a handful of operable guns. Yet the Union fleet continued to shy about rather than descend on Fort Hill. "Until now," as Burgwyn put it, "we have relied entirely on the game of Bluff."[45]

Yet there was a strong sense of confidence in the Rebel camps. "I think we will take the place," wrote Gus Jarratt, "if they will land below and come up we will give them a good thrashing." Capt. Stephen Wiley Brewer of Company E, 26th North Carolina, wanted to end the campaign. If the Confederates could not "whip them we Can Starve them out and they will be Bound to surrender." As the daily cannonading failed to bring a decisive break in the siege, Hill's men grew frustrated. Pvt. William Fleming of the 26th North Carolina wrote home, "we now have washington surrounded, and old Hill says he can take the place without the loss of a man at anytime he wants too. but I dont know what is the reason that he dont proceed, for we are all tired of lying here and listening at the cannons every day." Life in the siege camps at Washington was not pleasant. Burgwyn's men had not changed their underclothing for several weeks, and some were "near naked." The men only had one change of outer clothing, and "It is very near done."[46]

The weather finally turned dry and warm by the middle of the siege, but logistics remained a problem. Commissary officer Benjamin Wesley Justice spent nearly all day receiving and distributing rations for the 643 men of the 47th because provisions had to be transported all the way from Greenville each day.[47]

Pettigrew's men were disturbed by an alarm that Federal troops were approaching by way of Swift Creek, to the southwest of Fort Hill, on April 7. The 47th and 52nd North Carolina marched out to meet them, but it turned out to be a small force of cavalry that withdrew without making contact. This small mounted force was one arm of a major effort to relieve Washington. With his department commander isolated in the besieged town, Brig. Gen. Henry Prince had considered landing troops and attacking Hill's Point. After reconnoitering the area, he found that there was no practicable landing spot and that Leventhorpe's position at Blount's Mill was very strong. The bridge here could be partly disassembled to prevent troops from crossing, and Blount's Creek could not be waded because of its wide, swampy bottomland.[48]

Foster wanted Prince to advance overland from New Bern to relieve Washington, and he sent messages to that effect with the few ships able to run the blockade at Hill's Point. Rather than lead the column himself, Prince assigned Brig. Gen. Francis B. Spinola the task. It was a mistake he would regret, for the New York native was a political general with no military training or experience. Spinola's 6,400 men were divided into three brigades. Prince told Spinola he thought the relief expedition was doomed, and Spinola was fed information placing Hill's strength at 15,000 men. Thus it was with a heavy heart that the political general advanced northward. He decided to take the eastern road to Washington by way of Blount's Mill rather than the Swift Creek road.[49]

Confederate pickets detected Spinola's approach early in the afternoon of Thursday, April 9. Burgwyn was ordered at 1:00 P.M. to move to Leventhorpe's assistance. Major Jones took four companies of the 26th to reinforce the 11th North Carolina at Blount's Mill while Burgwyn took the remaining companies upstream to cover three fords. He found three companies of the 11th already there and assumed command of the combined force. Burgwyn was dissatisfied with the way Leventhorpe's officer had placed the men, so he carefully repositioned one company at the uppermost ford and three each at the other two, holding two companies in reserve. Four men of the 26th also filled in as gunners with an artillery piece of Graham's battery positioned at the mill.[50]

Leventhorpe was ready. His men were positioned atop slightly higher ground than Spinola's, and Company K of the 11th had removed enough planks from the bridge, which was a short distance downstream from the mill, to prevent anyone from dashing across it. He had four six-pounder guns in position and a total of 2,800 infantry, and Pettigrew was present as well. Spinola reached the bridge about 3:00 P.M. and began to skirmish with a Rebel company that was picketing the Union side of Blount's Creek. These Confederates fired for several minutes, then retired across the stream. The Bethel Regiment held the center of Leventhorpe's position, covering the road with its fire. As Amory's Federal brigade closed up to the creek, a two-hour artillery fight ensued. Part of Belger's Rhode Island battery and a section of thirty-two pounder guns poured canister into

Leventhorpe's well-fortified position from a distance of 450 yards. Only two infantry regiments, the 17th and 44th Massachusetts, came close enough to open fire. The rest of Spinola's large command could not find room to deploy. The Union general gave up, concluding that no effort to cross Blount's Creek could succeed without exhaustive casualties. The Federals disengaged at 5:00 P.M. and rapidly retreated toward New Bern, cutting trees to block the road behind them.[51]

Leventhorpe did not try to pursue. He just pushed out some pickets to the opposite side of the creek to guard against a night attack. Burgwyn, whose position was not threatened, sent out scouts that night and the next day to ascertain that Spinola was definitely gone. The ease with which the Rebels repelled the column was remarkable. "I never knew a more pusilanimous effort," mused Burgwyn. "They advanced very rapidly with many promises of sleeping in Washington that night & etc. & after a little skirmish, for it amounted to little more, they retreated in great haste & trepidation." Leventhorpe expressed a common disgust with the Yankees when he crowed to his wife that "the cowardly loons felled trees on the road & withdrew in the night." The losses had been very light on both sides. About thirty Yankees were killed and wounded, while Leventhorpe lost one killed and four wounded. Two of the Rebel casualties served in the 47th North Carolina, which came up to support Leventhorpe at the mill just as the engagement began. One soldier was wounded on the back of the neck by a shell fragment, and Pvt. Joseph Breedlove of Company G, an ambulance corpsman, was far to the rear at the field hospital, drinking from a spring, when a round tore off his leg, "just leaving it hanging by a narrow strip of skin." He died that night. Benjamin Wesley Justice was amazed at the effect of Spinola's fire on the environment. "The artillery shot through the mill house, shattered the trees in the swamp & raked the ground," he wrote. The 44th North Carolina came up "just in time to get a good shelling," in the words of Alexander S. Webb. The men stood in line all night, muskets at the ready, in case the Federals returned. Their lower legs were soaked with muddy water, making for a very uncomfortable night.[52]

Pettigrew's brigade decisively blunted this poorly led relief column, but the siege of Washington was doomed. Hill scoured the countryside for corn and bacon while his river blockade was crumbling. The steamer *Escort* ran past Fort Hill on the night of April 13 with reinforcements and repeated the trip two days later. Several boats had earlier passed the guns, but the *Escort* seemed to be the last straw. When he heard of the passage, Pettigrew wrote Hill with astonishing sarcasm, "So passes away the blockade. As somebody remarked this morning, with more truth than agreeability, 'The entertainment will now conclude with the laughable and amusing farce of "Running the Blockade." Parents may send their children with the assurance that the exhibition is perfectly innocent.'"[53]

Hill decided to give up. Burgwyn received orders to move out on the evening of April 15, but the march to Chocowinity was slowed by a torrential downpour. The men had to wade streams and constantly slipped in the muddy road, which was "visible only by the flashes of lightning & terribly cut up by the wheels of . . . numerous Artillery" and wagons. It took five hours to march eight miles. They bivouacked at the crossroads that night and the next day as well. "All the men were wet through & through & covered with mud from the crown of their heads to the sole of their feet," wrote Burgwyn. The brigade left the area for good on the evening of April 17, battling the mud as fiercely as before, and reached Greenville at noon on the eighteenth. The men had time to wash thoroughly and get a change of clothing, but their travels were not over. The next day Pettigrew sent them to Hookerton, a small town about twenty miles southwest of Greenville and ten miles north of Kinston on the south side of Contentnea Creek. There they established what they were led to believe would be a "permanent camp." Garnett's and Daniel's brigades also broke up their camps and retired.[54]

Foster summed up the Rebel operation by reporting that "after fourteen days of close siege of Washington General Hill had failed to obtain a single advantage or to advance one step nearer his object." This was painfully obvious to Hill's soldiers as well. Gus Jarratt believed he should have stormed the town and was frustrated that his regiment had marched 300 miles in the past month to no purpose. Lemuel Hoyle put it nicely when he told his mother, "Why Washington was not taken, I do not Know. Why the siege of Washington was raised when it was, I do not Know. Why we went to Washington, in the first place, I do not Know. Indeed upon the whole subject of the movement towards Washington I am pretty much of a 'Know Nothing.'"[55]

Burgwyn criticized Hill for relying too heavily on his artillery and for failing to prepare adequate supply lines. Burgwyn also faulted his commander for having no "definite plan. He should either have made up his mind to storm the place at once, or he should have been prepared to undertake a regular siege." Rather than divide his force north and south of the river, the general should have concentrated his strength for a decisive blow. "It seemed to me that Gen. Hill relied upon circumstances & events to suggest ideas & plans."[56]

Pettigrew must have felt frustrated with all the fruitless campaigning. He fired off a dispatch to Hill complaining about a number of problems after stationing his men at Hookerton. There were no adequate maps of the country, there was confusion about how much artillery he should have with his brigade, and there was a logistical problem to be solved. Despite the food-gathering mission, there were no stockpiles of provisions at either Greenville or Kinston. If he was to re-inforce either place at short notice, his men would not have enough to eat, "for in this country it is utterly impossible to support troops while they are march-ing." Pettigrew's concern for his men shone through when he noted that the "weather is very hard on troops on the march, and it is trying them too hard to add hunger to their other sufferings."[57]

At least one member of the 26th North Carolina complained publicly about the hardships. Pvt. William J. Laird of Company K wrote a letter to the *North Carolina Argus* in Wadesboro reporting that the men were suffering for want of food. The newspaper created a sensation when it reached the regiment. Capt. J. C. McLauchlin reported that his men "could be seen coming up from every quarter of my camp to my bivouac fire, their eyes flashing indignation, and their lips pouring forth profuse abuses upon" Laird's head. McLauchlin wrote a re-buttal to the newspaper and argued that most of his men did not suffer unduly from lack of provisions. Short rations and spoiled meat occurred sporadically and were always compensated for by a quick return to full supplies and edible fare. McLauchlin attacked Laird's character by noting that he was sick half the time and had eagerly volunteered to guard the company's baggage when Petti-grew started out to attack New Bern. McLauchlin encouraged the home folks to visit his company. "Our fare is coarse, it is true, but we have plenty, and all my men, except two or three croakers, who are always trying to lag behind, and shun every duty they can, are as contented and happy as soldiers can be—and they are in excellent health and spirits."[58]

Morale certainly was high, but conditions in the army were far from idyllic. The men were quite willing to go on with the war even though they longed for its end. W. E. Setser mused on the prospects of peace if it could be obtained on his own terms. "I wood like for pease to be made," he wrote home. "But I never want it made in this world in the yankes favor. I had as Soon live in Africa as to live under A Lincon Government."[59]

Leventhorpe took advantage of the short lull in operations to drill his con-scripts four hours a day separately from the other troops until an order to move out arrived on the morning of April 21. Yankees were reported to be advancing toward Greenville, where Daniel's troops were stationed. The brigade marched five miles to the northeast to Adams's Bridge, on Little Contentnea Creek, but the next day it discovered that the "reported advance was a hoax." Rather than return to Hookerton, the brigade was directed to Kinston, which it reached on April 29.[60]

While at Kinston, Burgwyn's 1,026 men were healthy but lousy. Burgwyn wryly noted that only his sergeant major and quartermaster among the staff officers "had the courage to examine themselves" for lice. The men had had no change of clothing since March 9 and had been living on one pound of meal or crackers and a half-pound of meat per day.[61]

The stay at Kinston proved to be short. Word reached the area on April 30 that a battle was brewing near Fredericksburg. The new commander of the Army of the Potomac, Maj. Gen. Joseph Hooker, had crossed the Rappahannock River to engage Lee's army. The Tar Heels were convinced Lee would "administer to him a most tremendous thrashing." Burgwyn was sure most of the troops in southeastern Virginia, eastern North Carolina, and South Carolina would be called up to help Lee, and he predicted the expected battlefield victory would lead to a Rebel invasion of Maryland and perhaps Pennsylvania.[62]

Ever since its organization, Pettigrew's brigade had operated in the comparative backwater of Virginia and North Carolina. It had few chances to distinguish itself. The men of the brigade had plenty of exposure to hard marching and short rations, and they had at least been fired at by gunboats and artillery. John Thorp, the historian of the 47th, accurately characterized the regiment's service as "arduous, but less conspicuous." It and the other regiments would be thrown into a much more demanding and dangerous theater of operations when Lee ordered them to join his famed army. Louis G. Young later wrote about this time. "The discipline of these Winter months in North Carolina was never wholly lost. It prepared the command for the bloody fields of Virginia and Pennsylvania, and served to gain for it the deathless fame which it acquired."[63]

Chapter 5

North to Pennsylvania

Although Burgwyn had predicted that his unit would return to Lee, the order to move out for Virginia was a surprise to everyone. The brigade left Kinston early on May 1 to form a line two miles from town in response to a reported Union move. Then instructions arrived to cook rations and be ready to leave for Virginia in the afternoon. The 11th and 26th, with Pettigrew and staff, boarded the trains that afternoon and reached Goldsboro in the evening. The other three regiments were left at Kinston for the time being in case the Federals were serious about attacking the place.[1]

A terrible accident happened between Goldsboro and Halifax. The train carrying the 11th North Carolina rammed into the cars loaded with the 26th North Carolina, which had stopped to let a mail train pass. Cpl. James W. Wright of Company C was appalled: "such a smash up I never saw in my life." Flatcars and boxcars were wrecked, and a man had his foot badly mauled. One soldier in Company E had his head caught between two cars, and it was "mashed all to pieces his brains was spattered all around him." Another man was caught between the cars at his hips and was badly crushed. Burgwyn lost one man killed, one mortally injured, and ten hurt. A few men in the 11th also were injured. The wreck delayed the two regiments, but they reached Petersburg by 11:00 that night. The men marched rapidly through, boarded the cars for Richmond, and reached the capital on the morning of May 3.[2]

The 11th and 26th missed the battle of Chancellorsville, which climaxed on the day they reached Richmond. The capital was essentially undefended, and a large force of Union cavalry under Maj. Gen. George Stoneman was descending on it. Lee requested that Pettigrew's men be sent to Hanover Junction, twenty miles north of the city, to protect the railroad bridge over the North Anna River. The request was quickly filtered down the chain of command to Maj. Gen. Arnold Elzey, commander of the Department of Richmond, who sent Major Jones's wing of the 26th North Carolina to the Richmond and Fredericksburg Railroad bridge over the North Anna River. Jones was instructed to defend the structure "to the last extremity." Elzey later ordered Pettigrew to send Burgwyn's wing as well. He also instructed Pettigrew to take charge of all forces at the bridges over both the North and South Anna and at Hanover Junction, which lay between the two streams. Here the Richmond and Fredericksburg line met the Central Railroad, which connected Hanover with Gordonsville in the piedmont to the northwest.[3]

Burgwyn reached the North Anna at noon on May 3 with his half of the regiment. He began to scout the terrain to acquaint himself with the position but received news that a small Federal mounted force was lurking in the area. He marched his men to the junction at Hanover, where he met Pettigrew, who took command of the area at dusk.[4]

The 11th North Carolina closely followed Burgwyn's regiment. It had to march through Richmond to retrain for the journey to Hanover Junction, and the relatively large regiment impressed the citizens who lined the streets. Someone asked which brigade was passing by. "The answer was 'It ain't anybody's brigade its the 11th North Carolina Regiment.'" This brought a knowing sigh from the civilians, and one of them said, "'Its a fine Regiment, but boys you'll never all get back.'" With this warning ringing in their ears, Leventhorpe's men reached Hanover Junction on the evening of May 3 and deployed to their guard posts.[5]

The remaining regiments of Pettigrew's brigade came up to join the 11th and 26th. Marshall's 52nd North Carolina left Kinston on May 2 and made it to Richmond the next evening without incident. It was held there to defend the city for five days, being stationed in the interior line of defenses, then moved to Hanover Junction on May 7. Marshall divided his regiment into battalions. Three companies were held as a reserve in camp near the junction, five companies were sent to the South Anna bridge, and two companies stood picket along the Richmond and Fredericksburg Railroad. The 26th North Carolina was concentrated at the North Anna bridge and the bridge over Polecat Creek a few miles north. The 44th North Carolina left Kinston on the night of May 3 and reached Richmond at 4:00 p.m. the next day. It spent the next several days camped on the capitol lawn in Richmond. Singletary's men were awakened on the night of May 6 to rush toward the Chickahominy Bridge on the report of a civilian who thought the Yankees were approaching. They found no enemy and were drenched with rain as they marched back in the dark.[6]

While at Richmond, the 44th North Carolina had the honor of escorting Stonewall Jackson's body on one short leg of its journey to its burial place in Lexington. Jackson had been accidentally shot at Chancellorsville and on May 10 had succumbed to complications resulting from his wounds. The next day his remains were transported by rail from Guinea Station south to Richmond. The 44th donned a "new uniform Dress," leading General Elzey to call it "the finest regiment he ever saw." The train was four hours late, so Singletary's men escorted the body of Col. James C. S. McDowell of the 54th North Carolina, who also had been mortally wounded at Chancellorsville, to the depot for shipment south. When Jackson's body arrived at 4:00 P.M., the regiment accompanied it from the depot to the governor's mansion. The remains lay in state at the capitol until they were shipped to the Shenandoah Valley. Although the men suffered under the warm sun in their dress uniforms, Alexander S. Webb assured his sister that "I wouldn't have missed escorting Gen Jackson's remains for any thing." A few days later the regiment moved to Hanover Junction.[7]

Faribault's 47th North Carolina remained near Kinston longer than any other of Pettigrew's regiments. On May 2 it marched toward Greenville, where Faribault took command of all the infantry, cavalry, and artillery and Capt. William C. Lankford took charge of the regiment. For more than two weeks the 47th sat idle in this backwater while its companions were guarding Lee's supply line at Hanover Junction. Finally orders arrived to leave for Virginia, and Faribault started the regiment on May 22. Three men deserted the first night out, and a fourth left before Faribault boarded his troops on the railroad cars at Tarboro the next day. The regiment rejoined the brigade on May 27 and was put to work on the fortifications at the South Anna Bridge. Faribault had issued a lot of new equipment just before leaving North Carolina, including socks, pants, drawers, shirts, jackets, caps, and shoes.[8]

The brigade spent nearly a month at Hanover Junction guarding Lee's supply line. Lee instructed Pettigrew to send what little cavalry was available to guard his flanks to the west and southwest, while the cavalry of the Army of Northern Virginia would screen him to the north and northwest. The men settled into a routine at Hanover Junction and marched in review for Pettigrew on June 1. "The dust was very disagreeable," wrote Burgwyn. "My Regt. did very well but showed the want of new clothes very much." A shipment of clothing arrived from Richmond on June 5. The pants were of varied colors and uneven quality, the jackets were a bit more uniform in color, but the caps were all the same style and color. Unfortunately his men preferred hats but had to accept whatever they could get.[9]

Since his men were outfitted in new clothes, Burgwyn thought they needed a new flag. The Confederate Congress had just adopted a new national flag, the Stainless Banner, so called because it consisted mostly of a white field with the battle flag of the Army of Northern Virginia in the upper left corner. The young colonel wanted one for his regiment, but the difficulties in acquiring it were enormous. He had to send the regimental flag home for safekeeping and obtained a battle flag of the Army of Northern Virginia pattern. The Confederate national flag he so much wanted never made it to the regiment.[10]

The young colonel also honed his ambition while at Hanover Junction. D. H Hill believed Burgwyn would be promoted as soon as Pettigrew was made a major general and given a higher command. Burgwyn even asked his father to "feel the N.C. delegation" in the Confederate Congress on this subject. He made no attempt to hide his ambition. "It is . . . a Cardinal point with me never to lose an opportunity," he wrote, but he also thought little of Pettigrew's chances for promotion. "He has done nothing to deserve it & he appears to hold himself too much aloof from everybody. To be sure he has a very fine Brigade, but everybody in the Brigade knows that he is not entitled to one particle of the credit for it." Burgwyn complained that Pettigrew rarely visited his regiments. "Although we receive orders by couriers enough to keep us continually bothered he personally judges of nothing & personally does nothing to increase the efficiency of the command."[11]

Leventhorpe also aspired to a brigade command, but he knew his limitations. He heard that a North Carolina cavalry brigade recently sent to Virginia wanted him as their commander, but he declined the honor. "I am an Infantry Soldier," the Englishman explained to his wife, "both in knowledge, & by preferance, & will never allow any further petition in my behalf." He had been similarly petitioned by the men of Pender's brigade, which Pettigrew had initially led, when Pender was moved up to command the Light Division. But Col. Alfred M. Scales, who was already leading the 13th North Carolina in that brigade, got the position instead.[12]

Lee took another step toward incorporating Pettigrew's brigade into his army when he proposed a major reorganization of his command. He created the Third Corps, to be commanded by Lt. Gen. A. P. Hill and consisting of three divisions, one of which was a new unit created partly from the regiments recently brought up from North Carolina. Maj. Gen. Henry Heth was to command it. Pettigrew's brigade; Heth's old Virginia brigade, now led by Col. John M. Brockenbrough; Brig. Gen. James J. Archer's brigade of Tennessee and Alabama regiments; and Brig. Gen. Joseph R. Davis's Mississippi brigade (with the 55th North Carolina attached) would constitute the division.[13]

Lt. Gen. Richard S. Ewell replaced Jackson as head of the Second Corps and marched westward into the lower Shenandoah Valley to pave the way for a new offensive into Northern territory. Lt. Gen. James Longstreet's First Corps moved northwestward to screen Ewell's advance, while Hill's corps was assigned the task of holding the heights at Fredericksburg and watching Hooker's movements across the Rappahannock. Hill was authorized to move Pettigrew's brigade up from Hanover Junction, and he immediately issued the necessary orders.[14]

The 26th left Hanover Junction on the morning of June 7, and a four-and-a-half-hour journey brought it to Hamilton's Crossing, two miles south of Fredericksburg. Burgwyn unloaded his men and joined the Confederate troops already in position. A small force of Federals had crossed the river downstream from Fredericksburg, and the 26th entered the earthworks to hold Hamilton's Crossing, where a wagon road intersected the railroad and ascended the river bluffs through a wide, deep gorge. The 52nd had the most difficulty moving to Fredericksburg, for the men were scattered at different posts and had to wait for rail transportation to arrive. The regiment reached Hamilton's Crossing late in the afternoon of June 8 and marched six miles south to man earthworks near the Rappahannock River. The 26th was also ordered to march south of the crossing to support the 52nd.[15]

The 44th North Carolina had started to board the cars at Hanover Junction when Pettigrew's adjutant told them the bad news: they were to stay put and continue to guard the railroad. Most of Singletary's men were severely disappointed. "Sorrowful at being left behind we sat up late that night to discuss the matter," recalled Sgt. William S. Long of Company G. They were tired of the "enforced inactivity of garrison duty" and wanted to be part of the northward movement. At least Alexander S. Webb had a change of heart two weeks later. Responding to news of the "hard times" Lee's men were having as they marched northward, he remarked at how "fortunate our Regiment was in getting sent" to Hanover Junction and staying there.[16]

Although there were no indications of a Federal offensive at Fredericksburg, the Confederates had to remain on their toes for several days to come. The Federal positions across the Rappahannock were clearly visible to the naked eye, and there were still a few Yankees on the west side of the river. Heavy picket duty was expected of Pettigrew's men to keep them at a safe distance. Pettigrew held the right flank of Hill's corps and was responsible for picketing the region north of the mouth of Massaponax Creek.[17]

There were complaints about Pettigrew's men from some of the more experienced soldiers of Lee's army. Joseph H. Saunders, an officer in the 33rd North Carolina of Brig. Gen. James H. Lane's brigade, Pender's division, noted that Marshall's men fired on the Federals all the time. Even when a Union officer came over with a flag of truce to ask them "to be more civilised and stop shooting, they told him if he did not hurry back they would shoot him and they intended to shoot every yankee that showed his head." Saunders believed they did not have the hardening experience of standing picket "where the yankees have the advantage of us and they do the shooting." The men of the 33rd knew what that was like and were willing to leave the enemy alone. Nevertheless there were some impromptu truces on the picket line, even though Pettigrew tried to ban them. Newspapers were exchanged, and Northern coffee was swapped for Southern tobacco. Pettigrew's company officers ignored this fraternization whenever possible.[18]

The band of the 26th found a great deal of professional company at Fredericksburg, for not only the 11th North Carolina but the 11th Mississippi and the 55th North Carolina also had bands. The Moravians singled out different units to play for on a regular basis. One day, close to dusk, they were serenading a battery when a civilian came out of a nearby house and asked them to stop, "as he feared we would draw the fire of the enemy's guns." The band members politely moved their concert to another location. Other households were more hospitable and offered the musicians delicacies such as soured sweet pickles for their performance. The band had much more music to play after they received a shipment of new scores from Salem in early June.[19]

Logistical matters became important as everyone began to realize they would likely join the rest of Lee's army in a strike north. The 11th North Carolina received a new battle flag of the Army of Northern Virginia pattern, and several of its companies were issued a wide variety of clothes. The brigade's transportation was upgraded as well. Pettigrew's quartermaster, Maj. G. P. Collins, reported that the 26th had eight wagons with teams of four horses, three wagons pulled by teams of two horses, and six wagons that were entirely worn out. The wagons were used to carry the regiment's ordnance, the headquarters equipment and papers, commissary stores, and company baggage. Although listed as "horse" wagons, they were all in fact pulled by a total of forty-two mules. The other regiments in the brigade had slightly fewer wagons than the 26th because of their smaller size. To cut down on the amount of transportation needed, Pettigrew issued an order to stop hauling officers' baggage. That included the personal belongings of the band, but the wily musicians made a deal with the quartermaster of the regiment so that Linebach could keep his valise, which served as "a common receptacle for various articles belonging to the crowd." Sam Mickey also managed to keep his box filled with sheet music, and two other carpet bags and a mess chest were secreted away in the wagons when no one was looking.[20]

Pettigrew told Leventhorpe of his concern that the brigade might be left behind and miss the Pennsylvania campaign, but his worry was wasted. The men were ordered from their picket posts south of Hamilton's Crossing to Marye's Heights on June 14 and bivouacked there that night. The brigade left Fredericksburg at 3:00 on the afternoon of June 15 and marched about nine miles before bivouacking just short of the Chancellorsville battlefield. It left the 44th North Carolina behind. Singletary's regiment remained at Hanover Junction to guard the railroad bridges and would miss the Pennsylvania campaign altogether. Capt. James S. Harris of the 7th North Carolina in Lane's brigade watched discerningly as Pettigrew's Tar Heels marched from Marye's Heights. "Pettigrew's regiments were full, well clothed and well armed, altogether they were a fine body of men."[21]

The soldiers got a taste of what was to come when they marched across the battleground at Chancellorsville on June 16. It was "a great sight to see," reported James W. Wright; "the timber was torn up very much and . . . graves a sight and dead horses[;] it was difficult getting along[,] the yankees and some of our men lying partly out of the ground." The band members of the 26th traveled with the wagons and thus crossed the battlefield that night. They could not see the things that stunned Wright, but they could tell they were in a charnel field by the foul, overpowering odor of rotting horse flesh rising in the darkness around them.[22]

The brigade marched hard to the west and reached Culpeper Court House on the evening of June 17. An order filtered down the chain of command for regimental officers to reduce their baggage to the minimum. The men were ordered to carry three days' worth of rations in their haversacks while another three days' worth was to be carried in the wagons. The band members were forced to sell their mess chest and give away some of the food they could not carry, but Julius Linebach managed to keep his valise.[23]

The march continued with the men up and on the road just before dawn every day. The hot sun caused sunstroke for some even as the brigade crossed the upper reaches of the Rappahannock River on June 18. Pettigrew crossed the Blue Ridge at Chester Gap on June 20. Marshall's family lived near the eastern foot of this dominating eminence, which was the eastern border of the Appalachian Highlands. In fact, Lee himself had dined with his family on the evening of June 17, but Marshall had no opportunity to pay even a short visit home.[24]

The brigade was greeted with bouquets of flowers in Front Royal. That night the men of the 26th unknowingly bivouacked near a rattlesnake den, however, and six of the creatures were killed. "There was not much traveling around that night," recalled J. A. Bush Sr. "Everybody got a place to lie down and kept quiet for the night." The next day the brigade crossed both forks of the Shenandoah

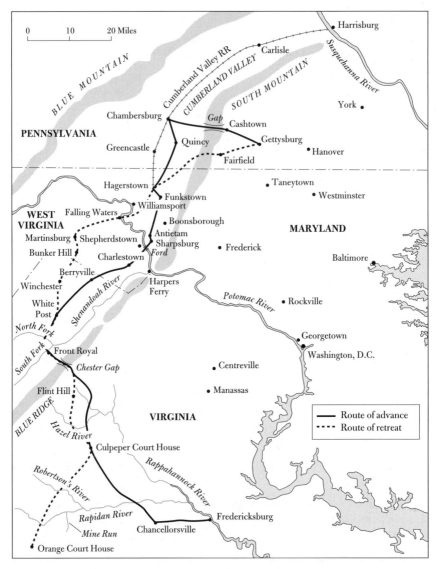

MAP 5.1 Pettigrew's Route to Pennsylvania

River where the two streams joined. The water was so deep it reached their armpits, but most of the men took off their outer clothing before they waded across. The Tar Heels stopped that evening near Berryville, ten miles northeast of Winchester and twenty-five miles short of the Potomac River. They had covered about fifteen to twenty miles each day, and Linebach admitted that his "feet were becoming pretty sore."[25]

When the brigade passed through Berryville on June 23, an overexcited woman wearing a Confederate flag shouted, "Hurrah for the rebels," and raced toward the marching column. She was so winded that she blurted out, "I never was in such a fix in my life. Whoop! I'm out of breath." Linebach noted with amusement that she was "well cheered by the men." The next morning the column passed through Charlestown, made famous as the scene of John Brown's trial and execution for his attack on the U.S. Army arsenal at Harpers Ferry nearly four years earlier. Pettigrew bypassed Harpers Ferry, which was still occupied by Federal troops, and bivouacked two miles from the south bank of the Potomac River near Shepherdstown.[26]

Pettigrew would have to launch his brigade across the river without the 44th North Carolina, which remained at Hanover Junction for the duration of the Pennsylvania campaign. Singletary kept two companies at the junction while dispatching Maj. Charles M. Stedman with four companies to the north. Lt. Col. Tazewell Hargrove posted one of the four remaining companies at each of the four bridges on the Richmond and Petersburg Railroad and the Central Railroad. Hargrove, an ardent secessionist who had been a delegate to the convention that took North Carolina out of the Union, had graduated from Randolph-Macon College in Ashland, near Hanover Junction. He remained with Company A at the Central Railroad bridge of the South Anna.

A small group of Federals suddenly swooped down on the bridges on the morning of June 26. The 11th Pennsylvania Cavalry and detachments of the 12th Illinois Cavalry and the 2nd Massachusetts Cavalry, totaling 1,050 men and commanded by Col. Samuel P. Spear, attacked Hargrove's Company A at the Central bridge over the South Anna. Hargrove had 40 men manning a fortification designed for ten times that number. He ordered them to evacuate the earthwork as untenable, moved them across the bridge, and posted them on the north bank of the river behind trees and other natural cover. The Tar Heels, armed with Mississippi rifles, put up a magnificent fight. They managed to blunt every attempt by Spear to cross the bridge from the south for two hours. Pvt. Joseph H. Cash, a sixteen-year-old farmer from Granville County, killed four Yankees who tried to set the bridge on fire and two more who ran across the span. Sgt. Alexander S. Peace took seven men into the river bottom to prevent the Yankees from setting fire to the south end of the thirty-foot-long bridge.

Spear then moved 400 men across an obscure ford pointed out to him by local slaves. He arranged this force for an attack on Hargrove's unprotected rear, but help arrived just in time. Hargrove had sent a courier racing toward Taylorsville for reinforcements when the fight started, and Capt. Robert Bingham's Company G came running up. Bingham placed his winded men behind an earthwork

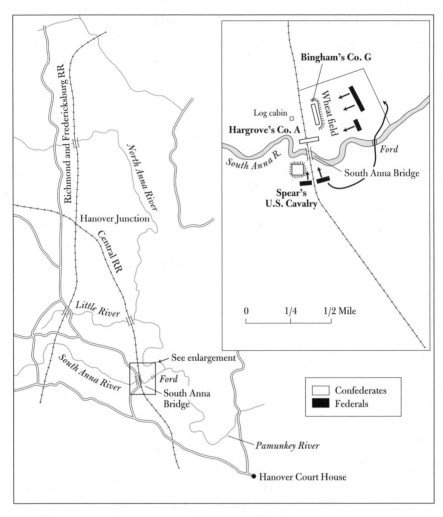

Bingham's Co. G

Log cabin

Hargrove's Co. A

North Anna River

South Anna R.

Wheat field

Ford

South Anna Bridge

Spear's
U.S. Cavalry

Richmond and Fredericksburg RR

Hanover Junction

Central RR

Little River

South Anna River

See enlargement

Ford

South Anna
Bridge

Pamunkey River

• Hanover Court House

0   1/4   1/2 Mile

Confederates
Federals

MAP 5.2 Hanover Junction and the Battle of the South Anna Bridge, June 26, 1863

previously dug beside the Central Railroad about 200 yards from the bridge, so as to protect Hargrove's rear. The Yankees decided to attack Company G head on, advancing over a level wheat field. Bingham waited until they were within forty yards before he shouted the order to fire. Bluecoated soldiers tumbled out of their saddles, and riderless horses careened over the field while the rest retreated in haste. Fifteen minutes later a second mounted charge was made and repulsed, and a third attempt was later blunted. While this was going on, Spear directed attacks on Hargrove's front, again with the intention of crossing the railroad bridge, but they were just as handsomely repulsed.

At this point Spear personally crossed the river and scouted the Rebel positions. Rather than driving frontally at Bingham's men, Spear ordered an assault along the bank of the river to slice into the gap between Bingham and Hargrove. This would allow the Federals to strike the left flank of Company A, which rested at the abutment of the railroad bridge, and the right flank of Company G. The Yankees slammed into the flanks of these two companies, but the Confederates put up an incredible resistance. Hand-to-hand fighting erupted with rifle butts, sword play, and pistol shots at close range. The antagonists were so closely intermingled at the bridge that Bingham ordered his men to cease firing for fear of hitting comrades in Company A. Hargrove refused to give up. He had made a small log cabin his headquarters and personally struggled with several Federal troopers on the porch. Pvt. Joe Cash came to Hargrove's assistance, bayoneting a "gigantic trooper" who was rushing to attack the lieutenant colonel, but another Yankee then shot Cash, who fell on the man he had just killed. When asked to surrender, Cash yelled, "I'll never do it, till my colonel tells me." Hargrove was sliced on the head and right arm by sabers, pricked on his breast by a bayonet, and knocked down by another saber blow to his head. He later counted eight saber cuts in his clothes, but he was not seriously injured, only overpowered and forced to give up.

After Company A was crushed, Spear turned his attention to Company G. Bingham's men were still mostly armed and ready to resume firing on the hundreds of bluecoated cavalry closing in on them, but Bingham decided it was useless to waste any more of his brave soldiers. The order was shouted to give up, and silence fell upon this little battlefield. Sixty years later an eighty-five-year-old Bingham proudly recalled, "We saved General Lee's communications with Richmond during the whole Pennsylvania campaign." Private Cash was dying on the porch of the little cabin when Bingham found him. "I put my hand on his head as he lay, beautiful in death, and felt and heard the broken bones scrape against each other like a crushed egg shell." Three Confederates were killed, twelve were wounded, and four were wounded and captured. Some were so seriously injured that Spear simply left them at the bridge with medicine and attendants. Sergeant Peace was hit in the lungs, the right side, and the groin, and a Yankee fired a pistol so close to him that his clothes caught fire. But Peace saw another man with eleven wounds and several others with the same number as his own. Most of the wounded were later recovered by the Rebels and shipped to Richmond, but Pvt. John Ruffin Buchanan was taken to a local house and nursed back to health by a compassionate woman. Peace paid a black man fifty cents to transport him to Richmond, where he received proper medical attention.

Eight officers and ninety-four enlisted men of the 44th North Carolina were

Lt. Col. Tazewell Lee Hargrove. He commanded two companies of the 44th North
Carolina in a bitter fight with Union cavalrymen to save Lee's supply line during
the Chancellorsville campaign. Hargrove spent the rest of the war in prison and
refused to take the oath of allegiance to the U.S. government for several weeks
after Appomattox. (Briggs Papers, SHC-UNC)

captured. Spear lost thirteen troopers, and he was sorely disappointed with his
limited success. More troops from the 44th had reinforced the guards at the
other three bridges, and Spear decided to call off the expedition. "Colonel Hargrove, you have ruined my reputation," he told the injured Tar Heel after the
fighting ended. "I came here to destroy all four of the bridges and the Junction,
and I must retreat after burning only one bridge, and capturing only this handful
of men. Your resistance is the most stubborn known to me during the whole
war."

Bingham had no regrets about his part in the battle. "Well, we did our duty," he wrote in his diary four days later, "and no action of our own could have altered the result." The Tar Heels found their captors to be magnanimous in victory. As the Federals marched the prisoners to Fortress Monroe, they "treated us like brothers. They expressed the greatest admiration for 'the magnificent fight we put up against such very great odds.'" The Federals shared their food as well. The enlisted men would soon be exchanged, for the cartel that had been arranged for that purpose months before was still operating. But the officers had a much longer imprisonment ahead of them.[27]

Pettigrew's men crossed the Potomac River the day before Hargrove and Bingham had their fierce battle. Each of the four regiments started early on June 25. The river was about 200 yards wide just downstream from Shepherdstown, where a ford enabled the men to walk across. Most of the soldiers stripped themselves of shoes, socks, pants, and underwear before wading through, but many men did not take off anything. Julius Linebach stumbled and fell on one knee as he began to walk up the Maryland side of the riverbank, "doing involuntary homage to the state." The band members finished dressing when a request came from brigade headquarters for "Maryland, My Maryland." The band played it and several other songs as the rest of Heth's division splashed across the Potomac.[28]

Pettigrew's men passed through Sharpsburg at noon, marched over the Antietam battlefield, and bivouacked just south of Hagerstown. As the 26th neared Northern territory, Lieutenant Colonel Lane decided to deal with a nagging discipline problem in a direct way. Several members of the regiment marching at the rear of the column under guard had been convicted of desertion and were awaiting execution. Lane rode beside them one day and asked, "'Are you in sympathy with the South, and if permitted to do so, will you help us fight in this next battle?'" The men replied, "'We will. We only wished to go home to see our folks.'" They were reprieved and resumed their places in the ranks.[29]

Perhaps Lane took this action because the regiment lost several men through desertion as it neared Northern territory. James Wright overheard many men talk freely of leaving before they reached Pennsylvania, and twenty-one made good on that threat. Nine left on June 16, the day the 26th crossed the horrid battlefield of Chancellorsville, and five deserted three days later. The rest decamped in smaller groups throughout the latter half of June. Seven of the twenty-one were conscripts. The 52nd North Carolina lost twenty-one men during the last half of June; the largest contingent, eight, left on June 20. However only one of the deserters appears to have been a conscript, and all but two returned to duty with the regiment after the campaign ended. Desertion was a far less serious problem in the other two regiments. Leventhorpe's Bethel Regiment lost twelve men in the last half of June; seven were conscripts. In contrast, only twenty-five men had deserted from the 11th during its entire period of service before that time. The 47th North Carolina apparently lost only two men to desertion in June. In comparison, Singletary's 44th North Carolina had seven desertions in the entire month of June while it guarded the bridges near Hanover Junction.[30]

The morale of these deserters stands in sharp contrast with those members of Pettigrew's brigade who were enthusiastic about the northern campaign. Lt. William B. Taylor of the Bethel Regiment hoped Lee's army would be allowed to lay waste to free soil. He wanted to "give the enemy a taste of the horrors of war," for "that is all that will close the war soon if anything will." The heady excitement of invading Northern territory affected many men in the brigade. One day Leventhorpe remarked to Pettigrew that he thought Lee's rear was dangerously exposed as the army headed northward. The brigade leader "replied in the quick manner which was peculiar to him, 'We have no rear.' I could not but smile at this idea, which, I may have observed, reminded me of Cortes' advance on Mexico."[31]

Brimming with confidence, Pettigrew's men crossed the Pennsylvania state line on June 26 and bivouacked on free soil. Many of them ignored orders and took chickens and vegetables wherever they could find them. The brigade marched fifteen miles on June 27, passing through Waynesboro, Quincy, Funkstown, Greenwood, and Fayetteville. Julius Linebach searched for "that standard Penn. product, apple-butter." He could not find any, but Alexander Meinung "got on the good side of an old lady by talking german with her" and procured some of the delicacy. All along the line of march the Confederates noted that the sturdy Dutch farmers were busy with their spring crops, reaping and storing their grain and cutting their hay. "They did not seem to be in the least frightened or dismayed by our presence, and were left by us in the quiet and undisturbed possession of their crops." But one elderly lady was anxious about her onion patch. She asked the men as they passed when the soldiers would "'get by.'" They replied that "'the line of march extended all the way back to North Carolina.'" The harried woman exclaimed, "'Lord bless our soul! I din't know thar was half as many men in the world.'"[32]

The brigade stopped to rest at Fayetteville, where the men were ordered to clean themselves and wash their clothes. Pettigrew had managed to bring his Tar Heels into Pennsylvania with very little straggling. As June 28 was a Sunday, the chaplains of the brigade held services. Minister Styring Scarboro Moore of the 26th North Carolina spoke on the text, "The harvest is passed, the summer is ended, and we are not saved." Underwood, the historian of the 26th, mused that this was "the last Sunday on earth to many a noble soul then beating with such high hopes and aspirations."[33]

The campaign reached a new stage when Hill's corps was ordered eastward to York, nearly fifty miles away, to threaten the line of communication between Harrisburg and Philadelphia. The men would pass through Gettysburg, which was the hub of a network of roads and rail lines between Fayetteville and York. Hill sent Heth's division to Cashtown, a small village at the eastern base of South Mountain on the pike from Chambersburg to Gettysburg, about eight miles west of the latter town. The rest of the corps would follow.[34]

Pettigrew's men moved from Fayetteville to Cashtown on June 29. From there the 52nd North Carolina was temporarily detached from Pettigrew and sent on a scout toward Fairfield, about six miles to the south. It camped there and fought a skirmish with the 8th Illinois Cavalry the next morning. Benjamin Franklin Little's Company E started the engagement and was reinforced by the rest of the regiment, which "swept around the town-dispersing the Cavalry." Marshall's men returned to Cashtown on the afternoon of June 30 to rejoin the brigade.[35]

While concentrating at Cashtown, Hill was told to reconnoiter toward Gettysburg to keep tabs on Federal movements. Heth delegated this task to his senior brigade leader, Pettigrew, with instructions not to bring on a general engagement. Heth also wanted Pettigrew to search for shoes that were rumored to be stored in the town. All reports indicated that only a few Pennsylvania militia troops were in Gettysburg, so little trouble was expected. Pettigrew's men mustered for pay on June 30 and then prepared for the march. The men were ordered to leave their knapsacks behind, and soldiers too weak to make a forced march were left at the bivouac. When Burgwyn gave the Moravian band the option of staying with the baggage, they took it. As the 11th, 26th, and 47th moved out at 6:30 A.M., the band members gathered the officers' tents for safekeeping and watched their comrades march toward an uncertain fate. A light rain fell nearly all day.[36]

Pettigrew took with him three guns of the Donaldsonville Artillery of Louisiana and several wagons to transport the shoes and other supplies he hoped to find in Gettysburg. The men marched well despite the weather. Pettigrew came across a picket line established by Col. W. S. Christian's 55th Virginia, belonging to Brockenbrough's brigade, only a mile and a half down the road. The North Carolinian asked the Virginian if he would bring his regiment along to Gettysburg. As Christian later recalled the conversation, the brigade leader admitted his men "were comparatively new," and he wanted to have "a veteran Regiment go with him." Christian could not refuse.[37]

Pettigrew halted the men at Seminary Ridge, about three-quarters of a mile from town, at 9:30, and sent out skirmishers at least 300 yards closer to Gettysburg. While the men rested, their officers gazed on the town through field glasses and interviewed the few civilians who ventured near. An hour after arriving, everyone saw the head of a Union cavalry column riding toward Gettysburg along Emmitsburg Road.[38]

Pettigrew sent word back to Heth, but the division leader was not impressed. He could not believe that a Federal force was so near and simply repeated his orders of the morning. Pettigrew was willing to enter Gettysburg if necessary, but he knew it would surely precipitate a hot battle; "the cost of the stores when gotten would have been dear," as Louis G. Young later put it. The brigade leader ordered his men to return to Cashtown. The Union cavalry followed them at a distance but did not threaten a fight. Young and Lt. Walter H. Robertson, also of Pettigrew's staff, stayed to the rear of the column to watch the Yankees. "This we easily did, for the country is rolling, and from behind the ridges we could see without being seen and we had a perfect view of the movements of the approaching column." The Federals stopped every time Young and Robertson rode out from behind cover to reveal themselves.[39]

Pettigrew did not withdraw all the way to Cashtown. He stopped at Marsh Creek, four miles from Gettysburg, placing one regiment on each side of the road and the third in line straddling the road, slightly in front. Here the men stayed for about two hours before Pettigrew ordered them to march farther west. He left the 26th behind to picket the west side of Marsh Creek and bivouacked the 11th and 47th between the tiny villages of McKnightstown and Seven Stars so they could come to Burgwyn's support at short notice. The 55th Virginia, the artillery, and the empty wagons moved on to Cashtown.[40]

Heth continued his obstinate refusal to believe Pettigrew when the brigade leader reached Cashtown that evening. The North Carolinian further explained that had his men entered Gettysburg and spread out to search for supplies, they would have been vulnerable to an attack that "might have proved disastrous to his command." Just then Hill reached Cashtown and rode up to the two officers, so Heth asked Pettigrew to repeat his report. Hill listened carefully but supported the division leader. Pettigrew brought up Young, who repeated the brigade leader's report and assured Hill that the column of horsemen he had observed during the countermarch to Cashtown was not a gaggle of militiamen but veteran troops. Hill "still could not believe that any portion of the Army of the Potomac was up; and in emphatic words, expressed the hope that it was, as this was the place he wanted it to be." While the aggressive Hill clearly wanted a fight, Heth could not believe a fight was possible, and Pettigrew was the only commander at Cashtown who was convinced that a battle was inevitable. The conference ended when Heth confidently asked Hill for permission to take his whole division to Gettysburg the next day to collect those fabled supplies. The corps commander said, " 'Do so.' "[41]

Archer's brigade was to lead Heth's advance on the morrow, so Pettigrew volunteered all the information he knew about the lay of the land near Gettysburg. Archer, who shared Heth's view that no trouble would be had on July 1, "listened, but believed not," according to Young. Hill also planned to send Pender's division to support Heth. The two divisions would be taking on a task better left to cavalry or small scouting parties; but there was no mounted force nearby to call upon, and Hill's effort to send a smaller infantry force to reconnoiter had already failed. Pettigrew deserved criticism for his handling of the mission on June 30. He retired too quickly to provide convincing evidence of the Union presence in town. Ever the amateur soldier, Pettigrew acted too cautiously, worried too much about losing his men, and adhered too strictly to the letter of his instructions. A short skirmish with the bluecoated horsemen would have convinced everyone that Gettysburg was not empty and that the Union army certainly was in the vicinity. All those months of monotonous duty in North Carolina had not been good training for service in a dangerous, high-stakes campaign such as the one Lee had undertaken in Pennsylvania.[42]

The cavalry force that Pettigrew sighted in Gettysburg was Brig. Gen. John Buford's division, two brigades with a total strength of 3,000 men. Pettigrew would have been slightly outnumbered, but he would have had the advantage of commanding infantry against cavalry. Buford was under orders from Maj. Gen. Alfred Pleasonton, commander of George G. Meade's cavalry, to watch enemy movements and hold the town if possible. The Federal troopers saw Pettigrew's men on Chambersburg Pike as they rode toward Gettysburg on the morning of June 30. Pettigrew had already left when Buford secured the town; a squadron of the 8th Illinois Cavalry shadowed the Confederate retreat, playing a game of observation with Young and Robertson, and then the Federals established a forward picket post on the east bank of Marsh Creek a few hundred yards from Burgwyn's regiment. Buford deployed his division and waited for dawn to disclose what was in store.[43]

The Tar Heels were "all worn out and broken down traveling through mud & water," remarked Henry Clay Albright. Burgwyn's men lost valuable sleep as they stood guard at Marsh Creek. Lieutenant Colonel Lane quickly found that his picket line had cut off two women from their homes. They appealed to him for help, and he assured them "that the Confederate soldier did not make war upon women and children, but ever esteemed it his duty and privilege to protect them." Lane advanced his picket line a bit to include the two houses and allow the ladies to go home.[44]

The brigade was about to enter its most famous and costly battle, but the men did not know it was coming. Historian Underwood later wrote of that night that "the men of Heth's Division quietly dreamed of home and loved ones in blissful ignorance of the momentous fact that [the enemy's] great army was almost within their hearing."[45]

Chapter 6

Gettysburg

Heth set out on the road to Gettysburg and picked up Pettigrew's brigade at 7:00 A.M. The Tar Heels tagged along in the rear of the column. The regiments left their knapsacks with the wagons, detailing a man from each company to guard them. The early morning rain stopped and the summer sun began to shine an hour later, but there was a great deal of humidity in the air for the rest of the day.[1]

After he crossed Marsh Creek, Heth could see Buford's cavalrymen positioned on McPherson's Ridge. He deployed on Herr's Ridge, the next rise of ground west of McPherson's Ridge, and pushed forward. Archer advanced to the right of the pike, and Davis went ahead to the left to do what Pettigrew had failed to accomplish the day before. At first they skirmished with the cavalry and then pushed across Willoughby Run toward the ridge. Archer's Tennessee and Alabama soldiers had moved into a small forest called Herbst's Woods, which covered a portion of the western slope of McPherson's Ridge, when suddenly they were hit in front and on the flank by Col. Solomon Meredith's Iron Brigade, which consisted of battle-hardened men from Wisconsin, Michigan, and Indiana. Archer's command was smashed and pushed out of the woods; it lost nearly 100 men as prisoners. To the north, Davis's brigade also was roughly handled and forced to retreat.[2]

Pettigrew had been marching at the rear of Heth's column all morning with the 47th first in line, then the 52nd, and the 26th and 11th marching last. Somewhere between Marsh Creek and Herr's Ridge the 47th was fired on by scattered Union pickets who had hidden in the woods 500 yards to either side of the pike. The Confederates reacted quickly to the threat. Colonel Faribault ordered Capt.

Campbell Iredell of Company C to take charge of fifty skirmishers, five men from each company, and charge to the right. Lt. George W. Westray of Company A took command of a similar number of men and charged to the left. They easily drove away the enemy. Then Faribault ordered the rest of the regiment to deploy to the right of the road and advance toward Gettysburg while Marshall's 52nd did the same to the left of the road. Both regiments encountered a few more cavalry skirmishers and lost four or five men who were slightly wounded, but they quickly dispersed the Yankees. The 26th and 11th were not engaged in this fight. Faribault and Marshall advanced only a short distance before it became apparent there was no more resistance, so they called in their skirmishers and returned to the pike. By this time the 26th and 11th had marched ahead and were now leading the brigade.[3]

The battle raged a mile in front. Pettigrew began to deploy his men, at first directing Burgwyn to move his regiment to the left of the pike, then quickly changing his order to move it to the right. The Tar Heels came under artillery fire as they maneuvered, causing "some little excitement," but Burgwyn calmed the men by riding along the column and shouting in a "clear, firm voice, 'Steady boys, steady.'" Pettigrew rode up on his horse, a "beautiful dappled gray," to oversee the deployment. He instructed Burgwyn to move in "'echelon by battalion.'" Burgwyn smartly executed the maneuver, uncovering the 11th as he moved south of the pike. The 11th, 47th, and 52nd deployed the same way. This took place on open ground two and a half miles from town. The brigade remained there for a half-hour as artillery fire took about a dozen men out of action. Then Pettigrew ordered his command to advance a half-mile to the top of Herr's Ridge; it stopped in a "skirt of woods" bordered by a fence. The men took position in the treeline, and from there they could see into the open across Willoughby Run. A wheat field lay in front of the 26th on the eastern slope of the ridge, and the run was bordered with "thick underbrush and briars." The 26th was posted on the left, then the 11th, the 47th, and the 52nd.[4]

Burgwyn's line partially covered what J. A. Bush Sr. called "a dutchman's horse lot." Soon an elderly man was seen leading a two-year-old colt away from the farm, and Lt. J. C. Greer jokingly called out to see if he would sell it. The man replied, "'I have no time to trade horses now. I is getting to de woods.'" Before he left, he told the Rebels that he was seventy years old and "never expected to see a battle line formed on his land."[5]

Pettigrew sent out skirmishers, who kept up a spirited fire for the next two hours. The fighting was particularly hot on Pettigrew's right, for Companies G and K of the 80th New York had been sent out to occupy the Harmon house, on the eastern slope of Herr's Ridge. Several members of the 47th North Carolina were hit in this firefight, including Lt. Col. John A. Graves, who was slightly wounded when a musket ball glanced off his sword scabbard and scratched his leg. Even the 26th became involved when Federal sharpshooters began to target it. The flagstaff was chipped, and a man in the color guard was wounded. Burgwyn asked for a volunteer to return this fire, and Lt. John Anderson Lowe of Company G came forward with a rifle musket. He crawled along a fence until he got to a spot where he could see the Yankees hiding behind the chimney of the Harmon house and opened fire. Pettigrew deliberately exposed himself to the Union skirmishers in an effort to raise the men's spirits while most of his men nervously waited for orders. It was already past noon, but no one in the brigade had a chance to eat.[6]

During this two-hour lull the Confederates positioned the rest of their available troops. Archer's mangled brigade, now under Col. Birkett D. Fry, took position on Pettigrew's right flank, while Brockenbrough's small Virginia brigade was placed between Pettigrew's left flank and the pike. It was obvious that Pettigrew's large, fresh brigade would have to carry the burden of the next attack.[7]

The ground that confronted Pettigrew offered some advantages to the Confederates. The only feature that separated the two lines was Willoughby Run, a comparatively small stream with a narrow bottom about fifty feet below the top of the ridges. Most of the eastern slope of Herr's Ridge was either cultivated or in pasture, and the same was true of the western slope of McPherson's Ridge. Only the trees of Herbst's Woods cluttered the landscape. McPherson's Ridge is comparatively steep as one begins to ascend it from the run. The ground begins to level off about a third of the way up the slope, and from that point the climb is not so steep.[8]

Pettigrew's opponents were the real obstacle, for they were some of the toughest troops in the Union army. The Iron Brigade was the anchor of the Federal defense. It was mostly deployed in Herbst's Woods and formed a salient in the Union line. This patch of trees was 300 yards wide on its western edge and 125 yards wide on the eastern edge. It extended all the way from the run nearly up to the crest of the ridge. Maj. Gen. Abner Doubleday, commander of the Federal First Corps, believed Herbst's Woods "possessed all the advantages of a redoubt," but it actually was a tactical sore spot for the Federals. The trees offered an avenue of protected passage for the Confederates, and they would be able to sneak up under cover. To prevent this approach, Meredith was forced to position his four available regiments forward in the western edge of the woods rather than on the top of McPherson's Ridge. The 7th Wisconsin was on the right, then the 2nd Wisconsin, the 24th Michigan, and the 19th Indiana made up this advanced position. To the south of the woods the 19th Indiana was forced to angle its line toward Col. Chapman Biddle's brigade, which was positioned entirely in the open and on the ridge. Biddle had the 151st Pennsylvania on his right, 400 yards to the rear of the 19th Indiana, then the 142nd Pennsylvania, the 80th New York, and the 121st Pennsylvania. Two batteries were positioned on the ridge to fire at Pettigrew's regiments.[9]

The fact that the Iron Brigade's left did not connect with Biddle would prove to be a weakness in the Union position, for it gave Pettigrew's men an opportunity to crack the line open. Biddle also was in a shaky position. There was no terrain feature on which he could anchor the left flank of the Federal line, although cavalry hovering to the south of Fairfield Road offered him some flank protection. The Iron Brigade had 1,100 men when the battle opened that morning. Biddle's brigade had 1,361 soldiers, but only the 80th New York had significant battle experience. The 121st and 142nd Pennsylvania had been at Fredericksburg and Chancellorsville but saw little combat there. The 151st Pennsylvania was a nine-month regiment that had never seen action. Just before the Rebels attacked, Biddle detached the 151st a bit to the right to act as a general reserve. The remaining three regiments on line totaled 820 men.[10]

Pettigrew was positioned 300 yards in front of the Iron Brigade. His men were deployed in echelon, the 26th on the left and forward, the 11th a few yards to the rear and right, and so on down the line. It appeared to the waiting Federals as if several battle lines were confronting them. The unusually large size of Pettigrew's command also fooled them into thinking that more than one brigade was about to strike. Pettigrew had 2,584 men ready to attack, double the average size of Lee's other brigades at Gettysburg. The 26th had 843 men, the 11th had 617 men, the 47th numbered 353 soldiers, and the 52nd took 567 men into action. The 26th confronted the 24th Michigan and part of the 19th Indiana, while the 11th would be able to hit the rest of the Hoosier regiment. The 47th and 52nd would deal with Biddle's men.[11]

Burgwyn was "quite impatient to engage the enemy" during this two-hour wait. Lieutenant Colonel Lane asked him for permission to go to the rear because he had been up all night with the pickets and felt ill after drinking muddy water. Burgwyn would not hear of it: " 'Oh, Colonel, I can't, I can't, I can't think of going into this battle without you.' " He offered Lane some French brandy to revive him. Lane recalled that there was plenty of time for religious services, but all the chaplains had gone to the rear. The men had to provide their own emotional comfort, exchanging "words of encouragement" and even a few jokes.[12]

It was 3:00 P.M., and the midafternoon sun was beating down on the men as the command "Attention" rippled along the line of the 26th North Carolina. The men "knew the desperateness of the charge we were to make," yet as Lane re-

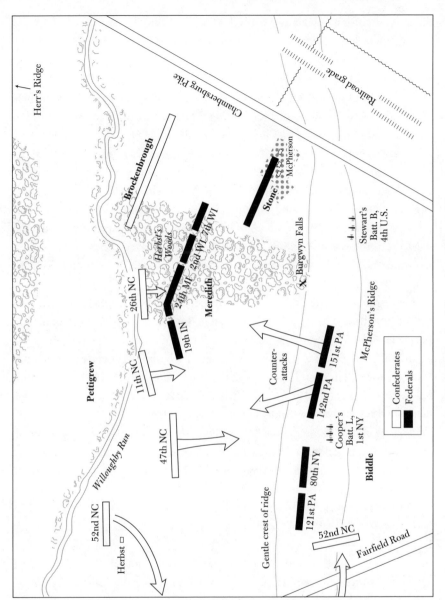

MAP 6.1 The Battle of Gettysburg, July 1, 1863

membered it, they quickly responded. More than 800 Tar Heels stood up and dressed their ranks. Burgwyn stepped to the center of the line, Lane took post on the right, and Major Jones placed himself on the left. Sgt. Jefferson B. Mansfield of Company E carried the flag four paces to the front, accompanied by his color guard of eight enlisted men. Federal skirmishers began to fire as the Rebels marched down the slope of Herr's Ridge, but only a few men were hit. An unidentified officer riding behind the regiment had his hat shot off in this fire, but it did not upset him. The officer, probably Louis G. Young, caught the hat before it fell to the ground and yelled, " 'Give 'em —— boys!' " Not surprisingly, the color-bearer was among the first to fall. Mansfield was shot in the foot and gave the colors to Sgt. Hiram Johnson of Company G. Johnson also was hit a few minutes later, and Pvt. John Stamper of Company A took charge and carried the flag toward the stream. A short distance before he entered the brush that lined the water, he was shot in the right shoulder. Pvt. George Washington Kelly of Company D seized the colors and pushed across.[13]

The regiment's ordered ranks began to bend and swerve when they reached Willoughby Run. The right wing crowded to the left, causing a crunch of men in the center. The brush and the water slowed many companies. The flag fell once again while the crossing took place. Private Kelly jumped over the water but tripped and fell. His friend Pvt. Larkin Thomas of Company F told him to get up, but Kelly thought he had broken his leg in the fall. He soon realized that shell fragments had hit him on the ankle and arm. Rather than fret about it, Kelly asked Thomas to find the fragments so he could take them home as souvenirs. Thomas would have none of that foolishness. He took the flag from Kelly and marched on.[14]

There was more delay as the regiment redressed its ranks on the eastern bank of Willoughby Run. Another obstacle appeared for at least part of the line. Louis G. Young of Pettigrew's staff was with the regiment and noticed that several men had stopped where they were sheltered by a cut in the base of McPherson's Ridge made by civilians who were mining marl. Young was trying to encourage these men to move out when fellow staff officer Capt. William Westwood McCreery rode up in a rather "joyous way." McCreery happily began to tell Young how his horse had been shot, but Young cut the story short by telling him "that we had no time to talk about such matters, that we must assist in getting the men forward." As McCreery rode off, Young's hat was twice shot off his head. The men responded quickly to his urgings, and the advance continued.[15]

The Iron Brigade was only forty yards away in the woods. There was relatively little underbrush obscuring the view, so as soon as the Tar Heels moved away from Willoughby Run, they were fair targets for the 24th Michigan. Its commander, Col. Henry A. Morrow, reported that Burgwyn's men "came on with rapid strides, yelling like demons." He gave the order to fire at will, and the most horrific battle the 26th would endure was joined. The fighting took place at ranges of twenty to forty yards as the advance slowed to a crawl. Larkin Thomas might have been killed by his comrade Sgt. J. T. C. Hood of Company F, for Thomas dashed in front of Hood with the flag just as the sergeant pulled the trigger of his rifle musket. Fortunately the weapon misfired because Hood had nervously placed two caps on the nipple. He fixed the gun and opened fire. Only a few minutes later, however, Thomas went down, hit in the left arm. He gave the flag to Pvt. John Vinson of Company G. Vinson was hit almost immediately. Pvt. John R. Marley of Company G took over and was killed a few moments later. The next brave man to take on this suicide mission was Pvt. William W. Ingram of Company K, who held up the flag in the rain of fire that came through the trees. To Lane on the right flank it "seemed as if the bullets were as thick as hailstones in a storm."[16]

The 11th North Carolina came to Burgwyn's aid at this time. The waiting Federals observed and admired Leventhorpe's advance. "The Rebel lines moved forward upon us in splendid style," reported Lt. Col. William W. Dudley of the 19th Indiana, "advancing across the oat fields which lay between us in a perfect line." The 11th slowed to cross Willoughby Run, but Leventhorpe soon discovered the exposed left flank of the 19th Indiana. The English colonel obliqued his line of approach to the left so he could take advantage of the opportunity. The Bethel Regiment marched up the open slope of McPherson's Ridge just south of Herbst's Woods and slammed into the Hoosiers, outflanking their line. For the next fifteen minutes the two opposing regiments were locked in a deadly exchange at a range of twenty yards. Leventhorpe was hit in the left arm by a rifle ball that shattered the bone; he also was badly injured in the hip and had to be carried off the field. Major Ross was mortally wounded at the same time. A canister ball struck his right side and "went nearly through him." He died four hours later.[17]

The flag became the focus of enemy fire. The color-bearer went down and Adj. Henderson C. Lucas picked up the flag to encourage the men. He moved out in front so they could clearly see him and was almost immediately hit. Lucas fell briefly, then rose and continued forward. He was shot again and this time could not get up, yet the stubborn officer refused to yield. He held the flag high only to have a bullet drill completely through his left arm. Then the colors lay a few paces in front of the battle line as Lucas lay dying. Inspired by his stunning devotion, the men moved forward as if propelled by a surge of adrenaline. Pettigrew also rode along behind the Bethel line and encouraged the men to push on. Lucas had enough strength to yell, " 'Boys, I have played out; go on to victory.' " Someone bent over to pick up the flag and was hit. When another soldier

Willoughby Run from McPherson's Ridge. Looking toward the advance of the 11th North Carolina near Herbst's Woods, the run is inside the line of trees. Note the open slope of the ridge where the 19th Indiana tried to stop the Bethel Regiment. (Courtesy of the author)

stooped to help that man, he too was killed. But then a third man scooped up the colors, and the regiment slowly pushed ahead.[18]

The 19th Indiana, which had already lost half its men, including eight color-bearers, was overwhelmed. The badly pressed Hoosiers fired as they retired. "You ought to have seen our brigade when it charged," Lt. William B. Taylor of the Bethel Regiment wrote his mother; "we drove the enemy like sheep." The withdrawal exposed the left flank of the 24th Michigan, and Morrow tried to refuse that wing to cover his position. But Burgwyn continued to apply heavy pressure on his front, so he also ordered a retreat. The Michigan men slowly moved about fifty yards farther up the wooded slope.[19]

By this time Lane was in a fog. The woods and the battle smoke obscured his view, so he raced toward the regiment's center to see how the fight was progressing. Burgwyn met him there and shouted, "It is all right in the center and on the left; we have broken the first line of the enemy." Lane reassured him that "we are in line on the right," and then he returned to his post.[20]

Another man then appeared before Burgwyn. Captain McCreery brought word from Pettigrew that the 26th "has covered itself with glory to-day." Just then color-bearer Ingram fell. Acting on an impulse, McCreery took the fallen banner, waved it high in the trees, and suffered the same fate as all who had touched it before. McCreery was shot through the heart and fell on the flag, staining it with his blood. McCreery, a twenty-six-year-old Virginian who had graduated from West Point in 1860, had joined Pettigrew's staff only seven weeks earlier. He had told a friend that if it was his fate to die in the war, "he wanted it to be when he had seized the colors from the dead colorbearers hand and *rallied the troops*—and that was exactly the way he was killed." Lt. George Wilcox of Company H rose to replace him. Wilcox tugged at the flag until he freed it from the weight of McCreery's body. He took only a few steps before he was hit in his right side and left foot. The regiment stalled again.[21]

It was well that at this time Morrow ordered his battered regiment to retire to its third line, about fifty yards behind the second. He lost his third color-bearer while defending this third line and estimated that no more than a fourth of the men he started with were still on their feet. A fourth color-bearer fell, and Morrow took the flag so he could rally the men. His Michigan soldiers were putting up an awesome fight.[22]

Pettigrew's right wing was waging a spectacular fight of its own. The 47th North Carolina started out smartly from Herr's Ridge. "The morale of the men was splendid," remembered Capt. John H. Thorp, "and when it advanced to its first grand charge it was with the feelings of conquerors." Capt. John D. S. Cook of the 80th New York left a vivid description of the regiment's advance.

> From the forest in front appeared a long brown line of the enemy's infantry. In poetry and romance the Confederate uniform is gray. In actual service it was a butternut brown, and on those fellows who faced us at short range was, owing to their long campaign, as dirty, disreputable and unromantic as can well be imagined. They exhibited no more of "the pomp and circumstance of glorious war" than so many railroad section hands. But they could shoot all right and as they stood out there in line in the open field and poured in a rapid fire of musketry they gave us no time to criticise their appearance.[23]

Faribault's Tar Heels began to take casualties immediately. A shell exploded in the company that occupied the right flank, killing three men and knocking down all the file closers. Still Faribault's men yelled as they stumbled across the run and climbed the open slope of McPherson's Ridge through the Herbst wheat field.[24]

When they were only seventy-five yards short of the crest, the Tar Heels could see "the heavy lines of Yankee soldiers with their guns shining and flags waving." These were the men of the 142nd Pennsylvania and the 80th New York, placed just behind the crest of McPherson's Ridge and thus not visible until the Rebels came within short range. For some time the two Federal regiments held Faribault's command while trading shots and bringing down numerous soldiers. The midafternoon sun caused the Tar Heels to sweat so heavily that perspiration made the ramrods slick, and it was difficult to ram the cartridges home. Many men simply inserted the ramrods in the barrel and then jammed them against the ground or a rock. "This, with the usual causes, undressed our advancing line; still all were yelling and pressing forward through the growing wheat breast high." Captain Iredell of Company C was so moved by the sight of one of his men falling mortally wounded that he rushed to his side. " 'My dear boy, I will try to avenge your hurt,' " he cried. Iredell grabbed the man's rifle musket and fired several rounds before he was hit in the arm and crumpled to the ground. He died later that day.[25]

Just as the 26th was helped by the flanking movement of the 11th, so was Faribault's regiment aided by the advance of the 52nd. Marshall's regiment had the longest journey, and therefore the Federals could see it for a longer time. Col. Charles Wainwright, an artillery officer, noted how Pettigrew's line overlapped his own and concluded the Federals could not hold the ridge. Marshall's men had unique difficulties to overcome. First, two companies of the 80th New York still occupied the Harmon farmstead. These brave skirmishers manned their post and fired into the surging mass of Rebels until Marshall surrounded them on three sides. Both Marshall and Pettigrew ordered the house burned, forcing the skirmishers to run for their lives up the valley of Willoughby Run to the south. A group of civilians who had been hiding in the cellar ran for their lives as well. A portion of the 52nd chased the skirmishers south and fought a squadron of the 8th New York Cavalry at Meals's orchard for about a half-hour before it returned to the regiment.[26]

After Marshall's men crossed Willoughby Run, they were threatened by other Union mounted units that hovered south of Fairfield Road. Marshall decided not to wait for an attack. Advancing south of the road, he ordered his men to form a hollow square and sent Company B to skirmish with the Federals. This was enough to discourage any assault. Company B held the troopers at bay until they retired of their own accord while the regiment reassembled its battle line and continued the assault. It was an unusual maneuver, but the 52nd did it "as promptly and accurately as if it had been upon its drill grounds."[27]

The 52nd advanced northward across Fairfield Road and crashed into the flank of the 121st Pennsylvania. This inexperienced regiment put up modest resistance for a time. Lt. Col. Alexander Biddle tried to change his regiment's front to the left to meet the attack, but the men were thrown into confusion by the raging fire. Biddle later reported that Marshall's men were "able to pour in a fire so much heavier than we could return that it was soon evident the position was no longer ours." The regiment began to fall apart, and the men ran for Seminary Ridge, a quarter-mile to the rear.[28]

Col. Theodore Gates's 80th New York had blocked the 47th for some time but now found itself caught in a crossfire from Marshall's men when the 121st Pennsylvania retreated. The regiment was badly outnumbered and outmaneuvered. The New Yorkers retired in order, stopping to fire now and then. During the course of this pursuit another Union cavalry threat appeared to Marshall's right. He did not stop the forward pressure but simply changed the front of his three right companies to scare it away. Archer's brigade, which could have protected Marshall's right, busied itself with idle skirmishing and was unable to keep pace with the Tar Heels.[29]

Brigade leader Biddle was in a frenzy. The dissolution of his command inspired him to lead a desperate counterattack by the inexperienced 142nd Pennsylvania. The left wing of the 47th North Carolina, the target of this assault, could plainly see a Federal officer riding forward with a flag held high. "The scattered Federals swarmed around him as bees cover their queen," wrote John Thorp. "In the midst of a heterogeneous mass of men, . . . he approached our left, when all guns in front and from right and left turned on the mass and seemingly shot the whole to pieces." The regiment left its colors on the field as it retired to Seminary Ridge. Biddle survived this attack, much to the admiration of his opponents in the 47th, only to be wounded later that day.[30]

With Biddle's brigade in retreat, the time had come for renewed effort on the part of the 26th and the 11th. Burgwyn's advance had stalled where Morrow's Michigan regiment held its third line. Much of Burgwyn's attention was devoted to making sure that the flag kept waving. Lieutenant Wilcox, the tenth man to hold it, fell soon after he dragged the flag from under McCreery's body. He was hit in the right side but managed to stay up and continued to move forward slowly. Then a second ball slammed into his left foot, forcing the lieutenant to stop. Burgwyn seized the moment. He took the flag from Wilcox but soon realized it was more of a responsibility than he could manage at the time. Lt. Thomas J. Cureton of Company B came to the rescue. He became aware of the need when Louis G. Young rode along to the rear of his company and ordered him to close up to the right toward the colors. Cureton looked in that direction and saw only two or three men where Company F should have been. Then he noticed Burgwyn running toward him with the flag in his hands. The colonel hurriedly asked him if one of his men could carry it, so Cureton ordered Pvt. Frank Honeycut forward.[31]

While Honeycut held the flag, Burgwyn turned his attention to the battle line. Lane came running over to reassure him that the right was in line. Burgwyn told him of the glowing message Pettigrew had sent by McCreery, and Lane lingered for a few moments near the center. Then Honeycut was shot in the head and instantly killed. Cureton and Lt. Milton B. Blair of Company I saw the flag on the ground, and both ran toward it. At that instant Burgwyn turned to the rear to see what had happened, exposing his right side to the enemy. His sword scabbard was "shot away"; at short range another rifle ball plunged into his side, cut through the lower part of both lungs, and brought the young colonel to the ground. Capt. William Wilson of Company B, one of the regiment's most promising officers, was shot within seconds only a few feet away.[32]

Lane later remembered this moment as "the crisis" of the day. He raced to Burgwyn's side and bent over, calling to him over the noise of battle, "'My dear Colonel, are you severely hurt?'" Burgwyn could not speak. He motioned to his side and pressed Lane's hand. The lieutenant colonel then took command of the regiment. He ran to the right and relayed Pettigrew's encouraging message to Capt. J. C. McLauchlin of Company K but decided not to tell him of Burgwyn's wounding for fear of disheartening the men. He told McLauchlin, "'Close your men quickly to the left. I am going to give them the bayonet.'" McLauchlin soon after was hit in the left hand and had his thumb amputated. Lane went to the left wing with the same message and then returned to the center.[33]

In the meantime, Cureton and Blair raced for the flag; Blair won and picked it up. Just then Lane arrived from his dash to the right and left and saw Blair step forward with the colors. "Blair give me them Colours," he shouted. The lieutenant passed them over with a sardonic quip, "You will get *tyred* of them. . . . No man can take these colors and live." Lane had no time to think about it. "'It is my time to take them now,'" he replied. Waving the flag, Lane turned to the regiment and shouted, "'26th, follow me.'" Those who were left standing yelled and moved forward. They slowly stepped over their dying colonel and the body of Honeycut and emerged from the woods near the top of McPherson's Ridge. Burgwyn had gotten his beloved regiment out of the trees and poised it for a decisive strike. Now it was up to Lane to complete the journey. The lieutenant colonel recalled, "Volleys of musketry are fast thinning out those left; only a skeleton line now remains." The sunshine was obscured by a thick pall of powder smoke from the rapid discharge of musketry, and the men who were in the middle of it felt almost as if it were as "dark as night."[34]

Lane did his job magnificently. He forced Morrow to retire from his third position to a fourth line in the open ground between McPherson's Ridge and Seminary Ridge. When division leader Heth later saw the ground, he remarked that the Federal dead at this third position "marked his line of battle with the accuracy of a line at a dress parade." But the casualties continued to fall in the 26th as well. Pvt. Thomas Perrett of Company G had fired fourteen rounds by this time. He dropped the butt of his gun to load a fifteenth time, and two balls slammed into his body. Sgt. William Preston Kirkman asked if the nineteen-year-

Col. John Randolph Lane. Badly wounded on July 1 while leading the 26th North Carolina after Burgwyn's death, Lane was also wounded in four subsequent battles but survived the war. (NCDAH)

old was wounded, and Perrett said yes. Rather than help him, Kirkman asked if he could use his gun, "a noted rifle which I had carried for more than a year." Perrett could not refuse him. "I pass him the gun. He advances only a few paces and falls mortally wounded." Kirkman died the next day. He was one of four brothers serving in Company G. Two were captured during the Gettysburg campaign and died in prison, and the other was reported missing during the battle and was never accounted for.[35]

At this crucial phase of the advance, Lt. Col. George F. McFarland led the 151st Pennsylvania in a counterattack against Lane's men. The unit brought 467 men forward. Its right wing fronted Herbst's Woods and the remnants of the 26th while the left wing fronted the 11th North Carolina to the south. McFarland pushed his men almost to the top of McPherson's Ridge and ordered them to fire at will. They held there long enough to give Biddle's regiments and the Iron Brigade time to pull back, but the 151st soon retired, suffering 72 percent casualties.[36]

The 26th built up a momentum going down the gentle eastern slope of McPherson's Ridge that was irresistible, while the 24th Michigan retired all the way to a fence on top of Seminary Ridge. Lane's 26th had taken only a few minutes to move across the 400 yards that separated the two ridges, but now it was running out of steam.[37]

As the Tar Heel attack petered out, the 26th lost its new leader. Lane was within thirty yards of the ridge top when he turned to urge his men on. Just then Sgt. Charles H. McConnell of the 24th Michigan leaned against a tree to steady his rifle musket and pulled the trigger. The ball penetrated the back of Lane's neck just below the cranial cavity and passed through his jaw and mouth. It was a horrible wound that crumpled the lieutenant colonel and caused him to lose the flag. Cureton saw Lane go down. He recalled that the lieutenant colonel "looked Back (like lots wife) and fell as limber as a Rag." Everyone assumed he was dead. Lane was the thirteenth color-bearer to be hit within thirty minutes. Capt. Stephen Wiley Brewer of Company E took the flag and carried it for the remainder of the fight. Only he and Blair managed to touch the colors without getting hit that afternoon.[38]

Pettigrew's brigade had done all it could in this short and vicious fight. By this time Pettigrew was no longer in charge of the brigade. Heth had received a stunning head wound early in the battle and turned over command of his division to the Tar Heel. Colonel Marshall took charge of the brigade while Lt. Col. Marcus A. Parks took over the 52nd North Carolina. Maj. John Thomas Jones assumed command of the 26th North Carolina after Lane went down. Pettigrew ordered all of his old regiments to stop advancing and return to Herr's Ridge for rest, for Pender's fresh division would take up the fight for Seminary Ridge. The 26th did not receive this order. Jones's men began to roam over the battlefield to collect ammunition from the Federal dead and wounded as they were "entirely out" of it. They were preparing to re-form for another attack when Pender's men "passed over them."[39]

After they caught their second breath, the men of the 26th realized they had some fight left, so they followed behind Pender's troops and marginally aided in the attack. Pender's division managed to clear the ridge after heavy fighting, and the 26th rejoined the other units under Marshall. All of them prepared to bivouac for the night in the skirt of woods that had been the starting point of the assault.[40]

It had been a stunning day for Pettigrew's men. This was the first sustained combat for any regiment in the brigade. Although the 26th had been under fire at New Bern and Malvern Hill, this day's battle was far heavier. It also was the first time the men attacked as a brigade, without the 44th North Carolina of course. The day's work also was the first time Pettigrew's men coordinated their combat role with the movements of supporting units on the field. All in all, it was a day of initiation for the men, despite the fact that they had been in service for a long while.

The brigade's losses were heavy. No prisoners were taken, but 1,100 of 2,584 men were killed and wounded. The 11th and 26th were "litterally cut to pieces," in the words of a man in the 47th North Carolina. Leventhorpe's regiment lost 250 of 550 engaged. It took 28 officers into the fight and lost 14 of them killed, while most of the rest were wounded. Company C had 36 of its 40 men shot down. The losses of the 47th and 52nd were lighter compared with the damages suffered by their companion regiments. Faribault's 47th lost 125 men in its tough fight with the 80th New York. Marshall's 52nd suffered 26 casualties, an unusually low figure because the 121st Pennsylvania put up relatively little fight. One man in Company H was reported as a deserter that day. He was held prisoner by the Federals and later joined a Northern volunteer regiment. The brigade staff also took a pounding; the acting inspector was killed, and the ordnance officer was wounded.[41]

The casualties of the 26th North Carolina were appalling. At least 549 of the 843 men engaged were casualties, for a loss rate of 65 percent. There were barely 216 men left for duty on the evening of the fight; some 40 men were straggling, and a number of others had been on detached duty and did not participate in the fighting. Company E took 82 soldiers into the battle and lost 18 killed or mortally wounded and 52 wounded, so only twelve men remained. Company A lost 11 killed and 66 wounded of 92 men engaged, leaving only 15 soldiers. Company F suffered almost legendary losses. Capt. Romulus Morrison Tuttle never forgot the suffering his Hibriten Guards endured that day. He took 87 men into action, having detailed 1 soldier to guard the company's knapsacks. Only 1 man went through the attack unhurt; 25 soldiers were killed and 61 were wounded. Three sets of twins served in Company F, and 5 of the 6 brothers were killed. Pvt. James Daniel Moore was the 85th man to be hit, shot in the neck and left leg. Sgt. Henry C. Coffey was the next man down, while only Sgt. Robert N. Hudspeth remained uninjured. Captain Tuttle, who was only twenty years old, was wounded in the right leg. Forty years later he still felt stunned by what had happened. "It is very hard to realize how men can be decimated so rapidly. My company was a splendid body of soldiers."[42]

Thirteen color-bearers were shot while holding the flag, but most of them survived the fighting of July 1. Sgt. Jefferson B. Mansfield of Company E endured his foot wound only to be captured later in the campaign. He was exchanged the following September. Sgt. Hiram Johnson of Company G had been wounded before, at Malvern Hill, and returned to duty from his Gettysburg injury by September 1863. He was wounded a third time in the fall of 1864 but was back on duty by the following February. Pvt. John Stamper of Company A was only twenty years old. He was transported to Richmond and hospitalized there for his shoulder wound. Given a sixty-day furlough to recuperate in August, he never bothered to return and was listed as a deserter. Pvt. George Washington Kelly of Company D also was captured later in the Gettysburg campaign and exchanged in September 1863. He recovered from his ankle and arm wounds, rejoined the regiment in the fall of 1864, and surrendered with the 26th at Appomattox. Pvt.

Larkin Thomas of Company F returned to duty with the regiment by January 1864, having survived his arm wound, and was captured in the war's closing days when he was left behind in a Richmond hospital. Pvt. John Vinson of Company G had enlisted as a substitute, had been wounded at Malvern Hill, and had deserted on March 29, 1863. He had been court-martialed and sentenced to be shot, but the sentence was later revoked. He survived his Gettysburg injury only to be wounded in the right leg and captured at the Wilderness. His leg was amputated by Federal surgeons, but he died on August 5, 1864. Pvt. John R. Marley of Company G was killed on July 1. Pvt. William Ingram of Company K was captured later in the Gettysburg campaign and exchanged in the winter of 1864, but he was absent sick for much of the remainder of the war. Captain McCreery of the brigade staff was killed. George Wilcox of Company H was captured on July 4 by Federal cavalry. He was immediately rescued and recuperated from his wound to return to duty by June 1864. He was captured again at the battle of Burgess's Mill on October 27, 1864, and escaped that night to return to his company. He was later transferred to a higher rank in Company H, 46th North Carolina. Colonel Burgwyn was killed, as was Pvt. Frank Honeycut of Company B, but Lieutenant Colonel Lane survived his wound.[43]

The magnificent fighting offered by Morrow's men was one reason why the 26th suffered so heavily. But another reason was the sheer size of the Confederate regiment. There were so many targets packed together for the Michigan men to hit, and the fighting took place at very short range. The nature of the ground forced Burgwyn to grind the advance slowly forward, pushing, shoving, and shooting, to win the day.

Burgwyn's loss drew more attention than that of any other man in the 26th. Lane was the first to go to his side after he fell, and George Wilcox was next to attend him. Wilcox was a short distance to the rear of the regimental line, seeing to his injured foot, when the colonel was hit. He looked up just in time to see through the thinned ranks that Burgwyn had fallen "flat of his back" on the green grass that bordered the eastern edge of Herbst's Woods. He lay under the shade of several oak trees. After the regiment moved on, Wilcox hobbled over to him and asked the colonel where he was hit. "He motioned to his side & tried to speak, but seemed, then in the agony of death." Wilcox could not understand what he was trying to say, but he called for help and waited with the colonel until it arrived. Burgwyn was bleeding internally, but there was no surgeon available to detect it.[44]

Pvt. William P. Elington of Company E and Pvt. Nevel B. Staten of Company B came to help the colonel. They placed him on a blanket and began to make their way to the rear, leaving Wilcox behind. Along the way Pvt. William M.

Herbst's Woods. This area, near the crest of McPherson's Ridge, is approximately where Burgwyn was mortally wounded. (Courtesy of the author)

Cheek joined the entourage. He had been knocked down by a shell explosion but had recovered enough to recognize Burgwyn. The colonel was able to speak by this time, and he asked Cheek to help Elington and Staten. Then an unknown lieutenant from a South Carolina regiment in Pender's division volunteered to help as well. He took hold of a corner of the blanket and walked some distance with the group. The shock of the wound had worn off enough so that Burgwyn began to feel a burning pain, and he asked the lieutenant to pour water over it. Everyone stopped and gently laid the colonel down so that canteens could be slowly emptied onto his side. Cheek took off Burgwyn's coat and reached for his watch, which was suspended around his neck by a silk cord. Just then the South Carolinian showed his true character by snatching the watch and walking briskly away with it. Cheek was so angry at this thievery that he raced after the officer. He stopped him with a rifle musket, cocked the hammer, and threatened to kill him "as sure as powder would burn" if he did not return the watch. Under this vigilant guard the cowardly man walked back to the party and handed over the precious memento. Then Cheek told him "he was nothing but a thief" and ordered him to leave, which he did. Burgwyn was pleased. He told Cheek "that he would never forget me, and I shall never forget the look he gave me as he spoke these words."[45]

The three soldiers picked up their colonel and continued slowly to the rear.

They had almost reached the top of Herr's Ridge when Louis G. Young came across the party. Burgwyn obviously was dying. Young tried to comfort him and gave him liquor from his flask. Burgwyn asked how the regiment fared and praised his men by saying that "they never would disgrace him." The colonel's last words were of resignation. "'The Lord's will be done. We have gained the greatest victory in the war.'" When Young told him that he despaired to see him wounded, Burgwyn replied, "'I have no regrets, I have fallen in the defense of my Country.'"[46]

Cheek decided to search for a stretcher to carry the young man. It took some time to find one, and when he approached with it, Burgwyn was in the last moments of his life. He could no longer talk, so Cheek cradled his hand in his lap as the group stood silently around. The end came two hours after he was hit; Burgwyn died "very quietly and resignedly." As J. J. Young later put it, "Here under the broad canopy of heaven he died as a patriot could only wish."[47]

The death of Burgwyn was one of the most poignant of the day, but hundreds of others suffered their own tragedies as well. Lieutenant Cureton recalled many years later that he wandered over to the seminary when the fighting ended. He was "completely exhausted in Climbing that Hill through the woods under Such circumstances." He found a number of young women who had taken refuge in the basement of the seminary. Just above them the ground floor of the building was filled with wounded Federals. The women were frightened by the presence of Lee's men, so Cureton assured them no harm would come. Southerners "did not war on women," he said.[48]

As the remnant of the brigade retraced the route of the attack, the full horror of it hit the men. Very many "of our Wounded had not yet been Carried to the Hospital," recalled Cureton. "The Enemys dead and wounded lay Mixed with their wounded Crying piteously for water which we freely gave. . . . our dead were lying where They had fallen, but the 'Battlefield Robbers' had been there plundering the 'dead.' They Seemed to have respected neither the enemys or our own dead." The men were completely worn out when they reached Herr's Ridge that evening, but they still wandered out at odd hours of the night to help the wounded in the field hospitals scattered across the countryside.[49]

Cureton may have heard a strange sound emanating from Herbst's Woods as he marched back to the bivouac, but he paid little attention to it. Louis G. Young heard it too and knew it came from the wounded. The South Carolinian had never heard such a sound before. "It was so distressing that I approached several with the purpose of calming them if possible, and to my surprise I found them foaming at the mouth as if mad, and evidently unconscious of the sound of their voices." The effect probably resulted from the excessive heat of the day and the tremendous thirst that always accompanied battle wounds. Young could do little for them. His effort to calm them with soothing words was not even acknowledged, so he moved on.[50]

The ambulance corpsmen worked feverishly to bring in the wounded, but there were too few aides to handle everyone in a timely manner. Most of the injured had to make their own way to the field hospitals or simply lay where they fell. Thomas Perrett did pretty well for himself after being hit with two bullets and giving up his prized rifle, just as Lane led the 26th to the top of McPherson's Ridge. Perrett lay on the ground for some time to make sure the fighting was going away, then he stood up. Before he moved toward the rear, he noticed a stuffed knapsack on the ground, dropped by a Federal, and slung it across his shoulder. It was well that he had this "instinctive desire for plunder," for a stray bullet slammed into the knapsack, saving him from a third wound. Perrett managed to walk only a short distance before he weakened and collapsed. He was later carried to a barn near Chambersburg Pike and spent the night on a bed of fresh straw.[51]

Heth saw much of the fighting before he was wounded and reported that the brigade "fought as well, and displayed as heroic courage as it was ever my fortune to witness on a battle-field." Louis G. Young was both an observer and a participant in the assault; he termed the fighting of July 1 the "deadliest" of any he had seen in the entire war. The 47th North Carolina, which had suffered less than the 11th and 26th, was "intoxicated with victory" as it bivouacked for the night. "Many were the incidents narrated on that beautiful, moonlight night," according to John Thorp. Another member of the regiment, William H. Blount, predictably used the attack as proof of the Confederate soldier's character. "In this fight we showed the superiority of Southern Soldiers over yankee hirelings."[52]

What exactly had the brigade accomplished? Its attack lasted about thirty minutes, by Louis G. Young's estimate. It tore up the Iron Brigade, smashed Biddle's brigade, and captured McPherson's Ridge. But the Federals fell back about 400 yards and had to be driven away from Seminary Ridge by Pender's division. There was no time left for anyone to go farther, to take the high ground south of town that would become the focus of the next day's battle. In hindsight it is clear that the Rebels had their best chance of winning the battle of Gettysburg on July 1, but they failed to do so.[53]

Chapter 7

Fire and Blood

Everyone in Pettigrew's brigade awoke on the morning of July 2 with a deep sense of the pressing need to put their regiments back together. Pettigrew ordered regimental officers to call up all the detailed men, slightly wounded soldiers, and cooks. These desperate measures could not replace the men lost on July 1, but they helped to bolster regimental strengths. It was a surprise for many that the brigade "seemed as ready for the fray on the morning of the third day, as it had been on that of the first."[1]

Caring for the wounded proved to be a gargantuan task. The 26th North Carolina alone had close to 500 injured men who needed immediate attention. Asst. Surg. William W. Gaither worked hard all night of July 1 and all day of July 2 supervising the removal of the injured from the field and treating their wounds. The small number of attendants slowed the care of the wounded soldiers even further, but Gaither refused to rest until all had been seen and made comfortable.[2]

Thomas Perrett slept well in his hospital bed of straw but still felt weak. An unnamed surgeon came by on the morning of July 2 to examine his double wound. Perrett was convinced the doctor was drunk, for he decided to make a "few incissions looking for the stray ball." Perrett adamantly refused. "The Doctor, however, still persists in his murderous designs, and insolently informs me that he proposes to cut out the ball whether I like it or not." The battle heated up considerably at this point. "I am about mad enough to fight a whole medical college," recalled Perrett, "with war of words between us becoming fast and furious; each combatant unable to find adjectives sufficiently [to] express his feelings. The Doctor finally retires from the field taking a farewell shot as he leaves that, 'a man so obstinate ought to die.'" But Perrett lived to survive the war, although he carried one of the bullets in his body for the rest of his life.[3]

The sorrowful task of burying the dead was begun. Armed with poor spades, squads of twelve men from the division pioneer corps roamed the battlefield. One such squad buried sixteen corpses that night and thirteen more on July 2, then they picked up arms and equipment for the rest of the day. Egbert Ross's body was buried on the night of July 1 with "a piece of plank" as a headboard; his name and rank were scratched on the board so the major's grave could be identified.[4]

Major Jones had placed a guard over Burgwyn's body all night to prevent anyone from robbing it. The remains were carried from Herr's Ridge to the north side of Chambersburg Pike for burial. An empty gun case was used as a coffin. Then Maj. G. P. Collins, Capt. J. J. Young, Sgt. Jesse T. Ferguson of Company C, and Pvt. Mac F. Boyte of Company B wrapped the body in a red woolen blanket and dug a hole. Captain McCreery, Captain Wilson of the 26th, and Captain Iredell of the 47th were buried next to Burgwyn under a large walnut tree. The interment took place, in Pettigrew's words, "with as much honor & ceremony as the hour permitted."[5]

After a day of desperate preparation the men of Pettigrew's brigade thought they were going back into action. Lee resumed his attacks that evening with assaults by Longstreet's corps on the right and Ewell's corps on the left. Anderson's division of Hill's corps launched uncoordinated attacks in the center. Pettigrew was instructed to move Heth's division forward to act as a reserve for Anderson. At 4:00 P.M., just as Longstreet and Ewell began their famous assaults, the brigade marched from its bivouac at Herr's Ridge and took position immediately behind the artillery, sheltered by the crest of Seminary Ridge. Here the men saw "a grand pyrotechnic display" as the Rebel guns blasted away and the noise of musketry rolled across the valley.[6]

Fortunately for Pettigrew his division was not ordered into action that evening. Marshall wanted the brigade's musicians to be with his men, but he had some difficulty prying them away from the field hospitals. The brigade surgeon, Dr. William C. Warren, sent Sam Mickey with a note to Marshall explaining how important they were to his work and asking that they be allowed to stay. Mickey found Marshall's headquarters and handed the note to Capt. Stephen Wiley Brewer, who was acting as an aide to Marshall. Brewer consulted with the new brigade leader and brought back instructions for the musicians to remain with Dr. Warren for the time. Thomas J. Cureton was amazed; he wondered if Pettigrew "was going to take their Horns from [them] and give them muskets also — He seemed so determined to recruit his ranks."[7]

Marshall later decided that the morale of his men demanded the bands's presence. The musicians of both the 26th and the 11th gathered their instruments and marched to Seminary Ridge, arriving there at 6:00 P.M. amid the noise and smoke of battle. They began to perform literally in the middle of combat. "It seemed to do the men good, as they cheered lustily when we played," thought Julius Linebach. The concert lasted for nearly an hour. Cureton recalled thirty years later that "a Gloom had settled over the entire regiment at the loss of their Comrades," which the performance helped to dispel. Just after the bands finished and headed back to Herr's Ridge, a stray shell burst where they had played. Linebach found that several men whom he had tended earlier that day had died while he was performing, and many more still needed attention. He worked feverishly until 11:00 P.M., then slept a few hours and awoke at 3:00 A.M. of July 3 to resume his merciful task.[8]

The brigade received no help from the Quaker conscripts of the 52nd North Carolina. Thomas Hinshaw and his brother Jacob were allowed to stay with the regimental wagons on June 30 because they had no weapons. They met Lt. James Daniel Wells, who earlier had treated them so harshly for their pacifism, on July 2. Wells told them "he could not blame us much for not fighting." The battle of July 1 must have mellowed his outlook. The lieutenant sent them forward to the field hospitals to help the wounded, but Hinshaw and his brother were stopped twice by guards along Chambersburg Pike and sent to a provost marshal for not having passes. They tried to find the regiment, but it had already moved up to Seminary Ridge. The two stopped to rest with several other stragglers and pushed on after dark.

The Hinshaws now reached a turning point in their military careers. Until this time they had never considered deserting. The other men rapidly walked into the darkness toward the battlefield, but the brothers "sat down by a fence and rested some time. And not feeling bound to follow after them, or thinking it our duty to do so, turned to the right and traveled some distance, I suppose near a north course." The two wandered throughout the night of July 2 and finally found a Quaker family about seven miles from Gettysburg. The brothers had their clothes washed for the first time since they left Fredericksburg. After resting for a couple of days, they set to work in the fields helping their rescuers harvest wheat. They were, for a time, out of the war they so religiously hated.[9]

After nightfall put an end to the fighting on July 2, Pettigrew's brigade bivouacked in line of battle behind Seminary Ridge. Early the next morning Thomas J. Cureton and Capt. Samuel P. Wagg of the 26th North Carolina walked forward to get a better view of the no-man's-land between the lines. It was a "beautiful Valley covered with Grass," remembered Cureton, "no trees or anything[,] not even a Hill to protect a charging line from artillery."[10]

Lee decided on a daring move that day. He would mount a large assault on the Union center with Maj. Gen. George Pickett's Virginia division, Pettigrew's four brigades, and two brigades of Pender's division, now led by Maj. Gen. Isaac R. Trimble. The strength of Pettigrew's brigade, still led by Marshall, was estimated at 1,500 to 1,700 men. Altogether some 12,000 Confederates would take part in the attack. The initial order called for Pettigrew to support Pickett with Heth's division, but that was soon changed so that both divisions would advance in line. This canceled order later gave rise to the erroneous impression that Pettigrew was supposed to play second fiddle to the Virginians.[11]

Pettigrew spread the word to his brigade leaders, telling Colonel Fry, who still commanded Archer's brigade, that a heavy artillery barrage was to precede the assault. " 'They will of course return the fire with all the guns they have; we must shelter the men as best we can, and make them lie down.' " Fry gave the necessary instructions.[12]

The Federals were outnumbered two to one in the section of line to be attacked. Brig. Gen. John Gibbon's Second Division of the Second Corps held the line to the left of an angle in the stone fence atop Cemetery Ridge, with Brig. Gen. Alexander Hays's Third Division to the right. Col. Thomas M. Smyth's brigade had only 830 soldiers in its 14th Connecticut, 1st Delaware, and 12th New Jersey, with Capt. William A. Arnold's Battery A, 1st Rhode Island Light Artillery, between it and Gibbon's division. Col. Eliakim Sherrill's New York brigade was posted to Smyth's right and rear. To the right front of Sherrill was the 8th Ohio, providentially placed to be on the flank of any attacking force.[13]

The landscape of this memorable assault was brutal in its simplicity. "The ground over which we had to pass was perfectly open," complained staff officer Louis G. Young, "and numerous fences, some parallel and others oblique to our line of battle, were formidable impediments in our way." A fence that stretched from Seminary Ridge toward the Federal line divided Pettigrew's division from Pickett's, while two fences parallel to the line of battle were along both sides of Emmitsburg Road, which ran at a slight diagonal across the front of both attacking divisions. From the road the Confederates would have to march up a gentle ascent toward the Federal line behind a low stone fence. Young rightly called this slope "a natural glacis," for it forced the Rebels to march straight into the fire of the defenders. But Pettigrew and Trimble would be fired on by a concentration of Federal artillery obliquely to their left on Cemetery Hill.[14]

Another feature in front of Pettigrew's brigade was the Bliss farm, which lay between the opposing lines. The brigade would have to march through a wide, shallow swale, the beginning of Stevens's Run, which was about fifty feet lower than the top of Cemetery Ridge. On the Confederate side of the bottom of this swale stood the Bliss barn and, a few yards north, the farmhouse. The barn, an imposing structure, had been the focus of heavy skirmishing on July 2 and 3. A ten-acre orchard lay just west of the barn. At least a portion of Pettigrew's brigade would have to pass through and around these obstacles.[15]

There was nothing in the landscape to give Pettigrew's men an advantage. Their only prospect of a tactical victory was to exploit the angle in the Union line. The stone fence extended westward about eighty yards before continuing south, forming a small and modified bastion in the line. The brigade had been able to exploit a much larger angle in the Union line on McPherson's Ridge two days before, but this was a much less pronounced irregularity that could easily be corrected if Gibbon's troops withdrew from the angle to form a continuous line with Smyth's brigade to the right.

When word of the impending bombardment spread along the division line, each brigade moved forward from its bivouac about 100 yards to take position 50 yards behind the crest of Seminary Ridge. The right of Pettigrew's division was just north of Spangler's Woods, the assembly area of Pickett's brigades. Lee and Longstreet reported that Pettigrew formed his men in two lines rather than one, that he placed half of each regiment about 100 yards behind the rest. But there is no support for this contention from anyone in the division, and there certainly seemed to be no advantage in deploying this way. Pettigrew formed his men in the traditional one-line formation with Fry, Marshall, Davis, and then Brockenbrough from right to left. Trimble's two brigades were placed 150 yards behind Pettigrew's. Within Marshall's brigade, the 47th North Carolina was on the right, touching Fry's left flank; then the 26th was next, followed by the 52nd and 11th. Just in front of Pettigrew's division was the line of artillery, placed in the edge of the open valley separating the opponents.[16]

There would be a lot of controversy over the decision to use Pettigrew's men this day, given their heavy losses on July 1. John Thomas Jones reported that the 26th North Carolina had scrounged up 230 men for duty, a far cry from the more than 800 who had attacked the Iron Brigade. "Captains and Lieutenants were in command of regiments on the 3d," Jones reported. The brigade chaplains were in the field hospitals ministering to the wounded, so the Tar Heels had to be content with overhearing services in Pickett's division.[17]

The guns opened at 1:00 P.M., and it seemed to Cureton that "the very ground trembled . . . [as] if an *Earth Quake*" had struck. Thomas W. Setser was impressed, writing home, "we lade in twenty Steps of our batters, and the hole

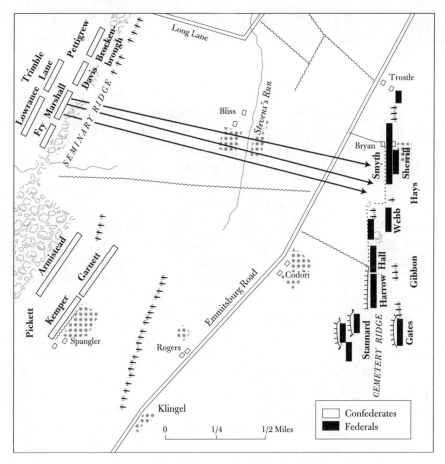

MAP 7.1 The Battle of Gettysburg, July 3, 1863

grown Shuck. the yankes kill five horses rite in fronte of mee at wone Shot, and
I cante tell how meny Caseearns tha blode up." The heat was so oppressive that
several men fainted just before the attack began. The sounds and tremors of the
barrage were felt behind the lines as well. Julius Linebach and a colleague were
walking to the wagon train for more rations for the wounded when the guns
opened up. "The very ground seemed to quiver under us from the awful concussion from the many heavy guns," he recalled.[18]

By 2:00 P.M. the barrage had ended, and the order to advance was given. Pettigrew signaled to Fry but personally spoke the order to his old brigade. Riding
up to Marshall's command, "with the Bright look he ... always wore in the Hour
of danger," Pettigrew said, "'Now Colonel for the Honor of the Good Old North
State forward.'" Marshall turned and repeated the command to his brigade. In

the 47th North Carolina, Colonel Faribault yelled, "'Attention, Battalion,'" and the order was echoed by Lieutenant Colonel Graves. "Every man sprung into line and was ready to go forward, the men knew not where, for the ridge just in front of the Forty-seventh Regiment obstructed the view of the Regiment beyond twenty-five yards." The men of Marshall's brigade marched with even step. "We all moved off in as magnificent style as I ever saw, the lines perfectly formed," reported Jones of the 26th North Carolina. Lt. Julius Rowan Rogers saw the same style in the ranks of the 47th North Carolina. It advanced "in good order and without any confusion." Even when the 47th passed the artillery line and could easily see the open field crisscrossed with fences that lay ahead, they did not hesitate; "no one faltered, but a good, steady quick-step was kept up."[19]

The only hitch in the advance so far was caused by a misunderstanding on the part of Davis. Pettigrew had cautioned him repeatedly during the bombardment to pay attention to the movement of Marshall's command to his right. Davis mistook other troops for Marshall's men and failed to advance with them. When Pettigrew rode out from the woods with his staff members behind his old brigade, he suddenly realized that neither Davis nor Brockenbrough were up. He told Louis Young to ride back "with all speed" and bring Davis, but Young had barely turned his horse around when Davis realized his mistake and rushed his Mississippi regiments forward. They advanced more quickly than the rest of the division and kept up this pace even after coming abreast of Marshall. The confusion in Brockenbrough's command was even worse. A misunderstanding caused half of this small force to remain in the trees while two regiments went forward alone. The tardy units started late but never caught up with the others. Young asked Pettigrew if he should see to the Virginia unit. No, Pettigrew replied; the brigade "might follow, and if it failed to do so it would not matter." Young thought Brockenbrough's command "was in a chronic state of demoralization, and was not to be relied upon; it was virtually of no value in a fight."[20]

When Pettigrew's men passed 100 yards beyond their own guns, the Federal artillery opened fire with shell, many of which burst exactly on target. The 47th saw "great gaps" opening in its ranks "at almost every five or ten steps," but men would always scramble to fill the holes as soon as they were made. A shell burst near Pettigrew, wounded his horse, and forced the division leader to continue on foot. The color-bearers of the 26th North Carolina were once again prominent targets. Sgt. W. H. Smith of Company K began the assault with the flag but was wounded fairly early. He was captured that day and died on July 18 of his injuries. Sometime later his replacement, Pvt. Thomas J. Cozart of Company F, was killed while carrying the flag, and Stephen Wiley Brewer replaced him.[21]

Just ahead was the Bliss farm. Pettigrew's skirmishers rejoined the battle line, and the Federal skirmishers fired a few rounds at the moving mass before retiring across the valley. Lt. James D. Newsom of Company H, 47th North Carolina, was among the first hit by this small arms fire. He was only slightly injured in the shoulder, but his fighting blood was aroused. Newsom ran over to Capt. Sidney Wilford Mitchell and shouted, "'Captain, they have wounded me, but I want to lead Company H.'" It was an odd request that Mitchell could hardly grant.[22]

The division halted to correct its alignment on the Bliss farm, now empty of Federal skirmishers. Davis's brigade continued to career almost out of control on the left and surged ahead of the rest of the division, but Fry's and Marshall's commands merely dressed their lines without wavering. Although he had started earlier, Pickett was forced to make a sharp left oblique to hit the Federal line on a narrow front from the angle to a small copse of trees just south of it. Pettigrew had only to move forward and dress to the right to maintain general alignment with Pickett.[23]

The brigade marched through the southern half of the Bliss orchard and crossed the swale that gave rise to Stevens's Run, crowding to the left all the time. Louis G. Young oversaw the left wing of the division and found that the line bunched up in several places because of this crowding. The trouble was "soon remedied by the thinning of the ranks, done by shot and shell," he recalled.[24]

Marshall's men continued to fall at a steady pace. Capt. John W. Brown of Company I, 47th North Carolina, was stunned by the explosion of a shell and was taken to the rear. His replacement, Lt. John Wiley Jones, was hit in the thigh and crumpled to the ground but was able to lift his sword and cheer the men on as they passed around him.[25]

Pettigrew lost his left flank as the division approached Emmitsburg Road. Brockenbrough's confused command broke under the hail of artillery fire and ran before it reached that point. Davis's hard-charging brigade made it to the road, but most Mississippians stayed a short time and then retreated. Pettigrew saw this from his position behind Marshall's command and sent an aide, Capt. W. B. Shepard, to rally them, but he could do nothing to stem the tide. By now Young was on foot. His mare was injured by three fragments of shell, and Young sent her to the rear with a wounded man aboard. He confessed years later that "the thoughts of my heart were more with the spirited animal which had borne me bravely through many perils, than with my hurt comrade." Pettigrew told Young to urge Trimble forward. The latter general sent Lane's brigade obliquely to the left to cover the ground left vacant by Davis and ordered Col. William L. J. Lowrance's North Carolina brigade to push faster straight ahead to support Marshall.[26]

Meanwhile, the rest of Pettigrew's command hit the fences. Crossing them

The approach of Pettigrew's brigade on July 3. The Tar Heels started from the tree line in the distance and passed over the Bliss farm toward this spot, occupied by Col. Thomas M. Smyth's Union brigade. The location of the Bliss orchard is indicated by the small trees on the far right. (Courtesy of the author)

"broke up the alignment, which, under the heavy fire, it was difficult to correct." The 14th Connecticut took this opportunity, when Pettigrew's men were most vulnerable, to rise up and open fire. The full force of its battle line let loose at about 175 yards, and the effect was devastating. The Tar Heels tumbled to the ground as Marshall's brigade endured its second slaughter of the campaign. From the ranks of the 14th Connecticut it looked like "the men dropped from the fence as if swept by a gigantic sickle swung by some powerful force of nature. Great gaps were formed in the line, the number of slain and wounded could not be estimated by numbers, but must be measured by yards." Some Federals were armed with breech-loading rifles, and the rest had stockpiled rifle muskets, loaded and ready for rapid firing.[27]

Many Confederates were shot while literally in the act of crossing the fences. Lieutenant Newsom of the 47th North Carolina, who had already been hit in the shoulder, was struck by a bullet as he put his foot on a rail. He was badly injured but survived. The only remaining officer in Company I, Julius Rowan Rogers, felt the impact of a ball on his left leg as he crossed. Rogers fell off the fence and lay stunned on the ground for a few minutes. Then he realized he could continue and saw that the 47th already was forging ahead toward the crest of Cemetery Ridge, so he hobbled after it.[28]

There were no more well-dressed ranks; the effort made in negotiating the road and its fences took care of that. Many soldiers pushed on singly or in small groups, but other members of the brigade failed to advance beyond Emmitsburg Road. In this atmosphere of confusion it was possible for many of them to lie in the roadbed to escape the rain of bullets. Lt. Col. J. McLeod Turner of the 7th North Carolina, Lane's Brigade, was later wounded and lay on the ground near some of these men who were members of the 11th and 26th. They claimed that they had been "compelled to stop at the road" because of the heavy fire. Perhaps half of the brigade, about 700 men, crossed the pike and continued toward the Federal line. It was not cowardice but prudence that led the others to hug the relative safety of the roadbed.[29]

Troops who did cross the thoroughfare took enormous casualties. So many Tar Heels fell right after crossing the road that Trimble thought "they seemed to sink into the earth under the tempest of fire poured into them." Despite the barrage of noise coming from the Federal line, Trimble heard a wounded Tar Heel yell, "'three cheers for the old North State.'" He was answered by a round of shouting from the men who were still pressing on. Trimble was astonished at the sight of Pettigrew's soldiers marching so steadily into the face of that fire. "'Charley,'" he said to an aide, "'I believe those first fellows are going into the enemy's line.'"[30]

The 26th North Carolina opened fire after it crossed Emmitsburg Road. The fire it received in turn seemed to intensify as it closed with the enemy. "The storm of lead which now met us is beyond description," recalled Jones soon after the battle. "The smoke was dense and at times I could scarcely distinguish my own men." By the time fragments of the regiment reached a point fifty yards from the stone fence, the 26th was "reduced to a Skirmish line by the Constant falling of the Men at every Step." The 1st Delaware, on the left front of the regiment, held its fire until the Rebels were too close to miss. The "advancing enemy was staggered," reported a Federal officer, and "thrown into confusion."[31]

The advance was stumbling to a halt but not before the angle in the stone fence was cleared. The Federals retreated out of the angle as soon as they realized that Pettigrew's command might outflank them, thus eliminating any chance of a decisive breakthrough. While a small part of Fry's brigade and some of Pickett's command entered the angle and stalled, some of Marshall's men advanced farther. But because of the higher stone fence and the more pronounced slope that faced them, the men could not close with the enemy. Small groups of Pettigrew's brigade slowly came to a stop only yards from the Yankees and stoically endured the killing while their officers, or whoever was left in authority, tried to figure out what to do. Capt. Joseph J. Davis of Company G, positioned nearly on the extreme left of the 47th, wondered how to respond to Sgt. Jesse M. Gilliam when he reported that all officers of his Company K were shot down. What should he do? Davis caught a glimpse of gray movement to the left and assumed that Lane was on the way to help. " 'Our supports are coming and we can whip them yet,' " he yelled to Gilliam over the din.[32]

Trimble tried to help. Lane had taken his brigade obliquely to the left to re-place Davis, but a mix-up diluted his strength. The 7th North Carolina and the right wing of the 37th North Carolina continued to advance straight ahead be-hind Marshall with Lowrance's brigade, separating themselves from their own brigade. Lane had ridden all the way across the valley on horseback and was a perfect target. Capt. John Thorp of Company A, 47th North Carolina, happened to look to the left and witnessed what took place. Lane was urging his men for-ward by waving his hand when Thorp saw "a large spurt of blood" leap from his horse. The poor animal was mortally wounded and began to plunge up and down. To Thorp it seemed as if "rider and horse went down in the smoke and uproar." Actually Lane did not fall but jumped from his dying animal before it collapsed.[33]

Much of Lowrance's command went beyond Emmitsburg Road but was un-able to help Marshall push farther. Most of Lane's brigade failed to go past that fatal line. All forward progress to the left of Marshall stopped. Trimble was se-verely wounded and later had his left leg amputated, and Pettigrew also was hit. Still walking behind his old command, the division leader was struck in the left hand by canister and suffered a painful injury when the bones were smashed.[34]

Marshall's brigade approached the stone fence at a diagonal, with the right wing closer than the left. The 11th and 52nd North Carolina took fewer men across Emmitsburg Road while the 26th and 47th brought more men close to the stone fence. Lieutenant Colonel Graves held many men of the 47th together in a strong cluster and led them to within forty yards of the Federals before he too was forced to stop.[35]

Pettigrew's brigade had already lost its commander when the attack reached high tide. Marshall had kept pace with the men, riding his horse all the way. While they were crossing Emmitsburg Road, he turned to Capt. Stockton Heth, the wounded division leader's son and aide. " 'We do not know which of us will be the next to fall,' " he said. Just a few minutes later two balls plunged into his forehead and killed him. Lt. Col. Marcus Parks, commanding the 52nd North Carolina, was shot about the same time in both thighs and was later captured. Maj. John Q. Richardson was mortally wounded while leading the left wing of the 52nd and slowly died where he fell, while Capt. Benjamin F. Little of Com-

Col. James Keith Marshall. Colonel of the 52nd North Carolina, he appears in the left rear of this view of cadets at Virginia Military Institute. Marshall led the brigade when Pettigrew took charge of Maj. Gen. Henry Heth's division. He was killed when he reached Emmitsburg Road during the charge on July 3. (Preston Library, Virginia Military Institute, Lexington)

pany E watched a few feet away, nursing his own wounded arm. The regiment now was led by its junior captain, Nathaniel A. Foster of Company F.[36]

The most stunning episode of the brigade's drive toward the fence involved the 26th North Carolina. A small group from this regiment surged to within twenty yards of the fence. The no. 4 gun of Arnold's Rhode Island battery was doubleshotted with canister and primed for firing, but Pvt. William C. Barker seemed reluctant to pull the lanyard. Sgt. Amos M. C. Olney yelled at him, "'Barker, why the d—l don't you fire that gun! pull! pull!'" Barker instantly obeyed, "and the gap in that North Carolina regiment was simply terrible." Among those who fell under this point-blank fire was Capt. Samuel P. Wagg of Company A. He and Lieutenant Cureton had examined the field of his death early that morning. Wagg was "'shot through with grape'" when only "'a few feet'" from the gun's muzzle.[37]

26th North Carolina marker. It commemorates the farthest advance of the regiment during Pickett's Charge on July 3. The lone gun of Arnold's Battery A, 1st Rhode Island Light Artillery, was positioned on the far right of this view.
(Courtesy of the author)

There came a time, a few minutes after they arrived at high tide, when the survivors of Marshall's brigade realized there was no point in staying. John Thomas Jones came to this conclusion after seeing that no support was on its way and asking "myself what we should do." He estimated that only sixty men were on their feet in the 26th North Carolina, "and [with] that small number diminishing every moment," he hesitated. Jones gave the order to retire. Somewhere among the clustered remnants of the 26th, Thomas J. Cureton heard shouting from the left. He saw that "the entire left of the line was gone." The 8th Ohio and other Federal units were advancing and firing into the brigade's flank. The Rebel advance crested for only a short while in front of the stone fence. Louis G. Young did not think it was as long as twenty minutes, while Lt. Gaston Broughton of the 26th recalled staying only about ten to fifteen minutes at the high-water mark. Henry Clay Albright of Company G thought the hail of small arms fire was even more dangerous while the 26th retreated than when it advanced.[38]

Benjamin Franklin Little, his arm badly injured, continued to lie on the ground fifty yards from the fence. Several men of his regiment were even closer when shot. He heard no order to retreat, but that did not surprise him. "Officers and men were about that time mowed down so rapidly, and the fighting so hot, that orders could not be heard if given." Years later, when defending the Tar Heels against accusations by Virginians that they did not properly support Pickett, Little sarcastically wrote, "The only 'giving way' that I could see on the part of Pettigrew's Brigade was the 'giving way' by falling to the earth, killed or wounded."[39]

Lieutenant Colonel Graves still held control of about 150 men of the 47th North Carolina displaying remarkable but misplaced bravery some forty yards from the stone fence. The entire group, including Graves, was soon captured. Julius Rowan Rogers managed to escape despite his injured leg. He admired the stamina of his comrades. "The Forty-seventh acted bravely, cooly and none faltered," he wrote after the war. "All did their duty and acted the part of brave soldiers." The regiment lost its flag because the bearer and all members of the color guard were shot down. Pvt. Robert A. Weeden of Company K "seized the colors and bore them aloft" but was soon wounded in the thigh and captured. He died three weeks later.[40]

Many members of the brigade decided to remain on the field, taking shelter in the roadbed, rather than risk their lives by retreating across the open valley. While they waited to be captured, Pettigrew walked calmly to the west, nursing his injured hand. Louis G. Young met and walked with him for a time. Young and Shepard were the only division staff Pettigrew had available on the battlefield, and he quickly sent both men on various errands. Thomas J. Cureton encountered Pettigrew and asked if he could be of assistance. The division leader thanked him and "offered me his *unwounded arm*" as the two continued toward the crest of Seminary Ridge. There, Pettigrew instructed Cureton to collect as many men of the division as he could behind the artillery. The lieutenant soon assembled "a pretty good Skirmish line."[41]

The men of Smyth's brigade were wild with joy. They continued to fire at the retreating Rebels "as long as they were within range." Many Confederates hid behind rocks, rises in the ground, and even dead bodies, and they raised their handkerchiefs in token of surrender. The 14th Connecticut had only 100 men engaged in the battle but collected 200 prisoners. Cpl. Christopher Flynn of Company K picked up the flag of the 52nd North Carolina, which was "new, without number or inscription," because it had been issued only two months before.[42]

Capt. James M. Kincaid of the 52nd was severely injured in the left thigh and left on the field. Cpl. Alexander McNeil of the 14th Connecticut talked with him and brought coffee while they waited for a stretcher. Kincaid had been very understanding of the Hinshaw brothers, the Quaker conscripts in his company, who at that moment had already deserted and were looking for a friendly home. McNeil also was impressed by Kincaid. "He was a sensible Intelligent man. He told me the South had been rough and harsh with North Carolina troops all through, since the War commenced. He told me that it was because the State of

North Carolina did not Secede quite soon enough to suit some of the other Slave States. He told me, too, that the State of South Carolina ought to be sunk. That, he said, was where the trouble started." Kincaid would not live to see the end of the war. He died in a field hospital at Gettysburg on August 27.[43]

Another example of friendship across the lines occurred when the flag of the 26th North Carolina fell into Union hands. The third color-bearer, Stephen Wiley Brewer, was seriously wounded and captured. He would survive the injury and his imprisonment at Johnson's Island to be exchanged in February 1865. His replacement, Pvt. Daniel Thomas of Company E, was the last holder of the banner that had attracted so much death at Gettysburg. He was wounded too but kept hold of the flag. Stranded at high tide, Thomas was talked into giving up by members of the 12th New Jersey. They yelled, " 'Come over on this side of the Lord,' " as he walked up to the stone fence and crossed into captivity, accompanied by Sgt. James M. Brooks of Company E. Thomas would be exchanged with Brewer, but Brooks was released in the spring of 1864. He would be wounded during the Petersburg campaign and captured one week before Appomattox, but he survived this second stint as a prisoner and returned home.[44]

The brigade would never again be in such terrible shape as when it reached the end of this catastrophic attack. Survivors of the assault hobbled in throughout the rest of the day. Some were unhurt but lay on the field until darkness offered a cover for retreat; others were too badly wounded to return quickly and thus "crawled from the field of carnage." Pettigrew fretted that evening about the attack. He had met Lee soon after it ended and exchanged a few memorable words with him. Lee had ridden to Pettigrew's starting point when he learned that Brockenbrough's brigade had broken apart and retreated. "General Lee," the Tar Heel excitedly said, "I am responsible for my Brigade, but not for the Division." It was a childish remark; as division leader, he should have shouldered responsibility for the entire command, but Lee was not bothered. He leaned down from his saddle and said, "General Pettigrew, it is all my fault." To many others Lee said the same thing, but he added a more personal note by saying, " 'General, I am sorry to see you wounded; go to the rear.' " The division leader could not restrain his anger and frustration before his own men. He told John Thomas Jones, who now led the brigade, that the failure to bring up adequate support doomed the assault. " 'My noble brigade had gained the enemy's works,' " he erroneously cried, " 'and would have held them had not ——'s brigade given way.' " Jones refused to report whose men Pettigrew blamed, but they probably were Davis's. " 'Oh! had they have known the consequences that hung upon their action at that moment, they would have pressed [on].' "[45]

Flag of the 26th North Carolina, captured at Gettysburg. Acquired by the regiment
in May 1863 and carried by fourteen men on July 1, this flag was taken across the stone
fence on July 3 by color-bearer Pvt. Daniel Thomas when he found himself stranded
at high tide and gave himself up. It lay in storage at the U.S. War Department
until transferred to the Museum of the Confederacy in 1906.
(MC; photo by Katherine Wetzel)

But other members of the brigade more accurately gauged the situation.
Quartermaster Young of the 26th North Carolina called it "a second Fredericksburg affair, only the wrong way." Louis G. Young diplomatically wrote that
"it must remain always a sealed question, whether or not Cemetery [Ridge]
could have been taken with the forces engaged." Lieutenant Blount of the 47th
North Carolina put it more strongly in a letter to his fiancée: "I think it was the
will of Heaven that we should fail."[46]

The 26th North Carolina suffered more than any other regiment of the
brigade from this unwise assault. The regiment had 843 men ready to attack the
Iron Brigade at 3:00 P.M. on July 1. Fifty hours later only 67 men and 3 officers re-

mained on their feet. About 100 of the 250 men who went into the assault were captured, many of the others were killed or injured, and the rest simply wandered back to the regiment during the night and the next day.[47]

The surgeons of the brigade were ordered forward that evening to be nearer the battlefield. Julius Linebach found the wounded scattered about, and there were plenty of bodies as well. Linebach was horrified by one corpse that had "become bloated out of all human shape." He worked with the wounded until 1:00 on the morning of July 4, then he went to sleep.[48]

J. A. Bush Sr. of Company I, 26th North Carolina, suffered horribly on the field. He was hit with five bullets "in less than five minutes" only a few yards from the stone fence and lay in the open the rest of the day. He nearly bled to death and then was almost hit again by Yankee skirmishers who were taking potshots at a wounded officer. The injured officer tried to crawl back to his own lines and came dangerously near Bush, who angrily told him to go away. The officer finally saved himself by heading for the Union side, but Bush continued to lie where he fell. He suffered immensely for lack of water. Sgt. Alexander Dunlap of Company H heard him call out and told him he had a canteen, but his leg was broken by a bullet and he could not walk. Bush tried to stand up, but the loss of blood made him so weak he fell on his back and rolled down the grassy slope. It was a fortunate turn of events, for Bush landed near a dead man who had a half-full canteen strapped around his body. Bush nursed his supply all night. Later that evening, under cover of darkness, a lieutenant of the 152nd Pennsylvania found him and shared some water but made no effort to carry him over the fence and to the Federal rear.[49]

The daunting task of counting the casualties and repairing the damage to the brigade was begun that evening. Jones found himself thrust into its command with every disadvantage. "Our brigade is in a bad fix," he soon reported to his father, "with no other field officers except myself and very few company officers." The brigade lost roughly half its strength in the charge, and three of the four regimental colors were lost. A total of seventeen men in the 26th North Carolina became casualties when they carried the flag during the two days of fighting. Only the 11th North Carolina retained its flag.[50]

Pettigrew's performance as a division commander was undistinguished. The failure of Davis and Brockenbrough to press home their attacks was not directly his fault; he can only be blamed for not making sure they as well as Fry and Marshall had their commands in hand. Knowing that Brockenbrough's Virginians were unreliable, he nevertheless placed them in the most exposed part of his formation and then paid no special attention to them. Pettigrew demonstrated personal bravery in staying so close to his division—closer than did Pickett. One of his staff members had been killed and one wounded on July 1, and another was mortally injured on July 3. Louis G. Young also was slightly hurt on the latter day. "My right ear was touched & my clothes & hat cut in sundry places," he reported to his mother. The division suffered enormously on July 3. It lost 470 killed, 1,893 wounded, and 337 men who were not wounded taken prisoners, all during the hour that it took to advance toward Cemetery Ridge and return. The total of 2,700 casualties represented 60 percent of its strength. Pickett's loss rate was 67 percent, and Trimble's was 52 percent. But if only Davis's, Marshall's, and Archer's brigade losses are tabulated, the rate was 70 percent in Pettigrew's division.[51]

Marshall's brigade lost 1,753 of 2,584 men engaged in the two days of fighting. That amounted to 67.8 percent of the total. The killed numbered 240, and 17 men whose fates were never determined were listed as missing. The wounded totaled 603 men. Of that number, 73.6 percent eventually returned to duty, while 13.4 percent were discharged. Another 11.1 percent of the wounded died of their injuries. But there were many other men who were wounded and captured, and nearly all of them fell in the assault of July 3. They totaled 584; 33.7 percent eventually returned to serve in their regiments before the war ended. Another 34.9 percent of those who were wounded and captured were discharged into civilian life, and 30.1 percent of the men who went to a prison camp with wounds died in captivity. That figure was nearly three times higher than the number of men who were wounded but remained in Confederate hands.

A total of 309 men were captured without being wounded. Nearly half of them, 41.1 percent, were released and sent to their homes in the South either before the war ended or after Appomattox. Nearly a quarter of the captured, 22.3 percent, were released from prison in time to return to duty, and 33.3 percent of the prisoners died in captivity. A total of 893 men wound up in a Federal prison, either wounded or unhurt. This was exactly half of all the casualties the brigade suffered at Gettysburg and 34.5 percent of the brigade's strength in the battle. One man was listed as having joined the Union army while in prison. One interesting item in the service records shows that three men of the 26th North Carolina gave up during the campaign and fell into Union hands. Whether they deserted or simply collapsed from exhaustion is unclear.

The statistics for the wounded were even more astounding. A total of 1,187 men were injured in the two assaults. That was 67.7 percent of all the casualties and 45.9 percent of the total number of men who entered the battle. The number of soldiers killed, 240, represented 13.6 percent of the total casualties and 9.2 percent of the number engaged.[52]

The 26th North Carolina lost more men than any other Confederate regiment at Gettysburg. In fact, it lost more men than any other Rebel regiment had in its ranks at the beginning of the battle. Several men offered conflicting estimates of the number of casualties. Underwood, the historian of the regiment, placed them at 708. Capt. Henry Clay Albright, who briefly commanded the regiment after the assault of July 3, recorded the figure 711 in his diary. The official loss was placed at 687, which was more than 81 percent of its strength, the fourth highest percentage lost by any Confederate regiment in the battle. The 26th also had the greatest number killed, 172, and the greatest number wounded, 443. It officially listed 72 men captured or missing, which was the fourteenth highest number in the Rebel army at Gettysburg. It is not surprising that the Union regiment that suffered the greatest total loss and the highest number of men killed or wounded at Gettysburg was the 24th Michigan.[53]

The enormity of the losses hit some families in a particularly vicious way. Pvts. Joseph and W. E. Phillips of Company F, twin brothers, were killed on July 1. W. E. Phillips had also been wounded at Malvern Hill exactly one year earlier. The Kirkman family of Chatham County lost four sons at Gettysburg. They all served in Company G and ranged in age from nineteen to twenty-five years. George E. Badger Kirkman was killed on July 1. Henry Clay Bascom Kirkman, a student before the war, was wounded in the left foot on July 3 and taken prisoner, only to die on September 1, 1863. Wiley Prentiss Kirkman was taken prisoner on July 5 and died at Point Lookout of scurvy one month before Lee surrendered. William Preston Kirkman, a teacher before the war, was wounded on July 1 and died one or two days later. The suffering must have been unimaginable in the Kirkman household and no doubt was intensified by the fact that the father of these men, George Kirkman, was a physician who was given no opportunity to take care of his boys.[54]

The losses within each company of the 26th told the tale more intimately. Only 14 men of Company A took part in the assault of July 3, and 10 of them were killed or missing. Lt. Gaston Broughton's Company D took 25 men into the assault and lost 5 killed, 6 wounded, and 6 men missing, a total of 17. All but 2 of the 12 men that Capt. Stephen Wiley Brewer of Company E led into the attack were killed or wounded. The story of Company F was particularly heartbreaking. It had suffered dreadfully on July 1, and only one man came out of the attack on McPherson's Ridge unhurt. Sgt. Robert Hudspeth did his best to build up the company; he found four or five men who were on detached duty with the ambulance corps or as pioneers and took them into the attack on July 3. One of them, Thomas Cozart, was killed while carrying the flag, and the others were lost as well. Hudspeth also was "knocked down by the bursting of a shell." Thus literally every man in the company was a casualty. Henry Clay Albright took twenty-two soldiers of his Company G into the assault, but only eight returned. He and Lt. John Anderson Lowe were "more or less wounded." Company H lost half of the dozen men who made the charge.[55]

The 11th North Carolina was a close second to the 26th in this grim race for distinction. It lost 366 men in the two days of battle, 108 of them killed and another 200 wounded. In all three categories the Bethel Regiment ranked second among the Confederate units at Gettysburg. It lost 59 percent of its men, making it eighteenth among Lee's regiments in loss ratio. Fifty-eight men were missing or captured. Company A took 100 men into the fighting of July 1 and ended up with 9 left on the evening of July 3. Company I lost 76 of the 78 men it took into the battle. Capt. Francis Bird's Company C protected the colors on July 3. It had taken 38 men into the fight two days before and lost 34 of them. Bird led the 4 remaining soldiers in the attack on Cemetery Ridge. When the flag bearer was shot, Bird personally took charge of the colors and brought them out of harm's way. The staff was severed, but he was able to carry both parts of it to safety. The regiment suffered for a long time from the loss of officers. As the regimental historians later put it, "This defective organization continued to mar the efficiency of the regiment to the end of the war." Yet the 11th continued to function effectively although it never was as sharp as it was on July 1.[56]

The 47th North Carolina was "cut all to pieces," moaned Sgt. Alexander H. Harris of Company I. Colonel Faribault was wounded in the shoulder and foot. Lieutenant Colonel Graves was wounded and died in prison the following March. Maj. Archibald D. Crudup was hit in the breast, neck, left arm, and left hip on July 3 and taken prisoner. He was released in March, but his health was "'completely shattered'" by the multiple wounds he received at Gettysburg, forcing him to resign from the army. The senior company leader had to command the regiment for the time being. The 47th lost 217 men, the seventeenth heaviest loss of any Confederate regiment in the battle. It also ranked seventeenth in the number of men killed, 53, and seventh in the number of soldiers wounded, 159.[57]

The losses in the regiment traumatized the survivors. "My company is completely annihilated," reported Sergeant Harris. Pvt. A. Hiram Rochelle had joined Harris's Company I only four months before the battle and was lucky to come out of it alive. A shell fragment bruised his leg, "but I can hobble about and hope I shall soon be well," he informed his father. The carnage stunned this neophyte soldier. "You never saw anything like it, thousands of killed and wounded all over the ground. Our Regiment is ruined forever, nearly all killed, wounded and missing."[58]

As in the 47th, all the regimental officers of the 52nd North Carolina were killed, wounded, or captured. The total number of casualties on July 3 amounted to 302 men, with 51 killed, 123 wounded and captured, 43 wounded and escaped from the field, and 85 captured or missing. Company I lost 45 of its 55 men in the assault. Right after the battle, George H. Coke wrote feelingly to a physician friend about the attack: "I have never in my life, Doctor, witnessed such slaughter as there was in our Brigade, all the field officers killed or wounded, all of the Captains in our Regiment Killed or wounded, and nearly the entire Regiment killed, wounded or captured."[59]

The whole campaign into Pennsylvania had been a rude awakening for the brigade. Working in the backwater of North Carolina for so long had inured the men to hard marches, but they were stunned by the intensity of fighting. The survivors of Gettysburg would form the hard corps of men on which the fighting history of Pettigrew's brigade would be based. Lt. Lemuel J. Hoyle of the 11th North Carolina movingly informed his mother that "we have at last had to pass through the ordeal of fire and blood." But Louis G. Young was convinced that this rite of passage was necessary to hone the brigade into an efficient weapon. "The bloody ordeal through which it passed on 1 and 3 July, 1863, was terrible," he wrote, "but it prepared it for its subsequent career, which has added lustre to the name of the State."[60]

FIRE AND BLOOD

Chapter 8

Back to Virginia

The attack of July 3 was Lee's last effort at Gettysburg. He accepted its result and planned a careful withdrawal from Pennsylvania. The men of Pettigrew's brigade tried to portray themselves as undaunted in spirit when they wrote of this moment years later. Pettigrew told everyone that they had been very close to a smashing victory, "that had we succeeded . . . no doubt our army would have been on the road to Washington and perhaps negotiations for peace would then be on foot."[1]

Lee's first priority was to save his wounded. A wagon train was organized, and Brig. Gen. John D. Imboden's cavalry brigade was to accompany it across the Potomac. The heavens opened on July 4 to drench the entire area around Gettysburg with a monsoonal rain as conveyances of all kinds mobilized on Chambersburg Pike. As the assemblage grew larger, the storm worsened, and all afternoon rain poured on the wounded who lay exposed in open wagons.[2]

Dr. William C. Warren, the surgeon of Pettigrew's brigade, instructed his helpers to make a list of the wounded and put as many as possible into the train. The band members helped in this merciful task and were to accompany the wounded to Virginia, but Warren decided to stay behind to care for men too badly injured to be removed. The train, which stretched for seventeen miles along the pike, was ready to go at 4:00 P.M. Julius Linebach described it as "a motley procession of wagons, ambulances, wounded men on foot, straggling soldiers and band boys, splashing along in the mud, weary, sad and discouraged." The infantry started out that evening, too. Pettigrew's brigade moved "through mud and water full knee deep" until the men reached South Mountain at dawn on July 5.[3]

Imboden pushed the wagons without rest, crossing South Mountain and by-passing Chambersburg to chart the straightest course to the Potomac. He left the pike and rumbled through Greencastle at dawn on July 5. This was the most try-ing day, for Federal cavalry harassed the train unmercifully, riding between the mounted guards in an effort to cut out and commandeer wagons. Several mem-bers of Pettigrew's brigade were taken prisoner. John Randolph Lane escaped by jumping out of the wagon and mounting a horse. Although his throat was so in-flamed by the wound he received on July 1 that he could not speak or eat, Lane mustered enough strength to ride out of harm's way. He took no nourishment for nine days after his injury, but he confounded the surgeons and survived his hor-rible wound. Collett Leventhorpe was not so lucky. His ambulance was taken by swift-riding Federals, and the Englishman was whisked away to a Yankee prison with 300 other Rebels from his part of the train. This killed any chance that Lev-enthorpe might take command of the brigade when he recovered. Lemuel J. Hoyle and four men of his company were taken, but Hoyle was recaptured by Imboden's troopers only ten minutes later. Pvt. Charles A. Nutall of the 47th North Carolina was less fortunate. He was wounded on July 1, but his ambulance broke down only twenty miles from the battlefield, where he waited for two days and nights without food or water. Then someone transported the wounded men to a nearby house where they recuperated for three weeks before Federal troops found them. Nutall was paroled and went home in November 1863 only to find that his young daughter had died a month before his release.[4]

Some men evaded capture after almost heroic efforts. The driver of an ambu-lance carrying Adj. Henderson C. Lucas of the Bethel Regiment turned into a side road and raced the horses for a mile before slowing down. He was now safe but separated from the train. Before rejoining the caravan, the wounded officer was jostled over the countryside for three days with no food and only one cup of coffee scavenged by a black servant. In the long run it made little difference, for Lucas died a few days later. At times the Rebel escort went to extraordinary lengths to help the wounded. Sgt. Alexander H. Harris of the 47th North Car-olina had been hit in the leg and shoulder on July 3. Federal cavalrymen took his wagon from the train and dashed off with it "at a rapid rate, jostling us almost to death." But Imboden's men gave chase so vigorously that the Yankees gave up. The Federals unhitched the horses and made off with them, leaving the wagons stalled in the road. "Thus we were recaptured," reported Harris.[5]

The train reached Williamsport on the afternoon of July 5 only to find the Potomac swollen with the heavy rain. Imboden hastily made a couple of ferries by lashing flats together and began the slow process of crossing the walking wounded over the river. The more seriously injured were taken from their uncomfortable wagons and placed in private homes.[6]

Everyone feared for their safety when the Federal cavalry caught up with Imboden on July 6. Two divisions of Yankee troopers threatened the train, and Imboden resorted to extraordinary means to defend it. With only 2,000 men available, he called on the teamsters and the lightly wounded for help. They added 700 rifles to Imboden's strength and were commanded by several slightly wounded officers from the train. Skirmishing took place all afternoon with shells flying into the mass of parked wagons from time to time, but the arrival of more Rebel cavalry at dark saved the train.[7]

After this scare subsided, the Moravians attempted to rejoin their regiment. The brigade was still somewhere in the Maryland countryside on its way to the river, but no one knew its location. Shoes were found for the barefoot musicians as the rain continued to pour and the water steadily rose. The bottomland where the wagons were parked was becoming a swamp, so the band moved to the top of the river bluff and set up its tent. The musicians sent word to Major Jones for instructions and received an order to rejoin the 26th. They learned on the way that the regiment was moving, and no one seemed to be able to tell them how to find it; so the Moravians decided to spend the night of July 10 with the brigade wagon train.[8]

Pettigrew's brigade had spent the preceding few days slogging through the mud. Heth's division reached Hagerstown on July 7 and stayed in the vicinity for some time, allowing Heth to recover from his head wound and resume command. This forced Pettigrew to return to the brigade and Jones to resume command of the 26th North Carolina. Pettigrew had taken time from his duties to scribble a letter to Governor Vance briefly informing him of the regiment's role in the battle. "It covered itself with glory," he assured its old commander. "They drove certainly three and we have every reason to believe five Regiments out of the woods with a gallantry unsurpassed."[9]

The brigade caught up with its wagon train on July 11 near Hagerstown, but Pettigrew shifted his position several times during the next few days as Lee sought the best defense of the river crossing while waiting for the water to subside. The Tar Heels formed a battle line on July 12 near Hagerstown to meet a threatened attack, but it never materialized. They also performed picket duty, exchanging sporadic fire with the Federals and losing a few casualties. The 47th North Carolina reported one killed and five wounded, while the 52nd North Carolina lost three wounded in this manner. The earthworks that Lee built near Williamsport were so well constructed that the Yankees chose not to challenge them.[10]

The Potomac was still high but had receded enough by July 13 to allow Lee to cross. He was eager to get home, realizing that even the strong earthworks at Williamsport would not keep the army safe indefinitely. Ewell's corps was to ford the river at Williamsport, while Longstreet and Hill were to cross at a pontoon bridge at Falling Waters, about six miles downstream from the town. The river curved sharply toward Virginia here, forming a progressively narrow finger of land on the Maryland side that could be defended as a bridgehead. Heth's division was assigned to cover the crossing with Maj. Gen. J. E. B. Stuart's cavalry to act as a screen. But the mounted force assigned this task mistook the rear of Longstreet's column for that of Hill's corps and crossed the bridge before its job was done. As a result Heth was unaware that there were no Confederate horsemen between his men and the Federal cavalry that was dogging every Rebel move.[11]

Pvt. Thomas Bailey of the 47th North Carolina helped to build the bridge at Falling Waters. A member of the division pioneer corps, he worked from July 7 to 12 carrying planks on his shoulders for a half-mile to accumulate material to make pontoons. Then the pioneers constructed a dirt causeway across the Chesapeake and Ohio Canal, which ran along the river's edge, and dug down the riverbank to form a ramp leading to the causeway. The crossing was ready by 10:00 A.M. on July 13. The tired pioneers then turned their attention to digging some earthworks for Heth's covering force. Six small artillery emplacements were made two miles from the crossing by dusk that day. Then the pioneers were the first to use their bridge, crossing to the Virginia side at night.[12]

Heth received orders to move out on the evening of July 13. His men marched into the pitch-black darkness; the mud was ankle deep, and the roads were "in a horrible condition." Stragglers fell out only to be caught by the Federal cavalry. Heth deployed at 10:00 A.M. on Tuesday, July 14, on a commanding ridge about two miles from the bridge, at the base of the peninsula that jutted westward toward Virginia. His left rested on the Chesapeake and Ohio Canal, and the rest of his division extended to the south for one and a half miles. He had no guns to fill the two small artillery emplacements on both sides of the road. An open field three-quarters of a mile long lay in front of his men, with a patch of woods beyond it. Pettigrew's brigade of about 800 men straddled the road in Heth's center. Pettigrew rested his right wing against a large garden that bordered the road and was enclosed with a slat fence. Archer's brigade was deployed to his right, and the rest of Heth's division was arranged to the left. Pickets were placed on the division's left wing to guard against any Union force that might approach along the river, but no pickets were put in front.[13]

The men fell out of ranks to sleep, exhausted by the all-night march through

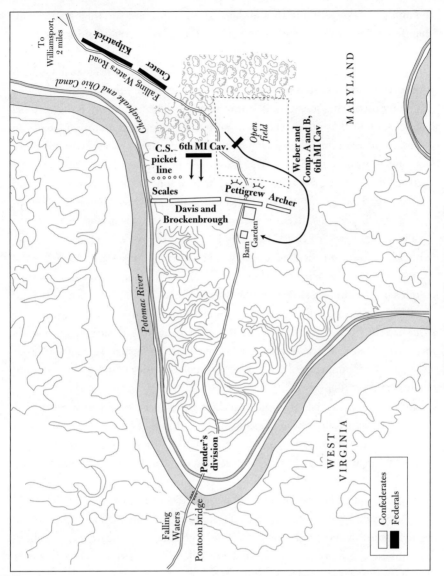

To Williamsport, 2 miles

Kilpatrick

Custer

Falling Waters Road

Chesapeake and Ohio Canal

MARYLAND

C.S. picket line

6th MI Cav.

Open field

Weber and Comp. A and B, 6th MI Cav

Scales

Pettigrew   Archer

Davis and Brockenbrough

Barn

Garden

Potomac River

Pender's division

WEST VIRGINIA

Falling Waters

Pontoon bridge

Confederates
Federals

MAP 8.1 The Battle of Falling Waters, July 14, 1863

the muddy darkness. Only an hour later Heth, Pettigrew, and their staffs sat on their horses near the gun emplacements, on the brigade's right, and saw a squad of some forty-five cavalrymen emerge from the woods. They boldly showed the Union flag, but Heth assumed they were Rebels. He had no idea that all Confederate cavalry had disappeared from his front and was angry that the officer was so flagrantly displaying a captured Union banner. Fearing that some eager Rebel might shoot, Heth cautioned everyone around him to hold their fire and made up his mind to arrest the officer commanding the detachment. Pettigrew was more uncertain; he ordered Louis G. Young to rouse the brigade. The mounted troops rode to within 175 yards of the Confederate position, stopped, drew sabers, and then charged straight up the road toward the two generals. Now it became apparent that they were Yankees who had caught the Rebels napping.[14]

These were men of Brig. Gen. Hugh Judson Kilpatrick's cavalry division, which had followed the Rebel retreat that morning. Maj. Peter A. Weber led Companies B and F of the 6th Michigan Cavalry in the vanguard with Kilpatrick and his brigade leader, Brig. Gen. George A. Custer, riding immediately behind him. When the advance reached the woods fronting Heth's division, Kilpatrick, who had pushed his division in fear that the Rebels would escape, impulsively ordered Weber to attack. The major deployed his 100 men and advanced. Louis G. Young later commented that it was "difficult to believe that sane men would attack as this small body of cavalry did."[15]

Pettigrew's men rushed to pick up their guns, many of which were already loaded but had become damp from the rain that had fallen all night. Weber wisely directed his troopers to ride around Archer's sleeping brigade and to strike Pettigrew's rear by moving between Pender's and Heth's divisions. A wild fight erupted as the Tar Heels about-faced to fire into the approaching horsemen. Jones called it "the funniest affair I have ever been in. The men clubbed their guns and knocked the yankees off their horses. One man knocked one off with a fence rail and another killed a yankee with an ax." The fight lasted about five minutes. Twenty-nine Federals were killed, wounded, or taken prisoner. Major Weber was among those slain.[16]

This short but vicious fight claimed Pettigrew as its most significant casualty. According to commonly accepted stories of his wounding, the general exchanged shots at point-blank range with Major Weber or with a Federal sergeant, and both antagonists went down in the melee with fatal wounds. But reality was nearly as dramatic. Heth and his staff dismounted immediately after the fight began and went to the rear through the garden. Pettigrew was not so fortunate. His horse reared at the first fire, and he fell off because two battlefield injuries had weakened his limbs. His left hand had been smashed on July 3 and was in a sling, while his right arm was still weak from his injury at Seven Pines. Unhurt from the fall, he got up and placed himself at a corner of the garden to encourage the men. Pettigrew noticed a Yankee corporal, on foot between the garden and a barn to the rear, who was taking potshots at everyone. He called on his men to shoot him, but they were too busy to hear; so the brigade leader pulled out a small pistol and walked close to get a better shot at the Yankee. The corporal fired first, shooting Pettigrew in the left side just above the hip and through the back. The Yankee was later killed, reportedly by Pvt. Nevel B. Staten of the 26th North Carolina, who used a "big stone" to crush his breast. Staten had been one of the men who had helped to carry the dying Burgwyn from the field on July 1. He was later killed at the Wilderness.[17]

The battle of Falling Waters was not yet over. Kilpatrick ordered an attack by the rest of the 6th Michigan Cavalry, which arrived just as the remnants of Weber's command retired. Brockenbrough's brigade repulsed the Michigan troopers in hand-to-hand combat. A third assault by the rest of Custer's brigade forced Heth to retire from the ridge.[18]

Jones resumed command of the brigade and led it well under difficult circumstances. After retreating 300 yards, he "turned and gave them a volley which sent them back. I then fell back as fast as I could," he later told his father, "but not before I was flanked on the left and several of my men taken." The pressure was so great that "there was more or less demoralization at the last," according to the historian of the 26th North Carolina, which was the last regiment of the brigade to cross. He estimated that up to 1,500 stragglers were left on the Maryland side, but Lee placed his loss at only 500 men.[19]

The losses in Pettigrew's brigade alone amounted to 261 men, 32.6 percent of those engaged. Of that number, 247 were captured, and 11 additional men were listed as wounded and captured. Only 3 men were wounded and remained in Confederate hands, while no one was identified as killed or missing. Casualties were heaviest in the Bethel Regiment, with 79 captured and 1 wounded. The 52nd North Carolina suffered a total of 72 casualties (67 captured, 4 wounded and captured, and 1 wounded), while the 26th North Carolina lost 57 captured and 2 wounded and captured. The 47th North Carolina suffered the least, with 44 captured, 4 wounded and captured, and 2 wounded.[20]

The brigade managed to evacuate its wounded commander, although the surgeon thought he was too seriously injured to be moved. Pettigrew refused to be left on the field, so four men were hastily detailed to carry him on a stretcher across the pontoon bridge. The bearers were affected by Pettigrew's suffering. He tried to cheer them by saying, "'Boys, don't be disheartened. May be I will fool the doctors yet.'" He rested on the Virginia side that night and was placed in an ambulance the next morning. His prospects were grim. When Pettigrew learned that the bullet had perforated his bowels, he prepared for the worst, giving instructions for the disposal of his effects. Louis G. Young offered to take any personal message to Pettigrew's family, but the general said there was nothing he could do except make sure he did not fall into enemy hands. When the doctors assured him the wound was not necessarily mortal, he began to hope for recovery.[21]

For the first time since June 24, Pettigrew's men spent the night on Confederate soil. They marched five miles into Virginia and bivouacked for the night. Heth felt guilty about his mistaken identification of Weber's command and apologized to Louis G. Young that night, expressing deep regret about Pettigrew's wounding. William Blount of the 47th North Carolina was proud that most of his comrades escaped. "Lee was willing to sacrifice our brigade to save the army, but I tell you we had no notion of being taken." The band members of the 26th had forded the Potomac near Williamsport and crossed into Virginia the day before the fight at Falling Waters, riding in empty wagons to weigh them down so they would not be taken downstream by the current.[22]

The brigade started early on the morning of July 15 and reached Bunker Hill that evening, where it settled for the next six days. Major Jones sent the Moravian bandsmen to serenade Heth and Lee. Their effort was well received. The army commander "acknowledged it with thanks sending us word that he hoped we would play a good deal while the men were resting," noted Julius Linebach. Lee also recognized that the style of these Moravian musicians was different from that of the army's other bands.[23]

Jones lost his position once again when Lt. Col. William J. Martin rejoined the Bethel Regiment at Bunker Hill on July 15. As senior officer, Martin took command of the brigade. There were only about 500 men left following the grueling retreat over the Potomac. Only two weeks earlier the brigade had gone into combat at Gettysburg with well over 2,500 men. J. S. Bartlett of the 11th Carolina had missed Gettysburg due to illness. When he saw what was left of the brigade, he was taken aback. "The ranks had been thinned until it seemed that only a skeleton of an army had returned."[24]

Pettigrew's fate was sealed by the primitive surgical techniques of his day; surgeons simply did not have the skills or technology to repair traumas to the bowels and other delicate organs. Lee had ridden by his side part of the way from the Potomac River to Bunker Hill and expressed sorrow at seeing him wounded. Pettigrew replied " 'that his fate was no other than one might reasonably anticipate upon entering the army, and that he was perfectly willing to die for his country.' " He was placed in the home of a man named Boyd at Bunker Hill and was made as comfortable as possible.[25]

Because Pettigrew seemed to improve on the morning of July 16, his staff members decided to give him several messages, including a request to recommend someone to take over the brigade. This meant it was necessary to tell him he would never be fit for service. Pettigrew took this harsh news "calmly" and admitted that he "had supposed so" all along. An Episcopal minister visited him at the Boyd house and asked if he would take Communion one last time. The general hesitated, modestly insisting that he was not "good enough" to do so. Several surgeons examined his wound during the day and expressed some hope, but Pettigrew obviously was much worse by the afternoon. He passed the night in peace and awoke briefly at 6:25 on the morning of July 17 to say, "'It is time to be going.'" Then he died of peritonitis, "as can only die the good & great," thought Young.[26]

It would take some time for Lee to find a suitable replacement for Pettigrew, for he considered the Tar Heel "a brave soldier" and "accomplished officer." Pettigrew was widely respected and loved, but not for his generalship. He had been in only two major battles and one small engagement and was wounded in all three actions. While his decisions at New Bern the preceding March killed any chance of capturing Barrington's Ferry, his work at Gettysburg had been more reliable. The best that can be said of his generalship was that he died before it could blossom. The respect he received was mostly due to his personality. The love he commanded may have made Heth jealous; at least staff officer George P. Collins believed so. Collins thought Pettigrew's command had not been treated well since it joined the division. Lee lost a good brigade leader who had the potential to evolve into a good division commander.[27]

After the war Maj. John Cheves Haskell expressed the prevailing sentiment well when he remembered Pettigrew, who had been his friend and colleague in the New Bern campaign. The general had all the attributes of a good soldier, "uniting with the brightest mind and an active body a disposition which made him the idol of his men and a courage which nothing could daunt." Yet Haskell also offered some gentle criticism that went to the heart of Pettigrew's limitations as a field commander. "He was so full of theoretical knowledge that I think it really impaired his usefulness, but experience, which he was getting fast, would have corrected that."[28]

Louis G. Young would never forget Pettigrew. He was convinced that the brigade's sterling war record was the result of his personal influence. Pettigrew "had in a few months made of his brigade as fine a body of infantry as ever trod the earth, and his men would have followed him wherever he led, or gone wherever he told them to go, no matter how desperate the enterprise."[29]

The Tar Heels had only a few days to mourn his passing before orders came to move out of Bunker Hill. Lee moved his army to Culpeper Court House, seventy miles south, to block a Federal move east of the Blue Ridge. The brigade left Bunker Hill on July 21 and marched by way of Winchester; it crossed the Shenandoah River on a pontoon bridge the next day. The band played for the citizens of Front Royal as the brigade passed through town. It took four hours to cross the Blue Ridge on July 23, then the men rejoined Heth's division at Flint Hill. There was sporadic skirmishing, mainly long-range artillery fire, as the column marched toward Culpeper on July 24, but Heth managed to cross the Hazel River that day without serious opposition. The division crossed the Rappahannock on July 25 and camped outside Culpeper.[30]

The extended stay at Culpeper allowed Louis G. Young to write a long letter to Pettigrew's sister about her brother. "I can only mingle my tears with yours for the loss of him for whom I would gladly have lain down my life to save," he wrote. Young assured her that Pettigrew had Roman Catholic leanings although he had still been a faithful attendant of the Church of England. The serious-minded general had shown indications that "he would no longer give only the part but the whole of his time to the service of the Almighty," if he had lived.[31]

Major Collins attended to the disposal of Pettigrew's effects. In addition to an umbrella, three pairs of white gloves, and three hair brushes, Pettigrew's camp possessions included a service of white china, cologne, gilt spurs, a small bathing tub, a white necktie, and a champagne basket. His will, made out eight years earlier, specified burial at Bonarva, one of the family plantations in eastern North Carolina.[32]

Pettigrew's body reached Raleigh and lay in state at the capitol during the morning hours of July 24. A large Confederate flag draped the coffin, which was covered with "wreaths of flowers and other tributes of feminine taste and tenderness." A funeral procession followed by religious services on the capitol lawn followed, then the remains were transported to Bonarva, where they were laid to rest. Public eulogies ignored the facts of his military career and focused instead on his personality. "We cannot but think that in the warm personal attachment of his men to him," commented a newspaper editor, "in his *ability to inspire Love*, he showed that he was possessed of the very highest attributes of genius."[33]

Henry King Burgwyn's family also had to deal with the sacrifice of a beloved member. Numerous well-wishers tried to console them. J. J. Young wrote, "In some way I have ever felt uneasy whenever he went into battle & always cautioned him to be cautious. My forebodings, alas, have proved too true & I have lost one of my best friends." William H. S. Burgwyn, an officer in the 35th North Carolina, was posted in the Richmond area and initially learned of his brother's death from a man passing through town on sick leave. William heard another

James Johnston Pettigrew's frock coat.
(Copyright North Carolina Museum of History)

James Johnston Pettigrew's sash.
(Copyright North Carolina Museum of History)

rumor the next day that Harry was alive, but he learned the sad truth on July 14. He wrote consolingly to his mother about the older brother he "had just begun to appreciate for his good and noble qualities." His parents had received definitive news of Henry's death on July 13 when a friend telegraphed the bad news.[34]

Public eulogies followed in the *Raleigh Register*. "The life, career, and death of young Burgwyn," wrote the editor, "convey a lesson to the youth of this Confederacy which cannot be too well studied and thoroughly profited by." The administration of the University of North Carolina sent a resolution of sympathy to the family, while the Virginia Military Institute sent a copy of Henry's diploma with Stonewall Jackson's signature on it.[35]

The family of James Keith Marshall did not learn of his fate until three months after Gettysburg. They heard many false reports that he had been taken prisoner and was in the North, until a letter from one of their relatives brought confirmation that he was dead.[36]

The brigade left hundreds of men in Pennsylvania. Thomas W. Setser of the 26th North Carolina was wounded in the thigh on July 1 and managed to return to the Confederacy, but he informed his family that cousin W. E. Setser was not so lucky. "I am . . . a live and well whiles hundreds of my fellows Soldiers has fell lifeless corps all a round mee and I was spaird but I cante See how it was." Thomas put Eli in an ambulance on the morning of July 4 and said goodbye. "I hate to tell you what he Said, . . . Tom tell my folks how it was. he Said that he was a going to die and he node it, and Said he was willing to die and he wanted mee to tell you how it was. he was shot in too or three places in the arme, and one or too holes threw his Coate, and one Came wente threw his thie and broke the bone all to pecis." Eli died later that day before the train moved out. Thomas returned to duty by January, but he deserted on March 29, 1865, and took the oath of allegiance five days before Lee's surrender.[37]

Many other men who barely survived the battle were in enemy hands. The nature of the assault on July 3 meant that hundreds of Tar Heels were wounded and captured. J. A. Bush Sr. of the 26th North Carolina had been hit by five bullets on July 3. Two days later he managed to get to his feet and walk a bit using a ramrod as a cane. He could only take eight steps at a time, but this slow pace brought him to the Federal picket line. Bush was moved from a house to a field hospital where, on July 7, he received the first food he had eaten in four days. Bush was transported by train to Baltimore, Philadelphia, and David's Island in New York, where he rapidly recovered. He was paroled on September 5 and returned to the South for exchange. Bush made up for his captivity with a long furlough to his North Carolina home, arriving September 19 and staying until February. In the meantime he taught in a local school and married his sweetheart.[38]

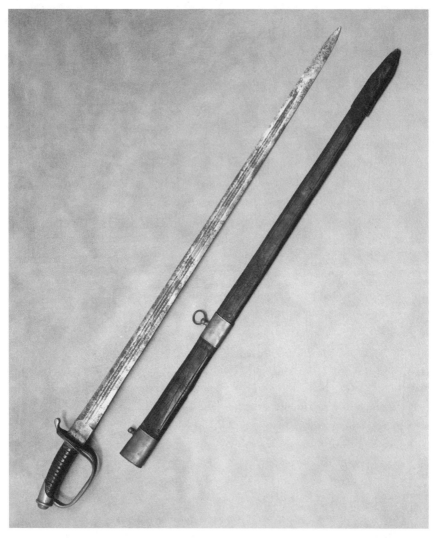

Henry King Burgwyn's sword and scabbard.
(Copyright North Carolina Museum of History)

Benjamin Franklin Little was severely wounded at the height of Pettigrew's charge on July 3. A bone in his left arm was completely broken by a musket ball, and he lay immobilized only a few yards from the stone fence while hundreds of rounds sailed over his head. The Yankees took him to the Sixth Corps field hospital a few miles from Gettysburg, and his arm was amputated by Dr. L. W. Oakley, who treated him with whiskey toddies. Oakley even wrote a letter to reassure Little's wife that her husband was well. The short stump hurt badly for a couple of days, but Little kept the bullet that wounded him (it landed in his shirt) as a souvenir. He gave it and his wedding ring to a comrade for safekeeping. Little was taken from the genial care of Dr. Oakley and transferred to Point Lookout, Maryland. His stump was not yet healed, but it progressed well in prison. He was released for exchange on March 6, 1864, and was promoted to lieutenant colonel of the 52nd a month later, but his missing arm prevented him from taking the field. He resigned on July 15, 1864, and never saw action after Gettysburg.[39]

The prisoners helped one another as best they could. Lt. Orren Hanner of the 26th North Carolina disposed of the remains and effects of fellow officer John R. Emerson when he died at David's Island. Hanner arranged to have Emerson's remains embalmed and placed in a vault in New York City and gave his pocketknife and comb to the dead man's brother, who also was imprisoned on David's Island. But friendly aid could not eliminate the boredom and fear associated with life as a wounded prisoner. Lt. W. J. Kincaid of the Bethel Regiment never fully recovered from his injury and feared he would remain "a cripple" forever. "I am dreadful tired of prison life," he complained from Johnson's Island in late December 1863. "We get no news from the outside—know but little what is transpiring."[40]

Some prisoners managed quite well in captivity. Sgt. J. T. C. Hood of Company F, 26th North Carolina, had been hit in the thigh and foot on July 1. He had been picked up by the Federals on July 6 at the field hospital near Marsh Creek. Imprisoned at David's Island in New York harbor, Hood worked in the kitchen and received numerous gifts of food from local Copperheads. He received a new suit of clothes and was even allowed to attend church services. Hood was paroled with 500 other prisoners the next winter, went home on furlough, and returned to his regiment in February 1864.[41]

Pvt. Albert Stacey Caison of Company I, 26th North Carolina, had a much more grueling time in prison. He was hit in the hand and hip only thirty yards from the stone fence on July 3, his retreat was cut off, and he was forced to surrender. Caison was transported to Fort McHenry in Baltimore and received his first ration, three hardtack, on July 6. The first treatment of his wounds took place two days later. Caison was soon transferred to Fort Delaware, which was a filthy place. The barracks were alive with vermin, and the water was unfit even for bathing. Conditions were better at Point Lookout, where seventeen men shared one tent, and at least Caison could bathe. The Yankees at Lookout treated their prisoners harshly. They were black soldiers and had no love for the Rebels. Women visitors often called out to the guards, "How are Jeff Davis's cattle getting on?" The prisoners's clothes wore out, and there were no replacements. Caison was barefoot and shirtless for months, and there were only two blankets for every three men. He later wrote, "If I were to tell half of the suffering and in-dignities to which we were subjected they would fill a good-sized volume." Cai-son stayed at Point Lookout for seventeen months and weighed only ninety pounds when he was paroled in March 1865.[42]

Collett Leventhorpe was the highest-ranking member of the brigade in Fed-eral hands. His left arm had only one broken bone, but it discharged fragments for nearly three months. Gangrene developed in part of the flesh, and a Federal surgeon advised amputation; but Leventhorpe absolutely refused. The surgeon then cauterized it with nitric acid. Leventhorpe even refused anesthetic, later telling a friend "that he would have died, rather than let an enemy see that a Con-federate Officer could not endure anything without a complaint." The colonel was held at Fort McHenry near Baltimore and later at Point Lookout. Friends living in England sent money to help him buy necessities while he was in prison. Leventhorpe was exchanged by April 1864 and returned to duty, but he would never again serve with the brigade.[43]

The fate of the rank and file who were wounded depended on their stamina and the willingness of Federal authorities to release them. Pvt. Daniel McCaskill of Company H, 26th North Carolina, was hit in the right hip on July 3 and fell into Union hands. The bullet passed cleanly through his leg, and for days after-ward the hole ran freely with fluid, bits of bone, and a great deal of pus. McCas-kill seemed to improve by mid-August, according to his Federal surgeon, but he died of his wound on November 17. Pvt. P. S. Bobbitt of Company G, 47th North Carolina, was badly wounded on July 3. A bullet sliced through his bladder and exited through his back. Urine drained through the back hole, "an exhausting diarrhea" afflicted him, and Bobbitt could keep nothing in his stomach. When the Federal surgeon tried to attach a catheter, he found a blockage in the urethra but managed to poke the device through it. The catheter immediately filled with pus. Bobbitt continued to weaken and died on August 20. Another man suffered an apparently simple wound that developed serious complications. Pvt. Cyrus A. McLure of Company E, 11th North Carolina, had his left forefinger fractured by a bullet at Falling Waters, where he was taken prisoner. The finger was easily amputated in the field, but McLure later developed an abscess on his palm. The surgeon was able to relieve this infection, but McLure's general health deterio-rated. His stomach grew irritable, his pulse quickened, and he became very fee-ble. McLure recovered enough to be paroled in late September.[44]

The wounded men who made it safely to Virginia with the ambulance train suffered much less mental anguish than did the wounded prisoners, but they still had to endure a great deal of physical suffering. Thomas Perrett was badly injured on July 1, but he survived the harrowing trip south. He was deposited in a church at Winchester where he lay without pillow or blankets for three days. The wounded were fed "some badly cooked corn bread and poor quality of tea, without cream or sugar." Perrett was then transported to Winder Hospital in Richmond. He remained there for a month until he received a furlough to visit his North Carolina home. Perrett returned to duty later that year and was again wounded at the Wilderness. He was back in the ranks by November 1864 but decided that the Confederacy was a dead letter. He deserted on February 22, 1865.[45]

The Federals also captured the two Quaker conscripts of the 52nd Carolina. Thomas and Jacob Hinshaw left the regiment on July 2 and found refuge at a Quaker farm near Gettysburg. There they worked in the fields until July 10, when Union cavalrymen took them into custody. The pair was taken to Harrisburg, Philadelphia, and then to Fort Delaware by July 15. Their Northern Quaker neighbors worked hard to secure their release. Thomas Evans, Samuel Hilless, and James B. Greaves went to Washington to implore Lincoln and Secretary of War Edwin Stanton, and they were more successful than anyone could have imagined. A telegram from the capital reached Fort Delaware on July 25, and the Hinshaws were sent on their way. They reached Hilless's house in Wilmington, Delaware, even before Hilless returned from Washington. The brothers left Wilmington two days later to gather with more Friends in Philadelphia. Here the Northern Quakers provided the two with needed articles and housed them at least until early August. The rest of their story remains a blank, for Thomas wrote his memoir while staying in Philadelphia. The two were listed as having been captured rather than deserting. Presumably they managed to return to their families in North Carolina. Lieutenant Wells, their chief enemy in the regiment who had softened his attitude at Gettysburg, was later captured at the Wilderness and spent the rest of the war in prison.[46]

While the Tar Heels recovered from the campaign, a bitter controversy brewed over their role in Pickett's Charge. Newspapers in Richmond began publishing reports that Pettigrew's division had not properly supported the Virginians, that it had retreated too soon and doomed the assault. Because many observers confused Pettigrew's brigade with Heth's division, they assumed that all of Heth's men were Tar Heels. Many Southerners desperately sought a scapegoat to explain away the bloody failure of July 3 and divert responsibility from Lee. Unfortunately the men of Pettigrew's brigade were the chief object of this unfair second-guessing by armchair generals.[47]

Brigade members tried their best to set the record straight. John Thomas Jones wrote to his father that Pettigrew's division was not ordered to support Pickett but was "in the same line. That we never came up is all a lie. Tell a man in this army that North Carolinians failed to go where Virginians went and he would think you a fool." Jones wrote a long letter to Henry King Burgwyn Sr. about the brigade's role in the attack. The elder Burgwyn published Jones's letter in the *Richmond Daily Enquirer* without asking the major's permission. Jones was surprised to read his missive in the same paper that had initially spread the erroneous reports.[48]

North Carolina newspapers took the lead in defending the brigade. The *Raleigh Daily Progress* noted "with much more pain than astonishment" the developing controversy. "The brigade is in command of its Junior Major. Each of its regiments is a broken and disjointed skeleton, numbering scarcely enough men to retain a distinct organization. . . . Hundreds, nay thousands, of what but a few weeks since was the largest and perhaps the finest command in the service, sleep their last sleep upon the battle field, or lie suffering and mutilated in the hospitals of the enemy. And yet it is of these brave men and of this noble brigade that base hirelings dare speak in terms of contempt and scorn."[49]

Historians quickly began to mimic the line of the Virginia clique as well. Samuel Pollard's *The Second Year of the War*, published late in 1863, drew heavily on Richmond newspaper accounts. The inaccuracies incensed the men of Pettigrew's brigade so much that they held a meeting of representatives from all the regiments. The delegates voted to take the offensive. They asked Louis G. Young, who was on leave in South Carolina, to write an account of the brigade's role in the assault, which later was published in the *Enquirer*, in several North Carolina newspapers, and in pamphlet form. Young's account was a substitute for an official report by Pettigrew. It accurately portrayed the unit's contribution and became the foundation of two articles Young would later write about the brigade's part in the battle. But the damage had already been done. The charges against the North Carolinians would never go away but continued to return like a throbbing toothache to torment the survivors of Pettigrew's brigade well into the twentieth century.[50]

Lee paid no attention to this matter, for he could not afford to waste any time while putting the army back together. On the day that Pettigrew died, he requested the transfer of the 44th North Carolina back to the brigade. Martin held the command only temporarily, and Lee wanted Col. Thomas C. Singletary of the 44th to take charge of it. "I have no other officer whom I can put in command of the brigade," Lee wrote. The 44th left Hanover Junction on July 25 and reached the brigade three days later, when Singletary took command.[51]

The 44th North Carolina had been temporarily attached to Brig. Gen. John R. Cooke's North Carolina brigade and had been quietly doing guard duty since the spirited battle at the South Anna Bridge on June 26. All eighty-five enlisted men who had been captured at the South Anna Bridge were paroled on June 29 at Fortress Monroe. Five of the six officers taken were held until the end of the war.[52]

The officers became embroiled in a controversy that threatened their lives. Federal authorities assembled twenty-four Rebel officers as hostages when the state of Georgia threatened to hang Col. Abel D. Streight's Union officers for attempting to incite a slave insurrection following their capture at the end of a daring raid behind Confederate lines. The six officers of the 44th and eighteen other prisoners taken at Gettysburg, including Lt. Levi C. Gentry of Company A, 26th North Carolina, were sent to Fort Norfolk, where accommodations were dreadful. The prisoners were housed in a tiny room with stifling air and poor food, but soon the men were transferred to Fort Delaware and then to Johnson's Island in Lake Erie.

Streight's men were not hanged, and the threat of death was removed from the Rebel officers as well; but they went from stifling heat in Virginia to subzero temperatures in Ohio as summer gave way to fall and then winter. Capt. Robert Bingham countered the boredom by reading Charles Dickens and making jewelry out of gutta-percha. He was among a group sent to Point Lookout, Maryland, for exchange in February 1864. But then the Federals stopped the exchange system in order to prevent the Rebel army from gaining more able-bodied soldiers. Bingham managed to sneak through the pipeline when a Southern woman, the sister-in-law of the doctor at Point Lookout, took a fancy to his jewelry. She talked the doctor into letting him go on one of the last boatloads of wounded prisoners sent to Richmond.[53]

The transfer of the 44th once again made the brigade complete. Singletary prepared to inspect his new command on July 29, but the review was canceled. Instead, soap was issued to counteract the lice that infected the brigade camp. Julius Linebach recalled that there "was no such thing as keeping clear of them. Officers and men were equally afflicted. One of our captains was compelled to sacrifice his beard, which was long and heavy, on account of the pests." The men received mail from home for the first time since the beginning of the raid into Pennsylvania. The Tar Heels set out on August 3 for Orange Court House, twenty-five miles to the south. They crossed the Rapidan River on August 4 and pitched camp at Orange the next day. This would be the area of their operations for the next eight months.

The band members began to tire of the demands made on them that summer. There was a constant round of calls from officers whom they could not afford to offend. They serenaded Hill and Heth, Heth's wife and staff members, and any civilians either general wanted to impress. On the night of August 12 the overworked Moravians took a long and bumpy ride into the countryside, serenaded a group of ladies for two hours, were offered only cake and ice cream by the audience, and finally made it back to camp at nearly dawn, "tired, hungry & sleepy, feeling that if our officers had had a good time, we had fully paid for our enjoyment and theirs as well."

It seemed to the band members that they were being taken for granted. The original officers of the 26th who had nurtured the band were all gone, while the current officers began to renege on the special arrangement the band had made with Vance. The musicians still were not regularly enrolled soldiers, and their pay, which was supposed to come from the private funds of the officers, was in arrears. As Linebach put it, "The reg. was considerably in our debt."

The Moravians tried to find a way out of the 26th North Carolina, but Heth absolutely refused to approve a transfer. He even suggested they might be eligible for conscription. The division leader advised them to enlist in the 26th so they could be formally assigned to it as a band. Regimental commander Jones reported that their names had already been submitted to Col. Peter Mallett, the conscription officer in North Carolina, but no action had yet been taken. This coercion "greatly surprised" and deeply hurt the bandsmen. They seethed with resentment but decided that to revolt openly would make the situation worse.

The band members contacted Mallett to suggest a transfer to the conscript camp at Raleigh, and they asked Vance for help as well. They were hampered by the fact that it was unclear exactly who among the regimental officers was their chief enemy. Jones seemed friendly enough, but the musicians did not know if they could trust him. The exchange of letters between the band, the governor, and the conscript officer proceeded slowly, for no one seemed to have the authority to approve the transfer except those who wanted to keep the band with the brigade.[54]

About this time the atmosphere in camp was electrified by a thunderbolt from home. William Holden, the editor of the *Raleigh North Carolina Standard* and organizer of the Conservative Party, printed a bombshell when he argued in his paper that the war was a mistake. He reported that in several counties meetings had been held in which civilians who were tired of the conflict called for an end to conscription and a negotiated settlement of the war. In the wake of the traumatic defeat at Gettysburg, such conciliatory talk aroused the Tar Heels in Lee's army. Many of them obviously agreed with Holden, as desertion began to increase in Pettigrew's brigade by late July. But the majority of the men who survived the battle continued to keep faith in the cause.[55]

"The large majority of the soldiers from N.C. now in this army, condemn & repudiate the sentiments of the Standard & the peace metings & the craven hearted peace men at home," roared Benjamin Wesley Justice of the 47th North Carolina. They "do not desire peace at the price of chains & slavery. We feel justly ashamed of our native state." Despite the losses at Gettysburg, Justice concluded, "we prefer death on the field, the glorious death of a patriot soldier." John Thomas Jones assured his father that the desertions were only taking place in North Carolina regiments. "The Standard has certainly had a bad effect on some of our troops," he admitted, but it was temporary. "If we ever are subdued it will be the fault of the people at home and not the armies."[56]

A convention was held at Orange Court House on August 12, 1863, consisting of two delegates from each North Carolina regiment in Lee's army. Surgeon Gaither of the 26th served on the committee that ran the meeting. It assigned the task of drafting resolutions to another committee, which included Capt. Richard W. Singletary of the 44th. These men worked hard and presented their drafts to the convention by midafternoon. Capt. James D. McIver of Company H, 26th North Carolina, had been opposed to holding the convention at all, fearing it would honor Holden by bringing him "too much into notice." But he served as a delegate anyway and listened to "several violent speeches" denouncing the Tar Heel editor. Eight resolutions were adopted. The delegates deplored the peace meetings and rejected all calls for a negotiated settlement. They bitterly denounced Holden and called on the government to suppress his newspaper, expressing complete faith in Vance's administration. Many North Carolina regiments, including the 11th, held separate conventions and issued their own resolutions, most of which duplicated the views of the general convention.[57]

The concentrated effort on regimental and company levels to repair the damage done at Gettysburg continued despite the Holden controversy. Capt. Lemuel J. Hoyle of Company I, 11th North Carolina, had been "trying to reorganize and get things into 'ship shape' again, but the work does not progress very rapidly." He had only one noncommissioned officer to help him manage a company of thirty-four men. All of his company books were lost during the retreat from Pennsylvania. Other members of the brigade found that the work of recuperating from Gettysburg went much faster with new recruits filtering in and the slightly wounded returning to duty. A member of the 26th North Carolina assured the folks at home that "soon we will have a respectable regiment again." Benjamin Wesley Justice believed that the desertions "purged the army of much worthless & hurtful material."[58]

Major Jones was disappointed that he was not allowed to command the brigade, even though he handled it well at Falling Waters. Because there was no immediate move to promote him, he also had little hope of permanently commanding the 26th. Lane would need several months to recover from his Gettysburg wound, and as long as there was a likelihood that he would return, Jones would lead the regiment only temporarily. "Had Gen. Pettigrew lived I think I would have been Col of the 26th without a doubt," Jones wrote home. "He as good as told me so several times after the battle. He seemed to take a great fancy to me after the fight at Gettysburg."[59]

The lull at Orange Court House gave the Tar Heels an opportunity to attend to personal business. William C. Allen of Company K, 26th North Carolina, applied for a leave of absence to visit his family in Anson County. He had been slightly wounded at Gettysburg, and his wife had recently lost her parents. She was "the only white person on the farm to controll a large family of negroes." Allen wanted to see to her welfare before he began another campaign. His request was granted.[60]

James D. McIver had a complicated problem. He read in the *Raleigh News and Observer* that his name had been mentioned as a candidate for the state legislature. The twenty-nine-year-old graduate of Davidson College was "completely *blocked* up, as to what I had better do." He did not know if his popularity was general or if a few friends had placed his name in nomination as a compliment. McIver decided to inform the newspaper that he accepted the candidacy as a matter of duty and he hoped that no one would vote for him on the assumption that he favored an end to the war. McIver was deeply concerned that the electorate know he was not an original supporter of secession but allied himself with that faction only when Lincoln called for troops to suppress the rebellion. His commitment to Southern independence was strong, and he felt the *Standard's* course was deplorable. "If those at home, who favor reunion, knew half as much about the yankees as I do, they would blush to think of such a thing." The candidate did not even know when the election was to be held, but he felt sure he could remain in the army and get a furlough when the legislature was in session.[61]

Within two weeks of accepting his nomination, McIver received disturbing news that made him withdraw his candidacy. He learned that his cousin John McIver had spearheaded the nomination, but the mood of Moore County was decidedly rebellious. No one associated with the army or the secession movement was likely to receive a vote due to widespread disgust with conscription and the war effort in general. McIver decided to pull out of the race. He managed to break into politics several months later when he won election as county court solicitor of Moore County and resigned his commission in June 1864.[62]

While various members of the brigade tended to their personal business, desertion increased. The problem was more severe in some companies than in others. Capt. Henry Clay Albright was greatly distressed by the loose talk in his company. "I can now put little or no confidence in any of the so called 'Chatham Boys,' they all speak favorably of desertion (with few exceptions) and assure they will endeavour to get home after they draw their pay." Lemuel J. Hoyle also found his spirits sagging under the weight of military defeat and desertion. "This seems to be the dark day of our young nation," he wrote his mother, "but I try to keep in as good spirits as possible."[63]

The brigade witnessed a rise in its desertion rate as a result of the Pennsylvania raid. The heightened statistics bracketed the battle of Gettysburg. Sixty-seven men left Pettigrew's command in June because they chose not to participate in the campaign. Twenty-one left in July in the immediate wake of the battle. Then the desertion rate shot up to sixty-three in August, when the men had lots of time to ponder the significance of their defeat. The desertion rate peaked that month and then suddenly plunged in September. It had been at a modest rate, 2.5 percent in June and 4.2 percent in July, but reached 12.6 percent in August before returning to normal levels.

Gettysburg provided several men with an opportunity to violate their oath to serve the Confederacy. Two soldiers of Company I, 26th North Carolina, were listed as having "acted badly" in the battle. Both were taken prisoner; one of them died in captivity, but the other was exchanged and reduced in rank from sergeant to private. Four other men were listed as having deserted during the campaign. Several men in the 26th North Carolina used their Gettysburg wounds as an excuse to go home without permission. Fourteen members of the regiment either deserted from Confederate hospitals while recuperating from their injuries or simply failed to report back to the regiment when they were well enough to travel. A small percentage of them eventually returned to duty. In contrast, only one other man in the brigade, a member of the Bethel Regiment, committed this military violation.[64]

Some of the men who deserted their regiments in the summer of 1863 did so with the intention of taking care of their families and then returning. The historian of the 26th North Carolina insisted there were "numerous cases" of this phenomenon. One such man was Goodwyn Harris, who had been drafted at age forty in January 1863. He had a wife and eight children and deserted sometime before Gettysburg because his "better informed Judgment was over Ruled by my sympathy for my family an there well fare." The authorities adopted a lenient policy toward men such as Harris; he not only was allowed to return to his company but was never officially listed as a deserter. Harris served faithfully until wounded at Bristoe Station and then was assigned to light duty at Weldon for the remainder of the war.[65]

Another temporary deserter, Cpl. Seth P. Dula of the 26th, fought well at Gettysburg but deserted soon after his return to Virginia. He returned to the regiment after nearly three weeks at home. " 'What in the world did you mean by doing this?' " Major Jones asked him. " 'You have put me in a devil of a fix.' " Dula explained that he ran away because " 'he heard his wife had had a little one, and he could not resist going home to see it.' " Jones relented and allowed him to return to duty with no punishment. Dula's family had seen him for the last time. He was killed at Bristoe Station less than three months after his French leave.[66]

Deserters were usually treated with leniency in all Tar Heel regiments, partly because the authorities recognized that punishment did not seem to deter others and partly because it was difficult and time-consuming to assemble courts-martial. Moreover, the definition of desertion was flexible enough to allow company and regimental officers a lot of latitude. They often delayed for months before listing a man as a deserter, giving him ample time to prove that his absence was only temporary. They also seemed to have dealt with returning deserters unofficially rather than going through the trouble of filling out paperwork and taking officers from their pressing duties to hear cases.[67]

Brigade officers, however, worked hard to retrieve the real deserters. There were standing offers of reward for anyone who located them and brought them back alive. Three deserters from the 52nd North Carolina were returned by a man named Lindsay Morris on August 9. He received thirty dollars for each man. All three were allowed to return to duty. Pvt. Enoch Manus had deserted in June 1862 and died of disease in September 1864. Pvt. Micajah Robbins had deserted only two weeks after being drafted. He was captured at Bristoe Station and spent nearly the rest of the war in prison. Pvt. John B. Harper deserted three times and was arrested and returned each time. He was captured on October 27, 1864, at the battle of Burgess's Mill and died in prison only three days after Lee surrendered.[68]

While the officers worked to refill the ranks, quartermasters tried to find enough clothing "to supply deficiencies" in their men's outfits. Nearly every company of the 11th and 44th ordered a wide range of goods, from shoes, jackets, pants, underwear, shirts, and socks to caps, fly tents, axes, and spades. They received enough to outfit about twenty-five men. Quarterly returns of property already in the hands of the men indicated that the other regiments in the brigade had no clothing to spare. There were two pairs of underwear and two shirts for each soldier in Company F, 52nd North Carolina, but only half as many knapsacks and canteens as needed. Company commanders managed to fill most of the glaring holes in the supply picture by October.[69]

Gettysburg was the biggest event in the history of the brigade. The battle rudely inducted the men into the demanding mode of warfare practiced by Lee and made their reputation as a hard-fighting and long-suffering unit. The 26th North Carolina, in particular, emerged from Gettysburg with an almost legendary status among Confederate regiments because of its heavy losses. The brigade was initiated into the brotherhood of battle shared by all the units that served in the Army of Northern Virginia and would become one of Lee's workhorse units as a long familiarity with battle lay in its future.

Chapter 9

Bristoe Station, Mine Run, and the Winter of '64

The need for a permanent commander to replace Pettigrew became more apparent as the brigade rebuilt itself. Singletary had never seen combat, and his 44th North Carolina had not yet been tested in battle. Jones had performed very well in Pennsylvania and was a good administrator, but he was only a major and could not be advanced over the heads of the more senior officers in the brigade without a lot of complications. The best choice would be an outsider who had all the qualifications already in hand.[1]

Such a man was Col. William Wheedbee Kirkland. He was assigned to the brigade on September 7, 1863, and assumed command four days later. Kirkland was born near Hillsborough, North Carolina, the grandson of a Scots immigrant. He studied for a time at West Point but did not graduate. Kirkland served as a lieutenant in the marine corps for five years and resigned in August 1860. He was elected colonel of the 21st North Carolina, participated in the operations that led to the battle of First Manassas, and took a heavy part in Jackson's Valley campaign. He received his first wound when he was shot through both thighs at the first battle of Winchester on May 25, 1862. This kept him out of action for a year, during which he temporarily served on the staff of Maj. Gen. Patrick Cleburne in the western Army of Tennessee. This unusual "vacation" was arranged because Kirkland had married a niece of Lt. Gen. William J. Hardee in 1859. He returned to duty with the regiment and participated in the fighting on July 2 at Gettysburg, winning promotion to brigadier general for his long and reliable service.[2]

Kirkland made few changes in the brigade staff, retaining Louis G. Young as the moving force in it. He brought Capt. Fred Nash from the 27th North Carolina as ordnance officer. The men were pleased with their new leader, called him "highly acceptable," and believed he would "prove a good humane General." Sgt. Maj. Alexander S. Webb of the 44th North Carolina thought him "quite a nice, young looking man." No one expected Kirkland to replace Pettigrew in their hearts. "He comes to us with a good reputation," noted William Blount, "and I think he will make a good officer. We will like him but not as much as we did the lamented Pettigrew."[3]

On the day that Kirkland took command of the brigade, the Moravians marched to his headquarters and found a musical party already in progress. Since a string ensemble was performing inside the house, the Tar Heels stayed outside and played between dances until the early morning hours, when the party finally broke up.[4]

Kirkland came close to leading his new command into battle for the first time on September 15. A Federal cavalry raid at Rapidan Station, the point where the Orange and Alexandria Railroad crossed the river, brought an order to move the brigade quickly to the threatened bridge. The men marched six miles and came up just in time to see the clash of mounted troops from a distance. They occupied fortifications on the south side of the river covering the railroad bridge while Kirkland put his headquarters in the house of station master John William Peyton. The fighting was limited to the troopers and ended as quickly as it developed. Kirkland's men bivouacked at the station that night and returned to their camp the next day. The raid on Rapidan Station convinced Lee that a larger force was needed to guard the bridge, so Kirkland moved his command from Orange Court House there on September 20. The men stayed until October 8, but they were never threatened.[5]

Kirkland loved the Moravians and the music they made. The band members serenaded the new brigade leader and his wife at every opportunity. He arranged to have an aria from Giuseppe Verdi's opera *Il Trovatore* transcribed for their instruments and used the Moravians as a brigade band on many occasions. The brigadier's interest could be overbearing at times. He wanted a musician "to blow calls on brigade drill," and Julius Linebach was selected for the job. Kirkland sent him a copy of the tactical manual, but Linebach did not have enough time to learn the calls. "There were so many, and I could not know what commands he would give, that I was much in the condition of the small boy, going to school without knowing anything of his lessons." The drill was an ordeal. Linebach was placed on a horse and rode beside Kirkland to the reviewing field. When the brigadier gave an order, it was repeated by regimental and company

Brig. Gen. William Wheedbee Kirkland. The second commander of the brigade, Kirkland was wounded at Bristoe Station and Cold Harbor. Because of his need to recuperate from those injuries, he led the brigade for less time than its other two commanders. (NCDAH)

officers, and then Linebach blew the call as a signal for the movement to begin. Sometimes he could recall the correct notes, but usually he made something up. "For two hours the farce was kept up," he remembered. Kirkland obviously noticed, for he never asked the band to do this again.[6]

Kirkland soon had an opportunity to lead his new brigade into action. Lee was compelled to send Longstreet's corps to Gen. Braxton Bragg's Army of Tennessee near Chattanooga, reducing Lee's strength to 45,000 men. Maj. Gen. George G. Meade decided to move his Army of the Potomac forward to prevent the further transfer of Rebel troops to the West. He advanced slowly and took position in a wide array of places as far south as the Rapidan River, but he made no serious attempt to press Lee. Then word arrived of the great battle at Chickamauga on September 19 and 20, where Bragg and Longstreet defeated the Federal Army of the Cumberland in northern Georgia and forced it to take refuge in Chattanooga. Two corps were taken from Meade and immediately transported to Tennessee, reducing his strength to 76,000 men. Lee decided to take advantage of this by striking. He hoped to outflank Meade's positions by marching to the west and cutting off at least a portion of his army.[7]

Hill's corps would attempt the flanking march by crossing the Rapidan on October 8 with as much secrecy as possible. Kirkland's men broke camp at Rapidan Station early in the morning and were well on their way to Orange Court House when dawn broke. Regimental commanders allowed barefoot men the option of staying in camp with no shame attached. Seventeen men among the eighty-seven members of Company G, 44th North Carolina, had no shoes, but none volunteered to remain behind. The brigade camped near Orange that night and continued the march on October 9, crossing the Rapidan and taking a number of small roads to hide its line of advance. Shielding themselves by moving between the Blue Ridge and the smaller ridges to the east, the men marched "through woods, fields & country roads, moving rapidly but taking long rests." A patriotic lady passed out discarded army shoes as the column marched past her farmhouse. On the morning of October 10 the brigade reached Madison Court House, where it rested for two hours as pioneers worked to rebuild several bridges. Then Kirkland's men were off again, passing Culpeper and crossing the Rappahannock. The brigade reached Warrenton on October 13.[8]

But Meade learned of Lee's movements and began to retire toward Centreville, just east of Manassas Junction. The Federal army forded Broad Run at Milford, one mile north of the Orange and Alexandria Railroad crossing of that stream and only a few miles west of Manassas, on October 14. The Second Corps, under Maj. Gen. Gouverneur K. Warren, brought up Meade's rear. His lead units marched along the railroad right-of-way and along a high ridge just east of the line.

Hill set out at 5:00 A.M. on Wednesday, October 14, with Heth's division in front. The van of his column reached a range of low hills on the west side of Broad Run and could see the tail end of a Federal column on the other side. "I determined that no time must be lost," reported Hill, and he formed Heth's men for battle. The Federals were getting away and Lee was not available for consultation, so the impetuous corps commander decided to attack.

Heth formed on both sides of Greenwich-Milford Road, one and a half miles north of Bristoe Station on the Orange and Alexandria Railroad. Kirkland's brigade with about 1,500 men was placed on the left with Brig. Gen. Henry H. Walker's brigade, formerly commanded by Brockenbrough, to its rear. The Tar Heels dropped their baggage and filed silently into the woods, careful not to make noise by breaking tree limbs. Brig. Gen. John R. Cooke's North Carolina brigade, recently added to the division, formed on the right. Cooke's was one of the largest brigades in the service with 2,500 men. Archer's and Davis's brigades were held in reserve. When Hill gave the word to advance, Heth told Walker to move his small command forward and place it on Kirkland's left, on the run. Everyone had to advance through the woods for about 300 yards. The small pine trees, about as thick as a walking cane, were closely packed. Walker had started the advance 100 yards behind Kirkland, and he found it impossible to move his men quickly enough through this growth to extend the division line to Kirkland's left. When Heth's men emerged from the woods, they saw the rapidly retreating Federals on the other side of Broad Run opposite Kirkland's left. Orders went out to all brigade commanders to push across the stream.

Before Heth could continue the advance, Cooke sent word that another Yankee force had appeared to his right, along the railroad. Bluecoated skirmishers were advancing toward the division. If this force was large, it would be the height of folly to continue advancing. Heth sent word of this new development to Hill, who told him to wait. This halt was a sobering experience for Sgt. William S. Long of the 44th North Carolina. "You do not know how dry one gets just at this point nor how hard it is to talk." He could only converse "in half whispers" with his comrades. "One thinks of his childhood, of the little things he did that were better he had not done," such as shooting blow darts at his neighbor's geese and pigs and pilfering milk and cream from the springhouse. Long resolved to make amends for these youthful transgressions if he survived.

While Long made peace with his past, Hill displayed no intention of calling off the pursuit. He ordered Anderson to deploy troops to cover Cooke's right flank and then sent word to Heth to continue the advance. The ten-minute halt was not long enough to give Walker's men time to form on Kirkland's left, so Heth moved out about 2:00 P.M. with only two brigades.

Hill's plans altered immediately. Anderson's men could not deploy quickly enough to screen Cooke, so the Tar Heel began to wheel his brigade to the right as a swarm of Union skirmishers assembled in the field to the south. Kirkland naturally conformed his movements to Cooke's and wheeled to the right. Neither Heth nor Hill wanted this to happen, but both commanders later understood the necessity for it. As a result the Confederates were attacking in a different direction and against a different enemy than anticipated. They would have to advance alone, for Walker had gone astray. The Virginia brigade continued advancing eastward across Broad Run while the two Tar Heel brigades wheeled to the south.

The Federal target was now Brig. Gen. Alexander S. Webb's division, the van of Warren's Second Corps. Webb's men had been marching along the ridge when they saw Confederate troops emerging from the woods more than a mile to the north. They hurried down the slope to take position behind the railroad embankment and sent out the 1st Minnesota as skirmishers. Webb deployed two brigades, Col. Francis E. Heath's, consisting of the 19th Maine, the 15th Massachusetts, the 1st Minnesota, and the 82nd New York, and Col. James F. Mallon's, which contained a mixture of Massachusetts, Michigan, and New York regiments. Heath and Mallon deployed behind the embankment just in time to meet the Rebels.

Webb had earlier told Heath to cross Broad Run, but only half of his brigade had crossed when Warren ordered the movement stopped, for Cooke and Kirkland were nearing the railroad embankment. Heath rushed his men back to the west side of the run, but he left Lt. T. Fred Brown's Battery B, 1st Rhode Island Light Artillery, on the east side. Brown's four Napoleons were therefore in a good position to enfilade Kirkland's left flank. Heath managed to place his men just in time to cover Kirkland's front, although his right-most regiment, the 82nd New York, was 150 yards short of the bridge. Webb's right was in the air, offering a tempting opportunity if Kirkland could exploit it. With the addition of a third brigade that managed to deploy before the Rebels hit, Webb had only 3,000 men to oppose Cooke's and Kirkland's 4,000 troops, but he had a decided advantage in artillery. Brown's cannons were supported by at least two other batteries partway up the ridge slope.[9]

The battle opened at 2:15 P.M. when the 1st Minnesota started firing at Cooke's brigade. A battery of Maj. David G. McIntosh's battalion was ordered to advance behind Cooke and Kirkland, but no one informed either brigade leader of this movement. Most of the ground was open and undulating with a few patches of old pine trees in the way. Cooke's men on the right had higher and more uneven ground to cover than Kirkland's on the left, as the land sloped eastward toward the run. The railroad embankment was five to ten feet high and served as an excellent breastwork for Webb's men, while the ridge slope provided superb artillery placements at least forty feet higher than the embankment. As Cooke and Kirkland advanced, the rest of Warren's corps stretched in line for a mile beyond Cooke's right. All the terrain advantages lay with the Federals. Heth called it an immensely formidable position that could not have been stronger without the labor of several hours of digging.[10]

Cooke and Kirkland were preceded by a line of skirmishers that halted on the last rise of ground fifty yards in front of the railroad. One shell burst took out fifteen men in the 47th North Carolina. The brigade stopped briefly partway to the railroad to re-form its line, then grimly continued the advance. Kirkland's men had done the same thing three and a half months before against Cemetery Ridge, and they had the grit to try it again.[11]

Kirkland faced Heath's brigade and Mallon's right flank, and his men quickly saw that their line overlapped Heath's right. About forty skirmishers from the 47th North Carolina refused to rejoin the battle line as it came up and instead crossed the front of the brigade to surge around the 82nd New York. They were followed by the 11th North Carolina, Kirkland's left-most regiment, and probably part of the 52nd North Carolina as well. The Tar Heels managed to climb the embankment and fire into the New Yorkers' flank and rear, but it was a temporary success. They received a withering series of canister rounds from Brown's

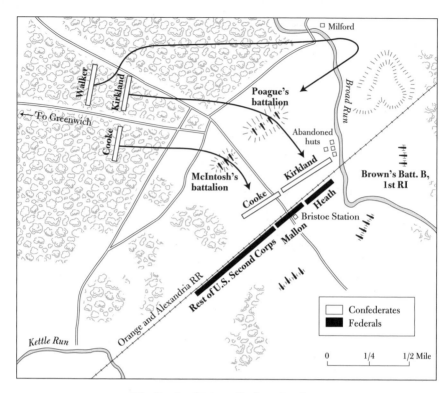

MAP 9.1 The Battle of Bristoe Station, October 14, 1863

battery, while the 82nd held firm, forcing the Rebels to retire. Heth noted, however, that some Tar Heels were "unwilling to expose themselves" and remained to be captured.[12]

At this critical stage of the assault both Cooke and Kirkland were severely wounded. Cooke's leg was crushed, and Kirkland suffered a fracture of the ulnar bone in his left arm. Their commands stalled only forty yards from the embankment and exchanged fire with the Yankees for several minutes. Some members of the 26th North Carolina went forward to the railroad and were driven back at the point of the bayonet. Meanwhile, Colonel Singletary of the 44th North Carolina took Kirkland's place, and Col. Edward D. Hall of the 46th North Carolina replaced Cooke. The two realized immediately that the attack was doomed. After "a painful suspense," orders were shouted to withdraw.[13]

Confusion had begun to set in by this point. Thomas Bailey of the 47th North Carolina noted that the different companies were losing their formations because the men were exhausted. They had already marched fourteen miles that day and had eaten no food. A din filled their ears; "nearly every man of strong voice was bawling out something of which I could distinguish the following: 'Cease Fire,' 'Lie down,' 'Don't shoot, you are shooting our own men,' 'Charge!' 'Fall Back!' and the like, so that it was impossible to recognize the voice of our commander unless very near him." Finally, near the Federal line, "it seemed to be pretty generally concluded that an order from someone in authority had been given to fall back and our Brigade retired suddenly."[14]

The field was now commanded by Union artillery, and the Tar Heels suffered many casualties while pulling back. Lieutenant Colonel Martin of the 11th North Carolina was hit twice, suffering a broken arm and a head injury. Capt. William Lowndes Grier of Company H took temporary command of the regiment. During the retreat a man in Company K saw the carcass of a large cat that had gotten caught in the hail of bullets and joked, "'Now boys you can see the horrors of War; here is an old spotted cat shot to pieces.'"[15]

The 44th North Carolina was seventy-five yards from the Federal position when its flag bearer was shot. Sergeant Long of Company G retrieved the colors but soon was met by Lieutenant Dupree, of Kirkland's staff, who put his hand on Long's shoulder to get his attention. Immediately after telling Long to retreat, he was nearly decapitated by an artillery round. Long quickly secured some of Dupree's personal belongings and ran back to plant the colors in a rotting log several hundred yards from the Federal line, yelling, "Rally on the flag 44th, rally on the flag." Only about 120 men did so, for Maj. Charles M. Stedman had already taken about 200 men back to the pine woods. Long sent a corporal to inform Stedman what he had done, and the major brought his contingent to join the rest in the open field. Long was nearly killed while rallying the men. He was struck by a shell fragment and a spent bullet, but neither drew blood. He later found seventeen bullet holes in his coat and pants.

The regiment paid a price for re-forming in the field, as Union artillery and skirmish fire took its toll. Long saw a shell explode as it hit a man who lay only ten feet away; "there was a flash, a burst of smoke, a roar, a shower of rags, flesh & dirt and next morning it looked as tho a chinese laundry had been burning joss paper and setting off fire crackers, for all the rags were red." Long witnessed another gruesome death when a sharpshooter's bullet struck a man in the abdomen. The unfortunate soldier grabbed his stomach, jumped up and down several times, then fell on his side and continued to jerk his legs until unconsciousness brought peace. One of the four men who carried him to the rear was hit in the head. Both casualties later died of their wounds.[16]

To the right, Cooke's brigade also retreated. The Federals followed up by sending out skirmishers, who quickly rounded up several hundred prisoners. Many of Kirkland's men were taken when they sought shelter in the huts of an abandoned Federal camp near the bridge. Five of McIntosh's guns were also captured because Singletary and Hall had overlooked them in their rushed retreat.[17]

Columbus A. Tuttle of Company F, 26th North Carolina, was one of the men taken in the Federal huts. He had been slightly wounded before the regiment reached the railroad and again while fighting on the embankment; the latter bullet fractured the bone of his left arm. Tuttle was taken to the Union side of the railroad, where he was exposed to Confederate artillery fire. A Union officer who took offense when Tuttle sought cover in a ditch tapped him with a riding crop and yelled, "You d — d Rebel get up and stand." Tuttle reluctantly stood up and endured the fire. Despite his wounds he escaped and returned to the regiment that night.[18]

The harried brigade leaders tried to re-form their commands, but Singletary was "shocked by the bursting of a shell" and lost control of his men. Regimental officers made their own decisions. The 44th North Carolina re-formed to support Hall, and two other regiments formed on Walker's left when the Virginia brigade recrossed Broad Run to support the battered Tar Heels, who had fallen back at least 600 yards before they re-formed. Now Archer's and Davis's men advanced Heth's division line as far as 400 yards short of the Federal position before they halted. The 47th North Carolina went forward as skirmishers and pushed the Yankee skirmishers back to the railroad in Kirkland's front. The fighting sputtered to an end by 4:00 P.M.[19]

"I have Come threw a nother Storm of iron hail Safe and unhurt," wrote Thomas W. Setser, "it was a purty hard little fite while it lasted." James A. Patton of the 47th North Carolina wrote, "I saw men shot down all around but thank be to God I came out safe."[20]

Confederate losses totaled 1,302 men. Kirkland's brigade lost 602, or 40 percent of its strength, while Cooke suffered a 27 percent loss with 700 casualties. Missing men made up a very large percentage of the casualties. Kirkland's command lost 277 prisoners, or nearly half of its total casualties. This had nothing to do with a breakdown of morale but was the result of the tactical situation. When the attack failed, they decided that exposing themselves while retreating over the open field was foolish and took a rational course of action to save themselves.[21]

Jones's 26th North Carolina lost 16 killed and 83 wounded. Company F reportedly lost 32 of its 34 men engaged, repeating the horror of Gettysburg. Not all of the injuries to soldiers in the 26th were caused by bullets or shells. Pvt. George Glenn of Company B sprained his left instep due to "Chargeinge over guleys & holes." The service records of the 26th indicate that a total of 84 men were captured. The 26th also lost its flag for the second time in the war. Pvt. Charles Gilbert of Company C was killed while carrying it toward the railroad embankment. The colors were later picked up by Cpl. M. C. Hanscom of the 19th Maine. Either the 47th or the 52nd North Carolina lost its flag as well, taken from the color-bearer's hands by Cpl. Thomas Cullen of the 82nd New York.[22]

Martin's 11th North Carolina lost relatively few men, only 4 killed and 11 wounded, despite its exposed position on the embankment. This was the first major battle for the 44th North Carolina; it lost 23 killed and 63 wounded. Pvt. Carney C. Williams of Company E was captured, but he refused to accept his imprisonment as a safe way to ride out the war. Williams escaped from the hospital of the Old Capitol Prison in Washington, D.C., in March 1864 and made his way south in time to rejoin his unit for the start of the spring campaign. The 47th North Carolina, under Capt. William C. Lankford of Company F, suffered lighter losses, with 5 killed and 37 wounded. Capt. Eric Erson's 52nd North Carolina lost 3 killed and 21 wounded. The prisoners recognized their captors. When taken to the rear, they noticed the white trefoil badges of the Second Corps and remembered who had repulsed them at Cemetery Ridge. "'There are those damned white clubs again,'" they muttered.[23]

The survivors of Bristoe Station spared no words in condemning the attack. Louis G. Young called it an "ill-judged" and "imprudently ordered" assault that took two good brigade commanders and hundreds of soldiers out of action. Charles Stedman of the 44th North Carolina termed it "a bloody and disastrous engagement." The most public condemnation by a member of Kirkland's brigade was published anonymously in the *Raleigh North Carolina Standard*. "I am fully convinced that some body, high in command, is greatly to be blamed, and if justice were done, would be cashiered." He summed up everyone's feelings by concluding, "I consider every man killed and wounded on the 14th instant, an unnecessary sacrifice, and that too, when Southern men are so precious."[24]

Heth was not the officer "high in command" whom the anonymous writer accused of incompetence. Yet the division leader refused to point the finger at anyone. Heth wrote in his report that no one could "attach blame to these two brigades for meeting with a repulse. My confidence in these troops is not shaken by the result, and I feel satisfied on fields to come they will vindicate the high reputation they have gained on many a hard-fought battle-field."[25]

A. P. Hill was responsible for the bloody mistake at Bristoe, and Lee fully realized it when he reached the field that evening. The army leader was angry and reproachful. He scolded Hill with harsh language even as the litter bearers searched for the wounded and Kirkland's men tried to sleep on the field. The cries of the wounded could be heard all night, leading William S. Long to venture out as far as he felt safe to retrieve several of them.[26]

Kirkland's brigade advanced just as dawn began to creep out on October 15; officers told the men not to stop or fire until the line reached the railroad. But when they drew near the deadly embankment, it became apparent that the Federals had fled in the night to Manassas Junction. There was nothing to do but take care of the wounded and clean up the field. Sgt. William S. Long, who now led Company G, 44th North Carolina, suddenly realized that his side was sore; a bullet hole indicated a flesh wound. When he reported to the surgeon, he was asked when he had received the wound; he replied that it had occurred yesterday. The surgeon responded, " 'I've got a whole lot of fellows here to look after that found out they were hurt last night, so you will have to wait." The surgeon finally examined him at noon but could not find the ball. Long carried it under his skin for many years to come.[27]

The dead were lying like lumps of clay on the sodden ground, for it had rained in the night. Thomas Setser took care of his sergeant, John A. Tuttle, who had died of a bayonet wound while trying to cross the embankment. "I borried him the beste I could, and cut his name on a pice of plank and put it to his grave," Setser reported. Lee's frustration had not cooled overnight. He surveyed such scenes and stung Hill with his sharp tongue. The corps leader accepted full responsibility for the assault. " 'Yes it is your fault,' " Lee retorted. " 'You committed a great blunder yesterday. Your line of battle was too short, too thin, and your reserves were too far behind.' " When Hill asked for further instructions, Lee replied, " 'Bury these poor men.' " Hill offered a weak apology in his report. "I am convinced that I made the attack too hastily, and at the same time that a delay of half an hour, and there would have been no enemy to attack. In that event I believe I should equally have blamed myself for not attacking at once." Many of "these poor men" whose loss Lee mourned had been survivors of Gettysburg, where the army leader had ordered a murderous assault that cost many more men than Hill's blunder at Bristoe Station.[28]

Lee tarried on October 15 and then set his men to work destroying the Orange and Alexandria Railroad as they retired southward. Kirkland's brigade, still led by Singletary, left the battlefield at dusk on October 15 and bivouacked five miles away that night. The Tar Heels marched another ten miles on October 16 before deploying along the tracks to begin the work of destruction. Each regiment was assigned a 200-yard section, but the men worked sluggishly because it rained all day, with thunder and lightning. The Tar Heels marched three more miles that evening over very muddy roads in the dark, and they continued to wreck the railroad all the way to Rappahannock Station, which they reached on October 17.

Singletary sent his wounded across the rain-swollen river on boats, since the railroad bridge had been burned by the Federals earlier in the campaign. Julius Linebach roamed through some abandoned Federal camps nearby and found heaps of bottles, empty cans, and leftover food scraps. He was not squeamish about picking through this garbage and saving what was edible. The infantry fired their muskets into the air on October 18, for many were still loaded from the battle and needed to be cleaned. The men crossed a newly built pontoon bridge in a drenching rain on October 19, marched two miles, and then camped.[29]

The emotional impact of Bristoe Station was enormous. Thomas W. Setser was one of only two men left in Company F, 26th North Carolina. "It is a lonsom time . . . now," he wrote home. "When I look a round and See nun of our boys, and think what has becom of them, I cante helpe but cry, and it looks like our time will come next, but I hope not for I wante to see this war come to a close." The regiment received a number of draftees so that there were seven men in Company F by mid-November, but Setser noted that "tha come in Slow."[30]

John Lane visited the regiment in mid-November while he was still recuperating from his Gettysburg wound. He was appalled by what he discovered. "'I found the regiment so low in spirits and few in number that the day I reached camp, was, I believe, the saddest day to me of all the war." Lane plunged wholeheartedly into the effort to bring the regiment back to life. Even though his wound was not completely healed, he reported himself ready for duty and was promoted colonel of the 26th, replacing John Thomas Jones, who was made lieutenant colonel. Capt. James T. Adams of Company D became major after he recovered from his July 1 wound. Lane would be the soul of the regiment. "'I went to work with all the will I could possibly bring to bear to recruit, drill and equip my regiment and restore it to something like its former numbers and efficiency.'" When Kirkland, who was recovering from his Bristoe wound, told Lane that the 26th might have to be consolidated with another regiment, he redoubled his efforts. Only by replenishing its numbers could he avert this merging and subsequent loss of unit identity. He was successful, thanks to the aid of company officers and the support of Jones and Adams.[31]

In the other regiments, harsher measures were used to bring the men back to a sense of their duty. A deserter from the 47th North Carolina was executed on November 1. The entire brigade marched "at slow time" to the site and formed on three sides around the twelve-man firing squad, the condemned, and his coffin. Julius Linebach was sickened by what happened. "The impact of the balls seemed to raise the man off his feet, and he fell backwards, and was dead almost instantly."[32]

The physical wants of the soldiers continued to present problems. There was never enough equipment, supplies, or food to satisfy everyone. Firewood was so scarce that eighteen men of the 44th North Carolina were put in the guardhouse for stealing fence rails. The weather was already turning cold, and there were too few axes in the regiment for everyone to cut their own wood. Alexander S. Webb reported that nearly half of the 44th were barefoot, and many of his comrades needed more clothes.[33]

The work of refitting was interrupted by a new Federal move. Meade once again advanced on the Confederates after a three-week delay following his victory at Bristoe. He rebuilt the Orange and Alexandria Railroad from Manassas to the Rappahannock and captured the crossing in a well-planned assault on November 7, forcing Lee's army to retire to the Rapidan. Kirkland's brigade crossed the river and camped near Orange Court House, providing pickets at various fords along the stream.[34]

Meade hesitated after his brilliant victory at Rappahannock Station, giving the armies a respite, and President Davis visited Lee's army to review both corps. Benjamin Wesley Justice saw the president and his army commander in person when he attended services at the Episcopal Church in Orange on November 22. Justice sat near enough to observe them closely. Davis had a "thin, bony face that reminds one so forcibly of a postage stamp as to excite a smile," he thought. Lee was "burly & 'beefy' and fat" with a "large and full and round" form. "His face is massive in its proportions, his nose slightly aquiline, his hair and beard are in the transition state from grey to snowy, his crown almost utterly bald, the back of his neck full and fat, indicating more of the animal in his nature than the lean, intellectual President. He holds a high head and is the very impersonation of dignity and manly power." Justice was close enough to Lee to observe that "a bunch of coarse, bristly, black hair grows seemingly out of the orifice of each ear." Lee's artillery chief, William Nelson Pendleton, gave the sermon, and Hill, Anderson, and other high-ranking officers filled the pews.[35]

When Meade resumed the offensive, he crossed the Rapidan downstream and moved westward on Orange Plank Road and Orange Turnpike, hoping to reach at least the west side of Mine Run before the Rebels could react. The plan could only work if the Federals moved quickly, but they were delayed for two days by heavy rain and took a full day to cross the river on November 26. Lee responded the next morning by sending Ewell eastward on Orange Turnpike and Hill on Orange Plank Road. A heavy frost made the ground slippery. "The men often fell with gun, knapsack, & equipments on the hard, glossy earth," reported Benjamin Wesley Justice. Both corps crossed Mine Run and met the enemy well short of his objective. Heth's division was once again in the lead of Hill's corps and deployed when it met Yankee skirmishers. Walker's Virginia brigade straddled the road, while Kirkland's brigade, still commanded by Singletary, moved out to his right and Davis deployed to his left.[36]

Fortunately Heth inspected his division just before he gave the order to advance. "I found, to my astonishment, [that] Kirkland's brigade [was] out of position, having gone half a mile or more too far to the right." He had to postpone the advance and try to bring the errant Tar Heels back to their assigned post, but night fell and put an end to the skirmishing before he could do this.[37]

The reason Kirkland's brigade was out of place was entirely due to Singletary. He had fortified himself against the cold by becoming drunk and was incompetent to command that day. Perhaps he also remembered how a shell explosion had stunned him at Bristoe Station and needed bolstering for that reason as well. At any rate, Heth placed him under arrest when he learned of his condition. The brigade re-formed with the rest of the division, having received some rounds of artillery fire that injured Capt. Ambrose B. Duvall of Company A, 26th North Carolina. The 47th North Carolina "lost a man or two" as well.[38]

To the rear, Benjamin Wesley Justice tended his commissary wagons and observed the preparations for battle. He saw many soldiers reading their old letters and "then tearing them into small bits & scattering them to the winds. I saw a bright tear glistening in more than one manly eye as they read, perhaps for the fiftieth time, those precious lines from absent dear ones." Justice saw blood dripping from the ambulances that brought the injured of Walker's brigade to the field hospitals. One man, wounded in the foot by a shell fragment, "moaned piteously" when the surgeon took off his shoe and stuck his fingers into the wound. Lee, Hill, and Heth rode by and stopped to inquire of the man's injury. Justice even saw Singletary being led away under armed guard and without his sword. The most memorable sight of the day was the place where a soldier had been mangled by a shell. While the man was lying flat on the ground, a shell fragment had crushed his skull and torn up his knapsack. "I reached the spot soon after & the scene was sickening. Brains were scattered in clots on the ground, on his gun, & on his torn knapsack. A large clot lay in the road near by. Shreds of his clothing hung on the bushes around."[39]

That evening Lee and Hill withdrew a mile and a half to the west side of Mine Run, where both corps dug in. They constructed the strongest field fortification that Lee's army had yet made in the war, with traverses to protect the angles and thick parapets dug from the gravelly soil. The bluff on the west side of Mine Run was moderately steep, parts of the stream were swampy, and the men cut down trees for nearly a thousand yards in front of the works. When Meade saw these formidable earthworks, he hesitated and tried to devise a plan to deal with this new development.[40]

The men of Kirkland's brigade contributed to the strength of this heavily fortified position. At first Heth's division was placed in reserve; then it was shifted to cover the right when Warren's Second Corps tried to flank that wing. Heth was able to reposition his men and dig works before the slow-moving Federals could outmaneuver Hill. Kirkland's brigade moved into position along Orange Plank Road after dusk; the 47th North Carolina was posted to the left of the road and drew Union artillery fire, which did little damage in the dark. Heth shifted a bit farther to the right at dawn on November 30, while another division extended the line to his right.[41]

Meade had planned a massive assault on the Rebel works that morning, but it never took place. Warren surveyed the Confederate position and was stunned by its strength. Showing a great deal of courage, Warren called off the attack at the last moment. Nothing happened that day except some skirmishing and artillery firing. Heth was very disappointed. "Had Warren attacked, his left and left center would have met my division. I was hoping he would attack; in order that I might square accounts with him for his treatment of me at Bristoe Station."[42]

All that day the soldiers idled away their time. Col. George H. Faribault returned from a leave to recuperate from his Gettysburg wound and resumed command of the 47th North Carolina, but he was immediately told to take charge of the brigade in the absence of Singletary, who was sobering up and still under arrest. Justice related an episode that was emblematic of the tactical stalemate. A flock of wild turkeys flew over the brigade, and the pickets of both sides took potshots at it. One turkey was hit and fell dead in the no-man's-land between the lines, a little closer to the Federals than to the Rebels. No Confederate ventured forth to retrieve it, but a lone Unionist braved the open ground and crawled toward the prize. He was shot and killed before he reached it. None of his comrades dared to follow. For the rest of that day everyone on both sides of the run could see the dead soldier and the turkey lying in full view as silent reminders that war meant cruel killing.[43]

Justice awoke on December 1 to find that the temperature had plunged below freezing. The water in his bucket was solid ice, and the beef had to be thawed beside the campfire before it could be cooked for breakfast. His beard turned white with frost when Justice went out to chop wood for the fire. The men filled the trenches constantly; a fourth of them were on duty at any given time and were relieved by another fourth so that everyone eventually stood their watch. They had orders to expect a night attack. The cold weather led officers to order barefooted men to the rear on December 1, but that plan backfired. Justice saw several men deliberately throw away their shoes to escape the front lines.[44]

Meade evacuated his position on the night of December 1, ending the Mine

Run campaign. The overall result was that Lee had averted a potential disaster and wound up with a tactical draw. He sent his army back to the old Rapidan line. Kirkland's brigade lost only six men wounded, four of whom belonged to the 26th North Carolina. "It was the most complete back down on the part of the yankees I ever saw," thought Gus Jarratt.[45]

The Tar Heels finally settled into winter quarters after Mine Run. They camped three and a half miles south of Orange Court House and near the railroad. Log huts were constructed with clay daubing, and tents were used as roofs. Some of the structures were ten feet by twelve feet in dimension, with wooden hinges for the doors and flour barrels as flues for the wooden chimneys. Bed ticking filled with dried leaves added to the comfort of the residents. Many men in the 26th North Carolina preferred to live in their tents, but the Moravian musicians added wooden shingles to the roof of their log hut.[46]

Food was a problem for the men. A half-pound of pickled beef, "or 'spiked Mule,'" was issued to each man on Christmas Eve. Bellfield King of the Bethel Regiment wrote home, "I recken if they dont give the Soldiers more to eat there is a heap of them will come home and I would not be much surprised if I want one of them I am not going to stay here and perish to death." Asst. Quartermaster John M. Tate of King's regiment declared, "I am hungry all the time, and feel now, like I could devour a whole *ham* and a *roast turkey*, with vegetables in proportion." Food was becoming so scarce in the area that the soldiers simply stole what they could find. A cow belonging to a freedman was taken by members of the 11th North Carolina. He complained to the brigade officers, who tried to search for it, but the cow had already been butchered. The thieves concocted an elaborate plot to shift blame to Davis's Mississippi brigade as they enjoyed their unauthorized ration.[47]

Pvt. Lambert Augustus Bristol of Company B, 11th North Carolina, was fed up. "Nothing to eat, nothing to drink and out of soap. I am very bare footed, I haven't had rest and shoes since I came back from Gettysburg. I have been doing duty all the time, but if they don't soon give me a pair, I will resist doing duty, for I am not going to stand guard bare footed any longer." Bristol tried to get a leave of absence when he heard that Lee was offering a thirty-day furlough to any soldier who brought in a recruit. He asked his brother to talk a man named John Shell into joining; he even offered to bribe Shell with twenty-five dollars, but the scheme fell through.[48]

Members of the brigade who managed a furlough had varied experiences. For some it was a harrowing visit. Columbus A. Tuttle of Company F, 26th North Carolina, was recuperating from his Bristoe wound in Caldwell County. He rode out one day to visit a lady friend and was waylaid by five horse thieves. Tuttle broke away from them but was chased for two miles before he evaded his pursuers. The next day he gathered four friends and tracked the thieves, took them by surprise, and scattered them in the woods. Tuttle caught all their horses and rewarded his comrades with a new mount apiece.[49]

Thomas Bailey of the 47th North Carolina had a much more pleasant time on furlough. He took his wife completely by surprise when he knocked on the door of their house in Davidson County. Elizabeth Ann, who had been his stepsister before their marriage, yelled out, "'Who's that?'" Thomas responded, "'Somebody you are looking for.'" She opened the door and exclaimed, "'Lord, is that you?'" Bailey enjoyed his stay and eventually survived the war.[50]

The work of refilling the ranks continued apace in the 26th North Carolina. Lane worked energetically to herd draftees into the regiment. The 26th would never regain the strength it had before Gettysburg, but it recovered nearly half that number during the winter. Progress was much slower in the Bethel Regiment. Lewis Warlick returned to the 11th after recuperating from his wound and capture at Gettysburg. He found the regiment "looking quite different to what it did when I left, new officers have taken the places of those who were killed and many strange faces are in ranks who have been enlisted since I left, upon the whole its not the regiment it once was but hope it will do better than it looks."[51]

Despite the material shortages, many members of Kirkland's brigade insisted that the morale of the soldiers remained high. "The result of this struggle is as certain as the rising of the morrow's Sun," wrote William H. Blount; "our independence is a fixed fact, our Separation from the yankee people is eternal." Gus Jarratt agreed with Blount about the hopeful mood of the soldiers, telling his mother that they "are all in fine spirits and have no idea of ever being whipped."[52]

The brigade was called out of its cozy quarters on February 3 to relieve Cooke's brigade on the picket line. The men marched to the Rapidan and took their places. The next day they came under sporadic skirmish fire. For forty days they held the line, alternately fishing and skating on the frozen river when off duty, until they were relieved by another brigade. They learned of a Federal advance toward Madison Court House, and all regiments, except the 52nd North Carolina, rushed toward that place on March 1. When they got within four miles of the town, the Tar Heels discovered that the Unionists had retreated. They bivouacked that night and then returned to their picket posts, "exhausted and dispirited, cold, muddy and hungry, as cross as a wet hen," in Thomas Bailey's words. The brigade returned to its winter quarters at Orange Court House on March 14.[53]

The band members of the 26th North Carolina received a furlough that winter and hurried to Salem. They spent several days serenading the citizens and skating on the frozen pond of the local paper mill. Then they met Governor Vance at a political rally in Wilkesboro on February 22. Fifteen hundred people gathered to hear Vance rail against defeatism, but neither the Moravians' music nor Vance's fiery rhetoric moved them. Julius Linebach thought most of the crowd disagreed with the governor. "The people of Wilkes County were rather illiterate,—of the mountaineer class, and did not take kindly to anything that interfered with their freedom of thought and action. They had no 'niggers' to fight for, and did not believe in being shot at for the sake of any body else's." The musicians gave a concert at the Blind Institute in Raleigh on March 3 and raised $480, with which they bought new clothes from the state quartermaster to replace their ragged uniforms before they returned to Orange.[54]

Kirkland returned for duty on February 20, while the men were still on picket duty along the Rapidan. He had been hospitalized at Gordonsville before he was shipped to Richmond for surgery, and then he went to Georgia for a long recovery. Singletary's fate now hung in the balance. He had been found guilty of dereliction of duty for his drunkenness at Mine Run and was to be cashiered out of the army, but Lee suspended the sentence until President Davis could be informed of the circumstances and make his wishes known. The case dragged on for some time. Heth wrote to the authorities on February 24 asking that Singletary be allowed to return to the 44th North Carolina as it was short of officers. They relented. His sentence was suspended, and the errant colonel resumed command of his regiment.[55]

With Kirkland back in place, a major effort was made to resupply the brigade with all manner of equipment and clothing. Large quantities of caps, shoes, pants, underwear, blankets, and shirts were ordered by special requisition and distributed to the needy men. The quartermaster of the 44th North Carolina also received a number of axes, picks, and the material to make shoes. A property return filed by Francis Bird for the 11th North Carolina indicated a total of 352 rifle muskets of .58 caliber and 19 muskets of .69 caliber in the regiment. The 11th had 171 bayonets, enough for only about half the men, although it possessed 243 bayonet scabbards. There were about enough cartridge boxes (306) and cap pouches (304) but not enough cartridge box belts (198). The men were well supplied with knapsacks and haversacks, but about 100 of them had no canteens. The ammunition on hand amounted to 18,765 rounds of .58-caliber cartridges and 685 rounds for the .69-caliber muskets.[56]

The concentrated effort to rebuild the brigade led to a harsh crackdown on desertion. The long stay in winter camp gave the authorities time to try and execute a number of men guilty of this crime. Two soldiers of the 52nd North Carolina were shot on February 1. The squad fired once but failed to kill them, and one man screamed horribly in pain. A second and then a third firing was necessary, the last at only five paces from the victims, before the bloody work was done. The affair shocked the men of the brigade. Corporal Wright called it "an awful sight to behold, a terror to all deserters or ought to be. I dont think I will ever bring such a disgrace on my family and relations."[57]

The ceremony was repeated on February 18 when a soldier of the Bethel Regiment and one from the 44th North Carolina were shot for desertion. Again the condemned did not die at the first round but had to be killed at close range by the officer in charge of the firing squad. As they grew in number, the executions became a severe trial for Chaplain Richard S. Webb of the 44th North Carolina. He had the "unpleasant" duty of ministering to four condemned men. Two of them went to the stake with good spirits, saying, "Farewell boys, meet me in a better world," to their assembled comrades. When he visited another batch of prisoners, five of whom were under a sentence of death, Webb thought it was "melting to ones heart to hear their earnest prayers."[58]

James Wright came closer than he expected to the process of killing when two men of the 26th North Carolina were scheduled for execution. He was detailed with four other soldiers to guard the condemned men, one of whom served in his own company. They were manacled in ball and chains. "O Fanny you don't know how bad I felt to see them in that condition and having to guard them the last night that they had to live I looked at them eat dry bread by itself and felt so bad I gave them some roasted potatoes and butter it done me good to see them eat it[;] one of them [George Washington Owens of his company] talked very calm and talked to me about his future state[.] he did not fear being shot. he appeared to give satisfaction to all that talked with him." The two were executed on March 24.[59]

These men were some of the nearly 200 Tar Heel soldiers who were shot for desertion during the war. Several hundred more were sentenced to death but received a reversal of that sentence. William Blount managed to add to the latter number. Robert C. West, a forty-four-year-old private, and Edwin Rose, a fifty-year-old substitute, had deserted and were in arrest. Blount wrote "a strong appeal" on their behalf and sent it up the chain of command. According to Blount, Lee himself authorized the lieutenant to make a decision in this case. Blount obviously relished this moment. "I went to the guard house and told them I had come with a full pardon. That I would give their lives to their families. They were perfectly delighted. Called me by every kind name that they could think of. They said that they never would forget me." West and Rose returned to duty and were captured at the battle of Burgess's Mill on October 27, 1864. West was exchanged a few months later and was captured a second time at the end of the Petersburg campaign. Both men survived the war.[60]

Near the end of this series of killings a fierce winter storm descended over the area, blanketing large regions of the South with a deep covering of snow. It started falling at Orange Court House late on the morning of March 22 and did not stop for twenty-four hours. The average depth was twelve inches, but in places the snow drifted to four feet. When the storm ended on the morning of Wednesday, March 23, the sun came out and shone brilliantly on the white landscape. The men began to play, tossing snowballs at the members of other commands. Inevitably one thing led to another, and the desire for an organized fight grew irresistible. Kirkland challenged Cooke's brigade to a "general engagement" to begin at 2:00 P.M. Word quickly spread, and ladies from the area gathered to watch. Col. William MacRae of the 15th North Carolina led Cooke's men, while Kirkland led his own brigade. Both men organized their commands as if they were preparing for battle. MacRae placed the 48th North Carolina on his right, then his own regiment, followed by the 27th and the 46th. Kirkland put the 44th and 26th on his right and distributed the rest of his regiments to form his left wing. The men of both commands made as many snowballs as they could and stuffed them into their haversacks. The two sides arrayed their battle lines 500 yards apart, separated by a ravine.

When everyone was ready, a signal was given and the snow began to fly. Kirkland immediately ordered an attack by his right wing across the ravine at double-quick. His men charged "with a yell, Such as we made upon the field of Gettysburg." Cooke's skirmishers were driven back as the 44th and 26th slammed into their opponents, crushing the 46th North Carolina. The regiment "acted shabbily," according to Samuel Hoey Walkup, and its commander and colors were captured; but MacRae responded with an attack by his right wing. The 48th and 15th closed with the remaining three regiments of Kirkland's brigade, and a fierce fight erupted. The "white balls flew as fast as men, hurried with excitement and a desire to win the day, could throw them," reported William H. Blount. At first this contest was purely in fun; but the "excitement of actual battle seized them," and they began to put rocks into their snowballs, which caused many injuries.

MacRae pushed his men forward and won the day. His 48th North Carolina "literally demolished the 52nd and drove them from the field," according to Walkup, who commanded the victorious regiment. He later flanked the 47th and 11th, forcing them back as well. What was left of Kirkland's brigade raised a flag of truce and gathered around MacRae, but they had no desire to surrender. They pulled MacRae off his horse and "roughly handled" the colonel, taking him prisoner under false pretenses. The fighting continued for a time as Kirkland escaped capture only by riding off the field. After two hours the men became exhausted, and the battle sputtered to an end. Many of them, including William Blount, were bruised and sore for days to come. Blount had been hit many times by snowballs and received "a bad lick in the eye," but he was not seriously injured. A few men suffered broken bones. Kirkland's brigade had captured MacRae, two colonels, several majors, two flags, and many prisoners, but most of the brigade was routed and lost one flag, that of the 52nd.

The hard-fought contest was one of the most memorable moments of the war for these men. Lemuel Hoyle feared it might be the source of "hard feeling" between the two commands, and the historian of the 26th North Carolina indicated that to be the case. The bitterness created between some members of both brigades "took time and comradeship, battles, privation and sufferings to destroy." But the snow battle also had a positive effect, sealing the bond between these two Tar Heel units that had its origin in their joint attack at Bristoe Station. Cooke's and Kirkland's brigades would be inseparable from this point on, often cooperating with each other on battlefields to come. In fact MacRae, who had so effectively crushed Kirkland's left wing, would assume command of Pettigrew's old brigade only four months later.[61]

Another major event of the winter was a revival of religious interest. This occurred not just in Kirkland's brigade but in the entire Army of Northern Virginia. The resurgence of faith began when the brigade built a log chapel near the center of Kirkland's camp. Lt. William P. Oldham of the 44th North Carolina was put in charge of fifty men detailed from the brigade to build this thirty-foot by forty-four-foot structure. The 26th North Carolina band played at its dedication on January 22. There were only two chaplains in the brigade by this time. William S. Lacy, a Presbyterian, served in the 47th North Carolina, and Richard S. Webb, a Methodist, served in the 44th North Carolina. Hoyle, who was already very religious, called both of them "excellent young men" who seemed to be zealous in their work. Both held regular meetings at the chapel, which were not well attended at first, but then more and more soldiers wandered by to listen and pray. Before long they were asking to be baptized. It made no difference which denomination they attended in civilian life; soldiers from all the Protestant faiths found a common spirit surrounding the chapel. Services were held there every day at noon and in the evenings.[62]

Chaplain Webb was excited by the revival. The twenty-eight-year-old cleric informed his mother, "I'm very much interested in my work" and "think I will be perfectly contented to remain here and labor with the soldiers." The revival peaked in April when the number of soldiers baptized exceeded 100. Webb could not consider a furlough, for the men "begged me not to leave them, saying that it would not be long before they would have to march & perhaps go into battle." So the preacher proposed marriage to Jennie, his regular correspondent, through the mail. He could offer her little money, only a fulfilling life serving God. It was Webb's first proposal, made to a woman who also was his cousin. Jennie must not have felt the call as strongly as Webb, for she turned him down.[63]

Many soldiers felt inspired by the religious spirit flowing through the camps. "I feel that a glorious day is about to dawn," exulted William H. Blount. "Our Soldiers are humbling themselves before God and asking Christ Jesus to come and reign over them. When all, both Soldiers & people look to God, He will give us peace and independence." When President Davis set aside a day of prayer and fasting, nearly the whole brigade flocked to the little chapel. Only about half the attendees could fit into the structure; the rest remained outside to pray. "Sinners were attentive," reported Lemuel Hoyle, "and a feeling of solemnity seemed to pervade all." One could excuse James W. Wright for concluding that "a great change is taking place in our Brigade. I feel like we will be victorious on the battlefield. I feel like the God of battles will help us out in our great difficulty and deliver us from our enemies."[64]

Men who were not moved by the spirit could rely on the entertainment provided by Governor Vance. He visited the camps in early spring to campaign for reelection in the upcoming gubernatorial contest. Samuel Hoey Walkup of Cooke's brigade knew him before the war but was not impressed with his speaking style. The content of one talk on March 28 was "tolerably good," he thought, but Vance delivered it in a way that had "too little seriousness and too much buffoonery." The governor spoke to Cooke's and Kirkland's brigades two days later. Before he began, Vance said to Walkup, "'Well Col. we used to be good old Whigs together. I want you to Amen for me when I say good things." Walkup found several good things in the speech, but he still thought Vance was hardly "dignified enough for the Governor of N.C. before Va. Genls. J. E. B. Stuart, Heth and others of our own State." Moravian musician Edward Peterson agreed with Walkup. He noted that Vance joked about the similarity in Jeb Stuart's name and his own nickname, Zeb. "It was somewhat silly I thought at the time."[65]

Vance's style was well received by most men, even if it embarrassed a few. When addressing Kirkland's brigade, he began by joking that Lee had so many men in northern Virginia, there were hardly any Confederates left south of Richmond. Then he addressed the crowd by yelling, "Halo tar heels," and asked them if they wanted to hear him. The governor received a loud cry to go ahead. Vance made a good impression on many. Henry Clay Albright of his old regiment professed to "love him as a father" and was willing to "pay the most profound attention to what he says[,] being perfectly willing to risk Z. B. Vance in anything pertaining to our young Republic." Francis Bird of the Bethel Regiment believed that most soldiers would vote for him, especially since his opponent was none other than the hated William Holden. Albright proclaimed himself willing to die in the streets of Raleigh to prevent Holden from taking office if he was elected, "for in doing so I would only be fighting *abolitionism* and *traitorism*."[66]

By April the executions had run their bloody course and the snow had disappeared. The revival was culminating that month with ever more conversions, and Vance had come and gone. The slow arrival of spring forced everyone to turn their attention to the coming campaign. Kirkland ordered his men to engage in target practice. They painted the outline of a man on a large plank and shot at it from a long distance to hone their firing discipline. The officers also addressed the fact that an inordinate number of soldiers were absent without leave. There was a fine and shifting line between a soldier who was absent without leave and a true deserter, for his company officers could not know his intentions or guess how long he intended to be on his unauthorized furlough. This gray area gave a lot of leeway to the officers, and they usually decided to be as lenient as possible on the men. Anyone who returned voluntarily was not punished. There are many notations in the service records that a soldier was absent without leave but no indication that any official action was taken against him. The officers desperately needed men in the ranks, and they also had families back home. Few of them were so hard-hearted as to punish a man for wanting to help his loved ones. All told, about a third of the men who were listed as deserters from North Carolina regiments in the war voluntarily returned to duty. The returning men combined with draftees to bring regimental strengths up to their most respectable level since July 1, 1863. The 26th North Carolina had 760 men by the opening of the spring campaign, and the 47th North Carolina was "pretty full again."[67]

The brigade moved its camp on April 27 because wood was becoming scarce and the water supply was too polluted in the old quarters. It moved only a couple of miles to a pine grove near Clark's Mountain, where Lee established his quarters.[68]

Orders soon arrived for the men to pack their surplus clothes, the first preparation for the coming campaign. Rumors flew through the camps that Lee would invade Pennsylvania again, which either excited or worried the soldiers, depending on their view of the previous summer's work. Corporal Wright thought "the boys are wiling to go this time or at least a portion of them is," but Lemuel Hoyle thoroughly disapproved. "It seems to me that the two disastrous campaigns, already made into the enemy's country, ought to be sufficient to teach our authorities the impolicy of invasion."[69]

The promotion of Ulysses S. Grant to command all Union armies was an ominous sign for the future. The North's most successful general would make his headquarters with the Army of the Potomac and try his hand against Lee. The Tar Heels were ready for him. "If Grant advances upon *us* . . . I will almost wager my heart that he gets such a thrashing as he has never before carried," wrote Henry Clay Albright. John Thomas Jones also felt the army was in good shape and could handle anything Grant brought against it. He hoped Lee would take the offensive, defeat Grant, and threaten Washington so as to force the Federals to evacuate all their troops from Virginia.[70]

Jones had an opportunity to advise Lee, if he so dared. He and Lane took the band to serenade the army leader on April 22 at his headquarters tent near the foot of Clark's Mountain. The performance was well received, and Lee told Lane, " 'I don't believe we can have an army without music.' " The Virginian spoke privately with Lane and Jones when the playing was over, expressing a desire to strike Grant early in the campaigning season and keep him as far north as possible. Jones found the army commander to be in "the highest of spirits"; he seemed to "think our prospects have never been so bright."[71]

Chapter 10

From the Wilderness to Cold Harbor

More than 118,000 Federal troops crossed the Rapidan River on May 4 to initiate the overland drive toward Richmond, and Lee's 62,000 men responded immediately. Grant penetrated the Wilderness, an area of second-growth timber west of the Chancellorsville battlefield and several miles east of Mine Run. He hoped to get through the tangled terrain, which was intersected by a network of roads, before Lee approached, but the Virginian struck early in an attempt to hold the Rapidan line.[1]

Kirkland's brigade left its winter camp at Orange Court House on the afternoon of May 4, 1864, with Heth's division in the van of Hill's corps as it marched eastward on Orange Plank Road. Kirkland camped at the old Confederate earthworks at Mine Run that night. The fighting began the next day, Thursday, May 5, and it would hardly stop until the end of the war nearly a year later. Kirkland's men were awakened by the beating of a long roll at dawn and set out, leading the division's advance. Federal pickets, troopers of the 5th New York Cavalry, appeared a mile ahead near Parker's Store, and Kirkland deployed Faribault's 47th North Carolina to push them back. The regiment went into battle line and sent out skirmishers at 9:00 A.M., driving the Yankees a mile or two before stalling. Faribault was forced to send out more companies as needed until the entire regiment was deployed on the skirmish line, so Kirkland sent Singletary's 44th North Carolina to reinforce the 47th.[2]

The 26th North Carolina, then the 11th, and finally the 52nd were sent to the ever thickening line of Rebel skirmishers. The Unionists made their toughest stand at the eastern edge of Widow Tapp's field, taking shelter in the tree line behind fences and logs, but Kirkland's men continued to push the outnumbered troopers another mile before they were relieved at noon by Cooke's brigade. Kirkland's Tar Heels disengaged and retired a short distance to rest. They had advanced five miles through some of the thickest vegetation imaginable and were exhausted.[3]

Cooke's men pushed on to the intersection of Orange Plank Road and Brock Road, where they were stopped by Brig. Gen. George W. Getty's division of the Sixth Corps. Getty delayed a counterattack to await the arrival of the Second Corps, now under its old commander, Maj. Gen. Winfield S. Hancock. A lull ensued on this part of the battlefield as Heth brought up the rest of his division. He ordered Cooke to re-form his line astride the road and placed Davis's brigade on his left with Walker's brigade to Cooke's right. Kirkland was ordered to remain in reserve behind Cooke. The terrain was generally level with a few swells or ravines to break up the monotony. The most serious impediment was the vegetation. Heth called it "a dense growth of small and large timber intermixed." One had trouble seeing more than a few yards in any direction.[4]

During the lull, Heth sent Maj. Eric Erson's 52nd North Carolina to the rear in response to an urgent call from the wagon train at Parker's Store that Federal cavalry were about to descend on it. The 52nd rushed back five miles only to find that the threat had evaporated. Erson rested his troops a bit and then started back at a more leisurely pace. As they neared Kirkland's brigade, they encountered a stream of walking wounded along Orange Plank Road, men who were "seeking the rear for shelter and relief," in the words of the regimental historian.[5]

Those responsible for the care of the wounded had a chance to observe the army's high command in action during this lull. Moravian band member Edward Peterson and other hospital attendants rested in the woods to the rear, close to a gathering of Lee, Hill, and artillery chief William N. Pendleton. Peterson observed their demeanor: "They seemed to be considerably excited & at one time, I believe, they were somewhat nonplussed." Lee interrogated captured Federal cavalrymen through Pendleton, the latter "stepping back a few paces to inform Lee of which answers he had got, & then step forward, & ask another." But Pendleton got more than he could handle when a Yankee trooper told him that 50,000 cavalrymen were arrayed along Orange Plank Road. "I thought he rather got the Gen." with that answer, wrote Peterson, as "he never asked any other questions" of that man.[6]

Getty was ready to advance astride Orange Plank Road by 4:15 P.M., and he hit Heth squarely. Hancock sent two divisions to support both of his flanks while retaining a third division south of the road. The Federals easily pushed Heth's skirmishers back but stopped and fell to the ground only fifty yards short of the

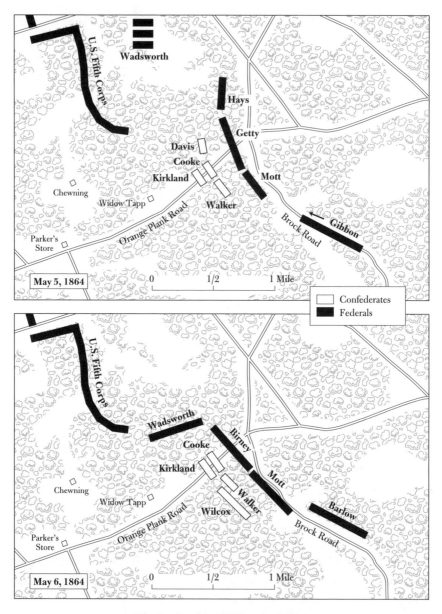

MAP 10.1 The Battle of the Wilderness, May 5–6, 1864

Rebel battle line as a torrent of fire met them. For two hours a static fight raged in the woods. It was almost entirely an infantry battle, for the Yankees deployed only one section of artillery in the road, the only open space to operate cannon. Heth's men occupied a slight rise of ground and thus had a small terrain advantage. When the Federals rose to attack, they were faced with a "rapid and constant fire of musketry," which cut them "down with such slaughter" that they had to retire to their starting point.[7]

Heth counted a total of seven failed assaults on different parts of his line, forcing Kirkland to send in help as needed. He did not fight the brigade as a unit but detached each of his four remaining regiments. The right of the 44th North Carolina rested on the road, and the 26th North Carolina was positioned to its right. The 47th North Carolina was placed on the far left, and the 11th North Carolina was on the far right.[8]

Lane's regiment received orders from Kirkland to move forward. The men ran at the double-quick down Orange Plank Road, as Lane was instructed by Cooke to support the 46th North Carolina. The Tar Heels "went into position in splendid order," according to Henry Clay Albright. They came under the most severe musketry Albright ever experienced. The men fell to the ground for cover and opened a hot fire in return. From time to time parts of the line seesawed back and forth as Federal units attempted to advance. On one such occasion the 26th was forced to fall back but did so "in as good order as possible" through the dense foliage. The regiment stopped after a few yards and poured fire into the advancing Federals. "I never have seen and heard such musketry in my life," remarked James W. Wright; "it looked like a man could not live." Lane was slightly wounded in the thigh, and Jones took command of the 26th.[9]

Shortly after Lane moved forward, Singletary's 44th North Carolina advanced along the north side of the road to support Cooke. The Tar Heels found that the roadbed was "swept by an incessant hurricane of fire, and to attempt to cross it meant almost certain death." A three-inch rifled gun belonging to Richard's battery of Poague's battalion was placed in the road, and the gunners and horses took many hits. Soon there were not enough of either to work the gun or pull it to safety. At this critical stage Lt. Robert Winship Stedman of Company A, 44th North Carolina, volunteered to lead a detachment of forty brave men from the regiment in an effort to drag the gun away. Stedman was helped by William O. Slade Jr., Heth's acting engineer officer, and Lt. Murray Forbes Taylor of Hill's staff. This small group ran into the hail of bullets and pulled the weapon off the road, but they paid a dear price for it. Only three of the forty-three men escaped injury; Stedman was badly wounded by a canister round fired directly down the road from the Yankee guns. Heth later recommended him for promotion, but it was not approved. Stedman returned to duty later that summer only to be wounded in August and then captured in October. He survived his captivity and the war.[10]

Faribault's 47th North Carolina was at first positioned on the brigade's left but then shifted to the right, south of the road. It received orders to move forward and "went in and mingled with Cooke's men in the fight." They endured the same hail of close-range musketry as did the 26th and the 44th. Lt. Julius Rowan Rogers of Company I recalled that the "black-jack saplings were skinned by the bullets like a young apple tree is in the spring of the year by the rabbits." Martin's 11th North Carolina also advanced to Cooke's support. In its enthusiasm the regiment actually charged over the men of MacRae's 15th North Carolina, who were lying on the ground. MacRae was astonished at their impetuosity and sneered at his fellow Tar Heels, " 'Go ahead; you'll soon come back.' " Perhaps he remembered the thrashing Kirkland's brigade had given him in the snowball battle only two months before. The ardor of the Bethel Regiment was cooled when the men realized the Federals were only a few yards away and showed no sign of retiring. As they retreated, they stepped back over the 15th North Carolina and lay down immediately behind MacRae's men. Later remembering MacRae's prediction about returning, the commander of the Bethel Regiment sheepishly remarked, "And sure enough we did."[11]

The 52nd North Carolina arrived too late to take part in the fight. It reached the scene of action from its futile trek to Parker's Store about 5:00 P.M., when the battle still raged, but there was no room to deploy. The rest of Kirkland's brigade was already forming a second line behind Cooke. The men of Erson's regiment could hardly see anything of the fight even though it took place only a few yards away, but they could hear the overpowering roar of it. There was "one continuous roll of muskety" coming from the darkening woods ahead. Kirkland instructed the regiment to lay on Orange Plank Road to his rear so it could be quickly shifted wherever needed.[12]

Heth had been battling an overpowering force of the enemy for more than an hour, one division against three, when Maj. Gen. Cadmus Wilcox's division of Hill's corps came up at 5:30. Although his men were nearly out of ammunition, Heth attacked with Wilcox in support. Getty's division was forced to fall back about fifty yards, and the men of Kirkland's brigade had an opportunity to see how well their own fire had affected the Yankee ranks. The 11th North Carolina occupied the Union position and took shelter behind "a line of dead Federals so thick as to form a partial breastwork." The Confederate attack stalled as dusk began to darken the sky. The Bethel Regiment stayed behind this gruesome fortification for several minutes; it was "a novel experience and seems ghastly enough in the restrospect," according to the regimental commander.[13]

Heth's attack was a mistake; when it stalled, Hancock's corps counterattacked and forced the Rebels to retire. They kept going past their point of departure, giving up the swell of ground that had served them so well, but managed to hold about 500 yards to the west. It had been a close call. "I should have left well enough alone," Heth wrote in his memoirs.[14]

Nightfall put an end to the fighting. The losses of Kirkland's brigade were not generally recorded for this day's fight, but Company K of the 26th North Carolina lost one killed and ten wounded. Company F reportedly lost nineteen of its twenty-six men that day. This company had suffered similarly on July 1 at Gettysburg and at Bristoe Station, but there is no reason to believe this loss ratio was typical of the 26th. Company K of the 47th North Carolina lost three killed and several wounded, but neither the losses nor the strengths of any other companies in the regiment were recorded. The fighting did not reach the level of ferocity of Gettysburg, but it was vicious and costly. The field hospital of the 26th had been moved back nearly to Mine Run during the action; both the surgeons and the bandsmen tended the wounded all night.[15]

The fighting exhausted the survivors of Kirkland's brigade, but no one gave an order to re-form the ranks. Everyone simply slept where they were when the firing stopped. Heth tried to convince Hill to bring order out of the chaos, for his division was "terribly mixed up." He asked Hill three times for instructions about where to re-form his men, only to be told that Longstreet was scheduled to arrive before dawn to relieve the corps. Heth stayed up all night hoping to see the vanguard of Longstreet's men appear on Orange Plank Road, but it never happened. When dawn broke, the corps was just as disorganized as it had been the evening before.[16]

Hancock planned a major attack that morning to clear Orange Plank Road. Maj. Gen. David G. Birney's division of the Second Corps replaced Getty's command and advanced along the road, while Brig. Gen. James S. Wadsworth's division of the Fifth Corps attacked north of it. Wadsworth placed three brigades in line and kept one brigade in reserve. One of his frontline units, Brig. Gen. Lysander Cutler's brigade, consisted of several regiments from the old Iron Brigade that had met the men of Kirkland's brigade on July 1 at Gettysburg. The rest of Wadsworth's division was a mixture of New York, Pennsylvania, and Wisconsin regiments. Wadsworth was to head nearly due south and hit the left of Kirkland's and Cooke's brigades, connect with Birney's right, and advance westward.[17]

Kirkland's men awoke at dawn, and the Federals stepped off at 7:00 A.M., forcing the Confederates to hammer together a defensive position quickly. The Tar Heels were shifted south of the road, facing north, when it became apparent that a large force was approaching from that direction. Already the brigade was receiving stray bullets, probably from Birney's division to Cooke's front, as it patched together a battle line. Davis's brigade was supposed to take position to Kirkland's left, but the woods were so thick that it was difficult to tell if the Mississippians were there.[18]

Erson's 52nd North Carolina had time to make crude breastworks of the material in this "dense forest of small gum ash Burchs and Briers," according to John A. Foster. While the rest of the brigade tried to form, Kirkland paced restlessly back and forth in front of his command, "casting his eyes towards his men and toward the advancing enemy." Most of the men lay flat on the ground. They had no artillery support, and it was impossible to see any infantry units to the right or left.[19]

Kirkland could stand the tension no longer. He ordered Louis G. Young to go to the left and find out if Davis was in place. Young had just returned that morning from a two-month sick leave spent in the hospital at Lynchburg. Even though the woods were thick, he rode his horse, picking his way through the undergrowth. Young found Wadsworth's battle line where Davis was supposed to be; the Federals had succeeded in getting the drop on Hill. About the same time, Kirkland's brigade was hit in front by Wadsworth's command, and a fierce firefight broke out. Young was desperate to get back to Kirkland so the brigade leader could extricate the men from this flanking movement. Even though Federal soldiers were only a few yards away, he wheeled his horse around and was fired on. One bullet penetrated his right arm just below the elbow, exited the arm, and grazed his stomach. Young urged his horse on, but the animal, which was probably wounded, lurched into a tree, knocking Young out of the saddle. The staff officer stood up and looked back to see several Yankees firing at him as they moved up, but he managed to run fast enough to escape and find Kirkland. There he communicated the "truly embarrassing position" of the brigade and went off to be treated for his wound. Both bullets that touched him cut twenty-two holes in his clothing. Young went back into action with a quickly applied bandage, but Kirkland later ordered him to the rear.[20]

The Tar Heels fought for a time before they began to give way. Enfilading fire came from the left, and the 52nd North Carolina even received some fire to its rear, from the right wing of Wadsworth's command advancing beyond Kirkland's left flank. The Bethel Regiment experienced a great deal of confusion as it tried to form on the left of the brigade. Martin recalled that when the brigade broke, "the unformed line was rolled up as a sheet of paper would be rolled without the power of effective resistance." It seemed as if all the "advantages of yesterday's hard fighting [were] about to be lost."[21]

Fortunately for Kirkland, Wadsworth could not fully exploit his advantage because his left became entangled with Birney's right. Unit cohesion broke down in both divisions as bluecoated infantrymen blundered into one another. Kirkland's regiments pulled back through the wooded terrain along Orange Plank Road, each one suffering a greater or lesser degree of confusion. The 47th North

Carolina initially retreated in good order, but its ranks disintegrated as the regiment pulled itself through the brush. The 44th North Carolina tried to stand the longest. Nine men were shot down holding the flag, according to a postwar account by Robert Bingham. The tenth man to take the colors, Cpl. George W. Barbee of Company G, carried them safely through the rest of the fighting and the war. A note in the regimental records indicated that Company I, 26th North Carolina, "fought until not a cartridge was left." Heth later noted that only Cooke's brigade retreated without confusion that morning.[22]

The Rebels continued until they reached Widow Tapp's field, where Cooke's, Davis's, and at least part of Kirkland's brigades re-formed a battle line and held for a time. Wadsworth and Birney occupied the eastern edge of the clearing just as the van of Longstreet's corps arrived to save Lee's army. The fresh veterans attacked with vigor and recaptured all the ground lost that morning, although Longstreet was accidentally wounded by his own men.[23]

Kirkland's brigade played only a supporting role for the rest of the day. It took position near the northwest corner of Widow Tapp's field and faced north to confront a new threat, the Ninth Corps of the Army of the Potomac, which cautiously advanced southward between the two roads. Because the fighting along Orange Turnpike to the north took place farther west than Widow Tapp's farm, Hill's corps formed the shoulder of a bulge extending eastward along Orange Plank Road. Kirkland's was the left-most brigade of Heth's division, with Wilcox's division to his left. As the Ninth Corps put more units in line and slowly felt its way south, Kirkland shifted farther west during the afternoon, winding up about a half-mile west of Widow Tapp's field and about a quarter-mile north of Parker's Store. His men built some crude breastworks to better defend their position.[24]

After two days of terrific fighting, both armies had achieved nothing more than a tactical stalemate. Gus Jarratt thought "the old 26th never fought better." Kirkland's brigade lost 3 missing, 21 killed, 102 wounded, 2 wounded and captured, and 55 captured, for a total of 183. The total strength of the brigade was never reported, but the 26th North Carolina had about 760 men just before the battle. It lost 69 men, about 9 percent of its strength. The Bethel Regiment suffered 27 casualties, and the 47th North Carolina lost 28 men. The service records indicated only 14 losses in the 44th North Carolina; apparently many members of Captain Stedman's artillery retrieval detachment failed to report their slight wounds. The 52nd North Carolina lost only 6 men to battlefield injuries but 39 to capture. The latter were mostly lost on the morning of May 6 when Kirkland's line was flanked and crumpled by the Union advance.[25]

The brigade's most important casualty was Lt. Col. John Thomas Jones. He was hit sometime during the fighting of May 6 as he lay on the ground with the 26th North Carolina. Maj. James T. Adams took over the regiment until Lane returned on May 7. Jones was taken a short distance behind the lines, where regimental surgeon Gaither found that a bullet had nearly penetrated his body, appearing just under the skin on its way out. He extracted the ball, "gave him a heavy dose of morphia," and put the officer into an ambulance for transportation to the field hospital. Gaither rode with Jones to watch his condition. Jones himself insisted on being moved despite the danger. Sam Mickey, the leader of the regimental band, stayed up all night with Jones, but he was much worse the next morning. When Gaither told him there was no hope, he replied with "a most yearning expression . . . , 'It must not be. I was born to accomplish more good than I have done.'" He died at 10:40 on the morning of May 7.[26]

Many soldiers took Jones's death hard. Julius Linebach remembered, "We all felt very much depressed, as we considered him the best friend we had in the reg't. We were so busy, however, that we could not brood much over the catastrophe." Jones's cousin, Pvt. Lloyd T. Jones of Company F, 26th North Carolina, lamented the officer's death. "Poor John[,] I Knew after he was gone, I would not have no other friend that would favor me in the least from dutys of any Kind. I Lost all when I lost him." Sam Mickey went to Orange Court House to have a coffin sent back to the hospital. Jones's remains were placed in it and transported back to Orange, where they were interred in a military graveyard. Mickey went to great lengths to mark the grave.[27]

Another ranking officer who went down in the fighting on May 6 was Thomas C. Singletary, who was hit in the left leg. Considering his checkered career, the brigade was better off without him. Singletary spent about a month in the hospital at Lynchburg but was sent home when Federal forces threatened that mountain town. He contracted dysentery while in North Carolina and extended his sick leave until December 1864. The troublesome commander went on another leave in late February and never returned to service. Given Kirkland's propensity for getting wounded, it was fortunate that Singletary was not on duty to replace him in the demanding campaigns that followed the Wilderness.[28]

The morning of May 7 found Kirkland's men in the same place as the evening before. The brigade moved several times that day for short distances as division and corps commanders readjusted their lines. The men sometimes rested and sometimes dug earthworks between these moves. Late that evening, about eight o'clock, a rumor ran up and down the line that the Federals were moving away. "The rebel yell was raised at some point on the right of the line," wrote the historian of the 26th North Carolina. It was "at first, heard like the rumbling of a distant railroad train, it came rushing down the lines like the surging of the waves

Lt. Col. John Thomas Jones. Shown here in his uniform as a private in the 1st North Carolina (six months). Jones would later rise to command the 26th North Carolina. He was mortally wounded on the second day at the Wilderness. (Society for Historical Preservation of the 26th Regiment North Carolina Troops, Inc.)

upon the ocean, increasing in loudness and grandeur; and passing, it would be heard dying away on the left in the distance. Again it was heard coming from the right to die away again on the distant left. It was renewed three times, each time with increased vigor. It was a yell like the defiant tones of the thunder storm, echoing and re-echoing. It caused such dismay among the Federals that it is said their pickets fired and ran in."[29]

Grant certainly was moving out but not away. He opted for a short flanking movement around the Confederate right, with Spotsylvania Court House and its junction of roads as the target. Lee anticipated this move and responded quickly. Maj. Gen. Jubal A. Early temporarily took command of the Third Corps on the morning of May 8 to replace the ailing A. P. Hill. He set the troops in motion that afternoon, with Kirkland's brigade moving about five miles before bivouacking for the night in an open field. It continued the next day, entering Shady Grove Road and approaching Spotsylvania directly from the west at noon. Kirkland's men were ordered to dig earthworks just east of the junction that evening.[30]

The men were not called on to fight, for there were as yet no Federals east of the town. But new movements far to the west would soon bring Heth's division into action. Grant sent Hancock's Second Corps forward to feel out Lee's left flank for a possible turning movement on May 9. Hancock crossed the Po River, a small stream that curved generally on a north-to-south axis, late that afternoon

John Thomas Jones's vest.
(Copyright North Carolina Museum of History)

and kept the river to his left. The Federals took position on the west side of Block House Bridge, where Shady Grove Road crossed the Po, and extended their line westward. As nightfall put an end to their advance, the Unionists were poised to turn Lee's left in the morning.[31]

Lee ordered Early to take a division and drive the Yankees away. He set out at dawn on Tuesday, May 10, with Heth's division in tow. The men marched westward along Shady Grove Road as far as Block House, then turned south and moved past the Old Court House, crossed the Po, and turned west onto a road that paralleled Gladys Run. Here the division formed a battle line and advanced northward, crossing the shallow stream and its swampy, wooded bottomland. They encountered an open field as they approached Shady Grove Road, and the advance stopped. Everyone lay down as the artillery opened on the Union position.[32]

By the time Heth was ready to pounce, Hancock had already pulled much of his strength back to the north. Grant had decided that day to abandon the turning movement to Lee's left in favor of concentrating his strength for a massive assault on the center. To keep the Rebels off balance, he instructed Hancock to leave one division behind while withdrawing the other two. Brig. Gen. Francis C. Barlow's command was selected as the delaying force. It was stretched along Shady Grove Road for two and a half miles from Block House Bridge westward, facing south. The Federals built crude breastworks just south of the road for protection.[33]

Heth's division was deployed in two lines. Kirkland was on the right of the first line, with Davis to his left. Behind Kirkland was Walker's brigade, and Cooke was positioned to Davis's rear. Barlow's right wing lay directly ahead, with Col. Paul Frank on the right and Brig. Gen. John R. Brooke to his left. Kirkland faced Brooke, whose 3,000 men had not yet seen heavy fighting that spring. His brigade consisted of a mixture of Pennsylvania and New York units with one Delaware regiment. There were dense woods to the rear of both Frank and Brooke, and massed Union artillery lay only a mile to the north, on the other side of the Po.[34]

After some preliminary bombardment, Heth gave the order to attack at 2:30. Skirmishers from Kirkland's and Davis's brigades went into the open field, followed by the battle line. They "attacked vigorously," in the words of Federal general Brooke, yelling at the top of their lungs and firing as they advanced. The fire from the two Union brigades was heavy enough to bring the Rebels to a halt in the open field, but Kirkland re-formed his ranks and pushed on. As John A. Foster of the 52nd North Carolina put it, the Tar Heels "charged up on them in thare brest works and drove them out thare brest works and got in them ourslves and raleighed." Frank's brigade in front of Davis's broke first, while Brooke's

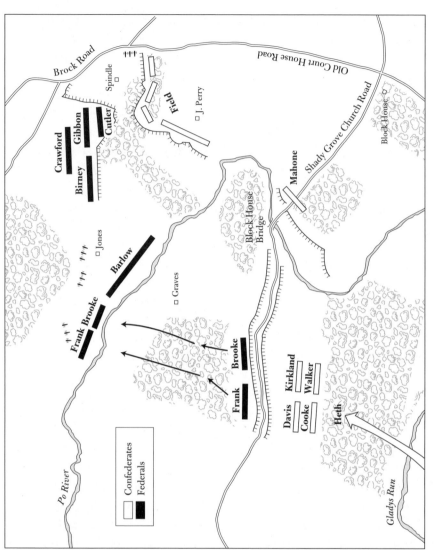

Brock Road

Old Court House Road

Spindle

Field

J. Perry

Cutler

Gibbon

Crawford

Birney

Shady Grove Church Road

Block House

Mahone

Block House Bridge

Jones

Barlow

Frank Brooke

Graves

Brooke

Kirkland

Walker

Frank

Davis

Cooke

Heth

Po River

Confederates

Federals

Gladys Run

MAP 10.2 The Battle of Spotsylvania, May 10, 1864

Yankees held on more stubbornly; but both brigades finally retreated to another line of breastworks on the north side of Shady Grove Road and made another stand. Once again, Kirkland's men ground to a halt.[35]

By now the fighting had set fire to the dense woods immediately behind Brooke's command. The dry leaves and trees began "burning furiously," in Hancock's words, trapping the Federals between two different kinds of blazes. The Yankees gamely held on despite the hopelessness of their situation, until the breastworks themselves started to burn. Orders were shouted along the blue line to retreat over the Po, and Brooke's regiments fell back through the burning forest to escape. The scattering soldiers managed to cross the river.[36]

The fire proved to be the Federals' best cover and Heth's worst obstacle. Kirkland's brigade jumped into the abandoned Federal works, but the blazing forest just beyond proved too much for it. The men stepped back a few paces and re-formed their ranks in Shady Grove Road as Cooke's brigade moved up to their right. The Tar Heels rested and watched in awe as Federal dead and wounded were consumed by the fire only a few yards away. Soon the Rebels were ordered forward once more, entering the cleared area to the east and north to avoid the burning trees. Here they came under intense artillery fire from the massed Union batteries on the north side of the Po. The attack up to this time had been entirely a contest of infantry fire, but now the Confederates advanced into an artillery barrage. James W. Wright of the 26th North Carolina marveled at the repeated explosions of shell overhead: "it appeared like nothing could live." Heth's attack ended in this open area just south of the river. Kirkland's brigade got close enough to the cannon so that the 52nd received at least one round of canister. Heth retired to Shady Grove Road and occupied the Yankee breastworks about 5:00 P.M., rebuilding them to defend against a possible attack from the north.[37]

It had been a splendid day for Kirkland's men. This was the first successful attack they conducted during the war that did not wreck the brigade. Henry Clay Albright proudly wrote in his diary, "We did it most handsomely after some very hard marching." The 44th North Carolina took possession of an abandoned Union gun, the first artillery piece lost by the Union Second Corps in the war. Lee was so pleased with the assault that he authorized Heth to issue a congratulatory order to his men.[38]

Once again, because of the absence of brigade and regimental reports, the strengths and losses of Kirkland's units on May 10 remain obscure. Company K of the 26th North Carolina reported a loss of one killed and one wounded, while Company F of the same regiment had thirteen men engaged in the assault and lost four of them. Meanwhile, Company K of the 47th North Carolina lost only two men wounded. The most interesting casualty in the brigade was Lt. James

G. M. Jones of Company D, 26th North Carolina. A bullet hit his left breast pocket but was deflected by a daguerreotype of his girlfriend. Jones would be out of action until September, recovering from the shock of the impact. He was captured in October and spent the rest of the war in prison. The best news was that he eventually married the woman whose picture saved his life.[39]

Another casualty of this attack suffered horribly before he died. Lee Gibson was hit by a shell in the knee; it "mangled his leg most horribly . . . all the bones smashed, the whole knee-bone, was all shattered to pieces, leg only hanging to the skin." Edward Peterson was a witness to his suffering in the field hospital and saw the agony endured by Gibson's brother, Abe, a member of the band. Gibson lived less than a day. He was buried in a blanket with a layer of cedar bushes below and another layer of cedar above the body. As Chaplain Richard Webb prayed over the grave, Abe wept bitterly. "Death is busy all around," Peterson mused. "I used to think, I couldn't bear the idea of seeing a man die, but I'm hardened to it now. I can look on quite comfortably now."[40]

The men had little time to savor their victory. They were roused from their bivouac along Shady Grove Road the next morning and marched back to Spotsylvania Court House. Kirkland's brigade spent the rest of May 11 in the earthworks east of town under a steady rain, and the muddy water that accumulated in the bottom of the trenches became "verry disagreeable" to John A. Foster. Benjamin Wesley Justice told his wife the men were in good spirits but feeling the burden of constant marching and fighting. "The excitement & confusion are great," he admitted. "The suffering of the wounded indescribable; the mental anxiety & solicitude almost insupportable. It *must* end before many days."[41]

There was to be little relief from the demands of this campaign. On the night of May 11 the 26th North Carolina received orders to be ready for a march. It was to guard a train of ninety-five wagons to collect forage near Milford Station, about fifteen miles to the southeast. The men rode in the empty wagons all night and loaded them with 2,000 bushels of corn while the rain poured all day on May 12. Then they left Milford Station on May 13 and returned to Spotsylvania that evening, bivouacking in the courthouse yard. The regimental wounded were shipped to Richmond and Orange Court House, reducing the hospital duties of the Moravian band. Its leader, Sam Mickey, lost his cornet during the Spotsylvania campaign. He had hung it from a tree limb while sleeping, and someone stole it. "This worried us all a good deal," remembered Linebach, "for we could not play very much without him." Mickey was able to borrow another horn from the 44th North Carolina band.[42]

The brigade was awakened on the morning of May 12 by a barrage of artillery fire, the beginning of a massive dawn attack on the Mule Shoe Salient in the center of Lee's line. The Ninth Corps, just to the left of Kirkland's position, supported this assault. Kirkland's brigade was missing the 26th North Carolina, which was still on its mission to Milford Station. The Tar Heels expected to be attacked all day as the Ninth Corps hit the line just to their left and Union artillery continued to lob shells into their position. Kirkland's right flank rested on Fredericksburg Road while Cooke held the line to his right. The rain turned the trenches into mud pits. Several soldiers of the 44th North Carolina leaped onto the parapet to get a better view of the fighting to the north, daring the shells to strike. Unfortunately several of the projectiles did find targets. Major Stedman of the 44th was wounded in the right foot seriously enough to be taken out of action for more than three months. Pvt. John M. Allen of the 52nd North Carolina was killed "by a cannonball striking his head." Company C, 47th North Carolina, lost its commander, Lt. Alexander H. Harris, who was hit in the ankle by a shell. His leg was later amputated, and Harris died on June 8 at a hospital in Lynchburg. Still, the overall losses were slight. Most of Kirkland's men remained safely behind their works and waited for this long, dreadful day to end.[43]

Lee gave up the Mule Shoe Salient that night and retired to a new line of works constructed at its base. The two exhausted armies now settled down for several days of rest. The 26th North Carolina rejoined Kirkland's command on May 14, but it found no room in the trenches and remained slightly to the rear as a reserve. Day after day the hapless soldiers had to endure the same monotonous round of skirmishing, the occasional cannon shot, and the continual torrent of rain that fell in the muddy trenches. This went on from May 13 through 17. The only thing that enlivened the scene was music. Kirkland wanted all three of his regimental bands to "come forward & play" on May 14. Lane had by now returned to resume command of the 26th, and he liked the idea as well. He instructed the Moravians to play right behind the trenches nearly every day for the rest of their time at Spotsylvania.[44]

The calm was briefly interrupted on the morning of May 18 when "a tremendous Shelling" took place for two hours. The firing was a diversion for a weak infantry assault on the Confederate position at the base of the Mule Shoe Salient, which made no headway. During the middle of this firestorm, members of the 26th North Carolina witnessed a memorable sight. Lee happened to be riding near the regiment, which was still held in reserve, when a few rounds seemed to come near him. "As quick as a flash the members of his staff placed themselves around him to protect him with their own bodies. . . . The troops were visibly affected, as General Lee with his staff, still surrounding him, rode off." The shelling wounded four men in Company C of that regiment, indicating that the army commander was indeed in danger.[45]

When the firing stopped later that morning, a gloomy calm once again descended over the lines. James W. Wright walked around to see the sights and reflected on what his comrades had been through since May 5. "Our men are anxious for the yankees to advance," he admitted to his family. They were tired of waiting in mud-soaked trenches and wanted the campaign to reach a climax. The corporal from Company C put his trust in divine providence. "I still hope God will protect me as he has done. it is him alone that has thus far protected me[;] he is my only hope."[46]

The brigade's losses were nearly as high as at the Wilderness. Seven men were killed, 80 were wounded, and 38 were captured, for a total of 125 casualties. Two regiments, the 26th and the 52nd, lost a lot more men captured than the other three. Since there was little opportunity for the Federals truly to capture them, given the tactical situation, it is safe to assume that many of these men simply deserted or allowed themselves to be taken. Both regiments had a larger proportion of conscripts than the rest of the brigade. Pvt. Solomon D. Swain of the 44th North Carolina certainly did desert. The service records note that he "gave himself up voluntarily to the Union pickets near Spotsylvania Court House." Swain was not a draftee but a transfer from the 28th North Carolina who had been serving in the 44th since December 1863. He died of pneumonia at Elmira Prison two months before the war ended. About half the men listed as captured in the 26th were "lost" between May 15 and 19, exactly when Swain deserted, indicating that this latter phase of the fight at Spotsylvania was the most dreary for those who possessed marginal motivation to fight.[47]

The Spotsylvania phase of the Overland campaign finally ended when Grant continued his swings to Lee's right on the night of May 20. The Confederate general quickly moved his army on a shorter line of march to protect the vital railroad junction at Hanover, between the North and South Anna Rivers. This was familiar ground to Kirkland's men, who had spent a month here one year before, guarding the railroad junction. Kirkland's men crossed the North Anna on May 22 at Butler's Bridge, and that afternoon they reached Anderson's Station on the Virginia Central Railroad west of Hanover Junction.

The two armies began to grapple the next day. Warren's Fifth Corps crossed the North Anna at Jericho Mill, and Lee ordered Hill, who had reassumed command of his corps, to drive it back. He dispatched Wilcox's division, which struck Warren that evening, catching the Federals by surprise. But Wilcox was outnumbered more than two to one, and soon the attack ground to a halt. Heth was ordered up to support Wilcox. Kirkland's men marched three miles along the railroad right-of-way from Anderson's Station to Noel's Station, then turned north. When Heth reached the battlefield, he deployed his division to Wilcox's rear and allowed Wilcox to move most of it farther to the right to cover the much longer Federal line. Most of the fighting was over by the time Heth showed up. He might otherwise have made all the difference in driving the Fifth Corps back across the river, for several of Warren's units had panicked when the Rebels hit them.

Lee decided to dig in that night. The center of his line was an inverted V on the south bank of the North Anna River at Ox Ford. From here the right wing stretched to the southeast, and the left went south to Little River, a small stream that lay between the North and South Annas. Heth's division marched from the battlefield back to Anderson's Station during the night and helped to dig this line. Kirkland's brigade was placed on the army's extreme left, the left flank resting on Little River.[48]

The 26th North Carolina managed to avoid most of the digging. It spent the night standing picket and rejoined the brigade on the morning of May 24, after Kirkland had already reached his place in the fortified line. The Moravian musicians tried to brighten the men's spirits by playing "Here's Your Mule," but the soldiers appreciated the opportunity to bathe and fish in Little River even more.[49]

Kirkland's men faced no immediate threat, but Lee worried about a flanking movement to his left. Heth took his division across Little River on May 25 to screen that wing. Kirkland's command splashed across at 1:00 in the afternoon, marched a mile, and began to fortify. The bandsmen of the 26th were not needed at the hospital, so they played for the regiment while the men worked. Linebach felt sorry for one civilian whose yard and potato patch were scarred by a long line of trench. The Tar Heels used his fence rails and some timbers from his buildings to strengthen the fortifications.[50]

As Heth fortified south of Little River, Grant ordered a cavalry division to threaten Lee's left. It was an attempt to divert the Rebels' attention from his next side step to the south, but it was not much of a demonstration. The horsemen moved only as far as the north bank of Little River in a driving rain before they returned to the North Anna. As a result, Kirkland's brigade made it through the entire North Anna campaign without firing a shot. It lost very few men, a total of seventeen. Six were wounded by the odd artillery round or light skirmishing, and eleven were captured. Again the 26th North Carolina lost the lion's share of those captured, six of eleven, perhaps because men deliberately allowed themselves to be taken.[51]

The Tar Heels now had time to evaluate what had happened to them thus far in the spring. Lemuel J. Hoyle was astonished at the prolonged intensity of the campaigning. "It is unlike any other fight, and Grant is unlike any other general," he wrote home, "but I am inclined to the opinion that it will yet be ended in our fortifications around Richmond." The mood in the brigade generally was good. Julius Linebach assured his Salem friends that "though Grant is nearer Richmond than he was three weeks ago, he is only so geographically, and is no nearer having this army whipped than when the first gun was fired."[52]

The Federals evacuated their works on both sides of the North Anna on the night of May 26. Grant crossed the Pamunkey River, formed by the union of the two Annas, two days later, and Lee moved to block him. Kirkland's men left their trenches at 10:00 on the morning of May 27 and camped for the night near Ashland. They continued the march until they were within twelve miles of Mechanicsville before bivouacking for the night. They were nearing the scene of McClellan's defeat in the Seven Days campaign two years earlier. Lee took a defensive position behind Totopotomoy Creek about seven miles southwest of Grant's crossing of the Pamunkey on May 29. As Kirkland's men dug earthworks in the level, sandy soil, the Moravian band members stood on a parapet near the 26th North Carolina and played for them as the sun went down.[53]

Hill's corps moved farther south as Grant continued to shift to his left. Kirkland's brigade left its trenches at 10:00 P.M. on the night of May 31 and moved three miles to the right, taking position at Hundley's Corner near Pole Green Church in works already constructed by the Stonewall Brigade of Early's Second Corps. Located about two miles northwest of Bethesda Church, the Corner was a significant intersection. Roads extended from the junction to connect with both Hanover Town and White House. The latter point was seventeen miles away and an excellent forward base of supplies for Grant's army. To the west the road extended from the Corner directly to the Confederate capital. Kirkland's Tar Heels would be directly in Grant's path.[54]

Probing actions took place on June 1. Opposite Kirkland's command, orders went out for Brig. Gen. John Gibbon's division of the Union Second Corps to divert Confederate attention from moves on other parts of the line. Gibbon assigned the task to Col. H. Boyd McKeen's brigade. Two regiments and part of a third, including four companies of the 36th Wisconsin, were selected. This regiment had been organized only a few months before and was completely untested in battle. In fact it had just reached the front on May 18. The Wisconsinites made up the center of the attacking force, while the 7th Michigan was on the right and the 42nd New York was on the left. All of the men had to attack for a quarter-mile over an open, level field to reach the Confederate entrenchments, aiming at the right of Cooke's and the left of Kirkland's commands. They would have no artillery support.

There was no sense of impending doom among Kirkland's hardened veterans as they contemplated the approach of this little band. The brigade line was just north of the road extending southeast toward White House, with Cooke's brigade to the left. A small grove of trees stood sixty yards in front of Cooke's right wing, but the rest of the ground was completely open. Late in the afternoon the fresh young men of the 36th Wisconsin started enthusiastically on their first assault, but there was no eagerness among the veterans to their right and left. The Wisconsin commander said they were from "old & demoralized regiments whose influence is anything but good." The 42nd New York failed to attack at all while the 7th Michigan jumped out of its works and ran a short distance into the field. Then it dropped to the ground, fired a shot or two, and retired. The green Wisconsin troops, 240 strong, ignored the example of their tested comrades and blindly marched forward.[55]

The Confederates had no difficulty dealing with these men. At a range of only 200 yards the Rebel artillery opened on them. At a range of only 50 yards the Rebel infantry opened fire. The prospect of punishing such a small, exposed group excited the men of Kirkland's brigade. The 47th North Carolina, posted on Kirkland's left, was in "splendid fighting trim on this occasion," exulted the unit's historian. Company commanders instructed the ranks to "fire by file," but they had to restrain the men from opening too soon. When the musketry blazed away, "it was so steady and accurate, for our men were perfectly cool," that the Federals went down in droves. "I must confess that I felt sorry for them," admitted J. L. Henry of the 26th North Carolina. His regiment was on the right, not directly targeted by the attack, and thus he had a perfect view of the proceedings.[56]

Soon after the infantry began firing, the Wisconsin soldiers dropped to the ground for protection. Groups of them jumped up now and then to run back, only to receive volleys from Cooke's and Kirkland's men. About twenty-five Wisconsin soldiers took shelter in the patch of woods while the rest simply lay where they were for nearly three hours until darkness offered them an opportunity to retreat in relative safety. Dusk also gave Cooke an opportunity to send out skirmishers from the 15th North Carolina and round up the twenty-five Federals who were still hiding in the woods.[57]

The battalion from the 36th Wisconsin lost 70 percent of its strength in this little assault. The prisoners were "new hands" at war, as J. L. Henry put it, and he found them to be happy to be out of the conflict. "If Grant keeps charging Lee he will soon have his forces massed in the Infernal Region," thought Henry. There were barely any casualties in Kirkland's brigade. The 26th North Carolina lost four men wounded in the hot skirmishing along the lines that day. So many sharpshooters' bullets sailed over the entrenchments that the regimental band was forced to move back to the hospital for its own safety. A total of about twenty

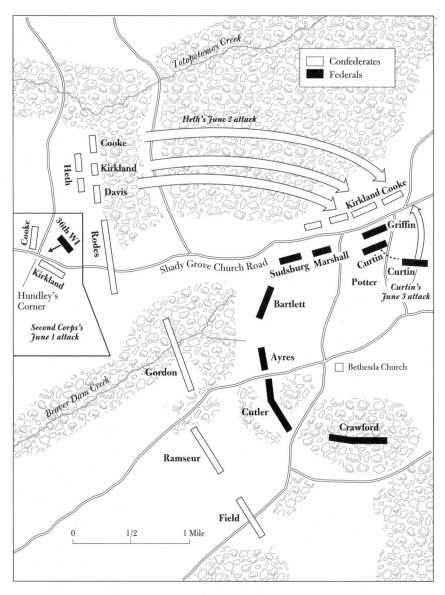

MAP 10.3 The Battle of Cold Harbor, June 1–3, 1864

wounded men from the different regiments appeared in the hospital the next day, all victims of the skirmishing.[58]

The fighting shifted slightly to the Confederate right as Grant worked his army farther south. All of the Second Corps had left the Union right flank by the evening of June 1, leaving the Ninth Corps to hold that area. Likewise most of

FROM THE WILDERNESS TO COLD HARBOR

Hill's corps was shifted to the far Confederate right, leaving only Heth to hold Lee's left and Early's Second Corps to Heth's right. There was no activity for most of the day on June 2, but then the Ninth Corps received orders to readjust its lines in preparation for a major assault by the whole army the next morning. This movement began at 1:00 P.M. as the Federals pulled out of their forward line, leaving a number of skirmishers in them, and marched in column to the rear and to the south. The Ninth Corps refused its right flank to better protect the northern end of Grant's line.[59]

"The Yankees are gone from our front," wrote J. L. Henry of this development. Early was determined to take advantage of it. He approached Heth with a suggestion that the two cooperate in an immediate attack. Early was to send two divisions along the road from Hundley's Corner toward Bethesda Church, while Heth would support them with one brigade to the north. Heth had already concocted the idea for an advance and told Early he would attack with his whole division, not just one brigade. This suited the combative corps leader, and the arrangements were made. All units would have to wheel to the southeast, since the Federal right flank was consolidated in that direction. Heth was to begin first because he had a longer distance to march, and then Early's men would start.[60]

Heth advanced Cooke on his left, then Kirkland and Davis to Cooke's right. Kirkland's men jumped out of their trenches at 3:00 P.M. and headed east, then south. They easily occupied the Federal works and took a few skirmishers, but Heth soon lost connection with Early to the south—if he ever had a connection from the beginning—and the attack turned into a disjointed, stumbling lurch toward the enemy. Heth's men moved on for two miles under a rainstorm that suddenly rolled across the area before they encountered significant resistance. Col. Simon G. Griffin's brigade of Maine, New Hampshire, and Vermont troops, of Brig. Gen. Robert B. Potter's division, quickly retraced its steps when word arrived of the Rebel advance. The Federals were able to reach an old trench dug by the Fifth Corps several days earlier and since abandoned; they fired into Kirkland's skirmishers as the Tar Heels approached and drove the Federals back.

Kirkland's battle line made it to Shady Grove Church Road and was now facing mostly south. It was no more than a "country road that skirted a wood," in William S. Long's words, but it provided a landmark in this flat landscape. The skirmishers returned, telling everyone that "Hell's broke loose over there & we are in for it now." Kirkland wanted to push on, so he ordered his men to re-form and advance into the woods. They failed to drive Griffin's New Englanders and returned to the road. It was rapidly getting dark, and the Tar Heels collected fence rails and dug a trench to fortify their position.[61]

Darkness did not put an end to the fight. As evening turned into night, the

Union artillery opened, and a heavy line of skirmishers appeared in Kirkland's front. The Federals were able to approach within forty yards of his position because of the woods, and Kirkland's men fired in the direction of the noise as the Yankees crashed through the brush. It was a blind fight in the ever darkening forest. The Tar Heels must have wondered why they were there, but at least Heth maintained a sense of humor. When a shell came screaming too close for comfort, the men "craned their necks" to avoid it. The division leader playfully told a staff officer "'to go stop that battery—tell them they are firing into my men.'" Ironically it did stop soon afterward, probably because the Federals were lodged so close to Kirkland's command. The flow of bullets in both directions was "terrific," according to Henry Clay Albright, but in the dense woods neither side inflicted a lot of damage on the other. Kirkland, however, was hit in the right thigh and badly injured, and Colonel Faribault of the 47th North Carolina temporarily replaced him. This was the third time in the war that Kirkland was wounded, and the second time since he assumed command of the brigade. The Tar Heels stayed in their improvised earthworks along Shady Grove Church Road all night. Early's command fought a sharp battle with the Ninth Corps and took several hundred Federal pickets, but it failed to do any decisive damage.[62]

Losses were light on June 2. Colonel Lane was injured slightly in the hand and side but remained on duty, and casualties within the 26th were unevenly borne by the different companies. While only three men were wounded in Company K, the ever suffering Company F lost half of its twelve men engaged in the attack. The Bethel Regiment lost one man killed and six men wounded. Capt. Lawrence Ruel Anderson, commander of the 44th North Carolina since Singletary had been injured, was killed in the abortive assault, but only two men of Company K in that regiment were wounded. The 47th North Carolina lost a similar number of men. Lt. Julius Rowan Rogers also was wounded. Kirkland recognized him when he arrived at the field hospital and directed his care, saw to his dressing, and arranged to have him sent immediately to a hospital in Richmond. "Had it not been for his kindness I doubt much if I should now be living, for I was out of my head for several days after I was wounded." Rogers recovered and returned to the regiment in time to take part in the battle of Reams Station.[63]

Grant initiated a general attack in the early morning hours of Friday, June 3, with the Ninth Corps assaulting the Confederate left about 7:00 A.M. Col. John I. Curtin's brigade of Potter's division struck Cooke's brigade and came to within seventy-five yards of the Rebel works before it was stopped. Curtin's Massachusetts, New York, Pennsylvania, and Rhode Island regiments dug into the earth where they halted and opened a heavy skirmish fire on the Rebels. Part of Curtin's line covered the left wing of Kirkland's command, to Cooke's right, but the brigade was not generally engaged. On its front the Federals took the skirmish pits, and everyone was subjected to a sniping fire that increased in intensity as the day passed. It "amounted almost to a battle," in Heth's words. The men had to keep their heads down in the trenches as much as possible and were unable to send skirmishers to annoy the enemy.[64]

This would be the last day of heavy fighting on the Cold Harbor line. That night Heth was instructed to pull out and rejoin Hill's corps on the right. Details were sent out to collect all the bayonets and canteens that could be found lying around, as these were the articles most desperately needed by the brigade. Kirkland's men left their trenches at 3:00 A.M. on June 4 and marched to the right before resting for the evening. The men continued to relax all day on June 5 as well.[65]

The rest gave Lemuel Hoyle an opportunity to reflect on what had happened. "One month ago today this terrible, this awful, battle began," he wrote to his mother; "hundred upon hundreds have fallen in the bloody conflict—thousands of loving hearts are now lacerated, torn & bleeding, and the voice of mourning comes up from every quarter of our suffering & afflicted country, and still the work of death goes on with no more prospect of a termination than there was at the beginning. Grant is a murderer and butcher and seems determined to persist in his efforts to take Richmond and 'crush' us out, no matter at what sacrafice of human life. Any other Yankee General would have given it up before now."[66]

The brigade moved out at 11:00 P.M. on June 5 to occupy its assigned section of trenches on the Confederate right. It was still in the works when dawn appeared. The men kept their heads behind the parapet during the daylight hours because the Federals were very close. The brigade pulled out of the works at midafternoon, marched two miles farther to the right, and began to make a new line of works complete with bombproofs. Many men had only their bayonets to use as digging tools. They worked all afternoon and all night while heavy skirmishing took place only a few yards away. The sniping continued on June 7, broken only by a truce to allow the Unionists to recover their wounded and bury their dead.[67]

The brigade suffered 101 casualties at Cold Harbor. Seventeen men were killed, 70 were wounded, 3 were wounded and captured, and 11 were captured. These were sustainable losses, but the survivors were "all very tired and dirty."[68]

Faribault's men remained in their newly constructed works until the evening of June 9, when they were ordered to cross the Chickahominy River. Marching three miles eastward, they relieved Robert Ransom's division at the picket posts above Bottom's Bridge. Lee expected Grant to continue the short turning movements that had become his trademark during the past month, and the Chickahominy was the next obstacle to be crossed. Federal pickets were nearby, but

Faribault's men had no difficulty keeping the peace. They were quite friendly with the Yankees. More than half of the brigade was on the picket line at any one time.[69]

The men found this duty agreeable. "We like our present position very well if we could stay here," wrote James W. Wright. "I dont think we would have much fight." They received good rations of bread, bacon, coffee, sugar, peas, and rice — more than they needed in fact. Daniel Liles of the 26th North Carolina traded corn bread and tobacco with Union pickets for a good canteen, crackers, coffee, and sugar. The ample food supply contrasted sharply with the rations issued to Ransom's men, and the discrepancy was so apparent that they became despondent. Ransom, the former brigade commander of the 26th North Carolina, complained to the authorities. He argued that his command was doing exactly the same kind of duty as Kirkland's brigade and ought to be fed the same.[70]

John Lane earned his rations during this period. The energetic colonel of the 26th crawled through the swamps tending to his picket posts, and his life was saved by quick-thinking soldiers on two occasions. Pvt. Laban Ellis of Company E fired at a Federal picket who tried to shoot Lane. His bullet hit the Federal's gun and knocked it from his shoulder just as the Yankee pulled the trigger. The Northerner surrendered and told Lane, "'Your man saved you.'" On another occasion Pvt. Ira L. Nall of Company E accompanied Lane on a scout of the terrain in front of the picket line. Nall noticed a Federal soldier taking aim at his colonel from only "a few feet away." He instantly realized he did not have time to shoulder his weapon, so he simply fired without doing so, killing the Yankee before he could squeeze his trigger.[71]

But the long tour of picket duty in the swamps also gave rise to fraternization. The 52nd held a section of the picket line opposite the 4th Rhode Island of the Fifth Corps, and the two regiments quickly worked out an arrangement. Neither side would fire on the other unless an attack was under way. This was quite a contrast to the attitude of the 52nd only a year earlier, when the Tar Heels had just joined Lee's army and manned their first picket line close to the enemy. Soon the two sides were exchanging Southern tobacco and corn bread for a variety of Northern items, including coffee, sugar, hardtack, knives, and combs.[72]

This fraternization in turn gave rise to increased opportunities for desertion. On June 11 Pvt. Johnson Broyhill of Company F, 52nd North Carolina, cautiously approached a picket post manned by Rhode Islanders under Lt. Henry Gawthrop. Broyhill "asked several questions as to how he would be treated if he came in," reported Gawthrop. One of his sergeants answered all the Tar Heel's concerns and talked him into giving up. Broyhill crossed the log that spanned the stream separating the two picket lines, telling the Yankees that half his regiment would desert if given the chance. The twenty-year-old farmer from Wilkes County was released on June 27 after taking the oath of allegiance. Another officer of the 4th Rhode Island reported that about thirty Rebels deserted to his regiment during these days on the Chickahominy.[73]

The time spent in this backwater soon came to an end, for Grant had no intention of simply crossing the Chickahominy. He planned a major sweep to cross the James River and attack Petersburg. This important city was the key to Richmond; if its rail connections were to fall, the capital would be doomed and Lee's army would have lost its anchor in Virginia. The Federal army pulled away from Cold Harbor on the night of June 12 and began to cross the James two days later. Lee was in the dark as to its position or intentions. All he could do was begin shifting his divisions across the Chickahominy to keep them between Richmond and Grant's supposed position.[74]

Kirkland's brigade was relieved of its picket duty on the night of June 12 by the City Battalion of Richmond. The brigade moved out in the darkness, crossed White Oak Swamp the next morning, and bivouacked beside the Charles City Road. The men were only about six miles from the battlefield of Malvern Hill, where the 26th North Carolina had fought its second engagement. They were roused on the morning of June 14 to dig earthworks. When that was done, the brigade rested for four days. No one seemed to know exactly where the Yankees had gone, but there was an air of quiet and peace between the Chickahominy and the James that belied the fierce fighting that was about to begin on June 15 just east of Petersburg.[75]

The Overland campaign was over. After six weeks of bitter fighting, the men of Kirkland's brigade were tired but in good spirits. They had been engaged in two days of battle at the Wilderness, one spectacular assault at Spotsylvania, a near-engagement at the North Anna, and three days of fighting at Cold Harbor. The brigade lost its casualty-prone commander and suffered a total of 426 losses in six weeks of campaigning. These included 3 missing, 45 killed, 258 wounded, 5 wounded and captured, and 115 captured. The Wilderness was the costliest fight of the Overland campaign for Kirkland's command, with 183 losses. Then Spotsylvania took the second highest toll, 125 men. Given the paucity of information about regimental strength, it is impossible to gauge accurately the proportion of casualties to men engaged. It is not unreasonable to assume that about 1,500 men started the campaign, at most, and therefore Kirkland's brigade lost at least one-third of its strength.[76]

Chapter 11

Petersburg

During the middle of June, when the fate of Petersburg and Lee's army hung in the balance, Kirkland's brigade picketed the swampy regions bordering the Chickahominy and played no direct role in the fighting. Beginning on June 15 the Federals cracked the Rebel defenses east of town that Kirkland's men had helped to build two years earlier, but they could not exploit their advantage. By the time the fighting ended on June 18, both armies had arrived on the scene, Petersburg was saved, and the war would continue for another ten months.[1]

Kirkland's men received word that the Federals had crossed the James River on June 17 and left that evening for White Cross, where they bivouacked. The brigade set out early on June 18 for what would be one of the worst marches of its history. The men crossed the James on a pontoon bridge near Drewry's Bluff and struck the pike between Richmond and Petersburg. "This was the hardest day's marching we have had during the present campaign," wrote Henry Clay Albright. "I think I never was so tired in all my life." The sun blazed down on the dusty surface of the pike to make the worst conditions for marching. It was "almost like going through a furnace," thought Julius Linebach. There was a lot of straggling as a result. The men reached the railroad six miles north of Petersburg, boarded a train, and rode five miles farther. Then they jumped off and marched the rest of the way to the Appomattox River.[2]

The Tar Heels now had a chance to see to their personal comfort. Benjamin H. Freeman of the 44th North Carolina took a thorough bath and donned his first clean shirt and underwear since May 2. "I threw away the ones I pulled off," he wrote home. New jackets, shoes, and pants were issued to the men along with good rations of bread, coffee, and sugar. There was very little meat in the rations, but the authorities made up for that by issuing large amounts of rice. The regiments were required to do picket duty in small holes dug into the ground before the line of earthworks. The pickets had to be changed during the night because the Federals were too close to allow it in daylight.[3]

The brigade was shifted to the far right of Lee's line by June 22 and placed near the point where one of Lee's most important supply lines, the Weldon Railroad, crossed Boydton Plank Road southwest of town. The Confederate States Lead Works was located here on the west side of the railroad. On the first day in this place the Moravian musicians were ordered to the brigade's extreme right and told to play as loudly as they could to give the impression that more troops were stationed there. Only three days after arriving at their new post, the men of the 52nd North Carolina were temporarily detached from the brigade to guard bridges on the pike north of Petersburg. They returned shortly.[4]

Beginning on June 22 Grant sent the Fifth and Sixth Corps on a raid to cut the Weldon Railroad, about the same time that Kirkland's brigade was moved to the extreme right. The Unionists tore up a section of track before two divisions of Hill's corps arrived to drive them away in a sharp battle. Kirkland's brigade was in position to support the attacking force, but it was not engaged. It remained the right-most infantry unit of Lee's army for some time to come.[5]

A turning point in the history of the brigade came in late June when a new commander was named to lead it. Kirkland's recovery from his Cold Harbor wound would take some time, and Faribault simply was not able to hone the brigade into a sharp fighting instrument. Col. William MacRae of the 15th North Carolina was ordered to replace Faribault on June 27. He was no stranger to the brigade, having led Cooke's men in their snowball battle against Kirkland the preceding March. He was appointed temporarily to the rank of brigadier general with the understanding that his tenure as commander of the brigade might be temporary as well, depending on how soon Kirkland recovered. MacRae accepted these provisions, tied up his business in the 15th, and reported for duty on June 29.[6]

MacRae arrived as the brigade was setting out to accompany a wagon train bringing supplies to Lee's army. Grant's temporary break of the Weldon Railroad forced the Rebels to haul corn from Stony Creek, a station some twenty miles south of Petersburg, around the rupture. Kirkland's men expected to be gone three days. MacRae rode up just as the brigade moved out of its camp, and he immediately took charge of the men. Faribault had allowed the boys to ride in the empty wagons, but MacRae refused to accept this. He gruffly ordered them out and set the column moving at a brisk pace to the south. Staff officer Louis G.

Young was impressed. MacRae's "quick manner" and his "stringent regulations for the march" gave him "the opportunity of establishing his control" on his first day in command. "Officers and men felt that laxity of discipline was at an end, and to the consequent grumbling in camp by a few, succeeded an absolute faith in the commander. His exact discipline prepared them for the trying ordeal through which they were to pass from now to the end."[7]

MacRae's first march with his new brigade was indeed a trying ordeal. The heat was awful those last days of June, and the short excursion to Stony Creek turned into a "terrible" experience, according to Lemuel Hoyle. Quite a few men broke down and fainted from the heat and exhaustion, but they managed to bring the corn to Lee's army without interference from the Federals. They ate a mountain of corn pone baked by the Moravian band of the 26th North Carolina and then had a cool bath in the Appomattox River.[8]

The next four weeks gave MacRae an opportunity to become acquainted with his new command. He retained most of Kirkland's staff, including Louis G. Young. Kirkland had taken his aide-de-camp with him, so MacRae appointed Lt. Joseph E. Porter. MacRae kept Kirkland's other appointee, Capt. Fred Nash, but he was later transferred by the War Department to another brigade. Capt. Alexander T. Cunningham replaced Nash as ordnance officer. A new surgeon, Dr. John Wilson, was acquired as well; but Maj. W. J. Baker remained as commissary, and Maj. George P. Collins stayed on as assistant quartermaster.[9]

Many members of the brigade already knew MacRae. Charles M. Stedman had first noticed him at the battle of Bristoe Station. "He won the love and admiration of all who upon that day witnessed his splendid conduct," recalled Stedman. MacRae returned the favor by telling Stedman that he noticed the bravery of the 44th North Carolina on that occasion as well. This regiment became his favorite while he commanded Kirkland's brigade, and he often stayed near its colors while under fire.

MacRae led a life very different from that of either Pettigrew or Kirkland. His Scots ancestors had fought in battles dating back to the thirteenth century, including Culloden and Waterloo, and had served in several Highland regiments of the British army. William MacRae was born in Wilmington on September 9, 1834. His father, Alexander, had served in the War of 1812 and, at age seventy, had led a battalion of infantry in the early months of the Civil War. Alexander made his mark in life mostly by working as a civil engineer and serving as president of the Wilmington and Weldon Railroad. William followed in his father's footsteps. He moved to Philadelphia at age sixteen to learn how to build locomotives and returned to Alexander's railroad several years later to work as a machinist.

William later studied civil engineering and worked with his father and brothers on railroads throughout the South.

The war brought the MacRae clan into action. All of William's eight brothers served either in the army or the navy; one even joined a Federal unit. William enrolled as a private in the Monroe Light Infantry, which became Company B, 15th North Carolina, but was quickly elected its captain. He soon was promoted lieutenant colonel of the regiment and saw action at Malvern Hill, Second Manassas, and South Mountain. MacRae temporarily commanded his brigade, led by Brig. Gen. Thomas R. R. Cobb, at Sharpsburg. The 15th was transferred to Cooke's brigade in the fall of 1862 and fought at Fredericksburg. Soon after, MacRae was promoted colonel of his regiment. Cooke's command was shifted to South Carolina to guard supply lines for much of the spring and summer of 1863 before it was brought back to Lee's army.

Like Pettigrew, MacRae was a bachelor who devoted his life to his work. MacRae was a practical and frank person, befitting his engineering talents. He hated to see anyone advance his career for reasons other than "actual merit" and was "very pronounced in his views about such matters." This was one reason he had risen slowly. Modest and "unobtrusive," his "chief aim was to do his duty," according to Stedman. "I have yet to hear of a single instance where merit alone has procured a Brigadier Generalship in our army," MacRae wrote a year before he became commander of the brigade. "Take the Brigadiers in our service as a class[.] I do think they are a greater set of asses than any other grade in the army can boast." He wrote his brother Don that it "would be less chimerical . . . to dream of striking a rich gold mine in 'Endor' than to hope for me ever to attain the position of Brig. Gen. I am as high now as merit can carry me." He liked to report the good things his superiors said of him, but he also insisted that he cared "little for the oppinion of the world generally." Only the "approbation of my Brothers & what few friends I may have" meant anything to him.[10]

MacRae was fully aware that his new brigade might be taken from him very soon. He reminded brother Don that he did not yet have a permanent general's commission and Kirkland was due to report by August 1. Although only a temporary commander, MacRae organized a corps of sharpshooters for the brigade. This tactic was taken up by other brigade leaders as well. They realized that the task of skirmishing had become enormously important now that the opposing armies were constantly within striking distance of each other. The corps consisted of eighty men selected for their performance under fire. Each member wore a gold cross sewn onto his left sleeve, and the names of each battle he fought in were also sewn onto his clothing. Charles Stedman later reported that the sharpshooters were armed with repeating rifles, but there is no evidence to support that claim. They were given special privileges to instill a strong sense of unit pride. Capt. Thomas Lilly of Company K, 26th North Carolina, was named commander of the corps. Lieutenants were drawn from each of the other regiments in the brigade except the 44th North Carolina.[11]

It was almost inevitable that the men of Kirkland's brigade would like their new leader. Lane evaluated him thusly: "His voice was like that of a woman; he was small in person, and quick in action. . . . He could place his command in position quicker and infuse more of his fighting qualities into his men, than any officer I ever saw. His presence with his troops seemed to dispel all fear, and to inspire every one with a desire for the fray." Another member of the brigade recalled that MacRae "changed the physical expression of the whole command in less than two weeks, and gave the men infinite faith in him and themselves, which was never lost." His disciplinary policy was as strict as that of Pettigrew, thought the commander of the Bethel Regiment, but much stronger than that of Kirkland. Perhaps that was why the men responded so magically to MacRae's touch. Their spirit and tone had deteriorated during the several months that Kirkland had commanded the brigade.[12]

The men remained in reserve behind Heth's division line for several days after they returned from Stony Creek. They were ordered into the trenches near the Weldon Railroad on July 8 and endured heavy artillery fire during the morning and skirmishing during the night. The same occurred the next day as well. MacRae was ordered to move his command five miles south along the railroad track; it stayed there for two days and then returned to its old position.[13]

Payday arrived soon after this abortive move down the railroad. The members of the 26th Regimental Band had to wait several days before their officers found the money to pay what Julius Linebach called "our pitifully small wages." By late July the Moravians were hardly in any condition to be seen, as their clothes were absolutely worn out. Linebach warned in a letter home that he would "soon be reduced to the condition of the little niggers one often sees, who can boast of the possession of but a single garment." He had only one complete shirt and a pair of drawers. "All other garments I possess only in part." His coat sleeves were reinforced with so many strips of extra material that they were multicolored. Of his pants he wrote, "It is not worth while to say where they have given out,— if I have not for some time been flying a flag of truce in the rear, it was because my drawers happened to be whole at the right place." Linebach's footwear was in worse condition. "Socks, heel-less and toe-less, and shoes,— one having sole & body tied together with strings and the other badly run down & bursted."[14]

Linebach would have to string up his uniform and prepare for action. Grant

Brig. Gen. William MacRae. The third and last commander of the brigade, MacRae was its most brilliant battlefield leader and an unsung hero of Lee's army during the Petersburg campaign. (NCDAH)

sent the Second Corps to the north side of the James on the evening of July 26 to divert Lee's attention from an attack planned on the Ninth Corps front, where the Federals had dug a mine to blow a hole in Lee's line. When fighting broke out at Deep Bottom the next morning, Lee was forced to shift Heth's division to bolster his left wing. MacRae received the order to march at 1:00 P.M. on July 27 and set out an hour later. The men reached the pike between Petersburg and Richmond and "marched verry hard" northward. They crossed the James on a pontoon bridge at midnight and reached the lines at Deep Bottom just after dawn. It had been a difficult twenty-mile march on corn bread and fat bacon. The brigade engaged in heavy skirmishing for a couple of hours on the afternoon of July 28 and constantly expected an attack; but the battle of Deep Bottom was winding down, and the men busied themselves with strengthening fortifications.[15]

In the middle of all this excitement, a vote was taken among the North Carolina soldiers of Lee's army. In MacRae's command the balloting for governor went heavily in Vance's favor. He won 200 votes in the 26th, compared with only 14 for William Holden. The Bethel Regiment handed Vance a similar majority, 199 of 232 votes cast. The 44th North Carolina tallied 93 votes for Vance and 18 for Holden, while the 47th North Carolina counted 35 votes for the governor and none for his opponent. The 52nd North Carolina cast 72 ballots for Vance and 20 for Holden. Vance received more than 13,000 of the 15,000 votes cast by soldiers in the field. The *Raleigh Daily Confederate* noted that a lot of exhausted stragglers could not keep up with their regiments on the march to Deep Bottom and never had an opportunity to vote. If not for that, the editor speculated, Vance's majority would have been even greater.[16]

But there were indications that the Holden vote was artificially limited by the candidate's antiwar stance. Two men deserted from the 52nd North Carolina that night because they had not been allowed to vote for Vance's opponent. When Hancock questioned them about this important issue, they said that only the character of company-level officers determined whether Holden supporters were allowed to cast their ballots. Only seventeen men in Company K, 44th North Carolina, were willing to vote, and they all cast ballots for Vance. It is quite possible that those who refused to vote were Holden supporters.[17]

The confrontation at Deep Bottom ended on July 29 when the Second Corps slipped back across the James after nightfall. The mine was exploded early the next morning with devastating results. It tore a gap in the Confederate line, but the follow-up assault was tragically botched, giving Lee a chance to hurry reinforcements to the breach. Bloody counterattacks sealed the hole by evening. MacRae's brigade was recalled to the south side of the James as a result of the attack. The men left their position on New Market Road at noon and crossed the river at Chaffin's Bluff on July 30. They struck the railroad about four miles away and waited for a train, boarding the cars at 10:00 P.M. The engine rolled so slowly that it was the middle of the night before they marched over the Appomattox River and through town. The hurried move wore on the men. Julius Linebach's old clothes nearly disintegrated under the pressure, and his "greasy haversack" soiled them. His face was "discolored by heat, dust & perspiration." Many men broke down under the oppressive sun. The brigade finally reached its assigned place in the trenches near the mine explosion at dawn on July 31. It had missed the terrible fighting at the crater, much to the relief of Gus Jarratt.[18]

The brigade was shoved into the trenches immediately to the right of the crater, where the Federal fortifications were only 150 yards away. After three days the men were pulled out and sent to the left to act as a reserve. Here they bivouacked in a ravine near the same Camp French that had been their home for so many months in 1862. Federal artillery and even infantry fire often sailed over their heads. One band member's music book was hit by a bullet while he used it as a pillow. The short rest in the ravine ended when MacRae relieved Cooke's brigade in the trenches at 10:00 P.M. on August 9. The men came under constant short-range fire the next day and returned it with vigor. Benjamin H. Freeman proudly wrote home, "I shot a Yankee a few minutes ago." He called this part of the line a "trublesome" place; "you can not raise your head above the brestworks what it is shot at." They had to approach and leave the line by using covered ways.[19]

The opposing lines were too close to allow MacRae to throw out his pickets; thus the skirmishing was done by the main battle line. One-third of the men had to be on duty in the trenches at all times, manning the fire steps by shifts. Artillery opened each morning at 3:00 A.M. and fired until dawn. Then the mortars pummeled shells into the works. The fortifications were strong against field artillery, but only bombproofs dug into the earth behind the lines could protect the men from mortar shells. "We have to ly in our trenches day and knight, rain or shine, hot or cold," reported a member of the 26th North Carolina. "Thair is som killed or wounded more or less every day by mortar shells or sharp shooters. The men have becom so careless, they don car much for any thing."[20]

Chaplain Webb of the 44th North Carolina found plenty of brigade members who were happy to avoid enemy fire. "They burrow in the ground the same as rats," he informed his sweetheart, Jennie; "the whole earth is full of caves, and when they hear a mortar shell coming, every man gets to his hole." Webb also caught his first sight of a black man in a U.S. uniform. Black regiments serving in the Ninth Corps opposed MacRae's brigade on this part of the line. "These negroes sometimes will jump out and dance and hollow to our men, calling them rebels, saying they are as free as we are."[21]

Despite the dangers, these veteran troops grew accustomed to duty in the trenches. The historians of the Bethel Regiment noted that the men "learned to sleep as soundly and as peacefully in these trenches as they were accustomed to do in camp. One can get used to anything." Indeed, J. S. Bartlett admitted that duty in the trenches became boring after a while. To amuse themselves the men took potshots at the green walnuts hanging from one of the few trees left standing in the vicinity. They cooked a disgusting meal of "growley," a mixture of hardtack, water, and meat grease, on open fires. Now and then the Federal snipers amused themselves by firing at the smoke and knocking dirt into the frying pan. MacRae kept his men in the trenches for three days before pulling them out on August 13 for rest. An inspection report indicated that there were 1,593 men in the brigade. The Bethel Regiment had 393, the 26th had 294, the 44th counted 338, the 47th had 356, and the 52nd fielded 212. The Tar Heels returned to the trenches on August 18 to continue the cycle of recuperation and duty that was typical of an army defending fortified lines.[22]

Kirkland recuperated quickly and expected to return to his command by early August. This did not please Louis G. Young, who had come to appreciate MacRae's talents. Young told his mother that MacRae was "so much more intelligent than my own commander, that his society affords much greater pleasure &

profit, which his other good qualities attach me to him, notwithstanding my efforts to avoid it." Young had been so deeply hurt by Pettigrew's death that he did not want to become devoted to MacRae, but he could not resist it. There was a widespread feeling in the brigade that MacRae should stay, even though some soldiers, such as Benjamin H. Freeman, still felt some loyalty to Kirkland.[23]

Kirkland was ready for duty by August 13, but by then the authorities had decided MacRae should continue in command. Just as Pettigrew had had to give way to Pender, Kirkland had to accept the fact that his injury had opened the way for a more energetic leader. Even though MacRae had not yet fought a battle with the brigade, he had so improved its efficiency and morale that his superiors knew he was the right man for the job. His temporary rank of brigadier general became permanent and was postdated to June 22. Gen. Pierre Gustave Toutant Beauregard had earlier requested that MacRae serve in his command on another part of the Petersburg line. When that was no longer an option, he asked for Kirkland instead. Thus this well-meaning officer retained his rank and command level and was assigned to lead James Martin's brigade in Hoke's division. Few members of MacRae's brigade, as the unit formally became known, really regretted Kirkland's departure.[24]

Kirkland had a full career throughout the rest of the war. His brigade was stationed in the trenches north of the James River until December 1864, when it was transferred to Wilmington. This important port city was under threat by a large Union force, and Kirkland took a prominent part in the ultimately futile effort to save it. He participated in the final battles in North Carolina at Wise's Fork and Bentonville during March 1865.[25]

Of the three permanent commanders of the brigade, Kirkland marked its history the least. He was a very competent but unremarkable leader. Personally brave, he failed to excel in administration or tactical prowess or in promoting a strong esprit de corps among the men. This was partly the result of his tendency to get wounded. Kirkland was severely injured at Bristoe Station, only a month after he took charge of the brigade, and did not return until the following February. He was again wounded at Cold Harbor only four months later. Kirkland was absent recuperating from battle injuries for six of the eleven months he led the brigade. With that disadvantage, even a man of more energy and talent would have found it difficult to make his mark on the command.

The men would soon see their new commander in battle. Grant decided to make another try at the Weldon Railroad in late August, and he sent the Second Corps once again to Deep Bottom while moving Warren's Fifth Corps to the track. Warren's men easily planted themselves around Globe Tavern, about eight miles from town, on August 18. Their success brought an immediate response. Hill ordered Heth to take two brigades and drive the Yankees away, unaware that four divisions were assembled at Globe Tavern. Heth formed Davis and Walker at the W. P. Davis house, where Vaughan Road angled to the southwest from the Weldon Railroad and its parallel, Halifax Road. South of the Davis house was a large cornfield, then a belt of thick timber, then a clearing surrounding Globe Tavern. The Rebels overran two lines of hastily constructed breastworks, but a Union counterattack pushed them back to the cornfield. Another attack was launched on August 19 with five brigades, but Warren received help from the Ninth Corps. Davis and Walker duplicated their actions of the previous day, with a temporary Rebel success followed by a Union counterattack.[26]

Hill refused to give up. Another, larger effort took a day and two nights to prepare. Warren tightened his defensive position, razing the two lines of crude breastworks in the woods and building a much stronger line of earthworks in the clearing. The Unionists placed the new fortification on top of a gentle slope and cut more timber from the southern edge of the belt of trees to increase their field of fire. Warren even ordered telegraph wire to be stretched between the stumps in front of his defenses to trip up attacking Rebels.[27]

Cooke and MacRae replaced Davis and Walker on the battlefield. MacRae's men had spent the previous days manning their usual hot spot to the right of the crater, enduring "a ceaseless fire day and night." A man in the 26th North Carolina reported that he "couden look over the breste works with oute beeing shot in the head." At times the level of skirmish fire and artillery practice was "giste like a Reglar fite." At least one or two men were struck each day in Lane's regiment, and the casualty figures were likely the same in MacRae's other units.[28]

The men left their cramped ditches on the night of August 20 through the covered way to a ravine about a quarter-mile to the rear. There they formed a marching column and set out at a brisk pace despite their fatigue. They reached the vicinity of the Davis house before dawn and slept in their blankets among the trees until daylight. Seeing the cornfield, many hungry soldiers roused themselves and slipped away to pick whatever ears were still lying in the marched-over field. J. S. Bartlett built a little fire, peeled the shuck halfway, and roasted the corn by laying it directly on the burning embers. Orders were shouted to assemble before his breakfast was ready.[29]

The Confederate battle plan for Sunday, August 21, called for Heth to attack along the railroad with three brigades, while other Confederate units would slash into the Union left. The Rebel guns opened at 7:30 A.M., just as MacRae's men moved into the cornfield. Union artillery immediately opened in reply, and the Tar Heels dropped to the ground. Many later recalled this as one of the worst shellings they ever endured. T. W. Setser of the 26th thought he "would bee kill ever minute, for the ball giste ploude the ground all a round mee."[30]

MacRae's brigade was in place west of the railroad, and Brig. Gen. Matt W. Ransom's North Carolina brigade of Maj. Gen. Bushrod Johnson's division, led by Col. John L. Harris, was placed east of the track. Cooke's men took position behind Harris as a reserve. The Federals had left a skirmish line, manned by the Purnell Legion of Maryland and the 146th New York, in the partially demolished line of works just inside the northern edge of the thicket. Warren's battle line waited in its newly constructed works some 700 yards south. Col. Frederick Winthrop's brigade of New York and Maryland volunteers, along with several regiments of regular infantry, held the trenches west of the railroad.[31]

The initial Confederate attack on Warren's left was repulsed, but Heth ordered his men forward anyway. The sky was clear after several days of intermittent rain. MacRae sent his corps of sharpshooters ahead and ordered his men to charge. They had no difficulty pushing the Maryland and New York skirmishers out of the line of razed works; "tha run as soon as we got in Site of them," crowed T. W. Setser. Then the Tar Heels plunged into the thicket. John Foster of the 52nd North Carolina called this an attack "through the open field and woods mud and swamps." MacRae easily took the second line of razed works, located just inside the southern edge of the timber.[32]

MacRae now surveyed the open field, crisscrossed with wired stumps, leading to the heavy earthworks. Harris's men were nowhere to be seen; their progress had been slowed by the trees and stiff Union skirmishing. Louis G. Young put it well after the war when he wrote, "The brigade found itself alone in front of the works, too weak to go on and too near to retreat"; so MacRae gave the order to advance. His men immediately came under a hail of cannon fire. Young wrote that they "rushed for the works and would have gone there, probably to their destruction," if the artillery fire had not been so heavy. There was a moment when the urge to take on the heavy odds conflicted with their desire to survive the battle of Globe Tavern. Some of the sharpshooters reached a shallow ravine near the Union line, but the brigade could not follow them. The men stopped, hesitated, and then retired quickly to the edge of the trees.[33]

MacRae's men took shelter behind the partly demolished line of Union works just inside the southern edge of the tree cover. For the rest of the day the Tar Heels sheltered themselves from the rain of shells that Warren's guns pumped into the woods. "I tell you tha made the grape and Canister fly," reported T. W. Setser; "tha was a lode of grape Struck the breste work rite in front of mee, kill a man on my lefte and nock mee down, and wounded Captain [Romulus M.]

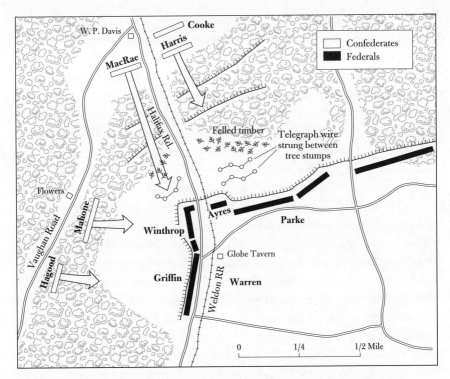

MAP 11.1 The Battle of Globe Tavern, August 21, 1864

Tuttle, but never hurte mee eny hardley." Tuttle was severely injured in the left side but survived his wound. The Richardson brothers of Company B, 26th North Carolina, were not so lucky. A shell hit the works and broke through directly in front of them as they lay side by side. Sgt. Brinkly J. Richardson was decapitated, and Pvt. E. R. Richardson was horribly mangled. The top of his head was smashed by a chunk of wood, "cutting an ugly gash & fracturing the skull, & also striking his eye." At times Confederate artillery also dropped a few shells unintentionally onto MacRae's position, shielded as it was from their view by the belt of trees.[34]

The boom of cannon and the spattering of rifle fire continued all day as the summer sun filtered through the trees. Harris's brigade came up to the edge of the woods sometime after MacRae's did so, but there was no opportunity to push forward and attack over the open ground. Toward evening the Bethel Regiment sent pickets westward into the woods and captured several Federal skirmishers. There was no other contact between MacRae's men and the bulk of Winthrop's command. The Tar Heels waited until dusk gave them an opportunity to withdraw. Colonel Martin of the 11th North Carolina later commented that Warren missed an excellent opportunity to gobble up the brigade.[35]

The withdrawal was easy for almost everyone except Woodson Garrett of Company G, 11th North Carolina. He had become a brigade sharpshooter because his brother Esau had been wounded in the lungs at Gettysburg, was captured, and died a few days later. This loss changed his personality; "he brooded over it and became sullen and embittered," commented Lt. Duncan C. Waddell, "and it seemed that the only object in life he had was to revenge his brother's death. He became reckless and was never so well pleased as when in battle." Garrett was so exhausted that he fell asleep in the shallow ravine occupied by the sharpshooters that night and was left behind in the retreat. When the Federals reoccupied the ground at dawn, Garrett put on a Union uniform he had earlier taken from a dead Yankee and carefully made his way toward the Confederate lines. The Davis cornfield was a no-man's-land between the contending forces, but Garrett told the Federals he wanted to search for roasting ears when they told him it was too dangerous to venture there. Finding a drunken Yankee looking for breakfast among the cornstalks, Garrett cajoled him into walking with him so he could use him as cover. When the man finally realized that the pair were reaching the Rebel position, he resisted, but Garrett drew his gun and forced him on. He managed to evade capture and bring in a prisoner at the same time. Garrett raised his hat in token of surrender when he neared MacRae's command and was allowed to come in.[36]

Garrett's escape was a memorable ending to an otherwise dismal fight. The Tar Heels did not return to the crater but were assigned a spot familiar from the early days of the Petersburg campaign, near the lead mine. Lee would need to mass more strength on his far right than before, given Grant's tendency to move west.[37]

The toll of casualties was muted by the circumstances of the battle. Much of the time the men were taking shelter on the ground, in the Union trench, or under the cover of trees. Colonel Lane was hit in the right leg but retained command of the 26th. Pvt. Jesse Souther of Company C was hit on his breast by a shell fragment, "tearing him open so his bowels and lungs fell out." MacRae's brigade lost 10 killed, 30 wounded, and 6 captured, for a total of 46, according to the service records. But other reports show that the 26th North Carolina lost 6 killed and 21 wounded, the Bethel Regiment suffered 30 casualties, and the 44th North Carolina lost 7 killed and 21 wounded. There are no comparable estimates for the remaining two regiments. If these reports are accurate, then the brigade lost well over 100 men. Band member Edward Peterson told his brother that records listed a total of 103 men brought to the brigade hospital, 15 of whom died of their injuries by the next day.[38]

"I shall long remember this Sunday morning," exclaimed Edward Peterson. He worked in the field hospital where the doctors "had their hands full again, in amputating arms, & legs, some of the men were most horribly mutilated, by shell, inflicting terrible wounds." Peterson watched in amazement as the surgeons worked on E. R. Richardson, the man whose head was smashed by a chunk of log. "I saw them cut his scalp open, & examine his skull & I saw it was all full of cracks, like ice will crack if you throw a stone on it." Eighteen-year-old Richardson died a few hours later. Peterson examined a piece of skull that the surgeons had cut out of another man's head. It "would have weighed half a pound," yet the patient was alive and doing fairly well. Another soldier had his leg "mashed into a jelly," which had to be amputated. The man died, but "no one knew where he belonged to, at last he was claimed in the 44th reg." Other soldiers had their feet and hands shot away by artillery rounds, and a member of the 26th North Carolina lost an arm. He nevertheless was in good spirits and only regretted that it was his right arm. "I assisted in dressing him in a new shirt, before he was sent off." Peterson also helped to bury the dead in "rough pine, flat top coffins" that had been shipped to the field hospital that morning.[39]

Chaplain Webb had visited the Third Corps guardhouse that Sunday morning to minister to prisoners, not knowing that a battle was in prospect. As soon as the sound of artillery fire drifted up from Globe Tavern, Webb rushed to the brigade hospital and found several men he had baptized the previous winter among the wounded. When a severe rainstorm came over the area that night, the wounded suffered even more. They were lying on the open ground, the few scattered candles were quickly extinguished by the rush of wind, and hail and rain pelted them without mercy. Because it was pitch dark, no one could move "for fear you would hurt some one, and I could but stand still and lift up my heart in prayer to the Ruler of the storm."[40]

Barely recovered from the fight, the brigade dug new works to extend Lee's right wing and picketed the no-man's-land between it and Warren's corps. A member of the 44th North Carolina deserted from his picket post on the night of August 22; perhaps he was disgusted with the heavy fighting that seemed to have resulted in no gain and decided to take himself out of the war. He passed on information about MacRae's location to a Federal provost before being shipped off to prison.[41]

Another deserter was not so fortunate. Pvt. David W. Wells of Company C, 26th North Carolina, had decamped twenty months earlier but was not arrested until July 1864. A court-martial sentenced the twenty-one-year-old Wilkes Countian to death, and he was executed on August 23. The Moravian band played at the event. "So you see," wrote Edward Peterson to his brother, "its killing time in the army, the Yankees kill our men, & we also kill them, to get rid of them. These are strange times, not so?"[42]

The killing would continue, for Grant ordered the Second Corps to make another lodgment on the tracks south of Globe Tavern to widen the breach in Lee's supply line. Hancock's men tore up track as they went and were grouped in a defensive position around Reams Station by August 24. They were separated from Warren's corps and the rest of Meade's army and were protected by inadequate earthworks. The fortifications here, forming a three-sided position encompassing a small space, had been built by the Sixth Corps in June and were badly eroded. The western face was nearly a mile long and lay just west of the track. Depot Road bisected the middle of this western face, and there was a long traverse stretching west to east south of the road. The track ran through a cut as much as thirteen feet deep north of Depot Road and over an embankment up to six feet high south of the road. Both features made it difficult for the Federals to move reinforcements up to the fortifications, but they also provided ready-made shelter for a second line of infantry behind the works. The result was that Hancock's 6,500 infantry and 2,000 cavalry were constricted in a small defensive position like settlers cowering in a circled wagon train. Lee decided to strike this isolated corps with eight brigades, including Cooke's and MacRae's.[43]

MacRae's men were doing their normal duty of picketing and digging earthworks on August 24 when the order arrived to prepare for the field. They started at 4:00 P.M. and marched steadily along Squirrel Level Road and then Vaughan Road to avoid detection by Federal pickets. Heth ordered them to bivouac at midnight near Armstrong's Mill on Hatcher's Run. The men rolled into their army blankets while the supply wagons caught up with them sometime during the night, but that did not prevent the hungry soldiers from stripping a "thriving crop of corn" from a nearby field the next morning. Benjamin Wesley Justice was astonished by their efficiency; "not a ear, not a stalk, scarcely a blade was to be seen" after they finished. The soldiers gobbled up the corn and fed the stalks to the draft animals.[44]

Heth's two brigades started from Armstrong's Mill just after dawn on Thursday, August 25. They stopped for rest at Gravel Run about noon. Here a courier from Hill rode up and delivered an order for haste. The wagons were left behind, and the infantry took the road and pushed ahead. Wilcox's division was already engaged at Reams Station, and Heth's men were needed. They could hear the sound of sharpshooting when they were still a mile from the battlefield, and they arrived on the scene at 3:00 P.M.[45]

Two hours earlier Wilcox had sent three of his brigades to attack the Federal west face north of Depot Road. Hancock had little difficulty repelling this assault. Now sharpshooters from several brigades were sent to skirmish with the Federals while Heth positioned his men and worked out a plan of attack with Wilcox. Hill was on the field but felt very ill, so the responsibility for managing the battle fell onto Wilcox's and Heth's shoulders. Fortunately Heth was careful to involve Cooke and MacRae in the planning. Based on the optimism of his two brigade leaders, Heth assured Hill that the Federal position could be taken.

The approach to the Federal lines was complicated by a belt of pine trees that extended northward from Depot Road and through which most of the attacking force would have to crawl. Beyond the trees was a cornfield nearly 100 yards wide fronting the Union works. The belt of trees ended about 100 yards north of Depot Road but did not continue south of it. There the flat land was much more open for a longer distance before the Federals, with only a few clumps of pines to break up the landscape. Heth and Wilcox deployed in and around the woods. Cooke took position to the north of Depot Road; his left wing was in the belt of trees, but his two right regiments, the 15th and 46th North Carolina, were in the open ground. To his left Lane's brigade, temporarily under Brig. Gen. James E. Conner, was completely deployed in the trees. MacRae placed his men to the right and rear of Cooke, astride Depot Road and entirely in the open. The 47th North Carolina was on MacRae's right, the 44th North Carolina was in the center, and the Bethel Regiment was on the left. But the exact positions of the other two regiments were not reported. MacRae was at least 300 yards from the Union line.[46]

While this deployment took place, MacRae sent out his corps of sharpshooters to help Wilcox's skirmishers. For nearly two hours the Rebel marksmen kept up a harassing fire that exhausted the Union infantry and forced them to keep their heads down behind the earthworks. Rebel artillery also advanced to within 250 yards of the Federal position. It did little damage except to force the Union gunners to return fire and thus expose them behind the poorly constructed earthworks. This exhausted their ammunition and their strength.[47]

MacRae personally reconnoitered the ground. His engineering talents enabled him to analyze the lay of the land, and he had the ability to visualize what his men needed to do. He took charge of the right wing of the brigade and told Louis G. Young to see to the left. Young was to do exactly as his commander, walk up and down the line and tell the men that "beyond the wood was an open field over which they must pass before reaching the enemy; that while advancing . . . they must be quiet, but when the field was reached, the charge would begin, and then every man must yell as though he were a division in himself, dash for the enemy's works, and not fire until there." Young was impressed with their reaction to this news. "As I looked into the eyes of the men while giving them these unusual instructions, it was easy to see that the works would be taken."[48]

MacRae carefully pointed out to the men of the right wing what they should do. " 'Don't fire a gun,' " he cautioned, " 'but dash for the enemy.' " This brought a shout of " 'All right, General; we will go there.' " Stedman recalled that the soldiers "were in high spirits, jesting and laughing, and ready to move on an instant's notice." Even Heth could tell that the Tar Heels were unusually eager for the fight. "The coolness and determination as evinced by all and expressed by many officers and men as I passed down the line, a few minutes before the attack was made, carried with it a conviction of success."[49]

The Federals opposite MacRae's brigade were far less enthusiastic for the fray. All the units were filled with recent draftees and substitutes, and the old veterans were tired. Lt. Col. K. Oscar Broady's brigade of Brig. Gen. Nelson A. Miles's division held the line from the position of the 10th Massachusetts Battery northward. The Bay State gunners were somewhere between the traverse and Depot Road. Broady placed the 7th New York Heavy Artillery on his left, then the 145th Pennsylvania and the 66th New York. The last regiment was at Depot Road. Two more of Broady's regiments were on the skirmish line, and two others were in a secondary line to the rear at the railroad embankment. Maj. John B. Byron's Consolidated Brigade, recently made by combining the old Second and Third Brigades of Miles's division, was positioned north of Depot Road. The former Third Brigade held the left of Byron's line from Depot Road northward and consisted of the 7th, 39th, 52nd, 57th, 111th, 125th, and 126th New York. The former Second Brigade, consisting of three more New York regiments, made up the right wing of Byron's Consolidated Brigade. A secondary line at the railroad cut, consisting of Lt. Col. Horace P. Rugg's brigade of Gibbon's division, was several yards behind Byron's weak line. MacRae's attack would hit Broady's right and Byron's left.[50]

The Rebel artillery had been firing for fifteen minutes when the infantry began its final preparation for the attack. A peculiar urge led the division commander to walk up to the skirmish line while the sharpshooters were firing. He decided that a battle flag was needed there to inspire the troops and ordered Lieutenant Waddell of the 11th North Carolina to have one brought up. Soon the colors of the 26th North Carolina arrived, and Heth insisted on taking the flag himself. Color-bearer Thomas Minton of Company C refused to give it up. " 'General, tell me where you want the flag to go and I will take it. I won't surrender up my colors.' " Heth's repeated orders were met with the same obstinate refusal. Finally recognizing that Minton had him stymied, Heth took him by the arm and said, " 'Come on then, we will carry the colors together.' " The division leader was as good as his word. He remained on the skirmish line until the attack started and helped Minton wave the colors to and fro as an inspiration for the

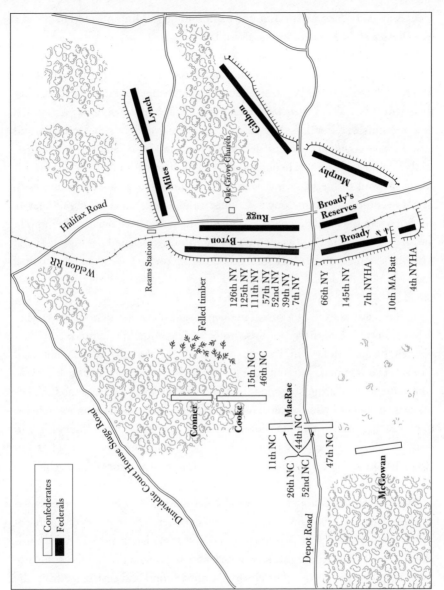

Confederates
Federals

Dinwiddie Court House Stage Road

Weldon RR

Halifax Road

Reams Station

Oak Grove Church

Felled timber

Lynch

Miles

Gibbon

Murphy

Rugg

Byron

Broady's Reserves

Broady

126th NY
125th NY
111th NY
57th NY
52nd NY
39th NY
7th NY

66th NY
145th NY
7th NYHA
10th MA Batt
4th NYHA

15th NC
46th NC

Conner

Cooke

MacRae

11th NC
26th NC
52nd NC
44th NC
47th NC

Depot Road

McGowan

MAP 11.2 The Battle of Reams Station, August 25, 1864

men. Both color-bearers survived the battle, although Minton would be killed a month later at the battle of Burgess's Mill.[51]

Orders arrived to start the infantry assault after the artillery had fired for about a half-hour. It was nearly 5:30 and not much daylight was left, but the men of MacRae's brigade never began an attack with such utter confidence in their ability to win. They were instructed to wait until Cooke's and Conner's men started before setting out, but those two brigades were delayed by the belt of pines and already were taking many casualties. MacRae waited impatiently for his compatriots to clear the woods. He noticed that the 15th and 46th North Carolina, directly in front of his left wing, were also waiting. His Scots blood aroused, MacRae could stand it no longer. Conner's and Cooke's men were mercilessly shot down in the tangled woods and needed help. MacRae decided to jump in and help the advance in his own way. "The thought flashed through General MacRae's mind that this had gone far enough," Young later recalled. "'I shall wait no longer for orders,'" he told the staff officer, "'give the order to advance at once.'"[52]

The brigade started at a run. The men forgot their instructions and began yelling "in their eagerness" to press home the assault. No one fired; they "absolutely dashed along," in Young's words. This irresistible force compelled Cooke's two regiments directly in front of MacRae's left wing to attack as well. Intermittent small arms fire sailed toward them, but most of it was too high because the Federals had become demoralized by two hours of sniping and refused to expose themselves to aim accurately. Yet there was enough artillery fire and musketry coming obliquely from better Federal units on either side of Depot Road to force the 15th and 46th North Carolina to retreat before they reached the earthworks.[53]

Even this was not enough to deter MacRae's brigade, which was determined to climb the parapets at any cost. Now the full benefit of two hours of sniping at the Yankees paid off. The Federal guns ran out of canister, and MacRae's hard-driving troops had an opportunity to race over the open ground with comparatively few casualties. The 47th North Carolina found stiff resistance from the 66th New York, immediately south of Depot Road, and was forced to stop only a few yards short of the works in order to open fire. The color-bearer was shot down, and Lt. Thomas Taylor of Company K grabbed the flag. The rest of MacRae's command found a weak spot in the defenses. The draftees and substitutes who filled the left wing of Byron's Consolidated Brigade continued to shoot wildly into the air. MacRae's desperate Tar Heels sensed this was the key to the battle and homed in on them. Charles Stedman remembered that his comrades in the 44th North Carolina "mounted the entrenchments and precipitated themselves amongst the Federal infantry." The Yankees "seemed to be dazed by the vehemence of the attack, and made a very feeble resistance after their ranks were reached." The left wing of the Consolidated Brigade fled without ceremony. This weakened the resolve of the 66th New York, whose flank was now exposed, and the 47th North Carolina resumed its advance. Lieutenant Taylor planted the flag on top of the parapet in triumph.[54]

All of MacRae's brigade was now firmly lodged in one section of the Union position, but only the first line had been breached. Two regiments from the secondary line, the 36th Wisconsin and the 20th Massachusetts of Rugg's brigade, offered at least some resistance from the railroad cut less than fifty yards away. The 66th New York also had fallen back to the railroad embankment, where it held firmly, blocking the Tar Heels from advancing farther. Unable to exploit his success by proceeding forward, MacRae instructed his right wing to extend the breach by advancing southward. He ordered the men to move in three columns, one to go in front of the parapet, one to move quickly along the top of the earthwork, and another to advance down the trench itself. This inspired maneuver outflanked the rest of Broady's brigade, regiment by regiment, and cleared a long stretch of the works. The Tar Heels had to stop at the traverse where the 4th New York Heavy Artillery held firm, protected by the embankment that ran diagonally to the east.[55]

The Carolinians attacked the 10th Massachusetts Battery, which was trying to enfilade the trench line and chew up the advancing Tar Heels with its few remaining rounds of canister. MacRae ordered the guns taken, and the 44th North Carolina responded. The Yankee artillerists were unsupported by infantry, but many of them refused to surrender and had to be physically subdued. The battery commander bravely remained on horseback, shouting encouragement to his men. MacRae, Robert Bingham, and Capt. William P. Oldham of Company K, 44th North Carolina, were among the first to reach the guns. They tried to take the commander prisoner, but a stray bullet mortally wounded the Yankee. The guns were secured, and a number of sharpshooters turned them eastward to fire on the Federals. They had been given artillery training and knew how to handle the cannon. In fact Captain Oldham enjoyed the artillery practice so much that he yelled with delight every time a gun went off. MacRae looked for a time with amusement on this scene and remarked, "'Oldham thinks he is at a ball in Petersburg.'"[56]

Despite the great success MacRae had enjoyed thus far, his brigade might never have broken through the Union position if not for the support of Cooke and Conner. MacRae actually was in a vulnerable position and could have suffered disaster if the Federals had mustered the willpower to counterattack. But

Cooke's and Conner's men crossed the cornfield, penetrated a small gap to the right of Broady's brigade, and made a lodgment in the earthworks. They widened the breach after several minutes of tough fighting and then pushed eastward, collapsing the Yankee line. MacRae also was aided by the advance of Brig. Gen. Samuel McGowan's South Carolina brigade to the south, which forced the 4th New York Heavy Artillery to retire from behind its traverse. Soon the whole western face of the Federal position was in Rebel hands. Hastily mounted counterattacks failed to stop the Rebel advance, so Hancock ordered a general retreat at 6:30, only an hour after the battle had begun, and retired eastward under cover of darkness.[57]

It was the most spectacular victory MacRae's men had ever seen. The Federals lost about 600 killed and wounded and more than 2,000 taken prisoner, while the Rebels suffered 720 casualties. Hill's men picked up 3,100 small arms, captured 9 cannon, and secured 12 flags. Three privates and noncommissioned officers of the Bethel Regiment and Capt. Macon G. Cherry of the 44th North Carolina were credited with taking four Union flags. Pvt. Robert W. Massey of the 47th North Carolina was credited with a more gruesome accomplishment; he "'slew a Major in single combat, on his refusing to surrender.'" The Second Corps abandoned a mountain of equipment and personal belongings in its hasty flight. Benjamin Wesley Justice recorded the scene for his wife: "We also captured . . . numerous horses, pistols, swords, saddles, guns, & an infinity of smaller plunder, such as knapsacks, clothing, oil cloths, blankets, pocket knives, razors, rings, pictures, watches, lady's veils, silk dresses, & c. Numbers of our men were wearing the flashy uniforms of the yankee artillerists & the fine hats of officers a few days after the battle."[58]

Justice noted that Cooke and MacRae "captured fully as many prisoners as they carried men into the fight." Brigade members were jubilant over the way Hancock's demoralized draftees gave up. They "threw down their guns and commenced waiving their hats and came meeting of us going to our rear," reported James W. Wright. Once they had surrendered, they were willing captives. "No guard was required to accompany prisoners to the rear," recalled Justice, "for they rushed along in crowds. One officer says he thought the hurrying crowd of prisoners was a successful charge of the enemy." The highest-ranking officer captured was Francis Walker, Hancock's chief of staff, who surrendered to Lt. William Emmett Kyle of the sharpshooters.[59]

The losses in MacRae's brigade were not heavy, but they cut deeply into the ranks. Eleven men were killed, fifty were wounded, and one was captured, for a total of sixty-two casualties. The Bethel Regiment lost fourteen men, including John C. Warlick, who was wounded. He thought Reams Station was "the prettiest fight we were ever in." Warlick went home to recuperate from the injury to his left arm, and a civilian doctor cut out the ball three weeks after the battle. The most serious loss in the regiment was Lt. Col. Francis Bird. He was shot in the temple only forty yards from the earthworks and died the next morning. Bird was a "very gallant officer & much beloved by the men," thought Lemuel Hoyle. His death left Colonel Martin as the only field officer with the regiment. The ranking captains could not be promoted to fill this void because they were all prisoners and the authorities dictated that promotions be based on seniority. Martin recalled after the war that this was ordinarily a wise policy, but it "worked very great injury to many regiments situated as ours was."[60]

The 26th North Carolina lost two killed and eight wounded. Lane once again topped the list, with his fifth and second-most-serious wound of the war. A shell fragment hit his left breast near his heart, fractured two ribs, broke a third, and tore "open the flesh to the bones, making a fearful wound six inches long and three wide." A piece of flesh as large as Edward Peterson's hand hung by a flap from his chest. It was sewn back by the surgeons, but Lane was out of action until November and was succeeded in command of the regiment by Lt. Col. James Theophilus Adams. The new leader also had a tendency to get wounded. As captain of Company D he had been shot in the right hip at Malvern Hill and had been injured in the left shoulder at Gettysburg on July 1. A twenty-five-year-old native of Wake County, Adams filled Lane's shoes admirably and remained with the regiment for the remainder of the war.[61]

The 47th North Carolina lost more men, three killed and sixteen wounded, than any other unit in the brigade, because of the fierce fire poured into the unit by the 66th New York. The list of casualties "included an over-proportion of our very best men." The New Yorkers dealt a blow out of proportion to the numbers they shot down. "Men who seemed to posess charmed lives; who struck so quick, and were so cool and daring to pass the danger line, were struck down almost in a body. Many of them returned after recovery, but the regiment was notably weakened after this." The 44th North Carolina lost nine wounded, and the 52nd North Carolina suffered three killed and seven wounded.[62]

The suffering only increased the elation felt by MacRae's men when they received compliments for their work. Heth was tremendously impressed by what he saw. "The charge and its results has proved to me that nothing is impossible to men determined to win." Lee was so moved by reports like this that he wrote to Governor Vance praising the Tar Heel troops involved in the battle. "I have frequently been called upon to mention the services of the North Carolina soldiers in this army, but their gallantry and conduct were never more deserving of admiration than in the engagement at Reams' Station." He sent a similar message to the Secretary of War and commented to Lane some time later that the Tar Heels "had by their gallantry not only placed North Carolina, but the whole Confederacy, under a debt of gratitude, which could never be repaid." The *Petersburg Express* waxed eloquent in an editorial praising the North Carolina brigades at Reams Station. "Too much praise cannot be awarded to these veteran commands for the intrepid manner in which they marched up to their work and accomplished it. . . . In every battle in which they have engaged, they have acquitted themselves nobly." But perhaps the most telling praise came from a Northern officer taken on the battlefield. In the wake of the affair he told an officer of the 47th, "'Lieutenant, your men fight well; that was a magnificent charge.'"[63]

MacRae's men had played the key role in cracking open Hancock's position and defeating the famed Second Corps. This was due entirely to MacRae himself; he deserved as much credit for the victory as anyone else on the battlefield. His clear-headed examination of the ground, personal instructions to the troops, and evident determination to succeed at any cost inspired them with confidence. Neither Pettigrew or Kirkland could have done this. MacRae had finally come into his own as a superlative field commander in Lee's army. "Our Brigade is proud of our new Brigadier & I believe he is proud of his new command," crowed Benjamin Wesley Justice. "He is exceedingly plain in appearance, but is a model officer & a gentleman."[64]

Everyone had reason to compliment themselves. Several men attempted to share the glory with Cooke's and Conner's brigades, noting that "the gallant 'tar heels' made short work of it." James Wright wrote his wife and father that "our boys done brave," while John Foster recorded in his diary that "it was a compleat victory on our side." No one put it more succinctly than T. W. Setser. "I tell you we giv them Sut," he wrote home.[65]

Heth's men left the battlefield on the night of August 25 and marched partway back to town, bivouacking five miles west of Rowanty Creek. They entered Petersburg the next day in a triumphal procession. Heth asked the Moravian band to meet the troops outside town and sent in the prisoners and then Cooke's brigade. Heth told the musicians to play in front of Cooke's men, while he, his staff, and three men who had captured Yankee flags marched in front of the band. As he stared at the Union flags waving in front of him, Edward Peterson remarked, "We had many a time, celebrated the 4th of July, with those colours waving over us, on the music stand in the square. How changed now, we exalting now in having captured them." After blaring Cooke's men into town, the musicians moved back in the column to play at the head of MacRae's men.[66]

MacRae camped his men at the end of Sycamore Street but moved them to a hill near Halifax Street the next day. Here they had an excellent view of the fiery streaks of shells and mortar rounds that arched over the siege lines at night. Edward Peterson marveled at this "magnificent sight . . . like rockets thro' the air in a bow, they pass very slowly, . . . taking several seconds in passing." MacRae's Tar Heels were able to rest until August 29, when orders arrived to go back into the trenches and resume the duty of siege work.[67]

The smashing success on August 25 did not alter the fact that Grant's Fourth Offensive, as the fighting at Globe Tavern and Reams Station came to be called, was at least a partial defeat for the Rebels. T. W. Setser had rejoiced over the victory at Reams Station, but his overall morale was weakening. "Olde grante Still holes the weldon rail rode, and I exspect will for Some time at, for I think he will bee very hard too git off the Rail Rode, So I think we will hav pice this winter, and that is the oppinion of the moste of the men." Setser hoped the war would end during the coming winter. The erosion of his morale would continue until he deserted on March 29, 1865. Setser spent a few days in a military prison and then left for home on April 4, five days before Lee's surrender.[68]

James Wright of the 26th North Carolina brooded a great deal that summer about the loss of comrades. "You don't know [how] I feel when so many of my fellow men have been slain and my life yet spared by an allwise God," he confessed to his wife and father. "We have to do much hard duty," Wright continued, "the boys are very tired, but I hope this campaign and war will soon come to a close."[69]

Chapter 12

Rebel Autumn

For more than a month after their victory at Reams Station, MacRae's men dug into the sandy clay that surrounded Petersburg. They constructed a second line of works behind the main line of fortifications east of Weldon Railroad until September 16, when they moved into a new area of operations. Lee worried that Grant might use his lodgment on the railroad to strike at Boydton Plank Road, an important part of his wagon train link between Stony Creek Station and Petersburg. From the plank road the Federals could continue on to cut the South Side Railroad, the last Confederate supply line from the west.

The Tar Heels marched southward along Boydton Plank Road for five miles, deployed skirmishers, and began to dig a line protecting it. Another one of Heth's brigades and three brigades from Maj. Gen. Charles W. Field's division had nothing more than "primitive logworks barely covered with earth" after four days of digging. But Lee wanted another, more forward line constructed, so the five brigades were ordered east on September 20 to Squirrel Level Road. This route ran southwestwardly and was three miles east of Boydton Plank Road and a mile west of the Weldon Railroad. The Rebels dug a line of works crisscrossing the road down to a large open expanse called Peebles' farm and on to a crossroad known today as Route 673. The entire line was about three miles long and was also crudely constructed by the tired soldiers. MacRae's brigade was on the southern end of the Squirrel Level Road Line. Here they built a redoubt and named it Fort MacRae.[1]

The works did not progress more rapidly because a draining exhaustion afflicted everyone in September. James W. Wright of the 26th North Carolina confessed to his wife that "when I think of what I have passed through I am almost lost in meditation to think how many has fallen on my right and left in front and near me." Wright's mother died at this time, and his application for an eighteen-day furlough was refused. It hurt the corporal deeply. "I have been with the regiment in every engagement and on every march that it has been in," he complained to a relative, and he found it hard to continue fighting for a government that could not allow him a few days to tend to his family affairs. "It is with a hesitance that I take up my gun to go to battle to fight for such people. I don't think I will ever expose myself as I have done to keep from being taken prisoner[.] I don't think I will do much more till I get a furlough[.] I have paid for one and I think I ought to have it." Wright felt terribly depressed and alone in the army; he wanted to see his father one last time and encouraged his wife to teach his son "to be a good boy." He worried about survival, his own and that of his comrades. "I feel quite bad to see so many of the boys wounded. it looks like a bad chance for any to escape, being hurt in some way[.] it looks like my chance to get home is very bad[.] I feel like giving up all hopes of seeing you all any more but then I feel like I will yet be spared to get home some time again." Wright was later captured at Burgess's Mill and died of diarrhea at Point Lookout on January 31, 1865.[2]

Even Benjamin Wesley Justice, who did no fighting but served as a commissary officer in the 47th, felt depressed by the ever lengthening conflict. "I am very lonely of late, & inclined to be low spirited," he wrote to his wife. The "sufferings & privations & anxieties of this dreadful war are fast wearing out my buoyancy & elasticity of spirit. I have no joys save in calling up the bright, rosy images of the buried past." In September band member Edward Peterson expressed his disgust with the war. He blamed "some blind leaders" for starting the conflict and misleading "the ignorant masses" into supporting it. Peterson noted the disparity of numbers and resources between North and South, and he wondered where the Confederacy could possibly find enough men to carry on "this miserable war."[3]

The continuous campaigning stressed many soldiers to the limit. Lt. Jones Watson of Company G, 11th North Carolina, faced charges of cowardice for walking to the rear during the battle of Reams Station. He had been suffering from respiratory trouble for more than a year and could not keep up with the hard-charging brigade. Asst. Surg. James P. McCombs of the Bethel Regiment refused to believe his story and preferred charges against him. A court-martial convicted Watson on September 5, and he was cashiered. Watson's father wrote letters to various North Carolina newspapers trying to explain his son's case. It might have worked, for Lieutenant Watson joined the 3rd North Carolina Cavalry on October 16 and served faithfully to the end of the war.[4]

A small group of about twenty-five men regularly attended services offered by the chaplains during September. With the return of Chaplain Abram N. Wells to the 26th North Carolina there were three ministers in the brigade. They took turns preaching so that a service was held each night. Few of the attendees offered themselves for baptism, however, because of the constant round of duties.[5]

Changes in staff officers took place in the brigade during September. Maj. William J. Baker, the brigade commissary, was transferred to a post in Raleigh. Benjamin Wesley Justice was glad to see him go, for the two had never gotten along; but Justice was disappointed in his efforts to take Baker's place. Another staff officer nearly left his post in the 26th North Carolina when Governor Vance pushed for Capt. J. J. Young to be made director of the state's new soldiers' home. Young hated to leave his regiment, but he dutifully sent his resignation to the secretary of war. Fortunately for him and the well-being of the regiment his resignation was rejected.[6]

Controversy over the placement of Union prisoners in Charleston, which was shelled daily by the Federals, led the Yankees to make an example of 600 Rebel officers held at Fort Delaware, and several members of the brigade were included. Lieutenant Colonel Hargrove of the 44th North Carolina, Capt. Jesse Kneeder Kyle of the 52nd, Lt. Murdoch McLeod of the 26th, and Lt. David A. Coon and Lt. Elisha Wesley Dorsey of the Bethel Regiment were among the prisoners. They left Fort Delaware on August 20 and were placed in a stockade in front of Battery Wagner on Morris Island, which the Yankees had captured the previous September. The Rebels were to be a human shield guarded by black soldiers of the 54th Massachusetts. Seventeen Rebel shells landed among them, but fortunately none exploded. The "Immortal Six Hundred" endured the privations and danger until October 23, hearing the screech of Union and Confederate shells arching over their heads all the while. Their point made, the Federal authorities shipped the prisoners to Fort Pulaski, where they were released at the end of the war.[7]

The fate of these prisoners was out of MacRae's hands, but he did all he could to care for the men still in the field. A report by Hill's inspector general indicated that the brigade was still a magnificent fighting unit despite the low morale of some men. Col. William J. Martin still led the Bethel Regiment; Maj. James T. Adams commanded the 26th; Maj. Charles M. Stedman led the 44th; Maj. William C. Lankford was in charge of the 47th; and Lt. William W. Carmichael commanded the 52nd in the absence of any higher-ranking company officers. MacRae's strength at the end of September was quite high. He had a total of 1,757 men present in the field, but only 1,231 were ready for active duty.

Hill's inspector, Maj. R. J. Wingate, was impressed with MacRae's and

Cooke's commands. He called them by far the best brigades in Heth's division. They were "in specially good order and commanded by two most excellent officers, who are strict disciplinarians, but who have great influence over their men in camp and on the field." The sanitary conditions of the brigade camp were only fair, but the Tar Heels' clothing and equipment were in excellent shape. Wingate noted that MacRae devoted himself "with great energy to the comfort and efficiency of his command and the improvement and strengthening of his line."[8]

It was well that the brigade maintained its fighting trim, for Grant launched another offensive in late September aimed at the area that MacRae occupied. While the Army of the James attacked the Rebel defenses north of the James River on September 29, a cavalry force probed west of Weldon Railroad to locate the Confederates. MacRae and Archer were still working on the Squirrel Level Road Line but were screened by cavalry pickets. The Ninth Corps and part of the Fifth Corps prepared to attack the next day, but Lee learned of the move and assembled a strike force of six brigades southwest of Petersburg on the evening of September 29. All the infantry were pulled out of the Squirrel Level Road Line, including MacRae's brigade, and concentrated at Battery 45, a strong earthwork located where the Petersburg city defenses crossed Boydton Plank Road. By nightfall the incomplete works along Squirrel Level Road were occupied by cavalry, and the Tar Heels went to sleep wondering where they would be sent the next day.

On Friday, September 30, the Fifth Corps moved northwestward and struck the line where it crossed Peebles' farm early in the afternoon. To their surprise they found dismounted troopers instead of infantrymen, and the line of works was soon in their hands. The Federals continued the advance up Church Road to Pegram's farm a quarter-mile away. Here the Ninth Corps assembled to continue the offensive while the Fifth Corps dug works. A quarter-mile north of Pegram's house lay thick woods that separated Pegram's farm from Jones's farm. About a mile farther northwest was Boydton Plank Road. As the Ninth Corps advanced up Church Road and emerged onto the "open, undulating country" of Jones's farm, its advance slowed to a crawl. The commanders had no idea where the Rebels were lurking, and the thick woods that bounded the farm could easily hide several brigades. To the northwest of Jones's house, the headwaters of the upper fork of Old Town Creek crossed Church Road a half-mile short of its junction with Boydton Plank Road. The earthworks that MacRae's men helped build were on the north side of the upper fork. Duncan Road also ran northwestward along the western side of this large expanse of farmland and connected with Boydton Plank Road.

Hill ordered Wilcox's division and two brigades of Heth's division, MacRae's and Archer's, to move rapidly along Boydton Plank Road and stop the Federals before they breached the line of works. Wilcox placed Lane's brigade on the right of Church Road and McGowan's brigade to the left. MacRae was instructed to deploy behind Lane, while Archer was placed behind McGowan; both units of this second line positioned themselves en echelon to the first. If the Unionists had advanced with confidence and brought the full weight of their force to bear, the plank road might well have been taken. Instead a lone brigade led by Simon Griffin advanced into the open ground west of Church Road. To his left and rear was John Curtin's brigade deployed in two lines, and to Curtin's left and rear was Brig. Gen. John Hartranft's brigade deployed near the southern edge of Jones's farm.

The Confederates struck these wary Yankees at 5:00 P.M. Wilcox enveloped both flanks of Griffin's brigade and sent it reeling down Church Road. Lane and McGowan pursued, leaving their supports to take care of the other Federal units on the field. Lane left behind the 33rd North Carolina, which accidentally became separated from his brigade, so MacRae aligned his command with it and advanced southward along the western side of the road. On the way, his right wing encountered Curtin's first line. The Federals in this line, which consisted of the 51st and 58th New York and the 45th Pennsylvania, noticed the Tar Heels moving past their right flank and opened fire on them.[9]

This touched off one of the most unique and successful attacks the brigade ever made. The left wing was moving too fast to give immediate support, so it was up to Colonel Martin of the Bethel Regiment to take charge. "The situation was critical," he later remembered, and "there was no time to ask for orders"; so he shouted for the 11th and the 52nd, which was next to his regiment on the right, to charge the Yankees. The 52nd had already begun to slow and become disordered because of the fire being poured into its flank, but both regiments quickly changed front to the right and attacked. Martin turned in the best day of his military career, pushing the Federals westward. They stopped twice to fire into their tormenters but were driven farther from support and toward Rebel cavalry positioned on the far Confederate right.[10]

Meanwhile MacRae angled the 26th, 44th, 47th, and 33rd toward the southwest and into the right flank of Curtin's second line. The attack took the Federals by surprise and rolled up their formation. The 48th Pennsylvania and the 21st and 36th Massachusetts offered less resistance than did Curtin's first line and were easily broken apart and sent flying from the field. Then MacRae crashed into Hartranft. This brigade was deployed in one line and was well led, but it had a sorghum field immediately in front of its right wing that shielded the advancing

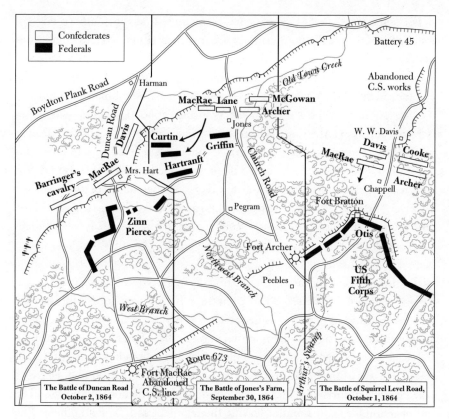

Battery 45

Abandoned
C.S. works

Boydton Plank Road

Harman

Old Town Creek

MacRae Lane   McGowan
                 Archer

Jones

W. W. Davis

Davis

Davis

Curtin

MacRae

Cooke

Griffin

Archer

Duncan Road

MacRae

Mrs. Hart   Hartranft

Chappell

Barringer's
cavalry

Church Road

Fort Bratton

Zinn
Pierce

Pegram

Otis

Fort Archer

Fort MacRae

Northwest Branch

Peebles

US
Fifth
Corps

West Branch

Route 673

Arthur's Swamp

Fort MacRae
Abandoned
C.S. line

The Battle of Duncan Road
October 2, 1864

The Battle of Jones's Farm,
September 30, 1864

The Battle of Squirrel Level Road,
October 1, 1864

MAP 12.1 The Fifth Offensive, September 30–October 2, 1864

Rebels from Hartranft's view. His Michigan, Ohio, New York, and Pennsylvania
troops maintained their formation and conducted a fighting retreat even though
Confederate cavalry attacked their left. MacRae pushed Hartranft from Jones's
farm, then he marched his men northward to help Martin's two regiments bot-
tle up Curtin's first line. These were the most unlucky Yankees on the battlefield.
Pressed unmercifully by Martin from the east, blocked by cavalry on the west,
and now attacked by MacRae from the south, most of them gave up. About 600
men of this first line were taken prisoner. All but 16 soldiers of the 350 in the 51st
New York fell into Rebel hands. The 45th Pennsylvania took 230 men into action
and lost 4 killed, 15 wounded, and 185 taken prisoner.

The result of this spectacular victory on Jones's farm was that Boydton Plank
Road and the South Side Railroad were saved. The Ninth Corps retired to Pegram's farm to regroup as nightfall put an end to further fighting, but there was
little likelihood Wilcox and Heth could have seized the farm even if there was
more time. They had only limited strength to throw at the two Union corps.[11]

For some time after MacRae's men reassembled on the southern edge of Jones's farm, they had an opportunity to savor their stunning victory and wander over the field picking up souvenirs. Benjamin H. Freeman found envelopes, canteens, socks, shirts, eating utensils, and gloves scattered over the farm. His comrade in the 44th, Alexander S. Webb, later wrote a letter home on Union patriotic stationery. "The 44th kept up its former good reputation," Webb reported, "and Gen'l MacRae declared on the field, it was the best Reg't he ever saw." Webb recognized that the Federal regiments were filled with draftees and substitutes, "new issue" as he called them, which enabled the Rebels to defeat such a large force with comparatively few men. "We had things pretty much our own way," he crowed. Pvt. Joseph A. Ingram and Pvt. Adolphus A. Welsh of the 26th were credited with capturing Yankee flags. Perhaps one or both of them simply picked up the colors of the 51st New York of Curtin's first line, which were reported lost by its commander.[12]

The highest-ranking casualty in the brigade was Colonel Martin of the Bethel Regiment, who was struck down right after his brilliant leadership against Curtin's brigade. When the Confederates assembled on the southern edge of Jones's farm, they came under intense Union artillery fire. Martin was forming his regimental line when a shell fragment "carried away a large slice of his left thigh." He was borne to the rear in a blanket, but the surgeon did not believe he had a chance of surviving. Martin confounded this prediction, but he would be out of action for many months, leaving the regiment with no field officer. The senior captain, James Madison Young of Company K, took charge of the regiment while Martin recuperated. Not until the night of April 1, 1865, the eve of the final day of fighting at Petersburg, would the colonel return to his command.[13]

The 26th North Carolina lost several men on September 30. The regimental hospital moved forward behind the men as they marched to Jones's farm but found the Union artillery too active to set up its operating tables near the fighting. The 44th counted one killed, eleven wounded, and one missing.[14]

Wilcox and Heth maintained their position on the southern edge of Jones's farm for three hours before they received word from Hill to pull back toward Petersburg. Reconnaissance of the Federal right wing, which occupied the captured Squirrel Level Road Line, indicated it was vulnerable, so Hill determined to hit it early the next morning. He desperately wanted to reclaim all lost ground; if that could not be done by a frontal attack along Church Road, then it must be done by a flank attack along Squirrel Level Road. MacRae and Archer left Jones's farm about 9:00 P.M. and marched in the pouring rain to Battery 45, where they rested for the remainder of the night. Then Davis and Cooke joined them, and Heth took his entire division down Squirrel Level Road on the morn-

Col. William Joseph Martin. A professor at several colleges before and after the war, Martin was severely wounded at Jones's farm while commanding the 11th North Carolina. He was one of the most effective regimental leaders in the brigade. (North Carolina Collection, University of North Carolina, Chapel Hill)

ing of Saturday, October 1. The rain had stopped in the night, but the ground was sloppy with mud.[15]

If MacRae's Tar Heels expected another easy victory, they were sorely disappointed. Warren's Fifth Corps held the line and was prepared for an attack. His right was anchored at Confederate Fort Bratton, which was redug so the Federals could fire up Squirrel Level Road. A new line was hastily dug eastward from the redoubt so Warren could connect with Fort Wadsworth on the Weldon Railroad. There was no open flank here, but there were well-dug earthworks that incorporated Confederate work with Yankee engineering. Lt. Col. Elwell Otis's brigade held this flank. He placed the 15th New York Heavy Artillery and the 11th U.S. in the trench to the left of Fort Bratton. The 5th and 146th New York occupied the redoubt, and the 14th U.S. was in the newly constructed trench to the right.

Heth deployed his division at W. W. Davis's house, a short distance up Squirrel Level Road from Fort Bratton, and sent out his sharpshooters. They met the Federal skirmishers just north of Chappell's house, located a few hundred yards from the Union line. Heth advanced his men behind the sharpshooters; MacRae's brigade, with Davis's behind it, was in the first line to the right of the road. Archer deployed to the left of the road with Cooke in support. The men drove through the belt of trees separating Davis's homestead from Chappell's house to find that the sharpshooters had just cleared the abatis ringing the southern edge of the woods. Heth had his first view of the Yankee defenses, and it made him pause.

Orders went out for a reconnaissance in force to feel out the strength of the Union line. MacRae moved out at 9:00 A.M. on this hazardous mission, but the 44th and 52nd on his right flank apparently misunderstood the order. Stedman and Carmichael believed they were to make an all-out attack, so their men shouted and rushed ahead. MacRae ordered the two regiments to slow down, but the men were buoyed by their easy victory the day before and ignored all orders. It is possible that they recognized the futility of making a halfhearted effort to develop the enemy's strength. Any advance over the open ground in front of the earthworks would be costly, and the men probably wanted to sell their lives dearly or not advance at all. At any rate, MacRae rode ahead to share their fate, leaving his other three regiments behind.[16]

The attack was doomed from the start. With no support to its left, the 44th received a cascade of fire onto its flank as well as from its front. Rain began to fall even as the assault petered out well short of the Union earthworks. Heth decided to give up all hope of rolling up the Union line. He later wrote that even if he could have taken Fort Bratton, his losses would have been so heavy that his division could not have gone any farther. Heth retired to W. W. Davis's house in the rain and held for the rest of the day as Federal skirmishers pestered his tired men.[17]

The first of October was a miserable day for the men of MacRae's brigade. With rain continuing to drizzle down, they took cover from the harassing fire and wondered why they had been ordered to attack. The temperature was dropping, indicating that fall was approaching. It was "as disagreeable a time, as I almost ever spent," thought Alexander S. Webb. His 44th lost quite a few men in their unwise assault and during the sniping of the afternoon. Webb was astonished when Sgt. Whitson B. Shemwell, who was only five feet from him munching on a piece of bread, was suddenly struck in the heart by a ball. He "died the quickest I ever saw any one." Stedman was slightly injured when a bullet hit one of his spurs and glanced away, forcing him to recuperate for a few days. Capt. Robert Bingham took charge of the regiment in the meantime.

Nightfall finally put an end to this miserable affair. Heth pulled away from the Davis homestead and sent Cooke and MacRae to Battery 45. Davis and Archer marched on to Jones's farm in case the Ninth Corps resumed its advance the next day. Wilcox's division was withdrawn to Petersburg. More troops would have to be dispatched to Boydton Plank Road the next day to reinforce Davis and Archer, but the two North Carolina brigades of Heth's division needed rest before they could be expected to go.[18]

The 44th suffered the most on October 1. Chaplain Webb thought it was "the worse cut up they have been the entire campaign." Stedman told hospital workers that "his men were just mowed down, they having to charge thro' an open field." Benjamin H. Freeman thought the attack on October 1 was "the hot[t]est place I was ever in before." He was shot through the muscle of his left arm and had the ball extracted from near his shoulder blade in a field hospital. His injury led to a pleasant stay at Richmond's Winder Hospital, where Freeman dined on a feast of good food not found in the trenches.[19]

The 26th North Carolina suffered the loss of one of its best officers. Henry Clay Albright was struck in the head by a bullet during the afternoon skirmishing. He had earlier said to a friend, " 'Oh, how I dread this day,' " when there seemed to be a prospect of an attack on the Federal works. Now he was transported to Winder Hospital, where his injury was found to be very serious. Albright drifted in and out, "senseless" one moment and then regaining possession of his mind. At one point he insisted on being moved to a ward filled with enlisted men so he could be close to them. As time went by a friend named M. Murchison kept Albright's father, a doctor, informed of his son's condition. Three weeks after the battle, Murchison frankly reported that "hee may git upe agane with close atention with out that he ise gon." He was "senceless yeat he seames to know noe body but me." Albright died on October 27 as his regiment fought one of its greatest battles at Burgess's Mill.[20]

The Federals made one final effort to reach Boydton Plank Road, resulting in yet another fight for MacRae's brigade. Meade rather than Grant pushed this last lunge into action. Brig. Gen. Gershom Mott's division of the Second Corps was to advance west on Route 673, swing north to reach Duncan Road, and move on to Boydton Plank Road west of Jones's farm while the Ninth Corps advanced to clear Pegram's farm. With only two brigades of Heth's division in the way, the Yankees could win a smashing victory if they pushed ahead with vigor and determination. Pegram's farm was easily cleared on the morning of Sunday, October 2, but the Ninth Corps was tired and wary. Mott advanced from Fort MacRae and along Duncan Road to a point three-fourths of a mile south of Mrs. Hart's house, where the Rebel earthworks crossed the road.

The cautious Union advance gave Hill time to shift more units to the threatened area. Cooke and MacRae were sent marching at once, and the former deployed his men to the right of Archer and Davis, who were near Church Road. MacRae was still on the move when the van of Mott's division suddenly appeared on Duncan Road and a Rebel courier raced to the Tar Heel column to deliver the alarming news. MacRae ordered his men to double-quick down Duncan Road to Mrs. Hart's. They approached the earthworks before the New Jersey troops of Brig. Gen. Robert McAllister's brigade reached them. The Tar Heels replaced some regiments of a cavalry brigade in the works and opened fire on the Federals, who traded a few rounds with them and fell back to the woods.[21]

The episode struck Louis G. Young as amusing. He later described it as "the unique incident of two opposing forces running to reach the same point, the point being in this instance the very works we had recently built." For some time after this initial clash, both sides consolidated their positions. The Rebel line was lengthened and strengthened. MacRae held the far right most of the afternoon, with cavalry screening his flank and the line to his left filling out with the shifting of more infantry. MacRae's men straddled Duncan Road and were fronted by Brig. Gen. Byron R. Pierce's brigade, composed mostly of troops from New York and Pennsylvania. The gray-coated soldiers worked like beavers to improve the fortifications, while the Yankees formed a solid, wavy battle line stretching from west of Duncan Road all the way to the east of Church Road. The Rebels were outnumbered, but there was hardly any desire on the Union side to push ahead, particularly when clear signals arrived from Meade that the army leader did not want another round of futile bloodshed.[22]

The stalemate was interrupted at midafternoon when Mott prepared a reconnaissance in force toward the Rebel line. He instructed Pierce to send his brigade up Duncan Road toward Mrs. Hart's house. Pierce assembled the 1st Massachusetts Heavy Artillery and the 141st and 84th Pennsylvania in a ravine 300 yards from MacRae's men and placed Lt. Col. George Zinn in charge of the strike force. His other regiments were arrayed to the rear and on both flanks as supports.

The Yankees attacked at 3:00 P.M., but they were hit by artillery fire from the left where the Rebels had placed guns to enfilade any movement up Duncan

Road. MacRae's Tar Heels poured a hail of lead into Zinn's attackers, glad of the opportunity to pay back the bluecoats for their rough treatment the day before. Zinn's regiments made it to within fifty yards of the earthworks before they broke and fled to the ravine. Heavy skirmishing continued along Duncan Road for the rest of the day. That night the Yankees withdrew to build a permanent line of works encompassing Pegram's farm and Peebles' farm, while Heth's tired soldiers continued to strengthen their Boydton Plank Road Line.[23]

"Our brigade was attacked again yesterday," wrote Chaplain Webb, "but easily repulsed the enemy only having three or four wounded from the brigade." No one was lost in Webb's regiment, the 44th North Carolina. In fact only 63 Confederates were lost in the fighting on October 2, compared with 142 Union casualties. What could have been a smashing breakthrough to the South Side Railroad turned into the most pathetic Union effort of the Fifth Offensive, which shuddered to an end after three days of fighting.[24]

MacRae's command suffered a total of 137 casualties in the Fifth Offensive, including 1 missing, 16 killed, 114 wounded, 2 wounded and captured, and 4 captured. The Bethel Regiment lost 3 killed, 25 wounded, and 2 captured, while the 26th North Carolina lost only 3 killed and 8 wounded. The 44th North Carolina suffered the most, with 1 missing, 5 killed, 37 wounded, 2 wounded and captured, and 1 captured. The 47th North Carolina lost 3 killed, 16 wounded, and 1 captured, while the 52nd North Carolina lost 2 killed and 28 wounded.[25]

Surgeon Warren of the 26th worked with the wounded until October 5, when he sent the last of them to area hospitals. Julius Linebach had grown so accustomed to nursing that he felt a regular hand at it by now. In fact, he fancied that he could do as well as any surgeon. Linebach noted how differently men reacted when under anesthesia; some swore and others sang. One injured soldier prayed "at the top of his voice, during the whole time that his leg was taken off." In addition to helping the wounded, the Moravian musicians were assigned the task of burying the severed limbs, unless the ambulance or pioneer corps was available to do it.[26]

To Cpl. James W. Wright, who missed the fighting because of illness, it seemed as if something had gone wrong. The "Brigade is badly cut up. bad management somewhere somebody to blame." He could not understand why his comrades had to fight to retake a line of works they had evacuated the day before. This reference to the bloody repulse along Squirrel Level Road illustrated a common feeling among the men. They did not "like the idea at all that they put up those strong works for the Yankees to fight behind," in Edward Peterson's words. There also was a general feeling in the command that the Tar Heels had done more than their share of fighting. "For two months our Brigade has experienced constant and great hardships, especially lately," wrote Louis G. Young.[27]

Heth's division extended the line of works along Boydton Plank Road from Duncan Road all the way to Hatcher's Run, a distance of about five miles, during the next three weeks. MacRae's men constantly worked on laying out new sections, strengthening old sections, and moving their camp short distances every few days. The brigade consistently remained on Heth's right and thus was the last infantry unit in Lee's Petersburg line. Guard and picket duty filled their time when they were not digging. At first there were occasional raids between the picket lines; one such foray by the Federals netted at least one prisoner from the Bethel Regiment. But picket duty gradually became less dangerous. With the Yankees a half-mile away, the pickets got out of the habit of shooting; instead they more often exchanged newspapers with the Federals.[28]

The need for more men was so pressing that the authorities began to clean out the hospitals and send recuperating soldiers to the front. Lemuel Hoyle was appalled at the sight: "some who have been wounded in battle and made permanently lame, come hobbling in on Sticks & c. I do think it is perfectly outrageous, and the men who send them must have neither hearts nor consciences."[29]

Grant put his army in motion once again on Thursday, October 27. Four columns set out, with the Second Corps as the main strike force. It crossed Hatcher's Run east of Heth's division and struck out to the west on Dabney's Mill Road, easily turning the Rebel flank. This road ran parallel to the run and intersected Boydton Plank Road a half-mile south of where it crossed the stream. Halfway between the junction and the stream crossing was the intersection of White Oak Road, which ran west. This was Hancock's key objective. He could cut Lee's wagon train link by gaining control of Boydton Plank Road and then march along White Oak Road toward the South Side Railroad. By early afternoon Hancock was positioning his units around the junction of White Oak Road and Boydton Plank Road, defending against a possible Rebel attack from the north and the west. Then someone realized that an abandoned road crossed Hatcher's Run and joined Dabney's Mill Road several hundred yards east of Boydton Plank Road. This unused road crossed the stream over a dam that Confederate cavalrymen had earlier built to flood the bottomland, which was thickly grown over with trees. The road ascended the creek bluff and entered a large cornfield spanning the high but uneven ground. This open area encompassed the intersection with Dabney's Mill Road and extended to Boydton Plank Road. A small ravine to the north near the Mill Road drained into Hatcher's Run, and a barn was nestled in it. On the Confederate side the abandoned road ran north from the dam on Hatcher's Run toward the rear of Heth's new line of fortifications, the line that ended on the north bank of Hatcher's Run.

Byron Pierce's brigade of Mott's division was ordered to cover this abandoned road. Pierce sent two guns of Battery C, 5th U.S. Artillery, to the crest of the bluff and sighted them north. He also sent the 5th Michigan and 93rd New York under Col. John Pulford to support the guns. Pulford deployed these units to the right of the cannons and partly in the thick trees, facing northeast so as to front anyone advancing along the abandoned road. Pulford later formed the rest of his brigade on the left of the artillery, facing north. He sent three companies of the 5th Michigan forward on the right of his command as skirmishers. They had been gone only fifteen minutes when firing broke out.

By four o'clock, about the time this skirmishing started, Grant and Meade had decided to cancel Hancock's further push west of the Boydton Plank Road. There obviously was a force of Rebel troops north of Hatcher's Run, but no one yet knew of the ominous presence on the abandoned road. Grant wanted Hancock to maintain his position until the next day, hoping he might lure the Confederates into attacking across the open ground north of the run where Federal artillery could punish them. The army leaders rode off just as skirmish fire began to heat up in front of Pulford's isolated command.[30]

Heth had been shifting units, including MacRae's, all day to lengthen his line to the right. When he learned that the Federals had crossed the run, he organized a counterstrike. Col. David Weisiger's Virginia brigade and Brig. Gen. John C. C. Sanders's Alabama brigade of Maj. Gen. William Mahone's division would advance with MacRae along the abandoned road so conveniently located behind the fortifications. The generals did not know exactly what lay in the cornfield at the end of that road, but there was every reason to believe they could hit the rear or flank of Hancock's force. At the same time all other Rebel units around the periphery of the Second Corps would attack.

Heth personally led the attacking force part of the way along the abandoned road, for he knew it well; then he left Mahone in charge. The men had no difficulty marching over the dam and through the woods. Near the open high land, Mahone sent forward his skirmishers and formed his battle line. Sanders was unable to keep pace and dropped so far behind the column that his men were not engaged. Weisiger held the left, and MacRae held the right of Mahone's line. The Tar Heels numbered 1,050 men, and the Virginia brigade probably was about equal in strength.[31]

Mahone struck at 4:30 P.M., with MacRae's men yelling as they started to ascend the short bluff. The Rebels hit the Federal line squarely on its angle, where the artillery was taken in flank. The Yankees were forced to give way in a hurry, leaving the two guns behind. Pierce's infantrymen retreated all the way to Boydton Plank Road and started to reassemble west of it. The Confederates followed

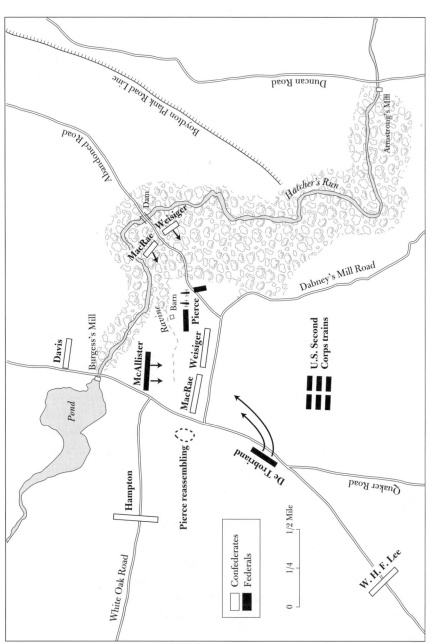

MAP 12.2 The Battle of Burgess's Mill, October 27, 1864

up this retreat and soon found themselves literally in the middle of Hancock's position, with Yankees to the north, west, and south. The limber chests and most of the horses belonging to the two abandoned guns had been evacuated, but two men of Company K, 11th North Carolina, impulsively seized the remaining horses and hitched up the lone caisson to haul it back across the run.[32]

As MacRae and Weisiger advanced nearly to Boydton Plank Road, they looked south and saw the Second Corps wagon train parked below Dabney's Mill Road. Both commanders redirected their fronts roughly ninety degrees to face south and advance toward this tempting target. Their line extended nearly to Boydton Plank Road on the right and almost to the abandoned road, the avenue of their advance, on the left.

But the Rebels were unable to continue. They had penetrated the right wing of Hancock's position and had gotten deep into the middle of his formation, where they could be hit with counterattacks from two directions. The outcome of the battle hung in the balance. If Mahone could be supported by timely assaults conducted by supporting Confederate units along Boydton Plank Road and White Oak Road, a magnificent triumph like that at Reams Station might be possible. If not, Mahone would have to fight his way out of the trap.[33]

J. S. Bartlett of the Bethel Regiment recalled that his comrades could easily see when they surveyed the cornfield that "we had only knocked a gap out of the Yankee line." The Federals quickly mounted counterstrokes before supporting Confederate units could come to Mahone's aid. Robert McAllister's brigade was positioned just east of the Boydton Plank Road and White Oak Road junction, facing north, when he learned of the Rebel attack. Wasting no time, McAllister ordered his men to about-face and advance south. He charged with his New York, New Jersey, and Massachusetts troops across the rugged terrain that drained into Hatcher's Run. Small gullys and thick hazel brush were in the way, and the ravine with the barn in it was the last obstacle. McAllister's men were therefore delayed long enough so that the Tar Heels faced about and opened fire. The new recruits and draftees that filled McAllister's ranks could not stand the punishment and broke. Soon the Federals, veterans and recruits alike, were scampering back into the ravine for safety. McAllister could not rally them in the bottom of the ravine but managed to patch together a line on the western side of it.[34]

A more serious counterattack came from the front. Brig. Gen. Regis de Trobriand had his brigade positioned along Boydton Plank Road, facing west, when the battle started, and he changed front to the rear. Advancing to the northeast with his New York, Indiana, and Pennsylvania men, who cheered as they swept across the mostly level farmland, he hit MacRae and Weisiger obliquely. The Rebels held and engaged in a fierce, stand-up exchange of musketry. The pressure was tremendous. Stedman recalled the "deafening shouts and obstinate fighting" of the men as they struggled without support from the other Rebel columns. MacRae was magnificent, inspiring the soldiers to their utmost. "No help came whilst his men toiled, bled and died," wrote Stedman. The flag of the 44th North Carolina fell several times and finally wound up in the hands of Cpl. William T. Tillman, a member of the color guard. When he was shot, another man stooped to pick up the colors. Tillman touched his arm and said, " 'Tell the General I died with the flag.' " He was later left for dead on the battlefield, but the flag was saved. The 26th also lost its color-bearer, Pvt. Thomas Minton of Company C, who was killed. The flag was left behind on the field to be picked up by a Federal soldier, the third time the regiment lost its colors in battle.[35]

Soon McAllister made another advance across the ravine and threatened MacRae. There seemed to be every danger that the Rebels might be boxed in and forced to surrender. Concern mounted in the ranks, and Lemuel Hoyle worried "that we would never get out—that we would all be either killed or captured." His regimental officers "did not know what to do, some talked of surrendering, some of forming where we were and fighting to the last, others of cutting our way out. The latter alternative was adopted." MacRae took the lead. On foot throughout the attack, he pointed to the rear and shouted instructions to the officers near him, and they passed the word to their men. Soon the brigade was advancing to the rear.[36]

When the Tar Heels realized what was happening, reported another member of the Bethel Regiment, "we did not falter; we about faced and cut our way out." On the way the brigade passed the two abandoned guns, still in their original location. J. S. Bartlett acted on a whim when he saw the cannons. He had been helping a wounded man of his company along but "turned him loose" and picked up a sassafras sprout. He used it instead of a metal rod to spike one of the guns and then rejoined the ranks. The wounded man made it to safety, but Bartlett's sassafras hardly disabled the gun. Charles Stedman insisted that his brother, Lt. Robert W. Stedman, disabled the guns before continuing the retreat. Robert was captured later that day and spent the rest of the war in Northern prisons. Bartlett also remembered looking over his shoulder just before entering the wooded bottomland to see a Federal artillery officer riding in front of the pursuing infantrymen. He held a guidon high in the air to rally the troops until a hail of Rebel bullets snapped the staff in two just above his hand. Bartlett slipped into the trees and did not wait long enough to see if the officer fell. All of the Yankee prisoners taken by Mahone's command on the way in were lost on the way out. Lemuel Hoyle estimated the number at 700.[37]

The victorious Federals mounted no pursuit but contented themselves with

Flag of the 26th North Carolina, captured at Burgess's Mill. The third flag of the 26th to be lost in action, it was left on the battlefield when color-bearer Pvt. Thomas Minton was killed and the brigade retreated to the starting point of its attack. (Copyright North Carolina Museum of History)

mopping up the battlefield. Units from Pierce's brigade marched into the ravine, where a number of Rebels had taken refuge in the barn, and captured 200 prisoners and a flag. MacRae's men were relieved to make it off the battlefield. "That was the hardest fight I have been in for some time," reported Gus Jarratt; "it was not so hard either[,] for the yankees did not half fight but the Brigade lost more heavily than it has for some time." Jarratt had contemplated surrendering rather than running, "but he thought of home & what he would suffer & concluded to risk it," in his father's words.[38]

MacRae's men hurried through the wooded bottomland of Hatcher's Run and reassembled on the north side. No one knew what had happened to color-bearer Minton, so Lieutenant Colonel Adams went back into the trees to find him while his 26th North Carolina re-formed its ranks. The men were understandably depressed by their repulse and the loss of the flag. In fact they used the colors of the 44th North Carolina as a rallying point. When Adams returned without Minton or the flag, he saw their gloomy faces and decided to take drastic action. Adams jumped onto a stump and shouted, "'Twenty-sixth, rally on your commander. He is here if his colors are lost.'" It worked wonders. The men raised a cheer and readied themselves for further orders.[39]

Heth wanted to continue attacking the next morning, but it became unnecessary when Hancock evacuated his position soon after the fighting ended. If the Rebels had waited another day, they would not have needed to attack at all, for the Second Corps was scheduled to give up its lodgment on Boydton Plank Road by noon of October 28. The Federals left their dead and a number of badly wounded men on the field, which was drenched with a rain shower that night.[40]

Heth was lavish with praise for MacRae's "gallant" soldiers and the "distinguished service they rendered." Stedman continued to glorify the men long after the war by writing, "No brigade in Lee's army ever made a more glorious fight than did MacRae's." But the general could not savor any of these compliments. He fumed for days after the battle about the heavy losses his men suffered. "MacRae complained bitterly about his superiors in command allowing him to be cut to pieces when it could have been prevented," remembered the historian of the 47th.[41]

MacRae's casualties were enormous. Thirteen men were killed, 34 were wounded, 6 were wounded and captured, and 415 were captured, for a total of 468 losses. Forty-four percent of the brigade's strength was lost in only two hours of fighting. When the ordnance officer of Lane's brigade, Joseph D. Joyner, visited the 47th North Carolina soon after the battle, he "found very few acquaintances, the yankees having gobbled them up. The yankees were very badly thrashed, but it is to be lamented that McRae's Brigade suffered so much on account of mismanagement."[42]

The Bethel Regiment lost 9 wounded and 98 prisoners. Lemuel Hoyle's company I suffered 11 casualties, all of whom were captured. The 26th North Carolina lost 3 killed, 5 wounded, 1 wounded and captured, and 59 captured. Gus Jarratt took 16 men of his Company C into the battle and lost 6 of them captured and 1 killed. The flag of the 26th was picked up on the battlefield by Sgt. Alonzo Smith of the 7th Michigan; for this he was later awarded a Congressional Medal of Honor. Another medal went to Sgt. Daniel J. Murphy of the 19th Massachusetts for picking up the flag of the 47th North Carolina. The 44th North Carolina lost 2 killed, 8 wounded, 4 wounded and captured, and 101 captured. Company G left the battlefield with only one survivor, a sergeant; it lost 18 men. The 47th North

Carolina lost 4 killed, 9 wounded, 1 wounded and captured, and 123 captured, while the 52nd North Carolina suffered 4 killed, 3 wounded, and 34 captured.[43]

The brigade lost its second largest contingent of prisoners during the war at the battle of Burgess's Mill, named for a building near the point where the Boyd-ton Plank Road crossed Hatcher's Run. Most of the 421 men who were held by the Federals, 71 percent, were released by the end of the war. Eighty-nine of them, 21 percent, died in prison. Only 29, or 6 percent of the prisoners, rejoined their units for further service during the war. The tactical situation accounted for this heavy loss of men; 90 percent of the brigade's total casualties at Burgess's Mill were those captured by the Federals.[44]

MacRae's men continued to occupy the extreme right of Heth's line from Mrs. Hart's house southward. Fifty draftees arrived to replace men lost in the lat-est round of fighting; twenty-nine of them entered the 26th North Carolina. There was much digging for them to do. The Rebel line had to be strengthened because, with Grant's continual edging to the right, fewer and fewer Rebel sol-diers were available to man the ever lengthening fortifications. "I think if we work much longer, we will have the works so that the yankees can't get in even if there was no men in them," wrote Gus Jarratt. The picket lines were close to each other, but there was no firing. The men "take a friendly talk most any time."[45]

Heth told members of the brigade that he had no intention of calling on them to fight for some time, if he could avoid it. The division leader realized the Tar Heels needed to recuperate after fighting six days in two months, winning three of those engagements and losing the rest. Their total losses in these encounters amounted to 713 men. Staff officer Young noted, "Recruits, conscripts, & ab-sentees are daily coming in and before we are put into another battle, I hope our number will be very respectable." By late November the losses at Burgess's Mill had been recovered, and brigade strength was once again up to 1,279 men.[46]

Between digging earthworks and standing picket, the Tar Heels began to build winter quarters just behind the fortifications. Lemuel Hoyle's company found lit-tle lumber to make bunks, shelves, and tables, yet the "boys say 'when we get our shanties done, just let it snow.'" Julius Linebach and two other band members made their own winter hut by digging a pit two feet deep and using logs as walls above ground. Tent flies served as a roof. The enterprising musicians constructed a fireplace and chimney at one end and a pantry at the other, but anyone hoping to receive food and clothing from home was likely to be disappointed. Conditions were worsening in Lee's army as fall set in, and "a regularly organized band of thugs and pickpockets" besieged the depot at Petersburg. They stole the personal belongings of soldiers and even ransacked packages from home. The thieves "have reduced the business to a system," noted Hoyle, "and anyone arriving on the train must keep a very sharp lookout."[47]

The Moravian band kept itself busy as usual. They were visited by Prof. William H. Hartwell, the leader of the 11th Mississippi band, whose acquaintance they had made many months before. Hartwell was a music professor, and his bandsmen inspired the admiration of the Moravians. The Tar Heel players continued to serenade Heth and Hill and received a shipment of gray pants and blue jackets on December 1, just in time for winter.[48]

MacRae had to deal with administrative matters regarding his staff. Previously, all brigadier generals were allowed two assistant adjutant generals, but the War Department issued new regulations forcing them to release one. MacRae lost Capt. Fred Nash, who was reassigned to Brig. Gen. Seth Barton's Virginia brigade. Louis G. Young was his remaining assistant adjutant general, and MacRae hoped to encourage him to accept a lieutenant colonelcy in one of the brigade's regiments so he could appoint his brother in Young's place. The faithful staff officer deserved promotion. "All the Generals from Genl. Lee down are anxious that he should be promoted," MacRae informed his brother. But the officers in the regiment refused to waive their right to the lieutenant colonelcy, so the plan fell through. MacRae had no opportunity to appoint a commissary officer for the brigade when Major Baker was reassigned to a post in Raleigh. All such staff appointments were now being made by the War Department.[49]

The leadership of MacRae's regiments continued to be borne by many officers of company rank. Only the 26th (Major Adams) and the 44th (Major Stedman) were led by regimental officers. Capt. James M. Young was in charge of the Bethel Regiment, Capt. Sidney W. Mitchell commanded the 47th, and Capt. William W. Carmichael continued to lead the 52nd. Many companies had a similar problem. Company D of the 52nd North Carolina had forty-three men on its rolls, but fifteen of them were prisoners of war. The company had been led by noncommissioned officers since Gettysburg. Sgt. Philip A. James was anxious about the coming winter season, for morale was sinking in the company. "I am afraid that thare is a heap of our men is a going to run away in the Spring for Som of them is a going to the yanks every night."[50]

The Tar Heels paid attention to the presidential election held that fall in the North. With the Democrats running on a platform proclaiming that the war was a failure and should end through negotiation rather than military power, many Southerners saw Lincoln's defeat as their last chance for victory. But a string of Union battlefield triumphs in Georgia and the Shenandoah Valley doomed the Democratic effort. Louis Young took the news with resignation. "Now that it is clearly established by Lincoln's election, that the war is to be prosecuted with vigour, all take it quietly, and remain determined to hold out to the end." But many members of the rank and file rejected Young's approach. Twenty deserters showed up in the Federal provost marshal's office soon after the election. One of the twenty was a member of MacRae's brigade.[51]

Desertion, in general, was not yet a serious problem for the brigade. From seven to fifteen men had deserted each month from June to December 1864. Four soldiers had fled the 26th North Carolina in the first three weeks of November, perhaps because of Lincoln's reelection. The real drain of manpower would not begin until the dead of winter, when the food supply seriously declined. Yet punishment was meted out for those who did desert and were caught. Pvt. Joshua Starney of the Bethel Regiment was executed on December 4, the only member of Company D ever shot by his own comrades. John C. Warlick remembered years later that "it was my sad duty to help shoot him. I aimed a bullet at his heart." Lemuel Hoyle, Warlick's company commander, was in charge of the firing squad.[52]

The Tar Heels made one more strike at the Yankees before the year was out. Grant tried to widen the break of the Weldon Railroad by sending elements of the Second and Fifth Corps to destroy the tracks below Stony Creek Station as far as Hicksford, only ten miles short of the North Carolina border. More than 20,000 Federal troops left the Petersburg lines on Wednesday, December 7, and camped at the Nottoway River that night. Confederate cavalry rode to the crossing of the Meherrin River to block them. Hicksford was on the south side of the stream, and Belfield was on the north bank. On December 8, as the Federals tore up rails and burned ties from the Nottoway River to Jarratt's Station, eight miles north of Belfield, Lee dispatched Hill with portions of three divisions to deal with them. Heth had to wait until Maj. Gen. John B. Gordon's troops relieved him in the trenches and then led MacRae's brigade and other troops out at 4:00 P.M. They marched on Boydton Plank Road and camped three miles south of Dinwiddie Court House on the night of December 8. When Gordon's troops were shifted elsewhere on December 11, the 13th Georgia occupied the space held by MacRae's men.

The Federals continued to tear up track south of Jarratt's Station on December 9, but they stopped when they neared Belfield. Grant did not want a major fight on this expedition, so Warren assessed the Rebel cavalry position and decided to return to Petersburg the next morning. Hill arrived at Hicksford that night with the van of his hard-marching column, but Heth was far to the rear. MacRae's men resumed their tramp at dawn of December 9 and crossed the Nottoway River later that day. They bivouacked eight miles short of Hicksford that night as a heavy sleet storm descended over the area.

The weather turned the roads into icy ribbons as the Federals started early on December 10 for the north. The Confederate infantry moved from their bivouac, assuming the enemy were still on the railroad at Jarratt's Station. Heth was ordered to attack any Federals he found there with his own and Wilcox's divisions, while Mahone struck for a point four miles south of Jarratt's. It came to nothing. At the station Heth found only a few cavalrymen who ran away at the first sound of firing. Hill ordered his infantrymen to cross the ruined tracks and march eastward in search of the elusive Federals. Heth made it to Rowland's farm on the night of December 10 and resumed marching east the next morning, but an order from Hill arrived to call off the pursuit and return to the Petersburg lines by way of Boydton Plank Road. MacRae bivouacked at the plank road's crossing of the Nottoway River on the night of December 11. His tired men spent the next night three miles south of Dinwiddie Court House and returned to their winter huts on the evening of December 13.[53]

The Tar Heels had endured a forced march under terrible winter conditions but "did not get a fight," as an officer of the 52nd later put it. Sixteen miles of track were destroyed, forcing Rebel engineers to work until March to restore the line all the way to Stony Creek Station. MacRae's men had marched a total of 100 miles in five days "through snow, rain and excessive cold." It was "quite a severe march" by everyone's estimation, but losses were very light. The 44th North Carolina had two men wounded and one captured, and the 47th North Carolina lost one wounded; but it is unclear how these losses occurred. The other three regiments suffered no casualties.[54]

The long campaign that had begun on May 5 had slowly reached a critical phase. There was increasingly little reason for MacRae's Tar Heels to hope that the war might be won as their rations thinned and the bitter cold whipped around their log huts. The last winter of the war was upon them.

Chapter 13

The Road to Appomattox

The brigade drilled and stood picket duty for some time after its strenuous march to Hicksford. Winter quarters were comfortable, and for the time rations were more or less adequate. There were no complaints regarding clothing, for Governor Vance made certain that plenty of good cloth was available for his troops. Furloughs were granted to every fifty men in the brigade beginning in late December, and desertions were irregular. When Pvt. John R. Foster of the 26th North Carolina deserted in the early morning hours of December 31, Federal general Nelson Miles doubted if he could trust his information. Foster had been wounded at Gettysburg and Cold Harbor; he had deserted earlier in the war but returned without punishment. Now he told Miles of Rebel preparations for a dash on Union picket lines, but the Yankee simply passed him on to an adjutant general. Foster spent a few days in custody and then was released after taking the oath of allegiance.[1]

The lines of earthworks were a half-mile apart, and the pickets did not feel compelled to fire on one another. Lieutenant Blount of the 47th North Carolina reported that "we have [a] friendly line, and we neighbors act with great decorum." Like many other Confederate units, MacRae's brigade built a dam on a small stream in front of their works to flood the area and prevent a Union attack. The dam had to be repaired when a rainstorm washed part of it away.[2]

Julius Linebach was delighted when Colonel Lane returned to command the 26th North Carolina on December 14 after recovering from his Reams Station wound. The musicians were desperate to go home for Christmas and encouraged friends to send a petition to Governor Vance so they could give concerts to benefit the state hospital, but MacRae disapproved the request for leave. The brigadier later ordered the Moravians and the bands of the Bethel Regiment and the 44th North Carolina to take turns playing every night from eight until ten o'clock, leading Linebach to assume it was a punishment for asking to go home.

There was little else to enliven the winter camps. Gus Reich sometimes gave his magic show for the soldiers, "making nonsensical speeches" to entertain the men further. Linebach noted that he "would always have a good audience of deadheads." A very strange bit of entertainment arrived one day when a civilian named R. O. Davidson made speeches to the soldiers about his idea to build a flying machine designed to drop aerial bombs on the Union trenches. Linebach derided him as "a crank" and his ideas as "absurd." The man disappeared, never to return.

Rations began to worsen after Christmas, with the band members reporting no meat except an occasional ration of old beef too tough to digest. Hardtack often was their only fare. Word arrived that the citizens of Richmond were planning to bake mountains of bread for the soldiers to celebrate the holidays, causing a stir of excitement in the camps. But Linebach was devastated when the results of this well-meant effort arrived on January 3, for there were only "a few mouthfuls" for each soldier. "Instead of cheering the men, and putting new enthusiasm into them, this pitiful effort only made more plain the desperate condition of affairs in the Southern Confederacy, & had rather a depressing effect." The men went on half-rations ten days later.[3]

While everyone complained that the bread ration was too low, Benjamin Wesley Justice also reported that soap was in short supply. He tried to make a substitute out of "offal & spoilt Beef," but it is difficult to believe that such a concoction could be effective. Justice correctly stated that a "corps of soapmakers would be a blessing to the army." Surgeon Warren reported that the ambulance mules were poorly fed, but rest of the brigade's logistical needs were adequately met. It had plenty of ammunition for the .58-caliber rifle muskets that all regiments were using, and the men's clothing was in pretty good condition.[4]

The dawn of 1865 was a good time to take stock of the losses in MacRae's brigade since the Wilderness campaign. It suffered a total of 1,132 casualties in that time. The killed amounted to 95, the wounded to 479, and the captured to 554. The losses suffered in 1863 were even heavier, with 17 missing, 282 killed, 810 wounded, 617 wounded and captured, and 820 captured, for an appalling total of 2,546 casualties.[5]

The men found it more difficult to find enough firewood with the deepening of winter. They had to walk "a long ways off and no wagon to hall it in to us and scanty rations to feed the men on." Benjamin H. Freeman reported the desertion of seven men from the brigade picket line on the night of January 27. "I expect that all will run off before long," he concluded. Many of them willingly gave information to the Yankees. Federal generals learned the location of each of Heth's brigades, stretched as they were from Burgess's Mill toward Jones's farm. MacRae's men were on Heth's far left, connecting with Wilcox's division near Claypoole Road, with brigade headquarters at Mrs. Hart's house on Duncan Road.[6]

The possibility that regiments might have to be consolidated created a great deal of debate in the brigade. The western armies had been doing this for some time as a solution to the chronic shortage of replacements for the ranks. Now Lee's army was facing the prospect as well. No one wanted it, but consolidation seemed almost inevitable. William Blount reported that the news had "caused some excitement among the 'Star & Bar' gentry but most of them . . . are willing to acquiesce in it with a patriotic self abnegation." MacRae's regiments were never consolidated, but some companies were combined. Lt. William N. Snelling led Companies A, C, and D of the 26th North Carolina during the last few months of the war.[7]

The thoughts of many soldiers turned to peace that gloomy winter. Benjamin H. Freeman saw an opinion poll circulating through the 44th North Carolina early in February. It was forwarded by Senator Robert M. T. Hunter of Virginia, one of three commissioners sent by the Confederate government to discuss peace terms with a Federal delegation at Hampton Roads. There were two questions on it: Should the South accept an honorable peace, and if so, on what terms? Should the South accept peace on any terms? Freeman noted that five of his company marked yes, apparently to the first question, and no one marked no to either question. The results were predictable, given the deteriorating condition of the army and the increasingly hopeless situation at Petersburg.

The conference was unproductive. The Southern delegation refused to accept the abolition of slavery, even though the Confederate Congress was on the verge of approving the arming of blacks to fight in the Rebel army, and the talks broke up. Many Tar Heels paid little attention to this fleeting hope for an end to the war. Freeman went skating on the frozen surface of the pond at Burgess's Mill, and the chaplain of the 47th North Carolina preached as often as he could in the winter camps. A chapter of the Young Men's Christian Association had been created in the regiment early in 1864, but it was disbanded during the winter, "the members of it having been knocked out," in the words of the regimental historian. Julius Linebach often sat in front of his quarters at night, watching the shells arch overhead. "It was much like an exhibition of sky rockets, very pretty to look at," he remembered, but he also wondered if some of these "blazing meteors would bring destruction, suffering or death, to some one, perhaps helpless & innocent women or children." There were few unalloyed joys that winter at Petersburg.[8]

In January the 44th North Carolina decided it needed a new flag. The old one had been so riddled with shell and bullets that its staff was spliced and the fabric was shredded. It was now so small that other regiments had difficulty seeing it during brigade drills. Since the 44th was the center regiment of MacRae's command, it was imperative that it have a new color. The old one was presented to Robert Bingham's wife, Della Worth Bingham, in a formal ceremony on January 1. She had won the hearts of the men for her devoted attention to their needs in the field. Her husband also was a favorite in the regiment. He kept the flag at his home for the rest of his long life.[9]

The war heated up when Grant launched another attempt to cut the wagon train link between Stony Creek Station and Petersburg. In the early morning hours of Sunday, February 5, the Fifth Corps made a dash for Boydton Plank Road while the Second Corps screened its movement by taking position where Duncan Road crossed Hatcher's Run at Armstrong's Mill, well in front of the Confederate Boydton Plank Road Line. Thomas Smyth's brigade anchored the Second Corps' left at the swampy bottomland of the run and stretched northwest along Duncan Road for a half-mile before turning east to Rocky Branch, which paralleled the road. To the east Mott's division was positioned to face north and connect with the Petersburg line, but a gap existed between his command and Smyth just east of Rocky Branch.[10]

Sleet began to fall as the Confederates responded to this move. Cooke, Archer, and MacRae moved out of their works and formed in the no-man's-land between the lines. MacRae was absent on sick leave, and it is uncertain who led the brigade; but Lane had seniority, and Louis G. Young seems to have superintended many of its movements that day. The men marched southward to hit the Second Corps at Armstrong's Mill. Cooke's and Archer's brigades, the latter commanded by Brig. Gen. William McComb, formed the first line, with MacRae's Tar Heels in reserve behind McComb's troops. Federal artillery began to fire at about 4:00, and Cooke received most of it. Many rounds fell among MacRae's ranks as well. The brigade sharpshooters had been loaned to Cooke so he could screen his right flank during the bombardment.

The punishment became too great for McComb's men, who bolted and ran through the ranks of MacRae's command. The Tar Heels allowed them to pass and then redressed their ranks and advanced to take their place next to Cooke. For a few minutes the two North Carolina brigades awaited the order to attack. Expectancy built to an uncomfortable level. Young walked over to Cooke and encouraged him to join MacRae's men in an unauthorized charge, but Cooke refused to do so. "I returned to the brigade to find it anxious to advance, and disappointed that it was not permitted to do so," remembered Young. He vividly recalled the image of Major Stedman of the 44th North Carolina, who approached the staff officer with his sword raised high, "calling out in loud tone, 'Our men are ready to advance and only await the command.'" Young did not oblige him, although he was "very much tempted" to do so. He regretted this reluctance for the rest of his life.[11]

When the order to attack finally came, only Cooke's brigade was sent in. His plucky Tar Heels charged three times and were repulsed with heavy loss. After ninety minutes of fighting, during which MacRae's men stood idle, the first day of the battle of Hatcher's Run came to an end. The Rebels prepared to retire to their former position just after dusk when Young received a serious wound that put him out of action for the rest of the war. It is doubtful that his brigade could have made much of a difference in the attacks. The Federals were more numerous and had a good defensive position. Hill had so much faith in MacRae's tactical skills that he believed Hatcher's Run would have been a victory if he had been on duty. As it was the brigade emerged from this sorely mishandled affair with few losses. Two men were killed, eighteen were wounded, and five were captured, for a total of twenty-five casualties.[12]

The struggle along the banks of Hatcher's Run was not yet over. A large Rebel force attacked the Fifth Corps south of the stream on February 6 but failed to break it. The next day another assault was planned in the same sector, and MacRae's men were ready to support it. The Tar Heels started out at dawn under a light fall of sleet and snow, but they were not engaged. As MacRae's men filed back into their winter quarters that night, Lee decided to call off further attacks. The Federals extended their line to Hatcher's Run and were now in a position to turn the corner and extend it westward across Boydton Plank Road.[13]

William Long was a casualty of this campaign, although he never came under fire. He had recuperated from his Cold Harbor wound well enough to return to the 44th North Carolina in December. The injury to his thigh worsened over the next month, and the surgeon advised Long not to go on the march to Hatcher's Run. But the plucky lieutenant asked him to bandage it very tightly and set out. The column encountered a spot in the road where a man's body had been mangled by a shell, leaving a bloody mess. Long jumped over the spot and tore open the wound. It bled so freely that he fainted and would have died if he had not received quick attention.

Long was thereafter assigned a soft post in the rear. He became adjutant of Libby Prison, a former tobacco warehouse in downtown Richmond, on February 27, 1865. He lived in a tent at the corner of Twenty-first and Cary Streets. His wound often forced him to rest in a chair while he filled out forms, and he even had to be carried about on occasion. When his wound healed enough to give him mobility, Long watched the workings of the Confederate Senate and frequently visited the War Department in his off-duty hours.

Although his duty was mostly undemanding, Long hated one part of it: taking Union prisoners who had just arrived from Andersonville, Salisbury, and Belle Island to City Point for exchange. They were malnourished, sick, and dying. He dreamed of them for months afterward. "A thousand times worse than a bloody field of battle was this mass of hopeless suffering men," he remembered decades later. "The[y] followed me with their helpless appealing stare, uttering no word of complaint, listless, hopeless." Long left Libby when Richmond fell and made his way to Georgia, hoping to find a position on some general's staff until Lee's surrender put an end to the war.[14]

The worsening conditions back on the Petersburg line led to a dramatic increase in the desertion rate following the battle of Hatcher's Run. The Federals continued to gather information on Rebel troop dispositions from MacRae's deserters. By now the Sixth Corps under Maj. Gen. Horatio G. Wright had taken position near MacRae's command, and its officers carefully sifted through the sometimes detailed reports passed to them by the Tar Heels.[15]

Widespread dissatisfaction was tempered by the ever hopeful spirits of a few. William H. Blount had always maintained an impressive if sometimes naive optimism. He tried to assure everyone at home that "the spirit of the army is improving," even though rations were "very Slim." Blount was willing "to live on half rations of bread until we gain our independence." He argued that the rank and file shared his optimism, that one could see a growing determination on the faces of the men. "We expect to enter upon the coming campaign in a blaze of enthusiasm," he crowed. "We intend to do our whole duty, put forth every effort."[16]

Thomas Bailey of the 47th North Carolina also refused to become depressed. "I don't see any of our men who look like starving though some would eat twice as much as they get," he reported. When brandy was issued on March 3, many men did not want their share and sold it to more thirsty comrades. The going rate was $5 a gill, amounting to $160 a gallon, yet several men bought enough to become drunk. Bailey also reported the creation of a division flag for Heth's command, undoubtedly issued to boost morale. It consisted of a blue field with a white cross in the middle.[17]

Despite Blount's and Bailey's comments, there is no doubt that the brigade was suffering its worst morale of the war. Desertion was the surest proof of it. Many years later Louis G. Young tried to cover up the fact by arguing that the brigade displayed remarkable cheerfulness, valor, "daring spirit," and discipline during the last few months of the Petersburg campaign. Young wrote of the men's "faithfulness unto death" and rightfully pointed out that the brigade deserved "to rank with the best troops of any clime, any country, any time." But no amount of postwar memorializing could obscure the fact that there was widespread demoralization among the men.[18]

MacRae returned to duty soon after Hatcher's Run, and there were rumors that he would be promoted to major general and take command of a division. MacRae had become the firm foundation of his command's remaining morale. Stedman wrote that "Nature had endowed him with a type of personal courage which made him absolutely indifferent to danger, and his calmness amidst a hurricane of shot, shell and musketry, was as great as when seated at his breakfast table in his tent or reviewing his command at dress parade." MacRae imparted that steadiness to his men; they "seemed to imbibe his spirit." He initiated a petition to North Carolina's delegates in the Confederate Congress, asking them to address the problem of civilian morale on the home front. MacRae and most of his subordinate officers were convinced that despairing letters from home were the chief cause of desertion, an opinion they shared with Lee.[19]

The 26th North Carolina lost the service of its Colonel Lane in mid-March when the lingering effects of his many wounds began to trouble him. He left the field for the last time and traveled to hospitals at Salisbury and Danville for treatment, while Adams resumed command of the regiment.[20]

The enlisted men found it more difficult to be dismissed from duty because of injuries. Benjamin H. Freeman had returned from his wound received during the Fifth Offensive, but he was not completely fit. The injury was healed, but he could not use his arm normally. Company officers detailed him to camp chores and to serve as courier, but the authorities postponed giving him a discharge because of the manpower shortage.[21]

The 47th North Carolina became the topic of discussion for a while when a woman named Mollie Bean was arrested on the Danville Railroad on the night of February 17 wearing a uniform. She claimed to have served in the regiment for more than two years and to have been wounded twice, but upon examination she was found to be "manifestly crazy." Bean was held at Castle Thunder for the time being. The authorities did not believe her story. "It will not, we presume, be pretended that she had served so long in the army without her sex being discovered," commented the editors of a Richmond newspaper.[22]

The long-discussed decision to arm slaves to fight in the Rebel army came to a climax in early March. When newspapers reported the congressional debates over this issue, Benjamin H. Freeman thought it was a bad idea; it would "not do for the White Soldiers[;] they say that they won't stay here[.] I think that this war will brake up in a row before it is done." When the decision was final a few days later, Freeman could only hope that the black soldiers would not be sent anywhere near MacRae's brigade, "for I dont want to fight with the negroes."[23]

Whether the decision led anyone to desert is impossible to say, but the rate continued to climb. Fourteen men left MacRae's command on the night of March 14. "A few have been caught & brought back while attempting to go home," reported Benjamin Wesley Justice, "but numbers go over to the yankees every night. And what speaks worse for the spirit of the army, is that the men on the picket line fire off their guns into the air & will not try to shoot down those who are in the act of deserting to the enemy." They continued to pass information to the Federals, though most of it was vague and inaccurate.[24]

The desertions were at a normal level in January, when 14 men left the brigade. They increased significantly in February, when 43 men deserted. March was the worst month; 42 men left the Bethel Regiment alone, 15 deserted from the 26th North Carolina, and 17 left the 47th North Carolina. Added to the number who deserted from the other two regiments, MacRae lost 89 men that month, more than 13 percent of his strength. The desertion rate plummeted in April only because Lee's line was broken at Petersburg and the war came to a swift end. A total of 155 men deserted from the brigade in 1865.

Men who deserted and reached their North Carolina homes had to deal with vigorous efforts to retrieve them. Columbus A. Tuttle of the 26th North Carolina related an episode that occurred in Caldwell County that winter. He was at home on furlough and volunteered to catch two deserters who were hiding in a cabin. Tuttle gathered a squad of six men, surrounded the building at night, and frightened the runaways into bolting for the door. They were easily subdued, although one of the men had to be shot in the shoulder. "Their wives cursed us for everything they could think of," he recalled.[25]

Brigade strength remained relatively high during the winter despite the desertion problem. MacRae had 1,386 men in late December, 1,267 in late February, and 1,411 in March. Regimental strengths in March amounted to 338 men in the 11th North Carolina, 268 in the 26th North Carolina, 278 in the 44th North Carolina, 321 in the 47th North Carolina, and 206 in the 52nd North Carolina.[26]

Despite the desertions, a majority of men in MacRae's brigade remained on duty. Most of them seem to have had little if any hope of a successful conclusion to the war, but they could not bring themselves to leave the army. They were willing to continue fighting out of a sense of hopeless duty to the cause or because they did not want to be stigmatized as cowards or because they feared punishment. A small proportion of men in the brigade remained optimistic against all signs to the contrary. A hard core of them meant to fight to the bitter end, while most remaining soldiers were ready for the war to end soon.

The end began as moderate spring weather appeared. Orders reached the brigade on the night of March 24 to be ready to move at dawn. No instructions arrived the next day, but everyone heard artillery firing to the left as Lee launched his last offensive of the war. Fully a third of his army captured Union Fort Stedman far to the left of MacRae's position. The Confederates briefly held it and even penetrated a short distance to the Federal rear, but they had no strength to hold the fort. Before the end of the morning, Fort Stedman was once again in Yankee hands.

This brought trouble for other parts of the line. Union artillery and pickets fired along MacRae's front as the Second Corps and, to its right, the Sixth Corps easily captured the Confederate picket line halfway across no-man's-land at 10:30 A.M. The artillery fire was so heavy that Julius Linebach was forced to stop reading a book that had absorbed his attention all morning and take shelter behind the earthworks. The winter huts were pummeled with shell, and many of them were demolished. The band's huts were not damaged, but a paper window was blown out by the concussion of a shell. Linebach was fascinated by this bombardment. He had rarely been under fire and took great interest in watching the puff of the Union cannon a mile away and then dodging the explosion several moments later. He heard the whistle of the shells as they arched overhead and noticed that the old veterans laughed when a newer soldier impulsively ducked his head at the sound of projectiles that had already passed.[27]

Mrs. Hart did not like the shelling. The brigade's line ran through her yard as it crossed Duncan Road, and she hid in the cellar when the artillery began to roar. She probably did not hear the skirmish that ensued when MacRae's sharpshooters counterattacked at 2:00 that afternoon. The strike was led by Col. John M. Stone, commander of Davis's Mississippi brigade. MacRae accompanied the sharpshooters, who numbered two officers and forty enlisted men, when they broke through a section of the Union picket line and turned to the right. Stone's 2nd Mississippi turned to the left, but both columns achieved limited success. Major Stedman estimated that they were outnumbered three to one. The Tar Heels skirmished for the rest of the day while other troops from Stone's brigade strengthened the picket line. It had been an exciting adventure for Stone, who took off his hat at one point and yelled, "'I would rather command those boys than have a commission as Brigadier General.'" The commander of the sharpshooters, Lt. William Emmett Kyle, was seriously wounded in this engagement. He was taken to a hospital in Petersburg but soon left, despite the protests of his surgeon, when he learned that his corps had no officers left on duty. Kyle's concern was commendable, but he was too badly injured to remain in the field. Capt. John H. Thorp of the 47th North Carolina was named his replacement on March 29. MacRae was satisfied with the appointment. He liked Thorp and once commented that he "'will do as much fighting and talk as little of it as any officer in our army.'"[28]

The brigade lost 123 men on March 25; 107 of them were captured, and 2 were wounded and captured. An additional 14 men were wounded. The 11th North Carolina lost 27, the 26th North Carolina lost 18, the 44th North Carolina lost 20, the 47th North Carolina lost 28, and the 52nd North Carolina lost 30.[29]

The events of March 25 broke the stasis into which the armies had settled since the Hatcher's Run campaign of early February. There was also an air of inevitability about the outcome of the next round of fighting. Heth was forced to stretch his line ever farther to the right as Lee expected another effort by the Federals to gain Boydton Plank Road and move on to the South Side Railroad. MacRae's command left the Hart house at 10:00 P.M. on March 29 with McGowan's South Carolina brigade and proceeded down the Boydton Plank Road. It was raining heavily as the men stumbled through the dark on the muddy thoroughfare. They bivouacked near Hatcher's Run and warmed themselves beside piles of burning brush. The Tar Heels crossed Hatcher's Run at daylight on March 30 and marched to a new line manned by Maj. Gen. Bushrod R. Johnson's division, filing into the trenches as Johnson's men moved to the right. Lee himself met MacRae's and McGowan's men as they took position in the works under the ever falling rain. The line ran along White Oak Road and was located about four miles south of the South Side Railroad. MacRae held the left of the line near its junction with Boydton Plank Road, and McGowan was to his right. The rain continued into the night of March 30.[30]

Back on the Boydton Plank Road Line, Lane's North Carolina brigade shifted to its right, and McComb's Tennessee brigade shifted to its left to cover the gap left by the removal of MacRae and McGowan. The Moravian band had accompanied Adams's regiment for a few hours on March 30; then it was sent back to the winter huts at Mrs. Hart's house to cook bread for the soldiers. The musicians baked all day and loaded their food onto wagons to be hauled to the regiment. More Rebel troops were moved to the White Oak Road line on March 30. Scales's North Carolina brigade moved up to replace MacRae on the left, where the line joined Boydton Plank Road, and MacRae's rain-soaked men shifted a bit to the right. Heavy Union artillery fire, as well as rain, fell on the lines that night.[31]

MacRae came close to getting involved in an attack on March 31. A large cavalry force under Maj. Gen. Philip Sheridan was moving from Dinwiddie Court House toward the South Side Railroad, with Warren's Fifth Corps approaching the White Oak Road Line to shield his right. Lee shifted McGowan's brigade to the far right and sent it and three other brigades, in succession, to conduct a slashing attack. MacRae was ordered to wait until the offensive rolled to his part of the line. The advance was an immediate success, catching the Federals by surprise and rolling them back, but then it petered out. Brig. Gen. Henry A. Wise's Virginia brigade, immediately to MacRae's right, was the last unit to go in. A spirited Union counterattack drove the Rebels back to the White Oak Road Line by dark, but at least the Yankees were prevented from crossing that important road and heading for the rail line. Except for his sharpshooters, who skirmished all day, MacRae's men were not engaged in the battle of White Oak Road.[32]

The next day, April 1, saw critical moves to bring the Petersburg campaign to a close. Sheridan's cavalry and Warren's Fifth Corps captured the important road junction of Five Forks, five miles west of MacRae's position. This gave the Federals a clear avenue to the South Side Railroad, which they could easily cut the next day. The Second Corps had already advanced up Boydton Plank Road the previous day, while the Fifth Corps was fighting its seesaw battle with the Rebels. It fronted the Confederate White Oak Road Line and readied for action on April 2.[33]

The Confederates had to shift units around to meet this developing threat. Johnson's division evacuated the right wing of the White Oak Road Line to hold the South Side Railroad as long as possible the next day. This forced all remaining units—McGowan's, MacRae's, and Scales's brigades—to extend to the right. When Heth left to tend to other parts of the attenuated Confederate line, he placed McGowan in charge of the White Oak Road Line; Cooke was told to take charge of the Boydton Plank Road Line for some distance north of its junction with White Oak Road. The Federals were very active all night of April 1, and the Confederates lost much sleep. MacRae's brigade suffered 16 men captured and 1 wounded when the Second Corps advanced in the night and took part of the Confederate skirmish line. The 26th North Carolina lost 1 wounded and 4 captured, the 44th North Carolina lost 9 captured, and the 47th North Carolina lost 3 captured. The Federals were ready to lunge toward White Oak Road at dawn.[34]

To make matters worse, MacRae was forced to detach a large portion of his overworked brigade. Heth ordered him to send the Bethel Regiment and the 52nd North Carolina, under Lt. Col. Eric Erson, to report to Cooke, who needed men to fill out the thin line along Boydton Plank Road. Erson pulled the two units out of line and marched them up the road on the night of April 1. Cooke placed them in their former position between McComb and Lane at 1:00 A.M. on April 2. The 11th filled trenches to the left of the 52nd and next to a ravine that flowed into Arthur's Swamp, not far from the Jones's farm battlefield. Erson's left rested at Mrs. Hart's house, and his two regiments straddled Duncan Road. The 28th North Carolina of Lane's brigade was positioned to Erson's left. MacRae had earlier detached 220 men to a heavy picket line near the Claypoole house and now could muster only 280 soldiers to hold his part of the White Oak Road Line. He was forced to stretch his command so thin that there was only one Tar Heel for every six feet of linear space in the trench. Erson commanded another 280 men in the two regiments along the plank road.[35]

MacRae's command was divided, outnumbered, and exhausted when Grant launched his final offensive at Petersburg. He ordered three major attacks on different parts of the line, two of which would hit the separated wings of MacRae's brigade. The first and most successful was conducted by the Sixth Corps; it easily penetrated the line held in part by Erson's two regiments. The second, more cautiously conducted by the Second Corps, gently pushed the Tar Heels out of the White Oak Road Line. There was little MacRae's men could do to stop either of these blue juggernauts.

The Sixth Corps had prepared thoroughly for the grand attack. Three divisions deployed in a wedge-shaped column; 14,000 men were to be thrown against only 2,000 defending Rebels just before dawn. The point of this wedge hit Lane's brigade, just to Erson's left. The left wing of the formation approached Erson a few minutes later. It consisted of Col. J. Warren Keifer's Maryland, New York, Ohio, and Pennsylvania brigade and Col. William S. Truex's New Jersey, New York, Pennsylvania, and Vermont brigade, both of Brig. Gen. Truman Seymour's division. The Tar Heels could hear the firing and yelling to their left, so they angled their muskets in that direction to open fire. They did not notice Keifer and Truex advancing silently to their front. In fact, J. S. Bartlett of the Bethel Regiment failed to see any Yankees until they began to cross the works only a few yards to his left. "I looked around and saw that there was no one there except myself and the Yankees. I might not have known that they were there [but] they had been yelling and shooting at the boys who ran before I did. Well, I felt very light and was anxious to see how fast I could run, so I set out for a foot race and when I quit running, I looked back and could not see a Yankee any where." Bartlett later remarked with a great deal of relish that "Richmond and Petersburg were both gone and so was I, and I kept going."[36]

John C. Warlick of the Bethel Regiment fired rapidly to the front as the Federals approached. They seemed to be "as thick as black birds," he recalled later. Warlick then saw shadowy figures come from the left. They appeared to be

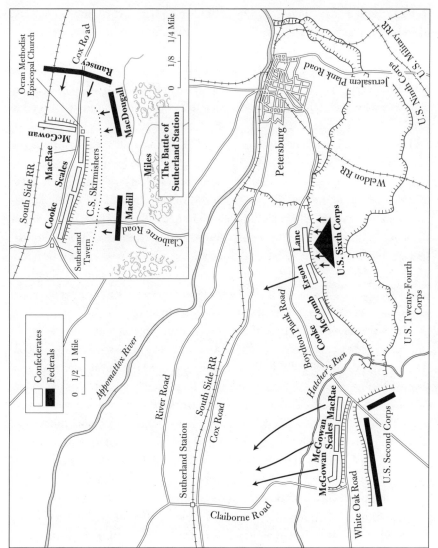

MAP 13.1 The Petersburg Campaign, April 2, 1865

Confederates
Federals

0   1/2   1 Mile

Inset: The Battle of Sutherland Station

Ocran Methodist
Episcopal Church

Cox Road

Ramsey

MacDougall

McGowan

South Side RR

Cooke   MacRae
         Scales

C.S. Skirmishers

Sutherland
Tavern

Madill

Claiborne Road

Miles

The Battle of
Sutherland Station

0   1/8   1/4 Mile

Main map labels:

Petersburg

Jerusalem Plank Road

U.S. Ninth Corps

U.S. Military RR

Weldon RR

Lane

U.S. Sixth Corps

Erson

Cooke
McComb

Boydton Plank Road

U.S. Twenty-Fourth
Corps

Hatcher's Run

McGowan
Scales   MacRae
McGowan

White Oak Road

U.S. Second Corps

Claiborne Road

Sutherland Station

Cox Road

South Side RR

River Road

Appomattox River

Rebels, "until a Capt. who was in front of his men with sword drawn whacked me over the head twice[;] before I realised my situation his men were right at his heels with fixed bayonets, how easily they could have pinioned me to the wooden breast works, the old Capt ordered me to get over the breast works & get to the rear[;] well I did too." The 52nd North Carolina tried to hold at the works "for some length of time," according to Erson, before it too was forced to flee.[37]

The Moravian band also was caught up in this assault. Heavy skirmishing began after 1:00 A.M. on April 2 near the Hart house. Two hours later a wounded Rebel picket vaulted over the parapet where the musicians were taking cover. He told them to go to the rear as the Yankees were massing and the Confederates could not hold them. They immediately went to the huts and packed their few belongings, then moved to the rear for some breakfast and rest. Even at this distance a few stray bullets sailed overhead and struck the trees. Dawn began to break. Linebach had just suggested to his comrades that they move farther back to escape the bullets when he looked toward the works and saw "a long blue line, sparkling with flashes of musketry," crawl across the parapet.

The bandsmen quickly picked up their bags and instruments and ran across the countryside, clambering over fences and struggling across soft, muddy fields. They stooped to avoid the bullets that ranged over the landscape and even dropped some packs to lighten their load. Linebach was forced to give up a bag of cornmeal he had carefully preserved for weeks. They passed a wagon train while the teamsters desperately tried to hitch up their mules to join the retreat. The musicians did not intend to stop until they were well out of harm's way.[38]

The Sixth Corps breakthrough completely cracked open the western part of Lee's line at Petersburg. The Federals turned to the left and ranged down Boydton Plank Road, scooping up large numbers of prisoners and forcing many Confederate units to abandon their positions. Some of the fugitives retired to the north, where the Rebels had an inner line of works protecting the western approaches to town, while others, including the 11th and 52nd, simply fled west.

The other wing of MacRae's brigade, led by MacRae along the White Oak Road, fared a bit better. The Second Corps advanced slowly on the morning of April 2, fearing a repetition of the slashing attack that had befallen the Fifth Corps on March 31. There was heavy skirmishing until MacRae received the order to withdraw due to the Sixth Corps success up the plank road. He got his command across Hatcher's Run "with slight loss" as the Second Corps pressed forward. MacRae moved north as fast as possible toward Sutherland Station, some five miles away on the South Side Railroad. Heth put Cooke in charge of the growing concentration of troops at the station and told him to hold out long enough to allow the wagons parked there to get away; then he was to retreat to the west. Heth rode off to find Lee. He had received word that A. P. Hill had been killed earlier that day, and he was to take charge of the Third Corps. The troops at Sutherland's could not expect any help, for the Federals had crossed the South Side Railroad to the east and cut them off from Petersburg. The city could hold out for one more night, but the Rebels at Sutherland Station were on their own.[39]

Cooke had what was left of MacRae's brigade, his own command, Scales's brigade, and McGowan's brigade to protect the trains. Some 1,200 Rebels began to dig in on the brow of a slight ridge, in an open field. Lacking spades, they used their bayonets "and such other means as were at command." Rails from nearby fences reinforced the earthwork. Their line ran just south of Cox Road, which paralleled the South Side Railroad, and was about a half-mile long. McGowan's command formed a refused left flank; his men stretched northward to cross the tracks, while Sutherland Tavern was the anchor of the right flank. MacRae had only three regiments with him, for the 11th and 52nd were retreating westward. His left connected with McGowan's right at Ocran Methodist Episcopal Church. They had an open field of fire for some 700 yards, then a small stream lay at the bottom of the shallow rise on which the line was positioned. Across the valley was another ridge with a few trees. Cooke deployed a heavy line of skirmishers to cover his weak front, which needed about 5,000 men to be at peak strength. MacRae sent out his remaining sharpshooters and detailed more men from the line to make a total of 100 skirmishers contributed by his brigade. Thirty were from the 47th North Carolina. The position was formed by 11:00 A.M.[40]

It would be tested by Nelson Miles's division of the Second Corps, which crossed the abandoned Rebel works south of Hatcher's Run and moved up Boydton Plank Road. Leaving that road and approaching Sutherland Station along Claiborne Road, Miles quickly ordered an attack on the thin gray line that lay on the other side of the valley. Brig. Gen. Henry J. Madill's brigade struck up Claiborne Road a bit after noon and hit Cooke's and Scales's brigades. This hastily organized assault was blunted and repulsed by the Rebels, and Madill was wounded. A second attack was quickly launched at 1:00 P.M. by his replacement, Col. Clinton MacDougall, who struck MacRae and McGowan on the Rebel left. The Federals rushed forward, "cheering as if already seeing victory." They drove in the Rebel skirmishers, and the Tar Heels opened fire at 300 yards, repulsing the attack with heavy loss. As MacRae's sharpshooters resumed their post in front, a few captured Yankees told McGowan's men that they had been told that only a skirmish line defended the station and everyone expected an easy victory. MacDougall also was wounded in this second attack.

The Federals could hardly afford to waste time and lives with these uncoordinated lunges. Miles blamed the "natural strength of the position," the impediment of the little valley, and the fact that Cooke could "concentrate his force opposite any threatened point." He retired about 800 yards to the wooded crest and took a couple of hours to organize a plan. Miles deployed a heavy skirmish line to overlap the Confederate right flank at Sutherland Tavern and divert Cooke's attention from his left wing. Part of this line actually clambered over the tracks, far from Cooke's right flank. Then Miles sent Col. John Ramsey's brigade on a wide flanking movement through a patch of woods and a shallow ravine to gain the railroad east of the station and hit McGowan.[41]

The plan worked beautifully. Ramsey attacked on the double-quick about 4:00 P.M.; his battle line crossed the railroad track and easily outflanked McGowan. MacRae tried to shift his sharpshooters to McGowan's left to shore up the flank, but he was too late. The South Carolinians were forced to retreat in haste, and Scales's brigade also broke a few minutes later, leaving the Tar Heels behind. MacRae ordered his men out of the crude earthworks as Cooke's command also disengaged and fell back. Many of MacRae's skirmishers were taken captive. They had maintained their loose formation against the first two Yankee attacks but were hit in flank and taken in the rear when the left wing caved in.[42]

The Confederates disengaged quickly. Some men ran fast while others retreated slowly, firing as they went. Still others "crouched motionless in their defences," according to an observer in McGowan's brigade. MacRae tried to reform his line several times to the north of the station, but he only collected a squad of six men and directed them in a fighting retreat toward the Appomattox River.[43]

Miles's division captured 600 Rebel prisoners, half of Cooke's force, in addition to two cannons and one flag. The remaining Confederates raced northward, but no one had prepared a way to move them across the Appomattox River. Some scrounged up a few small boats in the area or hastily made rafts. Most of them were forced to march up the south bank in hopes of finding something to get them across farther upstream. MacRae reported that his command "was badly scattered and crossed the River at different points in squads of three and four."[44]

Some of MacRae's men probably marched westward and simply stayed on the south side of the river, joining a throng of retiring Rebels from different parts of the abandoned Petersburg line. They struck out on the "nearest accessible road, and often through the woods," crossing Namozine Creek and Deep Creek along the way. The latter was fifteen miles from Sutherland Station. Members of the Bethel Regiment and the 52nd North Carolina were part of this flow of men.

They moved "with but little, if any, organization," in the words of the historian of the 52nd. J. S. Bartlett stopped late that evening at a house along the road and asked for food, as he had not eaten all day. A house servant offered him a piece of hoe cake and a slice of broiled ham, which he ate on the run.[45]

Ten miles from the station, Robert Bingham and many of his comrades in the 44th North Carolina found an abandoned ferry where an elderly black man was slowly hauling four men at a time on a "little skiff, even charging them for the service." Bingham calculated that it would have taken twelve hours to get his men over, and it was dusk already. Then he learned of an old ferryboat lodged on the opposite side of the river and believed he could glimpse it in the "dim, murky moonlight." MacRae told him to collect a crew of four men and commandeer the elderly man's skiff to retrieve the boat. When asked what he should do if the owner declined, MacRae told him to shoot the man. Fortunately Bingham did not have to take such drastic measures, although he did have to brandish a gun to force the ferryman to back down. The ferryboat was invaluable; it took 250 men across the Appomattox in only nine trips.

Bingham noticed that the color-bearer, Sgt. George W. Barbee, did not have the flag when he boarded the ferry. Barbee explained to the captain that he had torn it from the staff and wrapped it inside his shirt. The faithful soldier did not intend to let it fall into Union hands. " 'The Yankees never got any flag from the 44th Regiment, and my bones could not rest quiet if they were to get our Flag off my dead body,' " he told Bingham. The captain had a better idea. He took a sizable rock from the south bank of the river and told Barbee to wrap the colors around it. When the ferry was halfway across, Bingham quietly dropped it into the water. Barbee cried when he saw his precious flag, only a few months in service, slip into the darkness. "This man did not own a foot of land in the world," Bingham later moralized, "and did not know a letter in the book," yet he was a Confederate hero. Barbee had only been promoted to sergeant on March 31. He was captured the next day and released on June 23.[46]

The Moravian band had been separated from the brigade all day and continued to wander westward. The musicians stopped at a house for food and played "Lorena" in return for the homeowner's hospitality, "thereby ending our musical career as the 26th N.C. Regimental Band." A passing Rebel advised them to move on, as there were Yankees nearby who might hear the music. When they reached the Appomattox at Clark's Mill, they discovered that many soldiers had already crossed on small boats and then let them drift downstream. The bandsmen were lucky to find a craft nearby and crammed aboard. None of them knew how to handle the boat, and the current was swift; it carried them downstream at a rapid rate. The Moravians saved themselves by grabbing tree limbs when they drifted back to the south bank. Disappointed, they continued to walk upstream until they reached a high bluff. Tired and unsure of where the regiment had gone, the musicians made a momentous decision to stop and hide in the trees until the Federals passed. Then they would strike out for Weldon and home.

For two days the Moravians lived in the woods on the bank of the Appomattox. They could hear and see the Yankees pass by on Cox Road, but they were never discovered. Food was available at a nearby farmhouse until the housewife refused to help them. Her slaves had told the Federals of the bandsmen, and she was afraid of retribution. For another day or two the band lived in limbo, wondering when or if the Yankees would pay them a visit.[47]

It had been a disastrous day for MacRae's brigade. No one was listed as killed; but 10 men were wounded and captured, and 2 were wounded but remained in Confederate hands. An astounding number, 657, were captured by the Federals, making a total loss of 669. The brigade lost 52 percent of its strength on April 2, and the prisoners accounted for 98 percent of the casualties. This resulted from the breakup of the 11th and 52nd in the face of the Sixth Corps attack and the sudden collapse of the defensive position at Sutherland Station. There is little doubt that a number of Tar Heels deliberately allowed themselves to be taken prisoner. None of the captives returned to duty, for the war would end a week later. Most of them, 634, returned to their homes after only a few weeks in Union hands. Four percent of the captives died in prison.

The Bethel Regiment lost 1 wounded, 4 wounded and captured, and 194 captured, for a total of 199. The 26th North Carolina lost 2 wounded and captured and 73 captured, a total of 75. About half of the regiment's prisoners were taken at Hatcher's Run; the rest, at Sutherland Station. The 44th North Carolina lost 1 wounded and 145 captured, the 47th North Carolina lost 1 wounded and captured and 162 captured, and the 52nd North Carolina lost 3 wounded and captured and 83 captured.[48]

The engagement at Sutherland Station was the last battle of MacRae's brigade, but the survivors accompanied Lee's army all the way to the end at Appomattox. Richmond and Petersburg were evacuated on the night of April 2, and the remnants of the army streamed toward Amelia Court House. Located nearly forty miles northwest of Petersburg, it was the most convenient rendezvous point for the troops.[49]

The brigade continued to wander on April 3, a day that is blank in all surviving accounts. The service records indicate that 161 men were taken prisoner that day. Half of them were captured in the Richmond hospitals when the capital was occupied by Federal troops. They were too ill to be moved in the evacuation, and several died before they could be discharged. Lt. Benjamin Hickman Bunn of Company A, 47th North Carolina, was an exception. Wounded on March 25 in the fighting for control of the picket line, Bunn refused to fall into Yankee hands. He "rose from his bed, walked to Danville, and reached home on the day of Lee's surrender."[50]

The brigade members who had crossed the Appomattox followed its northern bank and joined Lee's columns at Goode's Bridge, twenty-five miles northwest of Sutherland Station and about eight miles short of Amelia Court House. The rest kept to the south side of the river and marched straight to the courthouse. Longstreet's and Ewell's commands trickled into town all day on April 4, while elements of Heth's division began arriving that evening. MacRae gathered about 150 men at Goode's Bridge by noon on April 4 and marched them to Amelia Court House by 4:00 P.M. More trickled in that night and the next day. Lee wasted time at Amelia vainly sending foraging parties into the countryside looking for food. Lt. John H. Robinson of the 52nd North Carolina put it well when he wrote that the "troops had now been forty-eight hours without regular rations and the prospect was disheartening."[51]

While MacRae's soldiers were scouring the countryside for food, the Moravian band members lost their chance to go home. They were convinced that if they returned to the regiment, they would be given guns and told to fight, which they adamantly refused to do, so they were determined to escape south. Late on the afternoon of April 5, the Moravians made their way toward Cox Road, where they quickly encountered a group of Federal soldiers. The Yankees confiscated their instruments, "the bitterest experience of all," moaned Julius Linebach. "I had learned to love my . . . cornet almost next to myself, and to see it go into the hands of another, & know that I should never see it again, was a hard, a very hard thing to endure." Sam Mickey saved his silver horn by hiding it in his haversack and taking another man's instrument, which was confiscated. No one searched his personal belongings.

The bandsmen marched until dark and ate the rations their captors shared with them. It was the best food they had eaten in many days. A Federal provost took charge of them on the morning of April 6 and added them to a lot of other prisoners bivouacked in an open field. Here the captives remained for a couple of days before marching to Petersburg.

Two musicians had become separated from the band when the Yankees broke through the Boydton Plank Road entrenchments on the morning of April 2. Edward Peterson and Gus Reich soon ran into a squad of Federals who seized Gus's bass drum and roughly beat it while yelling to the two Rebels, "'Keep step with the music.'" Peterson's slide trombone also was grabbed as a trophy. Everyone took shelter in a boxcar idled on the track of the South Side Railroad when

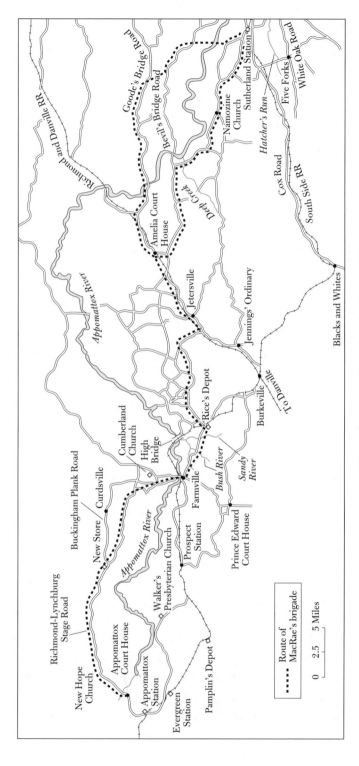

MAP 13.2 The Appomattox Campaign, April 2–9, 1865

Route of
MacRae's brigade

0   2.5   5 Miles

Richmond-Lynchburg
Stage Road

New Hope
Church

Appomattox
Court House

Appomattox
Station

Evergreen
Station

Pamplin's Depot

Walker's
Presbyterian Church

Prospect
Station

Prince Edward
Court House

Appomattox River

Buckingham Plank Road

New Store

Curdsville

Cumberland
Church

High
Bridge

Farmville

Bush River

Sandy
River

Appomattox River

Rice's Depot

Burkeville

To Danville

Jennings' Ordinary

Blacks and Whites

Jetersville

Amelia Court
House

Deep Creek

Namozine
Church

Sutherland Station

Cox Road

Hatcher's Run

South Side RR

Five Forks

White Oak Road

Richmond and Danville RR

Goode's Bridge Road

Bevil's Bridge Road

rain began to fall, and they found the floor covered with flour. The men, Union and Confederate alike, carried some of it to a nearby house and paid a woman a silver tankard, stolen from some nearby residence, to bake bread. Captors and captives alike had something to eat, and then the Yankees told the two musicians to go as they pleased when the rain stopped. Peterson and Reich wasted no time in heading for the regiment, but the two became separated. Reich later caught up with the 26th—he was the only bandsman to do so on the retreat—but Peterson met another errant musician, and the two simply walked home to North Carolina.[52]

The Confederates began to move out of Amelia Court House on the evening of April 5, taking the road south toward Jetersville to escape to North Carolina, but Sheridan's cavalry and two corps of infantry blocked them. Lee decided not to fight his way through but directed Longstreet, who assumed command of what was left of Hill's corps as well as his own, to head west to Farmville about twenty-five miles away on the South Side Railroad. There he hoped to feed his men and continue south. The rest of the army trailed behind Longstreet as he led the way.

The column reached Rice's Depot on the morning of April 6, tired and very hungry. Here Longstreet learned that the Federals had reached Burkeville only eight miles to the southeast. He deployed astride the railroad and ordered Wilcox to dig works south of the tracks, with Heth held in reserve, but the Federals simply advanced far enough to send out skirmishers. Other Union commands were not so cautious. The rear of Lee's column was crushed near Sailor's Creek late that afternoon. More than 7,700 troops were captured while MacRae's men waited near Rice's Depot for an attack that never came.

Longstreet and his weary soldiers continued toward Farmville that night. A particularly rough section of the road was before them. The crossing of Sandy River and Bush River had to be negotiated up and down "precipitous, rugged hills," and the starving draft animals could hardly pull the wagons. Heth ordered MacRae to help the trains, and the Tar Heels pushed and pulled all night to get them across the streams and into Farmville by noon on April 7. The famished soldiers snatched up their rations from the government storehouse, crossed to the north side of the Appomattox, and bivouacked on Cumberland Heights to prepare their food. The men ate heartily; thus far on the retreat the 47th North Carolina had been issued no food except two ears of corn for each man on one occasion. The rest of this diminishing army crossed farther downstream and formed a defensive position on the heights. It began with Longstreet's command on the south, paralleled the road northward from Farmville, and curved west around Cumberland Church. The Union Second Corps came up and formed opposite the center and left of this line, while Longstreet's men on the right were unopposed.[53]

MacRae's command was called on to deal with an emerging threat to the army's rear. Federal cavalry forded the Appomattox upstream from Farmville and advanced along Buckingham Plank Road. Brig. Gen. J. Irvin Gregg caught sight of Lee's wagon train at a road junction southwest of Cumberland Church at 4:00 P.M. He ordered his brigade to attack, and MacRae was called up. He rushed his men as fast as possible, but the crisis was averted before they arrived. Rebel cavalry stopped Gregg and saved the train. "We arrived in time to see them handsomely repulsed," reported MacRae, "but too late to participate."[54]

The increasingly hopeless state of affairs led the officers of the Bethel Regiment to hide their flag. They instructed Capt. Edward R. Outlaw of Company C to take charge of it. Outlaw secretly removed the color from its staff and replaced the silk covering so that no one would know it was missing. The color-bearer was instructed to pretend he still had the flag, and Outlaw hid it the next day.[55]

Lee moved his men from Cumberland Heights on the evening of April 7, hoping to reach Appomattox Station, get food, and continue west before turning south and heading for Danville. Longstreet and Maj. Gen. John B. Gordon, who had assumed command of the rest of Lee's army, marched along Richmond-Lynchburg Stage Road. The Rebels caught sight of the Blue Ridge Mountains forty miles to the west on April 8. That day Sheridan's hard-riding cavalry occupied Appomattox Station and secured the rations there. Sheridan positioned troopers to block the stage road west of Appomattox Court House and waited for the Union infantry to arrive. Lee's artillery train stopped two miles east of the courthouse by midafternoon, and the Federal troopers attacked it that evening. This prompted another call on MacRae's men. They had taken position in the rear of Longstreet's command, now the rear of Lee's army, that afternoon. The small force had formed a triangle straddling the stage road; MacRae placed the men six feet apart. When Mahone's command relieved them, the Tar Heels raced forward at the word that the artillery train was in danger, but they were too far away to reach the scene of action before the Yankee horsemen seized nearly thirty cannon and 200 wagons.

Lee ordered Gordon to attack in the morning and push Sheridan away. This last assault by the Army of Northern Virginia, on Sunday, April 9, cleared the stage road, but Federal infantry arrived just in time to throw the Rebels back and block Lee's escape. When the Second and Sixth Corps came up to Longstreet's rear, there was no usable road open to the Confederates. A cease-fire went into effect, and discussions were opened to negotiate a surrender.[56]

MacRae's men moved up to near the courthouse on the morning of April 9, expecting a battle. They filed to the right of the stage road and could even see Federal troops ahead, but MacRae yelled the order to halt and then waited. No one knew what this meant. Then, as if the weight of the world was upon him, MacRae quietly dismounted and lay on the ground. The men lay down too. "The sad news was quickly learned, and then followed that mighty expression of blasted hope, which a witness will never forget," wrote the historian of the 47th.[57]

The officers of the Bethel Regiment were ready for this moment. They sneaked off to a covered area in the woods and prepared a bonfire by raking together twigs and leaves. Here they burned their cherished flag, but not before tearing out pieces of it as souvenirs. It had been issued to the 1st North Carolina (six months) regiment and had never been taken while it flew over the 11th. "Sincere tears have often been shed around funeral pyres, but never more bitter and sorrowful tears bedewed any ashes than were shed over their dead flag." The only other regiment of the brigade that had never lost its flag was the 44th North Carolina, but it had already been quietly immersed in the Appomattox River. The other regiments apparently did not find it important to dispose of their colors; indeed, it is unclear whether they even had any left.[58]

The surrender negotiations in the McLean house that afternoon ended the war in Virginia. The Appomattox campaign had been a tough march for MacRae's men. At times during the retreat Lieutenant Colonel Adams of the 26th North Carolina commanded the brigade and Captain Cureton of Company B led the regiment. When the end came at Appomattox, the 47th North Carolina had no field officers and only two captains left.[59]

While MacRae suffered no battle casualties during the retreat, forty-five men were missing. Twenty-five were picked up by pursuing Federals on April 4. Five were taken on April 5, twelve the next day, one on April 7, and two on April 8. The 26th and 47th lost most of this number.

Losses for the entire period that brought the Petersburg campaign to an end and led to Appomattox were appalling. From March 25 to April 8 MacRae suffered a total of 1,015 casualties. The Bethel Regiment lost 264, the 26th North Carolina lost 148, the 44th North Carolina lost 208, the 47th North Carolina lost 249, and the 52nd North Carolina lost 146. None were killed and only 29 were wounded. Twelve of the latter also were taken prisoner. The captured, totaling 998, accounted for 98 percent of MacRae's losses. The brigade was quickly reduced to a shell of its former self in the last two weeks of the war.[60]

The only thing left to do was feed and surrender the men. The Federals provided food for Lee's army, a "herd of fat, young steers, and many wagon loads of crackers," according to a member of the 47th. The Rebels gobbled it up. Then complete rosters had to be made so that each man in Lee's army could be issued a parole. Under the surrender terms, the soldiers would not be sent to prison camps but would simply be allowed to return home as best they could after the paperwork was done and the formal surrender ceremony took place. Adams's 26th North Carolina still had 120 men, the largest regiment in the brigade. Martin's Bethel Regiment surrendered 74 soldiers, while Stedman's 44th had 70 men left. Capt. Robert H. Faucette's 47th North Carolina surrendered 72 men, and Erson's 52nd had only 60 soldiers remaining. MacRae surrendered 442 men, roughly equivalent to the combined strength of Cooke and McComb. Davis's brigade had mostly been captured on April 2 and had only 75 men left.[61]

MacRae praised his Tar Heels without reservation in his last report. "The officers and men who remained with the command after the battle of Sutherland Station have displayed the most commendable courage & fortitude. The hardships born by them from the 1st to the 9th inst have been unparalleled in the history of the war." If one extends that view to the long period before April 2, a select few deserved even higher praise for their dedication to the cause. Eight men of the 11th North Carolina who surrendered at Appomattox had also served in the 1st North Carolina (six months) and had fought at the battle of Big Bethel, the first land engagement of the war. They indeed were among the Tar Heels who were first at Bethel, farthest at Gettysburg, and last at Appomattox.[62]

The surrender ceremony on Wednesday, April 12, was a solemn affair. Gordon's corps began the process of formally laying down its arms at 6:00 in the morning by marching from the bivouac area east of the courthouse across a branch of the Appomattox River and up the hill into the village. There, three brigades of the Fifth Corps were aligned on both sides of Richmond-Lynchburg Stage Road. All day long the rest of Lee's 25,000 men marched up as the Federals stood silently and respectfully. Longstreet was next, and the remnants of Hill's corps were the last to come up. MacRae marched his men into the blue formation in midafternoon, one of the last Rebel brigades to lay down its arms. Like the others, MacRae gave the order for his Tar Heels to stop between the Union lines, turn to face the Federals, and then stack their arms and accoutrements. If there were any flags remaining, they were placed on the stacks. The 11th and 44th simply lay their bare staffs on the guns as a mute testimony to their determination never to let the enemy touch their colors. "There was no music," recalled a man in the 47th North Carolina. "'Twas silent—very sad."[63]

MacRae's men now had their long-awaited chance to go home. "Different parties took different routes to their desolate homes, and we bade each other a sad, in many cases a tearful, farewell," wrote the commander of the Bethel Regiment. J. A. Bush Sr. led his Company I of the 26th North Carolina from Appomattox on the evening of the surrender. They walked five miles and were forced to take shelter in an abandoned house when rain started to fall. "The next day every man looked out for himself. I had a few men with me and we stayed in a man's yard the second night. We thought it advisable to travel in less numbers, so that people would not dread to feed us as we came along."[64]

In this way, the proud regiments that made up the Pettigrew-Kirkland-MacRae brigade brought their history to a close.

Chapter 14

After the War

One of the three men who commanded the brigade was already gone when the surrender took place at Appomattox, but James Johnston Pettigrew's memory was burned into the mind of Louis G. Young. Young became a crusader, correcting every misapprehension he saw in print regarding the man he admired and loved. When Maj. Joseph A. Engelhard of Lane's brigade published a newspaper article implying that Pettigrew was to blame for the disaster at Falling Waters, Young leaped into the breach. "I was so bound to him in friendship and affection, that I rarely failed to observe him in the midst of scenes of excitement and danger," he wrote. Young clearly explained the details of the engagement. "In my judgment no blame rests on him," he concluded, "and it would be unjust to suffer the reputation of one to be tarnished, than whom few armies have known a more vigilant and capable officer."[1]

Collett Leventhorpe heartily agreed with Young. "Of all the noble army of martyrs who died for Southern independence none had more deeply at heart than he the cause for which he shed his blood. He gave himself up to it wholly, with all his fine energies, extraordinary talents, and the courage of a heart literally ignorant of fear." Leventhorpe considered Pettigrew "my 'beau ideal' of the patriot, the soldier, the man of genius, and the accomplished gentleman."[2]

There was no keeper of the flame for the brigade's second commander. William W. Kirkland moved to Savannah, where he entered business. Later he accepted a position in the post office in New York City. One of his daughters became a famous Broadway actress, but the former general lived a quiet life in the North until poor health forced him to enter the soldiers' home in Washington,

D.C. Kirkland died on May 12, 1915, and was buried in an unmarked grave just outside Shepherdstown, West Virginia.[3]

While Pettigrew had Young as his champion, William MacRae had Charles Manly Stedman. MacRae had been the best commander of the brigade, yet he would have been just as obscure as Kirkland if Stedman had not memorialized him. Stedman's main effort was a long biographical speech he gave in Wilmington in 1890 that included a detailed description of the battle of Reams Station. This was MacRae's brightest hour, and the speech caught so much public attention that it was reprinted several times.

MacRae was completely unconcerned about his image. He ended the war with almost nothing to live on but soon accepted a position as general superintendent of the Wilmington and Manchester Railroad. His organizational skills and native ability to lead men stood him in good stead, and the company was soon on sound financial footing. MacRae did a similar service for the Macon and Brunswick Railroad in North Carolina and the Western and Atlantic Railroad in Georgia. When his health deteriorated due to overwork, he resigned from business and moved to Florida to recuperate.

The general never married, but he always looked on his former comrades as his family. Once when a veteran of the brigade visited him in Wilmington, it became apparent that the visitor needed money. He had recently married and had no secure employment. " 'Is that all?' " MacRae retorted. " 'We lived on a good deal less during the war than my salary as a railroad superintendent. You can have one half of it, if your necessities demand it; tell your wife that you had more courage in Virginia than you show now.' " No wonder Stedman characterized MacRae as "a magnanimous man, cast in the heroic mould."

The former general escaped to Florida too late to save his life. He was progressively weakened by lung disease and decided to spend his last days in Wilmington. While traveling north, he was taken desperately ill with a congestive chill in Augusta, Georgia, and died on February 11, 1882. He was only forty-seven years old. His body was transported to Wilmington for burial in Oakdale Cemetery.[4]

Young noted the passing of the brigade commanders with a bittersweet line in his history of the unit, written in 1901. "Pettigrew and MacRae are gone. Kirkland lingers on the Border Land. . . . Those of us who remain are marching toward the setting sun."[5]

The brigade's regimental commanders ranged from the famous to the obscure. Zebulon Baird Vance turned in an impressive record as war governor of North Carolina and paid a price for it after Appomattox. He was arrested by Federal troops on May 13, 1865, while at his house in Statesville. The order for his imprisonment was initiated by President Andrew Johnson, another native of

North Carolina, who had succeeded Lincoln in the White House. Vance was never charged with a crime, but his arrest was the result of public outrage over the terrible conditions in the prison camp at Salisbury. For some time it looked as if the venerable governor might be used as a scapegoat by the Federal authorities, but evidence surfaced to exonerate him of personal responsibility. He was finally released on July 6, 1865. Vance considered leaving the country but instead applied to Johnson for a pardon, which he received nearly two years later. His vibrant spirit and innate political sense got him back on his feet quickly. Vance was elected governor again in 1876, after Radical Reconstruction had run its course in the Old North State. Later he entered the U.S. Senate. The first colonel of the 26th North Carolina died in 1894.[6]

The regiment's second commander, Henry King Burgwyn, was far from forgotten after his untimely death at Gettysburg. His father received a rare gift in September 1865 when a package arrived from Worcester, Massachusetts. It was sent by a former captain of the 25th Massachusetts and contained Burgwyn's diary. James Drennan had found it on the battlefield of New Bern and had kept it "with much care ever since with a view of returning it to him if he had lived." The family accepted it with grace and later retrieved the remains of their beloved son. Burgwyn's body was reburied in Oakwood Cemetery in Raleigh in the spring of 1867.[7]

The colonel's younger brother, William Hyslop Sumner Burgwyn, took it upon himself to be the keeper of the hero's memory. William had served as an officer in the 35th North Carolina, had seen action at Antietam and other engagements, and wound up on Thomas L. Clingman's brigade staff early in 1864. He was slightly wounded on June 1 at Cold Harbor and was taken prisoner on September 30 when Clingman's command tried to recapture Fort Harrison during Grant's Fifth Offensive against Petersburg. Burgwyn survived his imprisonment and lived a long life. By the 1890s he was writing to a number of people for their recollections of his brother's life and death, and he found many of them ready to talk. Regimental Quartermaster J. J. Young wrote, "I assure you most sincerely that the recollection of him will ever be sacred to me & I shall always feel the deepest interest in his surviving relations. The saddest thought to me, when thinking of the late war, is that so much of our best blood was spilled in vain."

The colonel also impressed the younger generation of the South. J. T. Murphy of Magnolia, North Carolina, wrote to William Burgwyn after the turn of the century to explain the impact of meeting his brother. Murphy was only nine years old when Henry Burgwyn and ten other officers of Pettigrew's brigade ate dinner at his father's house. He was so taken with the assemblage that he played soldier, drilling "every little negro (both male & female), with sticks for guns." The next year, when Sherman's cavalry came into the area, Murphy recalled making "an ignominious retreat into the dwelling house" and peeping out at the bluecoats.[8]

William was active in publicizing his brother's memory. He wrote articles for newspapers and eagerly offered information about the 26th and its commander to anyone who was interested. He was very proud of his brother when a specially commissioned portrait of the three commanders of the 26th—Vance, Burgwyn, and Lane—was presented to the government during the state fair of 1897. It is now displayed at the North Carolina Museum of History in Raleigh.[9]

John Randolph Lane lived longer than the other two commanders of the 26th. He was recuperating from his five wounds in a hospital in Danville, Virginia, when the regiment surrendered at Appomattox. Lane traveled to Greensboro and received a parole there on May 2. He went home to begin a long life as a successful businessman in Chatham County. Lane resided on Little Brush Creek while buying land, engaging in merchandising, and operating a cotton gin and gristmill. One year after Appomattox, the scarred veteran married Mary Ellen Siler and later fathered a daughter and a son. Lane never applied for a pension, but he was "conspicuous for his liberality and devotion to the old comrades of his immortal regiment," according to the historian of the 26th.[10]

Lane had been concerned with publicizing the exploits of the regiment even before the war ended. A report he wrote to the adjutant general's office in Raleigh found its way into the newspapers in August 1864. It listed and commented on the different officers of the 26th from its organization to the Petersburg campaign. Although ostensibly an official document, it was obviously written for public consumption. Lane found a ready ally in William H. S. Burgwyn, and the two contributed a great deal of information for George Underwood's history of the regiment. Burgwyn flattered Lane when the Cuban people rose in revolt against their Spanish masters in 1895. He was strongly sympathetic to their cause and told Lane, "If you & the old 26th could be landed in Cuba, and have a chance at the Spanish troops there, I reckon it would be a short matter for you to wipe them off the face of the earth. One charge such as you made at Gettysburg would drive them into the ocean or into a surrender."[11]

Sentiments such as these bolstered Lane's confidence. He told William Burgwyn that Vance and William's brother had always relied on him to handle important matters concerning the regiment, such as corralling draftees. Lane even encouraged William to write a full history of the regiment. William toyed with the idea of publishing a book on the unit, but he never followed through with the plan.[12]

The Three Colonels of the 26th North Carolina Regiment.
Painted by W. G. Randall, this triple portrait celebrates Zebulon Baird Vance
(right), Henry King Burgwyn (center), and John Randolph Lane (left).
(Copyright North Carolina Museum of History)

On a more personal level, Lane's most poignant memories of the war centered on the events of July 1, 1863. On that day he lost the commander he most admired and suffered the first and most serious of his five battlefield injuries. He gave a long address at Gettysburg on July 3, 1903, for a gathering sponsored by the North Carolina Society of Baltimore. In his speech he detailed the tragedy and the glory of that day, bragging that "a Yankee bullet ruined my throat and took away a part of my tongue and deprived me of my teeth." The Federal who fired that shot, Charles H. McConnell, also made the most of it. He gave lectures in a large tent, illuminated with electric lights, at the semicentennial reunion at Gettysburg in 1913. Musician Julius Linebach traveled to Gettysburg that year and was eager to hear McConnell's account of Lane's shooting, but the electricity failed the night the Union veteran was to speak. Linebach had to leave the next day and never heard the story from McConnell, but he received an Iron Brigade reunion ribbon, "which I prize as a valuable souvenir." There certainly was no animosity between Lane and McConnell. The two posed for a photograph with William H. S. Burgwyn in front of a monument to the 24th Michigan in Herbst's Woods.[13]

Lane became a legend among those who frequented reunions. He had a sincere and unaffected demeanor and often gave talks dressed in his old uniform. Bennett H. Young, a major figure in Confederate veteran circles in Kentucky, admired Lane and invited him to attend a Louisville gathering. Lane and 700 other Tar Heel Rebels accepted the invitation and journeyed to that city in 1900. They impressed the Kentucky veterans. Lane received a standing ovation when he was presented to the crowd, clad in his torn and dirty uniform. "His reception and the recognition of his sacrifices for his people touched the innermost depths of his brave soul," Young remembered, "and he often told me that he loved the people of Louisville with the same warmth with which he loved the men and women of his own State, and that he considered the week spent here as the happiest and pleasantest memory of his whole life." The Tar Heels returned the favor when they invited Young to attend their state gathering in Winston-Salem in 1908. Lane wept when he greeted Young and promised to return to Kentucky later that year, but it would be the last time the old soldier would see his friend. He died on December 31, 1908. "I never knew a kinder, braver, or more knightly man," wrote Young.[14]

Other regimental commanders were less visible in the postwar world. Collett Leventhorpe possessed a great deal of potential—he could easily have commanded the brigade—but his severe wounding and capture at Gettysburg forever crippled his career. The Englishman spent eight months in prison before he was exchanged. He resigned his commission in the Bethel Regiment and took charge of one of the state's two home guard brigades. His command consisted of four regiments filled with militia officers, government employees, and justices of the peace. Their primary task was to hunt and arrest deserters. After a time Leventhorpe was commissioned a brigadier general of state troops and led Confederate regiments in defending eastern North Carolina against an occasional Yankee raid. In December 1864 his men blunted an expedition aimed at capturing Fort Branch near Hamilton. He received a commission as brigadier general in the Confederate army in February 1865 and was placed in command of troops defending Raleigh when Sherman's army swept through the Old North State. His men retreated to Greensboro, where Leventhorpe received the news of Joseph E. Johnston's surrender to Sherman in late April.[15]

Leventhorpe busied himself with political issues and business after the war. He was sympathetic to the Ku Klux Klan during Radical Reconstruction and lived in New York for several years with his wife. Leventhorpe was a scholar; he fluently spoke French, Spanish, and Italian and appreciated literature and art. The Leventhorpes frequently visited England but settled in the mountains of North Carolina. He died in 1889 and left no descendants.[16]

Another commander of the Bethel Regiment, William Joseph Martin, resumed his career as a university educator after Appomattox. He was already teaching chemistry at the University of North Carolina at Chapel Hill in the fall semester of 1865. The onset of Radical Reconstruction hit the campus like a storm. The bitterness of this Northern policy, which included disenfranchisement of a large percentage of Southern whites and the granting of full citizenship rights to blacks, caused a student demonstration in the spring of 1867. The impetuous youths hoisted an old Confederate flag above one of the buildings and refused to attend classes. Martin quelled the uprising with a firm dignity. He reminded the students of his war service and of the severe wound he received at the battle of Jones's farm, and he told them that he meant it when he took the oath of allegiance to the U.S. government. With this testimony ringing in their ears, the rebellious students sheepishly took the flag down. But Martin saw the handwriting on the wall. He later resigned before the new Republican governor, William W. Holden, closed the university. It would reopen four years later but not with Professor Martin; he had moved on to found a high school in Columbia, Tennessee. He later returned to North Carolina to teach at Davidson College. He made Davidson his home for the rest of his life, teaching and serving as an administrator until poor health forced him to retire. Martin fathered ten children with his second wife, whom he had married in the middle of the war. He died in 1896.[17]

The last commander of the 26th North Carolina lived an obscure life after the war. James T. Adams performed very well while leading the regiment during the last few months of the conflict. He compiled a lengthy history of the unit for his niece so she could know what her uncle did in the war. Adams died in 1918, leaving behind a youthful photograph of himself taken during the war.[18]

Many other officers of the 26th entered politics. James D. McIver went from being county solicitor near the war's end to the state legislature, became a state solicitor, and served in the superior court. James C. McLauchlin was clerk of the Superior Court of Anson County for more than twenty years. James B. Jordan moved to Florida to work as clerk of the circuit court in Volusia County. Several other veterans, including George Willcox and Orren Alston Hanner, also served in the North Carolina legislature. Stephen Wiley Brewer was elected sheriff of Chatham County four times until his death in 1897.[19]

While these men eagerly embraced the political world, Benjamin Franklin Little of the 52nd North Carolina vigorously shunned it. A public meeting in Richmond County recommended him for the legislature, but he turned it down "most positively & emphatically." He much preferred to run his farm, but he was careful to do it in an honorable way. Little was perturbed by the widespread theft that characterized the first years of Reconstruction as the South was trying to rebuild its shattered economy. Fieldhands often stole large amounts of produce and sold it to mills in the middle of the night, leading to a great loss of revenue for the landowner. Little was willing to let his black laborers "pull Some roasting ears & take Some cotton &c for their own use," but he urged his neighbors to work together to stop outright theft. There were men in the area who were "ready like So many vultures to pounce upon every thing within their reach that can be turned into money, provisions or whiskey." But he meant to quit farming if he could not support his family "without taking advantage of either my hands or neighbors."[20]

Several officers of the 44th North Carolina stood out in the postwar history of the veterans. Tazewell Hargrove had a difficult time adjusting to the reality of a defeated South. He had spent the rest of the war in a Northern prison after he was captured at the South Anna Bridge in June 1863, and he refused to take the oath of allegiance to the U.S. government after Appomattox. One of his prison mates was Lt. George W. Finley, who had served in Pickett's division and was captured in the attack on July 3. He and Hargrove had been among the 600 Confederate prisoners held under Rebel fire at Charleston Harbor. Finley wrote an imploring letter to Hargrove when he returned to his home in Clarkesville, Virginia. He was saddened by what he saw; "we had no idea in prison of what is the real status." Confederate stragglers and deserters ranged through the countryside stealing property. "There is no law, no order anywhere, every man is the guardian of his own interests. The negroes bewildered by the sudden change in their condition are as yet quiet, most of them living as before with their owners. But this can not last long. Already there is some difficulty in controlling labor." Finley urged Hargrove to swallow his pride, take the oath, and return to his family and friends. The South was prostrate "before the blow so suddenly given us. Financially the country is a wreck. . . . Honest hearts, cool heads & stout arms with willing hands are sadly needed." The stubborn lieutenant colonel finally took Finley's advice and was released on July 24.[21]

Hargrove acquitted himself well in civilian life. He lived in Oxford, North Carolina, and worked as a lawyer, serving in the state legislature and as the state's attorney general. His wife, Mary Augustus Lamb, was the great-granddaughter of a man who had served in the state convention that ratified the U.S. Constitution. Hargrove died in 1889 and was buried in Townsville. His grave marker mentioned the only battle he fought during the war, identifying him as "The Defender of the South Anna Bridge." An acquaintance described him as the "most unreconstructed Rebel I ever knew."[22]

Robert Bingham, who had been released from prison much earlier than Hargrove, lived a full life as a prominent educator in the South. He came from a long line of teachers. His grandfather had taught in schools beginning in 1793, and his father had run Hillsborough Academy for nearly twenty years before opening his own school in 1844. Robert's older brother William took control of the Bingham School in 1864 and was succeeded by Robert when he died nine years later. The former captain of Company G led the school for fifty-four years and turned it into an impressive institution, "generally acknowledged to be the best private classical academy in the state and among the most prestigious of its kind in the South." Bingham was a progressive educator. He invited commissioned officers of the U.S. army to teach classes in military science, built the first gymnasium and swimming pool made specifically for an institution of secondary education in the South, successfully pleaded for the reopening of the University of North Carolina in 1874, and was an advocate of compulsory public education. Bingham also took the controversial stance of supporting free public schools for blacks even though he also supported school segregation. He pushed for the recruitment of women teachers and was instrumental in creating a teachers' college for women in Greensboro.

Poor health forced Bingham to retire in 1920. He spent the last few years of his life contemplating his war experience and wrote a long letter to his granddaughter about it so she could understand what he had been through. Bingham died in 1927, and the school he cherished most of his life closed its doors the following year, ostensibly to conduct extensive renovations of its physical plant. It never reopened.[23]

Charles Manly Stedman also taught the South's youth for a time after the war, in Chatham County, while he prepared for the bar exam. Stedman then practiced law in Wilmington and entered politics. He served as lieutenant governor of North Carolina and made two unsuccessful tries at the governor's office. Stedman's career moved forward when he was elected to the U.S. House of Representatives in 1910, and he was reelected nine times. The former commander of the 44th North Carolina retained that seat until his death in 1930 at age eighty-nine. He was the last Rebel veteran to serve in Congress.

Stedman also contemplated the meaning of the war and shared a similar conclusion about it with many other veterans. He agreed with Oliver Wendell Holmes Jr., who had served as an officer in the 20th Massachusetts and had gone on to a distinguished career as a jurist and Supreme Court justice, that wartime suffering had made better men of the veterans. "Was it to no purpose that your kinsmen died in the red glare of battle or perished amidst the festering horrors of the hospital?" asked Stedman in an address in Wilmington in 1890. Echoing Holmes, the Rebel veteran argued that suffering was necessary "to purify nations as well as individuals. It is from sacrificial flames that have arisen the noblest and grandest spirits, which have shed a halo of glory around humanity." Stedman worried, as did many Northern veterans, that the increased greed for wealth that accompanied rapid industrialization near the turn of the century might weaken the country's commitment to the ideals of "purer and better days." He wondered if the original principles of constitutional government and civic virtue would be jeopardized in the mad rush for money, with its attendant corruption and graft by public officials. Stedman called on all Americans to remember the sacrifice of the Civil War veteran and retain their faith in a "high and broad and lofty patriotism." Other veterans of the brigade would have agreed with Stedman, arguing as did Everard Hall of the 47th North Carolina that army service had brought out the best in each man who served.[24]

The officer corps of the five regiments produced few other visible veterans. All of them lived quiet, obscure lives after the war. Benjamin Wesley Justice, for example, went home and engaged in business and farming ventures. He became well known in the Raleigh area for teaching in Sunday schools. One day in 1871 he was helping to store cotton in the third story of a warehouse when he fell through the hatchway all the way to the first floor. On the way down his forehead hit a protruding corner of the second story, and his skull was fractured. The effects were not immediate; Justice even stood up and walked about, but the forty-four-year-old veteran was dead by noon.[25]

Maj. Charles Manly Stedman. Longtime commander of the 44th North Carolina,
Stedman eulogized brigade leader MacRae after the war. (North Carolina Collection,
University of North Carolina, Chapel Hill)

The private soldiers of Pettigrew's brigade mostly lived in obscurity as well,
but several of them left ample proof that they had full lives. James D. Moore of
the 26th North Carolina had been the eighty-fifth man shot in Company F on
July 1 at Gettysburg. A surgeon told him he had been struck by a projectile from
a cavalry carbine; where it came from remained a mystery to Moore until he
moved to Winnamac, Indiana, after the war. There he met a man named Hayes
who had served in the 24th Michigan and had an interesting story to tell. Hayes
had lost his Enfield rifle musket on the forced march of his regiment the night before the battle. He had picked up a carbine dropped on the field by a trooper be-

longing to Buford's cavalry division and fired it all day. Hayes recalled taking aim at the regimental colors at a distance of only twenty yards, and Moore reported being near the flag when he was hit. The two refused to let this incident stand in the way of their becoming good friends.[26]

Moore had an experience with two other members of the 26th while he was recuperating at home from his Gettysburg wound. While he was at his family's residence in Caldwell County, the house was attacked by Keith and Malinda Blalock and their gang. The Blalocks had joined Company F in March 1862 to avoid being drafted into Confederate service and intended to desert to Union lines at the first opportunity. They had become impatient, however, so Keith manufactured an excuse for a medical discharge, while his wife revealed her gender and was immediately sent home as well. The couple fled and formed a gang of deserters when home guardsmen pressured Keith to reenlist. The gang was scattered in a skirmish on Grandfather Mountain in October 1862, forcing Keith and Malinda to flee to Tennessee. There Keith became a recruiter for the 10th Michigan Cavalry and met George W. Kirk, who already was infamous as a guerrilla fighter and a guide for deserters and Unionists who wanted to make their way to Federal territory. Keith and Malinda recruited another guerrilla band and returned to North Carolina in the spring of 1863. They were motivated by a blend of Unionism and a desire to fight their personal and family feuds, and the Moore family was one of their worst enemies. Moore's father, Carroll, was seriously hurt in the attack on his house about September 1, 1863, but he fended off the gang, injuring Malinda and other attackers. When Keith raided the house again in the fall of 1864, he was shot in the head and lost an eye, and the Moore household was safe at last.

Malinda had been pregnant when she was wounded in the attack, and she gave birth to the couple's first child on April 8, 1864, while in Union-occupied Knoxville, Tennessee. Keith later signed up as a scout for the 10th Michigan Cavalry and recruited several of his gang members, including Malinda, who continued to disguise herself as a man, as his subordinates. The "scouts" seem to have done little for the regiment. They mostly raided homes belonging to their personal enemies in North Carolina, lived off the land, and spread terror across the Confederate home front. Keith was wounded twice in 1864 and severely injured in the hand in January 1865, but he survived the war.

The Blalocks' personal vendetta against their enemies deepened when Keith's stepfather was murdered and Keith killed a man in retaliation for it. He was arrested after the war but pardoned for his crime by Reconstruction governor Holden. Malinda resumed her identity as a woman as soon as the war ended. She was reunited with her son, who had been cared for by friends in Knoxville.

The couple owned a store and a farm, and Keith ran for the state legislature in 1874 but was defeated. The two lived briefly in Texas but again returned to their native land. Their enemies tried to get Keith's pension from the U.S. government revoked, arguing that his wounds were incurred on bushwhacking raids rather than in legitimate battles. This led to a court hearing in 1895 in which the pair marshaled supporting testimony from friends. They also carefully worded their statements to emphasize their supposed service to the Union and downplay their short time in the Confederate army. Keith was exonerated; he kept his pension, although the payments were reduced for a short time. Malinda died in her sleep in 1903, but Keith was killed in a strange railroad accident ten years later. He loved to race along the railroad tracks on a hand-powered car, desperately grabbing the last thrills of a long, tortured life lived mostly on the edge. One day he went too fast around a curve, and the car slid off the track, overturned, and crushed him to death.[27]

Moore never fully recovered from his Gettysburg wound, but he was well enough to return to duty in the spring of 1864. His stiff leg bothered him so much that he obtained a transfer to the 1st North Carolina Cavalry the following fall and participated in many engagements around Petersburg. He experienced an intense religious conversion one night in February 1865 when an older comrade spoke to him of his salvation. Moore lay in a fence corner praying and asking forgiveness of his sins as the older comrade comforted the nineteen-year-old soldier. When the war ended, he attended one year of school and became a cotton merchant and mill entrepreneur in Gastonia. He served in city government and became deeply interested in the Baptist church of the city. When Moore died in 1905, he was widely remembered as a man who had committed nearly his whole life to his faith.[28]

Moore's company commander, Romulus Morrison Tuttle, also devoted his life to religion. He had been wounded four times during the war. His right leg was fractured below the knee on July 1, 1863, and the wound never completely healed. He received a flesh wound in the breast on the first day of fighting at the Wilderness, and he was seriously bruised by a canister ball during the Petersburg campaign. Another serious injury occurred at the battle of Jones's farm when a rifle bullet smashed his left forearm, "shattering the larger bone and necessitating a resection of three or four inches." Tuttle attended Davidson College after the war and graduated in 1869. He preached for many years at various Presbyterian churches in Virginia.[29]

Another member of the 26th North Carolina, Albert Stacey Caison of Company I, had an experience with the Unionist guerrillas of the state. Wounded and captured on July 1 at Gettysburg, Caison was paroled in March 1865 and sent home. He arrived just before Union major general George Stoneman led a cavalry column into the mountains of North Carolina, and Caison was captured near Lenoir. The Yankees marched him and other prisoners twenty miles, feeding them only a half-ear of corn per man, before they turned them over to George W. Kirk's guerrilla band. Kirk pushed them even harder and ordered the execution of a Rebel lieutenant who had tried to escape. Caison was taken to Knoxville and given to the Federal authorities, who shipped him to Jeffersonville, Indiana, where Caison learned of Lincoln's assassination. He spent the next three months at Camp Chase, near Columbus, Ohio. Caison finally took the oath of allegiance on August 1 and returned home via Baltimore, Danville, and Greensboro, having endured two captivities and a grand tour of the North.[30]

Far different from Moore and Tuttle, Leonidas Lafayette Polk devoted his life to agricultural and political causes. Polk was descended from the same family line that produced President James K. Polk and Rebel lieutenant general Leonidas Polk. He already had begun a political career before the war by serving in the state legislature until his enlistment as a private in Company K, 26th Carolina. Polk was later promoted to sergeant major but transferred to a lieutenancy in the 43rd North Carolina by the spring of 1863. He was wounded at Gettysburg and resigned his commission in 1864 to reenter the legislature. Polk was the state's first commissioner of agriculture and the founder of the *Progressive Farmer*. He also was president of the National Farmer's Alliance. His entrepreneurial spirit led him to run a merchandise store in Anson County and to sell a cure for diphtheria in Northern cities. He died in 1892.[31]

W. W. Edwards of the 26th crafted a literary career after the war. He wrote popular stories for a publication called the *Messenger* in Siler City, North Carolina, under the pen name Buck.[32]

The war often changed the lives of the men who fought it while leaving others alone. Sgt. Alexander S. Peace had been severely wounded at the South Anna Bridge fight and eventually was transferred to the Invalid Corps. He resumed his studies at Trinity College in Durham, present-day Duke University. Peace was the only survivor among the eight men of his prewar class. James H. Sykes had enlisted in the 47th North Carolina at age eighteen as a substitute and was wounded on May 5, 1864, while fighting in the Wilderness. His left arm was fractured, and Sykes received a discharge the following February because the arm was paralyzed. He lived the rest of his life without being able to use it. George Mordecai Whitney of the same regiment was captured on July 3, 1863, and contracted a disease while in prison that killed him after the war. Ironically he had been a druggist in Wake County before the conflict. In contrast, William Walker Hartgrove was thirty-one years old and the father of four children when he enrolled in the Bethel Regiment. He was wounded at White Hall, on the first day of fighting at Gettysburg, and on June 1 at Cold Harbor. Yet he survived to surrender with Lee at Appomattox. He returned to his home on the Catawba River in Mecklenburg County to work as a carpenter. Hartgrove fathered eight more children with his first wife and two with his second spouse. He died at age seventy-four. The longest surviving member of Pettigrew's brigade apparently was James A. Kearns of the 44th North Carolina, who died in 1939 at age 103.[33]

John C. Warlick of the 11th North Carolina was born in 1841 and served faithfully throughout the war. He was captured during the Sixth Corps breakthrough on April 2, 1865, and paroled from prison two months later. Warlick reached home and immediately set to work harvesting wheat and courting Mary Lutes of Catawba County. They were married in January 1866 and produced ten children and seven grandchildren. Mary died in 1890, and John remarried two years later. His second wife, a member of the local school board, led him to become interested in public education. Warlick commented that he "did not get much [education] when I was growing up."

Warlick had a tough life. He had been bothered by rheumatism and "white swelling" of the knee ever since he was seventeen years old. He had thought army service might make it worse, "but I never enjoyed better health than during the war." A physician talked him into an operation to remove loose bone in the knee joint in 1899. The diagnosis was incorrect, and the operation, performed by three doctors in his own house, ruined his knee. Just before he was chloroformed, Warlick told the doctors "that what they were about to do felt more to me like going into battle, than anything I had ever experienced since the war, as I did not know whether I would come out alive." The anesthetic sickened him for days afterward, but no loose bone was found. The knee remained sore and stiffened so that he had to hobble around on crutches. Warlick considered suing the physicians but decided to let it pass as one more experience in a full life. He had supported himself by making brooms out of local Lincoln County material since 1875, and he took pride in being self-sufficient. In a letter to a former comrade he recalled that a man in his regiment had deserted during the Petersburg campaign, and "he did not come home untill after the war, & now I learn he has applied for a pension, what a shame."[34]

The band of the 26th North Carolina also tried to carry on in the postwar years. Its members had been taken prisoner on April 5 a few miles west of Petersburg and were marched to the city. There they received news of Lee's surrender, but hopes for a quick release were dashed when the Yankees marched them to City Point on April 12. The Moravians crowded aboard a steamer and reached the prison at Point Lookout, Maryland, the next day. Their personal belongings were taken, and black soldiers were set to guard them. A palpable air of tension hovered over the camp when Lincoln was assassinated, and Federal officers warned the prisoners not to give any provocation for the guards to shoot. It took several days for the tension to die down.

Julius Linebach was disgusted with his living arrangements. The tents were filthy and offered no privacy; "our condition was as near that of brutes as could well be imagined," he later wrote. The food was meager and of poor quality, mostly cod fish, soup, and bread. There were seven musicians in camp, including leader Sam Mickey and Linebach, and they were "in a chronic state of hunger." Three band members had become separated from the group on April 2; two were captured but immediately released, and all three made it home. One band member had been taken prisoner during the Gettysburg campaign and was in prison at Fort Delaware, while two others were on sick leave in Salem.

The Moravians endured Point Lookout, this "abominable hole," for nearly three months before the process of paroling them began in late June. Everyone was measured, weighed, and made to take an oath of allegiance to the Federal government. They were given their personal belongings except Linebach's oilcloth, which was kept because it was U.S. government issue. Unfortunately Linebach was the last bandsman to leave. The musicians were paroled alphabetically beginning with the letter A, and then the order of parole was switched to the letter Z, leaving for last those whose names began with a letter in the middle of the alphabet. When the blessed day finally arrived, Linebach boarded a boat for City Point. He then traveled by train to High Point, North Carolina, and met an old friend who also was on his way home from army service. The two set out for Salem and met Linebach's brother James, who had ridden out with food to meet his returning hero. When the musician reached home on July 2, he found his mother gravely ill. She died five days later.

The Moravians tried to continue performing as a group but found it difficult. They held a performance in late December 1865 to raise money to purchase new instruments to replace those taken by their captors the previous April. But there were fewer and fewer performances after that. Linebach admitted it "was not the same band after all. The 'esprit de corps' was wanting." During the war everyone had been bound by "the ever pervading sense of our mutual dependence on each other,—in that community of interest that made us feel that 'all we were brethren.'" Now they drifted into their separate lives. Edward Peterson, one of the two musicians who had left the group when the Petersburg line broke on April 2, had managed to walk back to Salem and arrived on Easter morning. He later married, raised a family, and worked in his brother's carpentry shop. His occasional performances ended with his death in 1906. William Henry Hall, who had lost his young son to disease just before the band came home for its first furlough, studied the confectionery business in Philadelphia and made candy in Salem for many years. Samuel T. Mickey, a tinsmith after the war, made a huge coffee pot to advertise his business. The pot is now a monument in Winston-Salem. W. Augustus Reich continued to entertain Salem with his magic tricks long after the conflict. Also a tinsmith, Reich made Christmas cake cutters and many other household utensils that filled the homes of his fellow Moravians. In 1904 Julius Linebach, the unofficial historian of the regimental band, finished writing a memoir based on his diary and letters. He also included a number of drawings of camp life done by band member Alexander Meinung, and the band books that the group had used during the war were carefully preserved as well. Linebach also served as secretary-treasurer of the Moravian Church, Southern Province, and died at age ninety-five. Julius Transou outlived Linebach by three months and was ninety-eight when he died; he was the last member of the 26th Regimental Band.[35]

Veterans of the brigade felt the need to memorialize their unit and preserve its history as they grew older. John Randolph Lane understood this very well. He noted that the private soldier did not fight for glory or recognition but that his "'identity is merged in that of his regiment; to him, the regiment and its name is everything. . . . He is jealous of the record of his regiment and demands credit for every shot it faced and every grave it filled.'" Thus the survivors of the 26th North Carolina often became obsessed with their unit's losses at Gettysburg, for that was the salient feature of its history. "'Scars are the true evidence of wounds,'" wrote Lane, "'and regimental scars can be seen only in the record of the casualties.'" Thomas Perrett, who was gravely wounded on July 3, tried to increase the casualty figures for the 26th at Gettysburg to correct what he called an "error in history. . . . I know whereof I speak, and know that history is wrong." In his effort to preserve his brother's memory, William H. S. Burgwyn contacted William F. Fox about pinning down the exact casualties on July 1. Fox outlined his extensive research, "for I am inclined to believe that in time this regiment will become as well known in history as the Light Brigade at Balaklava."[36]

George Underwood waxed poetic on the issue of casualty statistics in his history of the 26th. He believed that no other regiment had ever suffered such a loss in one engagement and argued that "honor should be given where honor was due. Such heroism as the Confederate soldier displayed cannot be in vain. Some good to the world must come from such sacrifice." Many people who read his history were impressed. A Union veteran named R. B. Brown was captivated by the "matchless story" of the 26th and its youthful colonel, and he hoped to meet the survivors of the regiment. A Southern boy who described himself as "very fond of the history of our Country" was also entranced by the unit's story. He wrote to William Burgwyn to express his admiration for Henry and received a picture of the colonel in return. "Papa says some day it will [be] a precious memory of a noble race that is dead," wrote the young man. Perhaps John Randolph Lane was not just mouthing a rhetorical flourish when he said to a group of veterans at Gettysburg, "All our State rings from end to end with eulogies of you. The youth of our schools and colleges recount your praises year by year." Lane broadened his view to include the whole country. "Your valor is coming to be regarded as the common heritage of the American nation. It no longer belongs to your State alone, it no longer belongs to the South; it is the high water mark of what Americans have done and can do. The day is soon coming and is already here, when your heroism will be as much admired in Maine as in Texas; in California as in Carolina."[37]

Nothing energized the veterans of Pettigrew's brigade more than the continued debate over responsibility for the failure of Pickett's Charge. This thorny problem refused to go away; it even grew worse after the war. Many people who had no connection with the brigade came to its defense out of state pride. Daniel Harvey Hill tried to counter the claims of the Virginia clique in his magazine, *The Land We Love*, and the Tar Heel publishers of another serial, *Our Living and Our Dead*, joined in the effort as well. Zebulon Vance appealed to the Southern Historical Society for help in correcting the slanted historical view promulgated by partisans of Lee, but that organization was dominated by Virginians who turned a deaf ear to the former governor. Even friends from other states who had witnessed the charge at close range defended the Tar Heels. Isaac Trimble and James H. Lane wrote powerful articles that set the record straight, but nothing seemed to override the stranglehold the Virginians had on the historical memory of that attack.[38]

Several survivors of the brigade joined in a flood of memory when the North Carolina press offered to publish their letters. Nearly 100 veterans of all Tar Heel regiments involved in the attack responded, but their testimony had little impact on the Virginians. Joseph J. Davis of the 47th North Carolina specifically criticized John Esten Cooke's biography of Lee as unfairly slamming the role of the Tar Heels in the assault. He enlisted the support of Charles S. Venable, one of Lee's staff officers, to speak out and correct public misconceptions of the attack. Davis assured Venable that Pettigrew's veterans felt "keenly the unjust and the untrue accounts" of that day and called the effort to make scapegoats of the Tar Heels "the grossest and most unpardonable injustice."

Other veterans of the brigade rose to their own defense. John C. McInnis had been hit four times near the stone fence. "We boys always called it Pickets newspaper charge," he recalled nearly a half-century later; "the Richmond Papers Blowed it and it has got into history." Another man, who identified himself as "H," argued that no one could have taken Cemetery Ridge with the resources available. "That we failed to carry the heights of Gettysburg is a matter of history; that we poured out the best blood [of] the State in the effort to do so is a matter of history, too. I know the line was too weak, and this is the only answer to the question as to why we failed; our failure affects not the character of the old Brigade; its conduct in the first day's fight proves its gallantry, its losses in the final charge proves its daring."[39]

The most stinging attack on the Virginians came from North Carolinian William R. Bond, who had been a classmate of John Thomas Jones and who had served in Daniel's Tar Heel brigade of the Second Corps at Gettysburg. He published a provocative booklet titled *Pickett or Pettigrew?* in which he excoriated Pickett's men, accusing them of "arrogance and self conceit" in their belief that "their division stood to Lee's army in the same relation, that the sun does to the Solar system." Bond noted that Pickett's brigades were fresh, but the 26th had suffered a crushing loss on July 1 and yet had the stamina to make a magnificent charge. "Whether any other regiment in our army *could* have done this I know not," Bond wrote.[40]

The best that the Tar Heels accomplished in their duel with the Virginians was a draw. This did not prevent them from feeling great pride in their accomplishments at Gettysburg and all the other battles they fought. Many of them wrapped their whole lives in the memory of their regiment. John Randolph Lane asserted, "My greatest glory is that I was so intimately associated with its history." Joseph J. Young was absorbed with love for his comrades, "and he could not do too much for them." Young preserved all the muster and pay rolls of the 26th and treasured them "as among the most valuable possessions to be bequeathed to his children." Edward R. Outlaw kept a piece of the Bethel Regiment flag he had torn off before burning it at Appomattox. The swatch was loaned to the state's history museum for display in 1920 and was buried with the captain the next year.[41]

The 26th North Carolina lost its first flag at Gettysburg. It was only three months old when fourteen men bore it through the attack of July 1 and Pvt. Daniel Thomas took it across the stone fence into captivity on July 3. The flag lay in a storage room of the U.S. War Department for forty-three years while sectional bitterness cooled and gave way to efforts at national reconciliation. In 1906 Congress voted to give it and 251 other Confederate flags to the Museum of the Confederacy. The regiment's second flag was lost at Bristoe Station, three months after Gettysburg, and it, too, was one of the War Department flags sent to the museum. The third regimental color to fall into Union hands was lost at Burgess's Mill, a year after Bristoe Station. Color-bearer Thomas Minton gave his life that day, and the flag eventually found its way to the North Carolina Museum of History, although by then only about two-thirds of the fabric remained intact. Another regimental flag from the brigade, that of either the 47th or the 52nd, was also taken at Bristoe Station and was one of the War Department colors sent to the Museum of the Confederacy in 1906.[42]

Veterans increasingly marked the passage of time as they grew older. J. A. Bush Sr. wrote, "I went into the army at nineteen years of age. I came out with a little more experience than I had when I left home." Thomas J. Cureton had trouble remembering his war experiences by 1890. "I am getting old and find it hard to Recollect so far Back or Confirm my Mind on it. Would like to have it all written up for truth of history." William S. Long was in the habit of jotting down memories of his battles on the anniversary of their occurrence in letters to his son. Regarding his vivid memory of Bristoe Station he wrote, "I may never feel in the humor to write again & yet I want you to know something of the things I have seen & done." When John C. Warlick attended a reunion of veterans of the 11th North Carolina in 1901, Lt. David A. Coon of Company I ordered the fifty-two veterans to fall in so he could take roll. Warlick wondered, "How can it be that 36 years have passed, it only seems a very few years."[43]

The memory of Pettigrew's brigade continued to shine brightly after the veterans were gone. The pages of the *Confederate Veteran* rang with its praise when Mrs. B. A. C. Emerson eulogized the 26th North Carolina in "The Most Famous Regiment." "Brave by nature and drilled almost to perfection by Lieutenant Colonel Burgwyn, it is easy to see why they were ready to make that matchless charge at Gettysburg."[44]

Many years later, another generation of Southerners honored these men by resurrecting an idea that had been born in the middle of the war. The Confederate Congress had voted on October 13, 1862, to issue a Medal of Honor for conspicuous courage in battle. It also authorized regiments to nominate members for inclusion in a Roll of Honor to acknowledge their participation in a particular engagement. While Richmond was flooded with nominations for both awards, the government never was able to follow through with them. It was up to the Sons of Confederate Veterans to complete the process in 1968. This organization voted to give the Medal of Honor to forty-three men named on the original Roll of Honor. It also compiled the remaining names to create the Roll of Honor officially as well. Henry King Burgwyn received the Medal of Honor for leading the 26th against the Iron Brigade at Gettysburg, and Tazewell Hargrove was awarded the Medal of Honor for his defense of the South Anna Bridge. The

47th North Carolina had ten men listed on the Roll of Honor for their participation in the battle of Reams Station. Two of them belonged to Company K because Company F chose not to nominate anyone. No other unit of the brigade selected nominees for the roll.[45]

A monument was erected in 1986 to the 26th North Carolina a few yards short of the stone fence, just to the north of the angle and in front of the position of Arnold's battery at Gettysburg. It commemorates the push of a small group of men from the regiment into the face of an artillery blast and positions the highwater mark of the Tar Heels in Pickett's Charge. That incident remains emblematic of the regiment's history and, in a larger sense, of the brigade's history as well.

Appendix

A Military Profile of the Pettigrew-Kirkland-MacRae Brigade

Nearly 100 members of Pettigrew's brigade left personal accounts of their wartime experiences. This is an unusually large number, especially for Confederate soldiers, yet that means that 8,156 other members of the brigade left no personal accounts. They do not have an opportunity to speak directly to us about their motives for fighting, their fears, their hopes, or their reflections on what the war meant to them.

But these men are not entirely obscure figures in the history of the brigade, for their service records reveal a certain amount of information about their lives and their role in the unit. Taken collectively, the service records offer interesting insights into many facets of the military history of the brigade that are unattainable from other sources. Fortunately the North Carolina Division of Archives and History has been engaged in a major undertaking to publish the full service records of each Tar Heel soldier in the Civil War. The massive effort, begun in 1966, takes information from the soldier's service record in the National Archives as a base (and it tends to be much more basic in content for Confederates than for Federals). Information gleaned from state records, from pension records, and even from the odd newspaper or personal account is added to that base. Fortunately the effort has progressed far enough through the list of Tar Heel units so that all five regiments of Pettigrew's brigade are represented in the volumes thus far published. This publication served as a major source of information for all chapters of this book, and it is the basis of most points made in this appendix.[1]

Another rich source of information on soldiers who failed to leave their own letters or diaries behind is what Civil War record keepers often referred to as a descriptive roll. It contains the vital statistics of Civil War soldiers, including their birthplace, age, marital status, and a physical description. Such descriptive rolls exist for many Union regiments; one such roll proved to be invaluable for my earlier study of the 12th Missouri Infantry (Union). It enabled me to construct what I called a sociomilitary profile of that unit when I combined the information in the descriptive roll with the information in the regiment's service records in the National Archives. Unfortunately it is impossible to do an identical project with Pettigrew's brigade, for there is no descriptive roll in existence. The service records in the National Archives do contain some descriptive information for these Tar Heels. Perhaps 10 percent of the men in Pettigrew's brigade had certificates of discharge or medical documents (often filled out by Union army personnel for wounded and captured Rebels) that contain some information about a man's age and physical appearance, but this is far too little to create a full profile. Therefore I have constructed a military profile, rather than a sociomilitary profile. I did find some information in the published service records about birthplaces and other aspects of the soldiers' personal lives, but I make no claims for completeness in this area due to the lack of completeness in the sources.[2]

It is not easy to research the service records, no matter how brief they tend to be, of more than 8,000 men. On some topics it seemed adequate to select randomly one company in each of the five regiments. For example, when I tried to understand how many men were promoted or demoted during their service and how many were listed as sick, it became apparent that the results would be too meager to justify investing time in examining all ten companies in all five regiments. Also, initial research into the available information on the men's ages at enlistment, their birthplaces, their occupations, and how many men shared surnames quickly revealed that the data was so consistent that one company in each regiment would be a sufficient sample. The companies selected at random were Company C, 11th North Carolina; Company E, 26th North Carolina; Company H, 44th North Carolina; Company K, 47th North Carolina; and Company A, 52nd North Carolina.

Topics such as the number of men discharged for any cause; the number of men who resigned, died from disease, or became casualties; those who served in other units; those who deserted or were executed; or the number who were disciplined for any reason seemed important enough and provided data varied enough to justify a full and complete search through all the companies of each regiment. The results of this sometimes tedious, sometimes fascinating research are presented in this appendix.

A total of 8,256 men are listed as having served in the five regiments of Petti-grew's brigade throughout the war, from the organization of the 26th North Carolina in May 1861 to the surrender at Appomattox on April 12, 1865. Of that number, 453 were officers, 817 were noncommissioned officers, and 6,986 were privates. The 11th North Carolina had 1,515 men (86 officers, 166 noncommissioned officers, and 1,263 privates); the 26th North Carolina had 2,175 men (120 officers, 179 noncommissioned officers, and 1,876 privates); the 44th North Carolina had 1,552 men (91 officers, 162 noncommissioned officers, and 1,299 privates); the 47th North Carolina had 1,589 men (83 officers, 145 noncommissioned officers, and 1,361 men); and the 52nd North Carolina had 1,425 men (73 officers, 165 noncommissioned officers, and 1,187 men).

BIRTHPLACES

The available information on birthplaces indicates that the regiments of Petti-grew's brigade were very much the product of the counties that gave rise to the companies. The vast majority of the men were born in a single county. In other words, the regiments were heavily American (virtually none of the men were born in foreign countries) and heavily North Carolinian (very few were born outside the state), and most of the companies had relatively few counties represented in their ranks. Only 313 of the 751 men who served in the five companies sampled had their birthplace listed; that is only 42 percent. Of that number, only one was born in a foreign country (Holland), and only two were born outside North Carolina (Virginia and Texas). Three of the five companies had high rates of men born in a single county. In Company E, 26th North Carolina, 77 percent of the men were born in Chatham County. In Company K, 47th North Carolina, 84 percent of the men were born in Alamance County, and in Company A, 52nd North Carolina, 79 percent of the men were born in Cabarrus County.

AGES

It is not surprising that the available information on the ages of the men at enlistment reveals that most of the soldiers were quite young. Of the 751 men who served in the five companies sampled, 549 had this information listed in their service records.

Relatively few of the men were underage or overage. Twenty-eight men in the sample were under eighteen, and twenty-four were forty years old or older. Many of those over forty were eventually discharged because they could not keep up

TABLE 1. Ages at Enlistment

Age (years)	Number of Men	Percentage of Sample
16–17	28	5.1
18–19	122	22.2
20–21	102	18.5
22–23	68	12.3
24–25	38	6.9
26–29	74	13.4
30–35	60	10.9
36–39	33	6.0
40–45	17	3.0
46–50	5	0.09
51–	2	0.03

with the physical pace of camp life or campaigning. Forty percent of the men were between eighteen and twenty-one years of age.[3]

The young age of most members of the brigade meant that their place of residence at the time of enlistment often was their parents' home. While the service records simply list the county of their residence (and it usually was the same county as the place of their birth), the census records indicate their precise residence. Recently a historian found the place of residence for 349 men who enlisted in the 26th North Carolina; 200 of them were living with their parents at the time of their enrollment. If that is typical, then 57 percent of the men in Pettigrew's brigade had no separate residence of their own.[4]

OCCUPATIONS

It is not surprising that most men were farmers. Of 265 soldiers in the five companies for whom an occupation is given, 221 (or some 83 percent) made their living in agriculture. Most of the rest were occupied in a variety of skilled and unskilled manual labor jobs. If one mixes modern with contemporary classifications, it would be possible to say that only 3 of the 265 men were middle class. Two of those listed their occupation as merchants, and one listed himself as a manufacturer. Eight of the 265 called themselves mechanics and thus, by modern standards, might be considered part of the industrial labor force. The remaining 13 percent of the 265 could be considered, also by modern standards, working class. The trend is definite: most men were farmers, a very few were middle class or industrial working class, and the rest represented a variety of trades, crafts, and unskilled labor.

A closer examination of the farm life of men in the 26th North Carolina reveals that the size and value of landholdings varied widely. Nearly a third of the farmers, or men who lived in farming families, owned no property of any worth. These men were farm laborers rather than yeoman tillers of the soil. Another 31 percent of the farmers owned property valued between $1 and $1,000. The rest, 36 percent, owned property worth more than $1,000. Most of the property owned by men who enlisted as sergeants and officers was on the higher end of this scale. A recent study shows that, of twenty-six officers and sergeants in the 26th North Carolina, twenty-two held property worth more than $1,000 and only four owned property worth less than that amount.[5]

The occupations of members across the brigade often reveal interesting perspectives on their lives. Company K of the 52nd North Carolina had a comparatively large number of students and teachers — two of each — in its ranks. All of them became casualties of the war. One student was killed on July 1 at Gettysburg, and the other student was furloughed for "insanity" but returned to duty in time to be captured at Burgess's Mill. One of the teachers was wounded at Globe Tavern, and the other also was captured at Burgess's Mill. Three plantation overseers joined Company A, 44th North Carolina, while one overseer and three sailors found their way into the ranks of Company C, 52nd North Carolina. The 47th North Carolina had several men who either had unusual occupations or were playing games with the enrolling officers. Twenty-five-year-old Pvt. William W. Crocker was variously listed as an artist and a farmer; he probably made a living by doing both. Lt. Pleasant P. Peace called himself a poet and physician. Pvt. Paschall A. Page listed his occupation as "gentleman," and Sgt. William Henry Hill called himself a "man of pleasure."

Some men signed the enlistment forms but never served. Ten such cases appeared in Company C, 44th North Carolina. They failed to report for duty after signing the enrollment forms and were subsequently dropped from the rolls. Pvt. Joel E. Foster of Company A, 26th North Carolina, signed the forms but never served because he soon after was elected to the secession convention. Presumably he voted to leave the Union. Pvt. John W. Baird of Company I, 26th North Carolina, died after he signed the forms but before he could report to camp.

RELATIVES

An interesting phenomenon is that there were many sets of close relatives serving in the same companies. Four Kirkman brothers enrolled in Company G, 26th

North Carolina. They were between eighteen and twenty-three years of age at enlistment, and all four were either missing, killed, wounded, or captured during the Gettysburg campaign; none returned home. A family named Jarman contributed three brothers to Company K, 26th North Carolina. All three men became battle casualties. Elijah was shot on July 1 at Gettysburg, captured during the retreat to Virginia, and died of his wounds on August 1, 1863. Charles was shot and captured on April 2 but survived to return home. John Robert was wounded at Bristoe Station but returned to his company and was among those who surrendered at Appomattox.

The Bethel Regiment had five Warlick brothers in its Company B; three of the five died. For Lewis Warlick the loss was increased by the fact that he also lost two sisters and his mother just before and during the war.[6]

There were many other sets of men in various companies who had the same last name and who came from the same county. It is difficult to tell if they were brothers, but they almost certainly were related to one another. Seven Braswells from Caldwell County served in Company F, 26th North Carolina. Six of them deserted, but two of the deserters returned to duty (one because he was arrested). One of the returnees deserted again for good, and the other was killed on July 1 at Gettysburg. The other Braswell died of typhoid fever. Three men named Rives joined Company E, 26th North Carolina, but all three were discharged after they provided substitutes to take their places in the ranks. One of the substitutes eventually deserted.

Seven men named Brewer served in Company E, 26th North Carolina. Four men named Church joined Company B of the same regiment on September 21, 1862, which identifies them as conscripts. Two of the Churches deserted, and the other two were wounded and captured in various engagements. Company C of the 26th North Carolina had five men named Souther, all from Wilkes County. Four of them were conscripts who enlisted on September 21, 1862; three of those conscripts deserted. Another Souther who had enlisted in June 1861 was wounded twice and captured twice. Company C also had ten men named Hall who hailed from Wilkes County. Two of them were conscripts who enlisted on September 21, 1862. The record of the ten was quite varied. Five were wounded or captured in battle, one was discharged for disability, and one died of disease. Two of the Halls were listed as absent without leave, and four deserted.

The 26th North Carolina did not have a monopoly on sets of relatives. The 52nd North Carolina also had large groups of men with the same surname. Seven Fosters served in Company F; all but one of them enlisted from Wilkes County. Four of the number probably were conscripts, judging by the dates of their enlistments. Five of the Fosters were wounded or captured in battle, but one deserted as well. Company F of the 52nd held the record for the largest number of men with the same name. Fourteen Browns were in its ranks. Seven of the fourteen deserted, but most of them eventually returned to duty, while one provided a substitute and went home. Ten of the Browns enlisted after the organization of the regiment and thus were probably draftees.

A comparison of surnames in the five sample companies reveals a consistent trend toward commonality. From 46 percent (Company A, 52nd North Carolina) to 68 percent (Company E, 26th North Carolina) of the enlisted men shared a surname with someone else in their company. While some of the names were Smith, Jones, and Davis, as one would expect in the Anglo-Saxon South, many were a bit out of the ordinary. There were eight men named Tickle in Company K, 47th North Carolina, and five men named Blackwelder in Company A, 52nd North Carolina.

SERVICE IN OTHER UNITS

A number of men in the brigade, 8 percent of the total, also served in other units. Some were members of the Bethel Regiment who had served in the 1st North Carolina (six months); others were transferred from other regiments in the latter part of the war; still others obtained transfers out of Pettigrew's brigade to other units (often cavalry regiments—apparently they had grown tired of marching). The numbers of men who served in other units varied. Only 5 percent of the 47th North Carolina were represented in this group, while 16 percent of the Bethel Regiment served in other units.

The Invalid Corps drew a few of the men in this category. Organized to make use of sick or wounded soldiers who could still perform some kind of duty, it mirrored a similar organization in the Union army but never grew as large as the Federal force. While more than 5 percent of the 12th Missouri (Union) served in the Northern Invalid Corps or its successor, the Veteran Reserve Corps, only 1 percent of Pettigrew's brigade served in the Confederate Invalid Corps. Two wounded men who could not perform service in the field were transferred to the "President's Guard" in Richmond, where they protected Jefferson Davis. Pvt. Duncan C. Murchison of Company G, 26th North Carolina, who had been wounded and captured at Gettysburg, was exchanged and detailed to this duty from September 1864 until February 1865. Pvt. Silas Matkins of Company K, 47th North Carolina, who also had been wounded at Gettysburg, was assigned the duty at the same time. Service in the Confederate navy also drew a small number of Tar Heels out of the ranks. Nineteen of them volunteered and obtained transfer papers from their regiments (none from the 44th but eleven from the 47th).[7]

WOMEN AND AFRICAN AMERICANS

Only one enlistee in the brigade was a woman, Sarah Malinda Blalock; her story has been told in Chapters 1 and 14. The confused woman who claimed to have served in the 47th North Carolina, as discussed in Chapter 13, was the victim of her own delusions. The only other woman soldier known to have served in a Tar Heel unit during the war was Lucy Matilda Thompson of the 18th North Carolina.[8]

Two African Americans were listed as serving in the brigade. George Ballantine was described in the service records as a "bodyguard for the family of Alsie Holland," serving in Company H, 47th North Carolina. What that meant is unclear, but the soldier referred to was certainly Pvt. Addison Holland of the same company. Holland was a twenty-six-year-old farmer from Wake County who enlisted as a substitute on March 7, 1862, and deserted on August 25, 1863. He returned sometime after October 1864, was captured on March 25, 1865, and survived the war. Tom Clark of Company H, 52nd North Carolina, had this short notation in his service record: "Negro. Worked as a servant during the war."

BANDS

Every Confederate regiment was authorized to have a band, but only three of the five units in Pettigrew's brigade managed to create one. Moreover, there never was a brigade band, even though such groups were common in the Union army after the summer of 1862. The Bethel Regiment had a band led by Elisha Todd. All of the fifteen men who were listed as musicians had previously served in a company of the regiment, and many of them were transferred to the band in September or October 1864. The 44th North Carolina had sixteen men who were listed as serving in its band, which was led by John Thomas Moore. Nearly all of its musicians were transferred to the band from various companies in the regiment from May through October 1864. The 47th North Carolina had only three men in its band, and the 52nd North Carolina had only four. All of these men were transferred from different companies of their respective regiments in the summer of 1864. It is obvious that both regiments attempted to form a band at this time but were unsuccessful.

The band of the 26th North Carolina had been formed, as we already know, much earlier. Samuel Timothy Mickey led the seventeen men who served in it. He not only directed their musical performances but often repaired instruments, established and maintained contact with other regimental bands in the army, tried to enlist the aid of respected musicians to teach his people, took care of sick bandsmen, auditioned men to recruit the best players, and arranged furloughs for his musicians.

The history of the Moravian band is amply documented through the writings of Julius Linebach, Mickey's own account, and the letters of Edward Peterson. Both Linebach and Peterson were decidedly unmilitary in their attitudes. They expressed pacifist sentiments, were critical of the suffering produced by the war, and were ambivalent about whatever glory other men saw in the conflict. Peterson referred to guard mounting as tomfoolery and mocked the band's assignment to play for regimental inspection. "I am so disgusted with military life I don't know what to do," he wrote in September 1862. Peterson recognized that the band members lived quite well compared with the enlisted men, yet he declared, "I can't content my self to this life." He was depressed by the depredations he witnessed during the Pennsylvania campaign and wondered how the war came about. Peterson made peace with his conscience by convincing himself that, as a musician, he was not part of the fighting force that did the killing. "I'm not to blame," he wrote. Peterson had little hope, save for a few times in the conflict, that the South could win. "She'll come out at the little end of the horn, any way you take it," he wrote in July 1864. The Yankees would "wear us out, in the end."[9]

PROMOTIONS AND DEMOTIONS

The Moravian band was an adjunct service, given its unique status and the attitudes of its personnel. The personal careers of the men who served in the regiments of Pettigrew's brigade and took military life seriously, however, could rise or fall depending on their performance and ambition. Twelve percent of the soldiers in the sample of five companies received promotions during the course of the war. In contrast, only 1 percent of that sample were punished with demotions.

DISCHARGES AND RESIGNATIONS

A full search of all the companies revealed that 619 men, or 7 percent of the total, were discharged for various reasons or offered their resignations. The numbers for each regiment were comparable. Of course, the resignations were all accorded to officers, who resigned for a number of reasons. Three men (two from the 47th and one from the 26th) resigned because of election to the North Carolina House of Commons. Several officers resigned because of ill health, the most common reason. Lt. George Williamson of the 47th North Carolina was wounded on the right side of the frontal bone on July 3 at Gettysburg. He was absent for most of 1864 trying to recover, but he was unsuccessful. Williamson resigned on March 9, 1865, due to epilepsy, which apparently was caused by the injury. Capt. Downing H. Smith of Company I, 44th North Carolina, suffered from rheumatism and diarrhea and asked for a transfer to the heavy artillery or cavalry, where he would have less marching to do. He was successful in obtaining his discharge in late December 1863. Capt. Everard Hall of Company C, 47th North Carolina, resigned because of bronchial infection and "deafness caused by the excessive use of quinine." Sidney P. Dula of the 26th North Carolina left the army not only because of declining health but because he had a wife and eight children, "the oldest only 15 years old, and a cripple for life." He was afraid they would be destitute if his health was ruined.

A small number of officers either resigned or were forced out of the army for reasons other than health or election to political office. Lt. Franklin Samuel Topping was only nineteen years old when he submitted his resignation from Company C, 44th North Carolina. Stedman endorsed it by writing, "From incompetence and cowardice this officer is worthless to his Regt. His resignation will be decidedly for the good of the service." It was accepted on August 2, 1864. Lt. Calvin Dickerson of Company B, 26th North Carolina, was court-martialed in November 1862 and was dismissed from the army for drunkenness. He later reenlisted in the 48th North Carolina and served well. Shot in the hand and thigh and taken prisoner on March 31, 1865, Dickerson had his leg amputated the next day and died in Union hands on May 7.

Enlisted men did not have the option of resigning from anything, but they received discharges for medical and other reasons. Pvt. John A. Ellis of Company F, 47th North Carolina, was released from the army on a "writ of habeas corpus," probably because he was under age. Another man in the 26th North Carolina, Pvt. John A. Deakin, was discharged because he "never acquired a domicile." Why that was done is a mystery. At least Pvt. William Ackroyd of the 26th was released for a logical cause. Born in Yorkshire, England, and a painter by trade, he was discharged after a year of service because he never became a naturalized citizen. Foreign nationals were not welcome in either the Union or the Confederate army. This did not stop Ackroyd; he later enlisted in the 61st North Carolina. Pvt. John Cooper, who also was a painter, was discharged from Ackroyd's company on the same day for the same reason.

Medical discharges were frequent. Pvt. William Brown of the 44th North

Carolina was wounded in the left hand on May 5 at the Wilderness. He was absent until October 1864 recovering from the injury, but the recovery was incomplete. He was discharged on March 25, 1865, because of "contraction of all the fingers into the palm of the hand." Other medical conditions that led to discharges included "want of physical vigor & development"; "natural infirmities of age" (for a man who was sixty-four years old when he enlisted and who was discharged nearly two years after enrolling); "mental derangement"; "epileptic fits and rheumatism"; "contortions of the muscles from rheumatism which has rendered his foot permanently deformed"; "cataract in his right eye & dim vision in his left"; blindness in one eye which caused "pressure on the nerve of the other"; "entire loss of voice & partial deafness" (in a twenty-six-year-old man); "deficiency in size"; "imperfect recovery from typhoid and he is neither mentally or physically fit for a soldier."

Battle injuries could leave a man maimed so that he could no longer perform duty. Pvt. Robert Laney of the 26th was wounded at Malvern Hill and was discharged three months later because of "permanent and rigid contraction of all the fingers of his left hand caused by [a] gunshot wound [and] subsequent unskillful surgical treatment." Accidents could cause similarly debilitating injuries. Pvt. Hamilton Ernest of the Bethel Regiment was hurt while wrestling with another man, who fell on him. He suffered "frequent paraxems of nervous depression" and unspecified damage to the left side of his chest, which led to his discharge. Pvt. Joseph Rufus Segraves of the 26th, an eighteen-year-old man, broke his left arm while the regiment was stationed on Bogue Island. He was released nearly a year later because of "stiffening of the left elbow joint caused by imperfect cure of fracture. The injury unfits him entirely for using a gun." Sometimes a condition tied physical disability with problems of mental development. Pvt. John Smith of the 26th was discharged in 1863, after exactly a year of service, for "hypertrophy of the heart, pulsations violently increased by slight muscular effort, general debility, & mental weakness, mental imbecility very marked."

SICKNESSES

Civil War service was notoriously bad for one's health. Twice as many men died from disease as from combat-related causes, as a general rule. A total of 1,137 men of the brigade, or 13 percent of the total enrollment, died of disease. The 44th North Carolina suffered the worst in this regard, with 289 men (18 percent of the total enrollment) dying of sickness. The lowest rate (11 percent) was suffered by the 26th. These figures do not include men who were captured in battle and then died in prison, for those deaths are attributable to battle casualties. In contrast to the national trend, the brigade lost a lower percentage of men to disease (13 percent) than to combat-related causes (14 percent).

Unfortunately the service records do not consistently provide information on how often a man was sick. There are very infrequent indications of this. For example, only 2 men in Company C, 11th North Carolina, of 134 men on the rolls, were officially listed as being absent sick at any time during their service. Obviously many more than that number were ill at some point in the war. The service records for Union regiments tend to be much more thorough in this regard.

DISCIPLINARY ACTIONS

Likewise, the service records for Pettigrew's men seldom mention disciplinary action taken against soldiers. In the sampling of five companies, only three men (in Company H, 44th North Carolina) had any action taken against them. Obviously much more was done than this spare statistic indicates. There were many minor infractions of military regulations that were dealt with informally or by the imposition of relatively small punishments that were never recorded. Again, a comparison with the 12th Missouri (Union) shows that Federal record keepers were much more conscientious in recording these actions.

Lewis Warlick was the object of one such disciplinary action, and he certainly did not think it was fair. He had been punished twice for allowing men in the Bethel Regiment to burn fencing. The punishment was the forfeiture of two months' pay, a typical minor punishment exacted by officers in the 12th Missouri (Union) as well. Warlick admitted he did not have the heart to stop the men or punish them before this action was taken against him, but afterward he vowed to harden his attitude in order to protect himself.[10]

DESERTIONS

Pettigrew's brigade suffered serious desertion problems at some points in its history, but its overall record in this regard was slightly better than the average in the Confederate army. A total of 869 men deserted, about 10 percent of the total enrollment. That compares with an average desertion rate of 12.2 percent in the Rebel army. Twenty-nine percent of the men who deserted from the brigade returned to duty voluntarily. Additionally, sixty-two deserters (7 percent of those who deserted) were arrested and returned. Some of them were tried and executed, but the vast majority were allowed to resume duty without punishment. At least thirty-two men who deserted (3 percent of the total) did so because they were in a hospital far from their regiment, recuperating from illness or a battle injury. They simply left the hospital and went home without permission, or they failed to return to the regiment from a sick leave or a furlough home to recuperate from battle wounds. In these cases, they were correctly listed as deserters.

Sixty-three men of the brigade deserted within two months of their enlistment, raising the possibility that they signed the enrollment forms simply to collect the small bounty. Twenty-six men deserted soon after they were transferred from other units, raising the possibility that their transfer was not voluntary or that they found it difficult to fit into their new regiments. Thirty-nine men (4 percent of the total) were repeat deserters, soldiers who took unauthorized leaves two, three, or even four times. A large number of deserters, 258, had enlisted in four of the regiments after the initial organization of those units, or in the 26th North Carolina after the institution of the Conscript Act. This raises the possibility that all of them were draftees. These men represented 29 percent of the deserters. Finally, twelve deserters were killed by militiamen or bounty hunters who tried to arrest them behind the lines, or they were executed by the military authorities after their arrest.

The lowest desertion rate in the brigade occurred in the 52nd North Carolina, with 9 percent of the men leaving. The highest rates (12 percent) took place in the 26th and 44th. The 52nd had the highest rate of deserters who returned, 53 percent, while the Bethel Regiment had the lowest rate, 19 percent. The brigade had a higher rate of returnees (29 percent) than was average in the Confederate army (20 percent).

The individual stories of some of these deserters tell us more about the subject than the statistics do. Pvt. Kizey Williams, twenty years old when he enlisted in the 26th North Carolina on October 1, 1862 (probably as a draftee), deserted the first time about October 31. He returned in February 1863 but deserted the second time on March 14, when his regiment was under Union naval gunfire at Barrington's Ferry. Williams returned at an unspecified date but was listed as a deserter for the third time later still. He died of typhoid pneumonia in a Richmond hospital on November 13, 1863. Sgt. Thomas R. Capel of the 52nd North Carolina was wounded on July 1 at Gettysburg but returned to duty within two months. He deserted on July 27, 1864, but was found dead in the Appomattox River nine days later.

Men who deserted and were hunted down by anyone interested in taking them back often did not survive the encounter. A member of the 26th, Pvt. Cornelius A. Wood, had been captured at New Bern and later exchanged; he was wounded and captured at Gettysburg, and was again exchanged on September 16, 1863. He apparently never returned from a furlough home and was reported absent without leave on January 1, 1864. Sometime before July 1 of that year he was "Killed by conscript guards." Another man of the 26th who resisted arrest was Pvt. Ben Lewis, a conscript who deserted one month after he enlisted in the fall of 1862. He was "Killed in woods . . . by men detailed to arrest deserters." Home guard officers killed Pvt. Noah Reeder of the 44th North Carolina on October 21, 1864, when they tried to arrest him. Of course, most of the deserters were never arrested or killed. Two men of the 26th even managed to find their way to Knoxville, Tennessee, where they took the oath of allegiance to the Federal government sometime after September 1863, when the city was occupied by Union troops.

Of the twelve men shot by deserter hunters or executed by order of a court-martial, only one was killed for something other than desertion. The strange case of Pvt. John Harrison raises a disturbing point. His service record shows that he was twenty-eight years old when he enlisted on November 28, 1862, in Company B, 44th North Carolina. This indicates that he probably was a draftee. Harrison was arrested in February 1863, court-martialed on September 10 of that year, and executed for "mutinous language" ten days later. Nothing more than this terse phrase in his service record indicates the reason for his execution. If the record is accurate, it raises the appalling possibility that the Confederacy actually shot one of its soldiers simply for saying the wrong thing at the wrong time.

One man who was listed as a deserter had a bloody war career. Pvt. John A. Fairless of Company C, 52nd North Carolina, enlisted on February 27, 1862, when talk of conscription was filling the air, but he failed to report for duty and was dropped from the rolls. Later, about July 1, 1862, he was officially designated a deserter. Fairless became the leader of a pro-Union guerrilla force headquartered at Wingfield. He and his band savaged the counties of Chowan, Bertie, Perquimans, Hertford, and Gates. In the words of the anonymous man who filled out his service record, the men "pillaged, plundered, burned, and decoyed off slaves." The rampage of these "Buffaloes," as Confederates in eastern North Carolina called pro-Unionists, came to an end when Fairless was killed by one of his own men in October 1862. His career is reminiscent of the activities of Keith and Malinda Blalock in the western part of the state.

AWOLS

A much less serious offense than desertion was absence without leave. Far fewer men of the brigade—372, or only 4 percent of the total enrollment—were officially listed as AWOL. The rate varied from 2 percent in the 47th North Carolina to 6 percent in the 44th and 52nd. Thirty-eight percent of brigade members who went AWOL returned voluntarily, and another 7 percent were eventually dropped from the rolls or officially discharged from their regiments. Twenty-eight percent of the AWOL cases were associated with sickness or exchange from a Northern prison. In other words, many of these men simply did not return to duty after a sick leave. The prisoner exchange system was such that men who were paroled and released by the enemy were not sent back to their regiments until the paperwork for their exchange was completed. Thus they sometimes failed to report to their units when the paperwork was done. The percentage of men who repeatedly went AWOL (3 percent) was about as high as for those who deserted more than once. Combining the numbers of the deserters and the men who were absent without leave shows that about 15 percent of the brigade were guilty of some form of unauthorized leave from their units.

CONSCRIPTS

It is not easy to understand exactly how many men in the brigade were drafted, for the service records do not list them as such. A lot of soldiers enlisted after the initial organization of their regiments. It is possible that a certain percentage of them were volunteers, but the Confederate government began to round up draftees aggressively after the passage of the Conscript Act in April 1862. The four regiments of the brigade that organized during that time were made up of volunteers, many of whom wanted to avoid the draft. But men who enlisted after their regiment was organized probably were conscripts. We definitely know that the large infusion of enlistees joining the regiments in September and October 1862 were draftees, for numerous personal letters from members of the brigade testify to that fact. Since there is no way to find out what percentage of those men who enlisted after the organization of their regiments were volunteers, I have assumed that all were draftees.

Thus the total number of men who were drafted would amount to 2,555, or 31 percent of the total enrollment of the brigade. The highest number, by far, was in the 26th North Carolina, which had 1,090 draftees (50 percent of its total enrollment). This regiment also enlisted 417 men after its organization in August 1861 but before the Conscript Act was passed in April 1862. These men obviously were volunteers, and they represented 19 percent of the total enrollment of the regiment. The proportion of draftees in all four of the other regiments of the brigade ranged from 22 to 25 percent.

The extraordinarily high percentage of conscripts in the 26th resulted from the vigorous efforts by regimental officers (especially Burgwyn and Lane) to keep the ranks as full as possible. Thus the regiment almost always was the biggest in the brigade. Yet Company F, 52nd North Carolina, also had a high concentration of conscripts compared with volunteers. Seventy-eight of 194 men in the company were draftees, amounting to 40 percent of the total. The desertion rate of the draftees in this company was significantly higher than that of the volunteers, 5 percent compared with 1 percent. But the conscripts who deserted tended to return to duty more frequently, 14 percent compared with 10 percent. The percentage of conscripts who went AWOL was exactly the same as the percentage of volunteers who were listed as absent without leave. A lower percentage of conscripts died of disease, 17 percent compared with 24 percent. Their fate in battle differed markedly as well. Thirty-two percent of the conscripts were captured, compared with 47 percent of the volunteers. Twenty-five percent of the conscripts were wounded, compared with 50 percent, but 10 percent of the draftees were killed in battle, compared with 7 percent of the volunteers. It is possible that the conscripts did not expose themselves as readily during battle or stand their ground while defending against an assault or thrust themselves into the forefront when conducting an attack. At any rate, they tended to survive battle more readily than did the volunteers.

SUBSTITUTES

The number of substitutes in the brigade was relatively small; only 205 (2 percent) of the total enrollment were identified as such. The Bethel Regiment had 4 substitutes; the 26th North Carolina had 29; the 44th North Carolina had 34; the 47th North Carolina had the bulk of the substitutes, 111; and the 52nd North Carolina had only 28. Forty-three members of the brigade were listed as having provided substitutes so they could go home. The number of substitute providers ranged from zero in the 11th North Carolina to eighteen in the 26th North Carolina.

Sometimes the substitutes enlisted to allow a family member to go home. For example, Pvt. Daniel Lowe entered the 52nd North Carolina at age eighteen to substitute for his father, Pvt. Isaac Lowe, a fifty-six-year-old farmer. Isaac had served five months before he was relieved by his son. Daniel was captured on May 6 at the Wilderness and was released from prison on May 19, 1865. Sgt. John W. Crews of the 52nd North Carolina provided Pvt. Yancey Crews as his substitute after only two months in service. John was forty years old and Yancey was seventeen; the two probably were father and son. Yancey was captured during Lee's retreat from Pennsylvania when he was left behind as a hospital nurse. He was released from prison after taking the oath of allegiance on February 2, 1864, and served in Company D, 1st U.S. Infantry.

The plight of the Quaker draftees in the 52nd North Carolina has already been detailed in previous chapters. Another Quaker was drafted into the 26th North Carolina, Pvt. John Hobson of Company G. He managed to obtain a discharge as a conscientious objector but died of typhoid on September 5, 1863, only two months after he enlisted and just before he could have gone home. Yet the 52nd seems to have garnered the lion's share of Quakers. Four enrolled in Company B in October 1862; three of them paid their $500 commutation fee and went home, and the other obtained a discharge as a conscientious objector. Five others enrolled in Company G on November 3, 1862. One paid his fee and left in February 1863, but the other four were either captured or were left behind as nurses during the retreat from Pennsylvania. Two more Quakers enlisted in the regiment but were never assigned to a company. One was discharged for infirmity, and the other paid the commutation fee. The Confederacy got no military service out of these men, which is a testament to their adherence to their principles.

CASUALTIES

The casualty statistics for the brigade are appalling. Of 8,256 men on the rolls, 4,830 were lost in battle, which amounts to 58 percent of the total. Twenty-one men were missing and never accounted for, 438 were killed on the battlefield, and 1,423 were wounded. A large number of soldiers, 651, were wounded and captured, and another 2,297 were captured without being injured. The total number of soldiers taken by the Federals, combining those who were wounded and captured with those who were only captured, amounted to 2,948. A grand total of 1,202 men died of combat-related causes; that number includes men who died in Northern prisons.

It is important to note that the number of men who were wounded or captured differs from the number of incidents of wounds and captures because a sizable lot of Tar Heels were wounded or captured more than once. Two hundred fifty-seven members of the unit accounted for a total of 536 incidents of battlefield injuries. Forty-seven men of the Bethel Regiment were wounded twice, and one was wounded three times. Ninety-seven men of the 26th North Carolina were wounded twice, 9 were wounded three times, and 2 were wounded four times. Nineteen men of the 44th North Carolina were wounded twice, while 40 men of the 47th North Carolina were injured twice and 2 were wounded three times. The 52nd North Carolina had 34 men who were injured twice and 6 who received three battlefield injuries.

The brigade also had 243 men who were captured more than once, accounting for 487 incidents of battlefield captures. Virtually all of them were captured twice; one man of the 52nd North Carolina was captured three times. The Bethel Regiment had 54 members who were captured twice, the 26th North Carolina had 63, the 44th had 35, the 47th had 53, and the 52nd had 37.

Nineteen men of the brigade held the unique distinction of having been wounded twice and captured twice in their army service. Nine served in the 26th North Carolina, with two each in the Bethel Regiment, the 44th North Carolina, and the 52nd North Carolina and four in the 47th North Carolina.

When totaling casualties for the brigade and its regiments, I used the number of men lost, not the number of incidents that occurred, for the two categories of wounded and of captured. It is important to tabulate the information in this way so as to be consistent with the other categories, since no one experienced getting killed, or being wounded and captured at the same time, more than once in the war. But in tabulating the fate of those men who were wounded and those who were captured, the number of incidents is used. This seemed necessary because I wanted to know what happened to every one of the wounded and the captured in each engagement.

A breakdown of the fate of the wounded reveals that 60 percent returned to duty after a few weeks or months of recuperation. Twenty-four percent were discharged from the army, and 12 percent died of their injuries. The remaining 4 percent have inadequate records regarding their fate. Those who were wounded and captured in the same battle fared far worse. Only 32 percent of them returned to duty with their regiments. Thirty-seven percent were released after being exchanged, but 28 percent died of their injuries. The statistics for men who were captured but not wounded are skewed by the fact that a large percentage of them were taken on April 2, 1865, and succeeding days, when the war was coming to a close. Thus many of them, 68 percent, were released directly into civilian life, while only 15 percent returned to duty with their regiments. Fourteen percent of the captured died in prison.

The service records provide consistent figures for casualties in most of the brigade's engagements — consistent, that is, with official reports and the information provided in letters, diaries, and newspapers. But for three campaigns there are significant differences, with the service records giving much lower statistics than other sources. At Globe Tavern, brigade losses amounted to only 46 in the service records but over 100 in other sources; at Reams Station the discrepancy was the same (62 in the service records compared with 120 in other sources); and during the Fifth Offensive the difference was 137 compared with 243. I cannot fully account for this, other than to hypothesize that the stress of

TABLE 2. Brigade Casualties

Missing	21	
Killed	438	(8.1% of casualties)
Wounded	1,423	(29.4% of casualties)
Returned	1,026	(60.2% of wounded)
Released	421	(24.7% of wounded)
Died	216	(12.6% of wounded)
No record	39	
Wounded and captured	651	(12.1% of casualties)
Returned	212	(32.5% of wounded and captured)
Released	242	(37.1% of wounded and captured)
Died	184	(28.2% of wounded and captured)
No record	13	
Captured	2,297	(47.5% of casualties)
Returned	401	(15.7% of captured)
Released	1,737	(68.3% of captured)
Died	364	(14.3% of captured)
No record	39	
Total	4,830	

continuous campaigning from late August to early October 1864 might have prevented officers and clerks from keeping their records up to date.

The 11th North Carolina suffered a total of 1,022 casualties, 67 percent of its enrollment, during the war. Seventy-nine men were killed, 301 were wounded, 140 were wounded and captured, and 502 were captured. Gettysburg was the biggest factor in this toll. Seventy percent of the men killed on the battlefield in the regiment's history were killed in that engagement. Gettysburg accounted for 88 percent of the wounded and captured in the unit's history. It also accounted for 66 percent of the wounded and 11 percent of the captured. Larger percentages of the captured were lost at Burgess's Mill (17 percent) and on April 2, 1865 (34 percent), but Gettysburg took the lion's share of all casualties in the Bethel Regiment.

The 26th North Carolina lost 1,307 of its 2,175 men, 68 percent. Eight men were listed as missing, 185 were killed, 443 were wounded, 212 were wounded and captured, and 469 were captured. Another way to look at this is to note that 2 percent of the regiment were missing, 8 percent were killed on the battlefield,

19 percent were wounded, 9 percent were wounded and captured, and 21 percent were captured. Separating the wounded from the wounded and captured can obscure the fact that 34 percent of the men who served in the 26th were injured on the battlefield; 31 percent were held in captivity by the enemy.

The 44th North Carolina suffered 693 casualties out of 1,552 men, or 44 percent. Two men were missing, 36 were killed, 214 were wounded, only 23 were wounded and captured (because the regiment missed Gettysburg, the battle that produced by far the largest number of losses in this category), and 418 men were captured. The large number of captured was boosted by the South Anna Bridge fight. Seventy percent of the captured were released into civilian life by the Federals, while 18 percent of the captured returned to duty with the regiment. Eleven percent of the prisoners died in captivity.

The 47th North Carolina had 1,589 men enrolled; 977 of them were counted among the casualties. Two were missing, 79 were killed, 273 were wounded, 123 were wounded and captured, and 500 were captured. The number of regimental members held as captives by the Federals amounted to 39 percent of the total enrollment; 24 percent of the enrollment were wounded, and 15 percent of the men died of combat-related causes. Sixty-one percent of the regimental members became casualties of war.

The 52nd North Carolina suffered a similar casualty rate, 59 percent of its 1,425 men. Nine members were missing, 59 were killed, 214 were wounded, 153 were wounded and captured, and 408 were captured. A total of 843 losses were suffered among 1,425 men. The men who were killed or who died of injuries or in captivity amounted to 231, or 16 percent of the total enrollment and 24 percent of the total number of casualties. Five hundred sixty-one men were held in captivity; that amounts to 39 percent of the total enrollment and 66 percent of the total number of casualties. Finally, 367 men were wounded, which represents 25 percent of the total enrollment and 43 percent of the casualties.

Without comparable statistics for other North Carolina regiments, or for other Confederate regiments, it is difficult to determine if the casualties suffered by the brigade were typical. I suspect they were not. The brigade saw unusually heavy action from Gettysburg until the end of the Petersburg campaign, and thus its loss ratios might have been higher than average among Southern units.

With so much exposure to battle, it is not surprising that a few members of the brigade would be hit in more than one engagement. Cpl. John B. Short of Company K, 26th North Carolina, was wounded at Malvern Hill and returned to duty by September 1, 1862. He was again wounded at Rawls's Mill on November 2 and returned by January 1, 1863. Wounded a third time at Gettysburg, Short was back on duty by January 1865. He was one of the few who surrendered at Ap-

TABLE 3. Regimental Casualties

	11th	26th	44th	47th	52nd
Missing	0	8	2	2	9
Killed	79	185	36	79	59
Wounded	301	433	214	273	214
Returned	194	372	116	192	162
Released	100	101	72	80	64
Died	43	72	38	35	28
No record	13	5	7	8	6
Wounded and captured	140	212	23	123	153
Returned	57	76	8	32	42
Released	32	86	11	52	62
Died	47	50	3	37	47
No record	4	0	1	2	2
Captured	502	469	418	500	408
Returned	107	111	82	47	54
Released	378	348	320	417	295
Died	66	66	50	85	97
No record	5	7	1	4	1
Total	1,125	1,487	747	1,072	928

pomattox. Cpl. James Martindale of Company E, 26th North Carolina, was hit in the chest on July 1 at Gettysburg but returned to duty in time for the battle of Bristoe Station, where he was again wounded. Martindale was promoted to his rank of corporal while recuperating from this injury. Back with the regiment by January 1864, he was wounded in the eye on May 6 at the Wilderness and recovered by July 1. Martindale was captured at Burgess's Mill, was held at Point Lookout, and was exchanged on March 30, 1865.

ACCIDENTS AND SUICIDES

The camps also took their toll of casualties. Twenty-one men in the brigade died or were injured by accidents or as the result of suicide. Eight of them were shot accidentally by other men or through their own careless handling of guns. Half of the eight died, while three others suffered the amputations of limbs or fingers.

Virtually all of these accidental injuries were recorded in the 26th and the 52nd North Carolina. Only one man, Pvt. J. Q. Taylor of Company A, 11th North Carolina, was identified as having committed suicide by deliberately shooting himself. He had enlisted on January 27, 1864, and thus was certainly a conscript. The suicide took place on October 24 of that year. One man in the 47th North Carolina was killed four days before the battle of Globe Tavern when a tree fell on him, and another man of the 26th was severely injured by the kick of a mule. Pvt. H. D. Wagoner of the 26th was unintentionally killed by Pvt. Meridith D. Stamper in April 1862 in a playful boxing match. Lt. William A. Summerow of the 52nd, apparently delirious with typhoid fever, died when he fell out of an upper-floor hospital window in Petersburg in August 1862.

PRISONERS OF WAR

Among the men who were captured, quite a few saw the inside of a Union prison more than once. Eight percent, or 243, of the 2,948 men who were held in captivity were taken more than once. Their numbers were fairly evenly distributed: 54 in the Bethel Regiment, 63 in the 26th, 35 in the 44th, 53 in the 47th, and 38 in the 52nd.

Although the brigade saw action in at least twenty engagements, only six accounted for a majority of the men captured in battle. At Gettysburg, at Falling Waters, at Bristoe Station, at Burgess's Mill, and on April 2 and 3, 1865, a total of 2,069 men were captured. That represents 70 percent of the total number of men captured in the brigade during the entire war. It is interesting to break down the fate of the men captured in these six encounters with the enemy. The highest percentage of men who returned to duty were taken at Falling Waters, 45 percent, while the lowest were those captured on April 2 and 3, literally 0 percent. Only 6 percent of those captured at Burgess's Mill returned to duty, while 18 percent of those taken at Bristoe Station and 22 percent of those captured at Gettysburg saw any service in their regiments again. The ratio of those who were released into civilian life was, of course, highest for the men captured on April 2 and 3 (95 percent and 72 percent, respectively), while it was lowest for Gettysburg (41 percent) and Falling Waters (34 percent). By far the highest ratio of prisoners who died were those captured at Gettysburg, 33 percent, because of the large number of men who were wounded and captured on July 3. The lowest ratio of death in captivity was suffered by those men captured on April 2, 4 percent. The men who were taken on April 3 had a much higher ratio of death, 9 percent, because a large number of them were captured while being treated for illness and

TABLE 4. Fate of Brigade Members Captured in Six Most Costly Battles

	Gettysburg	Falling Waters	Bristoe Station	Burgess's Mill	April 2, 1865	April 3, 1865
Number of captured plus wounded and captured	309	247	264	421	667	161
% returned	22	45	18	6	0	0
% released	41	34	64	71	95	72
% died	33	17	17	21	4	9
% with no record	4	4	1	2	1	19

wounds in Richmond hospitals. As a point of reference, 12 percent of all Confederate prisoners held by the North died in prison.

At best, prison life was dull and demoralizing; at worst, it led to high rates of disease and death. Quite a few members of the brigade took the oath of allegiance to the U.S. government. They then volunteered to serve in the Union army or disappeared into Northern civilian life. Of 2,948 men held in Union prisons, 30 took the oath before the end of the war, but beyond that their fate is unrecorded. Six men of the Bethel Regiment, 13 men of the 26th, 2 men of the 44th, 1 man of the 47th, and 8 men of the 52nd fall into this category. Sidney Briant of the 11th North Carolina, who had been captured at Burgess's Mill, declined the opportunity to be exchanged in March 1865. "I have no interest South," he proclaimed. Instead, Briant preferred to move to Ohio and "preform all of the doety's of a good citizen."

Another 130 men who took the oath of allegiance before the war was over volunteered for service in the Union army, thereby becoming galvanized Yankees. Eighteen men of the Bethel Regiment, 48 men of the 26th, 4 men of the 44th, 20 men of the 47th, and 40 men of the 52nd fell into this category. An additional prisoner from the 47th North Carolina volunteered to serve in the U.S. Navy. Most of the men were assigned to U.S. regular units, but several served in Southern state regiments, such as the 1st Maryland, which were part of the volunteer force of the Union army. The total of 161 men who took the oath of allegiance in prison amounted to only 5 percent of the total number of prisoners from the brigade.

At least two of the galvanized Yankees joined the Federal army simply to get out of prison, not because they had a genuine change of heart about the war. Sgt. James H. Robinson of Company B, 26th North Carolina, had been captured during the retreat from Gettysburg. He took the oath in January 1864 and was assigned to the 1st U.S. Infantry. Robinson deserted from that regiment near Elizabeth City, North Carolina, on August 1, 1864, and returned to duty with the 26th six days later. Pvt. James Simmons of Company I, same regiment, had a similar story. He also was captured during the Gettysburg campaign, joined a Union unit, but then "escaped from the enemy and rejoined the company" on February 3, 1865. At least one other member of the brigade, Pvt. John L. Wood of the 47th North Carolina, escaped from prison at Point Lookout about March 28, 1865, but there is no indication that he ever rejoined his unit.

UNIT EFFECTIVENESS

Despite the heavy losses on the battlefield, the brigade remained a strong, vibrant military force to the end. It retained its spirit and its organization while other brigades in Lee's army dwindled, and MacRae surrendered a goodly number of men at Appomattox. More famous units such as the Stonewall Brigade or the Louisiana Tigers, which had been powerful striking forces in the first half of the war, ended the conflict in obscurity. The Stonewall Brigade was devastated at Chancellorsville, and the Tigers were nearly wiped out in the battle of Rappahannock Station.

There was a certain degree of timeliness in this. These units, and others like them, had been the backbone of Lee's army in 1862 and 1863, but their time had run out due to battle losses and a dwindling supply of replacements during the last year of the war. Pettigrew's Tar Heels came into Lee's army when the stars of these better-known units were descending, and the North Carolinians had to take up the slack. They also suffered enormous battle losses in repeated engagements, but they could replenish those losses with a steady stream of conscripts. Also, the Tar Heel officers refused to give up on their units. Men such as John Randolph Lane, Charles Manly Stedman, and William Joseph Martin provided steady and enthusiastic leadership that inspired the rank and file. The morale of the brigade remained high enough, despite the crushing losses and demoralizing defeats, to allow the men to persevere. The brigade was among the handful of units that carried the burden of fighting in Lee's army to the end of the Petersburg campaign.

No other field army of the Civil War accomplished more on the battlefield with its limited resources than the Army of Northern Virginia, and much of the credit for this goes to the brigade commanders and their men. The brigades, especially by the time of the Petersburg campaign, were the heart and soul of Lee's army. They were the units that defended against the Union thrusts to extend the lines westward, as in the Fifth Offensive. They also were the units that provided the shock power in efforts to regain lost ground, as at Globe Tavern and Reams Station. The war in Virginia had devolved into a conflict where a few Rebel brigades were asked to stand or to attack in the face of Union divisions and corps, as Lee's available manpower was stretched to the breaking point. The brigades, such as MacRae's, which did this job well could be said to have prolonged the life of the Confederacy by several months. Maintaining a high level of combat efficiency on the brigade level was one of the keys to Lee's long survival at Petersburg. The fact that the town fell on April 2 was no reflection on the quality of the rank and file, just on the inexorable outcome of a war that had already been lost.

NOTES

ABBREVIATIONS

BCPL	Burke County Public Library, Morganton, N.C.
DCL	Davidson College Library, Davidson, N.C.
EU	Emory University, Special Collections, Atlanta, Ga.
GHM	Greensboro Historical Museum, Greensboro, N.C.
GHS	Georgia Historical Society, Savannah
GNMP	Gettysburg National Military Park, Gettysburg, Pa.
HSD	Historical Society of Delaware, Wilmington
LC	Library of Congress, Manuscripts Division, Washington, D.C.
MC	Museum of the Confederacy, Richmond, Va.
MHS	Minnesota Historical Society, Minneapolis
MMF	Moravian Music Foundation, Winston-Salem, N.C.
NARA	National Archives and Records Administration, Washington, D.C.
NCDAH	North Carolina Division of Archives and History, Raleigh
OR	*The War of the Rebellion: A Compilation of the Official Records of the Union and Confederate Armies.* 70 vols. in 128. Washington, D.C.: Government Printing Office, 1880–1901. Unless otherwise noted, all citations are to series 1.
PNB	Petersburg National Battlefield, Petersburg, Va.
SCL-DU	Duke University, Special Collections Library, Durham, N.C.
SHC-UNC	University of North Carolina, Southern Historical Collection, Chapel Hill
SP-MA	Moravian Archives, Southern Province, Winston-Salem, N.C.
USAMHI	U.S. Army Military History Institute, Carlisle Barracks, Pa.
UVA	University of Virginia, Special Collections, Charlottesville
VHS	Virginia Historical Society, Richmond
VMI	Virginia Military Institute, Archives, Lexington

1. Underwood, "Twenty-Sixth Regiment," 303–4.

2. Record of events, Companies A, B, C, F, G, H, I, and K, 26th North Carolina, Compiled Service Records, NARA; McGee, "Twenty-Sixth Regiment," 7–8, 11–16; "Webster's Company of Volunteers," 398–99.

3. Davis, *Boy Colonel of the Confederacy*, 7–8, 32–34, 39.

4. Underwood, "Twenty-Sixth Regiment," 306–7, 412; Dowd, *Sketches of Prominent Living North Carolinians*, 7–15; Tucker, *Zeb Vance*, 57–80, 109; Crofts, *Reluctant Confederates*, 34; Zebulon Baird Vance to C. C. Jones, February 11, 1861, and Vance to Hattie, July 4, 28, 1861, Vance Papers, SHC-UNC; Zebulon Baird Vance diary, May 3–5, 1861, Vance Collection, NCDAH; James G. Martin to Vance, August 27, 1861, in Johnston, *Papers of Zebulon Baird Vance*, 113.

5. Underwood, "Twenty-Sixth Regiment," 304–5, 408; Powell, *Dictionary of North Carolina Biography*, 4:12–13.

6. Edmund Jones, "Sketch of John T. Jones," Burgwyn Papers, NCDAH; John Thomas Jones to father, January 20, February 11, [March 4], May 21, 30, June 12, 20, 1861, Jones Papers, SHC-UNC.

7. Henry Clay Albright diary, n.d., Albright Papers, NCDAH; Albright to sister, August 10, 1861, Albright Papers, GHM; Wiley, *Life of Billy Yank*, 360; Mitchell, *Civil War Soldiers*, 3–4.

8. Noah Deaton to Miss Christian Ray, October 7, 1861, Ray Papers, SCL-DU; Jordan, *North Carolina Troops*, 7:564.

9. John Randolph Lane address, 1903, Lane Papers, SHC-UNC.

10. Henry King Burgwyn diary, August 28–September 1, 1861, Burgwyn Family Papers, SHC-UNC; Barrett, *North Carolina as a Civil War Battleground*, 14–17, 21.

11. Henry King Burgwyn diary, September 2–6, 1861, Burgwyn Family Papers, SHC-UNC; John A. Jackson to R. A. Cole, September 5, 1861, and Jackson to parents, September 7, 1861, Cole Collection, NCDAH.

12. Abstract of fuel issued September 30, 1861, and Captain W. W. Morrison to Vance, September 5, 1861, and Vance to Governor Clark, September 17, 1861, Regimental Letter Book, 26th Regiment North Carolina Troops, Muster Rolls and Regimental Records, Military Collection, Civil War Collection, NCDAH; requisition, Zebulon Baird Vance service record, 26th North Carolina, Compiled Service Records, NARA.

13. T. W. Setser to W. A. Setser, August 25, 1861, in Mast, "Setser Letters," pt. 1, p. 29; Underwood, "Twenty-Sixth Regiment," 307; requisition, Zebulon Baird Vance service record, 26th North Carolina, Compiled Service Records, NARA; John R. Lane interview, June 16, 1900, Burgwyn Papers, NCDAH.

14. Zebulon Baird Vance to wife, October 11, 1861, Vance Papers, SHC-UNC; John A. Jackson to R. A. Cole, October 22, 1861, Cole Collection, NCDAH; W. E. Setser to W. A. Setser, n.d., in Mast, "Setser Letters," pt. 1, p. 30; *Raleigh North Carolina Standard*, November 9, 1861; Vance to Governor Clark, November 15, 1861, 26th Regiment North Carolina Troops, Muster Rolls and Regimental Records, Military Collection, Civil War Collection, NCDAH; record of events, Companies D, F, H, and K, 26th North Carolina,

Compiled Service Records, NARA; John Quincey Adams to father, November 5, 20, 1861, Adams and Partin Family Collection, NCDAH; Hugh Ray to father, November 31, 1861, Ray Papers, SCL-DU.

15. Henry King Burgwyn diary, October 11, 1861, and January 23, 1862; Burgwyn to father, December 26, 1861, and January 19, 1862; and Burgwyn to mother, January 3, 1862, Burgwyn Family Papers, SHC-UNC; Underwood, "Twenty-Sixth Regiment," 308; John Quincey Adams to father, December 6, 1861, and January 15, 1862, Adams and Partin Family Collection, NCDAH; M. B. Blair to uncle, January 4, 1862, Blair Letters, NCDAH; Thomas W. Setser to W. A. Setser, January 13, 1862, in Mast, "Setser Letters," pt. 1, p. 31; N. A. Ray to Miss Christian Ray, December 27, 1861, Ray Papers, SCL-DU; Jordan, *North Carolina Troops*, 7:526.

16. Sauers, *"Succession of Honorable Victories,"* 17–69; Henry King Burgwyn diary, January 24, 1862; Burgwyn to mother, January 26, February 18, 1862; and Burgwyn to father, January 28, February 19, March 12, 1862, Burgwyn Family Papers, SHC-UNC; John Quincey Adams to father, January 29, 1862, Adams and Partin Family Collection, NCDAH; John Thomas Jones to father, February 3, 1862, Jones Papers, SHC-UNC; Orren Alston Hanner to Harrington, February 26, 1862, Harrington Papers, SCL-DU.

17. John Thomas Jones to father, February 18, 1862, Jones Papers, SHC-UNC; Orren Alston Hanner to Harrington, February 26, 1862, Harrington Papers, SCL-DU; William H. Glenn to mother, February 18, 1862, Glenn Papers, SCL-DU; Jordan, *North Carolina Troops*, 7:463–601.

18. Henry King Burgwyn to father, February 19, 1862, Burgwyn Family Papers, SHC-UNC; Vance to Allen Turner Davidson, March 4, 1862, in Johnston, *Papers of Zebulon Baird Vance*, 119–20.

19. Knouse and Crews, *Moravian Music*, 1–3.

20. Harry H. Hall, *Johnny Reb Band*, 3–10; Linebach diary, 5–6, SHC-UNC.

21. Linebach diary, 5–7, SHC-UNC.

22. Ibid., 8–10; Mickey account, SP-MA.

23. Sauers, *"Succession of Honorable Victories,"* 143–204; Henry King Burgwyn to father, February 24, 1862, Burgwyn Family Papers, SHC-UNC.

24. Sauers, *"Succession of Honorable Victories,"* 238–42; Davis, *Boy Colonel of the Confederacy*, 109–10; Henry King Burgwyn to mother, March 12, 17, 1862, Burgwyn Family Papers, SHC-UNC; "K, 26th" to editor, May 1, 1862, *North Carolina Argus*, May 15, 1862; Underwood, "Twenty-Sixth Regiment," 310–29; W. E. Setser to W. A. Setser, March 21, 1862, in Mast, "Setser Letters," pt. 1, p. 33; Vance to Lawrence O'Bryan Branch, March 17, 1862, in Johnston, *Papers of Zebulon Baird Vance*, 122.

25. "K, 26th" to editor, May 1, 1862, *North Carolina Argus*, May 15, 1862; Underwood, "Twenty-Sixth Regiment," 309.

26. Field visits to New Bern battlefield, February 24, 1994, and October 4, 1995; "K, 26th" to editor, May 1, 1862, *North Carolina Argus*, May 15, 1862; "Sketch of the Battle Field near Newbern," Clark Collection, NCDAH; Hopkins, "Battle of Newbern as I Saw It," 143; Underwood, "Twenty-Sixth Regiment," 309, 324; Davis, *Boy Colonel of the Confederacy*, 111–12; Zebulon Baird Vance to A. N. McMillan, March 17, 1862, *OR* 9:255; Vance to Lawrence O'Bryan Branch, March 17, 1862, in Johnston, *Papers of Zebulon*

Baird Vance, 123; W. A. Curtis, "Journal of Reminiscences of the War," 285; Henry King Burgwyn to mother, March 17, 1862, Burgwyn Family Papers, SHC-UNC; Adams to niece, December 7, 1911, Military Collection, Civil War Collection, NCDAH.

27. Zebulon Baird Vance to Hattie, March 20, 1862, in Yearns and Barrett, *North Carolina Civil War Documentary*, 39; Davis, *Boy Colonel of the Confederacy*, 115–17; Underwood, "Twenty-Sixth Regiment," 312–13, 315; Henry King Burgwyn to mother, March 17, 1862, Burgwyn Family Papers, SHC-UNC; Barefoot, *General Robert F. Hoke*, 45–46.

28. Underwood, "Twenty-Sixth Regiment," 313, 315; Oscar R. Rand to William H. S. Burgwyn, July 8, 1892, Burgwyn Papers, NCDAH.

29. Vance to Lawrence O'Bryan Branch, March 17, 1862, in Johnston, *Papers of Zebulon Baird Vance*, 124; Vance to Hattie, March 20, 1862, in Yearns and Barrett, *North Carolina Civil War Documentary*, 39; Underwood, "Twenty-Sixth Regiment," 316–17; Zebulon Baird Vance to A. N. McMillan, March 17, 1862, *OR* 9:256; record of events, Company H, 26th North Carolina, Compiled Service Records, NARA.

30. Underwood, "Twenty-Sixth Regiment," 318–20; John G. Foster to Lewis Richmond, March 20, 1862, *OR* 9:213; Oscar R. Rand to William H. S. Burgwyn, July 8, 1892, Burgwyn Papers, NCDAH; Sauers, *"Succession of Honorable Victories,"* 288–89.

31. Vance to Lawrence O'Bryan Branch, March 17, 1862, in Johnston, *Papers of Zebulon Baird Vance*, 124–25; Vance to Hattie, March 20, 1862, in Yearns and Barrett, *North Carolina Civil War Documentary*, 39; Underwood, "Twenty-Sixth Regiment," 323.

32. Henry King Burgwyn to mother, March 17, 1862, and Burgwyn to father, March 23, 1862, Burgwyn Family Papers, SHC-UNC; "K, 26th" to editor, May 1, 1862, *North Carolina Argus*, May 15, 1862; W. A. Curtis, "Journal of Reminiscences of the War," 286; Underwood, "Twenty-Sixth Regiment," 323–25; Barefoot, *General Robert F. Hoke*, 48; Vance to Lawrence O'Bryan Branch, March 17, 1862, in Johnston, *Papers of Zebulon Baird Vance*, 125.

33. Linebach diary, 11–14, SHC-UNC.

34. Underwood, "Twenty-Sixth Regiment," 329–30; Vance to Lawrence O'Bryan Branch, March 17, 1862, in Johnston, *Papers of Zebulon Baird Vance*, 125; Henry King Burgwyn to mother, March 17, 1862, Burgwyn Family Papers, SHC-UNC; Barefoot, *General Robert F. Hoke*, 48; John R. Lane interview, June 16, 1900, Burgwyn Papers, NCDAH; record of events, Company H, 26th North Carolina, Compiled Service Records, NARA; Linebach diary, 14–15, SHC-UNC.

35. W. E. Setser to W. A. Setser, March 21, 1862, in Mast, "Setser Letters," pt. 1, p. 33; Henry King Burgwyn to mother, March 17, 1862, Burgwyn Family Papers, SHC-UNC; Vance to Lawrence O'Bryan Branch, March 17, 1862, in Johnston, *Papers of Zebulon Baird Vance*, 126; Jordan, *North Carolina Troops*, 7:463–601; Vance to Hattie, March 20, 1862, in Yearns and Barrett, *North Carolina Civil War Documentary*, 40; J. J. Young estimate of losses at New Bern, 26th Regiment North Carolina Troops, Muster Rolls and Regimental Records, Military Collection, Civil War Collection, NCDAH.

36. Underwood, "Twenty-Sixth Regiment," 328; Special Orders No. 53, Department of North Carolina, March 17, 1862, *OR* 9:447–48; Sauers, *"Succession of Honorable Victories,"* 346–48.

37. Henry King Burgwyn to father, March 20, 1862, Burgwyn Family Papers, SHC-

UNC; Vance to wife, March 20, 1862, in Johnston, *Papers of Zebulon Baird Vance*, 130–31; W. E. Setser to W. A. Setser, March 21, 1862, in Mast, "Setser Letters," pt. 1, p. 33.

38. Underwood, "Twenty-Sixth Regiment," 328; Henry King Burgwyn to father, March 20, 1862, Burgwyn Family Papers, SHC-UNC; Zebulon Baird Vance to editor, March 26, 1862, *Raleigh North Carolina Standard*, April 2, 1862; requisition, May 5, 1862, Joseph R. Ballew service record, 26th North Carolina, Compiled Service Records, NARA.

39. Sauers, *"Succession of Honorable Victories,"* 309–40, 348; Henry King Burgwyn to father, March 20, 23, 28, April 1, 7, 1862, Burgwyn Family Papers, SHC-UNC; Zebulon Baird Vance to Hattie, April 29, 1862, Vance Papers, SHC-UNC; W. E. Setser to W. A. Setser, April 20, 1862, in Mast, "Setser Letters," pt. 1, p. 33; Isaac Augustus Jarratt to father, April 22, 1862, Jarratt-Puryear Family Papers, SCL-DU; Henry C. Albright to sister, April 17, 1862, Albright Papers, GHM; "K, 26th" to editor, May 1, 1862, *North Carolina Argus*, May 15, 1862; Mickey account, SP-MA; Linebach diary, 15–17, SHC-UNC.

40. Isaac Augustus Jarratt to father, April 22, 1862, Jarratt-Puryear Family Papers, SCL-DU; "K, 26th" to editor, May 1, 1862, *North Carolina Argus*, May 15, 1862; Henry King Burgwyn to father, April 23, 1862, Burgwyn Family Papers, SHC-UNC; Underwood, "Twenty-Sixth Regiment," 328.

41. Underwood, "Twenty-Sixth Regiment," 328–30; Jordan, *North Carolina Troops*, 7:463, 549, 589; Oscar R. Rand to William H. S. Burgwyn, July 8, 1892, Burgwyn Papers, NCDAH; Henry King Burgwyn to father, April 23, 1862, and Burgwyn to William, May 1, 1862, Burgwyn Family Papers, SHC-UNC.

42. See correspondence in Johnston, *Papers of Zebulon Baird Vance*, 132–39, 142–45; Vance to Hattie, April 29, 1862, Vance Papers, SHC-UNC.

43. Mickey account, SP-MA; Linebach diary, 16–22, SHC-UNC; Harry H. Hall, *Johnny Reb Band*, 13–16; Knouse and Crews, *Moravian Music*, 18.

44. McGee, "Twenty-Sixth Regiment," 60–61; Henry King Burgwyn to mother, May 11, 1862, Burgwyn Family Papers, SHC-UNC.

45. Stevens, *Rebels in Blue*, 3–4, 14, 19, 29–31, 34–39; Jordan, *North Carolina Troops*, 7:535, 543; Underwood, "Twenty-Sixth Regiment," 330–31; Powell, *Dictionary of North Carolina Biography*, 1:174–75; McGee, "Twenty-Sixth Regiment," 61; Henry C. Albright to sister, April 28, 1862, Albright Papers, GHM. Keith and Malinda made extravagant claims about their Confederate service in a successful effort to obtain a pension from the U.S. government after the war. They took credit for participation in the battle of New Bern, and Keith claimed to have led a squad of pickets in a skirmish with Union troops sometime between the battle and his discharge. Sam claimed to have been wounded in that skirmish. None of this is true.

46. See correspondence in Johnston, *Papers of Zebulon Baird Vance*, 145–49.

47. Sears, *To the Gates of Richmond*, 40–110; Henry King Burgwyn to mother, June 18, 20, 22, July 14, 1862, Burgwyn Family Papers, SHC-UNC; S. P. Dula to editor, July 3, 1862, *Raleigh North Carolina Standard*, July 16, 1862; Henry C. Albright to sister, June 19, 1862, Albright Papers, GHM; Linebach diary, 23–24, SHC-UNC; Mickey account, SP-MA.

48. Sears, *To the Gates of Richmond*, 184–89, 195.

49. Henry King Burgwyn to mother, July 14, 1862, Burgwyn Family Papers, SHC-UNC; Linebach diary, 26–28, SHC-UNC.

50. Henry King Burgwyn to mother, July 14, 1862, Burgwyn Family Papers, SHC-UNC; William H. Glenn to sister, July 14, 1862, Glenn Papers, SCL-DU; Underwood, "Twenty-Sixth Regiment," 332; John R. Lane interview, June 16, 1900, Burgwyn Papers, NCDAH.

51. Henry King Burgwyn to mother, July 14, 1862, Burgwyn Family Papers, SHC-UNC; Jordan, *North Carolina Troops*, 7:463–601; Robert Ransom to S. S. Anderson, July 19, 1862, *OR* 11(2):793.

52. Sears, *To the Gates of Richmond*, 194–213.

53. Henry King Burgwyn to mother, July 14, 1862, Burgwyn Family Papers, SHC-UNC; Sears, *To the Gates of Richmond*, 216; S. P. Dula to editor, July 3, 1862, *Raleigh North Carolina Standard*, July 16, 1862; Adjutant of 24th North Carolina to editor, July 17, 1862, *Raleigh North Carolina Standard*, July 26, 1862; Bush reminiscences, Shuford Collection, NCDAH; Underwood, "Twenty-Sixth Regiment," 332.

54. Henry King Burgwyn to mother, July 14, 1862, Burgwyn Family Papers, SHC-UNC; S. P. Dula to editor, July 3, 1862, *Raleigh North Carolina Standard*, July 16, 1862.

55. Henry King Burgwyn to mother, July 14, 1862, Burgwyn Family Papers, SHC-UNC; Sears, *To the Gates of Richmond*, 278–307.

56. Linebach diary, 28–29, SHC-UNC; Mickey account, SP-MA.

57. Sears, *To the Gates of Richmond*, 308–12; field visits to Malvern Hill, October 12, 15, 1994.

58. Sears, *To the Gates of Richmond*, 308–34; Henry King Burgwyn to mother, July 14, 1862, Burgwyn Family Papers, SHC-UNC; Bush reminiscences, Shuford Collection, NCDAH; Robert Ransom to S. S. Anderson, July 11, 1862, *OR* 11(2):794.

59. Robert Ransom to S. S. Anderson, July 11, 1862, *OR* 11(2):794; Gallagher, *Stephen Dodson Ramseur*, 42–44; Henry King Burgwyn to mother, July 14, 1862, Burgwyn Family Papers, SHC-UNC; Isaac Augustus Jarratt to mother, July 24, 1862, Jarratt-Puryear Family Papers, SCL-DU.

60. Robert Ransom to S. S. Anderson, July 11, 1862, *OR* 11(2):794; Isaac Augustus Jarratt to mother, July 24, 1862, Jarratt-Puryear Family Papers, SCL-DU; Henry King Burgwyn to mother, July 2, 14, 1862, Burgwyn Family Papers, SHC-UNC; William J. Clarke to editor, August 12, 1862, *Raleigh North Carolina Standard*, August 23, 1862; "K, 26th" to editor, July 15, 1862, *North Carolina Argus*, July 31, 1862; Henry C. Albright to sister, July 6, 1862, Albright Papers, GHM.

61. Henry King Burgwyn to mother, July 14, 1862, Burgwyn Family Papers, SHC-UNC; Robert Ransom to S. S. Anderson, July 11, 1862, *OR* 11(2):794.

62. Henry King Burgwyn to mother, July 2, July 14, 1862, Burgwyn Family Papers, SHC-UNC; Mickey account, SP-MA; Isaac Augustus Jarratt to mother, July 24, 1862, Jarratt-Puryear Family Papers, SCL-DU.

63. Sears, *To the Gates of Richmond*, 332, 335; Henry King Burgwyn to mother, July 14, 1862, Burgwyn Family Papers, SHC-UNC; Jordan, *North Carolina Troops*, 7:463–601; S. P. Dula to editor, July 3, 1862, *Raleigh North Carolina Standard*, July 16, 1862; Zebulon Baird Vance to Scott, July 25, 1862, Scott Papers, SCL-DU; Henry C. Albright to sis-

ter, July 6, 1862, Albright Papers, GHM; W. E. Setser to W. A. Setser, July 16, 1862, in Mast, "Setser Letters," pt. 2, pp. 26–27.

64. Henry King Burgwyn to father, July 2, 1862, and Burgwyn to mother, July 14, 1862, Burgwyn Family Papers, SHC-UNC; Linebach diary, 30–33, SHC-UNC; Isaac Augustus Jarratt to mother, July 9, 1862, Jarratt-Puryear Family Papers, SCL-DU.

65. Henry King Burgwyn to mother, July 14, 1862, Burgwyn Family Papers, SHC-UNC; Chatham to editor, July 21, 1862, *Raleigh North Carolina Standard*, July 23, 1862.

66. Stephen Wiley Brewer to R. B. Paschal, July 12, 1862, Brewer-Paschal Family Papers, SHC-UNC; Henry King Burgwyn to mother, July 27, 1862, Burgwyn Family Papers, SHC-UNC; correspondence in Johnston, *Papers of Zebulon Baird Vance*, 149–51; Yates, *Confederacy and Zeb Vance*, 17–18.

67. S. P. Dula to editor, July 3, 1862, *Raleigh North Carolina Standard*, July 16, 1862; Chatham to editor, July 21, 1862, ibid., July 23, 1862.

68. Linebach diary, 33–36, SHC-UNC; Mickey account, SP-MA; Harry H. Hall, *Johnny Reb Band*, 17, 19.

69. Zebulon Baird Vance to Scott, July 25, 1862, Scott Papers, SCL-DU; James W. Eason to cousin, August 3, 1862, Snead Papers, SCL-DU; Vance to wife, August 8, 1862, in Johnston, *Papers of Zebulon Baird Vance*, 151–52; Yates, *Confederacy and Zeb Vance*, 18; Davis, *Boy Colonel of the Confederacy*, 179–80.

70. Isaac Augustus Jarratt to mother, August 14, 1862, Jarratt-Puryear Family Papers, SCL-DU; Vance to Samuel Cooper, August 12, 1862, Zebulon Baird Vance service record, 26th North Carolina, Compiled Service Records, NARA.

71. Linebach diary, 37, SHC-UNC; Davis, *Boy Colonel of the Confederacy*, 185; John Thomas Jones to father, August 16, 1862, Jones Papers, SHC-UNC.

72. Vance to William A. Graham, August 17, 1862, in Johnston, *Papers of Zebulon Baird Vance*, 152–56; Underwood, "Twenty-Sixth Regiment," 334–35, 404–5.

73. Zebulon Baird Vance to Secretary of War Randolph, August 17, 1862, Henry King Burgwyn service record, 26th North Carolina, Compiled Service Records, NARA.

CHAPTER TWO

1. John Thomas Jones to Henry King Burgwyn, August 11, 1862, Burgwyn Family Papers, SHC-UNC; Warner, *Generals in Gray*, 253–54.

2. John Thomas Jones to Henry King Burgwyn, August 21, 22, 1862, Burgwyn Family Papers, SHC-UNC.

3. Henry King Burgwyn to mother, August 23, 24, 27, 1862, Burgwyn Family Papers, SHC-UNC.

4. Louis G. Young, "Pettigrew-Kirkland-MacRae Brigade," 555–56; A. C. Myers to wife, August 29, 1862, Myers Papers, NCDAH.

5. Linebach diary, 38–39, SHC-UNC; Henry King Burgwyn to mother, August 27, 1862, Burgwyn Family Papers, SHC-UNC; Mickey account, SP-MA; Isaac Augustus Jarratt to father, August 21, 1862, Jarratt-Puryear Family Papers, SCL-DU.

6. Powell, *Dictionary of North Carolina Biography*, 5:77–79; Francis W. Pickens to W. S. Pettigrew, May 18, 1864, Crawford Papers, LC; Wilson, *Carolina Cavalier*, 1–133.

7. Louis G. Young to mother, November 9, 1860, Read Collection, GHS; Young to mother, April 13, August 26, November 21, 1861, and Young to Uncle Robert, April 8, November 1861, April 28, 1861 [1862], Gourdin Papers, EU; Young to Robert Gourdin, November 1861, Gourdin Papers, SCL-DU; Woodward, *Mary Chesnut's Civil War*, 309–10; James Johnston Pettigrew to Samuel Cooper, March 1, 1862, Pettigrew Family Papers, NCDAH; Montfort McGehee to wife, April 12, 1862, Polk, Badger, McGehee Papers, SHC-UNC; John Wetmore Hinsdale diary, March 20, 23, April 3, 1862, Hinsdale Family Papers, SCL-DU.

8. Louis G. Young to mother, May 12, 1862, and Young to Henry, May 21, 1862, Gourdin Papers, EU; Sears, *To the Gates of Richmond*, 134–39; James Johnston Pettigrew to John Wetmore Hinsdale, August 1862, and Louis G. Young to Sir, June 2, 1862, Pettigrew Family Papers, SHC-UNC; Powell, *Dictionary of North Carolina Biography*, 5:78.

9. Louis G. Young to Sir, June 2, 1862, Pettigrew Family Papers, SHC-UNC; John Wetmore Hinsdale diary, June 1, 1862, Hinsdale Family Papers, SCL-DU; Louis G. Young to mother, June 2, 1862, Gourdin Papers, EU.

10. James Johnston Pettigrew to John Wetmore Hinsdale, August 1862; T. W. Hooper to Louis G. Young, June 3, 1862; and William J. Pettigrew to James Johnston Pettigrew, June 10, 1862, Pettigrew Family Papers, SHC-UNC; Powell, *Dictionary of North Carolina Biography*, 5:78; Welsh, *Medical Histories of Confederate Generals*, 170–71.

11. John Wetmore Hinsdale diary, June 3–4, 1862, Hinsdale Family Papers, SCL-DU.

12. Mother to Louis G. Young, August 15, 1862, Read Collection, GHS.

13. John Wetmore Hinsdale diary, June 4, 1862, Hinsdale Family Papers, SCL-DU; Louis G. Young to James Johnston Pettigrew, August 9, 1862, and Pettigrew to John Wetmore Hinsdale, August 1862, Pettigrew Family Papers, SHC-UNC; James Johnston Pettigrew to Louis G. Young, August 12, 1862, and Young to mother, August 9, 1862, Gourdin Papers, EU.

14. Louis G. Young, "Pettigrew-Kirkland-MacRae Brigade," 556; Louis G. Young to James Johnston Pettigrew, August 18, 1862, Pettigrew Family Papers, SHC-UNC; William D. Pender to Secretary of War Randolph, August 14, 1862; James Johnston Pettigrew to Secretary of War Randolph, August 29, 1862; and Louis G. Young to Uncle Robert, August 28, 1862, Gourdin Papers, EU.

15. James Johnston Pettigrew to John Wetmore Hinsdale, August 1862, and William J. Pettigrew to sister, September 5, 1863, Pettigrew Family Papers, SHC-UNC; James Johnston Pettigrew to Harper, September 4, 1862, Harper Papers, NCDAH.

16. James Johnston Pettigrew to Harper, September 4, 1862, Harper Papers, NCDAH; George W. Randolph to Porcher Miles, September 6, 1862, and Charles Venable to James Johnston Pettigrew, September 21, 1862, Pettigrew Family Papers, NCDAH; James Johnston Pettigrew to Carey, September 25, 1862, Pettigrew Family Papers, SHC-UNC.

17. Gordon, "Organization of Troops," 9–11; Sauers, *"Succession of Honorable Victories,"* 371–72.

18. Powell, *Dictionary of North Carolina Biography*, 4:226–27; Sauers, *"Succession of Honorable Victories,"* 371–72.

19. Jordan, *North Carolina Troops*, 3:1–2; J. S. Bartlett reminiscences, Bartlett Papers, SHC-UNC; Chapman, *More Terrible Than Victory*, 14–36.

20. Egbert A. Ross to sister, May 13, 1861, Ross Papers, SHC-UNC; Lewis Warlick to Cornelia, May 12, October 7, 1861, McGimsey Papers, SHC-UNC.

21. Jordan, *North Carolina Troops*, 3:2; W. J. Martin, "Eleventh North Carolina Regiment," 42–43; Martin and Outlaw, "Eleventh Regiment," 583–85; Chapman, *More Terrible Than Victory*, 51; Jordan, *North Carolina Troops*, 5:9, 20, 32, 40, 49, 57, 65, 75, 84, 96.

22. Powell, *Dictionary of North Carolina Biography*, 4:55.

23. Collett Leventhorpe to Marcus J. Wright, May 30, 1888, Wright Papers, SCL-DU; Powell, *Dictionary of North Carolina Biography*, 4:55; Martin and Outlaw, "Eleventh Regiment," 586–87.

24. Powell, *Dictionary of North Carolina Biography*, 4:231–32; Martin and Outlaw, "Eleventh Regiment," 587; Jordan, *North Carolina Troops*, 5:6, 9.

25. Orders No. 9, April 3, 1862; Regimental Orders, April 23, 1862; and General Orders, April 24, 1862, Leventhorpe Papers, SCL-DU.

26. Requisition, May 3, 1862, Collett Leventhorpe service record, and receipt, April 30, 1862, J. B. Lowrie service record, 11th North Carolina, Compiled Service Records, NARA; Lemuel J. Hoyle to mother, May 9, 1862, Hoyle Papers, SHC-UNC; Jordan, *North Carolina Troops*, 5:1, 37, 101; Francis W. Bird to sister, May 26, 1862, Winston Papers, SHC-UNC.

27. William G. Parker to Ema, June 10, August 6, 1862, Parker Papers, NCDAH.

28. Egbert A. Ross to sister, July 5, August 8, 1862, Ross Papers, SHC-UNC; Jordan, *North Carolina Troops*, 5:1; Powell, *Dictionary of North Carolina Biography*, 4:55; Collett Leventhorpe to Marcus J. Wright, May 30, 1888, Wright Papers, SCL-DU; Leventhorpe to wife, May 11, 1862, in "War Record of Genl Collett Leventhorpe," Military Collection, Civil War Collection, NCDAH; Regimental Orders, May 9, 17, 18, 23, 27, June 25, 1862, Leventhorpe Papers, SCL-DU.

29. Lemuel J. Hoyle to mother, September 18, 23, 29, October 10, 1862, Hoyle Papers, SHC-UNC; W. J. Martin, "Eleventh North Carolina Regiment," 42–44; Jordan, *North Carolina Troops*, 5:1; Collett Leventhorpe to Marcus J. Wright, May 30, 1888, Wright Papers, SCL-DU.

30. Stedman, "Forty-Fourth Regiment," 21; Stedman, "Forty-Fourth N.C. Infantry," 334; Jordan, *North Carolina Troops*, 10:399, 409, 418, 426, 434, 445, 454, 467, 475, 483.

31. Stedman, "Forty-Fourth Regiment," 21; *Confederate Reveille*, 63; General Orders 9, Department of North Carolina, November 28, 1861, George B. Singletary service record, 44th North Carolina, Compiled Service Records, NARA; General Orders No. 9, Department of North Carolina, November 28, 1861, *Supplement to the Official Records*, pt. 1, 1:332–33; Jordan, *North Carolina Troops*, 10:393.

32. Jordan, *North Carolina Troops*, 10:426; special requisitions, April 2, 1862, Lawrence Ruel Anderson service record, and April 3, 1862, William R. Beasley service record, 44th North Carolina, Compiled Service Records, NARA.

33. Franklin Scarborough to Samuel, March 23, 1862, and Scarborough to Mary, March 31, April 17, August 10, 1862, Scarborough Family Papers, SCL-DU; Benjamin H. Freeman to father, May 16, 1862, in Wright, *Confederate Letters*, 12; W. B. Gulick to Tazewell L. Hargrove, September 12, 1862, and Hargrove to father and mother, October 8, 1862, Briggs Papers, SHC-UNC.

34. Jordan, *North Carolina Troops*, 10:396–97; John H. Tillinghast to Will, May 7, 1862; Tillinghast to Emily, July 22, 1862; and Tillinghast to brother, November 9, 1862, Tillinghast Family Papers, SCL-DU; Powell, *Dictionary of North Carolina Biography*, 1:157.

35. Powell, *Dictionary of North Carolina Biography*, 5:431; Jordan, *North Carolina Troops*, 10:434; John H. Tillinghast to Will, May 7, 1862, Tillinghast Family Papers, SCL-DU.

36. Stedman, "Forty-Fourth Regiment," 24; John H. Tillinghast to sister, June 1, 1862, Tillinghast Family Papers, SCL-DU.

37. *Confederate Reveille*, 64; Wright, *Confederate Letters*, 69n; Jordan, *North Carolina Troops*, 10:244–363; Franklin Scarborough to father, June 8, 1862, Scarborough Family Papers, SCL-DU.

38. *Confederate Reveille*, 64; Jordan, *North Carolina Troops*, 10:396.

39. Thorp, "Forty-Seventh Regiment," 83; Lewis, "Life and Times of Thomas Bailey," 1, GNMP; Jordan, *North Carolina Troops*, 11:240, 247, 262, 272, 283, 293, 305, 315, 328, 340, 352.

40. Jordan, *North Carolina Troops*, 11:244.

41. Ibid., 11:240; Lewis, "Life and Times of Thomas Bailey," 1, GNMP; Thorp, "Forty-Seventh Regiment," 85.

42. Jordan, *North Carolina Troops*, 11:240, 245; T. H. Pritchard, "Death of Capt. B. W. Justice, Sept. 22nd. 1871," and Benjamin Wesley Justice to Ann, June 5, 1862, Justice Papers, EU; Thorp, "Forty-Seventh Regiment," 86.

43. Robinson, "Fifty-Second Regiment," 223; Jordan, *North Carolina Troops*, 12:417, 427, 438, 446, 454, 465, 480, 490, 501, 511.

44. Taylor, "Col. James Keith Marshall," 80.

45. Benjamin Franklin Little to Flax, April 19, 1862, Little Papers, SHC-UNC; A. C. Myers to wife, April 24, 1862, Myers Papers, NCDAH.

46. Taylor, "Col. James Keith Marshall," 78–80; Charles D. Walker, *Memorial*, 369–72, VMI; Jordan, *North Carolina Troops*, 12:393, 415, 503–4, 506, 508.

47. Jordan, *North Carolina Troops*, 12:454; Little, "Account of the Movements," 1, and Little to Flax, April 13, 19, 1862, Little Papers, SHC-UNC.

48. Jordan, *North Carolina Troops*, 12:452; A. C. Myers to wife, July 6, 1862, Myers Papers, NCDAH.

49. Benjamin Franklin Little to Flax, April 26, May 2, 1862, Little Papers, SHC-UNC; Jordan, *North Carolina Troops*, 12:393.

50. Jordan, *North Carolina Troops*, 12:393, 476; Robinson, "Fifty-Second Regiment," 226–27; Benjamin Franklin Little to Flax, July 11, August 8, 13, 21, 1862, Little Papers, SHC-UNC.

51. Benjamin Franklin Little to Flax, August 21, 1862, Little Papers, SHC-UNC.

52. Jordan, *North Carolina Troops*, 10:188; R. R. Crawford to James Johnston Pettigrew, October 25, 1862, Pettigrew Family Papers, NCDAH.

53. Henry King Burgwyn to mother, September 2, 1862, Burgwyn Family Papers, SHC-UNC.

54. Affidavit by Dr. L. P. Warren, December 25, 1862, and endorsements, John J. C. Steele service record, and Henry King Burgwyn to Secretary of War, September 4, 1862,

Oscar Rand service record, 26th North Carolina, Compiled Service Records, NARA; Jordan, *North Carolina Troops*, 7:481, 506.

55. Underwood, "Twenty-Sixth Regiment," 335; Jordan, *North Carolina Troops*, 7:463; Henry King Burgwyn to mother, October 14, 1862, Burgwyn Family Papers, SHC-UNC.

56. Henry King Burgwyn to John R. Lane, September 3, 1862, Burgwyn Papers, NCDAH; receipt, August 6, 1862, for G. H. Vipperman, 26th Regiment North Carolina Troops, Muster Rolls and Regimental Records, Military Collection, Civil War Collection, NCDAH; Jordan, *North Carolina Troops*, 7:560.

57. Linebach diary, 39, SHC-UNC; Harry H. Hall, *Johnny Reb Band*, 20–21.

58. Harry H. Hall, *Johnny Reb Band*, 21; Linebach diary, 40–41, SHC-UNC.

59. Harry H. Hall, *Johnny Reb Band*, 23; Linebach diary, 41, SHC-UNC.

CHAPTER THREE

1. James Johnston Pettigrew to Samuel G. French, [September] 1862, and Gustavus W. Smith to James Johnston Pettigrew, September 7, 1862, Pettigrew Family Papers, NCDAH.

2. Henry King Burgwyn to mother, September 13, 17, 1862, and Burgwyn to father, September 13, 1862, Burgwyn Family Papers, SHC-UNC; A. C. Myers to wife, September 17, 1862, and [Myers to wife, September 1862], Myers Papers, NCDAH.

3. James Johnston Pettigrew to Samuel G. French, September 17, 1862; Charles H. Dimmock to Pettigrew, September 19, 1862; and Francis Mahoney to Pettigrew, September 19, 1862, Pettigrew Family Papers, NCDAH; James Johnston Pettigrew to Samuel G. French, September 17, 1862, *OR* 18:744; Henry King Burgwyn to mother, September 18, 23, 1862, and Burgwyn to father, September 27, 1862, Burgwyn Family Papers, SHC-UNC; A. C. Myers to wife, September 24, 1862, Myers Papers, NCDAH.

4. James Johnston Pettigrew to brother, September 29, 23, 1862, Pettigrew Family Papers, SHC-UNC; Isaac Augustus Jarratt to brother, September 23, 1862, Jarratt-Puryear Family Papers, SCL-DU.

5. Stedman, "Forty-Fourth Regiment," 24; Thorp, "Forty-Seventh Regiment," 86.

6. A. C. Myers to wife, September 24, 1862, Myers Papers, NCDAH.

7. Taylor, "Col. James Keith Marshall," 81; Little, "Account of the Movements," 2, Little Papers, SHC-UNC; John A. Dix to Henry W. Halleck, October 3, 1862, *OR* 18:15; John J. Peck to D. T. Van Buren, October 9, 1862, *OR* 18:17–18; James K. Marshall to Samuel G. French, October 4, 1862, *OR* 18:18–19.

8. Taylor, "Col. James Keith Marshall," 81; Little, "Account of the Movements," 2–3, Little Papers, SHC-UNC; Robinson, "Fifty-Second Regiment," 228–29; Lewis Warlick to Cornelia, November 19, 1862, McGimsey Papers, SHC-UNC.

9. Jordan, *North Carolina Troops*, 5:1, 79–80; Regimental Orders, November 21, 1862, and Graham Daves to Collett Leventhorpe, December 11, 1862, Leventhorpe Papers, SCL-DU; Leventhorpe to wife, November 22, 1862, in "War Record of Genl Collett Leventhorpe," Military Collection, Civil War Collection, NCDAH.

10. Leonidas Lafayette Polk to mother, October 17, 1862, Polk Papers, SHC-UNC; Jordan, *North Carolina Troops*, 7:465.

11. Linebach diary, 41–45, SHC-UNC; Mickey account, SP-MA; Edward Peterson to sister, October 12, 1862, Peterson Papers, MMF.

12. Henry King Burgwyn to father, October 19, 25, 27, November 1, 1862, Burgwyn Family Papers, SHC-UNC; Leonidas Lafayette Polk to wife, October 31, 1862, Polk Papers, SHC-UNC.

13. Henry King Burgwyn to father, November 1, 1862, Burgwyn Family Papers, SHC-UNC.

14. Ibid., November 1, 8, 1862; John G. Foster to Henry W. Halleck, November 12, 1862, *OR* 18:21; Underwood, "Twenty-Sixth Regiment," 337–38.

15. Henry King Burgwyn to father, November 8, 1862, Burgwyn Family Papers, SHC-UNC; John G. Foster to Henry W. Halleck, November 12, 1862, *OR* 18:21–22; field visit to Rawls's Mill, October 2, 1995; Noah Deaton to friend, November 16, 1862, Ray Papers, SCL-DU; Underwood, "Twenty-Sixth Regiment," 338; Mickey account, SP-MA.

16. Henry King Burgwyn to father, November 8, 1862, Burgwyn Family Papers, SHC-UNC; John G. Foster to Henry W. Halleck, November 12, 1862, *OR* 18:21; Noah Deaton to friend, November 16, 1862, Ray Papers, SCL-DU; Underwood, "Twenty-Sixth Regiment," 338.

17. Henry King Burgwyn to father, November 8, 5, 1862, Burgwyn Family Papers, SHC-UNC; John G. Foster to Henry W. Halleck, November 12, 1862, *OR* 18:21; Noah Deaton to friend, November 16, 1862, Ray Papers, SCL-DU; McCallum, *Martin County*, 102; Benjamin H. Freeman to father, November 16, 1862, in Wright, *Confederate Letters*, 17; Mickey account, SP-MA; Lewis, "Life and Times of Thomas Bailey," 3–4, GNMP.

18. John G. Foster to Henry W. Halleck, November 12, 1862, *OR* 18:21.

19. McCallum, *Martin County*, 102–3; Benjamin H. Freeman to father, November 16, 1862, in Wright, *Confederate Letters*, 17; W. E. Setser to parents, November 15, 1862, in Mast, "Setser Letters," pt. 3, p. 10; Bush reminiscences, 2, Shuford Collection, NCDAH; Henry King Burgwyn to father, November 8, 5, 1862, Burgwyn Family Papers, SHC-UNC; John G. Foster to Henry W. Halleck, November 12, 1862, *OR* 18:21–22; Isaac Augustus Jarratt to father, November 10, 1862, Jarratt-Puryear Family Papers, SCL-DU; Underwood, "Twenty-Sixth Regiment," 339; Mickey account, SP-MA; Jordan, *North Carolina Troops*, 7:463–601.

20. Benjamin H. Freeman to father, November 16, 1862, in Wright, *Confederate Letters*, 17; Lewis, "Life and Times of Thomas Bailey," 4, GNMP; Isaac Augustus Jarratt to mother, November 15, 1862, Jarratt-Puryear Family Papers, SCL-DU; W. E. Setser to parents, November 15, 1862, in Mast, "Setser Letters," pt. 3, p. 10; Linebach diary, 45, 50, 53–54, SHC-UNC.

21. W. E. Setser to parents, November 15, 1862, in Mast, "Setser Letters," pt. 3, p. 10; Isaac Augustus Jarratt to father, November 18, December 5, 1862, Jarratt-Puryear Family Papers, SCL-DU; Henry King Burgwyn to Pollock, November 29, 1862, and Burgwyn to mother, December 8, 1862, Burgwyn Family Papers, SHC-UNC.

22. George Richards to Zebulon Baird Vance, December 19, 1862, in Yearns and Barrett, *North Carolina Civil War Documentary*, 135–36.

23. Benjamin Franklin Little to Flax, September 24, 26, 1862, Little Papers, SHC-UNC; Graham, "Adjutant-General's Office," 52.

24. Henry King Burgwyn to father, September 27, October 15, 1862, and Burgwyn to mother, October 14, 1862, Burgwyn Family Papers, SHC-UNC.

25. Jordan, *North Carolina Troops*, 12:485; Thomas Hinshaw reminiscences, Hinshaw Papers, SCL-DU.

26. Jordan, *North Carolina Troops*, 7:463–601.

27. Abstract of return of the Department of North Carolina, November 1862, *OR* 18:788; R. R. Crawford to James Johnston Pettigrew, October 25, 1862, Pettigrew Family Papers, NCDAH.

28. Peter Lyons to E. S. Gaillard, December 12, 1862, Confederate Inspection Reports, NARA.

29. John G. Foster to Henry W. Halleck, December 27, 1862, *OR* 18:54–55; Nathan G. Evans to S. W. Melton, December 20, 1862, *OR* 18:112–13.

30. Henry King Burgwyn to father, December 14, 1862, Burgwyn Family Papers, SHC-UNC; Robinson, "Fifty-Second Regiment," 229; Lemuel J. Hoyle to aunt, December 18, 1862, Hoyle Papers, SHC-UNC; Isaac Augustus Jarratt to father, December 15, 1862, Jarratt-Puryear Family Papers, SCL-DU; Gustavus W. Smith to Samuel G. French, December 16, 1862, *OR* 18:803–4.

31. Thorp, "Forty-Seventh Regiment," 86; John G. Foster to Henry W. Halleck, December 27, 1862, *OR* 18:56; Lewis, "Life and Times of Thomas Bailey," 5, GNMP.

32. Thorp, "Forty-Seventh Regiment," 86–87; John G. Foster to Henry W. Halleck, December 27, 1862, *OR* 18:56–57; Lewis, "Life and Times of Thomas Bailey," 5, GNMP.

33. Collett Leventhorpe to Marcus J. Wright, May 30, 1888, Wright Papers, SCL-DU; Lemuel J. Hoyle to aunt, December 18, 1862, Hoyle Papers, SHC-UNC; Beverly H. Robertson to A. L. Evans, December 9, 1862, *OR* 18:121–22; Francis W. Bird to sister, December 23, 1862, Winston Papers, SHC-UNC; Warlick, "Battle of White Hall."

34. Martin and Outlaw, "Eleventh Regiment," 587–88; John G. Foster to Henry W. Halleck, December 27, 1862, *OR* 18:57; Beverly H. Robertson to A. L. Evans, December 19, 1862, *OR* 18:121–22; Lemuel J. Hoyle to aunt, December 18, 1862, Hoyle Papers, SHC-UNC.

35. Collett Leventhorpe to Marcus J. Wright, May 30, 1888, Wright Papers, SCL-DU; Lemuel J. Hoyle to aunt, December 18, 1862, Hoyle Papers, SHC-UNC; Warlick, "Battle of White Hall"; Lewis Warlick to Cornelia, December 30, 1862, McGimsey Papers, SHC-UNC.

36. Beverly H. Robertson to A. L. Evans, December 19, 1862, *OR* 18:122; Collett Leventhorpe to Marcus J. Wright, May 30, 1888, Wright Papers, SCL-DU; Francis W. Bird to sister, December 23, 1862, Winston Papers, SHC-UNC; Lemuel J. Hoyle to aunt, December 18, 1862, Hoyle Papers, SHC-UNC; Chapman, *More Terrible Than Victory*, 64–67; Jordan, *North Carolina Troops*, 5:6–105.

37. Gustavus W. Smith to Samuel G. French, December 16, 1862, *OR* 18:803; Robinson, "Fifty-Second Regiment," 229.

38. Robinson, "Fifty-Second Regiment," 229–30; John G. Foster to Henry W. Halleck, December 27, 1862, *OR* 18:57–58; Thomas L. Clingman to A. L. Evans, December 21, 1862, *OR* 18:117–18; A. C. Myers to wife, December 18, 1862, Myers Papers, NCDAH.

39. Thomas L. Clingman to A. L. Evans, December 21, 1862, *OR* 18:117–18; A. C. Myers to wife, December 18, 1862, Myers Papers, NCDAH; Robinson, "Fifty-Second Regiment," 230.

40. John G. Foster to Henry W. Halleck, December 27, 1862, *OR* 18:58; Samuel Clarke Day to Irving Greenwood, December 28, 1862, Day Papers, MHS.

41. Nathan G. Evans to S. W. Melton, December 20, 1862, *OR* 18:113; Thomas L. Clingman to A. L. Evans, December 21, 1862, *OR* 18:118–19.

42. Samuel Clarke Day to Irving Greenwood, December 28, 1862, Day Papers, MHS; Thomas L. Clingman to A. L. Evans, December 21, 1862, *OR* 18:118.

43. Robinson, "Fifty-Second Regiment," 231; A. C. Myers to wife, December 18, 1862, Myers Papers, NCDAH.

44. Robinson, "Fifty-Second Regiment," 231; Samuel Clarke Day to Irving Greenwood, December 28, 1862, Day Papers, MHS.

45. Robinson, "Fifty-Second Regiment," 231; Samuel Clarke Day to Irving Greenwood, December 28, 1862, Day Papers, MHS.

46. Jordan, *North Carolina Troops*, 12:415–521; A. C. Myers to wife, December 18, 1862, Myers Papers, NCDAH; Little, "Account of the Movements," 3, Little Papers, SHC-UNC; Taylor, "Col. James Keith Marshall," 82; Robinson, "Fifty-Second Regiment," 231; Samuel Clarke Day to Irving Greenwood, December 28, 1862, Day Papers, MHS; Hale Wesson to father, December 25, 1862, Wesson Papers, EU.

47. Henry King Burgwyn to mother, December 18, 1862, Burgwyn Family Papers, SHC-UNC; Robert Bingham to Sally, February 7, 1863, Tillinghast Family Papers, SCL-DU; Thorp, "Forty-Seventh Regiment," 87; Linebach diary, 54–55, SHC-UNC; Jordan, *North Carolina Troops*, 10:396–493; Lewis, "Life and Times of Thomas Bailey," 5–6, GNMP.

48. Henry King Burgwyn to mother, December 18, 1862, Burgwyn Family Papers, SHC-UNC; Leonidas Lafayette Polk to wife, December 24, 1862, Polk Papers, SHC-UNC; A. C. Myers to wife, December 18, 1862, Myers Papers, NCDAH; Taylor, "Col. James Keith Marshall," 82; Robert Bingham to Sally, February 7, 1863, Tillinghast Family Papers, SCL-DU; Mickey account, SP-MA; Lewis, "Life and Times of Thomas Bailey," 6, GNMP; Henry C. Albright to sister, December 24, 1862, Albright Papers, GHM.

49. A. C. Myers to wife, December 18, 1862, Myers Papers, NCDAH; Henry King Burgwyn to mother, December 18, 1862, Burgwyn Family Papers, SHC-UNC.

50. Lemuel J. Hoyle to mother, December 27, 1862, Hoyle Papers, SHC-UNC; Henry King Burgwyn to father, December 20, 1862, Burgwyn Family Papers, SHC-UNC; abstract of field return, December 20, 1862, *OR* 18:807; Linebach diary, 57, SHC-UNC; Mickey account, SP-MA; Collett Leventhorpe to Mary Pettigrew, May 14, 1867, Pettigrew Family Papers, NCDAH.

51. Gustavus W. Smith to James A. Seddon, December 23, 1862, *OR* 18:808; Lemuel J. Hoyle to mother, December 27, 1862, Hoyle Papers, SHC-UNC.

52. Regimental Orders, December 28, 31, 1862, Leventhorpe Papers, SCL-DU.

53. General Order No. 26, December 28, 1862, Leventhorpe Papers, SCL-DU.

54. Robinson, "Fifty-Second Regiment," 232; Henry King Burgwyn to father, December 24, 1862, Burgwyn Family Papers, SHC-UNC; Little, "Account of the Movements," 4, Little Papers, SHC-UNC; Thorp, "Forty-Seventh Regiment," 87; Roger A.

Pryor to Gustavus W. Smith, January 6, 1863, *OR* 18:845; Jordan, *North Carolina Troops*, 11:244.

55. Jordan, *North Carolina Troops*, 12:476; Nathaniel A. Foster to William Rash, January 11, 1863, 52nd North Carolina Collection, MC.

56. Henry King Burgwyn to father, December 24, 28, 1862, Burgwyn Family Papers, SHC-UNC; Crabtree and Patton, *"Journal of a Secesh Lady,"* 331.

57. Henry King Burgwyn to father, January 2, 3, 6, 11, 1863, Burgwyn Family Papers, SHC-UNC; Leventhorpe to wife, January 10, 1863, in "War Record of Genl Collett Leventhorpe," Military Collection, Civil War Collection, NCDAH.

58. Linebach diary, 57–62, SHC-UNC.

CHAPTER FOUR

1. General Orders No. 5, January 23, 1863; brigade circulars, January 31, February 11, 1863; General Orders No. 12, February 21, 1863, Leventhorpe Papers, SCL-DU.

2. Jordan, *North Carolina Troops*, 7:493; Leonidas Lafayette Polk to Sallie, January 27, 1863, Polk Papers, SHC-UNC; Linebach diary, 65, SHC-UNC; Underwood, "Twenty-Sixth Regiment," 400–401; Mickey account, SP-MA; William H. Glenn to mother, January 27, 1863, Glenn Papers, SCL-DU.

3. Jordan, *North Carolina Troops*, 7:493.

4. William H. Glenn to mother, January 27, 1863, Glenn Papers, SCL-DU; McGee, "Twenty-Sixth Regiment," 84, 85n; Lewis Warlick to Cornelia, April 26, 1863, McGimsey Papers, SHC-UNC.

5. Lemuel J. Hoyle to mother, January 9, 1863, and Hoyle to Ema, January 10, 1863, Hoyle Papers, SHC-UNC; William G. Parker to Ema, February 11, 1863, Parker Papers, NCDAH; Lewis Warlick to Cornelia, December 30, 1862, McGimsey Papers, SHC-UNC.

6. Lemuel J. Hoyle to Ema, January 4, 18, 21, 1863, Hoyle Papers, SHC-UNC; Jordan, *North Carolina Troops*, 5:36; Francis W. Bird to sister, January 26, 1863, Winston Papers, SHC-UNC.

7. Lewis Warlick to Cornelia, January 25, 1863, McGimsey Papers, SHC-UNC; Regimental Order, January 29, 1863, Leventhorpe Papers, SCL-DU; Leventhorpe to wife, February 22, 1863, in "War Record of Genl Collett Leventhorpe," Military Collection, Civil War Collection, NCDAH; William G. Parker to Ema, January 28, 1863, Parker Papers, NCDAH; Robinson, "Fifty-Second Regiment," 232; A. C. Myers to wife, January 25, February 1, 1863, Myers Papers, NCDAH; J. N. Stallings to James Johnston Pettigrew, March 13, 1863, Pettigrew Family Papers, NCDAH.

8. Robert Bingham to Sally, February 7, 1863, Tillinghast Family Papers, SCL-DU; receipts, January 15, March 8, 1863, and invoice, February 25, 1863, James K. Marshall service record, 52nd North Carolina, and invoices, January 30, 1863, T. C. Singletary service record, and February 26, 1863, R. W. Singletary service record, 44th North Carolina, Compiled Service Records, NARA.

9. Samuel G. French to James Johnston Pettigrew, February 12, February 14, 1863, Pettigrew Family Papers, NCDAH; French to James A. Seddon, February 12, 1863, *OR* 18:874–75.

10. Abstract of field return, February 20, 1863, *OR*, 18:888; Robinson, "Fifty-Second

Regiment," 232; Lemuel J. Hoyle to mother, March 2, 1863, Hoyle Papers, SHC-UNC; Linebach diary, 66–67, SHC-UNC.

11. Lemuel J. Hoyle to mother, March 2, 1863, Hoyle Papers, SHC-UNC.

12. Cornelius Morris to wife, February 24, 1863, Confederate Papers, SHC-UNC; William G. Parker to Ema, March 10, 1863, Parker Papers, NCDAH.

13. Thomas Hinshaw reminiscences, Hinshaw Papers, SCL-DU.

14. General Order No. 3, January 15, 1863, Leventhorpe Papers, SCL-DU; Louis G. Young to James Johnston Pettigrew, February 10, 1863, Pettigrew Family Papers, NCDAH.

15. Louis G. Young to James Johnston Pettigrew, March 2, 1863, Pettigrew Family Papers, NCDAH.

16. Ibid., February 19, 1863.

17. Ibid., February 27, 1863.

18. Ibid., March 6, 1863.

19. Barrett, *Civil War in North Carolina*, 149–51; D. H. Hill to James A. Seddon, February 23, 1863, *OR* 18:890–91; James A. Longstreet to Robert E. Lee, March 19, 1863, *OR* 18:926–27.

20. Abstract of field return, March 10, 1863, *OR*, 18:916; Barrett, *Civil War in North Carolina*, 151.

21. Henry King Burgwyn to father, March 10, 1862, Burgwyn Family Papers, SHC-UNC; John C. Haskell to N. C. Hughes, March 16, 1863, *OR*, 18:190; James Johnston Pettigrew to D. H. Hill, March 17, 1863, *OR* 18:192; D. H. Hill to Pettigrew, March 10, 1863, *OR* 18:195; D. H. Hill to Pettigrew, March 10, 12, 1863, Pettigrew Family Papers, NCDAH.

22. Lewis, "Life and Times of Thomas Bailey," 8, GNMP; Linebach diary, 72–77, SHC-UNC; Henry King Burgwyn diary, March 12, 1863, Burgwyn Family Papers, SHC-UNC; James Johnston Pettigrew to D. H. Hill, March 17, 1863, *OR* 18:190–91.

23. *OR* 18:192–93; Linebach diary, 77–78, SHC-UNC; Henry King Burgwyn diary, March 13, 1863, Burgwyn Family Papers, SHC-UNC.

24. Barrett, *Civil War in North Carolina*, 154; James Johnston Pettigrew to D. H. Hill, March 17, 1863, *OR* 18:192–93; Henry King Burgwyn diary, March 14, 1863, Burgwyn Family Papers, SHC-UNC; William H. Blount to friend, March 26, 1863, Steed and Phipps Family Papers, SHC-UNC; map of Barrington's Ferry battlefield, Pettigrew Family Papers, NCDAH; Giles Frederick Ward Jr. to father, March 16, 1863, Ward Papers, SCL-DU.

25. Henry King Burgwyn diary, March 14, 1863, Burgwyn Family Papers, SHC-UNC; James Johnston Pettigrew to D. H. Hill, March 17, 1862, *OR*, 18:193.

26. James Johnston Pettigrew to D. H. Hill, March 17, 1862, *OR* 18:193; Henry King Burgwyn to mother, March 15, 1863, and Burgwyn diary, March 14, 1863, Burgwyn Family Papers, SHC-UNC.

27. Henry King Burgwyn to mother, March 15, 1862, and Burgwyn diary, March 14, 1863, Burgwyn Family Papers, SHC-UNC; Benjamin Franklin Little to Flax, March 17, 1863, Little Papers, SHC-UNC; Louis G. Young to mother, March 29, 1863, Gourdin Papers, EU.

28. James Johnston Pettigrew to D. H. Hill, March 17, 1863, *OR* 18:193–94; Thorp,

"Forty-Seventh Regiment," 87–88; Giles Frederick Ward Jr. to father, March 16, 1863, Ward Papers, SCL-DU.

29. James Johnston Pettigrew to D. H. Hill, March 17, 1862, *OR* 18:194.

30. John G. Foster to Henry W. Halleck, March 15, 1863, *OR* 18:184; James Johnston Pettigrew to D. H. Hill, March 17, 1863, *OR* 18:194; James A. Patton to wife, March 16, 1863, Patton Papers, EU; James F. Foulkes to James Johnston Pettigrew, March 14, 1863, Pettigrew Family Papers, NCDAH; Peterson letter (correspondent unknown), March 15, 1863, Peterson Papers, MMF.

31. Barrett, *Civil War in North Carolina*, 152–55; John G. Foster to Henry W. Halleck, March 15, 1863, *OR* 18:184; D. H. Hill to James A. Longstreet, March 16, 1863, *OR* 18:189; Leonidas Lafayette Polk to wife, March 17, 1863, Polk Papers, SHC-UNC; D. H. Hill to Pettigrew, March 14, 1863, Pettigrew Family Papers, NCDAH.

32. Henry King Burgwyn diary, March 14, 1863, Burgwyn Family Papers, SHC-UNC; *North Carolina Argus*, April 2, 1863; Isaac Augustus Jarratt to mother, March 17, 1863, Jarratt-Puryear Family Papers, SCL-DU; John G. Foster to Henry W. Halleck, March 15, 1863, *OR* 18:183–84; Barrett, *Civil War in North Carolina*, 156.

33. Henry King Burgwyn diary, March 15, 1863, Burgwyn Family Papers, SHC-UNC; Linebach diary, 80, SHC-UNC; James Johnston Pettigrew to D. H. Hill, March 17, 1863, *OR* 18:194; Benjamin Franklin Little to Flax, March 17, 1863, Little Papers, SHC-UNC.

34. Henry King Burgwyn diary, March 16–17, 1863, Burgwyn Family Papers, SHC-UNC; Linebach diary, 81, SHC-UNC; Lewis, "Life and Times of Thomas Bailey," 10, GNMP; James Johnston Pettigrew to D. H. Hill, March 17, 1863, *OR* 18:194; A. S. Webb to Ma, April 9, 1863, Webb Family Papers, SHC-UNC.

35. Barrett, *Civil War in North Carolina*, 157; D. H. Hill to Longstreet, March 17, 1863, *Civil War Times Illustrated* Collection, USAMHI; Lemuel J. Hoyle to mother, March 14, 27, 1863, Hoyle Papers, SHC-UNC; William G. Parker to Ema, March 24, 1863, Parker Papers, NCDAH.

36. James Johnston Pettigrew to D. H. Hill, [March] 17, 1863, *OR* 18:883; Linebach diary, 81, SHC-UNC; William H. Blount to mother, March 24, 1863; Blount to sister, March 24, 1863; and Blount to friend, March 26, 1863, Steed and Phipps Family Papers, SHC-UNC.

37. Linebach diary, March 21, 1863, SHC-UNC; Henry King Burgwyn diary, March 19–20, 1863; Burgwyn to father, March 22, 1863; and Burgwyn to mother, March 23, 1863, Burgwyn Family Papers, SHC-UNC; A. C. Myers to Joe, March 25, 1863, Myers Papers, NCDAH; Lemuel J. Hoyle to mother, March 27, 1863, Hoyle Papers, SHC-UNC.

38. W. E. Setser to family, March 24, 1863, in Mast, "Setser Letters," pt. 3, p. 11; Regimental Order, March 26, 1863, Leventhorpe Papers, SCL-DU; Linebach diary, 83–84, SHC-UNC; Henry King Burgwyn to mother, March 23, 28, 1863, Burgwyn Family Papers, SHC-UNC.

39. Barrett, *Civil War in North Carolina*, 156.

40. Robinson, "Fifty-Second Regiment," 233; Lemuel J. Hoyle to mother, April 25, 1863, Hoyle Papers, SHC-UNC; Henry King Burgwyn diary, March 30, 31, 1863, and Burgwyn to N. C. Hughes, April 26, 1863, Burgwyn Family Papers, SHC-UNC; Linebach diary, 85, SHC-UNC; Lewis, "Life and Times of Thomas Bailey," 10–11, GNMP.

41. Henry King Burgwyn to father, April 2, 1863; Burgwyn diary, March 31, April 1, 1863; and Burgwyn to N. C. Hughes, April 26, 1863, Burgwyn Family Papers, SHC-UNC; Lewis, "Life and Times of Thomas Bailey," 11, GNMP.

42. Henry King Burgwyn to father, April 2, 1863; Burgwyn to N. C. Hughes, April 26, 1863; and Burgwyn diary, April 2, 1863, Burgwyn Family Papers, SHC-UNC; Leventhorpe to wife, April 2, 3, 1863, in "War Record of Genl Collett Leventhorpe," Military Collection, Civil War Collection, NCDAH; Collett Leventhorpe to Mary Pettigrew, May 14, 1867, Pettigrew Family Papers, NCDAH.

43. Henry King Burgwyn to father, April 2, 1863, Burgwyn Family Papers, SHC-UNC; Barrett, *Civil War in North Carolina*, 157.

44. John G. Foster to Henry W. Halleck, April 5, 30, 1863, *OR* 18:211–12, 212–214; Barrett, *Civil War in North Carolina*, 157.

45. Henry King Burgwyn to father, April 6, 1863, and Burgwyn to mother, April 11, 1863, Burgwyn Family Papers, SHC-UNC; Benjamin Wesley Justice to wife, April 12, 1863, Justice Papers, EU.

46. Isaac Augustus Jarratt to father, April 4, 1863, Jarratt-Puryear Family Papers, SCL-DU; Henry King Burgwyn to father, April 6, 1863, Burgwyn Family Papers, SHC-UNC; Stephen Wiley Brewer to John J. Paschal, April 11, 1863, Brewer-Paschal Family Papers, SHC-UNC; William Fleming to W. A. Setser, April 13, 1863, in Mast, "Setser Letters," pt. 3, p. 11.

47. Benjamin Wesley Justice to wife, April 12, 1863, Justice Papers, EU; A. C. Myers to wife, April 8, 1863, Myers Papers, NCDAH.

48. Benjamin Wesley Justice to wife, April 12, 1863, Justice Papers, EU; Robinson, "Fifty-Second Regiment," 234; Henry Prince to John G. Foster, April 26, May 10, 1863, *OR* 18:230–35, 236.

49. Francis B. Spinola to Southard Hoffman, May 15, 1863, *OR* 18:251–52.

50. Henry King Burgwyn to N. C. Hughes, April 26, 1863; Burgwyn diary, April 9, 1863; and Burgwyn to mother, April 11, 1863, Burgwyn Family Papers, SHC-UNC.

51. J. S. Bartlett reminiscences, 2, Bartlett Papers, SHC-UNC; Francis B. Spinola to Innis N. Palmer, April 9, 1863, *OR* 18:245–46; Spinola to Southard Hoffman, May 15, 1863, *OR* 18:251–52; Louis G. Young to Uncle Robert, April 23, 1863, Gourdin Papers, EU; Leventhorpe to wife, April 10, 1863, in "War Record of Genl Collett Leventhorpe," Military Collection, Civil War Collection, NCDAH.

52. J. S. Bartlett reminiscences, 2, Bartlett Papers, SHC-UNC; Henry King Burgwyn to N. C. Hughes, April 26, 1863; Burgwyn diary, April 10, 1863; and Burgwyn to mother, April 11, 1863, Burgwyn Family Papers, SHC-UNC; Francis B. Spinola to Southard Hoffman, May 15, 1863, *OR* 18:252; Louis G. Young to Uncle Robert, April 23, 1863, Gourdin Papers, EU; Leventhorpe to wife, April 10, 1863, in "War Record of Genl Collett Leventhorpe," Military Collection, Civil War Collection, NCDAH; Jordan, *North Carolina Troops*, 11:317; Benjamin Wesley Justice to wife, April 12, 1863, Justice Papers, EU; William H. Blount to friend, April 26, 1863, Steed and Phipps Family Papers, SHC-UNC; A. S. Webb to brother, April 12, 1863, Webb Family Papers, SHC-UNC; Chapman, *More Terrible Than Victory*, 75–78.

53. Barrett, *Civil War in North Carolina*, 159, 161; James Johnston Pettigrew to D. H. Hill, April 15, 1863, *OR* 18:990.

54. Henry King Burgwyn diary, April 10–19, 1863; Burgwyn to N. C. Hughes, April 26, 1863; and Burgwyn to mother, April 19, 1863, Burgwyn Family Papers, SHC-UNC; Lemuel J. Hoyle to mother, April 25, 1863, Hoyle Papers, SHC-UNC.

55. John G. Foster to Henry W. Halleck, April 30, 1863, *OR* 18:216; Isaac Augustus Jarratt to mother, April 19, 1863, Jarratt-Puryear Family Papers, SCL-DU; Lemuel J. Hoyle to mother, April 25, 1863, Hoyle Papers, SHC-UNC.

56. Henry King Burgwyn to father, April 21, 1863, Burgwyn Family Papers, SHC-UNC.

57. James Johnston Pettigrew to D. H. Hill, April 20, 1863, *OR* 18:1004.

58. J. C. McLauchlin to editor, April 27, 1862, *North Carolina Argus*, May 7, 1863.

59. W. E. Setser to family, April 20, 1863, in Mast, "Setser Letters," pt. 3, p. 12.

60. Regimental Order, April 23, 1863, Leventhorpe Papers, SCL-DU; Henry King Burgwyn diary, April 21–29, 1863; Burgwyn to father, April 21, 23, 1863; and Burgwyn to mother, April 24, 30, 23, 1863, Burgwyn Family Papers, SHC-UNC; Isaac Augustus Jarratt to father, April 26, 1863, Jarratt-Puryear Family Papers, SCL-DU; Little, "Account of the Movements," 8, Little Papers, SHC-UNC.

61. Henry King Burgwyn diary, April 30, 1863; Burgwyn to father, April 21, 1863; and Burgwyn to mother, April 23, 1863, Burgwyn Family Papers, SHC-UNC.

62. Henry King Burgwyn diary, April 30, 1863, and Burgwyn to mother, April 30, 1863, Burgwyn Family Papers, SHC-UNC.

63. Thorp, "Forty-Seventh Regiment," 88; Louis G. Young, "Pettigrew-Kirkland-MacRae Brigade," 558.

CHAPTER FIVE

1. Henry King Burgwyn diary, May 1, 1863; Burgwyn to father, May 1, 1863; and Burgwyn to mother, May 1, 1863, Burgwyn Family Papers, SHC-UNC.

2. Henry King Burgwyn diary, May 2–3, 1863, and Burgwyn to mother, May 11, 1863, Burgwyn Family Papers, SHC-UNC; James W. Wright to father, May 2, 1863, Wright Collection, NCDAH; Francis W. Bird to sister, Winston Papers, SHC-UNC; Isaac Augustus Jarratt to mother, May 7, 1863, Jarratt-Puryear Family Papers, SCL-DU.

3. Robert E. Lee to James A. Seddon, May 3, 1863, *OR* 25(2):768; Special Orders No. 108, Adjutant and Inspector General's Office, May 5, 1863, *OR* 25(2):778; T. O. Chester to James Johnston Pettigrew, May 3, 1863, Pettigrew Family Papers, NCDAH.

4. Henry King Burgwyn diary, May 3, 1863; Burgwyn to father, May 6, 1863; and Burgwyn to mother, May 8, 1863, Burgwyn Family Papers, SHC-UNC; James W. Wright to father and mother, May 5, 1863, Wright Collection, NCDAH; James Johnston Pettigrew to Arnold Elzey, May 4, 1863, *OR* 18:1044; Isaac Augustus Jarratt to mother, May 7, 1863, Jarratt-Puryear Family Papers, SCL-DU; Edward Peterson to sister, May 4, 1863, Peterson Papers, MMF.

5. J. S. Bartlett reminiscences, 3, Bartlett Papers, SHC-UNC; Henry King Burgwyn to father, May 14, 1863, Burgwyn Family Papers, SHC-UNC.

6. Henry King Burgwyn diary, May 8, 1863, and Burgwyn to father, May 14, 1863, Burgwyn Family Papers, SHC-UNC; Little, "Account of the Movements," 8, Little Papers, SHC-UNC; Robinson, "Fifty-Second Regiment," 234–35; Francis W. Bird to sis-

ter, May 16, 1863, Winston Papers, SHC-UNC; A. S. Webb to sister, May 5, 1863, and Webb to Ma, May 7, 1863, Webb Family Papers, SHC-UNC.

7. Benjamin H. Freeman to father and mother, May 13, 1863, in Wright, *Confederate Letters*, 19–20; A. S. Webb to sister, May 12, 1863, Webb Family Papers, SHC-UNC.

8. Lewis, "Life and Times of Thomas Bailey," 13, GNMP; Jordan, *North Carolina Troops*, 11:244–363; special requisitions, May 12, 1863, Joseph Harris service record, W. H. Harrison service record, and R. H. Fossett service record, and record of events, Company H, 47th North Carolina, Compiled Service Records, NARA.

9. Arnold Elzey to James Johnston Pettigrew, May 8, 1863, *OR* 18:1052; Pettigrew to Elzey, May 14, 1863, *OR* 18:1061; Armistead L. Long to Pettigrew, May 19, 1863, *OR* 18:1065; Henry King Burgwyn diary, May 19–June 5, 1863, Burgwyn Family Papers, SHC-UNC.

10. Henry King Burgwyn to sister, May 10, 1863, and Burgwyn to father, May 14, 1863, Burgwyn Family Papers, SHC-UNC.

11. Henry King Burgwyn to father, May 31, 1863, Burgwyn Family Papers, SHC-UNC.

12. Leventhorpe to wife, June 4, 1863, in "War Record of Genl Collett Leventhorpe," Military Collection, Civil War Collection, NCDAH.

13. Robert E. Lee to Jefferson Davis, May 20, 1863, *OR* 25(2):810; Special Orders No. 146, Army of Northern Virginia, May 30, 1863, *OR* 25(2):840; Henry King Burgwyn diary, June 3, 1863, Burgwyn Family Papers, SHC-UNC.

14. Robert E. Lee to A. P. Hill, June 5, 1863, *OR* 27(3):859.

15. Henry King Burgwyn diary, June 7–8, 1863, and Burgwyn to mother, June 8, 1863, Burgwyn Family Papers, SHC-UNC; Robinson, "Fifty-Second Regiment," 235; Little, "Account of the Movements," 11, Little Papers, SHC-UNC.

16. William S. Long reminiscences, fol. 1203, Long Papers, LC; A. S. Webb to Ma, June 22, 1863, Webb Family Papers, SHC-UNC.

17. Benjamin Franklin Little to Flax, June 8, 1863, Little Papers, SHC-UNC; Henry King Burgwyn diary, June 9–11, 1863, and Burgwyn to mother, June 10, 1863, Burgwyn Family Papers, SHC-UNC; R. H. Finney to Pettigrew, June 13, 1863, Pettigrew Family Papers, NCDAH; Robinson, "Fifty-Second Regiment," 235.

18. Joseph H. Saunders to mother, June 15, 1863, Saunders Papers, SHC-UNC; Benjamin Franklin Little to Flax, June 9, 1863, Little Papers, SHC-UNC; W. E. Setser to W. A. Setser, June 9, 1863, in Mast, "Setser Letters," pt. 3, p. 13.

19. Linebach diary, 96–100, SHC-UNC.

20. Special requisitions, June 20, 1863, Collett Leventhorpe service record, and June 11, 1863, W. J. Kerr service record, L. Elias service record, J. B. Lowrie service record, and A. S. Haynes service record, 11th North Carolina, Compiled Service Records, NARA; R. H. Finney to James Johnston Pettigrew, June 13, 1863; G. P. Collins to Pettigrew, June 12, 1863; and Consolidated Return of Means of Transportation in Genl Pettigrew's Brigade, June 1863, Pettigrew Family Papers, NCDAH; Linebach diary, 101, SHC-UNC.

21. Collett Leventhorpe to Mary Pettigrew, May 14, 1867, Pettigrew Family Papers, NCDAH; Henry King Burgwyn to father, June 13–15, 1863, Burgwyn Family Papers, SHC-UNC; Robert E. Lee to Samuel Cooper, June 23, 1863, *OR* 27(3):925; Taylor, "Col. James Keith Marshall," 84; Underwood, "Twenty-Sixth Regiment," 341.

22. James W. Wright to father and mother, June 17, 1863, Wright Collection, NCDAH; Linebach diary, 102–3, SHC-UNC.

23. Henry King Burgwyn to mother, June 17, 1863, Burgwyn Family Papers, SHC-UNC; Linebach diary, 103, SHC-UNC.

24. Henry Clay Albright diary, June 18–20, 1863, Albright Papers, NCDAH; Linebach diary, 104–6, SHC-UNC; Little, "Account of the Movements," 12–13, Little Papers, SHC-UNC; Taylor, "Col. James Keith Marshall," 84.

25. Linebach diary, 104–6, SHC-UNC; Bush reminiscences, 3, Shuford Collection, NCDAH.

26. Linebach diary, 107–10, SHC-UNC; Underwood, "Twenty-Sixth Regiment," 342.

27. Stedman, "Forty-Fourth Regiment," 24–25; Robert Bingham to granddaughter, March 14, 1923, Bingham Papers, SHC-UNC; Jordan, *North Carolina Troops*, 10:396–493; Samuel P. Spear to D. T. Van Buren, June 28, 1863, *OR* 27(2):796; William S. Long reminiscences, fols. 1204–6, Long Papers, LC; Devine, "Defense of the South Anna Bridge," 179; Peace, "Fighting against Great Odds"; McRae, "Fight at South Anna Bridge"; Trudeau, "'Blackberry Raid,'" 7–9.

28. Little, "Account of the Movements," 14, Little Papers, SHC-UNC; Linebach diary, 108–10, SHC-UNC.

29. Linebach diary, 108–10, SHC-UNC; Robinson, "Fifty-Second Regiment," 235; Thorp, "Forty-Seventh Regiment," 88; Underwood, "Twenty-Sixth Regiment," 401.

30. James W. Wright to father and mother, June 17, 1863, Wright Collection, NCDAH; Jordan, *North Carolina Troops*, 7:463–601; McGee, "Twenty-Sixth Regiment," 94–95; Jordan, *North Carolina Troops*, 5:6–105, 10:396–493, 11:244–363, 12:415–521; Chapman, *More Terrible Than Victory*, 88.

31. Taylor to mother, June 22, 1863, GNMP; Julius Sidney Joyner to mother, June 29, 1863, Joyner Family Papers, SHC-UNC; Collett Leventhorpe to Mary Pettigrew, May 14, 1867, Pettigrew Family Papers, NCDAH.

32. Linebach diary, 110–11, SHC-UNC; Underwood, "Twenty-Sixth Regiment," 342; Mast, "'Trip That Didn't Pay,'" 10.

33. Linebach diary, 111–12, SHC-UNC; Little, "Account of the Movements," 14, Little Papers, SHC-UNC; Comte de Paris to W. Jones, March 23, 1878, Heth Papers, MC; Underwood, "Twenty-Sixth Regiment," 342.

34. A. P. Hill to R. H. Chilton, November 1863, *OR* 27(2):606–7; Pfanz, *Gettysburg—The Second Day*, 8.

35. Linebach diary, 113, SHC-UNC; Little, "Account of the Movements," 15–16, Little Papers, SHC-UNC; Taylor, "Col. James Keith Marshall," 84; Robinson, "Fifty-Second Regiment," 236.

36. Henry Heth to W. N. Starke, September 13, 1863, *OR* 27(2):637; Morrison, *Memoirs of Henry Heth*, 173; Underwood, "Twenty-Sixth Regiment," 342; Linebach diary, 113–14, SHC-UNC.

37. David G. Martin, *Gettysburg*, 25–26; W. S. Christian to John Warwick Daniel, October 24, 1903, Daniel Papers, UVA.

38. David G. Martin, *Gettysburg*, 26–27.

39. Louis G. Young, "Pettigrew's Brigade at Gettysburg, 1–3 July, 1863," 115–16; Underwood, "Twenty-Sixth Regiment," 342–343; Thorp, "Forty-Seventh Regiment," 88–89.

40. David G. Martin, *Gettysburg*, 28.

41. Louis G. Young, "Pettigrew's Brigade at Gettysburg, 1–3 July, 1863," 116–17; Morrison, *Memoirs of Henry Heth*, 173.

42. Louis G. Young, "Pettigrew's Brigade at Gettysburg, 1–3 July, 1863," 117; Haines, "A. P. Hill's Advance," 7.

43. Louis G. Young, "Pettigrew's Brigade at Gettysburg, 1–3 July, 1863," 115; David G. Martin, *Gettysburg*, 41–44, 47–48.

44. Haines, "A. P. Hill's Advance," 7; Henry Clay Albright diary, June 30, 1863, Albright Papers, NCDAH; David G. Martin, *Gettysburg*, 31; Underwood, "Twenty-Sixth Regiment," 342.

45. Underwood, "Twenty-Sixth Regiment," 343.

CHAPTER SIX

1. Henry Heth to W. N. Starke, September 13, 1863, *OR* 27(2):637; J. T. C. Hood statement, April 8, 1896, Burgwyn Papers, NCDAH; Elmore, "Torrid Heat and Blinding Rain," 10–11; Linebach diary, July 1, 1863, SHC-UNC.

2. Henry A. Morrow to J. D. Wood, February 22, 1864, *OR* 27(1):267; Henry Heth to W. N. Starke, September 13, 1863, *OR* 27(2):637; Shue, *Morning at Willoughby Run*, 99–168; David G. Martin, *Gettysburg*, 155–56.

3. Rogers, "Additional Sketch," 103–5.

4. Underwood, "Twenty-Sixth Regiment," 343–44; Henry Heth to W. N. Starke, September 13, 1863, *OR* 27(2):642–43; Caison, "Southern Soldiers in Northern Prisons," 159; Gragg, *Covered with Glory*, 97.

5. Bush reminiscences, 3, Shuford Collection, NCDAH.

6. David G. Martin, *Gettysburg*, 186–94; Hartwig, "Defense of McPherson's Ridge," 17, 23; Rogers, "Additional Sketch," 105; Hood, "26th Regiment at Gettysburg"; Underwood, "Twenty-Sixth Regiment," 350; Collett Leventhorpe to Mary Pettigrew, May 14, 1867, Pettigrew Family Papers, NCDAH.

7. David G. Martin, *Gettysburg*, 186–94.

8. Field visit to Gettysburg, March 23, 1997.

9. C. H. McConnell to William H. S. Burgwyn, August 3, 1903, Burgwyn Papers, NCDAH; Hartwig, "Defense of McPherson's Ridge," 17–18; Underwood, "Twenty-Sixth Regiment," 349–50; Hadden, "Deadly Embrace," 23.

10. Donald L. Smith, *Twenty-Fourth Michigan*, 129; Hartwig, "Defense of McPherson's Ridge," 16–17, 22.

11. Underwood, "Twenty-Sixth Regiment," 347–50; Busey and Martin, *Regimental Strengths at Gettysburg*, 173, 229; David G. Martin, *Gettysburg*, 350.

12. Underwood, "Twenty-Sixth Regiment," 350, 368–69.

13. John Randolph Lane address, 1903, Lane Papers, SHC-UNC; Hadden, "Deadly Embrace," 27–28; David G. Martin, *Gettysburg*, 350–51; Gragg, *Covered with Glory*, 123; Jordan, *North Carolina Troops*, 7:479.

14. John Randolph Lane address, 1903, Lane Papers, SHC-UNC; Hadden, "Deadly Embrace," 28; David G. Martin, *Gettysburg*, 351; Jordan, *North Carolina Troops*, 7:513.

15. Louis G. Young to William H. S. Burgwyn, August 22, 1903, Burgwyn Papers, NCDAH; Gragg, *Covered with Glory*, 124–25.

16. Louis G. Young to William H. S. Burgwyn, August 22, 1903, Burgwyn Papers, NCDAH; Henry A. Morrow to J. D. Wood, February 22, 1864, *OR* 27(1):268; Hadden, "Deadly Embrace," 28; Hood, "26th Regiment at Gettysburg"; Jordan, *North Carolina Troops*, 7:547, 555; David G. Martin, *Gettysburg*, 352; Underwood, "Twenty-Sixth Regiment," 374; John Randolph Lane address, 1903, Lane Papers, SHC-UNC.

17. Ladd and Ladd, *Bachelder Papers*, 2:941; Collett Leventhorpe to Marcus J. Wright, May 30, 1888, Wright Papers, SCL-DU; William B. Taylor to mother, July 29, 1863, in Mast, "Six Lieutenants," 12.

18. John M. Tate to editor, July 12, 1863, *Charlotte Daily Bulletin*, July 25, 1863; editorial, ibid., August 23, 1863; Collett Leventhorpe to Mary Pettigrew, May 14, 1867, Pettigrew Family Papers, NCDAH.

19. Gaff, "'Here Was Made Out Our Last and Hopeless Stand,'" 30; William W. Dudley to E. D. Townsend, n.d., in Ladd and Ladd, *Bachelder Papers*, 2:941; William B. Taylor to mother, July 29, 1863, in Mast, "Six Lieutenants," 12; Hartwig, "Defense of McPherson's Ridge," 23–24; Henry A. Morrow to J. D. Wood, February 22, 1864, *OR* 27(1):268.

20. John Randolph Lane address, 1903, Lane Papers, SHC-UNC.

21. Ibid.; Hadden, "Deadly Embrace," 28–29; Gragg, *Covered with Glory*, 123–25; Jennie Cooper Dawson to Kittie, September 27, ca. 1911, Rowland Collection, MC; Jordan, *North Carolina Troops*, 7:562.

22. Henry A. Morrow to J. D. Wood, February 22, 1864, *OR* 27(1):268.

23. Thorp, "Forty-Seventh Regiment," 89; Cook, "Personal Reminiscences of Gettysburg," 128.

24. Rogers, "Additional Sketch," 106.

25. Ibid., 106–7; Thorp, "Forty-Seventh Regiment," 89; Alexander Biddle to Abner Doubleday, n.d., *Supplement to the Official Records*, pt. 1, 5:151; Jordan, *North Carolina Troops*, 11:273.

26. David G. Martin, *Gettysburg*, 357; Hartwig, "Defense of McPherson's Ridge," 23; Collett Leventhorpe to Mary Pettigrew, May 14, 1867, Pettigrew Family Papers, NCDAH; Andrew Cross, *The War*, 26.

27. Robinson, "Fifty-Second Regiment," 236–37; Taylor, "Col. James Keith Marshall," 85.

28. Taylor, "Col. James Keith Marshall," 85; Hartwig, "Defense of McPherson's Ridge," 23; David G. Martin, *Gettysburg*, 360–61; Alexander Biddle to Abner Doubleday, n.d., *Supplement to the Official Records*, pt. 1, 5:151.

29. Taylor, "Col. James Keith Marshall," 85; Hartwig, "Defense of McPherson's Ridge," 23; David G. Martin, *Gettysburg*, 360–61.

30. David G. Martin, *Gettysburg*, 361, 409; Thorp, "Forty-Seventh Regiment," 90; Hartwig, "Defense of McPherson's Ridge," 23; Dreese, *151st Pennsylvania*, 43.

31. Jordan, *North Carolina Troops*, 7:562; George Wilcox to William H. S. Burgwyn, June 21, 1900, Burgwyn Papers, NCDAH; Thomas J. Cureton to John Randolph Lane, June 15, 1890, Lane Papers, SHC-UNC.

32. John Randolph Lane address, 1903, and Thomas J. Cureton to Lane, June 15, 1890, Lane Papers, SHC-UNC; Jordan, *North Carolina Troops*, 7:486; G. P. Collins to Henry King Burgwyn Sr., July 3, 1863, Burgwyn Family Papers, SHC-UNC; J. J. Young to Henry King Burgwyn Sr., July 31, 1863, Burgwyn Papers, NCDAH; Underwood, "Twenty-Sixth Regiment," 418.

33. John Randolph Lane address, 1903, Lane Papers, SHC-UNC; Jordan, *North Carolina Troops*, 7:589.

34. Thomas J. Cureton to John Randolph Lane, June 15, 1890, and Lane address, 1903, Lane Papers, SHC-UNC; J. J. Young to Henry King Burgwyn Sr., July 31, 1863, Burgwyn Papers, NCDAH.

35. Hadden, "Deadly Embrace," 29; Henry Heth to W. N. Starke, September 13, 1863, *OR* 27(2):639; Mast, "'Trip That Didn't Pay,'" 11; Jordan, *North Carolina Troops*, 7:554–55, 557.

36. David G. Martin, *Gettysburg*, 362–363; Hartwig, "Defense of McPherson's Ridge," 24; George F. McFarland to Abner Doubleday, March 16, 1864, in Ladd and Ladd, *Bachelder Papers*, 1:89–90; Dreese, *151st Pennsylvania*, 47–51.

37. Hadden, "Deadly Embrace," 30; David G. Martin, *Gettysburg*, 364; Henry A. Morrow to J. D. Wood, February 22, 1864, *OR* 27(1):268–69; Nolan, *Iron Brigade*, 243–47.

38. Hadden, "Deadly Embrace," 30; John Randolph Lane address, 1903, and Thomas J. Cureton to Lane, June 15, 1890, Lane Papers, SHC-UNC; Gragg, *Covered with Glory*, 135.

39. David G. Martin, *Gettysburg*, 366–67; John Thomas Jones to R. H. Finney, August 9, 1863, *OR* 27(2):643.

40. John Thomas Jones to R. H. Finney, August 9, 1863, *OR* 27(2):643; David G. Martin, *Gettysburg*, 368.

41. Louis G. Young, "Pettigrew's Brigade at Gettysburg, 1–3 July, 1863," 120; Alexander H. Harris letter, July 8, 1863, *Raleigh Daily Progress*, July 14, 1863; Collett Leventhorpe to Marcus J. Wright, May 30, 1888, Wright Papers, SCL-DU; John M. Tate to editor, July 12, 1863, *Charlotte Daily Bulletin*, July 25, 1863; Louis G. Young, "Pettigrew's Brigade at Gettysburg," *Our Living and Our Dead*, 555–56; George H. Faribault to editor, n.d., *Raleigh Daily Sentinel*, March 29, 1867; Taylor, "Col. James Keith Marshall," 88; Jordan, *North Carolina Troops*, 11:336.

42. John Randolph Lane address, 1903, Lane Papers, SHC-UNC; Louis G. Young, "Pettigrew's Brigade at Gettysburg, 1–3 July, 1863," 120; Underwood, "Twenty-Sixth Regiment," 359; J. T. C. Hood statement, April 8, 1896, and transcript of losses in Company F from *Richmond Examiner*, Burgwyn Papers, NCDAH; R. M. Tuttle, "Addenda," 3 [125]; Jordan, *North Carolina Troops*, 7:533, 544; R. M. Tuttle to Mr. Bright, June 3, 1903, Daniel Papers, UVA.

43. Jordan, *North Carolina Troops*, 7:479, 486, 513, 527, 547, 553, 555, 560, 562, 595. Three other men, Pvt. John D. Rollins of Company B, Pvt. James G. Melton of Company C, and Pvt. Smith A. Thomas of Company F, were identified in service records as having been wounded while carrying the regimental colors on July 1, but there is no supporting evidence from other sources to substantiate this information. All three returned to duty with the 26th. See ibid., 491, 501, 547.

44. George Wilcox to William H. S. Burgwyn, June 21, 1900, and J. J. Young to Henry King Burgwyn Sr., July 31, 1863, Burgwyn Papers, NCDAH.

45. Olds, "Brave Carolinian Who Fell at Gettysburg," 246; Jordan, *North Carolina Troops*, 7:492, 524.

46. J. J. Young to Henry King Burgwyn Sr., July 31, 1863, and William M. Cheek to William H. S. Burgwyn, April 18, 1906, Burgwyn Papers, NCDAH; G. P. Collins to Henry King Burgwyn Sr., July 3, 1863, Burgwyn Family Papers, SHC-UNC; Olds, "Brave Carolinian Who Fell at Gettysburg," 246.

47. Olds, "Brave Carolinian Who Fell at Gettysburg," 247; William M. Cheek to William H. S. Burgwyn, April 18, 1906, and J. J. Young to Henry King Burgwyn Sr., July 31, 1863, Burgwyn Papers, NCDAH.

48. Thomas J. Cureton to John Randolph Lane, June 22, 1890, Lane Papers, SHC-UNC.

49. Ibid.

50. Louis G. Young, "Pettigrew's Brigade at Gettysburg, 1–3 July, 1863," 119.

51. Mast, "'Trip That Didn't Pay,'" 12.

52. A. P. Hill to R. H. Chilton, November 1864, *OR* 27(2):607; Henry Heth to W. N. Starke, September 13, 1863, *OR* 27(2):638; Louis G. Young, "Pettigrew's Brigade at Gettysburg, 1–3 July, 1863," 119–20; Thorp, "Forty-Seventh Regiment," 90; William H. Blount to Bettie, August 2, 1863, Steed and Phipps Family Papers, SHC-UNC.

53. Louis G. Young, "Pettigrew's Brigade at Gettysburg, 1–3 July, 1863," 121.

CHAPTER SEVEN

1. Rogers, "Additional Sketch," 107; Underwood, "Twenty-Sixth Regiment," 362; Thomas J. Cureton to John Randolph Lane, June 22, 1890, Lane Papers, SHC-UNC.

2. Underwood, "Twenty-Sixth Regiment," 412–13.

3. Mast, "'Trip That Didn't Pay,'" 12.

4. Lewis, "Life and Times of Thomas Bailey," 15, 17, GNMP; William B. Taylor to mother, July 29, 1863, in Mast, "Six Lieutenants," 12.

5. G. P. Collins to Henry King Burgwyn Sr., July 3, 1863, and W. E. Taylor Jr. to Henry King Burgwyn Sr., August 2, 1863, Burgwyn Family Papers, SHC-UNC; J. J. Young to Henry King Burgwyn Sr., July 31, 1863, Burgwyn Papers, NCDAH; Louis G. Young, "Pettigrew's Brigade at Gettysburg," *Our Living and Our Dead*, 556; Underwood, "Twenty-Sixth Regiment," 408; James Johnston Pettigrew to Mrs. McCrary, July 9, 1863, Pettigrew Family Papers, SHC-UNC.

6. Henry Clay Albright diary, July 2, 1863, Albright Papers, NCDAH; Thomas J. Cureton to John Randolph Lane, June 22, 1890, Lane Papers, SHC-UNC; John Thomas Jones to R. H. Finney, August 9, 1863, *OR* 27(2):643; Thorp, "Forty-Seventh Regiment," 90.

7. Linebach diary, 121–22, SHC-UNC; Thomas J. Cureton to John Randolph Lane, June 22, 1890, Lane Papers, SHC-UNC.

8. Linebach diary, 123, SHC-UNC; Thomas J. Cureton to John Randolph Lane, June 22, 1890, Lane Papers, SHC-UNC; Underwood, "Twenty-Sixth Regiment," 399.

9. Thomas Hinshaw reminiscences, Hinshaw Papers, SCL-DU.

10. Thomas J. Cureton to John Randolph Lane, June 22, 1890, Lane Papers, SHC-UNC.

11. Stewart, *Pickett's Charge*, 114, 172–73; Louis G. Young, "Pettigrew's Brigade at Gettysburg," *Our Living and Our Dead*, 554; Ashe, "Pettigrew-Pickett Charge," 158.

12. Fry, "Pettigrew's Charge at Gettysburg," 92.

13. Stewart, *Pickett's Charge*, 114, 173.

14. Louis G. Young, "Pettigrew's Brigade at Gettysburg," *Our Living and Our Dead*, 555; Ashe, "Pettigrew-Pickett Charge," 143–44.

15. Field visit to Gettysburg, March 23, 1997; Christ, *Struggle for the Bliss Farm*, 4–5, 7, 34–77.

16. Rogers, "Additional Sketch," 107; Fry, "Pettigrew's Charge at Gettysburg," 92; Stewart, *Pickett's Charge*, 86–87; Trimble, "North Carolinians at Gettysburg," 57; Chapman, *More Terrible Than Victory*, 106, has a different placement of the regiments in Marshall's brigade.

17. Jones, "Pettigrew's Brigade at Gettysburg," 134–35; Thomas J. Cureton to John Randolph Lane, June 22, 1890, Lane Papers, SHC-UNC.

18. Thomas J. Cureton to John Randolph Lane, June 22, 1890, Lane Papers, SHC-UNC; Thomas W. Setser to W. A. Setser, July 29, 1863, in Mast, "Setser Letters," pt. 3, p. 15; William B. Taylor to mother, July 29, 1863, in Mast, "Six Lieutenants," 13; Linebach diary, 124, SHC-UNC; Fry, "Pettigrew's Charge at Gettysburg," 92.

19. Fry, "Pettigrew's Charge at Gettysburg," 92; Thomas J. Cureton to John Randolph Lane, June 22, 1890, Lane Papers, SHC-UNC; Rogers, "Additional Sketch," 107; Jones, "Pettigrew's Brigade at Gettysburg," 133.

20. Louis G. Young, "Pettigrew's Brigade at Gettysburg, 1–3 July, 1863," 124–25; William S. Christian to John Warwick Daniel, October 24, 1904, Daniel Papers, UVA.

21. Louis G. Young, "Pettigrew's Brigade at Gettysburg, 1–3 July, 1863," 125; Theodore G. Ellis to William P. Seville, July 6, 1863, *OR* 27(1):467; Rogers, "Additional Sketch," 107; Stewart, *Pickett's Charge*, 198; Underwood, "Twenty-Sixth Regiment," 374; Jordan, *North Carolina Troops*, 7:538, 599; Jones, "Pettigrew's Brigade at Gettysburg," 133.

22. Rogers, "Additional Sketch," 108.

23. Christ, *Struggle for the Bliss Farm*, 76–79; Louis G. Young, "Pettigrew's Brigade at Gettysburg, 1–3 July, 1863," 126; A. S. Haynes to editors, October 8, 1877, Grimes Papers, SHC-UNC.

24. Christ, *Struggle for the Bliss Farm*, 78; Louis G. Young, "Pettigrew's Brigade at Gettysburg, 1–3 July, 1863," 127.

25. Rogers, "Additional Sketch," 108.

26. Ashe, "Pettigrew-Pickett Charge," 146–47; W. B. Shepard to editors, September 18, 1877, Grimes Papers, SHC-UNC; Louis G. Young, "Pettigrew's Brigade at Gettysburg, 1–3 July, 1863," 127.

27. John B. Bachelder to A. M. Scales, October 29, 1877, and Henry C. Moore to editors, November 6, 1877, Grimes Papers, SHC-UNC; Page, *History of the Fourteenth Regiment*, 152.

28. Rogers, "Additional Sketch," 108–9.

29. Ashe, "Pettigrew-Pickett Charge," 147; J. McLeod Turner to editors, October 10, 1877, Grimes Papers, SHC-UNC.

30. Trimble, "North Carolinians at Gettysburg," 58.

31. Jones, "Pettigrew's Brigade at Gettysburg," 133; Thomas J. Cureton to John Randolph Lane, June 22, 1890, Lane Papers, SHC-UNC; Thomas P. Smyth to George P. Corts, July 17, 1863, *OR* 27(1):465.

32. Ashe, "Pettigrew-Pickett Charge," 151–52; Joseph J. Davis to editors, September 20, 1877, Grimes Papers, SHC-UNC.

33. Thorp, "Forty-Seventh Regiment," 91; James H. Lane to editors, September 7, 1877, and W. G. Morris to editors, October 1, 1877, Grimes Papers, SHC-UNC.

34. J. McLeod Turner to editors, October 10, 1877, Grimes Papers, SHC-UNC; Stewart, *Pickett's Charge*, 173, 238; Underwood, "Twenty-Sixth Regiment," 366.

35. George W. Whiting to Paris, April 27, 1869, Paris Papers, SHC-UNC; A. S. Haynes to editors, October 8, 1877, and Joseph J. Davis to editors, September 20, 1877, Grimes Papers, SHC-UNC.

36. Taylor, "Col. James Keith Marshall," 87; Marshall to uncle, October 6, 1863, VMI; Gragg, *Covered with Glory*, 192; Robinson, "Fifty-Second Regiment," 238–39; Benjamin Franklin Little to editors, September 20, 1877, Grimes Papers, SHC-UNC.

37. Trinque, "Arnold's Battery and the 26th North Carolina"; Jordan, *North Carolina Troops*, 7:467; Gragg, *Covered with Glory*, 199. Trinque argues that there is no compelling evidence that the 26th North Carolina was the target of Barker's blast and believes the focus was more likely the 16th North Carolina of Lowrance's brigade. I am not convinced by his evidence and still believe that the 26th was in front of Arnold's gun that afternoon. Trinque bases his argument on the Confederate flags picked up by members of the 14th Connecticut. The units to which they belonged indicate to him that the 26th North Carolina was north of the Connecticut regiment. But a further reading of Union sources makes it clear that Federal troops ranged widely over the battlefield to grab any flags they could lay their hands on after the Confederate repulse. Thus this is a poor foundation for any conclusion about the placement of Rebel regiments on the battlefield. Trinque says there is no evidence from the 26th North Carolina to confirm that the incident took place, but the service record of Captain Wagg, quoted in the text, offers compelling evidence that he was hit by canister fire only a few yards from the stone fence. There was no other artillery that could have fired and hit him in this spot other than the one that was placed in front of the regiment.

38. Ashe, "Pettigrew-Pickett Charge," 153; Jones, "Pettigrew's Brigade at Gettysburg," 134; Thomas J. Cureton to John Randolph Lane, June 22, 1890, Lane Papers, SHC-UNC; Gaston Broughton to editors, October 15, 1877, Grimes Papers, SHC-UNC; Henry Clay Albright diary, July 3, 1863, Albright Papers, NCDAH.

39. Benjamin Franklin Little to editors, September 20, 1877, Grimes Papers, SHC-UNC.

40. Rogers, "Additional Sketch," 109; Louis G. Young, "Pettigrew's Brigade at Gettysburg," *Our Living and Our Dead*, 556; transcript of George W. Whiting article, Paris Papers, SHC-UNC; Jordan, *North Carolina Troops*, 11:362.

41. Thomas P. Smyth to George P. Corts, July 17, 1863, *OR* 27(1):465; Louis G. Young, "Pettigrew's Brigade at Gettysburg, 1–3 July, 1863," 128–29; Thomas J. Cureton to John Randolph Lane, June 22, 1890, Lane Papers, SHC-UNC.

42. Page, *History of the Fourteenth Regiment*, 156, 158; Theodore G. Ellis to William P. Seville, July 6, 1863, *OR* 27(1):468.

43. Taylor, "Col. James Keith Marshall," 89; Jordan, *North Carolina Troops*, 12:480.

44. Underwood, "Twenty-Sixth Regiment," 374; Jordan, *North Carolina Troops*, 7:519, 521, 531, 538, 599; Rose, *Colours of the Gray*, 38.

45. Thorp, "Forty-Seventh Regiment," 92; Thomas J. Cureton to John Randolph Lane, June 22, 1890, Lane Papers, SHC-UNC; Stewart, *Pickett's Charge*, 256; Jones, "Pettigrew's Brigade at Gettysburg," 134; Joseph John Davis to Charles Scott Venable, July 30, 1889, Venable Papers, VHS; John Thomas Jones to father, August 17, 1863, Jones Papers, SHC-UNC.

46. J. J. Young to Zebulon Baird Vance, July 4, 1863, Burgwyn Papers, NCDAH; Louis G. Young, "Pettigrew's Brigade at Gettysburg," *Our Living and Our Dead*, 555; William H. Blount to Miss Bettie, August 2, 1863, Steed and Phipps Family Papers, SHC-UNC.

47. Thomas J. Cureton to John Randolph Lane, June 22, 1890, Lane Papers, SHC-UNC; Henry Clay Albright diary, July 3, 1863, Albright Papers, NCDAH.

48. Underwood, "Twenty-Sixth Regiment," 413; Linebach diary, 125, SHC-UNC.

49. Bush reminiscences, 3–4, Shuford Collection, NCDAH.

50. John T. Jones to father, July 17, 1863, Jones Papers, SHC-UNC; Busey and Martin, *Regimental Strengths and Losses at Gettysburg*, 310; Louis G. Young, "Pettigrew's Brigade at Gettysburg," *Our Living and Our Dead*, 555; Rose, *Colours of the Gray*, 31, 39.

51. Louis G. Young, "Pettigrew's Brigade at Gettysburg, 1–3 July, 1863," 131; Louis G. Young to mother, July 8, 1863, Gourdin Papers, EU; Stewart, *Pickett's Charge*, 263.

52. Jordan, *North Carolina Troops*, 5:6–105, 7:463–601, 11:244–363, 12:415–521.

53. J. J. Young to Zebulon Baird Vance, July 4, 1863, Burgwyn Papers, NCDAH; casualty list, 26th North Carolina, *Raleigh Daily Progress*, July 23, 1863; return of killed and wounded, Army of Northern Virginia, *OR* 27(2):333; return of casualties, Army of Northern Virginia, *OR* 27(2):344; J. J. Young to Zebulon B. Vance, July 4, 1863, *OR* 27(2):645–46; Busey and Martin, *Regimental Strengths and Losses at Gettysburg*, 264–66, 298–302; Underwood, "Twenty-Sixth Regiment," 373; Henry Clay Albright diary, n.d., 1863, Albright Papers, NCDAH. Slightly different statistics can be compiled from the service records of the 26th North Carolina. They list 109 killed, 298 wounded, 197 wounded and captured, 74 captured, and 6 missing, for a total of 684 lost on both days of the battle of Gettysburg. See Jordan, *North Carolina Troops*, 7:463–601.

54. Jordan, *North Carolina Troops*, 7:544, 554–55; Henry C. Kirkman to Dr. George Kirkman, August 6, 1863, and Owen to George Kirkman, December 8, 1863, USAMHI.

55. Gaston Broughton to editors, October 15, 1877, and George Wilcox to editors, October 1877, Grimes Papers, SHC-UNC; Underwood, "Twenty-Sixth Regiment," 359, 416; R. M. Tuttle, "Addenda," 3–4 [125–26]; R. M. Tuttle to Mr. Bright, June 3, 1903, Daniel Papers, UVA; Henry Clay Albright diary, July 3, 1863, Albright Papers, NCDAH; Henry C. Albright to sister, July 12, 1863, Albright Papers, GHM.

56. Busey and Martin, *Regimental Strengths and Losses at Gettysburg*, 298–301; *Raleigh Daily Progress*, July 29, 1863; A. S. Haynes to editors, October 8, 1877, Grimes Papers, SHC-UNC; Lemuel J. Hoyle to mother, July 2, 1863, Hoyle Papers, SHC-UNC; Louis G. Young, "Pettigrew's Brigade at Gettysburg," *Our Living and Our Dead*, 555–56; undated fragment of letter by Francis W. Bird, Winston Papers, SHC-UNC; Martin and Outlaw, "Eleventh Regiment," 590. Slightly different statistics can be compiled from the service records of the 11th North Carolina. They list 56 killed, 120

wounded, 131 wounded and captured, and 58 captured, for a total of 365 lost on both days of the battle of Gettysburg. See Jordan, *North Carolina Troops*, 5:6–105.

57. Martin and Outlaw, "Eleventh Regiment," 591; Jordan, *North Carolina Troops*, 5:6–7.

58. Alexander H. Harris letter, July 8, 1863, *Raleigh Daily Progress*, July 14, 1863; *Raleigh Daily Progress*, July 30, 1863; Jordan, *North Carolina Troops*, 11:244–45; Busey and Martin, *Regimental Strengths and Losses at Gettysburg*, 299–301. Slightly different statistics can be compiled from the service records of the 47th North Carolina. They list 46 killed, 121 wounded, 111 wounded and captured, 76 captured, and 2 missing, for a total of 356 lost on both days of the battle of Gettysburg. See Jordan, *North Carolina Troops*, 11:244–363.

59. Taylor, "Col. James Keith Marshall," 88–89; Busey and Martin, *Regimental Strengths and Losses at Gettysburg*, 300; George H. Coke to E. Warren, July 6, 1863, *Raleigh Daily Progress*, July 14, 1863. Statistics for the losses suffered by the 52nd North Carolina on both days of the battle of Gettysburg can be found in the service records. They list 29 killed, 64 wounded, 145 wounded and captured, 101 captured, and 9 missing, for a total of 348. See Jordan, *North Carolina Troops*, 12:415–521.

60. Lemuel J. Hoyle to mother, July 12, 1863, Hoyle Papers, SHC-UNC; Louis G. Young, "Pettigrew-Kirkland-MacRae Brigade," 558.

CHAPTER EIGHT

1. Thorp, "Forty-Seventh Regiment," 92.

2. Imboden, "Confederate Retreat," 422–23.

3. Ibid., 423–24; Linebach diary, 125–127; Henry Clay Albright diary, July 4, 1863, Albright Papers, NCDAH.

4. Imboden, "Confederate Retreat," 425; Underwood, "Twenty-Sixth Regiment," 370; Collett Leventhorpe to Marcus J. Wright, May 30, 1888, Wright Papers, SCL-DU; Collett Leventhorpe to Charles Colcock Jones, April 13, 1887, Jones Papers, SCL-DU; Lemuel J. Hoyle to mother, July 12, 1863, Hoyle Papers, SHC-UNC; Nutall reminiscences, *Civil War Times Illustrated* Collection, USAMHI.

5. *Charlotte Daily Bulletin*, August 23, 1863; Alexander H. Harris letter, July 8, 1863, *Raleigh Daily Progress*, July 14, 1863.

6. Imboden, "Confederate Retreat," 425; Mast, "'Trip That Didn't Pay,'" 12; Linebach diary, 129, SHC-UNC.

7. Linebach diary, 129, SHC-UNC; Imboden, "Confederate Retreat," 426–27.

8. Linebach diary, 130–32.

9. Morrison, *Memoirs of Henry Heth*, 178; James Johnston Pettigrew to Zebulon B. Vance, July 9, 1863, Pettigrew Family Papers, SHC-UNC.

10. Linebach diary, 132–33, SHC-UNC; Robinson, "Fifty-Second Regiment," 239; Thorp, "Forty-Seventh Regiment," 92; *OR* 27(2):337; Rogers, "Additional Sketch," 109; Henry Clay Albright diary, July 6–12, 1863, Albright Papers, NCDAH.

11. Robert E. Lee to Samuel Cooper, July 31, 1863, *OR* 27(2):310; J. E. B. Stuart to Walter H. Taylor, August 20, 1863, *OR* 27(2):705; field visit to Falling Waters, June 28, 1997.

12. Lewis, "Life and Times of Thomas Bailey," 18, GNMP.

13. Underwood, "Twenty-Sixth Regiment," 375, 377; Robinson, "Fifty-Second Regiment," 239–40; Morrison, *Memoirs of Henry Heth*, 178; Henry Clay Albright diary, July 13, 1863, Albright Papers, NCDAH; William H. Blount to Miss Bettie, August 3, 1863, Steed and Phipps Family Papers, SHC-UNC; letter from Brockenbrough's brigade, August 16, 1863, *Richmond Daily Enquirer*, August 24, 1863; Sion H. Oxford to R. M. Oxford, July 17, 1863, McCall Papers, SCL-DU; Louis G. Young, "Death of Brigadier General J. Johnston Pettigrew," 29–30.

14. Morrison, *Memoirs of Henry Heth*, 179; Louis G. Young, "Pettigrew-Kirkland-MacRae Brigade," 559; Martin and Outlaw, "Eleventh Regiment," 591; Louis G. Young, "Death of Brigadier General J. Johnston Pettigrew," 30.

15. Bush, "Sixth Michigan Cavalry at Falling Waters," 110–14; Louis G. Young, "Death of Brigadier General J. Johnston Pettigrew," 30.

16. Robinson, "Fifty-Second Regiment," 241; Morrison, *Memoirs of Henry Heth*, 179; John Thomas Jones to father, July 17, 1863, Jones Papers, SHC-UNC; Underwood, "Twenty-Sixth Regiment," 376; Louis G. Young, "Death of Brigadier General J. Johnston Pettigrew," 30–31; Bush, "Sixth Michigan Cavalry at Falling Waters," 114.

17. Rogers, "Additional Sketch," 110; Morrison, *Memoirs of Henry Heth*, 179; Louis G. Young, "Pettigrew-Kirkland-MacRae Brigade," 560; Louis G. Young letter, July 15, 1863, Pettigrew Family Papers, NCDAH; Underwood, "Twenty-Sixth Regiment," 376; Louis G. Young, "Death of Brigadier General J. Johnston Pettigrew," 31; Jordan, *North Carolina Troops*, 7:492; Gragg, *Covered with Glory*, 217.

18. Letter from Brockenbrough's brigade, August 16, 1863, *Richmond Daily Enquirer*, August 24, 1863; Louis G. Young, "Pettigrew-Kirkland-MacRae Brigade," 560; John Thomas Jones to father, July 17, 1863, Jones Papers, SHC-UNC; Bush, "Sixth Michigan Cavalry at Falling Waters," 114.

19. Letter from Brockenbrough's brigade, August 16, 1863, *Richmond Daily Enquirer*, August 24, 1863; John Thomas Jones to father, July 17, 1863, Jones Papers, SHC-UNC; Underwood, "Twenty-Sixth Regiment," 378; Martin and Outlaw, "Eleventh Regiment," 591; Robert E. Lee to Samuel Cooper, January 1864, *OR* 27(2):323; Bush, "Sixth Michigan Cavalry at Falling Waters," 114.

20. Jordan, *North Carolina Troops*, 5:6–105, 7:463–601, 11:244–363, 12:415–521.

21. Louis G. Young to Mary Pettigrew, August 1, 1863, Pettigrew Family Papers, SHC-UNC; Underwood, "Twenty-Sixth Regiment," 377; Louis G. Young letter, July 15, 1863, Pettigrew Family Papers, NCDAH.

22. Martin and Outlaw, "Eleventh Regiment," 591; Louis G. Young, "Pettigrew-Kirkland-MacRae Brigade," 560; Henry Clay Albright diary, July 14, 1863, Albright Papers, NCDAH; Robinson, "Fifty-Second Regiment," 241; Rogers, "Additional Sketch," 110; William H. Blount to Miss Bettie, August 3, 1863, Steed and Phipps Family Papers, SHC-UNC; Linebach diary, 134, SHC-UNC.

23. Henry Clay Albright diary, July 15, 1863, Albright Papers, NCDAH; Linebach diary, 135–37, SHC-UNC; Underwood, "Twenty-Sixth Regiment," 399.

24. Martin and Outlaw, "Eleventh Regiment," 591–92; Henry Clay Albright diary, July 1863, Albright Papers, NCDAH; W. B. Shepard to editors, September 18, 1877, Grimes Papers, SHC-UNC; J. S. Bartlett reminiscences, Bartlett Papers, SHC-UNC.

25. Underwood, "Twenty-Sixth Regiment," 377.

26. Louis G. Young to Mary Pettigrew, August 1, 1863, Pettigrew Family Papers, SHC-UNC; Louis G. Young, "Pettigrew-Kirkland-MacRae Brigade," 561; Welsh, *Medical Histories of Confederate Generals*, 171.

27. Robert E. Lee to James A. Seddon, July 17, 1863, *OR* 27(3):1016; George Collins to Mary, August 18, 1863, Pettigrew Family Papers, NCDAH.

28. Govan and Livingood, *Haskell Memoirs*, 52.

29. Louis G. Young, "Pettigrew's Brigade at Gettysburg, 1–3 July, 1863," 131; Louis G. Young, "Pettigrew-Kirkland-MacRae Brigade," 561.

30. Henry Clay Albright diary, July 21–25, 1863, Albright Papers, NCDAH; Linebach diary, 139–43, SHC-UNC; Robinson, "Fifty-Second Regiment," 241.

31. Louis G. Young to Mary, August 1, 1863, Pettigrew Family Papers, SHC-UNC.

32. Inventory of effects of James Johnston Pettigrew, July 24, 1863; copy of will of James Johnston Pettigrew, December 7, 1856; and J. C. Johnston to William S. Pettigrew, October 2, 1863, Pettigrew Family Papers, NCDAH.

33. *Raleigh Daily Progress*, July 18, 23, 24, 25, 31, 1863; undated fragment of letter by William S. Pettigrew, Pettigrew Family Papers, SHC-UNC; Underwood, "Twenty-Sixth Regiment," 377.

34. J. J. Young to Henry King Burgwyn Sr., July 11, 1863; William H. S. Burgwyn to mother, July 14, 1863; Samuel W. Meton telegram, July 13, 1863; Mary W. Barney telegram, July 14, 1863, Burgwyn Family Papers, SHC-UNC; Schiller, *Captain's War*, 89–91.

35. *Raleigh Register*, July 22, 1863; "Tribute of Respect," November 10, 1863, and Francis H. Smith to Henry King Burgwyn Sr., July 31, 1863, Burgwyn Papers, NCDAH; Francis H. Smith to Henry King Burgwyn Sr., April 9, 1864, Burgwyn Family Papers, SHC-UNC; Davis, *Boy Colonel of the Confederacy*, 72.

36. Taylor, "Col. James Keith Marshall," 88.

37. Thomas W. Setser to W. A. Setser, July 29, 1863, in Mast, "Setser Letters," pt. 3, p. 14; Jordan, *North Carolina Troops*, 7:545.

38. Bush reminiscences, Shuford Collection, NCDAH.

39. Benjamin Franklin Little to Flax, July 9, 20, August 24, October 14, 1863; Little diary, July 1863–March 1864; L. W. Oakley to Mrs. Little, July 9, 1863; and J. T. McLean to Mrs. Little, January 15, 1864, Little Papers, SHC-UNC; Jordan, *North Carolina Troops*, 12:415, 454.

40. Orren A. Hanner to Mrs. Emerson, August 12, 1863, in Mast, "Six Lieutenants," 10–11; W. J. Kincaid to C. S. Brown, December 27, 1863, Martin Collection, DCL.

41. Hood, "26th Regiment at Gettysburg"; Hood, "From Gettysburg to the Wilderness."

42. Caison, "Southern Soldiers in Northern Prisons," 160–62.

43. Powell, *Dictionary of North Carolina Biography*, 4:56; Collett Leventhorpe to wife, October 5, 1863, and February 8, 1864, Leventhorpe Papers, NCDAH; Edmund Jones speech, in "War Record of Genl Collett Leventhorpe," Military Collection, Civil War Collection, NCDAH; Welsh, *Medical Histories of Confederate Generals*, 138.

44. Medical Descriptive List, July 22, 1863, and Record of Death and Internment, November 17, 1863, Daniel McCaskill service record, 26th North Carolina; Medical Descriptive Lists, n.d., P. S. Bobbitt service record and J. J. Bunch service record, 47th

North Carolina; and Medical Descriptive List, n.d., Cyrus McLure service record, 11th North Carolina, Compiled Service Records, NARA; Jordan, *North Carolina Troops*, 7:566–67.

45. Mast, "'Trip That Didn't Pay,'" 9, 12–13.

46. Thomas Hinshaw reminiscences, Hinshaw Papers, SCL-DU; Jordan, *North Carolina Troops*, 12:480, 484, 485.

47. *Richmond Daily Enquirer*, July 25, 1863.

48. John Thomas Jones to father, August 17, 1863, and April 26, 1864, Jones Papers, SHC-UNC; Jones, "Pettigrew's Brigade at Gettysburg," 135.

49. *Raleigh Daily Progress*, August 1, 1863.

50. *Richmond Daily Enquirer*, July 28, 1863, and March 18, 1864.

51. Robert E. Lee to James A. Seddon, July 17, 1863, *OR* 27(3):1016; Samuel Cooper to Lee, July 24, 1863, *OR* 27(3):1038; Lee to Jefferson Davis, July 29, 1863, *OR* 27(3):1048–49; Linebach diary, 143, SHC-UNC; Francis W. Bird to sister, July 30, 1863, Winston Papers, SHC-UNC; John Tillinghast to Will, July 29, 1863, Tillinghast Family Papers, SCL-DU.

52. Troops in the Department of Richmond, July 20, 1863, *OR* 27(3):1029; Jordan, *North Carolina Troops*, 10:396–409, 454–66; Robert Bingham to granddaughter, March 14, 1923, Bingham Papers, SHC-UNC; *Harrisburg Evening Telegraph*, August 1, 1863.

53. Robert Bingham to granddaughter, March 14, 1923, Bingham Papers, SHC-UNC.

54. Linebach diary, 143–56, SHC-UNC.

55. *Richmond Daily Enquirer*, August 15, 1863; Linebach diary, 144, SHC-UNC.

56. Benjamin Wesley Justice to wife, August 9, 1863, Justice Papers, EU; John Thomas Jones to father, August 17, 1863, Jones Papers, SHC-UNC.

57. Alexander S. Webb to brother, August 8, 1863, Webb Collection, NCDAH; "X" to editor, August 12, 1863, *Richmond Daily Enquirer*, August 15, 1863; James D. McIver to John, August 14, 1863, McIver Papers, SCL-DU; resolutions, *Charlotte Daily Bulletin*, August 19, 20, 23, 1863.

58. Lemuel J. Hoyle to mother, August 1, 1863, Hoyle Papers, SHC-UNC; Thorp, "Forty-Seventh Regiment," 92; James D. McIver to John, August 14, 1863, McIver Papers, SCL-DU; J. A. P. to editor, August 17, 1863, *North Carolina Argus*, September 3, 1863; Benjamin Wesley Justice to wife, August 9, 1863, Justice Papers, EU.

59. John Thomas Jones to father, August 17, 1863, Jones Papers, SHC-UNC; medical certificates, September 10, October 19, 1863, John R. Lane service record, 26th North Carolina, Compiled Service Records, NARA.

60. Allen to Secretary of War, August 14, 1863, William C. Allen service record, 26th North Carolina, Compiled Service Records, NARA; Jordan, *North Carolina Troops*, 7:590.

61. Underwood, "Twenty-Sixth Regiment," 418; James D. McIver to John, August 14, 1863, McIver Papers, SCL-DU.

62. James D. McIver to John, September 1, 1863, McIver Papers, SCL-DU; Jordan, *North Carolina Troops*, 7:561.

63. Henry Clay Albright to brother, August 21, 1863, Albright Papers, NCDAH; Lemuel J. Hoyle to mother, August 17, 1863, Hoyle Papers, SHC-UNC.

64. Jordan, *North Carolina Troops*, 5:6–105, 7:463–601, 11:244–363, 12:415–521.

65. Underwood, "Twenty-Sixth Regiment," 400; Goodwyn Harris to Zebulon B. Vance, July 13, 1863, in Yearns and Barrett, *North Carolina Civil War Documentary*, 146; Jordan, *North Carolina Troops*, 7:579.

66. Underwood, "Twenty-Sixth Regiment," 401; Jordan, *North Carolina Troops*, 7:577.

67. Bardolph, "Confederate Dilemma," pt. 2, pp. 191–92.

68. Receipt, September 10, 1863, Enoch Manus service record, 52nd North Carolina, Compiled Service Records, NARA; Jordan, *North Carolina Troops*, 12:432, 436.

69. Receipt, September 30, 1863, Robert B. Lourie service record, 11th North Carolina; special requisition, September 30, 1863, L. Elias service record, 11th North Carolina; special requisition, September 30, 1863, Lemuel Hoyle service record, 11th North Carolina; special requisition, October 7, 1863, W. J. Kerr service record, 11th North Carolina; special requisition, October 5, 1863, R. C. Brown service record, 44th North Carolina; special requisition, August 10, 1863, T. M. Carter service record, 44th North Carolina; special requisition, August 17, October 5, 1863, M. G. Cherry service record, 44th North Carolina; special requisition, October 3, 1863, R. Singletary service record, 44th North Carolina; special requisition, October 5, 1863, D. H. Smith service record, 44th North Carolina; special requisition, October 5, 1863, R. G. Sneed service record, 44th North Carolina; special requisition, August 12, 1863, J. W. Brown service record, 47th North Carolina; quarterly return, September 30, 1863, J. J. Parlier service record, 52nd North Carolina; and clothing return, September 30, 1863, Thomas R. Capel service record, 52nd North Carolina, Compiled Service Records, NARA.

CHAPTER NINE

1. Special Orders No. 224, Army of Northern Virginia, September 7, 1863, *OR* 29(2):701.

2. Powell, *Dictionary of North Carolina Biography*, 3:371; Welsh, *Medical Histories of Confederate Generals*, 127.

3. Louis G. Young, "Pettigrew-Kirkland-MacRae Brigade," 562; John M. Tate to Mr. Britton, September 26, 1863, *Charlotte Daily Bulletin*, October 3, 1863; Henry Clay Albright to brother, September 1863, Albright Papers, NCDAH; A. S. Webb to brother, September 12, 1863, Webb Family Papers, SHC-UNC; William H. Blount to Bettie, September 15, 1863, Steed and Phipps Family Papers, SHC-UNC.

4. Linebach diary, 157–58, SHC-UNC.

5. Henderson, *Road to Bristoe Station*, 44–45; William H. Blount to Bettie, September 15, 1863, Steed and Phipps Family Papers, SHC-UNC; Linebach diary, 160, SHC-UNC; Robinson, "Fifty-Second Regiment," 241.

6. Linebach diary, 160, 163, 165–68, 172, SHC-UNC.

7. Henderson, *Road to Bristoe Station*, 32, 68–69.

8. Benjamin Wesley Justice to wife, October 14, 20, 1863, Justice Papers, EU; Linebach diary, 168–69, 172, SHC-UNC; William S. Long reminiscences, fols. 1209–12, Long Papers, LC; Henderson, *Road to Bristoe Station*, 70, 72, 84, 104.

9. Henderson, *Road to Bristoe Station*, 84, 140, 167, 169–70, 174, 176, 179; Alexander S. Webb to Francis A. Walker, October 16, 1863, *OR* 29(1):277; A. P. Hill to R. H. Chilton,

October 26, 1863, *OR* 29(1):426; Henry Heth to W. N. Starke, October 24, 1863, *OR* 29(1):431–33; William S. Long reminiscences, fols. 1215–16, Long Papers, LC.

10. Henderson, *Road to Bristoe Station*, 174–75; A. P. Hill to R. H. Chilton, October 26, 1863, *OR* 29(1):427; J. S. Bartlett reminiscences, Bartlett Papers, SHC-UNC; *Raleigh North Carolina Standard*, October 27, 1863; field visit to Bristoe Station, March 21–22, 1996.

11. Alexander S. Webb to Francis A. Walker, October 16, 1863, *OR* 29(1):277; Benjamin Franklin Justice to wife, October 14, 20, 1863, Justice Papers, EU; C. A. Tuttle, "Company F, 26th Regt. N.C. Troops at Bristow Station."

12. Henderson, *Road to Bristoe Station*, 179; Thorp, "Forty-Seventh Regiment," 93; Robinson, "Fifty-Second Regiment," 242; Martin and Outlaw, "Eleventh Regiment," 593; Alexander S. Webb to Francis A. Walker, October 16, 1863, *OR* 29(1):277; Henry Heth to W. N. Starke, October 24, 1863, *OR* 29(1):431.

13. Henderson, *Road to Bristoe Station*, 180; Welsh, *Medical Histories of Confederate Generals*, 127; Martin and Outlaw, "Eleventh Regiment," 593; Linebach diary, 173, SHC-UNC; *Raleigh North Carolina Standard*, October 23, 1863; C. A. Tuttle, "Company F, 26th Regt. N.C. Troops at Bristow Station."

14. Lewis, "Life and Times of Thomas Bailey," 25, GNMP.

15. Henry Heth to W. N. Starke, October 24, 1863, *OR* 29(1):431; Martin and Outlaw, "Eleventh Regiment," 593; *Raleigh North Carolina Standard*, October 23, 1863; J. S. Bartlett reminiscences, 6, Bartlett Papers, SHC-UNC.

16. William S. Long reminiscences, fols. 1219–22, 1234, Long Papers, LC.

17. Alexander S. Webb to Francis A. Walker, October 16, 1863, *OR* 29(1):277, 278; A. P. Hill to R. H. Chilton, October 26, 1863, *OR* 29(1):427; Edward D. Hall to R. H. Finney, October 22, 1863, *OR* 29(1):435.

18. C. A. Tuttle, "Company F, 26th Regt. N.C. Troops at Bristow Station."

19. Henry Heth to W. N. Starke, October 24, 1863, *OR* 29(1):431; Henry H. Walker to R. H. Finney, October 21, 1863, *OR* 29(1):433–34; Edward D. Hall to R. H. Finney, October 22, 1863, *OR* 29(1):436; Henderson, *Road to Bristoe Station*, 176, 181–82, 185–87; Linebach diary, 173, SHC-UNC; Lewis, "Life and Times of Thomas Bailey," 25, GNMP.

20. Thomas W. Setser to W. A. Setser, October 20, 1863, in Mast, "Setser Letters," pt. 4, p. 13; James A. Patton to wife, October 20, 1863, Patton Papers, EU.

21. Henderson, *Road to Bristoe Station*, 182; Louis G. Young, "Pettigrew-Kirkland-MacRae Brigade," 562; *Raleigh North Carolina Standard*, October 23, 1863; Underwood, "Twenty-Sixth Regiment," 379. Jordan, *North Carolina Troops*, 5:6–105, 7:463–601, 10:396–493, 11:244–363, 12:415–521, has different casualty statistics for the brigade, amounting to 42 killed, 198 wounded, 22 wounded and captured, and 264 captured, for a total of 526.

22. Underwood, "Twenty-Sixth Regiment," 379; R. M. Tuttle to Mr. Bright, June 3, 1903, Daniel Papers, UVA; C. A. Tuttle, "Company F, 26th Regt. N.C. Troops at Bristow Station"; Jordan, *North Carolina Troops*, 7:463–601; George Glenn to William H. Glenn, October 21, 1863, Glenn Papers, SCL-DU; John R. Lane interview, June 16, 1900, and Walter Clark to William H. S. Burgwyn, April 16, 1900, Burgwyn Papers, NCDAH; Thomas W. Setser to W. A. Setser, October 20, 1863, in Mast, "Setser Letters," pt. 4, p. 13; Alexander S. Webb to Francis A. Walker, October 16, 1863, *OR* 29(1):278; list of captured flags, *OR*, ser. 3, 4:816; Terry, "Mystery Flags of Bristoe Station," 13.

23. Martin and Outlaw, "Eleventh Regiment," 593; Robinson, "Fifty-Second Regiment," 242; Henderson, *Road to Bristoe Station*, 183. The service records indicate slightly different casualties for these regiments. The 11th North Carolina lost 3 killed, 10 wounded, 1 wounded and captured, and 41 captured, for a total of 55. The 44th North Carolina lost 16 killed, 60 wounded, 9 wounded and captured, and 53 captured, for a total of 138. The 47th North Carolina lost 3 killed, 38 wounded, 5 wounded and captured, and 47 captured, for a total of 93. The 52nd North Carolina lost 2 killed, 24 wounded, and 46 captured, for a total of 72. See Jordan, *North Carolina Troops*, 5:6–105, 10:396–493, 11:244–363, 12:415–521.

24. Louis G. Young, "Pettigrew-Kirkland-MacRae Brigade," 562; Stedman, "Forty-Fourth Regiment," 26–27; *Raleigh North Carolina Standard*, October 27, 1863.

25. Henry Heth to W. N. Starke, October 24, 1863, *OR* 29(1):432.

26. Henderson, *Road to Bristoe Station*, 189–91; J. S. Bartlett reminiscences, 6, Bartlett Papers, SHC-UNC; James A. Patton to wife, October 20, 1863, Patton Papers, EU; William S. Long reminiscences, fol. 1214, Long Papers, LC.

27. William S. Long reminiscences, fols. 1221–22, 1228, Long Papers, LC.

28. Henderson, *Road to Bristoe Station*, 190–93; Thomas W. Setser to W. A. Setser, October 20, 1863, in Mast, "Setser Letters," pt. 4, p. 13; A. P. Hill to R. H. Chilton, October 26, 1863, *OR* 29(1):427.

29. Henderson, *Road to Bristoe Station*, 194; Lewis, "Life and Times of Thomas Bailey," 26–27, GNMP; J. S. Bartlett reminiscences, 6, Bartlett Papers, SHC-UNC; Benjamin Franklin Justice to wife, October 14, 20, 1863, Justice Papers, EU; Linebach diary, 172–79, SHC-UNC.

30. Thomas W. Setser to W. A. Setser, October 20, November 13, 1863, in Mast, "Setser Letters," pt. 4, pp. 13–14.

31. Underwood, "Twenty-Sixth Regiment," 380–81.

32. Linebach diary, 180–82, SHC-UNC.

33. A. S. Webb to brother, October 26, 1863, Webb Collection, NCDAH; special requisitions, October 30, 1863, R. H. Fossett service record and J. W. Brown service record, 47th North Carolina, Compiled Service Records, NARA; Thomas W. Setser to W. A. Setser, November 13, 1863, in Mast, "Setser Letters," pt. 4, p. 14.

34. Graham and Skoch, *Mine Run*, 5–35; Robinson, "Fifty-Second Regiment," 243; Linebach diary, 185–89, SHC-UNC.

35. Justice to wife, November 22, 1863, Fredericksburg Battlefield; Graham and Skoch, *Mine Run*, 38.

36. Graham and Skoch, *Mine Run*, 40, 42–43, 46–49, 57; A. P. Hill to R. H. Chilton, January 27, 1864, *OR* 29(1):895; Henry Heth to William H. Palmer, January 20, 1864, *OR* 29(1):897; Benjamin Wesley Justice to wife, November 29, 1863, Justice Papers, EU.

37. Henry Heth to William H. Palmer, January 20, 1864, *OR* 29(1):897.

38. Benjamin Wesley Justice to wife, November 29, 1863, Justice Papers, EU; Isaac Augustus Jarratt to mother, December 3, 1863, Jarratt-Puryear Family Papers, SCL-DU; Jordan, *North Carolina Troops*, 7:467; Thorp, "Forty-Seventh Regiment," 93.

39. Benjamin Wesley Justice to wife, November 29, 1863, Justice Papers, EU.

40. A. P. Hill to R. H. Chilton, January 27, 1864, *OR* 29(1):896; Graham and Skoch, *Mine Run*, 69; field visit to Mine Run, March 21, 1996.

41. A. P. Hill to R. H. Chilton, January 27, 1864, *OR* 29(1):896; Lewis, "Life and Times of Thomas Bailey," 29, GNMP; Graham and Skoch, *Mine Run*, 69–71, 73, 78.

42. Graham and Skoch, *Mine Run*, 76–77, 80; Morrison, *Memoirs of Henry Heth*, 180.

43. Benjamin Wesley Justice to wife, December 1, 1863, Justice Papers, EU.

44. A. S. Webb to Ma, December 1, 1863, and Webb to sister, December 6, 1863, Webb Family Papers, SHC-UNC; Benjamin Wesley Justice to wife, December 1, 1863, Justice Papers, EU.

45. Graham and Skoch, *Mine Run*, 80–83, 90; Jordan, *North Carolina Troops*, 5:6–105, 7:463–601, 10:396–493, 11:244–363, 12:415–521; Isaac Augustus Jarratt to mother, December 3, 1863, Jarratt-Puryear Family Papers, SCL-DU.

46. Benjamin H. Freeman to father, mother, and sisters, December 30, 1863, in Wright, *Confederate Letters*, 31; Lemuel J. Hoyle to mother, December 27, 1863, Hoyle Papers, SHC-UNC; Jesse L. Moffitt to Hannah, December 12, 1863, Lawrence Papers, SCL-DU; Henry Clay Albright to brother, December 30, 1863, Albright Papers, NCDAH; James W. Wright to Fanny, January 17, 1864, Wright Collection, NCDAH; Richard S. Webb to Jennie, January 1, 1864, Webb Family Papers, SHC-UNC; Linebach diary, 201–5, SHC-UNC.

47. Lemuel J. Hoyle to mother, December 27, 1863, Hoyle Papers, SHC-UNC; Bellfield King to mother and Aunt Margaret, January 18, 1864, King Papers, SCL-DU; John M. Tate to John L. Brown, April 10, 1864, Young Papers, SHC-UNC; J. S. Bartlett reminiscences, 6–9, Bartlett Papers, SHC-UNC.

48. L. A. Bristol to brother, January, 1864, Bristol Letters, BCPL.

49. Columbus A. Tuttle, "Incidents Which Happened in Caldwell County," Reminiscences, Civil War Collection, NCDAH; Jordan, *North Carolina Troops*, 7:544.

50. Lewis, "Life and Times of Thomas Bailey," 30, 32, 36–37, GNMP.

51. James W. Wright to brother, February 12, 1864, Wright Collection, NCDAH; Lewis Warlick to Cornelia, March 22, 1864, McGimsey Papers, SHC-UNC.

52. William H. Blount to friend, January 1, 20, 1864, Steed and Phipps Family Papers, SHC-UNC; Isaac Augustus Jarratt to mother, January 17, 1864, Jarratt-Puryear Family Papers, SCL-DU.

53. Lemuel J. Hoyle to mother, January 23, 1864, Hoyle Papers, SHC-UNC; James W. Wright to Fanny, father, and mother, February 7, 1864, Wright Collection, NCDAH; record of events, Companies A, B, and G, 26th North Carolina, Compiled Service Records, NARA; Richard S. Webb to Jennie, March 16, 1864, Webb Family Papers, SHC-UNC; Lewis, "Life and Times of Thomas Bailey," 31, GNMP.

54. Linebach diary, 213–20, 226–27, SHC-UNC.

55. Welsh, *Medical Histories of Confederate Generals*, 127; Robinson, "Fifty-Second Regiment," 244; Henry Heth to Samuel Cooper, February 24, 1864, Thomas C. Singletary service record, 44th North Carolina, Compiled Service Records, NARA; Jordan, *North Carolina Troops*, 10:391.

56. Special requisition, March 4, 1864, M. G. Cherry service record, 44th North Carolina; special requisition, March 4, 1864, R. Singletary service record, 44th North Carolina; invoice, January 1864, W. L. Cherry service record, 44th North Carolina; special requisition, December 2, 1863, W. J. Kerr service record, 11th North Carolina; special requisition, February–March 1864 and second quarter 1864, W. J. Kerr service record, 11th North Carolina; special requisition, second quarter 1864, L. Elias service record,

11th North Carolina; special requisition, second quarter 1864 and February–March 1864, Lemuel Hoyle service record, 11th North Carolina; property return, March 27, 1864, Francis W. Bird service record, 11th North Carolina; and special requisition, March 1864, J. W. Brown service record, 47th North Carolina, Compiled Service Records, NARA.

57. James W. Wright to parents and Fanny, February 1, 1864, Wright Collection, NCDAH; William H. Blount to friend, February 1, 1864, Steed and Phipps Family Papers, SHC-UNC.

58. Benjamin H. Freeman to father and family, February 19, 1864, in Wright, *Confederate Letters*, 34; Richard S. Webb to Jennie, February 22, 1864, Webb Family Papers, SHC-UNC.

59. James W. Wright to father, mother, and Fanny, February 18, 1864; Wright to father and mother, March 20, 1864; and Wright to Fanny, March 24, 1864, Wright Collection, NCDAH; Jordan, *North Carolina Troops*, 7:503, 539.

60. Bardolph, "Confederate Dilemma," pt. 2, p. 200; William H. Blount to friend, April 26, 1864, Steed and Phipps Family Papers, SHC-UNC; Jordan, *North Carolina Troops*, 11:290, 292.

61. Walkup journal, 43–45, SCL-DU; Underwood, "Twenty-Sixth Regiment," 379–80; Lemuel J. Hoyle to mother, March 28, 1864, Hoyle Papers, SHC-UNC; William H. Blount to friend, March 24, 1864, Steed and Phipps Family Papers, SHC-UNC.

62. Lemuel J. Hoyle to mother, April 25, 1864, Hoyle Papers, SHC-UNC; Richard S. Webb to Ma, January 15, 1864, Webb Family Papers, SHC-UNC; Linebach diary, 213, SHC-UNC; Benjamin H. Freeman to father, mother, and sisters, April 26, 1864, in Wright, *Confederate Letters*, 38.

63. Richard S. Webb to Ma, February 13, April 16, 1864; Webb to Jennie, April 25, 1864; and Jennie to Webb, June 10, 1864, Webb Family Papers, SHC-UNC.

64. William H. Blount to friend, February 1, 1864, Steed and Phipps Family Papers, SHC-UNC; Lemuel J. Hoyle to mother, undated fragment, Hoyle Papers, SHC-UNC; James W. Wright to father and mother, April 24, 1864, Wright Collection, NCDAH; Benjamin H. Freeman to father and family, April 9, 1864, in Wright, *Confederate Letters*, 36.

65. Walkup journal, 46, SCL-DU; Edward Peterson to sister, May 17, 1864, Peterson Papers, MMF.

66. Jesse L. Moffitt to Hannah, April 3, 1864, Lawrence Papers, SCL-DU; Henry C. Albright to sister, March 29, 1864, Albright Papers, GHM; Francis W. Bird to sister, April 7, 1864, Winston Papers, SHC-UNC.

67. Underwood, "Twenty-Sixth Regiment," 381, 400, 413–14; Benjamin H. Freeman to father, mother, and sisters, April 26, 1864, in Wright, *Confederate Letters*, 37, 103n; Thorp, "Forty-Seventh Regiment," 93.

68. James W. Wright to father and mother, April 26, 1864, Wright Collection, NCDAH; Robinson, "Fifty-Second Regiment," 244; Linebach diary, 228–29, SHC-UNC.

69. James W. Wright to father and mother, March 20, 1864, and Wright to father, mother, and Fanny, April 17, 1864, Wright Collection, NCDAH; Lemuel J. Hoyle to mother, March 28, 1864, Hoyle Papers, SHC-UNC.

70. Henry Clay Albright to brother, April 16, 1864, Albright Papers, NCDAH; J. L. Henry to Bet, April 1864, Henry Papers, SCL-DU; John Thomas Jones to father, April 11, 1864, Jones Papers, SHC-UNC.

71. Linebach diary, 227, 229–30, SHC-UNC; Underwood, "Twenty-Sixth Regiment," 399; John Thomas Jones to father, April 26, 1864, Jones Papers, SHC-UNC.

CHAPTER TEN

1. Rhea, *Battle of the Wilderness*, 21, 34; Linebach diary, 230, SHC-UNC; record of events, Company K, 47th North Carolina, Compiled Service Records, NARA; Henry Clay Albright diary, May 4, 1864, Albright Papers, NCDAH.

2. Rhea, *Battle of the Wilderness*, 115–22; John A. Foster reminiscences, Foster and Foster Papers, SCL-DU; Linebach diary, 232, SHC-UNC; Henry Heth to William H. Palmer, December 7, 1864, *Supplement to the Official Records*, pt. 1, 6:703; Rogers, "Additional Sketch," 110–11.

3. Henry Heth to William H. Palmer, December 7, 1864, *Supplement to the Official Records*, pt. 1, 6:703; John A. Foster reminiscences, Foster and Foster Papers, SCL-DU; Thorp, "Forty-Seventh Regiment," 94; James W. Wright to father, mother, and Fanny, May 9, 1864, Wright Collection, NCDAH.

4. Rhea, *Battle of the Wilderness*, 134–36, 193; George W. Getty to C. A. Whittier, October 13, 1864, *OR* 36(1):676; Henry Heth to William H. Palmer, December 7, 1864, *Supplement to the Official Records*, pt. 1, 6:703–4; field visit to the Wilderness, July 12–14, 1995.

5. John A. Foster reminiscences, Foster and Foster Papers, SCL-DU; Robinson, "Fifty-Second Regiment," 244–48.

6. Edward Peterson to sister, May 17, 1864, Peterson Papers, MMF.

7. Rhea, *Battle of the Wilderness*, 222–25; Winfield S. Hancock to assistant adjutant general, Army of the Potomac, February 1865, *OR* 36(1):320; George W. Getty to C. A. Whittier, October 13, 1864, *OR* 36(1):677; Frank Wheaton to Peter T. Washburn, September 1, 1864, *OR* 36(1):681–82; Lewis A. Grant to Peter T. Washburn, August 27, 1864, *OR* 36(1):696–97.

8. Morrison, *Memoirs of Henry Heth*, 182–83; Henry Heth to William H. Palmer, December 7, 1864, *Supplement to the Official Records*, pt. 1, 6:704; Stedman, "Forty-Fourth Regiment," 27; Thorp, "Forty-Seventh Regiment," 94.

9. Henry Clay Albright diary, May 5, 1864, Albright Papers, NCDAH; James W. Wright to father, mother, and Fanny, May 9, 1864, Wright Collection, NCDAH; *Raleigh Daily Confederate*, May 26, 1864; Linebach diary, 232, SHC-UNC; Underwood, "Twenty-Sixth Regiment," 382.

10. Stedman, "Forty-Fourth Regiment," 27–28; Henry Heth to William H. Palmer, December 7, 1864, *Supplement to the Official Records*, pt. 1, 6:705–6; Cockrell, *Gunner with Stonewall*, 87–88; Jordan, *North Carolina Troops*, 10:399–400.

11. Rogers, "Additional Sketch," 111; Thorp, "Forty-Seventh Regiment," 94; Martin and Outlaw, "Eleventh Regiment," 595.

12. Robinson, "Fifty-Second Regiment," 244; John A. Foster reminiscences, Foster and Foster Papers, SCL-DU.

13. Henry Heth to William H. Palmer, December 7, 1864, *Supplement to the Official Records*, pt. 1, 6:704; Martin and Outlaw, "Eleventh Regiment," 596; Henry Clay Albright diary, May 5, 1864, Albright Papers, NCDAH.

14. George W. Getty to C. A. Whittier, October 13, 1864, *OR* 36(1):677; Rhea, *Battle of the Wilderness*, 234–36; Henry Heth to William H. Palmer, December 7, 1864, *Supplement to the Official Records*, pt. 1, 6:705; Morrison, *Memoirs of Henry Heth*, 182–83.

15. Record of events, Companies F and K, 26th North Carolina, and Company K, 47th North Carolina, Compiled Service Records, NARA; Underwood, "Twenty-Sixth Regiment," 416–17; John Randolph Lane address, 1903, Lane Papers, SHC-UNC; Linebach diary, 232, SHC-UNC.

16. Morrison, *Memoirs of Henry Heth*, 183–84.

17. Rhea, *Battle of the Wilderness*, 269–70.

18. Louis G. Young, "Pettigrew-Kirkland-MacRae Brigade," 563; Henry Clay Albright diary, May 6, 1864, Albright Papers, NCDAH.

19. John A. Foster reminiscences, Foster and Foster Papers, SCL-DU.

20. G. P. Collins to Mrs. Young, May 6, 1864; Louis G. Young to mother, July 29, 1864, and Young to Henry, May 7, 1864, Gourdin Papers, EU; Louis G. Young, "Pettigrew-Kirkland-MacRae Brigade," 563.

21. Henry Clay Albright diary, May 6, 1864, Albright Papers, NCDAH; Robinson, "Fifty-Second Regiment," 245; Martin and Outlaw, "Eleventh Regiment," 595.

22. Rhea, *Battle of the Wilderness*, 283–89; Thorp, "Forty-Seventh Regiment," 94; Robert Bingham to granddaughter, March 14, 1923, Bingham Papers, SHC-UNC; Jordan, *North Carolina Troops*, 10:456; Henry Heth to William H. Palmer, December 7, 1864, *Supplement to the Official Records*, pt. 1, 6:706; record of events, Company I, 26th North Carolina, Compiled Service Records, NARA.

23. Rhea, *Battle of the Wilderness*, 290–302.

24. Ibid., 326–37; Henry Clay Albright diary, May 6, 1864, Albright Papers, NCDAH.

25. Isaac Augustus Jarratt to father, May 12, 1864, Jarratt-Puryear Family Papers, SCL-DU; Jordan, *North Carolina Troops*, 5:6–105, 7:463–601, 10:396–493, 11:244–363, 12:415–521.

26. W. W. Gaither to Edmund Walter Jones, May 26, 1864, Jones Papers, SHC-UNC; *Raleigh Daily Confederate*, May 26, 1864; Linebach diary, 233, SHC-UNC; Underwood, "Twenty-Sixth Regiment," 410.

27. Linebach diary, 233, SHC-UNC; Lloyd T. Jones to Edmund Walter Jones, July 24, 1864, and W. W. Gaither to Edmund Walter Jones, May 26, 1864, Jones Papers, SHC-UNC.

28. W. J. Blow certificate, July 11, 1864, T. C. Singletary service record, 44th North Carolina, Compiled Service Records, NARA; Jordan, *North Carolina Troops*, 10:396.

29. Rhea, *Battles for Spotsylvania Court House*, 45–54; Henry Clay Albright diary, May 7, 1864, Albright Papers, NCDAH; John A. Foster diary, May 7, 1864, Foster and Foster Papers, SCL-DU; Underwood, "Twenty-Sixth Regiment," 383.

30. Rhea, *Battles for Spotsylvania Court House*, 46–54; Henry Clay Albright diary, May 8–9, 1864, Albright Papers, NCDAH; Robinson, "Fifty-Second Regiment," 246.

31. Rhea, *Battles for Spotsylvania Court House*, 109–12; John R. Brooke to assistant adjutant general, First Division, Second Corps, November 1, 1864, *OR* 36(1):408.

32. Rhea, *Battles for Spotsylvania Court House*, 134–36; John A. Foster diary, May 10, 1864, Foster and Foster Papers, SCL-DU.

33. Rhea, *Battles for Spotsylvania Court House*, 131–34; Winfield S. Hancock to assistant adjutant general, Army of the Potomac, September 21, 1865, *OR* 36(1):332.

34. John R. Brooke to assistant adjutant general, First Division, Second Corps, November 1, 1864, *OR* 36(1):406, 409; Rhea, *Battles for Spotsylvania Court House*, 133–34.

35. Winfield S. Hancock to assistant adjutant general, Army of the Potomac, September 21, 1865, *OR* 36(1):332; John R. Brooke to assistant adjutant general, First Division, Second Corps, November 1, 1864, *OR* 36(1):408; Rhea, *Battles for Spotsylvania Court House*, 137.

36. Winfield S. Hancock to assistant adjutant general, Army of the Potomac, September 21, 1865, *OR* 36(1):332–33; John R. Brooke to assistant adjutant general, First Division, Second Corps, November 1, 1864, *OR* 36(1):409.

37. John A. Foster diary, May 10, 1864, Foster and Foster Papers, SCL-DU; Underwood, "Twenty-Sixth Regiment," 411; Martin and Outlaw, "Eleventh Regiment," 596; James W. Wright to parents and wife, May 15, 1864, Wright Collection, NCDAH; Rhea, *Battles for Spotsylvania Court House*, 139–140.

38. Henry Clay Albright diary, May 10, 1864, Albright Papers, NCDAH; *Raleigh Daily Confederate*, May 26, 1864; Rhea, *Battles for Spotsylvania Court House*, 141; Morrison, *Memoirs of Henry Heth*, 187–88.

39. Record of events, Companies F and K, 26th North Carolina, and Company K, 47th North Carolina, Compiled Service Records, NARA; Underwood, "Twenty-Sixth Regiment," 420; Jordan, *North Carolina Troops*, 7:507.

40. Edward Peterson to brother, May 11, 1864, Peterson Papers, MMF.

41. John A. Foster diary, May 11, 1864, Foster and Foster Papers, SCL-DU; Benjamin Wesley Justice to wife, May 11, 1864, Justice Papers, EU; Rhea, *Battles for Spotsylvania Court House*, 226.

42. Henry Clay Albright diary, May 11–13, 1864, Albright Papers, NCDAH; Underwood, "Twenty-Sixth Regiment," 384; Linebach diary, 233–35, SHC-UNC.

43. Linebach diary, 234, SHC-UNC; Rhea, *Battles for Spotsylvania Court House*, 294–301; Henry Heth to William H. Palmer, December 7, 1864, *Supplement to the Official Records*, pt. 1, 6:707; John A. Foster diary, May 12, 1864, Foster and Foster Papers, SCL-DU; Stedman, "Forty-Fourth Regiment," 28; Jordan, *North Carolina Troops*, 10:396, 12:447; *Raleigh Daily Confederate*, June 14, 1864.

44. John A. Foster diary, May 13–16, 1864, Foster and Foster Papers, SCL-DU; Henry Clay Albright diary, May 14–20, 1864, Albright Papers, NCDAH; Linebach diary, 235, SHC-UNC.

45. James W. Wright to Fanny and parents, May 21, 1864, Wright Collection, NCDAH; Henry Heth to William H. Palmer, December 7, 1864, *Supplement to the Official Records*, pt. 1, 6:707; Underwood, "Twenty-Sixth Regiment," 384.

46. James W. Wright to Fanny and parents, May 21, 1864, Wright Collection, NCDAH; field visit to Spotsylvania, June 25, 1997.

47. Jordan, *North Carolina Troops*, 4:6–105, 7:463–601, 10:396–493, 11:244–363, 12:415–521.

48. Rhea, *To the North Anna River*, 212–54, 267, 303–19; Miller, *North Anna Campaign*, 12, 32, 34, 40, 50; Henry Heth to William H. Palmer, December 7, 1864, *Supplement to the Official Records*, pt. 1, 6:707–8; Chapman, *More Terrible Than Victory*, 172.

49. Henry Clay Albright diary, May 23–24, 1864, Albright Papers, NCDAH; Linebach diary, 236, SHC-UNC; Benjamin H. Freeman to father, mother, and sisters, May 26, 1864, in Wright, *Confederate Letters*, 40.

50. Miller, *North Anna Campaign*, 96, 125, 128; Henry Clay Albright diary, May 25, 1864, Albright Papers, NCDAH; Linebach diary, 237, SHC-UNC; Benjamin H. Freeman to father, mother, and sisters, May 26, 1864, in Wright, *Confederate Letters*, 39.

51. Rhea, *To the North Anna River*, 367; Miller, *North Anna Campaign*, 131–34; Jordan, *North Carolina Troops*, 5:6–105, 7:463–601, 10:396–493, 11:244–363, 12:415–521.

52. Lemuel J. Hoyle to mother, May 25, 1864, Hoyle Papers, SHC-UNC; Linebach diary, 237, SHC-UNC.

53. Furgurson, *Not War but Murder*, 38–43, 53–54; Henry Clay Albright diary, May 27–28, 1864, Albright Papers, NCDAH; Linebach diary, 238–39, SHC-UNC.

54. Furgurson, *Not War but Murder*, 83; Henry Heth to William H. Palmer, December 7, 1864, *Supplement to the Official Records*, pt. 1, 6:708; Henry Clay Albright diary, May 31, 1864, Albright Papers, NCDAH; Early, *War Memoirs*, 361.

55. Furgurson, *Not War but Murder*, 111; Brady, notes; Clement Warner to Herbert, June 5, 1864, in Mrs. Lathrop E. Smith, "My Recollections of Civil War Days," 33; Mullen diary, June 1, 1864, MC; field visit to Cold Harbor, August 10, 1996.

56. J. L. Henry to Bet, June 2, 1864, Henry Papers, SCL-DU; Thorp, "Forty-Seventh Regiment," 95; Ethelbert Fairfax to Ma, June 4, 1864, Fairfax Letters, MC.

57. Ethelbert Fairfax to Ma, June 4, 1864, Fairfax Letters, MC; Brady, notes; Mullen diary, June 1, 1864, MC.

58. Brady, notes; J. L. Henry to Bet, June 2, 1864, Henry Papers, SCL-DU; Henry Heth to William H. Palmer, December 7, 1864, *Supplement to the Official Records*, pt. 1, 6:708; Linebach diary, 239, SHC-UNC.

59. Furgurson, *Not War but Murder*, 122–23, 126–27; Ambrose E. Burnside to Seth Williams, November 26, 1864, *OR* 36(1):913; Brady, notes.

60. J. L. Henry to Bet, June 2, 1864, Henry Papers, SCL-DU; Furgurson, *Not War but Murder*, 124–25; Early, *War Memoirs*, 363; William N. Pendleton to Walter H. Taylor, February 28, 1865, *OR* 36(1):1049; Morrison, *Memoirs of Henry Heth*, 188–89; Henry Heth to William H. Palmer, December 7, 1864, *Supplement to the Official Records*, pt. 1, 6:708.

61. Henry Clay Albright diary, June 2, 1864, Albright Papers, NCDAH; Morrison, *Memoirs of Henry Heth*, 188–89; Henry Heth to William H. Palmer, December 7, 1864, *Supplement to the Official Records*, pt. 1, 6:708; E. G. Marshall to T. L. Crittenden, June 1864, *OR* 36(1):926; Byron M. Cutcheon to John D. Bertolette, October 23, 1864, *OR* 36(1):971; Furgurson, *Not War but Murder*, 127–30; Brady, notes; William S. Long reminiscences, fols. 1235–42, Long Papers, LC. Long's reminiscences are detailed and colorful, but much of them are unreliable and not supported by other accounts of the fight on June 2.

62. Furgurson, *Not War but Murder*, 130; Thorp, "Forty-Seventh Regiment," 96;

Henry Clay Albright diary, June 2, 1864, Albright Papers, NCDAH; Louis G. Young, "Pettigrew-Kirkland-MacRae Brigade," 563; Welsh, *Medical Histories of Confederate Generals*, 127; Robinson, "Fifty-Second Regiment," 246; Early, *War Memoirs*, 363.

63. Linebach diary, 240, SHC-UNC; *Fayetteville Observer*, June 13, 1864; record of events, Companies F and K, 26th North Carolina, and Company K, 47th North Carolina, Compiled Service Records, NARA; Benjamin H. Freeman to father, mother, and sisters, June 5, 1864, in Wright, *Confederate Letters*, 40; Rogers, "Additional Sketch," 111; Jordan, *North Carolina Troops*, 5:6–105.

64. Furgurson, *Not War but Murder*, 153–54; Ambrose E. Burnside to Seth Williams, November 26, 1864, *OR* 36(1):914; Henry Heth to William H. Palmer, December 7, 1864, *Supplement to the Official Records*, pt. 1, 6:709; Early, *War Memoirs*, 363; Henry Clay Albright diary, June 3, 1864, Albright Papers, NCDAH; Ethelbert Fairfax to Ma, June 4, 1864, Fairfax Letters, MC.

65. Henry Heth to William H. Palmer, December 7, 1864, *Supplement to the Official Records*, pt. 1, 6:709; Early, *War Memoirs*, 363; Henry Clay Albright diary, June 3–5, 1864, Albright Papers, NCDAH; Thorp, "Forty-Seventh Regiment," 96; Linebach diary, 240–41, SHC-UNC.

66. Lemuel J. Hoyle to mother, June 5, 1864, Hoyle Papers, SHC-UNC.

67. Henry Clay Albright diary, June 5–9, 1864, Albright Papers, NCDAH; Linebach diary, 241–42, SHC-UNC; John A. Foster diary, June 6–7, 1864, Foster and Foster Papers, SCL-DU.

68. Jordan, *North Carolina Troops*, 5:6–105, 7:463–601, 10:396–493, 11:244–363, 12:415–521; Francis W. Bird to sister, June 4, 1864, Winston Papers, SHC-UNC.

69. Henry Clay Albright diary, June 9–12, 1864, Albright Papers, NCDAH; Robinson, "Fifty-Second Regiment," 247; Linebach diary, 242, SHC-UNC.

70. James W. Wright to parents and Fanny, June 12, 1864, Wright Collection, NCDAH; McGee, "Twenty-Sixth Regiment," 146; Robert Ransom to Adjutant General, June 12, 1864, *OR* 36(3):898.

71. Underwood, "Twenty-Sixth Regiment," 387.

72. Rodman Smith to father, June 12, 1864, Smith Letters, HSD.

73. Henry Gawthrop to unidentified, June 12, 1864, and Gawthrop diary, June 11, 1864, HSD; Rodman Smith to father, June 12, 1864, Smith Letters, HSD; Jordan, *North Carolina Troops*, 12:468.

74. Trudeau, *Last Citadel*, 16–25.

75. Henry Clay Albright diary, June 12–14, 1864, Albright Papers, NCDAH; Linebach diary, 243–44, SHC-UNC.

76. Jordan, *North Carolina Troops*, 5:6–105, 7:463–601, 10:396–493, 11:244–363, 12:415–521.

CHAPTER ELEVEN

1. Trudeau, *Last Citadel*, 16–55.

2. Henry Clay Albright diary, June 17–18, 1864, Albright Papers, NCDAH; Linebach diary, 244–45, SHC-UNC; Robinson, "Fifty-Second Regiment," 247.

3. Benjamin H. Freeman to father, mother, and sisters, June 19, 1864, in Wright, *Con-*

federate Letters, 44; Henry Clay Albright diary, n.d., 1864, Albright Papers, NCDAH; inventory of effects, n.d., William Wyatt service record, 26th North Carolina, Compiled Service Records, NARA.

4. Stedman, "Forty-Fourth Regiment," 29; Linebach diary, 246, 249, SHC-UNC; Robinson, "Fifty-Second Regiment," 247.

5. Trudeau, *Last Citadel*, 58; George H. Sharpe to A. A. Humphreys, July 1, 1864, *OR* 40(2):563; Chapman, *More Terrible Than Victory*, 203–5; James W. Wright to parents and Fanny, June 29, 1864, Wright Collection, NCDAH.

6. Special Orders No. 151, Army of Northern Virginia, June 27, 1864, *OR* 40(2):694.

7. Benjamin H. Freeman to father and the rest, July 1864, in Wright, *Confederate Letters*, 44–45; James W. Wright to parents and Fanny, June 29, 1864, Wright Collection, NCDAH; Stedman, "Forty-Fourth Regiment," 29; Louis G. Young, "Pettigrew-Kirkland-MacRae Brigade," 563.

8. Lemuel J. Hoyle to mother, July 29, 1864, Hoyle Papers, SHC-UNC; Linebach diary, 250, SHC-UNC.

9. Stedman, *Memorial Address*, 14; Louis G. Young, "Pettigrew-Kirkland-MacRae Brigade," 564.

10. Stedman, *Memorial Address*, 5–9, 16; Stedman, "Forty-Fourth Regiment," 27; Powell, *Dictionary of North Carolina Biography*, 4:193–94; William MacRae to brother, June 18, 1863, August 16, 1861, and March 15, 1862, MacRae Papers, SCL-DU.

11. William MacRae to brother, July 9, 1864, MacRae Papers, SCL-DU; Stedman, *Memorial Address*, 12–13.

12. Underwood, "Twenty-Sixth Regiment," 385; Martin and Outlaw, "Eleventh Regiment," 597.

13. John C. Babcock to A. A. Humphreys, July 8, 1864, *OR* 40(3):75–76; John A. Foster diary, July 8–12, 1864, Foster and Foster Papers, SCL-DU.

14. Linebach diary, 253, 255–56, SHC-UNC.

15. Cavanaugh and Marvel, *Battle of the Crater*, 28–32; Lee to R. H. Anderson, July 27, 1864, *OR* 40(3):809; Lemuel J. Hoyle to mother, July 29, 1864, Hoyle Papers, SHC-UNC; Linebach diary, 256, SHC-UNC; Benjamin H. Freeman to father and family, July 29, 1864, in Wright, *Confederate Letters*, 48; John A. Foster diary, July 27, 28, 1864, Foster and Foster Papers, SCL-DU; Robinson, "Fifty-Second Regiment," 247; Henry Heth to William H. Palmer, December 7, 1864, *Supplement to the Official Records*, pt. 1, 7:330.

16. Linebach diary, 256, SHC-UNC; James W. Wright letter fragment, [July 29, 1864], Wright Collection, NCDAH; *Raleigh Daily Confederate*, August 3, 1864.

17. Winfield S. Hancock to A. A. Humphreys, July 29, 1864, *OR* 40(3):598; Benjamin H. Freeman to father and family, July 29, 1864, in Wright, *Confederate Letters*, 49, 98n.

18. Cavanaugh and Marvel, *Battle of the Crater*, 36; John A. Foster diary, July 30, 1864, Foster and Foster Papers, SCL-DU; Robinson, "Fifty-Second Regiment," 247; Linebach diary, 257, SHC-UNC; Lemuel J. Hoyle to mother, August 8, 1864, Hoyle Papers, SHC-UNC; James W. Wright to Fanny, August 2, 1864, Wright Collection, NCDAH; Edward Peterson to sister, August 1, 1864, Peterson Papers, MMF; Isaac Augustus Jarratt to father, August 3, 1864, Jarratt-Puryear Family Papers, SCL-DU.

19. R. M. Tuttle to William H. S. Burgwyn, September 29, 1900, Burgwyn Papers, NCDAH; Robinson, "Fifty-Second Regiment," 247; Benjamin H. Freeman to father and

mother, August 6, 10, 1864, in Wright, *Confederate Letters*, 49, 51; Linebach diary, 256–57, SHC-UNC.

20. J. S. Bartlett reminiscences, 11–12, Bartlett Papers, SHC-UNC; McGee, "Twenty-Sixth Regiment," 150–51.

21. Richard S. Webb to Jennie, August 13, 1864, Webb Family Papers, SHC-UNC.

22. J. S. Bartlett reminiscences, 12, Bartlett Papers, SHC-UNC; Martin and Outlaw, "Eleventh Regiment," 597–98; Robinson, "Fifty-Second Regiment," 248; Fred Nash inspection report, August 15, 1864, Confederate Inspection Reports, NARA.

23. Louis G. Young to mother, July 29, 1864, Gourdin Papers, EU; Benjamin H. Freeman to father and mother, August 10, 1864, in Wright, *Confederate Letters*, 52.

24. Louis G. Young to mother, August 15, 1864, and Henry Bryan to Robert Newman Gourdin, August 23, 1864, Gourdin Papers, EU; Powell, *Dictionary of North Carolina Biography*, 4:194; Pierre G. T. Beauregard to Samuel Cooper, August 17, 21, 1864, *OR* 42(2):1183, 1194.

25. Powell, *Dictionary of North Carolina Biography*, 3:371–72.

26. Trudeau, *Last Citadel*, 146, 157–62, 165–66; Horn, *Destruction of the Weldon Railroad*, 9, 55, 57–59, 61–65, 78–79, 84–85, 88; Henry Heth to William H. Palmer, December 7, 1864, *Supplement to the Official Records*, pt. 1, 7:473; field visit to Globe Tavern, July 7, 1994; Morrison, *Memoirs of Henry Heth*, 190–91.

27. Trudeau, *Last Citadel*, 170; Henry Heth to William H. Palmer, December 7, 1864, *Supplement to the Official Records*, pt. 1, 7:473; Frederick Winthrop to W. W. Swan, August 22, 1864, *OR* 42(1):475.

28. Louis G. Young, "Pettigrew-Kirkland-MacRae Brigade," 564; T. W. Setser to W. A. Setser, August 28, 1864, in Mast, "Setser Letters," pt. 4, p. 15; *Raleigh North Carolina Standard*, September 2, 1864.

29. Robinson, "Fifty-Second Regiment," 248; J. S. Bartlett reminiscences, 12, Bartlett Papers, SHC-UNC; T. W. Setser to W. A. Setser, August 28, 1864, in Mast, "Setser Letters," pt. 4, p. 16.

30. Trudeau, *Last Citadel*, 171; Horn, *Destruction of the Weldon Railroad*, 91–92; Frederick Winthrop to W. W. Swan, August 22, 1864, *OR* 42(1):475; J. S. Bartlett reminiscences, 12, Bartlett Papers, SHC-UNC; T. W. Setser to W. A. Setser, August 28, 1864, in Mast, "Setser Letters," pt. 4, p. 16; John A. Foster diary, August 21, 1864, Foster and Foster Papers, SCL-DU.

31. Horn, *Destruction of the Weldon Railroad*, 94, 99–100; Henry Heth to William H. Palmer, December 7, 1864, *Supplement to the Official Records*, pt. 1, 7:474.

32. Horn, *Destruction of the Weldon Railroad*, 96, 100; Trudeau, *Last Citadel*, 172; T. W. Setser to W. A. Setser, August 28, 1864, in Mast, "Setser Letters," pt. 4, p. 16; John A. Foster diary, August 21, 1864, Foster and Foster Papers, SCL-DU.

33. Louis G. Young, "Pettigrew-Kirkland-MacRae Brigade," 564; Horn, *Destruction of the Weldon Railroad*, 100.

34. Horn, *Destruction of the Weldon Railroad*, 101; John A. Foster diary, August 21, 1864, Foster and Foster Papers, SCL-DU; T. W. Setser to W. A. Setser, August 28, 1864, in Mast, "Setser Letters," pt. 4, p. 16; *Raleigh North Carolina Standard*, September 2, 1864; Robinson, "Fifty-Second Regiment," 248; Edward Peterson to brother, August 22, 1864, Peterson Papers, MMF; Jordan, *North Carolina Troops*, 7:490.

35. T. W. Setser to W. A. Setser, August 28, 1864, in Mast, "Setser Letters," pt. 4, p. 16; Horn, *Destruction of the Weldon Railroad*, 103; J. S. Bartlett reminiscences, 13, Bartlett Papers, SHC-UNC; Martin and Outlaw, "Eleventh Regiment," 599.

36. Waddell, "How Woodson Garrett Was Captured and Escaped from the Yankees," Reminiscences, Civil War Collection, NCDAH; Jordan, *North Carolina Troops*, 5:69.

37. John A. Foster diary, August 21, 1864, Foster and Foster Papers, SCL-DU; T. W. Setser to W. A. Setser, August 28, 1864, in Mast, "Setser Letters," pt. 4, p. 16.

38. Louis G. Young to mother, August 24, 1864, Gourdin Papers, EU; John A. Foster diary, August 21, 1864, Foster and Foster Papers, SCL-DU; Underwood, "Twenty-Sixth Regiment," 409; *Raleigh North Carolina Standard*, September 2, 1864; Jordan, *North Carolina Troops*, 7:504; James W. Wright to father and Fanny, August 27, 1864, Wright Collection, NCDAH.

39. Edward Peterson to brother, August 22, 1864, Peterson Papers, MMF; Jordan, *North Carolina Troops*, 7:490.

40. Richard S. Webb to Jennie, August [September 1], 1864, Webb Family Papers, SHC-UNC.

41. John A. Foster diary, August 22–23, 1864, Foster and Foster Papers, SCL-DU; John McEntee to A. A. Humphreys, August 23, 1864, *OR* 42(2):420.

42. Edward Peterson to brother, August 22, 1864, Peterson Papers, MMF; Jordan, *North Carolina Troops*, 7:506.

43. Horn, *Destruction of the Weldon Railroad*, 117, 119–20; Trudeau, *Last Citadel*, 176–79, 182.

44. John A. Foster diary, August 24, 1864, Foster and Foster Papers, SCL-DU; Benjamin Wesley Justice to wife, August 30, 1864, Justice Papers, EU; Horn, *Destruction of the Weldon Railroad*, 120–21; Lemuel J. Hoyle to mother, August 29, 1864, Hoyle Papers, SCH-UNC; Robinson, "Fifty-Second Regiment," 248.

45. Henry Heth to William H. Palmer, December 7, 1864, *Supplement to the Official Records*, pt. 1, 7:474; Benjamin Wesley Justice to wife, August 30, 1864, Justice Papers, EU; Robinson, "Fifty-Second Regiment," 248.

46. Horn, *Destruction of the Weldon Railroad*, 128–29, 137–38, 155–57; Henry Heth to William H. Palmer, December 7, 1864, *Supplement to the Official Records*, pt. 1, 7:474; Bearss, "Battle of Reams' Station," 17, PNB; field visit to Reams Station, August 30, 1995; Chapman, *More Terrible Than Victory*, 226.

47. Stedman, *Memorial Address*, 21–23.

48. Louis G. Young, "Pettigrew-Kirkland-MacRae Brigade," 565.

49. Thorp, "Forty-Seventh Regiment," 97; Stedman, *Memorial Address*, 20; Henry Heth to William H. Palmer, December 7, 1864, *Supplement to the Official Records*, pt. 1, 7:475.

50. Horn, *Destruction of the Weldon Railroad*, 122, 127, 157.

51. Ibid., 154–55; Adams to niece, December 7, 1911, Military Collection, Civil War Collection, NCDAH; Underwood, "Twenty-Sixth Regiment," 388–89. Chapman, in *More Terrible Than Victory*, 217–18, 335, argues that Heth's odd insistence on waving a regimental flag to inspire MacRae's men took place on August 21 at Globe Tavern. But Underwood is quite clear that it took place at Reams Station, and he is a very reliable source. Also, given the excitement that everyone felt just before the attack, it seems more likely that the incident took place at Reams Station than at Globe Tavern.

52. Louis G. Young, "Pettigrew-Kirkland-MacRae Brigade," 565–66; Henry Heth to William H. Palmer, December 7, 1864, *Supplement to the Official Records*, pt. 1, 7:475; Stedman, *Memorial Address*, 20.

53. Horn, *Destruction of the Weldon Railroad*, 156; Stedman, "Forty-Fourth Regiment," 30; Louis G. Young, "Pettigrew-Kirkland-MacRae Brigade," 565–66.

54. Horn, *Destruction of the Weldon Railroad*, 156–58; Stedman, "Forty-Fourth Regiment," 30–31; *Raleigh North Carolina Standard*, September 7, 1864.

55. Horn, *Destruction of the Weldon Railroad*, 158.

56. Ibid.; Stedman, *Memorial Address*, 21–22; Stedman, "Forty-Fourth Regiment," 31.

57. Horn, *Destruction of the Weldon Railroad*, 158, 162–63.

58. Ibid., 171; Trudeau, *Last Citadel*, 189; Henry Heth to William H. Palmer, December 7, 1864, *Supplement to the Official Records*, pt. 1, 7:478; Jordan, *North Carolina Troops*, 11:322; Benjamin Wesley Justice to wife, August 30, 1864, Justice Papers, EU; A. S. Webb to Ma, August 27, 1864, Webb Family Papers, SHC-UNC.

59. Benjamin Wesley Justice to wife, August 30, 1864, Justice Papers, EU; James W. Wright to father and Fanny, August 27, 1864, Wright Collection, NCDAH; T. W. Setser to W. A. Setser, September 2, 1864, in Mast, "Setser Letters," pt. 4, p. 16; Stedman, *Memorial Address*, 24.

60. Jordan, *North Carolina Troops*, 5:6–105, 7:463–601, 10:396–493, 11:244–363, 12:415–521; Benjamin Wesley Justice to wife, August 30, 1864, Justice Papers, EU; Lemuel J. Hoyle to mother, August 29, 1864, Hoyle Papers, SHC-UNC; John C. Warlick to E. R. Outlaw, December 1, 1901, Warlick Letters, SCL-DU; undated newspaper clipping, Winston Papers, SHC-UNC; Martin and Outlaw, "Eleventh Regiment," 599.

61. Jordan, *North Carolina Troops*, 7:463–601; T. W. Setser to W. A. Setser, August 28, 1864, in Mast, "Setser Letters," pt. 4, p. 16; Edward Peterson to sister, August 28, 1864, Peterson Papers, MMF; Underwood, "Twenty-Sixth Regiment," 389–90, 411; biographical sketch and Adams to niece, December 7, 1911, Military Collection, Civil War Collection, NCDAH. Peterson, in his August 28 letter, revealed a loss for the 26th different from that given in the service records—four killed and twenty-four wounded.

62. Jordan, *North Carolina Troops*, 10:396–493, 11:244–363, 12:415–521; Benjamin Wesley Justice to wife, August 30, 1864, Justice Papers, EU; Thorp, "Forty-Seventh Regiment," 97. A. S. Webb reported heavier casualties for the 44th North Carolina—two killed and twenty wounded—than do the service records; see A. S. Webb to Ma, August 27, 1864, Webb Family Papers, SHC-UNC.

63. Henry Heth to William H. Palmer, December 7, 1864, *Supplement to the Official Records*, pt. 1, 7:475; Horn, *Destruction of the Weldon Railroad*, 175; *Raleigh North Carolina Standard*, September 2, 1864.

64. Benjamin Wesley Justice to wife, August 30, 1864, Justice Papers, EU.

65. J. S. Bartlett reminiscences, 13, Bartlett Papers, SHC-UNC; Samuel Finley Harper to sister, August 26, 1864, Harper Papers, NCDAH; Stedman, *Memorial Address*, 21; James W. Wright to father and Fanny, August 27, 1864, Wright Collection, NCDAH; John A. Foster diary, August 25, 1864, Foster and Foster Papers, SCL-DU; T. W. Setser to W. A. Setser, August 28, 1864, in Mast, "Setser Letters," pt. 4, p. 16.

66. Henry Heth to William H. Palmer, December 7, 1864, *Supplement to the Official*

Records, pt. 1, 7:476; Linebach diary, 262–63, SHC-UNC; Edward Peterson to sister, August 28, 1864, Peterson Papers, MMF.

67. Linebach diary, 262–63, SHC-UNC; Edward Peterson to sister, August 28, 1864, Peterson Papers, MMF.

68. T. W. Setser to W. A. Setser, August 28, September 2, 1864, in Mast, "Setser Letters," pt. 4, p. 16; Jordan, *North Carolina Troops*, 7:545.

69. James W. Wright to father and Fanny, August 27, 1864, Wright Collection, NCDAH.

CHAPTER TWELVE

1. Robinson, "Fifty-Second Regiment," 249; Sommers, *Richmond Redeemed*, 180; Edward Peterson to niece, September 16, 1984, Peterson Papers, MMF.

2. James W. Wright to Fanny, September 2, October 2, 1864, and undated fragment, and James W. Wright to W. W. Wright, undated fragment, Wright Collection, NCDAH; Jordan, *North Carolina Troops*, 7:506.

3. Benjamin Wesley Justice to wife, August 30, 1864, Justice Papers, EU; Edward Peterson to sister, September 12, 1864, and Peterson to niece, September 16, 1864, Peterson Papers, MMF.

4. Chapman, *More Terrible Than Victory*, 234–35; Jordan, *North Carolina Troops*, 7:75.

5. Richard S. Webb to Jennie, September 27, 1864, Webb Family Papers, SHC-UNC.

6. Benjamin Wesley Justice to wife, September 1, 1864, Justice papers, EU; Young to James A. Seddon, September 13, 1864, J. J. Young service record, 26th North Carolina, Compiled Service Records, NARA.

7. Garrison, *Civil War Hostages*, 177–78, 180–82; MacRae, "Confederate Prisoners at Morris Island."

8. R. J. Wingate inspection report, September 1864, *OR* 42(2):1274–75; strength of MacRae's brigade, September 30, 1864, *OR* 42(2):1308; organization of Heth's division, September 30, 1864, *OR* 42(2):1309.

9. Sommers, *Richmond Redeemed*, 13–177, 201, 207, 235, 250–51, 268–69, 274–76, 282, 288.

10. Martin and Outlaw, "Eleventh Regiment," 600; Sommers, *Richmond Redeemed*, 288; John I. Curtin to Samuel Wright, October 17, 1864, *OR* 42(1):582.

11. Sommers, *Richmond Redeemed*, 288–89, 305; Martin and Outlaw, "Eleventh Regiment," 600; Lafayette W. Lord to T. Edward Ames, November 1, 1864, *OR* 42(1):585.

12. Benjamin H. Freeman to father, October 4, 1864, in Wright, *Confederate Letters*, 54; A. S. Webb to Ma, October 6, 1864, Webb Family Papers, SHC-UNC; Henry Heth to William H. Palmer, December 7, 1864, *Supplement to the Official Records*, pt. 1, 7:478; Lafayette W. Lord to T. Edward Ames, November 1, 1864, *OR* 42(1):585.

13. Martin and Outlaw, "Eleventh Regiment," 599–600; J. S. Bartlett reminiscences, 13, Bartlett Papers, SHC-UNC.

14. Linebach diary, 268, SHC-UNC; record of events, Company K, 26th North Carolina, Compiled Service Records, NARA; A. S. Webb to Ma, October 6, 1864, Webb Family Papers, SHC-UNC.

15. Sommers, *Richmond Redeemed*, 307–9; Henry Heth to William H. Palmer, December 7, 1864, *Supplement to the Official Records*, pt. 1, 7:477.

16. Sommers, *Richmond Redeemed*, 250, 316, 326–34; A. S. Webb to Ma, October 6, 1864, Webb Family Papers, SHC-UNC.

17. Sommers, *Richmond Redeemed*, 334–36; James Grindlay to C. E. La Motte, October 3, 1864, *OR* 42(1):478; Henry Heth to William H. Palmer, December 7, 1864, *Supplement to the Official Records*, pt. 1, 7:477.

18. Sommers, *Richmond Redeemed*, 336, 355, 375; A. S. Webb to Ma, October 6, 1864, Webb Family Papers, SHC-UNC; Jordan, *North Carolina Troops*, 10:490.

19. R. S. Webb to sisters, October 3, 1864, and A. S. Webb to Ma, October 6, 1864, Webb Family Papers, SHC-UNC; Edward Peterson to sister, October 3, 1864, Peterson Papers, MMF; Benjamin H. Freeman to father, October 4, 1864, in Wright, *Confederate Letters*, 54.

20. Underwood, "Twenty-Sixth Regiment," 389; D. C. Murchison to Dr. Albright, October 2, 20, 1864, and A. R. Johnson to Dr. Albright, January 5, 1864, Albright Papers, NCDAH.

21. Sommers, *Richmond Redeemed*, 360, 369, 378–79, 381, 385, 388, 393; Henry Heth to William H. Palmer, December 7, 1864, and Joel R. Griffin to Henry B. McClellan, October 12, 1864, *Supplement to the Official Records*, pt. 1, 7:477, 511.

22. Louis G. Young, "Pettigrew-Kirkland-MacRae Brigade," 566; Sommers, *Richmond Redeemed*, 393–96.

23. Sommers, *Richmond Redeemed*, 401–13; A. S. Webb to Ma, October 6, 1864, Webb Family Papers, SHC-UNC.

24. Sommers, *Richmond Redeemed*, 416; R. S. Webb to sisters, October 3, 1864, and A. S. Webb to Ma, October 6, 1864, Webb Family Papers, SHC-UNC.

25. Jordan, *North Carolina Troops*, 5:6–105, 7:463–601, 10:396–493, 11:244–363, 12:415–521. See Sommers, *Richmond Redeemed*, 495, for a different report of brigade losses, totaling 243. See also Edward Peterson to sister, October 3, 1864, Peterson Papers, MMF; Peterson reported that the 26th North Carolina lost 10 killed and wounded on September 30 at Jones's farm and 8 to 10 men on October 1 along the Squirrel Level Road.

26. Linebach diary, 268, SHC-UNC.

27. James W. Wright to Fanny, October 2, 1864, Wright Collection, NCDAH; Edward Peterson to sister, October 3, 1864, Peterson Papers, MMF; Louis G. Young to mother, October 6, 1864, Gourdin Papers, EU.

28. Henry Heth to William H. Palmer, February 1, 1865, *Supplement to the Official Records*, pt. 1, 7:479; Lemuel J. Hoyle to Mr. Lewis, October 13, 1864, and Hoyle to mother, October 20, 1864, Hoyle Papers, SHC-UNC; John G. Parke to A. A. Humphreys, October 4, 1864, *OR* 42(3):76; J. C. Babcock to A. A. Humphreys, October 8, 1864, *OR* 42(3):120.

29. Lemuel J. Hoyle to mother, October 20, 1864, Hoyle Papers, SHC-UNC.

30. Trudeau, *Last Citadel*, 219, 222–27, 234, 242–43; Henry Heth to William H. Palmer, February 1, 1865, *Supplement to the Official Records*, pt. 1, 7:481; Byron R. Pierce to J. P. Finkelmeier, October 30, 1864, *OR* 42(1):367; John Pulford to C. W. Forrester, October 30, 1864, *OR* 42(1):374; Benjamin M. Peck to C. W. Forrester, October 31, 1864, *OR*

42(1):388; Chapman, *More Terrible Than Victory*, 256 – 57; Francis A. Walker, *History of the Second Army Corps*, 622.

31. Trudeau, *Last Citadel*, 243, 246 – 47; Henry Heth to William H. Palmer, February 1, 1865, *Supplement to the Official Records*, pt. 1, 7:479 – 82, 484; Robinson, "Fifty-Second Regiment," 250; Powell, *Dictionary of North Carolina Biography*, 4:194; Chapman, *More Terrible Than Victory*, 256; Fred Nash inspection report, October 1864, Confederate Inspection Reports, NARA.

32. Trudeau, *Last Citadel*, 244 – 45; Robinson, "Fifty-Second Regiment," 250; Byron R. Pierce to J. P. Finkelmeier, October 30, 1864, *OR* 42(1):367; John Pulford to C. W. Forrester, October 30, 1864, *OR* 42(1):374; Chapman, *More Terrible Than Victory*, 258 – 60; J. S. Bartlett reminiscences, 14, Bartlett Papers, SHC-UNC.

33. Byron R. Pierce to J. P. Finkelmeier, October 30, 1864, *OR* 42(1):367; Chapman, *More Terrible Than Victory*, 259; Francis A. Walker, *History of the Second Army Corps*, 622.

34. J. S. Bartlett reminiscences, 14, Bartlett Papers, SHC-UNC; Robert McAllister to A. H. Embler, October 30, 1864, *OR* 42(1):396; Stedman, "Forty-Fourth Regiment," 32; Chapman, *More Terrible Than Victory*, 260; Francis A. Walker, *History of the Second Army Corps*, 622.

35. Regis de Trobriand to J. P. Finkelmeier, October 30, 1864, *OR* 42(1):359; Stedman, "Forty-Fourth Regiment," 32 – 34; Jordan, *North Carolina Troops*, 7:502, 10:444; Underwood, "Twenty-Sixth Regiment," 389; Robinson, "Fifty-Second Regiment," 250.

36. Lemuel J. Hoyle to mother, November 5, 1864, Hoyle Papers, SHC-UNC; Thorp, "Forty-Seventh Regiment," 98; Stedman, "Forty-Fourth Regiment," 31.

37. Letter from member of 11th North Carolina, October 29, 1864, *Raleigh Daily Confederate*, November 5, 1864; J. S. Bartlett reminiscences, 14, Bartlett Papers, SHC-UNC; Stedman, "Forty-Fourth Regiment," 32; Jordan, *North Carolina Troops*, 10:399; Lemuel J. Hoyle to mother, November 5, 1864, Hoyle Papers, SHC-UNC.

38. Regis de Trobriand to J. P. Finkelmeier, October 30, 1864, *OR* 42(1):360; Byron R. Pierce to J. P. Finkelmeier, October 30, 1864, *OR* 42(1):367; N. Shatswell to C. W. Forrester, October 30, 1864, *OR* 42(1):372; John Pulford to C. W. Forrester, October 30, 1864, *OR* 42(1):374; Robert McAllister to A. H. Embler, October 30, 1864, *OR* 42(1):396; Trudeau, *Last Citadel*, 245 – 47; Isaac Augustus Jarratt to John, November 14, 7, 1864, Jarratt-Puryear Family Papers, SCL-DU.

39. Underwood, "Twenty-Sixth Regiment," 412; Adams to niece, December 7, 1911, Military Collection, Civil War Collection, NCDAH.

40. Trudeau, *Last Citadel*, 249 – 51; Henry Heth to William H. Palmer, February 1, 1865, *Supplement to the Official Records*, pt. 1, 7:483 – 84; Robinson, "Fifty-Second Regiment," 250.

41. Henry Heth to William H. Palmer, February 1, 1865, *Supplement to the Official Records*, pt. 1, 7:484; Stedman, *Memorial Address*, 17; Thorp, "Forty-Seventh Regiment," 98.

42. Jordan, *North Carolina Troops*, 5:6 – 105, 7:463 – 601, 10:396 – 493, 11:244 – 363, 12:415 – 521; Louis G. Young to mother, November 17, 1864, Gourdin Papers, EU; Joseph D. Joyner to Mrs. I. H. Joyner, November 7, 1864, Joyner Family Papers, SHC-UNC.

43. Lemuel J. Hoyle to mother, November 5, 1864, Hoyle Papers, SHC-UNC; letter

from member of 11th North Carolina, October 29, 1864, *Raleigh Daily Confederate*, November 5, 1864; Isaac Augustus Jarratt to John, November 14, 1864, Jarratt-Puryear Family Papers, SCL-DU; Jordan, *North Carolina Troops*, 5:6–105, 7:463–601, 10:396–493, 11:244–363, 12:415–521; Richard S. Webb to sister, October 28, 1864, Webb Family Papers, SHC-UNC.

44. Jordan, *North Carolina Troops*, 5:6–105, 7:463–601, 10:396–493, 11:244–363, 12:415–521.

45. John C. Babcock to A. A. Humphreys, November 4, 19, 1864, *OR* 42(3):508, 659; Jordan, *North Carolina Troops*, 7:463–601; Isaac Augustus Jarratt to John, November 14, 1864, Jarratt-Puryear Family Papers, SCL-DU.

46. Lemuel J. Hoyle to Mr. Lewis, November 22, 1864, Hoyle Papers, SHC-UNC; Louis G. Young to mother, November 17, 1864, Gourdin Papers, EU; Fred Nash inspection report, November 24, 1864, Confederate Inspection Reports, NARA.

47. Lemuel J. Hoyle to Mr. Lewis, November 22, 1864, and Hoyle to mother, November 12, 1864, Hoyle Papers, SHC-UNC; Linebach diary, 271, SHC-UNC.

48. Linebach diary, 272, SHC-UNC.

49. Powell, *Dictionary of North Carolina Biography*, 4:194; William MacRae to brother, November 23, 1864, MacRae Papers, SCL-DU.

50. Organization of MacRae's brigade, November 30, 1864, *OR* 42(3):1240; P. A. James to A. C. Myers, December 6, 1864, Myers Papers, NCDAH.

51. Louis G. Young to mother, November 17, 1864, Gourdin Papers, EU; J. McEntee to A. A. Humphreys, November 22, 1864, *OR* 42(3):681.

52. Jordan, *North Carolina Troops*, 5:6–105, 7:463–601, 10:396–493, 11:244–363, 12:415–521; John C. Warlick to E. R. Outlaw, December 1, 1901, Warlick Letters, SCL-DU.

53. Trudeau, *Last Citadel*, 264–71, 277–79, 283; *Supplement to the Official Records*, pt. 1, 7:487–88; Linebach diary, 273–74, SHC-UNC.

54. Robinson, "Fifty-Second Regiment," 250; Trudeau, *Last Citadel*, 285; record of events, regimental staff and Company E, 26th North Carolina, Compiled Service Records, NARA; Lemuel J. Hoyle to mother, December 19, 1864, Hoyle Papers, SHC-UNC; Jordan, *North Carolina Troops*, 5:6–105, 7:463–601, 10:396–493, 11:244–363, 12:415–521.

CHAPTER THIRTEEN

1. Robinson, "Fifty-Second Regiment," 250; Lemuel J. Hoyle to mother, December 19, 1864, Hoyle Papers, SHC-UNC; Nelson Miles to Major Cairncross, December 31, 1864, J. R. Foster service record, 26th North Carolina, Compiled Service Records, NARA; Jordan, *North Carolina Troops*, 7:498–99.

2. William Henry Blount to friend, December 24, 1864, Steed and Phipps Family Papers, SHC-UNC; Linebach diary, 284–85, SHC-UNC.

3. Linebach diary, 274–79, 283–85, SHC-UNC.

4. Benjamin Wesley Justice endorsement on inspection reports, January 27, February 27, 1865; L. P. Warren endorsement on inspection report, February 27, 1865; and John H.

Robinson inspection report, February 27, 1865, Confederate Inspection Reports, NARA.

5. Jordan, *North Carolina Troops*, 5:6–105, 7:463–601, 10:396–493, 11:244–363, 12:415–521. Heth reported different losses for MacRae's brigade: 228 killed, 479 wounded, and 543 captured, for a total of 1,627; see report of casualties in Heth's Division, Heth Papers, MC; William Henry Blount to friend, January 16, 1865, Steed and Phipps Family Papers, SHC-UNC.

6. Benjamin H. Freeman to father, January 28, 1865, in Wright, *Confederate Letters*, 56; John L. Babcock to George G. Meade, January 15, 1865, *OR* 46(2):135; Greene, *Breaking the Backbone of the Rebellion*, 131n.

7. William Henry Blount to friend, January 16, 1865, Steed and Phipps Family Papers, SHC-UNC; Underwood, "Twenty-Sixth Regiment," 421.

8. Benjamin H. Freeman to father, February 1, 1865, in Wright, *Confederate Letters*, 58–59; Thorp, "Forty-Seventh Regiment," 98; Linebach diary, 289, SHC-UNC.

9. Stedman, "Forty-Fourth Regiment," 33–34; Bingham to granddaughter, March 14, 1923, Bingham Papers, SHC-UNC.

10. Trudeau, *Last Citadel*, 312, 314.

11. Thorp, "Forty-Seventh Regiment," 99; Trudeau, *Last Citadel*, 314–15; Louis G. Young, "Pettigrew-Kirkland-MacRae Brigade," 567–68.

12. Trudeau, *Last Citadel*, 314–15; Louis G. Young, "Pettigrew-Kirkland-MacRae Brigade," 568; Powell, *Dictionary of North Carolina Biography*, 4:194; Jordan, *North Carolina Troops*, 5:6–105, 7:463–601, 10:396–493, 11:244–363, 12:415–521.

13. Trudeau, *Last Citadel*, 318, 322; Robinson, "Fifty-Second Regiment," 251; Linebach diary, 287, SHC-UNC.

14. William S. Long reminiscences, fols. 1243, 1255, 1257–59, 1271, 1275, Long Papers, LC; Jordan, *North Carolina Troops*, 10:397.

15. Record of events, Company G, 26th North Carolina, Compiled Service records, NARA; Horatio G. Wright to Alexander S. Webb, February 21, 1865, *OR* 46(2):615.

16. William Henry Blount to Bettie, February 24, 1865, and February 1865, Steed and Phipps Family Papers, SHC-UNC.

17. Lewis, "Life and Times of Thomas Bailey," 72, GNMP.

18. Louis G. Young, "Pettigrew-Kirkland-MacRae Brigade," 568.

19. Underwood, "Twenty-Sixth Regiment," 394; Stedman, *Memorial Address*, 10; MacRae's brigade petition, February 24, 1865, Graham Papers, SHC-UNC; Greene, *Breaking the Backbone of the Rebellion*, 121.

20. Underwood, "Twenty-Sixth Regiment," 393, 409; Adams to niece, December 7, 1911, Military Collection, Civil War Collection, NCDAH.

21. Benjamin H. Freeman to father, mother, and sisters, March 15, 1865, in Wright, *Confederate Letters*, 62.

22. Jordan, *North Carolina Troops*, 11:363.

23. Benjamin H. Freeman to father, mother, and sisters, February 26, March 15, 1865, in Wright, *Confederate Letters*, 60–61.

24. Benjamin Wesley Justice to wife, March 15, 1865, Justice Papers, EU; Horatio G. Wright to Alexander S. Webb, February 21, 28, March 14, 20, 1865, *OR* 46(2):614, 732,

971, and 46(3):54; George G. Meade to Ulysses S. Grant, March 2, 1865, *OR* 46(2):785; Philip Schuyler to G. D. Ruggles, March 3, 6, 1865, *OR* 46(2):808, 858; Schuyler to Meade, March 14, 1865, *OR* 46(2):966.

25. Columbus A. Tuttle, "Incidents Which Happened in Caldwell County," Reminiscences, Civil War Collection, NCDAH.

26. Jordan, *North Carolina Troops*, 5:6–105, 7:463–601, 10:396–493, 11:244–363, 12:415–521; Louis G. Young inspection report, December 26, 1864, and John J. Robinson inspection report, February 27, 1865, Confederate Inspection Reports, NARA; Underwood, "Twenty-Sixth Regiment," 394.

27. Greene, *Breaking the Backbone of the Rebellion*, 177–79; Trudeau, *Last Citadel*, 337, 352, 366; Linebach diary, 290–91, SHC-UNC.

28. Benjamin H. Freeman to father, mother, and sisters, March 28, 1865, in Wright, *Confederate Letters*, 63; Stedman, *Memorial Address*, 12–13; Greene, *Breaking the Backbone of the Rebellion*, 177–79, 243–44.

29. Jordan, *North Carolina Troops*, 5:6–105, 7:463–601, 10:396–493, 11:244–363, 12:415–521.

30. William MacRae to R. H. Finney, April 11, 1865, Lee Headquarters Papers, VHS; Caldwell, *History of a Brigade of South Carolinians*, 207–8; Greene, *Breaking the Backbone of the Rebellion*, 215–17.

31. Greene, *Breaking the Backbone of the Rebellion*, 215–17, 221, 223; Linebach diary, 292, SHC-UNC; circular, Army of the Potomac, February 4, 1865, *OR* 46(2):370.

32. Greene, *Breaking the Backbone of the Rebellion*, 226–29; Calkins, *Appomattox Campaign*, 16–37; Chapman, *More Terrible Than Victory*, 283; William MacRae to R. H. Finney, April 11, 1865, Lee Headquarters Papers, VHS; Caldwell, *History of a Brigade of South Carolinians*, 209.

33. Calkins, *Appomattox Campaign*, 16–37; Chapman, *More Terrible Than Victory*, 284.

34. Caldwell, *History of a Brigade of South Carolinians*, 215, 218; William MacRae to R. H. Finney, April 11, 1865, Lee Headquarters Papers, VHS; Jordan, *North Carolina Troops*, 5:6–105, 7:463–601, 10:396–493, 11:244–363, 12:415–521.

35. William MacRae to R. H. Finney, April 11, 1865, Lee Headquarters Papers, VHS: Chapman, *More Terrible Than Victory*, 286: Martin and Outlaw, "Eleventh Regiment," 602; Greene, *Breaking the Backbone of the Rebellion*, 234, 283, 298, 336n.

36. Trudeau, *Last Citadel*, 367, 369–73; Chapman, *More Terrible Than Victory*, 288–89; Greene, *Breaking the Backbone of the Rebellion*, 319–24; J. S. Bartlett reminiscences, 16, Bartlett Papers, SHC-UNC.

37. Warlick to E. R. Outlaw, December 1, 1901, Warlick Letters, SCL-DU; Henry Heth to William H. Palmer, April 11, 1865, *Supplement to the Official Records*, pt. 1, 7:810–11; Eric Erson to John H. Robinson, April 11, 1865, *Supplement to the Official Records*, pt. 1, 7:813.

38. Eric Erson to John H. Robinson, April 11, 1865, *Supplement to the Official Records*, pt. 1, 7:813; Linebach diary, 292–94, SHC-UNC.

39. William MacRae to R. H. Finney, April 11, 1865, Lee Headquarters Papers, VHS; Henry Heth to William H. Palmer, April 11, 1865, *Supplement to the Official Records*, pt. 1, 7:810–11; Eric Erson to John H. Robinson, April 11, 1865, *Supplement to the Official*

Records, pt. 1, 7:813; A. A. Humphreys to Alexander S. Webb, April 2, 1865, *OR* 46(3):465; Trudeau, *Last Citadel*, 375–78; Calkins, *Appomattox Campaign*, 49–50; Greene, *Breaking the Backbone of the Rebellion*, 430–32.

40. Trudeau, *Last Citadel*, 393; Robinson, "Fifty-Second Regiment," 251; John R. Cooke report, April 11, 1865, *Supplement to the Official Records*, pt. 1, 7:814; Calkins, *Appomattox Campaign*, 48; Caldwell, *History of a Brigade of South Carolinians*, 218–19; Thorp, "Forty-Seventh Regiment," 99.

41. Trudeau, *Last Citadel*, 389, 394–96; Greene, *Breaking the Backbone of the Rebellion*, 433–38; Caldwell, *History of a Brigade of South Carolinians*, 220–22; Nelson A. Miles to C. A. Whittier, April 20, 1865, *OR* 46(1):711.

42. Trudeau, *Last Citadel*, 396–97; Greene, *Breaking the Backbone of the Rebellion*, 438–41; Nelson A. Miles to C. A. Whittier, April 20, 1865, *OR* 46(1):711; John Ramsey to R. A. Brown, April 14, 1865, *OR* 46(1):746; Henry Heth to William H. Palmer, April 11, 1865, *Supplement to the Official Records*, pt. 1, 7:811; Rogers, "Additional Sketch," 111–12; Thorp, "Forty-Seventh Regiment," 99.

43. Caldwell, *History of a Brigade of South Carolinians*, 223–24; William MacRae to R. H. Finney, April 11, 1865, Lee Headquarters Papers, VHS.

44. Trudeau, *Last Citadel*, 397; Calkins, *Appomattox Campaign*, 48; Eric Erson to John H. Robinson, April 11, 1865, *Supplement to the Official Records*, pt. 1, 7:812; John R. Cooke report, April 11, 1865, *Supplement to the Official Records*, pt. 1, 7:814; William MacRae to R. H. Finney, April 11, 1865, Lee Headquarters Papers, VHS.

45. Robinson, "Fifty-Second Regiment," 252; J. S. Bartlett reminiscences, 16, Bartlett Papers, SHC-UNC.

46. Bingham to granddaughter, March 14, 1923, Bingham Papers, SHC-UNC; Jordan, *North Carolina Troops*, 10:456.

47. Linebach diary, 295–96, SHC-UNC.

48. Jordan, *North Carolina Troops*, 5:6–105, 7:463–601, 10:396–493, 11:244–363, 12:415–521.

49. Calkins, *Appomattox Campaign*, 58.

50. Jordan, *North Carolina Troops*, 5:6–105, 7:463–601, 10:396–493, 11:244–363, 12:415–521.

51. Calkins, *Appomattox Campaign*, 75–76, 85; William MacRae to R. H. Finney, April 11, 1865, Lee Headquarters Papers, VHS; Chapman, *More Terrible Than Victory*, 300; Stedman, "Forty-Fourth Regiment," 32; Robinson, "Fifty-Second Regiment," 252.

52. Linebach diary, 297–98, 301, SHC-UNC. For a photograph of Mickey's cornet, which he saved from capture, see *Echoes of Glory*, 221.

53. Calkins, *Appomattox Campaign*, 85–86, 89, 91, 99, 105, 115–16, 124, 132–33; Caldwell, *History of a Brigade of South Carolinians*, 230–31; William MacRae to R. H. Finney, April 11, 1865, Lee Headquarters Papers, VHS; Thorp, "Forty-Seventh Regiment," 100.

54. Calkins, *Appomattox Campaign*, 133–134; Thorp, "Forty-Seventh Regiment," 100; William MacRae to R. H. Finney, April 11, 1865, Lee Headquarters Papers, VHS.

55. Martin and Outlaw, "Eleventh Regiment," 603.

56. Calkins, *Appomattox Campaign*, 138, 154–56, 162, 164–65; Martin and Outlaw, "Eleventh Regiment," 603.

57. Thorp, "Forty-Seventh Regiment," 100.

58. Martin and Outlaw, "Eleventh Regiment," 603. The Museum of the Confederacy has a remnant of a flag identified as part of the 44th North Carolina's. It is about twelve inches square, has one star, and is listed as having been carried by William S. Long. I cannot verify that this is an authentic flag of the regiment. Long had an overheated imagination, and he might have passed on unreliable information. The museum records indicate that Long carried the flag from Fredericksburg to Appomattox; there is no proof he ever was a color-bearer, and he certainly was not present during either campaign. It is possible, however, that this fragment is part of the unit's original flag given to Robert Bingham's wife in early 1865. The second regimental flag was cast into the Appomattox River during the retreat from Petersburg. See Rose, *Colours of the Gray*, 14.

59. Underwood, "Twenty-Sixth Regiment," 393; Adams to niece, December 7, 1911, Military Collection, Civil War Collection, NCDAH; Thorp, "Forty-Seventh Regiment," 100.

60. Jordan, *North Carolina Troops*, 5:6–105, 7:463–601, 10:396–493, 11:244–363, 12:415–521.

61. Calkins, *Appomattox Campaign*, 185; Thorp, "Forty-Seventh Regiment," 101; *Appomattox Roster*, 297, 299–300, 302–3; Underwood, "Twenty-Sixth Regiment," 394–95; organization of C.S. forces commanded by Gen. Robert E. Lee, n.d., *OR*, 46(1):1272. Starting with a brigade strength of 1,411 men in early March, I subtracted the total losses from March 25 through April 8 and came up with 396 men remaining by the time of the surrender. The difference with published statistics, 46 men, seems slight considering the normal fluidity of numbers when dealing with these issues.

62. MacRae to R. H. Finney, April 11, 1865, Lee's Headquarters Papers, VHS; William B. Taylor to mother, July 29, 1863, in Mast, "Six Lieutenants," 13.

63. Calkins, *Appomattox Campaign*, 190–92; Thorp, "Forty-Seventh Regiment," 101.

64. Martin and Outlaw, "Eleventh Regiment," 604; Bush reminiscences, Shuford Collection, NCDAH.

CHAPTER FOURTEEN

1. Louis G. Young, "Death of Brigadier General J. Johnston Pettigrew," 29, 31.

2. Collett Leventhorpe to Mary, May 14, 1867, Pettigrew Family Papers, NCDAH.

3. Powell, *Dictionary of North Carolina Biography*, 3:371–72.

4. Ibid., 4:194; Stedman, *Memorial Address*, 9, 15.

5. Louis G. Young, "Pettigrew-Kirkland-MacRae Brigade," 568.

6. Tucker, *Zeb Vance*, 411, 415, 427–29, 433, 460, 463, 477.

7. James Drennan to Henry King Burgwyn Sr., September 15, 1865, Burgwyn Family Papers, SHC-UNC; Underwood, "Twenty-Sixth Regiment," 408.

8. Jordan, *North Carolina Troops*, 9:427; T. L. Clingman to Henry King Burgwyn Sr., June 25, 1864; A. M. McKithan to T. L. Clingman, October 3, 1864; J. J. Young to William H. S. Burgwyn, October 3, 1889; and J. T. Murphy to William H. S. Burgwyn, June 1, 1907, Burgwyn Papers, NCDAH.

9. J. J. Young to William, October 3, 1889, Burgwyn Papers, NCDAH; William H. S. Burgwyn to Clement A. Evans, November 1, 1897, Lane Papers, SHC-UNC; Underwood, "Twenty-Sixth Regiment," 408.

10. Powell, *Dictionary of North Carolina Biography*, 4:13; transcript of article in the *Ran-*

dolph Tribune, Lane Papers, SHC-UNC; Underwood, "Twenty-Sixth Regiment," 409.

11. John R. Lane to James H. Foote, n.d., *Raleigh Daily Confederate*, August 20, 1864; William H. S. Burgwyn to John Randolph Lane, March 19, 1895, Lane Papers, SHC-UNC.

12. John R. Lane to William H. S. Burgwyn, May 14, 1900, Burgwyn Papers, NCDAH.

13. John R. Lane address, *Raleigh News and Observer*, July 5, 1903; Linebach diary, 49, SHC-UNC; Schiller, *Captain's War*, 175.

14. Bennett H. Young, "Col. John R. Lane and His Regiment"; Powell, *Dictionary of North Carolina Biography*, 4:13.

15. Collett Leventhorpe to Marcus J. Wright, May 30, 1888, Wright Papers, SCL-DU; Graham, "Adjutant-General's Office," 52; Collett Leventhorpe to James C. McRae, December 28, 1864, *Supplement to the Official Records*, pt. 1, 7:531–33; Powell, *Dictionary of North Carolina Biography*, 4:56.

16. Powell, *Dictionary of North Carolina Biography*, 4:56; Edmund Jones address, in "War Record of Genl Collett Leventhorpe," Military Collection, Civil War Collection, NCDAH; Chapman, *More Terrible Than Victory*, 320.

17. Powell, *Dictionary of North Carolina Biography*, 4:232; Chapman, *More Terrible Than Victory*, 318–320.

18. Norris, "Now Growing Old Gracefully"; Adams to niece, December 7, 1911, Military Collection, Civil War Collection, NCDAH; Mast, *State Troops and Volunteers*, 1:321.

19. Underwood, "Twenty-Sixth Regiment," 415–21.

20. Benjamin Franklin Little to Flax, March 18, 1868, and Little to Captain McFarlane, July 18, 1868, Little Papers, SHC-UNC.

21. Clemmer, *Valor in Gray*, 243n; G. W. Finley to Tazewell Hargrove, May 2, 1865, Briggs Papers, SHC-UNC; Jordan, *North Carolina Troops*, 10:396.

22. Devine, "Defense of the South Anna Bridge," 182.

23. Powell, *Dictionary of North Carolina Biography*, 1:157–58; Robert I. Curtis, "Bingham School," 329, 374–75; Bingham to granddaughter, March 14, 1923, Bingham Papers, SHC-UNC.

24. Powell, *Dictionary of North Carolina Biography*, 5:431; Stedman, *Memorial Address*, 26–27.

25. Transcript of newspaper article, 1871, Justice Papers, EU.

26. Underwood, "Twenty-Sixth Regiment," 369.

27. Stevens, *Rebels in Blue*, 52, 54, 57–64, 68–70, 77–79, 89–92, 105, 114, 117, 138, 161, 180, 191, 210, 211–12; Powell, *Dictionary of North Carolina Biography*, 1:174–75.

28. Marshall, *In Memoriam*, 16–17, 20–22, 30.

29. Underwood, "Twenty-Sixth Regiment," 417.

30. Caison, "Southern Soldiers in Northern Prisons," 163–64.

31. Underwood, "Twenty-Sixth Regiment," 421–22; Jordan, *North Carolina Troops*, 7:465; Noblin, *Leonidas LaFayette Polk*, 50–72, 144–46.

32. Underwood, "Twenty-Sixth Regiment," 422.

33. Peace, "Fighting against Great Odds," 371; Jordan, *North Carolina Troops*, 10:406, 11:273, 304; William Walker Hartgrove sketch, MC; Mast, *State Troops and Volunteers*, 1:246.

34. John C. Warlick to E. R. Outlaw, December 1, 1901, Warlick Letters, SCL-DU.

35. Linebach diary, 299–311, SHC-UNC; "Bandsman's Letters to Home from the War," 8; Harry H. Hall, *Johnny Reb Band*, 105; Stockton, "26th Regimental Band," 52–55.

36. Underwood, "Twenty-Sixth Regiment," 423; William F. Fox to William H. S. Burgwyn, September 30, 1889, Burgwyn Papers, NCDAH; fragment of Perrett letter, Perrett reminiscences, Reminiscences, Civil War Collection, NCDAH.

37. Underwood, "Twenty-Sixth Regiment," 422–23; R. B. Brown to William H. S. Burgwyn, November 24, 1903, and Marcy Mason to Burgwyn, August 10, 1898, Burgwyn Papers, NCDAH; John Randolph Lane address, 1903, Lane Papers, SHC-UNC.

38. Reardon, *Pickett's Charge in History and Memory*, 76, 132–33, 135–37; Reardon, "Pickett's Charge."

39. Transcripts of letters to newspapers regarding Pickett's Charge, Grimes Papers, SHC-UNC; Reardon, *Pickett's Charge in History and Memory*, 133; Joseph John Davis to Charles Scott Venable, July 30, 1889, Venable Papers, VHS; John C. McInnis to Marcus Cicero Stephens Noble, July 24, 1913, Noble Papers, SHC-UNC; George M. Whiting to editor, March 9, 1867, *Raleigh Daily Sentinel*, March 18, 1867; "H" to editor, n.d., *Raleigh Daily Sentinel*, March 29, 1867.

40. Bond, *Pickett or Pettigrew?*, 14, 30.

41. Underwood, "Twenty-Sixth Regiment," 403, 414; J. J. Young to William H. S. Burgwyn, October 3, 1889, Burgwyn Papers, NCDAH; Chapman, *More Terrible Than Victory*, 321.

42. Rose, *Colours of the Gray*, 31, 37–38; Terry, "Mystery Flags of Bristoe Station," 13.

43. Bush reminiscences, Shuford Collection, NCDAH; Thomas J. Cureton to John Randolph Lane, June 22, 1890, Lane Papers, SHC-UNC; William S. Long reminiscences, fols. 1196, 1231, Long Papers, LC; John C. Warlick to E. R. Outlaw, December 1, 1901, Warlick Letter, SCL-DU.

44. Emerson, "Most Famous Regiment," 352.

45. Clemmer, *Valor in Gray*, xv, xix–xxi, 241, 251, 447, 468.

APPENDIX

1. Jordan, *North Carolina Troops*, 5:6–105, 7:463–601, 10:396–493, 11:244–363, 12:415–521.

2. Hess, "12th Missouri Infantry"; 11th North Carolina, 26th North Carolina, 44th North Carolina, 47th North Carolina, and 52nd North Carolina, Compiled Service Records, NARA.

3. See McGee, "Twenty-Sixth Regiment," 4–5, for another perspective on the ages of those who served in this regiment.

4. Ibid., 19.

5. Ibid., 2–3.

6. Chapman, *More Terrible Than Victory*, 142, 314, has some conflicting information about the Warlicks. See also Lewis Warlick to Cornelia, April 26, 1863, and July 8, 1864, McGimsey Papers, SHC-UNC.

7. Hess, "12th Missouri Infantry," 62.

8. Richard Hall, *Patriots In Disguise*, 100–103.

9. Mickey account, SP-MA; J. Edward Peterson to sister, September 28, 1862, and July 5, 1864; Peterson to niece, March 30, 1863; and Peterson letter (correspondent unknown), July 9, 1863, Peterson Papers, MMF.

10. Lewis Warlick to Cornelia, July 21, 1864, McGimsey Papers, SHC-UNC.

BIBLIOGRAPHY

ARCHIVAL SOURCES

Burke County Public Library, Morganton, N.C.
  Elam and L. A. Bristol Letters
Chicago Historical Society, Chicago, Ill.
  Charles Frederick Gunther Collection
  Zebulon Baird Vance Papers
Davidson College Library, Davidson, N.C.
  William Joseph Martin Collection
Duke University, Special Collections Library, Durham, N.C.
  Alfred M. Foster and John A. Foster Papers
  Elizabeth Glenn Papers
  Robert N. Gourdin Papers
  John McLean Harrington Papers
  J. L. Henry Papers
  Hinsdale Family Papers
  Thomas Hinshaw Papers
  Jarratt-Puryear Family Papers
  Charles Colcock Jones Papers
  Willis H. King Papers
  Hannah R. Lawrence Papers
  Collett Leventhorpe Papers
  Rebecca Maria McCall Papers
  John McIver Papers
  Hugh MacRae Papers
  Nevin Ray Papers
  Scarborough Family Papers
  William Lafayette Scott Papers
  Thomas D. Snead Papers
  Tillinghast Family Papers
  Samuel Hoey Walkup Journal

Giles Frederick Ward Jr. Papers
John C. Warlick Letters
Marcus J. Wright Papers
Emory University, Special Collections, Atlanta, Ga.
Robert Newman Gourdin Papers
Benjamin Wesley Justice Papers
James A. Patton Papers
Hale Wesson Papers
Fredericksburg Battlefield, Fredericksburg, Va.
William Domas Brewer Letters
Benjamin Wesley Justice to wife, November 22, 1863
Georgia Historical Society, Savannah
Keith Read Collection
Gettysburg National Military Park, Gettysburg, Pa.
Mary E. Lewis, "The Life and Times of Thomas Bailey," 47th North Carolina
Regimental File
William B. Taylor to mother, June 22, 1863, 11th North Carolina File
Greensboro Historical Museum, Greensboro, N.C.
Henry C. Albright Papers
Historical Society of Delaware, Wilmington
Henry Gawthrop Letters and Diary
Rodman and Linton Smith Letters
Library of Congress, Manuscripts Division, Washington, D.C.
Clothing Receipts, Muster Roll, and Payroll, 11th North Carolina
Samuel Wylie Crawford Papers
Breckinridge Long Papers
Moravian Archives, Southern Province, Winston-Salem, N.C.
Sam Mickey Account
Moravian Music Foundation, Winston-Salem, N.C.
J. Edward Peterson Papers
Minnesota Historical Society, Minneapolis
Samuel Clarke Day Papers
Museum of the Confederacy, Richmond, Va.
52nd North Carolina Collection
J. W. Crawley Receipts
Randolph and Ethelbert Fairfax Letters
William Walker Hartgrove Sketch
Henry Heth Papers
Joseph Mullen Jr. Diary
Muster Rolls, 52nd North Carolina
Kate Mason Rowland Collection
National Archives and Records Administration, Washington, D.C.
Compiled Service Records of Confederate Soldiers Who Served in Organizations
from the State of North Carolina, RG 109
Confederate Inspection Reports, M935

Muster Rolls, 11th North Carolina, 26th North Carolina, 44th North Carolina, 47th
North Carolina, and 52nd North Carolina, RG 109
New-York Historical Society, New York
Lawrence O'Bryan Branch Letter
North Carolina Division of Archives and History, Raleigh
Adams and Partin Family Collection
Henry Clay Albright Papers
Blair Letters
Lawrence O'Bryan Branch Papers
William H. S. Burgwyn Papers
Civil War Collection, Miscellaneous Records
Reminiscences
Thomas Perrett reminiscences, box 71, folder 46
Columbus A. Tuttle, "'F' and 'I' of the 26th Regiment from 1861 to 1865," box
72, folder 21
———, "Incidents Which Happened in Caldwell County in 1864," box 72,
folder 21
———, "Pettigrew's Brigade at Gettysburg, July 3, 1863," box 72, folder 21
Waddell, W. C. "How Woodson Garrett Was Captured and Escaped from the
Yankees," box 70, folder 51
Military Collection
26th Regiment North Carolina Troops, Bounty Payroll, box 58
26th Regiment North Carolina Troops, Muster Rolls and Regimental Records,
1862–1864, boxes 49–53
44th Regiment North Carolina Troops, Bounty Payrolls, box 58
47th Regiment North Carolina Troops, Bounty Payroll, box 58
James T. Adams to niece, December 7, 1911, box 74, folder 1
Bounty Payrolls, 1862–1864, boxes 9–16
Muster Roll, Comp. F, 26th Regiment, North Carolina Troops, December 31,
1864, to February 28, 1865, box 85, folder 16
Orders, Muster Rolls, Requisitions, Morning Reports, Descriptive Rolls,
boxes 43–44
Pettigrew's Brigade, Quartermaster Returns, box 58
"War Record of Genl Collett Leventhorpe," box 71, folder 20
J. J. Young, Quartermaster Returns, Abstracts, and Vouchers, 1862–1865,
boxes 54–57
Henry Toole Clark Collection
Richard A. Cole Collection
Samuel Finley Harper Papers
A. C. Myers Papers
William G. Parker Papers
Pettigrew Family Papers
Lowry Shuford Collection
J. A. Bush Sr. reminiscences, box 70, folder 23
Zebulon Baird Vance Collection

Webb Collection
John Wright Collection
Petersburg National Battlefield, Petersburg, Va.
Edwin C. Bearss, "The Battle of Reams' Station"
University of North Carolina, Southern Historical Collection, Chapel Hill
J. S. Bartlett Papers
Robert Bingham Papers
Brewer-Paschal Family Papers
Willis G. Briggs Papers
Burgwyn Family Papers
Confederate Papers, Unit 15
William A. Graham Papers
Bryan Grimes Papers
Lemuel J. Hoyle Papers
Edmund Walter Jones Papers
Joyner Family Papers
John Randolph Lane Papers
Julius A. Linebach Diary
Benjamin Franklin Little Papers
Benjamin Franklin Little, "Account of the Movements of Co. E 52nd Regt
N.C. Troops from the time it left the County of Richmond up to Battle of
Gettysburg"
Cornelia McGimsey Papers
William James Martin Papers
Marcus Cicero Stephens Noble Papers
John Paris Papers
Pettigrew Family Papers
Leonidas Lafayette Polk Papers
Polk, Badger, McGehee Papers
Egbert A. Ross Papers
Joseph H. Saunders Papers
Steed and Phipps Family Papers
Zebulon Baird Vance Papers
Webb Family Papers
Edmund Jones Williams Letters
Robert Watson Winston Papers
Nancy Brown Young Papers
University of Virginia, Special Collections, Charlottesville
John Warwick Daniel Papers
McGregor Papers
U.S. Army Military History Institute, Carlisle Barracks, Pa.
Civil War Times Illustrated Collection
D. H. Hill to Longstreet, March 17, 1863
Charles A. Nutall Reminiscences
W. D. Patterson Letter

Henry C. Kirkman Letter, Gregory Coco Collection-Harrisburg Civil War Round
    Table Collection
Virginia Historical Society, Richmond
    Lee Headquarters Papers
    Charles Scott Venable Papers
Virginia Military Institute, Archives, Lexington
    F. Lewis Marshall to uncle, October 6, 1863
    Charles D. Walker, *Memorial, Virginia Military Institute*

NEWSPAPERS

Asheville (N.C.) News
Charlotte (N.C.) Daily Bulletin
Fayetteville (N.C.) Observer
Harrisburg (Pa.) Evening Telegraph
North Carolina Argus (Wadesboro)
Raleigh Daily Confederate
Raleigh Daily Progress
Raleigh Daily Sentinel
Raleigh News and Observer
Raleigh North Carolina Standard
Raleigh Register
Richmond Daily Enquirer

PUBLISHED WORKS

The Appomattox Roster. New York: Antiquarian Press, 1962.
Ashe, S. A. "The Pettigrew-Pickett Charge, Gettysburg, 3 July, 1863." In *Histories of
    the Several Regiments and Battalions from North Carolina in the Great War,
    1861–'65*, edited by Walter Clark, 5:137–59. Goldsboro, N.C.: Nash Brothers, 1901.
Atlas to Accompany the Official Records of the Union and Confederate Armies. Washing-
    ton, D.C.: Government Printing Office, 1891–95.
"A Bandsman's Letters to Home from the War." *Moravian Music Journal* 36 (spring
    1991): 5–8.
Barden, John R., ed. *Letters to the Home Circle: The North Carolina Service of Pvt.
    Henry A. Clapp*. Raleigh: North Carolina Division of Archives and History, 1998.
Bardolph, Richard. "Confederate Dilemma: North Carolina Troops and the Deserter
    Problem." Pts. 1 and 2. *North Carolina Historical Review* 61 (January, April 1989):
    61–86, 179–210.
Barefoot, Daniel W. *General Robert F. Hoke: Lee's Modest Warrior*. Winston-Salem,
    N.C.: John F. Blair, 1996.
Barrett, John G. *The Civil War in North Carolina*. Chapel Hill: University of North
    Carolina Press, 1963.
———. *North Carolina as a Civil War Battleground, 1861–1865*. Raleigh: North Car-
    olina Department of Cultural Resources, 1987.

Bond, W. R. *Pickett or Pettigrew? An Historical Essay*. Weldon, N.C.: Hall and Sledge, 1888.

Busey, John W., and David G. Martin. *Regimental Strengths and Losses at Gettysburg*. Hightstown, N.J.: Longstreet House, 1986.

———. *Regimental Strengths at Gettysburg*. Baltimore: Gateway Press, 1982.

Bush, Garry L. "The Sixth Michigan Cavalry at Falling Waters: The End of the Gettysburg Campaign." *Gettysburg Magazine*, no. 9 (July 1993): 109–15.

Caison, Albert Stacey. "Southern Soldiers in Northern Prisons." *Southern Historical Society Papers* 23 (1895): 158–65.

Caldwell, J. F. J. *The History of a Brigade of South Carolinians Known First as "Gregg's," and Subsequently as "McGowan's Brigade."* Philadelphia: King and Baird, 1866.

Calkins, Chris M. *The Appomattox Campaign, March 29–April 9, 1865*. Conshohocken, Pa.: Combined Books, 1997.

Cavanaugh, Michael A., and William Marvel. *The Petersburg Campaign: The Battle of the Crater, "the Horrid Pit," June 25–August 6, 1864*. Lynchburg: H. E. Howard, 1989.

Chapman, Craig S. *More Terrible Than Victory: North Carolina's Bloody Bethel Regiment, 1861–65*. Washington, D.C.: Brassey's, 1998.

Christ, Elwood W. *The Struggle for the Bliss Farm at Gettysburg, July 2nd and 3rd, 1863*. Baltimore: Butternut and Blue, 1994.

Clemmer, Gregg S. *Valor in Gray: The Recipients of the Confederate Medal of Honor*. Staunton, Va.: Hearthside, 1996.

Cockrell, Monroe F., ed. *Gunner with Stonewall: Reminiscences of William Thomas Poague*. Jackson, Tenn.: McCowat-Mercer, 1957.

The Confederate Reveille. Raleigh: Edwards and Broughton, 1898.

Cook, John D. S. "Personal Reminiscences of Gettysburg." In *Gettysburg Sources*, compiled by James L. McLean Jr. and Judy W. McLean, 2:122–44. Baltimore: Butternut and Blue, 1987.

Crabtree, Beth G., and James W. Patton, eds. *"Journal of a Secesh Lady": The Diary of Catherine Ann Devereaux Edmondston, 1860–1866*. Raleigh: North Carolina Division of Archives and History, 1979.

Crews, C. Daniel. *A Storm in the Land: Southern Moravians and the Civil War*. Winston-Salem, N.C.: Moravian Music Foundation, 1997.

Crofts, Daniel W. *Reluctant Confederates: Upper South Unionists in the Secession Crisis*. Chapel Hill: University of North Carolina Press, 1988.

Cross, Andrew. *The War: Battle of Gettysburg and the Christian Commission*. N.p., 1865.

Cross, J. F. "N.C. Officers in Prison at Johnson's Island, 1864." In *Histories of the Several Regiments and Battalions from North Carolina in the Great War, 1861–'65*, edited by Walter Clark, 4:703–12. Goldsboro, N.C.: Nash Brothers, 1901.

Curtis, Robert I. "The Bingham School and Classical Education in North Carolina, 1793–1873." *North Carolina Historical Review* 73 (July 1996): 328–77.

Curtis, W. A. "A Journal of Reminiscences of the War." *Our Living and Our Dead* 2 (May 1875): 281–90.

Davis, Archie K. *Boy Colonel of the Confederacy: The Life and Times of Henry King Burgwyn Jr.* Chapel Hill: University of North Carolina Press, 1985.

Devine, W. S. "Defense of the South Anna Bridge." *Confederate Veteran* 40 (May 1932): 178–82.

Dowd, Jerome. *Sketches of Prominent Living North Carolinians.* Raleigh: Edwards and Broughton, 1888.

Dreese, Michael A. *The 151st Pennsylvania Volunteers at Gettysburg: Like Ripe Apples in a Storm.* Jefferson, N.C.: McFarland, 2000.

Early, Jubal Anderson. *War Memoirs.* Bloomington: Indiana University Press, 1960.

Echoes of Glory: Arms and Equipment of the Confederacy. Alexandria, Va.: Time-Life Books, 1991.

Elmore, Thomas L. "Torrid Heat and Blinding Rain: A Meteorological and Astronomical Chronology of the Gettysburg Campaign." *Gettysburg Magazine,* no. 13 (July 1995): 7–21.

Emerson, Mrs. B. A. C. "The Most Famous Regiment." *Confederate Veteran* 25 (August 1917): 352–55.

Fletcher, Arthur L. *Ashe County: A History.* Jefferson, N.C.: Ashe County Research Association, 1963.

Fry, B. D. "Pettigrew's Charge at Gettysburg." *Southern Historical Society Papers* 7 (1879): 91–93.

Furgurson, Ernest B. *Not War but Murder: Cold Harbor, 1864.* New York: Knopf, 2000.

Gaff, Alan D. "'Here Was Made Out Our Last and Hopeless Stand:' The 'Lost' Gettysburg Reports of the Nineteenth Indiana." *Gettysburg Magazine,* no. 2 (January 1990): 25–31.

Gallagher, Gary W. *Stephen Dodson Ramseur: Lee's Gallant General.* Chapel Hill: University of North Carolina Press, 1985.

Garrison, Webb. *Civil War Hostages: Hostage Taking in the Civil War.* Shippensburg, Pa.: White Mane, 2000.

Gordon, Major A. "Organization of Troops." In *Histories of the Several Regiments and Battalions from North Carolina in the Great War, 1861–'65,* edited by Walter Clark, 1:3–49. Goldsboro, N.C.: E. M. Uzzell, 1901.

Govan, Gilbert E., and James W. Livingood, eds. *The Haskell Memoirs: John Cheves Haskell.* New York: G. P. Putnam's Son, 1960.

Gragg, Rod. *Covered with Glory: The 26th North Carolina Infantry at Gettysburg.* New York: Harper Collins, 2000.

Graham, Martin F., and George F. Skoch. *Mine Run: A Campaign of Lost Opportunities, October 21, 1863–May 1, 1864.* Lynchburg: H. E. Howard, 1987.

Graham, William A. "Adjutant-General's Office." In *Histories of the Several Regiments and Battalions from North Carolina in the Great War, 1861–'65,* edited by Walter Clark, 1:51–59. Goldsboro, N.C.: E. M. Uzzell, 1901.

Greene, A. Wilson. *Breaking the Backbone of the Rebellion: The Final Battles of the Petersburg Campaign.* Mason City, Iowa: Savas Publishing, 2000.

Hadden, R. Lee. "The Deadly Embrace: The Meeting of the Twenty-fourth Regiment, Michigan Infantry, and the Twenty-sixth Regiment of North Carolina Troops at

McPherson's Woods, Gettysburg, Pennsylvania, July 1, 1863." *Gettysburg Magazine*, no. 5 (July 1991): 19–33.

Hadley, Horton Strowd. *Chatham County, 1771–1971*. N.p.: Moore Publishing, n.d.

Haines, Douglas Craig. "A. P. Hill's Advance to Gettysburg." *Gettysburg Magazine*, no. 5 (July 1991): 4–11.

Hall, Everard. "Camp Life, with a Few Reflections Incident Thereto." *Our Living and Our Dead* 2 (April 1875): 157–64.

Hall, Harry H. *A Johnny Reb Band from Salem: The Pride of Tarheelia*. New York: Da Capo, 1980.

Hall, Richard. *Patriots in Disguise: Women Warriors of the Civil War*. New York: Paragon House, 1993.

Hartwig, D. Scott. "The Defense of McPherson's Ridge." *Gettysburg Magazine*, no. 1 (July 1989): 15–24.

Hayes, Johnson J. *The Land of Wilkes*. Wilkesboro, N.C.: Wilkes County Historical Society, 1962.

Henderson, William H. *The Road to Bristoe Station: Campaigning with Lee and Meade, August 1–October 20, 1863*. Lynchburg: H. E. Howard, 1987.

Hess, Earl J. "The 12th Missouri Infantry: A Socio-Military Profile of a Union Regiment." *Missouri Historical Review* 76 (October 1981): 53–77.

Hood, J. T. C. "From Gettysburg to the Wilderness." *Lenoir Topic*, July 1, 1896.

——. "The 26th Regiment at Gettysburg." *Lenoir Topic*, April 8, 1896.

Hopkins, George G. "Battle of Newbern as I Saw It." In *Personal Recollections of the War of the Rebellion: Addresses Delivered Before the Commandery of the State of New York, Military Order of the Loyal Legion of the United States*, 138–47. 3d series. New York: Knickerbocker Press, 1907.

Horn, John. *The Destruction of the Weldon Railroad: Deep Bottom, Globe Tavern, and Reams Station, August 14–25, 1864*. Lynchburg: H. E. Howard, 1991.

Hunt, Henry J. "The Second Day at Gettysburg." In *Battles and Leaders of the Civil War*, edited by Robert Underwood Johnson and Clarence Clough Buel, 3:290–313. New York: Thomas Yoseloff, 1956.

Imboden, John D. "The Confederate Retreat From Gettysburg." In *Battles and Leaders of the Civil War*, edited by Robert Underwood Johnson and Clarence Clough Buel, 3:420–29. New York: Thomas Yoseloff, 1956.

Johnston, Frontis W., ed. *The Papers of Zebulon Baird Vance*. Vol. 1. Raleigh: State Department of Archives and History, 1963.

Jones, John T. "Pettigrew's Brigade at Gettysburg." In *Histories of the Several Regiments and Battalions from North Carolina in the Great War, 1861–'65*, edited by Walter Clark, 5:133–35. Goldsboro, N.C.: Nash Brothers, 1901.

Jordan, Weymouth T., comp. *North Carolina Troops, 1861–1865: A Roster*. 14 vols. Raleigh: Division of Archives and History, 1966–97.

Knouse, Nola Reed, and C. Daniel Crews. *Moravian Music: An Introduction*. Winston-Salem, N.C.: Moravian Music Foundation, 1996.

Krick, Robert K. *Lee's Colonels: A Biographical Register of the Field Officers of the Army of Northern Virginia*. Dayton, Ohio: Morningside, 1979.

Ladd, David L., and Audrey J. Ladd, eds. *The Bachelder Papers: Gettysburg in Their*

Own Words. 3 vols. Dayton, Ohio: Morningside, 1994–95.

Linebach, Julius A. "Scenes at the Battle of Gettysburg." In *The Salem Band*, edited by Bernard J. Pfohl, 75–84. N.p.: Winston-Salem, N.C., 1953.

McCallum, James H. *Martin County during the Civil War*. Williamston, N.C.: Martin County Historical Society, 1971.

McRae, Robert P. "The Fight at South Anna Bridge." *National Tribune*, August 23, 1883.

MacRae, Walter G. "Confederate Prisoners at Morris Island." In *Histories of the Several Regiments and Battalions from North Carolina in the Great War, 1861–'65*, edited by Walter Clark, 4:713–19. Goldsboro, N.C.: Nash Brothers, 1901.

Marshall, W. F., comp. *In Memoriam: James Daniel Moore, 1846–1905*. Raleigh: Edwards and Broughton, 1907.

Martin, David G. *Gettysburg, July 1*. Conshohocken, Pa.: Combined Books, 1995.

Martin, W. J. "The Eleventh North Carolina Regiment." *Southern Historical Society Papers* 23 (1895): 42–56.

Martin, W. J., and E. R. Outlaw. "Eleventh Regiment." In *Histories of the Several Regiments and Battalions from North Carolina in the Great War, 1861–'65*, edited by Walter Clark, 1:583–604. Goldsboro, N.C.: E. M. Uzzell, 1901.

Mast, Greg. "'Sam' Blalock, 26th North Carolina Troops." *Military Images* 11 (July–August 1989): 10.

———. "Six Lieutenants: Vignettes of North Carolinians in America's Greatest Battle." *Military Images* 13 (July–August 1991): 6–13.

———. *State Troops and Volunteers: A Photographic Record of North Carolina's Civil War Soldiers*. Vol. 1. Raleigh: North Carolina Department of Cultural Resources, 1995.

———. "'Tha Kill So meny of us': 26th Regiment North Carolina Troops at Gettysburg." *Military Images* 10 (July–August 1988): 8.

———, ed. "The Setser Letters." Pt. 1. *Company Front*, December 1988–January 1989, 27–34.

———. "The Setser Letters." Pt. 2. *Company Front*, February–March 1989, 24–29.

———. "The Setser Letters." Pt. 3. *Company Front*, June–July 1989, 9–15.

———. "The Setser Letters." Pt. 4. *Company Front*, August–September 1989, 13–17.

———. "'A Trip That Didn't Pay:' The Gettysburg Reminiscences of Private Thomas Perrett, Company G, 'The Chatham Boys,' 26th Regiment North Carolina Troops." *Company Front*, April–May 1990, 9–13.

Miller, J. Michael. *The North Anna Campaign: "Even To Hell Itself," May 21–26, 1864*. Lynchburg: H. E. Howard, 1989.

Mitchell, Reid. *Civil War Soldiers: Their Expectations and Their Experiences*. New York: Viking, 1988.

Morrison, James L., Jr., ed. *The Memoirs of Henry Heth*. Westport, Conn.: Greenwood, 1974.

Murray, Elizabeth Reid. *Wake, Capital County of North Carolina*. Raleigh: Capital County Publishing, 1983.

Noblin, Stuart. *Leonidas LaFayette Polk: Agrarian Crusader*. Chapel Hill: University of North Carolina Press, 1949.

Nolan, Alan T. *The Iron Brigade: A Military History*. New York: Macmillan, 1961.

Norris, M. T. "Now Growing Old Gracefully." *Confederate Veteran* 20 (November 1912): 509.

Olds, Fred A. "Brave Carolinian Who Fell at Gettysburg." *Southern Historical Society Papers* 36 (1908): 245–47.

Page, Charles D. *History of the Fourteenth Regiment, Connecticut Vol. Infantry*. Meriden, Conn.: Horton, 1906.

Peace, A. S. "Fighting against Great Odds." *Confederate Veteran* 34 (October 1926): 370–71.

Pfanz, Harry W. *Gettysburg—The Second Day*. Chapel Hill: University of North Carolina Press, 1987.

Powell, William S., ed. *Dictionary of North Carolina Biography*. 6 Vols. Chapel Hill: University of North Carolina Press, 1979–96.

Reardon, Carol. "Pickett's Charge: The Convergence of History and Myth in the Southern Past." In *The Third Day at Gettysburg and Beyond*, edited by Gary W. Gallagher, 56–92. Chapel Hill: University of North Carolina Press, 1994.

———. *Pickett's Charge in History and Memory*. Chapel Hill: University of North Carolina Press, 1997.

Rhea, Gordon C. *The Battle of the Wilderness, May 5–6, 1864*. Baton Rouge: Louisiana State University Press, 1994.

———. *The Battles for Spotsylvania Court House and the Road to Yellow Tavern, May 7–12, 1864*. Baton Rouge: Louisiana State University Press, 1997.

———. *To the North Anna River: Grant and Lee, May 13–25, 1864*. Baton Rouge: Louisiana State University Press, 2000.

Robinson, John H. "Fifty-Second Regiment." In *Histories of the Several Regiments and Battalions from North Carolina in the Great War, 1861–'65*, edited by Walter Clark, 3:223–53. Goldsboro, N.C.: Nash Brothers, 1901.

Rogers, J. Rowan. "Additional Sketch: Forty-Seventh Regiment." In *Histories of the Several Regiments and Battalions from North Carolina in the Great War, 1861–'65*, edited by Walter Clark, 3:103–12. Goldsboro, N.C.: Nash Brothers, 1901.

Rollins, Richard, ed. *Pickett's Charge: Eyewitness Accounts*. Redondo Beach, Calif.: Rank and File, 1994.

Rose, Rebecca Ansell. *Colours of the Gray: An Illustrated Index of Wartime Flags from the Museum of the Confederacy's Collection*. Richmond: Museum of the Confederacy, 1998.

Sauers, Richard A. *"A Succession of Honorable Victories": The Burnside Expedition in North Carolina*. Dayton, Ohio: Morningside, 1996.

Schiller, Herbert M., ed. *A Captain's War: The Letters and Diaries of William H. S. Burgwyn, 1861–1865*. Shippensburg, Pa.: White Mane, 1994.

Scott, W. W. *Annals of Caldwell County*. Lenoir, N.C.: News-Topic, ca. 1930.

Sears, Stephen W. *To the Gates of Richmond: The Peninsula Campaign*. New York: Ticknor and Fields, 1992.

Shue, Richard S. *Morning at Willoughby Run, July 1, 1863*. Gettysburg: Thomas, 1995.

Smith, Donald L. *The Twenty-Fourth Michigan of the Iron Brigade*. Harrisburg: Stackpole, 1962.

Smith, Mrs. Lathrop E. "My Recollections of Civil War Days." *Wisconsin Magazine of History* 2 (1918): 28–36.

Sommers, Richard J. *Richmond Redeemed: The Siege at Petersburg*. Garden City, N.Y.: Doubleday, 1981.

Speer, Allen Paul, ed. *Voices from Cemetery Hill: The Civil War Diary, Reports, and Letters of Colonel William Henry Asbury Speer, 1861–1864*. Johnson City, Tenn.: Overmountain Press, 1997.

Stedman, Charles M. "Battle at Reams' Station." *Southern Historical Society Papers* 19 (1891): 113–20.

———. "The Forty-Fourth N.C. Infantry." *Southern Historical Society Papers* 25 (1897): 334–45.

———. "Forty-Fourth Regiment." In *Histories of the Several Regiments and Battalions from North Carolina in the Great War, 1861–'65*, edited by Walter Clark, 3:21–34. Goldsboro, N.C.: Nash Brothers, 1901.

———. *Memorial Address Delivered May 10th, 1890, at Wilmington, N.C.* Wilmington, N.C.: n.p., n.d.

Stevens, Peter F. *Rebels in Blue: The Story of Keith and Malinda Blalock*. Dallas, Tex.: Taylor Publishing, 2000.

Stewart, George R. *Pickett's Charge: A Microhistory of the Final Attack at Gettysburg, July 3, 1863*. Boston: Houghton Mifflin, 1959.

Stockton, Dr. Edwin L., Sr. "26th Regimental Band." *Moravian Music Journal* 26 (fall 1981): 51–57.

Supplement to the Official Records of the Union and Confederate Armies. 100 vols. Wilmington, N.C.: Broadfoot, 1995–99.

Taylor, Michael W. "Col. James Keith Marshall: One of the Three Brigade Commanders Killed in the Pickett-Pettigrew-Trimble Charge." *Gettysburg Magazine*, no. 15 (1996): 78–90.

———. "North Carolina in the Pickett-Pettigrew-Trimble Charge at Gettysburg." *Gettysburg Magazine*, no. 8 (January 1993): 67–93.

———. *"To Drive the Enemy From Southern Soil": The Letters of Col. Francis Marion Parker and the History of the 30th Regiment North Carolina Troops*. Dayton, Ohio: Morningside, 1998.

Terry, Mark R. "The Mystery Flags of Bristoe Station." *Company Front*, September 1999, 9–15.

Thorp, John H. "Forty-Seventh Regiment." In *Histories of the Several Regiments and Battalions from North Carolina in the Great War, 1861–'65*, edited by Walter Clark, 3:83–112. Goldsboro, N.C.: Nash Brothers, 1901.

Trimble, I. R. "North Carolinians at Gettysburg." *Our Living and Our Dead* 4 (March 1876): 53–60.

Trinque, Bruce A. "Arnold's Battery and the 26th North Carolina." *Gettysburg Magazine*, no. 12 (January 1995): 61–67.

Trudeau, Noah Andrew. "The 'Blackberry Raid.'" *Gettysburg Magazine*, no. 11 (July 1994): 7–18.

———. *The Last Citadel: Petersburg, Virginia, June 1864–April 1865*. Baton Rouge: Louisiana State University Press, 1991.

Tucker, Glenn. "Some Aspects of North Carolina's Participation in the Gettysburg Campaign." *North Carolina Historical Review* 35 (April 1958): 191–212.

——. *Zeb Vance: Champion of Personal Freedom*. Indianapolis: Bobbs-Merrill, 1965.

Tuttle, C. A. "Company F, 26th Regt. N.C. Troops at Bristow Station, Va, Oct. 14, 1963 [*sic*]." *Lenoir Topic*, June 24, 1896.

Tuttle, R. M. "Addenda: Unparalleled Loss, Company F, 26th Regt., N.C. Troops at Gettysburg, July 1, 1863." In *History of the Twenty-Sixth Regiment of the North Carolina Troops in the Great War, 1861–'65*, by George C. Underwood, 1–6 [123–28]. Goldsboro, N.C.: Nash Brothers, 1901.

——. "Company F, 26th N.C. Infantry." *Confederate Veteran* 3 (1895): 109.

Underwood, George C. *History of the Twenty-Sixth Regiment of the North Carolina Troops in the Great War, 1861–'65*. Goldsboro, N.C.: Nash Brothers, 1901.

——. "Twenty-Sixth Regiment." In *Histories of the Several Regiments and Battalions from North Carolina in the Great War, 1861–'65*, edited by Walter Clark, 2:303–423. Goldsboro, N.C.: Nash Brothers, 1901.

Walker, Francis A. *History of the Second Army Corps in the Army of the Potomac*. New York: Charles Scribner's Sons, 1887.

Warlick, J. C. "Battle of White Hall, N.C." *Confederate Veteran* 12 (April 1904): 178.

Warner, Ezra J. *Generals in Gray: Lives of the Confederate Commanders*. Baton Rouge: Louisiana State University Press, 1959.

The War of the Rebellion: A Compilation of the Official Records of the Union and Confederate Armies. 70 vols. in 128. Washington, D.C.: Government Printing Office, 1880–1901.

"Webster's Company of Volunteers." *Confederate Veteran* 23 (September 1915): 398–400.

Welsh, Jack D. *Medical Histories of Confederate Generals*. Kent, Ohio: Kent State University Press, 1995.

Wiley, Bell Irvin. *The Life of Billy Yank: The Common Soldier of the Union*. Baton Rouge: Louisiana State University Press, 1983.

Wilson, Clyde N. *Carolina Cavalier: The Life and Mind of James Johnston Pettigrew*. Athens: University of Georgia Press, 1990.

——. *The Most Promising Man of the South: James Johnston Pettigrew and His Men at Gettysburg*. Abilene, Tex.: McWhiney Foundation, 1998.

——. "The Most Promising Young Man of the South: James Johnston Pettigrew." *Civil War Times Illustrated* 11 (1973): 12–23.

Woodward, C. Vann, ed. *Mary Chesnut's Civil War*. New Haven: Yale University Press, 1981.

Wright, Stuart T., comp. and ed. *The Confederate Letters of Benjamin H. Freeman*. Hicksville, N.Y.: Exposition Press, 1974.

Yates, Richard E. *The Confederacy and Zeb Vance*. Tuscaloosa, Ala.: Confederate Publishing, 1958.

Yearns, W. Buck, and John G. Barrett, eds. *North Carolina Civil War Documentary*. Chapel Hill: University of North Carolina Press, 1980.

Young, Bennett H. "Col. John R. Lane and His Regiment." *Confederate Veteran* 17 (March 1909): 110–11.

Young, Louis G. "Death of Brigadier General J. Johnston Pettigrew, of North Carolina." *Our Living and Our Dead* 1 (September 1874): 29–32.

———. "The Pettigrew-Kirkland-MacRae Brigade." In *Histories of the Several Regiments and Battalions from North Carolina in the Great War, 1861–'65*, edited by Walter Clark, 4:555–68. Goldsboro, N.C.: Nash Brothers, 1901.

———. "Pettigrew's Brigade at Gettysburg." *Our Living and Our Dead* 1 (February 1875): 552–58.

———. "Pettigrew's Brigade at Gettysburg, 1–3 July, 1863." In *Histories of the Several Regiments and Battalions from North Carolina in the Great War, 1861–'65*, edited by Walter Clark, 5:113–32. Goldsboro, N.C.: Nash Brothers, 1901.

THESIS AND NOTES

Brady, Patrick S. Notes for a book on Cold Harbor.

McGee, David H. "The Twenty-Sixth Regiment North Carolina Troops, C.S.A." Master's thesis, Virginia Polytechnic Institute, 1992.

INDEX

Bristol, Pvt. Lambert A., 199
Broady, Lt. Col. K. Oscar, 250
Brockenbrough, Col. John M., 142, 144, 154, 165
Brooke, Brig. Gen. John R., 219
Brooks, Sgt. James M., 152
Broughton, Lt. Gaston, 150, 156
Brown, Capt. John W., 145
Brown, R. B., 322
Brown, Pvt. William, 336
Broyhill, Pvt. Johnson, 232–33
Buchanan, Pvt. John R., 111
Buford, Brig. Gen. John, 117
Bull, Col. Augustus A., 39
Bunn, Lt. Benjamin H., 298–99
Burgess's Mill, battle of, xiii, xvi, 182, 202, 259, 270–77, 325, 331, 347–49
Burgwyn, Col. Henry K., Jr., 2–4, 7–9, 13, 16, 18, 20, 23–24, 29, 31–35, 54–56, 61–66, 75, 78, 89–90, 93–99, 101–4, 115, 168–72, 308–10, 325, 341; at battle of Gettysburg, 120, 126, 129–30, 134–36, 139
Burgwyn, Henry K., Sr., 7, 176
Burgwyn, William H. S., 168–71, 308–9, 311, 322–23
Burnside, Maj. Gen. Ambrose E., 8, 12, 17
Bush, Sgt. J. A., Sr., 64, 107, 120, 154, 171, 304, 325
Butler, Maj. Gen. Benjamin F., 6
Byron, Maj. John B., 250

Caison, Pvt. Albert S., 173–74, 318–19
Capel, Sgt. Thomas R., 339
Carmichael, Maj. Abner B., 2, 13, 15, 17
Carmichael, Capt. William W., 260, 266, 278
Cash, Pvt. Joseph A., 109, 111
Casulties, xv, 343–50; in 1864, 282; in retreat to Appomattox, 303; in Bellfield-Hicksford raid, 280; at battle of Bristoe Station, 192–93, 386 (n. 21), 387 (n. 23); at battle of Burgess's Mill, 276–77; at battle of Cold Harbor, 227–28, 230–31; in fighting at Duncan Road, 269; at

battle of Falling Waters, 165, 174; in Fifth Offensive at Petersburg, 269, 400 (n. 25); at battle of Gettysburg, 132–33, 153–58, 171–75, 380 (nn. 53, 56); at battle of Globe Tavern, 246; at battle of Hatcher's Run, 285; at battle of Jones's Farm, 264; from March 25 to April 8, 1865, 303; at battle of the North Anna, 225; in Overland campaign, 233; in fall of Petersburg, 290–91, 298; at battle of Reams Station, 254–55, 398 (nn. 61, 62); at battle of Spotsylvania, 221–22, 224; at battle of Squirrel Level Road, 267; at battle of the Wilderness, 213, 215–16
Cheek, Pvt. William M., 134–36
Cherry, Capt. Macon G., 254
Christian, Col. W. S., 115
Clark, Gov. Henry T., 7
Clark, Tom, 334
Cleburne, Maj. Gen. Patrick, 184
Clingman, Brig. Gen. Thomas L., 72–75, 308
Coffey, Sgt. Henry C., 133
Coke, George H., 158
Cold Harbor, battle of, xiii, xvi, 226–31, 308, 320
Collins, Maj. George P., 40, 106, 139, 167–68
Colson, Thomas K., 51
Colson, Thomas K., Jr., 51
Connecticut units
—infantry
    14th, 141, 146, 151, 379 (n. 37)
Conner, Brig. Gen. James E., 249, 252–53, 256
Conscription, 17–18, 48, 55, 65–68, 85, 277, 341–42
Cook, Capt. John D. S., 127
Cooke, John E., 323
Cooke, Brig. Gen. John R., 176, 187–91, 200, 203–4, 209, 215, 219, 226–27, 229, 243, 249, 252–53, 256, 264, 267–68, 284–85, 291, 294–96, 304
Coon, Lt. David A., 260, 325

Foster, Maj. Gen. John G., 62–64, 69–73, 89, 91–92, 95, 98
Foster, Pvt. John R., 281
Foster, Capt. Nathaniel A., 78, 149
Fox, William F., 322
Frank, Col. Paul, 219
Freeman, Benjamin H., 234, 240, 242, 264, 267, 282–83, 287–88
French, Maj. Gen. Samuel G., 17, 62, 82
Fry, Col. Birkett D., 21, 141–42, 145

Gaines, Dr. William G., 39
Gaither, Surg. William W., 138, 216
Galloway, Col. Thomas, 40
Garnett, Brig. Gen. Richard B., 87, 92–93, 95, 98
Garrett, Esau, 246
Garrett, Woodson, 246
Gates, Col. Theodore, 128
Gawthrop, Lt. Henry, 232
Gentry, Lt. Levi C., 177
Georgia units
—infantry
35th, 37, 39
Getty, Brig. Gen. George W., 209
Gettysburg, battle of, xiii, xvi, 115–58, 184, 309, 311, 318, 320, 322, 324–26, 331–32, 336, 339, 345–50, 376 (n. 43), 379 (n. 37), 381 (nn. 58, 59)
Gibbon, Brig. Gen. John, 141, 226
Gibson, Abe, 222
Gibson, Lee, 222
Gibson, Capt. Leonidas R., 85
Gilbert, Pvt. Charles, 193
Gilliam, Sgt. Jesse M., 148
Glenn, Pvt. George, 192
Glenn, Pvt. William H., 9, 81
Globe Tavern, battle of, xiii, 242–48, 331, 344, 348, 351, 397 (n. 51)
Goldsboro, expedition to, 69–76, 79
Gordon, Maj. Gen. John B., 279, 302
Gorman, Brig. Gen. Willis A., 39
Graves, Lt. Col. John A., 50, 121, 144, 151, 157
Greaves, James B., 175

Greer, Lt. James C., 85, 120
Gregg, Brig. Gen. J. Irvin, 302
Grier, Capt. William L., 191
Griffin, Col. Simon G., 229, 262

Hall, Col. Edward D., 190, 192
Hall, Capt. Everard, 315, 336
Hall, William H., 30–31, 321–22
Hancock, Maj. Gen. Winfield S., 209, 213, 217, 219, 221, 240, 248, 254, 270–73, 276
Hanner, Lt. Orren A., 173, 313
Hanscom, Cpl. M. C., 193
Hardee, Lt. Gen. William J., 184
Hargrove, Lt. Col. Tazewell L., 49, 55, 109–12, 260, 313–14, 325
Harper, Pvt. John B., 182
Harris, Sgt. Alexander H., 157, 160
Harris, Lt. Alexander S., 223
Harris, Sgt. Francis C., 61
Harris, Goodwyn, 181
Harris, Capt. James S., 107
Harris, Col. John L., 244–45
Harrison, Pvt. John, 340
Hartgrove, William W., 319–20
Hartranft, Brig. Gen. John, 262–63
Hatcher's Run, battle of, 284–86
Haskell, Maj. John C., 87, 167
Hauser, Lewis A., 31
Hays, Brig. Gen. Alexander, 141
Hearne, James D., 51
Heath, Col. Francis E., 188–89
Henry, J. L., 227, 229
Heth, Maj. Gen. Henry, 104, 168, 177, 187–90, 193, 197–98, 201, 209, 211–13, 215, 219, 221, 224–25, 229–31, 243, 248–50, 252, 255–56, 261, 263–64, 266, 271, 276–80, 301, 397 (n. 51); at battle of Falling Waters, 161–66; at battle of Gettysburg, 115–17, 119, 130, 132, 139; in fall of Petersburg, 290–91, 294–95
Heth, Capt. Stockton, 148
Hill, Lt. Gen. Ambrose P., 104–5, 116, 162, 177, 186–88, 193–94, 196–97,

209, 213, 217, 262, 268, 278–79, 285, 295

Hill, Maj. Gen. Daniel H., 83, 91–93, 97–98, 104, 323

Hill, Sgt. William H., 331

Hilless, Samuel, 175

Hinsdale, John W., 38

Hinshaw, Jacob, 66–68, 83–84, 140, 175

Hinshaw, Thomas, 66–68, 83–84, 140, 175

Hobson, Pvt. John, 343

Hoggard, Sgt. William M., 81

Hoke, Lt. Col. Robert F., 13, 52

Holden, William W., 30, 178–79, 206, 239–40, 312, 317

Holland, Pvt. Addison, 334

Holmes, Oliver W., Jr., 315

Honeycut, Pvt. Frank, 129, 134

Hood, Sgt. J. T. C., 125, 173

Hoyle, Lt. Lemuel J., 46, 71, 76, 81, 83, 98, 158, 160, 179, 181, 204–6, 225, 236, 270, 274, 276–79

Hudspeth, Sgt. Robert N., 133, 156

Huger, Maj. Gen. Benjamin, 22–25

Hughes, Capt. N. Colin, 40, 80, 90

Hunter, Sen. Robert M. T., 283

Illinois units
—cavalry
8th, 115, 117
12th, 109

Imboden, Brig. Gen. John D., 159–61

Indiana units
—infantry
19th, 121–22, 125–26

Ingram, Pvt. Joseph A., 264

Ingram, Pvt. William, 125, 134

Ingram, Lt. William S., 64

Invalid Corps, 333

Iredell, Capt. Campbell T., 40, 120, 128, 139

Jackson, John A., 7

Jackson, Lt. Gen. Thomas J., 103, 171

James, Sgt. Philip A., 278

Jarman, Charles, 332

Jarman, Elijah, 332

Jarman, John R., 332

Jarratt, Capt. Isaac A., 27–29, 32, 35, 58, 65, 85, 91, 95, 199–200, 215, 240, 275–77

Johnson, Pres. Andrew, 307

Johnson, Maj. Gen. Bushrod R., 244, 290

Johnson, Sgt. Hiram, 124, 133

Johnston, William, 30–31

Jones, Lt. James G. M., 221–22

Jones, Lt. Col. John Thomas, 4, 9, 19, 32, 34, 55, 63, 96, 102, 132, 161, 164–66, 175–76, 179–80, 182, 184, 195, 207, 215–18, 324; at battle of Gettysburg, 139, 142, 144, 147, 150, 152, 154

Jones, Lt. John W., 145

Jones, Pvt. Lloyd T., 216

Jones's Farm, battle of, 261–65, 312, 318

Jordan, James B., 313

Joyner, Joseph D., 276

Justice, Capt. Benjamin W., 51–52, 95, 97, 179, 196–98, 222, 248, 254, 259–60, 282, 288, 315

Kearns, James A., 320

Keifer, Col. J. Warren, 292

Kelly, Pvt. George W., 124, 133

Kendall, Maj. James S., 18–19, 55

Kendall, Pvt. Julius A., 52

Kilpatrick, Brig. Gen. Hugh J., 164

Kincaid, Capt. James M., 67–68, 151–52

Kincaid, Lt. W. J., 173

King, Bellfield, 199

King's School House: skirmish at, 23–24

Kirk, George W., 317, 319

Kirkland, Brig. Gen. William W., xvi, 184–90, 201, 203–4, 212, 214–16, 219, 224, 226, 229–30, 233, 235, 241, 256, 306–7

Kirkman, George, 156

Kirkman, George E. B., 156

Kirkman, Henry C. B., 156

Kirkman, Wiley P., 156

Kirkman, Sgt. William P., 130–31, 156

17th, 72, 97
19th, 276
20th, 253, 315
21st, 13, 15
24th, 49
25th, 15, 75, 308
36th, 262
44th, 63, 97
54th, 260
Massey, Pvt. Robert W., 254
Matkins, Pvt. Silas, 333
McAllister, Brig. Gen. Robert, 268, 273–74
McCain, Capt. John C., 51
McCaskill, Pvt. Daniel, 174
McComb, Brig. Gen. William, 284, 304
McCombs, Asst. Surg. James P., 259
McConnell, Sgt. Charles H., 131, 311
McCreery, Capt. William W., 40, 124, 126–27, 129, 134, 139
McDowell, Col. James C. S., 103
McFarland, Lt. Col. George F., 131
McGowan, Brig. Gen. Samuel F., 254, 262, 290, 295
McInnis, John C., 323–24
McIntosh, Maj. David G., 189, 192
McIver, Capt. James D., 85, 179–80, 313
McIver, John, 180
McKeen, Col. H. Boyd, 226
McLauchlin, Capt. James C., 62–64, 99, 130, 313
McLeod, Lt. Murdoch, 260
McLure, Pvt. Cyrus A., 174
McNeil, Cpl. Alexander, 151
McRae, Rev. Cameron F., 4
Meade, Maj. Gen. George G., 117
Medical care, 75
Meinung, Alexander, 114, 322
Melton, Pvt. James G., 376 (n. 43)
Meredith, Col. Solomon, 119
Meyers, Sgt. Anderson C., 53, 75
Michigan units
—cavalry
6th, 164–65
10th, 317

—infantry
5th, 271
7th, 226–27, 276
24th, 121–22, 126, 131, 134, 156, 311, 316
Mickey, Samuel T., 10–11, 28, 30–31, 56, 106, 139, 216, 222, 299, 321–22, 335
Miles, Brig. Gen. Nelson A. 250, 295–96
Mine Run campaign, 195–99
Minnesota units
—infantry
1st, 182
Minton, Pvt. Thomas, 250, 252, 274–76, 325
Mississippi units
—infantry
2nd, 289
11th, 106
Missouri units
—infantry
12th (U.S.), 328, 338
Mitchell, Capt. Sidney W., 145
Moore, Carroll, 317
Moore, Pvt. James D., 133, 316–18
Moore, John T., 334
Moore, Rev. Styring S., 114
Morale, 6, 42, 45, 114, 259, 286–89, 350
Moravians, 9–10
Morell, Brig. Gen. George W., 25
Morris, Lindsay, 182
Morrow, Col. Henry A., 124, 126–27, 130
Mott, Brig. Gen. Gershom, 267–68
Murchison, Pvt. Duncan C., 333
Murchison, M., 267
Murphy, Sgt. Daniel J., 276
Murphy, J. T., 308–9

Nall, Pvt. Ira L., 232
Nash, Capt. Fred, 185, 236, 278
New Bern: battle of, 12–17, 339, 357 (n. 45); Hill's attack against, 86–91
New Jersey units
—infantry
9th, 3, 71–72
12th, 141, 152